SMALL BUSINESS

Planning and Management

Charles R. Kuehl
University of Missouri—St. Louis

Peggy A. Lambing
University of Missouri—St. Louis

The Dryden Press
Chicago   New York   Philadelphia   San Francisco   Montreal   Toronto
London   Sydney   Tokyo   Mexico City   Rio de Janeiro   Madrid

Acquisitions Editor: Mary Fischer
Developmental Editor: Penny Gaffney
Project Editor: Karen Vertovec
Design Supervisor: Jeanne Calabrese
Production Manager: Mary Jarvis
Permissions Editor: Doris Milligan
Director of Editing, Design, and Production: Jane Perkins
Field Staff Representative: Russ Boersma

Text and Cover Designer: Mark Feldman
Copy Editor: Thomas Kelly
Compositor: The Clarinda Company
Text Type: 10/12 Times Roman

Library of Congress Cataloging-in-Publication Data

Kuehl, Charles R.
  Small business.

  Includes index.
  1. Small business—Management.
2. Small business—Planning.
I. Lambing, Peggy A.   II. Title.
HD62.7.K84   1987   658′.022   86-4611
ISBN 0-03-071331-5

Printed in the United States of America
789-039-987654321

Address orders:
383 Madison Avenue
New York, NY   10017

Address editorial correspondence:
One Salt Creek Lane
Hinsdale, IL   60521

CBS COLLEGE PUBLISHING
The Dryden Press
Holt, Rinehart and Winston
Saunders College Publishing

Cover images: Cloud photo by Sharon
Hoogstraten. Silicon chip photo courtesy of
RCA. Light bulb over cityscape photo by
Martin Iger for the Duro-Test Corporation.

To our parents, Fran and Rae O'Rourke,
Otto and Natalie Kuehl

To Barb and Jerry
And to Emily, Laura, and Jenny

The Dryden Press Series in Management

Arthur G. Bedeian, Consulting Editor

Preface

Small business and entrepreneurship have generated considerable interest in the 1980s. It is no wonder. The small business sector has given our economy much of its recent vitality through the creation of new jobs and the development of new products and services. Beyond these economic contributions, small business provides unbounded opportunities for individuals to pursue dreams of independence and financial success. Small business seems to have captured the spirit of the times.

One purpose we had in writing this text was to heighten your interest in the exciting world of small business; another was to get you to consider small business ownership as a career; a final purpose was to describe the means by which a small business is planned and managed. To help accomplish these purposes, we have incorporated a number of features in the text:

Unique businesses.   We have included a number of descriptions of businesses that you are not likely to have encountered. Some are very clever, some are a little wacky, all of them are real.

Small business successes.   A wide variety of businesses are described throughout the text. They are in a number of industries and are located throughout the United States. They share only one characteristic: they are successful.

Cases.   Cases follow each of the text parts. The cases are provided to allow you to apply your understanding of the principles and techniques covered in the chapters to real-life situations and problems.

Glossary.   Because many readers will have little or no background in business, we have included a glossary. Definitions appear in the margins each time a new term occurs. In addition, we have provided definitions of many financial terms not used in the text.

The text is made up of five parts. The first part provides insights into the role of small business in the United States, describes the personality and background of a typical entrepreneur, and identifies the most commonly used routes into small business.

The second part is concerned with the early stages of planning a small business. The topics covered in this part are the nature of the market, site selection, and break-even analysis. The purpose of these planning efforts is to screen out ideas that have too little promise of developing into successful businesses. The ideas that survive this screening require additional examination; this is the subject of Part Three. The topics covered are projected financial statements, legal structure considerations, sources of financing, and feasibility studies.

The operation of a small business is the subject of Part Four; in it we cover a wide variety of management concerns. These concerns range from pricing to production, and their diversity clearly demonstrates the need for the owner of a small business to be a jack-of-all-trades.

The last part includes a number of areas of increasing importance to the entrepreneur: the role of the government, computerization, and insurance. In the final chapter, we discuss success and failure in small business, giving close attention to a number of myths concerning the failure rate of small businesses.

Available with this text are an *Instructor's Manual and Test Bank* and a student workbook. The *Instructor's Manual* contains chapter outlines, chapter objectives, answers to the end-of-chapter questions, and suggested sources for supplementary material for each chapter. We have also provided detailed analyses for all of the in-text cases. A separate section of the manual provides objective test questions for each chapter. The student workbook, *A Practical Guide to Small Business Planning and Management,* is designed to help students develop a deeper understanding of the issues involved in starting and managing a small business.

This text did not reach its final form through our efforts alone. A number of talented and knowledgeable people contributed to its development from the proposal state through the actual production. One very important group was the reviewers. Their comments, though occasionally unsettling, were insightful and useful, and the text is better because of their efforts. We thank them all.

Robert Brockhaus
St. Louis University

Richard Cuba
University of Baltimore

Charles Downing
Massasoit Community College

Paul Dunn
Northeast Louisiana University

R. Burton Fletcher
El Camino College

Eugene Gomolka
Virginia Polytechnic Institute and State University

Glen Grothaus
St. Louis Community College—Meramec

F. E. Hartzler
Emporia State University

Robert L. Holland
George Washington University

Susan Osborne Howes
Wichita State University

Herbert Johnson
Sam Houston State University

Rudolph Kagerer
University of Georgia

Judith Kamm
Bentley College

R. B. Keusch
East Carolina University

Richard LaBarre
Ferris State College

Jerre G. Lewis
Kirtland Community College

Pamela Little
North Harris County College

Louis Mansfield
Kankakee Community College

Joseph Platts
Miami Dade Community College

Thomas L. Powers
Eastern Michigan University

Charles Prentiss
Phoenix College

Richard Randall
Nassau Community College

Diane Robertson
Northern Illinois University

Nicholas Sarantakes
Austin Community College

Don Sexton
Baylor University

Connie Sitterly
Amarillo College

George Stevens
University of Central Florida

Al Travers
Indiana Vocational Tech—South Bend

Sandra Whitcomb
Pasadena City College

Kitty T. Wilkinson
Southwest Missouri State University

Harold Wilson
Southern Illinois University

Peter Wright
Southeastern Louisiana University

Our text contains four cases that we did not write. We would like to thank the authors of those cases:

- Donald F. Kuratko, Ball State University, and Norman J. Gierlasinski, Central Washington University: *Inner-City Paint Corporation*
- Ronald G. Greenwood, GMI Engineering and Management Institute: *The Case of the Tardy Employees*
- Donald F. Condit, University of Detroit: *Harvey Industries*
- Joseph T. Kastanin and Robin A. Alexander, University of Wisconsin-LaCrosse: *Folk Art Inc.*

We were also fortunate to have received support and encouragement from our colleagues at the University of Missouri—St. Louis. Dean Don Driemeier provided a variety of resources and his unique brand of interest in our progress. Associate Dean Dave Gustafson and Ms. Margaret O'Connor gave their support and counsel during a lengthy series of Saturday luncheon meetings. Finally, we would like to thank a group of secretarial friends, particularly Sharon Presnell and Diane Loesing, for all of their capable and cheerful assistance.

We would also like to acknowledge the efforts of the dedicated and patient people at The Dryden Press, especially Russ Boersma, Penny Gaffney, and Karen Vertovec. They made our task much easier than it otherwise would have been.

Charles R. Kuehl
Peggy A. Lambing
St. Louis, Missouri
September 1986

Contents

Part Four Directing and Controlling   244

PART

One

Small Business and the Entrepreneur

In Part One we will provide an introduction to the small business environment. We will emphasize the importance of small businesses to the economy, describe the type of person who becomes an entrepreneur, and discuss alternative methods of becoming an owner of a small business.

Perhaps the most important contribution of small business to our society is that it offers opportunities for success and independence to anyone and everyone. Notice that we said opportunities; no guarantees are offered, and risks can never be completely eliminated. Nonetheless, our nation's history includes countless stories of immigrants and others of modest backgrounds experiencing great success as entrepreneurs. In addition to offering opportunities to the individual, small business provides considerable vitality to the U.S. economy. The majority of new jobs in our economy are created by small business. As our society and economy change, small business changes with them. In Chapter 1 we will describe these and other contributions of small business. We will also define small business and describe the major types of endeavors in which the small enterprise is commonly found.

The entrepreneur is an unusual person. In Chapter 2 we will describe the characteristics of this individual. In some respects, the entrepreneur is no different from anyone else; in other respects, the differences are clear. The focus in this chapter will be on the differences, those traits which make the entrepreneur unique. To allow you to assess your own entrepreneurial tendencies we have provided ''The Entrepreneur Test.'' Additional topics covered in this chapter include a description of the reasons why people go into business on their own and an examination of the conditions or circumstances associated with the launching of most ventures.

The final topic covered in Part One is the various ways to enter small business. These routes are available: starting a business, buying an existing business, and buying a franchise.

Starting a business is the purist form of entrepreneurship for it involves spotting an opportunity and establishing a business to respond to it. It is also the most risky way to go into business and in Chapter 3 we will examine these risks and compare them to those associated with the other ways of entering. Buying an established business or a franchise reduces the level of uncertainty because we have more information with which to make decisions. We will discuss the advantages and disadvantages of buying a business, the factors influencing the price of the business, and the means of evaluating a franchise.

CHAPTER 1

Small Business in the United States

K E Y Objectives

1. To make clear the importance of small business to the U.S. economy.

2. To define the term *small business*.

3. To identify the types of business where small business is most often found.

4. To discuss why people start their own businesses.

For the first three-fourths of this century, the trend was toward bigness. Our cities, our governments, and our corporations were all growing, many of them to the point where social critics raised grave questions concerning the future of our society.

One writer described the emergence of the American Corporate State, a colossal network of huge corporations and government agencies.[1] It represented the logical culmination, as many people thought, of the trend toward large size. In this climate, small business generated little interest or enthusiasm. It was treated instead as an insignificant force in the economy, the product of earlier, simpler times. Indeed, one writer dismissed small business as "dead as a dodo."[2]

Entrepreneurial Economy
An economy in which small new businesses provide the basis for growth.

If it was dead, it has arisen from its ashes and we have seen the emergence of the age of the **entrepreneurial economy.** Now, in the 1980s, small business is resurging; it is a dynamic force in our society. In his May 1985 report to Congress, President Ronald Reagan stated, "New businesses, new industries, and new jobs have been produced by millions of entrepreneurs free to test new ideas in open markets. This growing and dynamic small business role must be continued if we are to maintain our national strength in the world economy."[3]

Why has this happened? What had caused small business to go from the brink of extinction, as some people saw it, to robust health? It is impossible to pinpoint all of the reasons, but we do know that, more than ever before, the world around us is changing, and as it does its institutions change as well.

---

[1]Charles R. Reich, *The Greening of America* (New York: Random House, 1970).
[2]J. K. Galbraith, *The New Industrial State* (Boston: Houghton Mifflin, 1967).
[3]*The State of Small Business: A Report of the President* (Washington: U.S. Government Printing Office, 1985), vii.

Unique Business   1.1

To Beef Up Your Ad Campaign . . .

A farm on the outskirts of Toronto makes space available for outdoor advertisers. Nothing unusual about that, right? Wrong. The space provided by Park Farm is on the side of one of its cows. The ads are 2-by-3-foot pieces of oilcloth strapped to the cow. For $500 you get Bossy's services for one year, and if she has a calf you get it "signed up" for free. For an extra $7 per month a cowbell will be included for additional hype.

The "mediacow" business was started as a form of diversification by the farm, which also produces conventional farm items such as corn, dairy products, and eggs.

Source: The Wall Street Journal, March 27, 1984, 37.

Some of the changes are rapid, some gradual, many profound. Nowhere are these changes more significant than in our economy. Here are some examples:

- Foreign competition is becoming increasingly troublesome in more and more industries. Our steel, textile, and automobile industries have seen a constant erosion in domestic markets in recent years.
- During the last 25 years we have shifted from an industrial society where blue-collar jobs predominated to an information society where technicians, clerks, and managers outnumber manual laborers.[4] From that point we have been known as the postindustrial society.
- Women are entering the labor force in greater numbers than men and by 1995 will outnumber men within the civilian force.[5]
- Deregulation by the federal government has had a dramatic impact in some industries, such as trucking and air travel.
- The record of annual improvements in productivity and standard of living that started after World War II ended in the deep recession of the early 1980s.

This is, of course, an incomplete listing, and further reflection tells us that much of our country's economic landscape is being altered. Many of the firms

---

[4]John Naisbitt, *Megatrends* (New York: Warner Books, 1982).
[5]*The State of Small Business: A Report of the President* (Washington: U.S. Government Printing Office, 1984), 234.

and industries that have had prominent roles in our culture are in jeopardy. They must change or perish. Amid all of this turbulence, small business is alive and well. It provides the enduring American success story. It may well be the biggest economic development of our age, broader in scope and deeper in significance than anything since the Industrial Revolution. In the post–World War II economy, we were creating fewer than 100,000 new businesses every year. We currently start 600,000 per year.

Included in this vast number of new businesses are many conventional enterprises, some that are unusual, and a few that are unique. We find these unique businesses interesting because they represent the true spirit of entrepreneurship as reflected in the uncommon creativity and initiative of their founders. We will provide descriptions of such businesses throughout the book, starting with Unique Business 1.1. The purpose of these descriptions is to give you some insight into the range of opportunities and activities on which people base businesses. We hope you enjoy them.

Contributions to Society

. . . .

The significance of small business in our economy goes beyond the annual number of starts. Consider the following contributions:

Jobs: During the 1970s and the 1980s, small business created approximately 80 percent of the new jobs in this country. During 1981 and 1982, U.S. businesses with fewer than 20 employees created 2,650,000 new jobs. This more than offset a 1,664,000 loss in jobs in large business, resulting in a net gain of nearly one million jobs.[6]

Innovations: The record of small business in discovering and bringing to the market new products and ideas is truly remarkable. Among the more notable products for which small business can be credited are the following:

- cellophane
- the jet engine
- the ball-point pen
- xerography
- penicillin
- insulin
- air conditioning

The list represents the tip of the iceberg. Despite the complexity and costs associated with modern-day research, small businesses have accounted for more than half of the major inventions in the past 30 years. The efficiency with which these innovations have been achieved makes the record all the

---

[6]*The State of Small Business*, 1984, 2.

A Tale of Two Cities

A British researcher, Jane Jacobs, has compared the English cities of Manchester and Birmingham as they developed during the mid-1800s. Manchester, with its planned economy, was seen as a model city, the wave of the future. Birmingham was not regarded so favorably; its economy was "messy," with many small household businesses starting and nearly as many failing. This broad base, however, led to the development of a strong sense of entrepreneurship within Birmingham. With this climate of entrepreneurship, the city prospered, while Manchester acquired "the efficiency of a company town," which brought about the stagnation of the city's economy.

Source: Jane Jacobs, *The Economy of Cities* (New York: Random House, 1969).

more remarkable. Small businesses produce 24 times as many inventions for each research dollar as do our largest businesses.[7]

Economic Resilience: Any economy in which change is taking place will witness the failure of some of the institutions that have served it so well in the past. The practices and culture of a hitherto successful organization, once the cornerstones of its success, prevent it from coping with environmental changes. This problem constantly plagues large organizations because with size comes a rigidity that makes change difficult. Small organizations also perish because of adverse environmental changes, but new ones arise in their wake. Illustration Capsule 1.1 gives a 19th century example of the importance of entrepreneurship to a local economy.

Opportunities for the Individual: In addition to its economic contributions, small business offers hope to the individual. Anyone whose dreams of independence cannot be accommodated by our existing organizations can start her own. The maverick and the outcast have a way out, as countless people in our country's history have discovered. See Illustration Capsule 1.2.

In a special issue on the changing face of America, *Time* magazine described the way in which immigrants from all over the world establish their own businesses here in the United States. Among the examples given are a

[7]U.S. Congress, Senate, Joint Hearings before the Select Committee on Small Business and other committees, *Small Business and Innovation*, August 9–10, 1978, 7.

Illustration Capsule   1.2

The American Dream

Writing in the "My Turn" column in *Newsweek* magazine, Bob Coleman comments on the role of small business in the history of our country. "Small Business has been a traditional path to independence for new Americans, and—happily enough—the same methods that worked for the Italians, the Irish and the Jews at the turn of the century are working for the Vietnamese, Koreans and Cubans today." Small business provides opportunity for those whom society has not provided with a place in its corporate or governmental worlds. Not all of the new generation of immigrants will succeed, but many are seizing the opportunity and many will "prevail by reason of hard work, tenacity and personal service, cliches that aren't cliches to [these] people."

In an editorial in the August 1983 issue of *Inc.* magazine, Milton Stewart comments on the role of entrepreneurship in our democracy:

> *Entrepreneurship, in part, protects the right to free expression. And the larger the entrepreneurial sector, the safer the right becomes.... This country's 14 million small businesses ... provide 14 million sources not only for economic opportunity but also for political liberty.*

Sources: Newsweek, November 14, 1983, 33; and *Inc.*, August 1983, 132.

Korean man who followed many of his countrymen in establishing a green-grocery in New York City; a native of the state of Gujarat in India who now operates a motel in California; and a Palestinian who has a small grocery store in San Francisco. Without the opportunity provided by small business, the hopes of these individuals may have been dim.

Women have also discovered the promise of entrepreneurship. In 1984, there were over three million female business owners, with the growth in the ranks proceeding in dramatic fashion. The number of women owning their own business increased by 46 percent during a recent 5-year period, with over a quarter of sole proprietorships now being held by women.[8]

By any measure, then, the small business is a vital component of our economic strength and promises to be through the foreseeable future. This book

[8]*The State of Small Business*, 1985, xv.

is about the men and women who are in business for themselves and about the way in which they start and operate their businesses. In this chapter we will first define what a small business is, then we will identify the areas in which they are most likely to be found, and finally we will discuss different types of small businesses and the payoffs they can bring.

Small Business Defined

. . . .

Small Business
Any business that is independently owned and operated and is not dominant in its field of operation.

A variety of definitions of **small business** may be found. We have selected two as illustrations.

Small Business Administration

Small Business Administration (SBA)
An independent agency in the U.S. government created in 1953 to help preserve free, competitive enterprise in the economy. The agency is engaged in a variety of activities including financing, procurement, and management assistance.

The definition of a small business given by the **Small Business Administration (SBA)** is detailed and complex.[9] It occupies 37 pages of SBA regulations. The definition takes into account a number of factors and results in a wide range of cutoff points for small business, examples of which are given below:

Industry	A Business Is Defined as Small if:
Construction	its average annual receipts for its preceding 3 fiscal years do not exceed $12 million
Manufacturing	
Meat packing	its number of employees does not exceed 500
Household laundry equipment	its number of employees does not exceed 1,000
Service	
Computer programming	its average annual receipts for its preceding 3 fiscal years do not exceed $4 million
Motion picture	its average annual receipts for its preceding 3 fiscal years do not exceed $8 million
Transportation	
Air	its number of employees does not exceed 1,500
Retail	
Department stores	its annual sales do not exceed $7.5 million
Variety stores	its annual sales do not exceed $2.5 million

---

[9]Small Business Act, Chapter 1, "Small Business Size Standards," part 121, 277–314.

Unique Business   1.2

The Old Folks at Home

Home Sitting Services Inc. of Denver, Colorado provides vacationers with live-in caretakers to feed the pets, water the plants, get the mail, etc. All of the house-sitters are retirees who receive room, food, and utilities plus an amount that does not disqualify them for Social Security entitlements. The chairman and founder was in his mid-70s when he started the company.

Source: Inc., July 1983, 19.

Committee for Economic Development

The SBA specifications, though precise, provide little insight into the character or nature of the small business concern. Another definition, much more useful in this regard, is that offered by the Committee for Economic Development.[10] This group defines as small any business that satisfies any two of the following criteria:

1. Independent management (usually the owner)
2. Owner-supplied capital
3. Mainly local area of operations
4. Relatively small size within the industry

Types of Businesses

While small businesses may be found in virtually every industry, certain types of business are more suited for the small organization than are others. Here we will describe the role of small business in four major sectors of the economy.

[10]*Meeting the Special Problems of Small Business* (New York: Committee for Economic Development, 1947), 14.

"One day, there will be no room for yet another chocolate-chip cookie, regardless of its quality."

Source: Drawing by Stevenson; © 1984 The New Yorker Magazine, Inc.

Retailing

Retail Store
An enterprise involved in selling directly to the final consumer.

Retailing
The activities involved in the sale of goods or services directly to the ultimate consumer for personal, nonbusiness use.

Service Enterprises
Firms engaged in providing a wide variety of services to individuals and businesses.

Using the SBA definitions of small business given above, the overwhelming majority (90 percent or more) of our country's nearly two million **retail stores** are small businesses. **Retailing** is the sale of goods or services directly to the consumer for personal use. Within this sector are such businesses as food stores, service stations, drug stores, and clothing stores. They are typically modest in scale, most of them having fewer than four employees. They are often prime examples of what is meant by the term ''mom and pop operations.''

Service

This is the most popular way to start in business. The number of new **service enterprises** was twice that of new retail firms during 1980 to 1982.

The range of service businesses is vast, from funeral service and dry cleaning to horse shoeing and providing charter jet transportation to entertainers.

Unique Business   1.3

The Duck Stops Here—but Not for Long

Not all businesses are started by the young and restless. Sometimes just being restless is enough. The president of Ugly Duckling Rent-a-Car System, Thomas Duck, Sr., of Tucson, Arizona, is 71. He's been around during his work years, having earned a paycheck in 26 different occupations. The moving about hasn't seemed to have hurt his self-confidence; he says, "I always felt I could fly if I just moved my arms properly."

Source: Adapted from Elden Graham, ''The Entrepreneurial Mystique,'' *The Wall Street Journal,* May 20, 1985, sec. 3, 1.

As the number of families with both spouses working increases, so does the demand for services. Until quite recently, for example, housecleaning services were used almost exclusively by the very rich. The demands on the time of the working wife changed all that, moving housecleaning from a luxury category to a necessity. This market opportunity has, of course, been noticed, and a number of maid-service businesses have emerged in recent years.

Because of gradual changes in our society, with increasing amounts of both leisure time and disposable income available to most individuals, and because most services cannot be mass-produced, this sector should experience continued growth and vitality in the future.

Construction

This type of business requires considerable training and experience to compete effectively. It is usually carried out under the terms of a contract. The contractor agrees to provide the materials and labor needed in the construction. Because most construction projects require a number of different operations, there are various types of construction contractors. The general contractor has overall responsibility for the project; in addition, subcontracts may be established with electrical, plumbing, and excavating firms.

Although entry is usually restricted to individuals with the needed backgrounds, the construction industry has a great number of very successful small firms.

Pop for Pampered Pets

If Fido seems to be down in the doggy dumps lately, why not treat him to some K-9 Kola? That's right: K-9 Kola, from R & Y Enterprises of Phoenix, Arizona. It's a noncarbonated, vitamin-fortified beverage with a fruity flavor that Ed Reed, co-owner of R & Y, likens to grape Kool-Aid. It comes in a six-pack and is priced at $4.99, with each can providing three servings.

Source: Inc., September 1984, 24

Manufacturing

Manufacturing
The production of goods for individual or organizational use.

Manufacturing is the production of goods for individual or organizational use. Because of the large amounts of capital needed to compete, many manufacturing industries are dominated by industrial giants—for example, the steel, brewing, railroad, and automobile industries. In many industries, however, size does not bring any important advantages. Consequently, hundreds of thousands of small manufacturers are able to compete effectively with any size competitor. Such firms might include saw mills, shoe factories, bakeries, bottling plants, cabinet shops, and concrete plants.

By now it should be clear that small business is an important factor in each of the economic sectors described above. The degree of importance varies considerably from sector to sector. In construction, nearly 70 percent of the industry's employees work for small firms; in manufacturing it is less than 20 percent. In both the retail and service industries, approximately half of the work force is employed by small firms. When all industry is included, the figure is 34 percent. That is, 34 percent of all the workers in all industries work for firms classified as small businesses.[11]

---

[11]*The State of Small Business*, 1984, 14.

Small Business Success 1

William Tao and Associates, St. Louis, Missouri

William Tao and Associates Inc. of St. Louis, Missouri is an internationally recognized leader in energy conservation engineering specializing in high-rise buildings, computer centers, and hospitals. WTA also offers computer software and computer-aided design services to design professionals.

Both Mr. Tao and his wife, Anna, were born in China. After they immigrated to the United States following World War II, they started their firm while Mr. Tao taught engineering part-time at Washington University. In 1956, the company had a staff of two; it now has approximately 100 employees, major projects in many states, Germany, and Saudi Arabia, and liaison offices in Taipei, Taiwan, and Singapore.

Among the many outstanding projects in which the company has participated is the McDonnell Douglas MCAUTO Computer Center, which won the prestigious Outstanding Engineering Project in the United States of 1983, and the Monsanto Research Center, which won the Outstanding Industrial Project Award in 1984.

Source: The Changing World of Smaller Business (New York: Price Waterhouse, 1982).

Making It Big in Small Business

While for most people the decision to go into business is based on a number of goals or dreams, one obvious part of virtually any entrepreneur's motivation is money. People start businesses to establish a livelihood or to supplement their existing one. But while entrepreneurs share an interest in having their business provide them with material success, the level of aspiration differs considerably from entrepreneur to entrepreneur.[12]

For some, the business is started as a substitute for an ordinary job. These business starts tend to be modest in scale of operations and limited in the

[12]Patrick R. Liles, "Who are the Entrepreneurs?" *MSU Business Topics*, Winter 1974, 5–14.

Illustration Capsule 1.3

Examples of Recent Public Stock Offerings

Entrepreneur	Company	Value of Entrepreneur's Stock at Offering (in Millions)
Allen E. Paulson	Gulfstream Aerospace Corp., Savannah, GA	$550.9
Andrew F. Kay, Mary M. Kay	Kaypro Corp., Solana Beach, CA	224.9
Russell Berrie	Russ Berrie Inc., Oakland, NJ	164.9
William Diaz	Columbia Data Products, Columbia, MD	114.9
J. B. Hunt	J. B. Hunt Transport, Lowell, AR	85.7
Milton Maltz	Malrite Communications Group Inc., Cleveland, OH	82.0
Terje Mikalson	Norsk Data, Oslo, Norway	78.3
Raymond G. Chambers	Gibson Greetings, Cincinnati, OH	66.0
Leslie Combs II	Spendthrift Farm, Lexington, KY	52.0

Source: Venture, April 1984, 48–56, and April 1985, 54–58.

Job Substitute
A business started by an individual as an alternative to working as an employee.

Attractive Small Company
A business that offers the founder a package of attractive pay plus various perquisites.

rewards they promise. Examples of these businesses are a small grocery store, a dry cleaning establishment, and a dairy bar. Although some of these provide a comfortable living if they are well managed, these businesses usually have only modest potential and can be labeled **job substitutes.**

Another type of venture, which shows considerably more promise than job-substitute firms, is the **attractive small company.** These firms are usually built on the specialized skills or talents of the founder. Within this category are service firms that provide consultation in areas such as market research, data processing, or engineering. Also found here are firms with specialized manufacturing capabilities. This type of venture, if successful, offers the

Entrepreneur	Company	Value of Entrepreneur's Stock at Offering (in Millions)
Seymour I. Rubinstein	MicroPro International, San Rafael, CA	47.6
Horace H. Irvine II	Hadeo Corp., Salem, NH	45.8
William E. Bindley	Bindley Western Industries Inc., Indianapolis	43.8
Philip E. Jakeway, Jr.	Wilfred American Educational Corp., New York	42.1
Vincent J. Coates	Nanometrics Inc., Sunnyvale, CA	41.9
Donald Panoz	Elan Corp., Ireland	39.6
Thomas R. Brown	Burr-Brown Corp., Tucson, AZ	36.6
Gene Bicknell	National Pizza Co., Pittsburg, KS	35.8
William H. Brady, Jr.	W. H. Brady Co., Milwaukee, WI	35.5
Leroy A. Pesch	Health Resources Corp. of America, Houston, TX	32.1
Carl E. Berg	Integrated Device Technology, Santa Clara, CA	31.3

Perquisite
Extra payment received because of one's regular work.

High-Potential Venture
A business that offers its founder(s) large financial rewards when it is sold to investors.

founder an attractive salary plus **perquisites** such as an expensive company car and tax-deductible travel opportunities, as well as the flexibility and freedom to work as she chooses.

One other category of small company can be identified, the **high-potential venture.** This is the type of firm on which the most ambitious of dreams are built, the type of firm that every founder hopes will allow her to make it big. If successful, such a firm provides its owner or owners with lifetime financial comfort and security. These firms, because of their spectacular growth prospects, attract the attention of the investing community, and with this attention occasionally comes the opportunity to "go public." This means the owner-

**Initial Public Offering
(IPO)**
The first public sale of a
company's stock.

ship of the company will be sold to the public through the sale of stock in
what is called an IPO, or **Initial Public Offering.** With this transaction the
entrepreneur relinquishes part or all of his company but receives what has
been labeled "megabucks" or "super money."

Illustration Capsule 1.3 lists the results of the public stock offerings of
some noteworthy high-potential ventures. The list only scrapes the surface; a
total of 302 entrepreneurs had the volume of their stock increase to $10 mil-
lion or more when their companies "went public" in 1983; another 73
reached that level in 1984.

Many of the 20 firms listed in Illustration Capsule 1.3 match the ideas that
people have about the spectacular growth companies of the 1980s, that is,
they are in high-technology and computer-based industries. Many are not,
however; Russ Berrie Inc. sells stuffed teddy bears; Gibson Greetings makes
greeting cards; Spendthrift Farm raises horses; and Malrite Communications
Group controls 17 broadcast stations. Notice the geographical distribution of
the companies. There are three California companies, two European companies, two from Ohio, and one each from 13 different states, with every sector
of the country represented. A similar kind of diversity can be seen in "The
Best Little Growth Companies in America," a listing of 100 small companies
in the May 27, 1985 issue of *Business Week*. Along with some outstanding
high-technology companies were a couple of television and movie producers,
a Russian translator, a restaurant chain, and an ice cream producer. Included
in the *Business Week* list were companies from 25 states.

Opportunity, it would appear, knows no industrial or geographical bound-
aries; the companies on the lists show wide diversity with regard to both type
of business and place. Indeed, the only common thread running through companies on both lists is success, and this will be the focus of our feature Small
Business Successes, in each of which we will describe a business that has
performed in extraordinary fashion. The feature, which will appear near the
end of each chapter, will reflect the wide diversity that characterizes small
business. The only thing these businesses have in common is success. In the
arena of small business competition, anyone who prepares well enough and
works hard enough has the opportunity to succeed. That is the only guarantee
you will find, the opportunity to succeed; but for the people whose businesses
we will be describing, that was enough.

K E Y   Objectives Reviewed

1. The small business sector of our economy makes critical contributions
    by providing new jobs, economic resilience, innovation, and opportu-
    nities for the individual.

2. The definition of small business provided by the SBA takes into account a wide variety of factors including the industry, the sales level, and the number of employees. The Committee for Economic Development identifies as small those businesses with independent management and limited scope.

3. Small businesses are found throughout our economy but are most commonly encountered in the retail, service, and construction industries.

4. People start businesses with varying levels of aspirations. Some see business ownership as simply an alternative to holding a job; others are interested in achieving more, sometimes much more, with their businesses.

Discussion Questions

1. Why is small business called the enduring American success story?
2. What part does small business play in providing our economy with resilience?
3. Why is the service sector likely to continue to grow?
4. Distinguish between the different types of small business according to the level of aspiration of the founder.
5. Describe the attitude toward business size as it existed in the 1960s and early 1970s. How is today's attitude different?
6. What is an IPO and what significance does it have for company founders?

CHAPTER 2

The Entrepreneur

Source: John Blaustein for McKesson Corporation. Used with permission.

K E Y   Objectives

1. To define the word *entrepreneur*.

2. To examine why people start their own businesses.

3. To describe the personality traits of the entrepreneur.

4. To provide insights as to whether you have entrepreneurial characteristics.

Entrepreneur
A person who takes initiative for a business project, organizes the resources it requires, and assumes the risks it provides.

The term *entrepreneur* has French roots; its literal translation is "undertaker" (*entre* being under and *preneur* being derived from the French verb *prendre,* to take). A more useful definition than the literal "undertaker" is one who has undertaken something. The term was used as early as 1775 in the writings of the French economist Cantillon.[1] Since that time a number of economists and other writers have proposed their definitions of what an **entrepreneur** is and does.[2]

The definition we will use here is one that considers the various things an entrepreneur does. The first element is that of taking initiative, that is, the entrepreneur is one who decides to get something moving. Hence it might be said that an entrepreneur is an initiator. Another common thread is that of putting together, or organizing the disparate elements needed to form a business. An entrepreneur is an organizer. Finally, any definition of entrepreneurship should mention the risk inherent in starting a business. Even the most careful, most optimistic individual must acknowledge the possibility of failure. So although the entrepreneur may guard against failure, she is a risk-taker by virtue of the uncertainty she is willing to accept.*

---

[1]Joseph A. Schumpeter, *The Theory of Economic Development* (Cambridge, Mass.: Harvard University Press, 1934).
[2]Each of the following has a unique definition of entrepreneurship: Jean Baptiste Say, *A Treatise of Political Economy* (New York: Kelley, 1827); Arthur A. Cole, *Business Enterprise in Its Social Setting* (Cambridge, Mass.: Harvard University Press, 1959); Orvis F. Collins and David G. Moore, *The Organization Makers: A Behavioral Study of Independent Entrepreneurs* (New York: Meredith Corp., 1970); and *The American Heritage Dictionary, Second College Edition* (Boston: Houghton Mifflin, 1982).
*Although most of the book will use a writing style that does not specify gender, in this chapter we will alternate between *he* and *she* in referring to the entrepreneur. We will do this for two reasons. First, individuals plan, start, and run companies, and we think using *he* or *she* helps drive this point home. Second, we want to underscore the point made in Chapter 1 about entrepreneurship being an opportunity that large numbers of women are discovering.

Unique Business   2.1

Business on the Move

Anthony Giordano Matawan, Jr., was the neighborhood answer man for lawn problems. He was an expert regarding the use of feeds, seeds, and weeds. Rather than limiting himself to business coming into his hardware store, he took the show on the road using a trailer hooked to his automobile. The idea flourished; the company now has 290 franchised outlets in 23 states. The average van—there are 700 of them nationwide—averages $100,000 in gross income each year.

Decorating Dan Systems of Indianapolis began in 1969 when Steven Bursten loaded samples of wall coverings, window treatments, flooring, and the like into his van and started visiting homes. Having the samples available for viewing in the customers' homes allows them to make more confident choices. The company now has 140 franchised outlets, which own 175 vans, each with the Decorating Dan logo on the side.

Source: Nation's Business, March 1984, 66.

Why People Go into Business

The definition given above describes the entrepreneur but it does not answer a very important and obvious question: What prompts people to go into business on their own? Why do people start businesses? Consider these facts:

1. The hours are extremely long. The time devoted to work is far greater for the entrepreneur than for managers in an employed status. As one observer put it, "Succeeding in business only requires that you work half days, and the nice part is it doesn't matter which 12 hours you choose."

2. Small businesses are risky. Many businesses fail during the first year. These failures can mean considerable financial loss to the entrepreneur, occasionally including large debts for which he is obligated. Risks are clearly present, and yet, as Chapter 21, "Small Business Successes and Failures," will indicate, the level and nature of these risks are often misunderstood and exaggerated.

3. Families of entrepreneurs suffer. The demands of building a business are often all-consuming. The long hours and constant preoccupation with the business force the family into a role of "playing second fiddle." Being an entrepreneur and a parent means making tough choices between the demands of a child ("I want you to watch me play soccer Saturday morning") and the business ("This report is going to have to be done this weekend").

5. Many of the comforts of conventional employment are nonexistent for the entrepreneur. Paid vacations, cost-of-living adjustments, and fixed working hours are seldom available to entrepreneurs.

The list could be expanded, but by now the point should be clear: there are many reasons not to go into business for yourself. Nonetheless, many people do; there were more than 600,000 business starts during each of the years from 1980 to 1984.[3] While a few of these businesses were started by other businesses, the great majority of these starts were by individuals. Why did so many people embark on such a difficult journey? We will explore that issue in two ways. We will first consider the attractions, real and imagined, that small business offers. We will then describe why some people, the entrepreneurs, respond to those attractions. Who are those people and what prompts them to move?

Independence

Perhaps the most important attraction of small business is independence. The question that must be considered here is independence from what? The entrepreneur has independence from the unreasonable boss, the poorly conceived performance-rating systems, the rigid rules of the bureaucracy inhibiting creativity and needed changes, and the many personnel regulations that give large organizations the predictability they need to function effectively. From all of these, the entrepreneur gains independence.

By many other measures, however, the independence people hope to experience by being their own boss is an illusion. Many people depend on the business owner, and with these dependencies come obligations on the part of the entrepreneur. She must pay employees and suppliers promptly and fairly. She must look after customer complaints and follow up sales leads. She must see that new employees receive proper training. Many others depend on her as well. The effect of all these dependencies is easy to understand: the freedom of the entrepreneur is restricted. It is not restricted in the way it was within a large organization, but it is restricted nonetheless.

---

[3]*The State of Small Business: A Report of the President* (Washington: U.S. Government Printing Office, 1985), 11.

The lure of independence was seen by de Tocqueville, the noted 19th century French sociologist, as a characteristic of the American. "In the United States as soon as a man has acquired some education and pecuniary resources, he either endeavors to get rich by commerce or industry or buys land in the bush and turns pioneer. All that he asks of the state is not to be disturbed in his toil, and to be secured of his earnings."[4] De Tocqueville made that observation in the 1830s; it remains an apt description of the entrepreneur of the 1980s.

Financial Success

For many it is clearly the lure of big money that prompts them to start a business. The idea that your earnings are limited only by your own levels of energy, dedication, and creativity holds great appeal for such people. It is to this dream that many magazine and newspaper ads ("Start your own business and become financially independent") are pitched. We know of no record of the success rate of businesses started in this way, but it appears that any business founded on such a fragile base has only dim hopes for long-term survival.

Yet many entrepreneurs are attracted by the promise of big returns, and for them the old bromide "You'll never get rich by working for somebody else" is enough. We have all heard stories of some individual whose timing, luck, and determination allowed him to amass a fortune. Most of us hope there is a pot of gold at the end of our rainbow. For some the rainbow is a corporate career, for others it is trips to Las Vegas, but for entrepreneurs it is small business ownership.

Job Satisfaction

Working for someone else can often mean being engaged in tasks that provide no sense of satisfaction. Motivation experts are convinced that the best way to combat job boredom is to enrich the job by building in certain characteristics. Among these characteristics are skill variety required, task identity, task significance, autonomy, and feedback.[5] The job of entrepreneur typically provides plenty of each of these characteristics, with the result being a level of work satisfaction that is a great deal higher than in most occupations.

This package of independence, financial success, and job satisfaction is one almost everyone would find attractive, and yet relatively few people actually start their own business. Who are the people who do so? To answer this question, our next section will describe the entrepreneur.

---

[4]Alexis de Tocqueville, *Democracy in America* (London: Oxford University Press, 1946).
[5]J. R. Hackman and G. R. Oldham, *Work Redesign* (Reading, Mass.: Addison-Wesley, 1980).

The Entrepreneur as an Individual

· ·

A great deal of time and effort has gone into the attempt to discover the traits that make the entrepreneur what she is. So far the results have been disappointing. As Donald Sexton put it at the 1983 meeting of the Academy of Management, "The study of psychological characteristics of entrepreneurs is one of the most researched and least understood areas in the field of entrepreneurship."[6]

A review of entrepreneurial personality research provides some insight as to why so little understanding has been achieved. First, the question of the bases of comparison must be raised. With whom should the entrepreneur be compared? The groups that have been used in the past include the general population; managers (managers in general, top managers, middle managers, successful managers, unsuccessful managers); and students (both business students and students in general). One study may compare entrepreneurs with the general population and find some promising distinctions; another may focus on the same personality traits but, using top managers as its basis for comparison, discover no discernable difference between the groups.

A similar question can be raised concerning the designation of entrepreneurs. The groups used here include business owners, "budding" entrepreneurs, "successful" entrepreneurs, university students with a major in entrepreneurship, and business owners who have participated in a management assistance program provided by the Small Business Administration. Each of these groups obviously has an entrepreneurial orientation, but there are great differences among them. Entrepreneurship students and business owners, for example, differ considerably in terms of age and experience. These differences will likely obscure many of the traits the two groups may have in common.

A final problem plaguing researchers in their attempts to determine the nature of the entrepreneurial personality is that of trait measurement. It is a rather inexact science; indeed, up until the mid-1970s, some researchers were willing to conclude that stable personality traits and dispositions do not even exist.[7] More recently, however, researchers have been able to point to evidence suggesting that human behavior is influenced by enduring traits.[8] These latest findings demonstrate a consistency or stability of traits that most of us would expect to find in the mature human personality and thus give hope for future research in an area that has proven difficult.

---

[6]Donald L. Sexton and Nancy Bowman, "Determining Entrepreneurial Potential of Students," *Academy of Management Proceedings* (1983): 488.

[7]Walter Mischel, "On the Future of Personality Measurement," *American Psychologist* 32 (April 1977): 246–254.

[8]Paul T. Costa, Jr., R. R. McGrae, and D. Arnberg, "Enduring Dispositions in Adult Males," *Journal of Personality and Social Psychology* 38 (May 1980): 793–800.

In summary, the attempts to learn the qualities of the entrepreneur have had some important shortcomings. This should not lead us to the conclusion that we know nothing about the topic, however; we do have some important findings available to us. Before we describe these findings and give you our own observations, however, we want you to take a test, or inventory, of your own entrepreneurial tendencies.

The Entrepreneur Test

One thing that becomes apparent to anyone who works with entrepreneurs is that they differ greatly from one another. They come in all shapes and sizes. Some are aggressive, some not; some are well educated, some poorly; some are gracious, some barely civilized. There seems to be no common thread, and yet certain activities often are found in their backgrounds, and certain outlooks or philosophies are frequently at the core of their personalities. We offer the test below as a crude assessment of how you measure up in these respects.

The test has no statistical substantiation and is included merely as a means by which you can compare yourself with what we have concluded are some important characteristics of the entrepreneur. The test has as its focus the composite, or typical, entrepreneur. Not all entrepreneurs are exactly like this, obviously, but the closer the fit, the more of the ''right stuff'' an individual would appear to have.

1. In goal-setting situations, such as improving your grade point average, running times, scores on video games, etc., which is your most likely strategy?
    A. Shooting for the sure thing to avoid failure
    B. Trying to reach a level of achievement that represents moderate risk
    C. Going all out for the biggest reward, despite the odds being stacked heavily against you

2. If someone suggests a goal she feels would be a good one for you, do you
    A. Pay little attention because you know what your capabilities are, or
    B. Incorporate the goal into your planning?

3. Do you occasionally sacrifice sleep, with no noticeable effects, to work on a project that interests you greatly?

4. In terms of birth order, where are you?
    A. Firstborn
    B. Middle child
    C. Last child
    D. Only child

5. Where did you get your spending money as a child of 12?
   A. Mowing lawns
   B. Baby-sitting
   C. Allowance from parents
   D. Providing services to neighbors
   E. Other

6. Do you insist on being told how you did on assignments you hand in to your instructors in class?

7. Which strikes you as the more reasonable statement?
   A. People make their own way in life. Pointing to bad luck or poor health as reasons for failure is the sign of a loser.
   B. Most of us have basically the same amounts of talent and ability. For some, though, things fall into place nicely; others run into troubles that they don't deserve. That's the way life is.

8. Are you currently considering starting your own business? How long have you been thinking about it?

9. What was your father's occupation? Was he an immigrant? Was he absent during much of your childhood?

10. When you are convinced of something, do you try to win over others, or do you usually feel it is futile to attempt it?

11. Which is the leading cause of small business failure?
    A. Economic depressions
    B. Economic recessions
    C. Poor planning by the owner
    D. Unreasonable bankers
    E. The influence of labor unions

12. Are you troubled by classes in which the grading system is not completely explained at the start?

13. If you had a proposal to start a business under the consideration of a financier, what would be your most likely course of action?
    A. Check with him frequently so you can go elsewhere if the decision is no.
    B. Allow the individual plenty of time to decide, because of the importance of her full commitment to the project.

14. Which statement do you most agree with?
    A. I can do better than most people on whatever I set my mind to.
    B. My abilities may not be exactly the same as those of other people, but the differences are not that great because everybody has strengths and weaknesses.

15. Which type of task would you prefer to be given?
    A. One in which the details have been taken care of in advance and the various contingencies explained to you.

B.   One in which a variety of things, which no one can anticipate, may come up.

16.   Over the next 5 years, do you see yourself as more likely to
A.   Get involved in a number of different types of businesses or activities to broaden your horizons, or
B.   Attempt to learn a great deal about one or two types of businesses?

We will not give you a scoring key because that might suggest more precision than should be attributed to the test. As to its interpretation, two things should be said. First, many successful entrepreneurs might "flunk," some rather badly. There is room for many personality types and personal interests in entrepreneurship, so no one must be forced into a mold. Second, and perhaps more important, is the message given by a close match between you and the typical entrepreneur. This may indicate that you would find work in a large corporation unsuitable. This suggests, then, that you may be well advised to consider carefully a career in small business. What we will do is explain what the items tell us about the various characteristics that we have concluded are associated with entrepreneurial personalities.

Internal Locus of Control

Internal Locus of Control
The belief of an individual that his or her future is within his or her control and that fate or other external forces should have little or no influence.

External Locus of Control
The belief of an individual that his or her future is not in his or her control but rather controlled by external forces such as fate or destiny.

Every small business requires planning; long-range, "big picture" planning and careful, detailed planning. For an individual to invest time and effort in planning, she must believe in its usefulness. The basis of such a belief is that, despite uncertainties of the future, plans can be achieved and that their achievement depends directly on the individual. Control, therefore, is in the hands of the individual. The name psychologists use for this philosophy is **internal locus of control.**

The competing explanation of why things turn out as they do is one we often hear and occasionally use. Fate, or some other force, determines what will happen. The other force takes on a variety of forms—the stars, politics, luck—but it is always outside of the individual and therefore beyond his control. The natural consequence of this philosophy (**external locus of control**) is that planning, because it involves making decisions for the future, is seen as futile. The view is appealing to many people because it relieves them of certain responsibilities of making their own way in the world and it makes failure an impersonal outcome. The entrepreneur will have none of this; she is clearly in control of her destiny.

One last word: there is a self-fulfilling quality in each of these philosophies. The individual who sees no point in planning is going to be buffeted about by fate from time to time. With no plans made for dealing with them, misfortunes will often be impossible to handle. The world is seen as a difficult, hazardous place. The planner, on the other hand, recognizes that there will be occasional setbacks, provides for them to the extent possible, and emerges from them with renewed confidence in his own abilities.

Source: Copyright Ford Button.

The quiz you just took had four items (numbers 5, 7, 10, and 11) that provide insights into your locus of control.

Item 5: Where did you get your spending money as a child of 12? The *C* response (allowance from parents) is wrong because relying on Mom and Dad, no matter how generous and dependable they may have been, shows less independence and self-reliance than the other choices.[9] Choices *A* (mowing lawns) and *B* (baby-sitting) can be modestly encouraging if you responded

---

[9]We will use ''right'' or ''correct'' in the sense that the response is consistent with the entrepreneurial personality pattern; such answers are obviously no better, objectively or ethically, than those we label ''wrong'' or ''incorrect.''

to requests for your services; they are *very* positive if you took the initiative by distributing flyers and the like to let people know you were available. Choice *D* (providing services to neighbors) shows the kind of "I'll-do-it-myself" tendencies often seen in entrepreneurs. Choice *E* (other) can be encouraging if the activity was one where you took it on yourself to get things started; if, on the other hand, you relied on someone else, this response is not part of the typical entrepreneurial mold.

Item 7: Which strikes you as the more reasonable statement? The *A* response, which said people make their own way, is preferable to *B* (for some people things fall into place nicely while others run into trouble).

Item 10: When you are convinced of something, do you try to win over others, or do you usually feel it is futile to attempt it? If you said it is futile, you made the wrong choice. The entrepreneur feels he can change things, including the opinions of others.

Item 11: Which is the leading cause of small business failure? This question had five answers that can be very detrimental to the health of a small business, but the individual with a high internal locus of control will choose *C* (poor planning by the owner).

Energy Level

Making a business succeed requires work—lots of hard work. Entrepreneurs typically have the energy level necessary to accomplish great amounts of work. They have the capacity to work long hours and get by with less sleep than most of us need. Without a reasonably high energy level, a prospective entrepreneur will find the demands of his business are overwhelming.

Item 3: Do you occasionally sacrifice sleep with no noticeable effects to work on a project that interests you greatly? A yes answer here, and to similar questions concerning whether your interests and enthusiasm prompt you to go "full tilt" for long periods, suggests a sufficient amount of drive. Answers of no, though they do not eliminate you from the running, are not encouraging. There are limits to everybody's energy and drive; your limits may be short of what your own business would likely demand.

The Need to Achieve

Need to Achieve
A psychological need found in many entrepreneurs that manifests itself in the individual preferring moderate risk, immediate feedback, and situations in which he or she sets his or her own goals.

If there is one human quality or trait that is nearly synonymous with entrepreneurship, it is the **need to achieve.** People with a high need to achieve tend to have the following behavioral characteristics.[10] First, they tend to prefer moderate risk situations to those with no risk or great risk. Higher achievers behave differently than others in some situations; for example, they are likely

---

[10]David C. McClelland, *The Achieving Society* (Princeton, N.J.: D. Van Nostrand, 1961).

Illustration Capsule   2.1

The Seeds of Achievement

McClelland has studied the child-rearing practices of families from which high achievers came. He found the parents of these high achievers set moderately high standards for them and were warm and encouraging in their attitudes toward efforts to achieve. The fathers were nondominating, allowing the children to try things out on their own. The role of the mother was supportive, bestowing rewards such as hugs and praise for achievement.

Source: David C. McClelland and David G. Winter, *Motivating Economic Achievement* (New York: The Free Press, 1969), 33–35.

to act in a certain predictable way when playing the children's ring-toss game. The high achievers will not stand so close to the peg that getting the ring over it brings no feeling of satisfaction because that is too easy, or so distant that the chances of success are remote. They search out the distance that represents a difficult but achievable goal; it is in this area that the risk is moderate.

The second characteristic of high achievers is that they like immediate feedback. They like to be able to determine for themselves how they are doing. Finally, they like to establish their own goals. They know their capabilities, having tested them often, and therefore prefer to determine their own objectives.

Item 1: In goal-setting situations, such as improving your grade point average, running times, scores on video games, etc., which is your most likely strategy? The *B* choice of accomplishing a level of moderate difficulty is better than either the safe choice *(A)* or the nearly impossible *(C)*.

Item 2: If someone suggests a goal she feels would be a good one for you, what do you do? If you pay little attention because you know what you can do *(A),* you chose correctly.

Item 6: Do you insist on being told how you did on assignments you hand in to your instructors in class? High achievers want feedback, as mentioned above, so a yes response is the right one.

The need to achieve can be described as the central need of most entrepreneurs; its development can be traced to childhood for most people (see Illustration Capsule 2.1).

Confidence

In the section describing the internal locus of control, we pointed out the importance of believing that you determine your own fate. This attitude is necessary but not sufficient for the prospective entrepreneur; he must also have confidence in his ability to make things turn out right. He has the feeling of mastery over whatever obstacles may present themselves during the course of the venture.

Two types of self-confidence can be identified. First there is a confidence based on the mastery of routine, day-to-day tasks. These tasks compose the "nuts and bolts" aspect of the business, and the prospective entrepreneur must have little or no question concerning her abilities here. The best advice is to let someone else train you, that is, learn the business as an employee, not as the owner of a business. Employee mistakes are often costly; owner mistakes are often catastrophic.

The other type of confidence is harder to describe and to judge. It is a general type of self-confidence in the ability to deal with any complex and unanticipated problems that may be encountered. This type of self-confidence has ebbs and flows. We can all remember periods of our life during which we would have taken on almost anything; at other times uncertainty seems to prevail. It appears that the entrepreneur must master the day-to-day requirements of the business and thus strengthen the basis for, and level of, general self-confidence.

Item 14: Which statement do you most agree with? Seeing your abilities as more or less equal to those of others *(B)* is not as consistent with the typical entrepreneur's self-image *(A),* which displays a clear sense of self-confidence.

Item 16: Over the next 5 years, which do you see yourself as more likely to do? The *B* response leads to the kind of in-depth understanding that is more likely to result in the needed level of self-confidence than will the "sampling" type of behavior mentioned in *A*.

Tolerance for Ambiguity

Ambiguity is the result of situations that are unstructured, or information that is unclear or incomplete. Some people find ambiguity not at all to their liking; they suffer psychological discomfort from it. But with the creation of any business a number of ambiguities arise, and therefore, dealing with these ambiguities is a basic part of the entrepreneurial task. Fortunately, for the typical entrepreneur this is not difficult. Because he has a high **tolerance for ambiguity,** the entrepreneur can accept the fact that the world is chaotic, unorganized, and unpredictable.

Tolerance for Ambiguity
The psychological characteristic that allows one to be untroubled by disorder and uncertainty.

Item 12: Are you troubled by classes in which the grading system is not completely explained at the start? **Item 15:** Which type of task would you prefer to be given? If being in a class or taking on a task in which you have to decide for yourself how to proceed does not bother you, your tolerance for ambiguity appears to be high.

Awareness of the Passage of Time

Another word for this might be impatience. Entrepreneurs want things to progress as rapidly as possible. If you have been thinking for 2 or 3 years about starting your own business, forget it. That is the advice some people who know entrepreneurship would give you. Your willingness to delay, albeit for important reasons, means that the ''hurry-up-and-get-it-done'' attitude is missing. Some would see that as a fatal flaw.

Item 8: Are you currently considering starting your own business? How long have you been thinking about it? If you said yes, you're thinking about your own business, good; if, however, you said you have been thinking about it for a number of years, it is not good.

Item 13: If you had a proposal to start a business under the consideration of a financier, what would be your most likely course of action? Choosing to give the financier plenty of time to decide *(B)* is not as good as pressing for an answer *(A)*.

Background Factors

Many people contend that we are what we are because of our backgrounds. In the case of entrepreneurs two factors appear to be significant: birth-order position and father's influence.

Our personality characteristics are greatly influenced by whether we are the oldest or the only child, the second, third, or subsequent child. There are some very desirable traits found in the second child, e.g., sociability, easygoing nature; or in the third child (often referred to by child psychologists as ''those glorious thirds''). Despite these worthy traits, the best spot for the entrepreneur is first. By every conventional measure, firstborns achieve more than later-born children. This is true here in the United States despite the fact that there are twice as many later-born children as firstborn.

Another important part of the backgrounds of entrepreneurs is the father. Chances for entrepreneurial success are best when the entrepreneur's father is or was:

1. An entrepreneur. The father's occupation provides the basis for imitating or modeling; hence, the offspring of entrepreneurs are most likely to start their own businesses.

2. An immigrant. Just as firstborns are given different nurturing, so are the children of immigrants.

3. Absent for at least part of the entrepreneur's childhood. The father's absence gives children responsibilities earlier. Those responsibilities can speed maturity and independence.

Notice that it is the role of the father that was cited as crucial. There are two reasons for this. First, until rather recently, the overwhelming number of businesses were started by men. The father, rather than the mother, served as a role model for the child who eventually went into business on her own. Second, the research examining the influence of parents on entrepreneurs has focused on the father. We have little in the way of research data to tell us how an entrepreneur-mother affects her children's interest in small business, or if certain characteristics of the traditional mother have an important influence on her children's likelihood to start a business. Is a harsh, demanding mother more likely to raise an entrepreneur, or should she be warm and encouraging? Is one style right for daughters and another for sons? Until these and similar issues are explored, we can only speculate on the role of the mother. For that reason our analysis here is limited to the role, or influence, of the father of the entrepreneur.

Item 4: In terms of birth order, where are you? Being the first or only child in the family is good.

Item 9: What was your father's occupation? Was he an immigrant? Was he absent during much of your childhood? The best combination, as suggested above, would be having an entrepreneur father who was an immigrant and occasionally absent.

Launching the Venture
. . . .

The personality of the entrepreneur is a bit different than that of others. The differences are such that the entrepreneur is more likely to take action than are the rest of us. This predisposition to action must nonetheless be triggered. Certain conditions seem to prompt the entrepreneur to make her move.

Timing

The first concern is when the venture is likely to be started. Liles points out the impact of changes in an individual's life on the capacity of that individual (as she perceives it) to start a business[11] (see Figure 2.1). The typical "free-choice period" begins in the mid- to late twenties as the combination of knowledge, experience, and confidence of the individual exceed the level needed to start a company. The period continues until the point where the individual's financial obligations, demands from the family, and nonbusiness interests bring reductions in the perceived capacity to start. About this time the individual adopts an attitude of wistful resignation toward the prospect of owning her own business. ("I always thought of owning my own business, but...the children will be starting college in a few years...there are so many things I want to do...")

---

[11]Patrick R. Liles, "Who Are the Entrepreneurs?" *MSU Business Topics* 22 (Winter 1974): 5–14.

Figure 2.1   The Free Choice Period for the Would-Be Entrepreneur

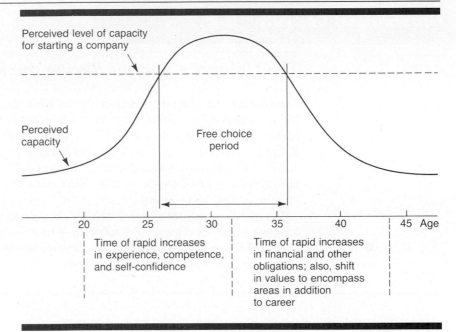

Perceived level of capacity
for starting a company

Perceived
capacity

Free choice
period

20   25   30   35   40   45 Age

Time of rapid increases
in experience, competence,
and self-confidence

Time of rapid increases
in financial and other
obligations; also, shift
in values to encompass
areas in addition
to career

Source: Adapted from Patrick R. Liles, "Who Are the Entrepreneurs?" *MSU Business Topics,* Winter, 1974, 5–14.

There are, of course, many exceptions to this pattern. These exceptions can be seen in the "early" starts made by entrepreneurs who are still in high school or college. Some individuals are simply too eager to let a lack of experience or background stand in the way of starting their own business. The other kind of exception concerns the "late bloomers." These are people who start a business at a time in their lives when their peers are starting or planning their retirements. A classic example of the late bloomer group is the founder of the Kentucky Fried Chicken restaurant organization, Colonel Harland Sanders (see Illustration Capsule 2.2).

Support

An entrepreneur who launches a venture seldom does it totally on his own. Entrepreneurs seem to require two types of support or assistance from those closest to them. Often this support is provided by the spouse. The first type of support is one that urges caution and care. The tendency of the individual who has decided to make it on her own in business is to "hip shoot." This tendency manifests itself in a number of ways; opportunities are magnified, problems are minimized, and complications are ignored entirely. A devil's

The Colonel's Special Recipe for Retirement

Colonel Harland Sanders had been in the food business for much of his life but, because of a loss in tourist trade due to the opening of a new highway, he sold his restaurant at a loss and went into retirement. He didn't find retired life to his liking and decided to sell franchises for his special 11-herbs-and-spices chicken. He opened the first franchise in Salt Lake City in the mid-1950s, and by 1963 more than 600 Kentucky Fried Chicken outlets had opened.

The company now has over 5,000 outlets around the world—all of this from the efforts and insights of someone who should have been enjoying "his golden years of retirement." For Colonel Sanders the years were not retirement, but they were indeed golden.

---

advocate is needed; someone who challenges assumptions and conclusions, and insists on being shown facts. The purpose of adopting this questioning attitude is to nip bad ideas in the bud. As a venture proposal develops, it absorbs large amounts of time, energy, and psychic involvement. Even a highly charged entrepreneur has limited amounts of these, so they must not be squandered on faulty projects. This role of caution should not be regarded as a negative one but rather as one that provides balance, rationality, and objectivity. These qualities are indispensable if sound planning is to take place.

After the plan has emerged from the careful scrutiny of the entrepreneur and her number one aide and the enterprise has been started, a different kind of support is likely to be needed. Once the excitement and euphoria of the start have worn off, some emotional propping up is usually needed. Few businesses do not encounter setbacks of some kind. When these setbacks come in bunches, the prospects for even a sound business can appear bleak to the individual closest to the scene. At these times the entrepreneur needs support from someone who can convince her that things still look good for the long term.

Support is not limited to the spouse of the entrepreneur. Friends, bankers, lawyers, accountants, and established entrepreneurs are all possible sources of support. Members of each of these groups can help in unique and important ways.

Small Business Success 2

Motion Designs Inc., Clovis, California

A hang gliding accident left sports enthusiast Marilyn Hamilton paralyzed from the waist down in August of 1978. She turned to two friends, Jim Okamoto and Don Helman, who applied the aerospace technology of hang gliders to design a wheelchair that would allow her to continue her active life-style. Back then, a lightweight, precision engineered wheelchair was hard to find, and the folding chair was only a dream. The industry had said it couldn't be done, but Marilyn, Jim, and Don set out to prove the industry wrong. The three friends consulted with medical professionals and other disabled individuals to perfect the chair that they call the "Quickie."

As Motion Designs began to take off, the three partners looked for professional and financial guidance. Growing pains became apparent. The company outgrew the original 400-square-foot shed, a 5,000-square-foot building, and a 17,000-square-foot building. Small business loans enabled Motion Designs to construct a 48,000-square-foot manufacturing headquarters that has undergone expansion to 96,000 square feet. Motion Designs has been able to share some of its success with the local economy by providing employment, supporting other local businesses, and contributing goodwill to society with a caring, quality product.

Source: Company press release.

Event

Most business starts require a trigger of some kind. This trigger, or precipitating event, can be negative or positive, but it results in the entrepreneur taking the step into business. A negative trigger is either a serious setback on the job or the actual loss of it. While the reaction of most people is to search for another job, the reaction of the entrepreneur is to free himself from such setbacks by starting his own company.

The other type of trigger is positive in that it pulls the individual into business. This happens when an opportunity emerges. This opportunity can be of a type that suddenly becomes available, e.g., because of the death of the owner, a business is up for sale. Probably a more common set of events, however, are those that evolve over time and result in an opportunity the entrepreneur recognizes as one she can grasp. Examples include the emergence of a new product in a market with which the individual is familiar; a change in supplier-customer relationships; and a shift in consumer spending patterns.

Other events that can serve as entries into business include marriage to the son or daughter of a business owner and inheriting a business. Though these are not uncommon routes into business, they are not available to very many prospective entrepreneurs. Our next chapter describes the more conventional methods of going into business.

K E Y Objectives Reviewed

1. An entrepreneur is someone who takes the initiative for the enterprise, organizes the resources it requires, and assumes the risks it provides.

2. Entrepreneurs start businesses to gain independence, financial rewards, and job satisfaction.

3. The personality traits of an entrepreneur typically include an internal locus of control, a high level of energy, a strong need to achieve, strong self-confidence, great tolerance for ambiguity, and an awareness of the passage of time.

4. Timing, the strong support of someone, and a precipitating event are major factors in launching a venture.

Discussion Questions

1. What kind of independence does the entrepreneur enjoy?

2. What makes it difficult to draw conclusions based on entrepreneurial personality research?

3. Distinguish between an internal locus of control and an external locus of control.

4. What are the characteristics of a high achiever? Why is this type of person attracted to small business?

5. What kinds of support does the entrepreneur appear to need?

6. Why is a high tolerance for ambiguity an important trait for an entre-preneur?

7. What appears to be the role of the father in the establishment of entre-preneurial tendencies?

8. What are the elements of the job of entrepreneur that make it a source of job satisfaction?

CHAPTER 3

Ways to Enter the World of Small Business

Source: Robert Keeling for Carson Pirie Scott & Co. Used with permission.

K E Y Objectives

1. To describe the ways in which new businesses are started.

2. To examine the process of buying an existing business.

3. To describe the concept of franchising and to identify the various types of franchises available.

4. To identify the advantages and disadvantages of each of the ways of going into business.

There are various ways to go into business. The way used most often is to start a new business; we discuss it first. The other methods, buying an existing business, or getting a franchise, will also be described.

Starting a New Business
. . . .

Opportunity Recognition
A means of finding the basis for starting a business that involves scanning the environment for developments that can be translated into economic opportunity.

Idea Generation
A method for starting a business based on an examination of the background, skills, and interest of the entrepreneur in light of what the market may support.

Serendipity
An opportunity for starting a business that emerges with no deliberate search by the founder of the business.

Starting a new business means starting from scratch, i.e., taking an idea and turning it into a business. This is the purest form of entrepreneurship. It requires discovering an opportunity or idea and responding to it. The process by which new business prospects develop takes three forms. The first two are the result of deliberate search efforts by the entrepreneur; they are **opportunity recognition** and **idea generation.** The other way in which new business prospects develop is by luck or accident; we will call it **serendipity.** Each of these is described below.

Opportunity Recognition

The entrepreneur is always on the prowl for developments that can be translated into economic opportunity. News of such an opportunity can come from a variety of sources, the following being some examples:

- Newspapers allow the entrepreneur to spot any societal or cultural trends that may be taking place.
- Business periodicals provide timely coverage of changes in the economy.
- Trade journals describe the events and environment of a particular industry. Trade shows are also useful in this regard.

Unique Business   3.1

Responding to the Itch of the Flea Market

In Houston, Mr. Eli More has established a Flea Market for automobiles. He rents 12 acres of paved ground, which is used by people who want to sell their cars. These sellers, who rent space by the day, week, weekend, or month, provided $250,000 in revenues to Houston Autofair Inc. during its first year. Owner More projected sales of $750,000 or more during the company's second year. He feels the company has succeeded because "people like sales that are simple, direct, and quick."

Over 10 million used cars are sold each year in the United States by individuals.

Source: Inc., June 1984, 22.

- Government publications can be another useful idea source. For example, patents available for public use are described in information provided by the U.S. patent office.
- Product-licensing information services are available through independent brokers, universities, and corporations throughout the country.

The key here is in the translation from the trend to specific opportunity. For example, consider the automobile as a source of business opportunities. It has been around in large numbers for more than 50 years, so you might think all of the automobile-related opportunities have been exploited. That is not the case, as the following examples indicate.

The increases in the prices of new cars and the spread of self-service gasoline stations mean that many people will be deferring the purchase of their next car but not providing adequate service to their current one. This points to an opportunity for automobile repair shop businesses. These conditions were noticed not only by many small operators but by at least one very large company as well. Shell Oil recently began promoting "Auto Care" as a service provided by its dealers.

The rise in terrorism has led to the development of firms that add armor to automobiles and of schools that teach defensive driving to chauffeurs.

A New Jersey company was founded to rebuild automobiles, particularly BMWs and Volvos. The founders, aware of the intense loyalty of the owners to these cars and increasing price levels of new ones, felt their service would be attractive to many of the people whose cars were due for "remanufacturing."

These kinds of societal, or environmental, trends are often so gradual as to escape notice. The entrepreneur with an ear to the ground may have a significant advantage due to early recognition. The opportunity recognition approach to new venture starts has an *outside-in* orientation; that is, the entrepreneur looks at the world to see what kinds of possibilities exist. When taken too far, this approach can lead to ways of getting into business that are clearly not advisable. Staff members of Small Business Administration offices and others who provide small business counseling regularly receive requests for advice in the form of questions such as, "What kind of business should I start?" or "What business will be most profitable in the coming years?" Such tactics are not likely to work because of the importance of the entrepreneur to the enterprise. The two must fit one another. Any opportunity must be closely examined in light of the background, skills, and interests of the entrepreneur.

Idea Generation

This approach is based on the notion that the key determinant of business success concerns the entrepreneur as an individual. The important thing, therefore, is to identify what the entrepreneur does best. Once that happens, a market test can be conducted to determine whether the idea shaped around that talent appears to hold promise as a viable business.

This is a process with *inside-out* orientation. It involves the use of the knowledge and information that the individual already has as a result of experiences and learning over the years. The difficult part is putting the knowledge and information to use in an effective way. As an example, a Milwaukee couple decided to get into a business of their own. He had a degree in architecture and she had arts and crafts skills from her days as a member of a 4-H club. This package of skills and training pointed them toward an interior design services business, which they established. Sometimes the indications are not so clear-cut. A gentleman in Los Angeles established a company that sells out-of-print records, through direct-mail marketing, to retailers and individuals. The founder, who spent over 20 years in management in the record industry, said he loves records and direct-mail marketing, so it was logical to come up with this concept.

Serendipity

Some ideas for businesses seem to present themselves with no deliberate search by the founder of the business. Some people refer to this as being in the right place at the right time. Included in this category are businesses that develop from a profitable hobby, those started due to the urging of business associates, and those started in response to an unsatisfied consumer need. A public school music teacher who lost her job because of budget cuts decided to set up shop in her van. She parks it next to the schools and the students come to her for their lessons. She likes the arrangement, and so do the parents and students. Her business was triggered by her response to a situation put before her. Another example of an unusual set of circumstances that gave rise to a successful business can be found in the origin of Federal Express, the air-freight company. The company founder, Frederick W. Smith, wrote a paper in an economics class at Yale University in which he proposed a freight distribution system using a central hub (Memphis) with next-day delivery throughout the country. He acted on his idea by starting the business, which reached the billion-dollar sales level faster than any other company.

One final note: business starts are often the direct result of creativity of the entrepreneur. Creativity allows us to identify and develop new and original responses to a familiar set of circumstances. Regardless of whether the business is based on a search of the environment for opportunities, the skills and interests of the individual, or an unanticipated development, creativity is always useful and can be critical. Though wide variations in creativity exist in individuals, creativity can be taught.[1] At least that is the opinion of many of the people who have studied the trait. Here are some of the ways they suggest to enhance the creative process:

- Start with a thorough understanding of the problem.
- Relax; stress inhibits the creative process.
- Generate as many alternatives as possible. The emphasis should be on generation, not evaluation; there will be plenty of time for that later.
- Use ''what if'' questions liberally. Imagining how things would be if certain circumstances were different can provide stepping stones to new ideas.
- Conduct brainstorming sessions. This is an effective way to generate possible solutions because it taps the creative potential of interaction within groups.
- Recognize that everyone both senses and knows. We all have an analytical side and an intuitive side; creativity is best when we use both. It is what some people mean when referring to the right side and the left side of the brain.

The individual who is creative enough to start a business from scratch will find it provides certain advantages relative to the other options of buying an existing business or a franchise. The next section describes those advantages.

Advantages of Starting a Business

Federal Express is an example of a business started from scratch that provided a return of spectacular proportions to its founder. While such returns are extremely rare, they are possible and therefore represent one advantage of creating a new venture. There are others more commonly encountered.

---

[1]For an excellent guide to creativity see Don Koberg and Jim Bagnall, *The Universal Traveler* (Los Altos, California: William Kaufman, Inc., 1976).

Clean Slate.   A small business started from scratch has the advantage of a "clean slate," whereas an existing business or a franchise comes with a history as well as an image held by customers and noncustomers. Not all of a company's past is positive, and not all of the people who have dealt with it in the past are satisfied. A new business has no past mistakes or customer complaints to plague it.

Open Choices.   An additional advantage to starting a new venture is the freedom afforded the entrepreneur in a wide variety of decisions. Location, for example, is part of what the entrepreneur buys when an existing business is purchased. Perhaps the business is in a deteriorating neighborhood or an antibusiness community. These difficulties are easily avoided by someone establishing a business but are often facts of life for an existing business.

Operating Flexibility.   Someone who starts a business can do things as she sees fit. These decisions may not always be sound, but there are no restrictions of the type provided by most corporations that grant franchises. The franchise agreement, as will be explained later, often includes a commitment, by the individual, to operate the business in a manner specified by the corporation. The product line, the operating hours, the materials used, the level of staffing, and the facility layout are examples of decisions made by the organization and not the individual.

The restrictions encountered by someone who purchases an existing business, though not as extensive as those of a franchise operation, can also be troublesome. The layout of the facility may be outmoded and very expensive to change; the operating hours can be changed, but doing so may bring on a negative reaction from customers. Starting a business means more flexibility because nothing has to be undone.

Disadvantages of Starting a Business

With the freedom to make the right choices, however, comes the freedom to make mistakes. The entrepreneur starting a new venture is constantly confronted with decisions for which no clear answers, and often little or no useful data, exist. It may be said that business starts require decisions for which neither all of the alternatives nor any of their consequences may be known. This uncertainty is the major disadvantage faced by the entrepreneur who starts a new venture. It may be seen in the little questions (how should our merchandise be arranged or what type of cash register should we use?) as well as the major (is this business really going to be able to survive?).

For many businesses, establishing relations with vendors is an important, but difficult, matter. A business that is starting small may face price disadvantages and a reluctance on the part of vendors to provide the same level of service as they do to their established accounts.

A final disadvantage, and perhaps the biggest for some businesses, is that of not having name recognition within the community or customer group. In a business such as a restaurant, where prospective customers have a wide variety of choices, not having an established name presents a formidable obstacle. This is one of the major reasons why establishing an independent (not franchised) restaurant has become increasingly difficult.

The uncertainty surrounding the major questions often brings with it a reluctance on the part of bankers, suppliers, and other important people to support the entrepreneur in the venture. Planning a new business is no easy matter, and neither is convincing others, whose support is essential, that nothing will go wrong. Because of these stumbling blocks, many entrepreneurs decide to buy an established business or a franchise. The next two sections will consider these options.

Purchasing an Established Business

For some the urge to create a new business is very strong. They are convinced that it will respond effectively to the needs or desires of enough people to allow it to become a viable business. For others this urge is not so strong, and yet they choose the independence of having their own business. The option chosen by many of these people is the purchase of an existing business. In this section we will examine the advantages and disadvantages of going into business in this way.

Advantages of Buying an Existing Business

There are three basic reasons for buying an ongoing business rather than starting a new one. Less risk is involved; less time and effort are required; and there is a chance to buy the business at a bargain price.

Less Risk.   Even a great deal of preliminary (or preentry) planning will not totally eliminate the risk incurred when a new business is started. Until the doors are opened and the customers arrive, doubts persist; maybe some factor that was overlooked entirely will emerge as an insurmountable barrier. For example, an entrepreneur had planned to start a restaurant across the street from an office and technical facility in which nearly 400 employees of a manufacturer worked. There was no other restaurant in the immediate area, so the entrepreneur reasoned that his lunch trade would provide the core of his business. Shortly before he made the final commitment to construct the building, he learned something that changed the picture entirely. The company allowed only one-half hour for lunch; hence, very few people left the office building to eat their lunch.

Another example of an obscure, but vital, factor concerns the location of a service station. People are much more likely to stop there on their way home from work, so a site on a one-way street that bears the traffic *in* to work will be far less attractive than one that can capture the homebound group.

Many subtle factors are at play when a business is first established. If one of them is sufficiently negative, the entire plan is jeopardized. Ongoing businesses provide far fewer unknowns and, therefore, represent less risk.

Less Time and Effort Required. The established business has developed relationships with groups and individuals on which it depends. Included here are groups such as customers, employees, suppliers, and professionals such as bankers and accountants. Even though the new owner will make changes in these relationships over time, they can remain on a business-as-usual basis until the opportunity for change presents itself.

Other time and effort advantages can be found in the inventory, furniture, layout, and physical facilities areas. All of these require someone's attention. Analyses must be conducted; decisions must be made; plans must be formulated and implemented. The process can take great amounts of time and effort. Once again, the buyer of an existing business can take time in deciding on any changes and simply allow the business to operate in its established way in the meantime.

Chance to Buy at a Bargain Price. Finally, there is the possibility of getting a bargain. The likelihood of this depends on four factors: the owner's financial sophistication, the owner's reason for selling, who is doing the selling, and the method of evaluation used.

Owner's Financial Sophistication. If the owner has little financial expertise or sophistication, a prospective buyer has a chance of discovering an undervalued business. Many owners will, of course, get assistance in determining the price, but some will not, and even those who do may not be given sound advice. A business broker would probably prefer making a sale at a bargain price to not making it at a premium price.

Reasons for Selling. Owners of businesses offer them for sale for a variety of reasons. It may be poor health, retirement to Florida, boredom, or greed. These are obviously just a few of the possible motives for selling, but each may have an important impact on the asking price. An owner whose health is troublesome may unload the business for less than it is worth; someone motivated by greed will not let it go for a dime less than highest possible price.

Determining the real reason for selling the business is difficult but obviously important. The best piece of advice may be *caveat emptor,* or let the buyer beware. No prospective buyer should make the assumption that the information given is the whole truth and nothing but the truth. A seller whose business is being threatened may somehow keep from lying but can hardly be expected to disclose everything. There is no substitute for a thorough investigation. The buyer must talk with customers, suppliers, employees, and competitors, must examine the business's records carefully, and must read as much about the market and industry as can be found. Though these efforts do not ensure against a mistake, they make one far less likely.

The Person Doing the Selling.   Buying a business from its founder can be a difficult experience. Most people who start and develop a business have a considerable emotional investment in it. The business has often cost them through the years in such things as family relations, leisure pursuits, and personal health. Selling is a major step, perhaps the biggest single move of a lifetime to these people. The chances of getting a bargain are not good, unless the owner sees in the prospective buyer those qualities the business needs. (These, of course, closely match the entrepreneur's own qualities.) Though this happy coincidence is always possible, dealing with the company founder typically brings difficulties.

In contrast, the family of a deceased company founder may be very cooperative and easy to negotiate with. Often, the family's chief concern is to get rid of the business while it still has its vitality. Such a set of circumstances is favorable for a prospective buyer.

Various Methods of Evaluation.   The prospective buyer must determine the value of the business as the first step in arriving at a bidding price. This process is inexact and takes on many forms, but there are two basic considerations that should be included: the value of the business's assets and its future earnings.

With the purchase of a business, the purchaser gets its assets. The value of these assets can be calculated in at least four ways. First, we can use the company's records; specifically, we would use the balance sheet to determine the **book value** of the assets. This figure is the price the company paid minus the depreciation that has occurred. Next, we can determine how much it would cost to replace the asset. This **replacement value** approach tells us whether it would be cheaper to buy the assets needed to start a business rather than buy an ongoing business that has those assets. Third, there is an approach that considers the **liquidation value** of the assets. This is the safest approach in arriving at a price to bid because it represents the amount the assets would bring if they were sold at auction.

Finally, there is the **appraised value.** This is the value of an asset according to someone who understands the supply of, and demand for, the item. Because this price takes into account both the seller's side and the buyer's, it typically is somewhere between the replacement value (which can be above the original price due to inflationary pressures) and the liquidation value.

To illustrate the differences between the four methods, we will use the purchase of a small automobile rental agency. Company accounting records show the book value of the cars to be $30,000 (five cars, each worth $6,000). The cars are each 2 years old, and since they have a useful life of 4 years, they are each worth one-half of their original cost of $12,000.

To replace the fleet of cars, we find we will have to spend $8,000 each. The replacement value of the assets, then, is $40,000.

As the next part of our investigation, we determine the liquidation value. If we decided after buying the business that it was a mistake and that we have

Book Value
The balance sheet figure for assets, which gives the price paid for them minus depreciation.

Replacement Value
The cost of buying new or equivalent items to replace existing assets.

Liquidation Value
The value of assets if they were sold at auction.

Appraised Value
The value of an asset according to an objective assessment from someone familiar with the market.

to sell out for whatever we can get, we would find the lowest price prevails. Each car is worth only $5,000, so the assets would bring only $25,000.

Finally, the appraised value is used, which in this case is $7,000 per car, giving a total of $35,000.

Which of the four is best? It is seldom the book value; this is an accounting entry and only rarely matches actual value. The replacement value is useful for the prospective buyer who has decided definitely to go into the business being considered. It is necessary to buy the business with its assets, or find them elsewhere. The liquidation value provides the best data for a "worst case" scenario. That is, an entrepreneur can take some comfort in being able to salvage this amount from the business if everything turns sour. Of course, the liquidation value figure changes, so the $25,000 figure in our example will decrease steadily over time. The appraised value is the most useful figure in negotiations between a buyer and seller who are both knowledgeable and interested in completing the deal.

The purchase of a business is usually more than the acquisition of a collection of assets. A business is capable of generating future profits. Consequently, another measure of the value of a business is its expected flow of future earnings. If it were possible to determine this flow with precision and certainty, we would have no problem setting the price for the business. The process that would be used is called **discounting future cash flows,** and it simply means we discount the value of future earnings according to a formula or table, because money to be earned in future years is not worth as much as what we are earning currently. For example, sixty-two cents invested at 10 percent interest will be worth one dollar in 5 years, so earnings of $20,000 projected for the fifth year after purchase of a company must be discounted to $12,400 ($20,000 × 0.62). Year 4 income of $20,000, also discounted by the 10 percent interest factor, is worth more, $13,600, because we will not have to wait as long to receive it.

Discounted Cash Flow The present value of future earnings, discounted by interest rates.

The reason we cannot make the valuation a strictly computational process like that just described is that we really do not know what the business's future earnings will be. We can, and do, use its past earnings record as an indication of future prospects, but it is only that, an indication. Changes in the environment, the industry, the market, or the company will affect the levels of future profitability. Consequently, the determination of value based on future profits, though very useful, requires more than computation. It requires that judgment be used, that assumptions be made, and that resulting figures be used with caution and in conjunction with figures determined by other methods of valuation.

There is one additional consideration in determining the value of an existing business, and it is often subject to wide disagreement between buyers and sellers. It is called goodwill, the intangible but important quality of those companies that have created for themselves a positive image in the eyes of customers and others. There is no question that the goodwill of customers is valuable to a business; the question is *how* valuable. Most businesses list it

Illustration Capsule   3.1

Determining the Price of a Business

- **Step 1** Determine the adjusted tangible net worth of the business. This is the total value of the firm's assets, using the appraised value, minus its debts. For our car rental firm, which has $5,000 in debts, this is $35,000 − $5,000 or **$30,000.**

- **Step 2** Estimate how much the buyer could earn annually with an amount equal to the value of the tangible net worth (from step 1), invested elsewhere at a level of risk similar to that of the business being considered. In addition to risk, this figure will reflect the current rate of interest. Let's use 10 percent here; that gives us **$3,000.**

- **Step 3** Add the normal salary for the owner-operator. That is, the income that the individual could be expected to earn elsewhere. We will estimate **$20,000.**

- **Step 4** Determine the average annual net earnings of the business over the past few years. This figure is before income taxes and the owner's salary have been subtracted. Our real interest is in the likely level of earnings for the next few years, so trends in past earnings are important. The car rental firm averaged annual net earnings of **$30,000.**

- **Step 5** Subtract the buyer's investment's earning power (step 2) and the owner-operator salary (step 3) from the business's average annual net earnings (step 4). This is the extra earning power of the business ($30,000 − $3,000 − $20,000), **$7,000.**

- **Step 6** Multiply the extra earning power by what is called the "years of profit" figure. This years of profit figure is intended to reflect the "uniqueness" of the business. How difficult and risky would it be to establish such a business? How long would it take to do so? How much goodwill has the business established? A well-established business might warrant using a 5 here; a company that has just started might suggest a 1. Here we will use a 2, giving us, for intangibles, **$14,000.**

- **Step 7** To arrive at the final price, we add the firm's adjusted tangible net worth and the value of its intangibles (steps 1 and 6). This gives us $30,000 and $14,000 for a total price of **$44,000.**

Source: Adapted with permission from Bank of America, NT&SA, "How to Buy or Sell a Business," *Small Business Reporter,* copyright 1969, 1982.

as an asset—an intangible asset, but an asset nonetheless. It is recognized as such because the business is more valuable as a result of what this positive view of customers bodes for its future earnings.

We have described the two basic considerations, assets and earnings, used in arriving at the price of a business. Illustration Capsule 3.1 demonstrates one method that takes into account both of these factors.

In summary, existing businesses offer less risk, savings in time and effort needed to start, and the possibility of buying a business for less than it is worth. Existing businesses do provide some disadvantages, however, and in our next section we will explore these.

Disadvantages of Buying an Existing Business

No business is entirely without problems. Businesses that are on the market, however, usually have more problems than those not up for sale, and these problems tend to be more troublesome. It is useful to think of these problems as either external or internal in nature.

External.   These difficulties can be due to a market too small to support the business. For example, for a Karate studio to succeed it must have as its market a community of considerably larger size than that needed for a hardware store. Exhibit 3.1 gives the population needed to provide an adequate customer base for various types of businesses.

Another external difficulty concerns the competition. If the competitors are strong and/or numerous, a business may be doomed to failure or to a marginal existence. The prospective buyer should ask the following: Who are my competitors? How do they compete on price? on quality? on service? Are there any new, aggressive competitors on the scene? Are any of the competitors backed by a large organization intent on gaining market share?

The final external consideration is the state of the economy of the market that the business serves. Communities that are large enough to support a certain type of business and that have only modest competition in that market may nonetheless be poor prospects because of their depressed economy.

Internal.   These are problems unique to the business. Location is one example. Anyone who buys an existing business in retailing must consider whether its location is prime and is likely to stay that way. The opening of a new highway or a new shopping mall can bring catastrophic results to a previously stable central city location.

The business' employee group may represent a disadvantage of buying a business. While the new owner can, of course, make changes, these changes are likely to be costly. Furthermore, if the company is unionized, any needed personnel action may be difficult to effect.

A final potential disadvantage concerns the business's image or reputation. This may be the most difficult to deal with because of the long memories of some customers. Winning back a customer can be a long and uncertain under-

Exhibit   3.1   Estimated Population Needed to Support Business Ventures

Kind of Business	Number of Inhabitants per Store	Kind of Business	Number of Inhabitants per Store
Food Stores		*Building Material, Hardware, and Farm Equipment Dealers*	
Grocery stores	1,534	Lumber and other building materials	
Meat and fish (seafood) markets	17,876	dealers	8,124
Candy, nut, and confectionery stores	31,409	Paint, glass, and wallpaper stores	22,454
Retail bakeries	12,563	Hardware stores	10,206
Dairy product stores	41,587	Farm equipment dealers	14,793
Eating, Drinking Places		*Automotive Dealers*	
Restaurants, lunchrooms, caterers	1,583	Motor vehicle dealers— new and used cars	6,000
Cafeterias	19,341	Motor vehicle dealers— used cars only	17,160
Refreshment places	3,622	Tire, battery, and accessory dealers	8,864
Drinking places (alcoholic beverages)	2,414	*Boat Dealers*	61,526
General Merchandise		*Household Trailer Dealers*	44,746
Variety stores	10,373	*Gasoline Service Stations*	1,195
General merchandise stores	9,837	*Miscellaneous*	
Apparel and Accessory Stores		Antique and secondhand stores	17,169
Women's ready-to-wear stores	7,102	Book and stationery stores	28,584
Women's accessory and specialty stores	25,824	Drugstores	4,268
Men's and boys' clothing and furnishing stores	11,832	Florists	13,531
Family clothing stores	16,890	Fuel oil dealers	25,425
Shoe stores	9,350	Garden supply stores	65,118
Furniture, Home Furnishings, and Equipment Stores		Gift, novelty, and souvenir shops	26,313
Furniture stores	7,210	Hay, grain, and feed stores	16,978
Floor covering stores	29,543	Hobby, toy, and game shops	61,430
Drapery, curtain, and upholstery stores	62,460	Jewelry stores	13,495
Household appliance stores	12,585	Liquified petroleum gas (bottled gas) dealers	32,803
Radio and television stores	20,346	Liquor stores	6,359
Record shops	112,144	Mail order houses	44,554
Musical instrument stores	46,332	Merchandising machine operators	44,067
		Optical goods stores	62,878
		Sporting goods stores	27,063

Source: Starting and Managing a Small Business of Your Own (Washington, D.C.: Small Business Administration, 1973).

taking. Businesses are often sold because of a reservoir of ill will that has built up over time. This ill will suggests that a fresh start may be preferable.

Franchising

Franchising
A continuous relationship in which the franchisor provides a licensed privilege to do business, plus assistance in organizing, training, merchandising, and managing in return for consideration from the franchisee.

The third and final route into business is **franchising.** Franchising is an arrangement by which the owner of a product, process, or service allows others to distribute the product. The owner is the franchisor; the distributor is the franchisee. The word can be traced to its original French meaning, "to be free from servitude." The first important use of franchising was in the automobile industry at the turn of the century, when the manufacturers (the franchisors) established their networks of dealers (the franchisees).

Franchising has become an increasingly popular means of going into business. Consider the following remark made in the U.S. House of Representatives: "The concept of modern franchising, particularly in its evolution since the late 1960s, has opened a remarkable door of opportunity for many of our country's prospective small businessmen." Retail franchising sales for 1982 were $339 billion, or nearly one-third of all U.S. retail sales. There are approximately 500,000 franchised business establishments in the United States.[2]

Types of Franchises

Product/Trade Name Franchising
Product distribution arrangements in which the franchisee is, to some degree, identified with a manufacturer's supplies.

Business Format Franchising
Franchising in which the franchisor establishes a fully integrated relationship that includes product, service, trademark, marketing strategy and plan, operating manuals and standards, quality control, and feedback procedures.

There are two types of franchising arrangements: product/trade name and business format. Within **product/trade name franchising,** three industries predominate. Automobile/truck dealerships, gasoline service stations, and soft drink bottlers accounted for 76 percent of all franchise sales during 1982.

The **business format franchise** takes on many different forms, ranging from muffler shops to real estate offices to restaurants and hotels. Using this arrangement, the franchisor usually establishes and maintains close touch with the franchisee with regard to marketing, operations, quality control, and reporting procedures.

Franchising versus Starting an Independent Business

Franchising as a way into business offers certain advantages in comparison with starting an independent business. These advantages may be categorized into those that are most relevant during start-up and those that benefit ongoing operations.

---

[2]U.S. Department of Commerce, *Franchise Opportunities Handbook* (Washington, D.C.: Government Printing Office, 1983).

Source: Reprinted by permission: Tribune Media Services.

Start-up.   Many services are provided that make the franchisee's job of getting the business started much easier. These services include site selection and facilities layout analysis; financial assistance (both directly from the franchisor and indirectly with other money sources more likely to agree to participate in financing the business); management training; and employee selection and training assistance.

In addition to these services provided by the franchisor, the franchising option provides a ready-made basis for judging profit prospects. The process by which the future profitability of a business is determined is difficult and uncertain. Whenever a new business is started, no one can say for certain how it will turn out. With a franchise purchase, however, the process is made much easier because a "Burger World" in Davenport is likely to fare about as well as the Burger Worlds in Des Moines and Dubuque. The franchise buyer cannot be certain of this, but the experiences of sister franchise outlets provide a sound basis for comparison.

A final start-up advantage concerns the instant recognition that comes from buying a franchise from an established nationwide chain. The lean early years that cause many businesses to fail are far less troublesome for the franchised outlet than for the independent business.

Ongoing Operations.   Continuing guidance is provided by many franchisors to safeguard quality and to maintain high levels of efficiency. Marketing benefits are also available through national and cooperative local advertising and promotion campaigns.

While franchising provides some very important advantages, it also means the entrepreneur will face some restrictions that an independent business would not present. These restrictions, or limitations, must be weighed against the advantages that a franchise brings.

Limitations Encountered in Franchising.   A person who starts a business often does so in the belief that a better way can be found. This "better way" is often simply a different way and, as such, has no place in the highly controlled system developed by many franchisors. The best example of this kind of regimentation is that of the McDonald's restaurant organization. The franchisee is not given free rein; indeed, the operations manual specifies even such minute details as when to oil the bearings on the potato slicer. The purpose of these regulations is to ensure that each outlet is run in a uniform, correct way.

This restriction on the owner's method of operating the business usually extends to the items included in the product or service line. It may be in the interest of a Ford dealer to expand the line to include a Japanese make of cars, but the contract may not permit it. This precludes the owner from shopping for bargains in the usual manner.

Financial costs represent another limitation. Franchises cost money, sometimes large amounts of money. Beyond the original cost of the franchise, profits are usually shared with the franchisor, and other fees (for advertising, management advisory services, etc.) are often required budget items.

A final limitation is the prospect of the company arbitrarily canceling the franchise. Although many states have franchise termination statutes, franchises in states without these laws can be vulnerable to such tactics. The oil shortage of the early 1970s, for example, prompted oil companies to cancel the franchise of many service stations.

In summary, the choice between going into business as the owner of a franchise or as an independent can be difficult. Many factors must be considered. The next section will provide an approach for considering these factors.

Evaluation of the Franchise Option

To determine whether franchising should be chosen as the route by which to go into business, a number of preliminary questions must be examined.

The first question a person must explore is personal: Does he have the qualities necessary to succeed as a franchisee? These qualities are a bit different from those of the typical entrepreneur as described in Chapter 2. The franchisee must be able to accept restrictions with which many entrepreneurs would have difficulty. The franchisee must be able to maintain extremely high levels of conformity of operations with the franchisor's procedures and standards. This appears to require more of a structured type of managing than the creative, innovative style of many entrepreneurs. We are not characterizing the franchisee as a docile yes man but rather as one who understands and accepts the legitimacy of close, detailed franchisor requirements. Not all prospective entrepreneurs do.

After settling the personality issue, we can turn our attention to the kinds of franchises available and to those that appear to be most promising. The 1983 *Franchise Opportunities Handbook* lists franchise opportunities.[3] The list comprises the following 40 categories. (Following the category title is the number of entries listed.)

---

[3] U.S. Department of Commerce, *Franchise Opportunities Handbook*.

Automotive Products/Service	89
Auto/Trailer Rentals	17
Beauty Salons/Supplies	19
Business Aids/Services	123
Campgrounds	4
Children's Stores/Furniture/Products	2
Clothing/Shoes	15
Construction/Remodeling Materials/Services	36
Cosmetics/Toiletries	7
Dental Centers	6
Drug Stores	6
Educational Products/Services	22
Employment Services	52
Equipment/Rentals	9
Food—Donuts	14
Foods—Grocer/Specialty/Stores	48
Foods—Ice Cream/Yogurt/Candy/Popcorn/Beverages	33
Food—Pancake/Waffle/Pretzel	7
Foods—Restaurant/Drive-Ins/Carry-Outs	261
General Merchandising Stores	3
Health Aids/Services	33
Hearing Aids	1
Home Furnishings/Furniture Retail/Repair/Services	38
Insurance	7
Laundries/Dry Cleaning Services	9
Lawn and Garden Supplies/Services	9
Maintenance/Cleaning/Sanitation Services/Supplies	41
Motels, Hotels	19
Optical Products/Services	5
Paint and Decorating Supplies	6
Printing	16
Real Estate	30
Recreation/Entertainment/Travel Services/Supplies	23
Retailing—Not Elsewhere Classified	84
Security Systems	5
Swimming Pools	4
Tools, Hardware	4
Vending	5
Water Conditioning	6
Miscellaneous Wholesale/Service Business	26

Future franchising opportunities will develop in a wide variety of industries. *Venture* magazine identified the following areas as showing promising growth in franchising:[4]

1. Personal computer stores

2. Real estate

---

[4]"The Newest Franchises Growth." *Venture*, November 1980, 56.

Small Business Success 3

Florida Food Industries, Winter Park, Florida

Cajun "dirty rice" and chicken livers augment the spicy fried chicken on the Popeyes' Famous Fried Chicken menu. L. David Horner, a banker with 20 years experience, had just been named president of Orlando's Southeast National Bank when he resigned to become an entrepreneur in 1976. He liked Popeyes' varied menu and the latitude the franchise allowed for creative marketing. In late 1977 he opened his first Popeyes in a converted Amoco station in Winter Park. He emphasized using fresh products and cooking to order and offered incentives to his employees: cash awards, training programs, and opportunities for advancement. New franchises were added, each with its own motif; one in Daytona Beach reflected Horner's love of the sea, with aquariums for wall dividers and a small museum of Florida treasure. Horner now owns 22 stores employing 800, and sales have increased from $107,000 in 1977 to $18 million in 1985. In 1982, *Inc.* magazine rated the company the fourth fastest growing firm in the nation, and readers of the *Orlando Sentinel* have named Florida Food Industries the best fried chicken restaurants in Orlando for three years running.

Source: Small Business Means Jobs (Washington, D.C.: S.B.A., 1984).

3.   Sporting goods stores

4.   Hair salons

5.   Video-related sales and service

6.   Energy-related stores or products

7.   Health food snacks

We have examined the personal qualities needed to run a franchised operation; we have identified the franchise opportunities available; and we have named some that provide unusual promise. Now we will explore the means by which the franchise itself may be evaluated.

Any evaluation must include a comparison of the franchise with one or more competing franchises. If you are interested in a particular ''Business Aids/Services'' franchise, compare it with some of the other 122 franchises

Exhibit   3.2   Checklist for Evaluating a Franchise

The Franchise

1. Did your lawyer approve the franchise contract you are considering after he studied it paragraph by paragraph?

2. Does the franchise call on you to take any steps that are, according to your lawyer, unwise or illegal in your state, county, or city?

3. Does the franchise give you an exclusive territory for the length of the franchise or can the franchisor sell a second or third franchise in your territory?

4. Is the franchisor connected in any way with any other franchise company handling similar merchandise or services?

5. If the answer to the last question is yes, what is your protection against this second franchisor organization?

6. Under what circumstances can you terminate the franchise contract and at what cost to you, if you decide for any reason at all that you wish to cancel it?

7. If you sell your franchise, will you be compensated for your goodwill or will the goodwill you have built into the business be lost by you?

The Franchisor

8. How many years has the firm offering you a franchise been in operation?

9. Has it a reputation for honesty and fair dealing among the local firms holding its franchise?

10. Has the franchisor shown you any certified figures indicating exact net profits of one or more going firms that you personally checked yourself with the franchisee?

11. Will the firm assist you with
    a.   A management training program?
    b.   An employee training program?
    c.   A public relations program?
    d.   Capital?
    e.   Credit?
    f.   Merchandising ideas?

12. Will the firm help you find a good location for your new business?

13. Is the franchising firm adequately financed so that it can carry out its stated plan of financial assistance and expansion?

Source: Franchise Opportunities Handbook (Washington, D.C.: U.S. Government Printing Office, 1982).

14. Is the franchisor a one-person company or a corporation with an experienced management trained in depth (so that there would always be an experienced person at its head)?

15. Exactly what can the franchisor do for you that you cannot do for yourself?

16. Has the franchisor investigated you carefully enough to assure itself that you can successfully operate one of their franchises at a profit both to them and to you?

17. Does your state have a law regulating the sale of franchises, and has the franchisor complied with that law?

You—The Franchisee

18. How much equity capital will you have to have to purchase the franchise and operate it until your income equals your expenses? Where are you going to get it?

19. Are you prepared to give up some independence of action to secure the advantages offered by the franchise?

20. Do you really believe you have the innate ability, training, and experience to work smoothly and profitably with the franchisor, your employees, and your customers?

21. Are you ready to spend much or all of the remainder of your business life with this franchisor, offering his product or service to your public?

Your Market

22. Have you made any study to determine whether the product or service that you propose to sell under franchise has a market in your territory at the prices you will have to charge?

23. Will the population in the territory given to you increase, remain static, or decrease over the next 5 years?

24. Will the product or service you are considering be in greater demand, about the same, or less demand 5 years from now than today?

25. What competition exists in your territory already for the product or service you contemplate selling?
    a.   Nonfranchise firms?
    b.   Franchise firms?

listed in the *Franchise Opportunities Handbook*.[5] Want a Cosmetics/Toiletries franchise? There are seven to choose from; compare one with another for such things as price, terms, and assistance provided.

Examination of the franchisor's disclosure statement (sometimes called a "prospectus") is an important part of the evaluation. The disclosure statement is required by the Federal Trade Commission and must be provided by the franchisor. It contains detailed information on 20 subjects, each of which may have an important bearing on the desirability of a franchise. Among the topics covered in this document are the backgrounds of the franchisor's officers, directors, and managers; bankruptcies in which the franchisor has been involved; obligations and restrictions faced by the franchisee; training provided to franchisees; financial statements of the franchisor; and a list of names and addresses of other franchisees.

Another part of the evaluation concerns your legal rights as a prospective franchisee. The Federal Trade Commission provides for

1. The right to receive the disclosure statement and documentation for any earnings claims, both at least 10 business days before signing any agreement or paying any money.

2. The right to receive sample copies of the standard franchise and related agreements at least 5 business days before signing. (This period, like that specified in item 1, is a minimum; most entrepreneurs will need more time to examine the copies.)

3. The right to receive any refunds promised by the franchisor.

4. The right not to be misled by the franchisor.

The United States Department of Commerce has issued a useful set of guidelines for the prospective franchisee. Exhibit 3.2 presents these guidelines.

Most franchisors are genuinely interested in seeing franchisees succeed, but before anyone agrees to the purchase of a franchise, the questions included in Exhibit 3.2 must be answered. To do less is to invite failure and disappointment.

K E Y   Objectives Reviewed

1. New businesses are started in three ways: through the outside-in approach called *opportunity recognition,* through the inside-out approach called *idea generation,* and through an unplanned set of circumstances, which we call *serendipity.*

---

[5]U.S. Department of Commerce, *Franchise Opportunities.*

2. Purchasing an existing business typically means less risk and requires less time and effort than starting a new business. It also provides the chance to buy the business at a favorable price. The evaluation of an existing business includes two basic considerations, the value of the business' assets and its future earnings.

3. Franchising provides another means of becoming a small business owner. It provides some important advantages in the start-up of the business as well as during operations. With this reduction in risk, however, come certain restrictions imposed on the entrepreneur.

4. Starting a new business provides the advantages of a clean slate and flexibility as to operations. The disadvantages can be seen primarily in the uncertainty surrounding any business start and lack of name recognition among customers. Purchasing an existing business reduces the risk level and the time and effort needed to get started. In addition there is a chance of buying a business at a bargain price. The disadvantages of buying a business can be external, with competitor or market problems as examples, or internal, with things such as poor facilities or unproductive employees. Franchising brings the advantages of wide name recognition and a proven method of operation; its disadvantages are primarily financial with original costs and ongoing charges often being substantial.

Discussion Questions

1. What are the processes by which new businesses are started?

2. What factors determine whether an existing business can be purchased at a bargain price?

3. Why is it difficult to establish a price for a business?

4. Summarize the advantages and limitations of starting a business by purchasing a franchise.

5. Why does the operation of a franchise require a different type of management than does an independent business?

6. Why is the opportunity recognition method of starting a business referred to as the outside-in approach? Why is the idea generation approach called inside-out?

Cases for Part One

Presnell Industries

Sharon Rawls had worked in her father's wholesale furniture store in Tiffin, Ohio since the age of ten. She had grown up with the furniture industry as a part of her life and had always dreamed of owning her own business in the industry.

On graduating from college with her degree in business administration, Sharon wanted to run her own business rather than accept a job with a major corporation. When speaking to a supplier, she was informed of a furniture manufacturing firm, Presnell Industries (also located in Tiffin) that was for sale. The current owner had several businesses and was not able to devote adequate time to the manufacturing firm. Because of this, the company had not been profitable, and the owner was willing to sell.

Sharon contacted the owner and arranged a meeting to discuss a possible buy-out. The owner provided financial statements and a list of existing customers. Although sales had increased every year, profits were consistently poor. A summary of the financial information is shown below.

	Sales	Profit
1985	$900,000	($42,000)
1984	890,000	13,000
1983	817,000	(14,000)
1982	734,000	(52,500)

The assets of the company were as follows:

Factory building	$316,000	(appraised value)
Factory equipment	135,000	(appraised value)
Accounts receivable	105,000	(actual amount owed by customers)
Inventory	45,000	(valued at cost)
Furniture	15,000	(book value)
Truck	10,000	(book value)

The company currently owed $325,000 to banks, suppliers, etc. The owner informed Sharon that he would want her to assume these liabilities if she bought the business. (She would be responsible for paying them as they become due; they would not all have to be paid immediately.) A few payments to banks and suppliers were late, but most had been paid on time.

Presnell Industries employed thirty people and was well known for producing quality furniture. To most people, Presnell appeared to be a very successful small business. Its customers (wholesale furniture stores) were pleased with the quality, quick delivery, and friendly service Presnell offered. The company had developed a good name, and sales volume was expected to continue to increase.

Sharon took the financial information and informed the owner that she would contact him to discuss the sale after she had closely analyzed the company. When Sharon reviewed the company operations further, it was obvious that a substantial amount of money could be saved if a few changes were made. Presnell's manufacturing facility (building and machinery) was located in one building in Tiffin, but office space was leased in Columbus, Ohio because the owner's other businesses were there. This not only resulted in such things as increased rent, utilities, and insurance, but also required substantial travel and delivery expense between the office and the plant. Because there was adequate space within the manufacturing facility for the office, Sharon determined that eliminating the Columbus office and related expenses could save $30,000. With several other changes, she felt the company could generate profits as follows:

1986	$8,000
1987	20,000
1988	35,000

Although Sharon felt confident that the business could become profitable, several people advised her not to buy the business because of the substantial losses it had incurred. If the changes Sharon had planned did not succeed in reducing expenses, she would be the new owner of a financially troubled company. If the business failed, she would ruin her credit rating and lose the money she had planned to invest. Then, at a very young age, she might have to declare bankruptcy.

Sharon's uncle, who also owned a business, advised her not to buy the manufacturing plant because of her lack of experience in manufacturing. Although she knew the wholesale furniture industry well, he stated, she did not know anything about manufacturing processes or costs and had no mechanical or engineering background to make decisions concerning machinery.

Sharon felt that the business needed a good manager, not a good engineer, and contacted the owner to inquire about his selling price. The owner insisted that the business only lost money because he did not have time to manage it properly. The assets, he argued, were worth a total of $626,000 and were in excellent condition. Therefore, he felt the business was worth a great deal of money, although he had not set a specific price.

Sharon was not sure if she should consider buying the business without looking at other companies that were for sale and their selling prices in order to make a knowledgeable judgment of the value of Presnell Industries. The owner of Presnell had indicated that several other people were considering buying the business, and he could not guarantee that the business would still be available if she took too long to decide. Therefore, Sharon was concerned that if she did not make a quick decision, someone else might buy the company.

Questions

1. Considering the large losses the company has shown for the past several years, do you think Sharon should consider purchasing the company?

2. Do you agree with Sharon's uncle concerning her lack of experience in the manufacturing industry?

3. Should Sharon buy Presnell Industries without looking at other companies available for sale?

4. What do you feel is a reasonable purchase price for this company?

Case IB   The Bushnell Empire

By the time Nolan Bushnell was 35 years old he had founded several companies, including Atari and Chuck E. Cheese Pizza Time Theatres, and had become a millionaire. Described as Silicon Valley's "boyish genius," Bushnell mixed technology and fantasy to create his companies, and people believed he could do nothing wrong.

Nolan Bushnell began his life in a very ordinary way as the son of a religious, middle-class family in the Great Salt Lake area. He later moved to California with his wife and children and was employed as an electronics engineer. His normal life ended, however, in the early 1970s, when his first business, Atari, began its rapid growth. At that point Bushnell also changed his home life, leaving his wife and children, flying around the country in his Lear jet, and sailing on his yacht. By the late 1970s, Bushnell was both very famous and very wealthy.

Source: Steve Coll, "When the Magic Goes," *Inc.*, October 1984, 83–97.

Atari

· ·

Bushnell's first business, Atari, began with his invention of the Pong game, one of the first video games available to consumers. Although Pong was a very simple video tennis game, it was so successful that it served as the springboard for Atari's development of more advanced video games. By 1976, only a few years after the company was founded, Warner Communications purchased Atari from Bushnell for $28 million.

Bushnell continued to serve as director of Atari. He had always maintained an easygoing management style. Employees came to work at all hours of the day, dressed in blue jeans and T-shirts. Brainstorming sessions to develop new ideas were often held at vacation resorts by the ocean. This unique management was often viewed as the reason for the highly creative ideas that resulted.

By 1977, though, the company was growing at a phenomenal rate, and Bushnell found it difficult to control. He had never been a good manager, but as long as Atari was profitable, few people questioned his style. By the late 1970s, however, this began to change. A new product line introduced in 1977 did not sell as well as had been expected. This left Atari with excess inventory and lower profits. Warner Communications and Bushnell began to argue over strategies. Eventually, Bushnell resigned his position as director and began to devote his attention to another of his ventures—Chuck E. Cheese Pizza Time Theatres.

Chuck E. Cheese Pizza Time Theatres

· ·

The first Chuck E. Cheese Pizza Time Theatre opened in May 1977 as part of Atari. Pizza parlor/theatre combinations were first started as part of Atari & Warner Communications, but growth was not as good as expected. After 18 months of operation only six restaurants existed.

When Bushnell resigned his directorship of Atari in 1978, he purchased the rights to Chuck E. Cheese Pizza Time Theatres and began to devote all of his time and energy to the company. The theatres combined video game machines, mechanical animals that performed shows on a stage, and a pizza parlor. As the market for video games grew, so did the sales and profits of Chuck E. Cheese.

Within two years after Bushnell began to devote his time to the company, the number of restaurants increased, and franchises became available for sale. By 1980, 88 theatres existed, and by 1982, there were 204 theatres in 35 states and three foreign countries. Once Chuck E. Cheese seemed to be operating successfully, Bushnell needed a new challenge. The pizza theatres no

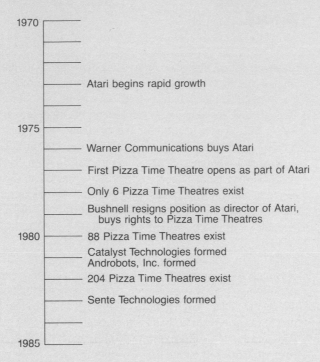

1970

Atari begins rapid growth

1975

Warner Communications buys Atari

First Pizza Time Theatre opens as part of Atari

Only 6 Pizza Time Theatres exist

Bushnell resigns position as director of Atari,
   buys rights to Pizza Time Theatres

1980   88 Pizza Time Theatres exist

Catalyst Technologies formed
Androbots, Inc. formed

204 Pizza Time Theatres exist

Sente Technologies formed

1985

longer seemed to need his full-time attention, so he hired a manager and devoted his energies to two new ventures—Catalyst Technologies and Andro-bot Inc.

Catalyst Technologies

Bushnell had never planned to have only one company. Long-range goals included many companies, and investors were willing to give Bushnell money for them because of his track record of success. Therefore, Bushnell began to develop a company, Catalyst Technologies, that would help new businesses get started. Catalyst Technologies would provide money, business plans, office space, accounting, and other services to new businesses. Then, when the business was established, Catalyst Technologies would provide more money needed for growth.

This was considered one of the most innovative ideas in Silicon Valley. In late 1981, Catalyst Technologies was started; another of Bushnell's companies, Androbot Inc., was its first sponsored company. By early 1982, Catalyst Technologies was sponsoring several businesses.

Androbot Inc.

At the same time he was developing Catalyst Technologies, Bushnell began to consider a business that would design, produce, and sell robots. Bushnell developed the company, lined up investors for $1 million, and began to pay engineers to develop the robots. The robots were to be "personal robots" that would be used in homes to perform such duties as household chores and fetching snacks. The selling price was to be about $2,000. In 1983, a sample robot taken to a trade show was the hit of the show. Bushnell, convinced that Androbot could be as successful as Atari or Chuck E. Cheese, instructed his engineers to develop ten different robots within the next year. The engineers and managers felt this would be an impossible task, so a compromise of four robots eventually resulted.

Sente Technologies

As Androbot Inc. appeared headed for success, Bushnell began to develop another business based on video games. When he had sold Atari to Warner Communications, he had agreed not to produce and sell video games for seven years. By October 1983, the seven years would be over, and Bushnell planned to reenter the video game market. To accomplish this, Bushnell purchased the assets of a video game software company, using them to establish a company named Sente Technologies.

Sente Technologies would be able to design video games and sell them to all of the Pizza Time Theatres. In addition, Bushnell planned to lease the video game machines and games to distributors and retailers.

Visions of an Empire

With the formation of Sente Technologies, Bushnell had the beginning of an empire. His businesses would all be interrelated, based on a combination of high technology and fantasy. In addition to the sales of Sente's video games to Chuck E. Cheese parlors, Bushnell dreamed of Androbot's robots waiting on the customers at the tables. Silicon Valley's "boyish genius" appeared to have a magic touch.

Questions

1. In what way is Nolan Bushnell a "typical entrepreneur"? What personality characteristics does he have that are typical of successful entrepreneurs?

2. What are Bushnell's strengths? Weaknesses?

3. What are the advantages of owning several interrelated companies (companies that buy and sell products to each other)? What are the disadvantages?

4. What was the major reason for the rapid success of the Pizza Time Theatres?

Case IC   The Path to Entrepreneurship

Eni Liu

. . . .

Eni Liu, the owner of Celestial Restaurant in St. Louis, did not grow up dreaming of her own restaurant. Originally from Taiwan, she began a career there as a journalist. In 1977, she came to the United States to obtain a doctorate in speech communications with the intention of returning to Taiwan to continue her career.

Meanwhile, however, her parents in Taiwan were playing matchmakers, arranging for her to meet a man named Paul Liu. Paul had moved to St. Louis to work as a chemical engineer with Monsanto Chemical Company. Eni and Paul eventually met and, after a short romance, became engaged. Eni moved to St. Louis and enrolled at the University of Missouri to study accounting, realizing that accounting positions usually paid more than those for speech communication majors. After graduation, Eni accepted a job with Ralston Purina.

In 1982, Paul and Eni became part of a partnership and opened Celestial Restaurant. The partners did not get along, though, and by January 1983, the partnership no longer existed. Eni, then 27 years old, resigned her job at Ralston Purina and took over as sole owner of Celestial Restaurant. The large restaurant maintains a modern atmosphere but serves gourmet Chinese food from five Chinese provinces: Peking, Hunan, Szechuan, Canton, and Shanghai. The management of this restaurant was not an easy task. There are few female bosses in Chinese restaurants, and several chefs refused to listen to her directions. Problems with chefs caused profits to be low, but Eni persisted. Eventually, a good chef was hired, and after several other changes, the restaurant became profitable.

———
Source: Kathleen Flood, "Restaurant Women," *St. Louis Dining* (St. Louis, Missouri: Portofino Publications, Inc., 1985), 12–15.

Eni's diversified background is a benefit in running the restaurant. Because of her accounting training, she is able to handle all the financial aspects of the business as well as manage the kitchen and seven employees. She also serves as hostess and can serve as cook if necessary.

Often referred to as the "Boss Lady," Eni ensures that her employees follow her directions and leaves no doubt that she is in charge. She will, however, do everything possible to help her employees, many of whom are recent immigrants. If necessary, she takes them to the hospital or to get a marriage license and helps them to learn the English language and American customs. Serving as an excellent role model, she warns employees not to waste their lives.

Eni's restaurant is not her only interest, though. Paul and Eni have two children, and Eni insists that her home life is her number one priority and that her marriage is the best thing in her life. Eni also has another interest, writing Chinese novels, which she often does after coming home from the restaurant. She also enjoys reading books on the economic policies of the United States.

Zoe Houk

. . . .

Zoe Houk began her restaurant career as a waitress while attending college. She worked for several restaurants, acquiring more and more knowledge about restaurant management with each job she held. Many of the restaurants were owned by young women, which made Zoe realize that owning her own business was not impossible. However, she still did not seriously consider restaurant ownership as a career for herself.

In the early 1980s she had been employed by Empire Cafe for about a year when Empire decided to open a second location. Zoe was chosen to manage the new cafe. Within a short time, though, the partners who owned Empire Cafe began to argue about business matters, and Empire Cafe closed its doors.

Zoe and her friend Steve Robinson knew that the cafe's clientele were disappointed when the restaurant closed and that potential for a new restaurant existed. After the Empire had been closed for three months, Zoe and Steve decided to open their own cafe, and seven months after Empire Cafe closed, Cafe Zoe opened.

As with all new business owners, though, Zoe and Steve soon faced unexpected challenges. In the first week of operation, they fired their chef and restaurant consultant. Zoe and Steve wanted a simple menu, but the chef wanted to prepare more elaborate dishes. New chefs were hired, and the simple menu was introduced.

Cafe Zoe began to develop an increasing customer base, which Steve and Zoe attribute to an interesting location and fresh, simple food that tastes good.

After only two years, the business is almost completely free of debt, and Zoe believes that the restaurant has not reached its potential.

Zoe has a lighthearted nature but is also a perfectionist. Her management is firm: she has been known to "maintain the posture of a tyrant." Zoe and Steve never vacation except to take short trips to Chicago. All free time is spent reading books about food or sampling dishes at other restaurants. A second location is planned in the near future.

Questions

1. Why do you think Eni has been successful despite her lack of experience in the restaurant industry?

2. How are Eni and Zoe similar to successful entrepreneurs? How are they different?

3. In what ways are Eni's and Zoe's experiences similar? In what ways are they different?

Case ID   A Doctor/Entrepreneur

Most people probably thought that Stanley Gold would grow up to be a doctor, but Stanley had other ideas. His father taught clinical pharmacology at Cornell University Medical College, and his mother chaired the physiology department at Hunter College. With two parents in the medical field, though, Stanley chose to be different and obtained a degree in electrical engineering from Columbia University. His father continued to push him toward his medical doctorate degree from New York University School of Medicine.

While serving in the Marine Corps in 1975, Gold began moonlighting in emergency rooms. He participated in a $2 million study of the emergency medical needs of patients in the Los Angeles County area. The results of the study indicated that very few people who thought they needed emergency care were actually in life-threatening situations. Gold realized that the large numbers of people who came to a hospital's emergency room and waited for hours for routine care were not satisfied with the service and they really did not need a hospital. Gold tried to bring about a change in the hospital system,

Source: Nancy Friedman, "Emergency, Inc.," *Inc.*, August 1985, 48–56.

but the hospital administrator instead encouraged Gold to open his own health care outlets.

Gold began observing the new walk-in clinics that had begun to open throughout the country. He found that they all had common characteristics, which included easy accessibility, availability 14 to 18 hours per day, and fast service at an economical price. Gold met another doctor who planned to open a walk-in clinic; that same day they decided to become partners in a new business.

Gold was eager to provide the medical care but was not prepared for the business aspects of running a clinic. He attended a seminar on how to operate a walk-in clinic and found it to be very unsettling. He discovered that the clinics were a very tough business in which the owners had to "watch pennies, count Band-Aids, and advertise." Gold also began to have disagreements with his partner over how the business would be operated, and the partners split up before the clinic ever opened.

Gold continued his plans to open the clinic and spent several months searching for the best location. Once the location was chosen and the clinic was open, problems continued. Gold assumed that Southern California needed a clinic open seven days a week, 18 hours each day. He spent $20,000 on a direct-mail campaign and coupons in local newspapers, plus $50,000 on grand opening advertising. Despite this incredible promotion, not one patient came during the first four hours the business was open. For the first three months, an average of 13 patients per day came to the clinic, well below expected levels. Gold also had problems because he originally decided that he would not accept patients who would pay for services through insurance programs. He had planned only to accept payment directly from customers, then let the patients seek reimbursement from insurers. This resulted in many potential patients being turned away when revenue was badly needed. After repeatedly turning away insurance patients, Gold reversed his decision.

Eventually, several other changes were made. The clinic's hours were cut from 18 to 16 hours on weekdays and to 12 hours on weekends. The expensive advertising was eliminated and replaced with personalized letters, which were more effective. The name of the center was also changed from American Emergicenter to Americare 1 Immediate Medicine. Gold felt that the reference to "emergency" in the name might give potential customers the wrong impression.

Experts say that the biggest problem with establishing clinics such as Gold's is that the owner always underestimates the time it will take for the people to accept it. Quick medical care was a relatively new concept when Gold established his business, and people were not used to that type of service. In future years, Gold feels that similar clinics will be as successful and as common as McDonald's hamburger outlets. But in reviewing all that happened, Gold said if he had to do it all over again, he would probably make the same mistakes.

Questions

1. In what ways do you think Gold's experiences are similar to those of first-time entrepreneurs?

2. What could Gold have done differently to avoid some of the problems he encountered?

3. Gold stated that if he had to do it over again, he would probably make the same mistakes. Why do you think he said that?

PART

Early Planning

In Part One we provided an introduction to small business; we described the entrepreneur; and we considered the ways in which an individual could enter small business. In Part Two we will discuss starting a business. Although some of the material presented will apply to buying an existing business or a franchise, the primary focus of this section will be the establishment of a new business. We will deal with those topics that must be examined before the business opens its doors.

Chapter 4 discusses the market of the small business. This topic is covered first to underscore its importance; without a market a small business cannot exist. Careful market analysis should be the foundation of any entry into small business, and yet too often it is not. In this chapter we will describe various types of markets and the purchasing decision processes within them. We will also describe the ways in which the overall market may be separated into components, or segments. This process of segmentation can allow a business to compete more effectively by serving a particular group in the best manner. The process for conducting market research is the final topic included in Chapter 4.

One of the most important influences on the fortunes of a small business is its site. Large companies go to great lengths to choose the best location, eliminating the majority of possibilities in the process. The importance of site for retail businesses is clear; convenience is an important consideration for most customers. For other types of businesses, location can be critical as well. Factors such as a site's trading area, its cost, its zoning restrictions, and the lease or buy options available can, and often do, make the difference between success and failure of the business.

After the market has been researched and the possible sites analyzed, the entrepreneur must systematically evaluate the chances of success of the business. This evaluation is the topic of Chapter 6. It is accomplished by using a simple yet powerful technique called break-even analysis. By taking into account the sales a business appears likely to generate and the expenses it will face, break-even analysis provides a means for screening out ideas that have little or no chance of succeeding from those that have enough promise to warrant a feasibility study, which is the culmination of the preentry planning process. We will cover feasibility studies in Part Three; for now, we turn to the early stages of planning for a small business.

CHAPTER 4

The Nature of the Market

Source: Photograph courtesy of Phillips Petroleum Company.

K E Y Objectives

1. To define the term *customer*.

2. To identify the types of markets.

3. To describe the individual as a consumer.

4. To identify the various kinds of organizational markets.

5. To describe market segmentation and its various bases.

6. To explain the process of market research.

In this part of the text we will discuss the things a prospective entrepreneur must do to evaluate a possible business start. In this chapter we start the process by describing what must be done to determine the level of sales the proposed company is likely to achieve. Sales projection is a critical issue that demands careful, unbiased analysis—anything less is an invitation to serious problems.

Reasons for Inaccurate Sales Projections

Unfortunately, many entrepreneurs make inadequate assessments about the sales levels their companies will achieve. There are two causes of this mistake. The first is that many people starting a business do not know how to analyze a firm's market. We will address this problem by acquainting you with some basic principles of marketing and by describing the market research process as it may be used in starting a small business.

The second reason for inadequate projections of sales is that many, perhaps most, prospective entrepreneurs are ''in love'' with their product or service and therefore can see no obstacle standing in the way of their companies' success. This second cause is attitudinal in nature and stems from the entrepreneur's positive bias toward the proposed business. This chapter should eliminate this problem by making it clear that blind faith in the future is not enough. Enthusiasm and confidence in preliminary planning are both essential, but they must be supplemented by rational analysis. This kind of analysis

Unique Business   4.1

Taking the Mystery out of Business

If you are pondering the imponderable and finding it troublesome, you may want to turn to Delphi Associates, a network of psychic consultants. One of the company's founders, Anthony White, a Stanford MBA, describes the services as business oriented and based on solid research. Delphi has worked with individuals and corporations to find missing objects, locate hidden assets, and predict commodity market movements. Its basic consulting fee is $100 per hour.

The firm is based in California.

Source: Inc., June 1984, 31.

---

examines all of the issues in light of the best information available, making as few assumptions as possible.

Rational analysis starts with the question of who will be the company's customers. Two things are found in a customer: interest and sufficient financial resources. If either is missing the individual can no longer be regarded as a prospective customer. A student in junior high school may have plenty of interest in a $270 pair of skis but inadequate resources since he has only $16 left from last summer's grass-cutting jobs. His wealthy 80-year-old aunt, on the other hand, has plenty of money but little inclination to ski. Consequently, neither fits our description of a customer.

In identifying a company's prospective customers it is useful to distinguish between individuals as consumers and organizations as consumers. This is the topic of our next section.

Types of Markets

The Individual as Consumer

This market is one in which goods or services are purchased for consumption by the individual or household. This market is vast, with a great number of identifiable subgroups (for example, executives, the elderly, blacks). In the United States, this market includes 225 million people when its broadest dimensions are considered. Serving them all is impossible for a small business; later in this chapter we will discuss the ways in which a part (or segment) of the market can be identified for possible entry by the firm.

Competing in any individual consumer market requires an understanding of the way in which buying decisions are made. Buying decisions are not always simple buy/don't buy choices. There are often a number of intermediate choices the consumer must make. Kotler provides an excellent example of this as he describes the way a woman proceeded toward the purchase of a Nikon camera.[1]

> *The buying process started with Betty feeling a need for some new activity. She tried to clarify the nature of her need and decided that she wanted some new form of self-expression (need-class decision). She considered various alternatives and decided that photography would be fun to try (generic-class decision). In considering the different classes of photographic equipment, she concluded that she wanted a camera (product-class decision). She decided that a complex 35-mm camera would be best (product-form decision). Among the brands she saw, Nikon gave her the most confidence (brand decision). She decided to go to dealer 2, who was reputed to run the best camera shop in town (vendor decision). She also thought of suggesting that her girlfriend buy a camera and take up photography but dropped the idea (quantity decision). She decided to buy the camera on the weekend (timing decision). And finally, she decided to pay for it using her credit card (payment-method decision).*

In addition to recognizing the complexity of the buying decision, any analysis of a consumer market must identify the various participants in the process. Consider, for example, the circumstances leading to a father's purchase of an electronic game for his 8-year-old daughter. He has been sent to the store by the child's mother, who has been hearing for weeks about the game owned by the daughter's best friend. The mother checked with the girl's older sister, a 12-year-old who, in her role of technical advisor, suggested Brand A rather than the Brand B owned by the 8-year-old's friend. Brand A is now on sale, and the father, therefore, finds himself closing in on the purchase of something in which he has no interest.

Who is the critical participant in all of this? The father was the *buyer;* he made the purchase and paid for the toy. The mother was the *decider;* she determined what, where, and when to buy. The 12-year-old daughter singled out Brand A as the choice to make; she had the role of *influencer.* The 8-year-old was the *initiator,* although her best friend may be guilty of complicity. The 8-year-old also has the role of *user.* Each of these participants must be identified as part of the analysis of the market an entrepreneur hopes to enter. Failing to sort out the roles and decision criteria of each of the participants can be a very costly error.

Finally, consumer markets may be analyzed as to the various influences on the buyer. These influences include the social class and reference groups to which a person belongs and his or her personal and psychological character-

---

[1]Philip Kotler, *Principles of Marketing* (Englewood Cliffs, N.J.: Prentice-Hall, 1980), 235–237.

istics. Buying behavior is often directly attributable to influences of this type, as will be discussed later in the section on market segmentation.

Organizational Markets

Many small businesses serve organizations rather than individuals or households. As buyers, organizations operate differently than individuals. They buy for different reasons, they use different criteria, and they tend to be much more formal (quotations, bids, and product specifications are often involved). Not all organizational markets are the same. Kotler has identified three types of organizational markets; we will use his typology here.[2]

Producer Market
A market comprising organizations that produce goods or services.

The Producer Market.   Examples of industries included in the **producer market** are manufacturing, construction, finance, insurance, and public utilities. The producer market is usually characterized by a small number of large buyers. The buying decision is the product of a formalized process in which many individuals play a part. The buying process varies considerably from situation to situation (see Exhibit 4.1).

Reseller Market
Organizations that purchase goods for resale to others. This market includes wholesalers and retail firms.

The Reseller Market.   The **reseller market** consists of organizations that purchase goods for resale to others. Included here are wholesalers and retail firms. These organizations may insist on the lowest possible price (as may be the case with a cut-rate store chain) or may regard price as an issue of only minor significance (as might a chic clothing store or boutique). Regardless of the importance of price, however, the buyers and buying systems in most reseller organizations are quite sophisticated and demanding. These buyers know their organizations' customers and will seek out those vendors who can help in serving them.

Government Market
All government units that purchase or rent goods or services to carry out the functions of government.

Open-Bid Buying
The buying process, used by the government, in which the contract is awarded to the supplier with acceptable quality, which offers the lowest price.

The Government Market.   The **government market** is vast; it consists of all government units that purchase or rent goods to carry out the functions of government. The federal government purchased about 60 percent of the total ($365 billion) purchased by units at all levels of government.

Not all government purchases are made using the same process or procedure. In the vast majority of cases the buying process is one in which the lowest-cost producer with acceptable quality is given the contract. This is known as **open-bid buying.** The $27 light bulb or $640 hammer are rare exceptions. Most suppliers find that the government's buying criteria and the competition for contracts severely limit profits.

Negotiated Contract
The buying procedure in which a government unit uses a company engaged in a project for which there is little or no effective competition.

The other type of buying procedure is the **negotiated contract.** Here a government unit works with a company engaged in a project for which there is little or no effective competition. Because these contracts are subject to review, any excessive profits may bring public criticism of the company and/or renegotiation of the contract.

---

[2]Philip Kotler, *Principles of Marketing,* 2d ed. (Englewood Cliffs, N.J.: Prentice-Hall, 1983), 166–187.

Exhibit 4.1	Types of Buying Situations

I. New or Unique Purchase

A requirement or problem that has not arisen before.

Little or no relevant past buying experience to draw upon.

A great deal of information is needed.

Must seek out alternative ways of solving the problem and alternative supplies.

Occurs infrequently—but very important to marketers because it sets the pattern for the more routine purchases that will follow.

May be anticipated and developed by creative marketing.

II. Straight Rebuy

Continuing or recurring requirement, handled on a routine basis.

Usually the decision on each separate transaction is made in the purchasing department.

Formally or informally, a "list" of acceptable suppliers exists.

No supplier not on the "list" is considered.

Buyers have much relevant buying experience, and hence little new information is needed.

Appears to represent the bulk of the individual purchases within companies.

Item purchased, price paid, delivery time, etc., may vary from transaction to transaction, so long as these variations do not cause a new source of supply to be considered.

III. Modified Rebuy

May develop from either new purchase or straight rebuy situations.

The requirement is continuing or recurring, or it may be expanded to a significantly larger level of operations.

The buying alternatives are known, but they are changed.

Some additional information is needed before the decisions are made.

May arise because of outside events, such as an emergency or by the actions of a marketer.

May arise internally because of new buying influences, or for potential costs reductions, potential quality improvements or potential service benefits.

Marketers who are not active suppliers try to convert the customer's straight rebuys into modified rebuys.

Source: From Marketing Science Institute Series, *Industrial Buying and Creative Marketing* by Robinson, Faris and Wind. Copyright © by Allyn and Bacon, Inc. Used with permission.

Market Identification

In the 1920s Henry Ford made a vast fortune by standardizing the production of the only car his company made, the black Model T. His concept of the market was one in which a dependable, low-priced car was what everyone wanted. He was right, but times have changed and the automobile market has changed, too. It has become very complex; one car type does not appeal to all, or even most, potential car buyers. Mass marketing has given way to market segmentation.

In this section we will describe **market segmentation,** identify its bases, and describe the use of a market grid.

Bases of Market Segmentation

Market Segmentation
The process of dividing the total market into parts, or groups, of buyers who have something in common with one another, which causes them to have similar buying patterns.

Market segmentation involves dividing the market into groups of buyers. Buyers within these groups have something in common with one another that causes them to have similar buying patterns. For example, the car marketing people may segment the market by assuming that different age groups have different preferences. While it is true that an elderly widow *may* buy a four-wheel drive, off-road vehicle, Detroit will bet against it by promoting its more conventional automobiles to the senior citizen market.

Even a less glamorous market, such as that of breakfast cereal, can be used to demonstrate the advisability of segmentation. Within the cereal-consuming group are people of all ages with varying health problems, reading and television interests, and degrees of interest in nutrition. Consequently, we are offered cereals that have fruit and fiber, that have no sodium and/or no sugar, that feature characters from TV programs, or that provide our every conceivable nutritional requirement. The cereal market, like the automobile market, is not homogeneous; it is a composite of many smaller markets. This is true of most markets; they comprise many consumers who have little in common with other buyers. A small business owner must segment the company's market; the entire market simply cannot be served. Deciding which segment or segments the business can best serve is the real issue. Three possible bases for market segmentation follow.

Demographic Segmentation
A form of market segmentation that groups people on the basis of geography or socioeconomic traits.

Demographic Segmentation.   **Demographic segmentation** groups people on the basis of geography or socioeconomic traits.

A small business may determine that its major appeal is to the suburban market. For some kinds of businesses (stores, restaurants), this has obvious site selection implications; for other kinds (magazines, lawn care services) this has important promotional effort implications.

Age, income, occupation, marital status, education, and social class are all socioeconomic factors. Usually a company is concerned with the effect that a combination of these factors will have. For instance, the important factors for car buyers seem to be age, income, and marital status. Several years ago, Pontiac found Sunbird buyers to be young, middle-income, and single, whereas LeMans buyers tended to be middle-aged, low-income, and married.

Exhibit 4.2 describes the effects of yet another demographic variable, the life-cycle stage.

Benefit Segmentation
Market segmentation that groups buyers of a product according to reason for purchase.

Benefit Segmentation.   **Benefit segmentation** takes into account the fact that the same product is purchased by different people for different reasons. The owner of a clothing store must decide if the store is going to appeal

Exhibit 4.2   An Overview of the Family Life Cycle and Its Influence on Purchases

Bachelor stage; young single people not living at home	Newly married couples; young, no children	Full nest I, youngest child under six	Full nest II, youngest child six or over six	Full nest III; older married couples with dependent children	Empty nest I; older married couples; no children living with them, head in labor force	Empty nest II, older married couples, no children living at home, head retired	Solitary survivor in labor force	Solitary survivor, retired
Few financial burdens.	Better off financially than they will be in near future.	Home purchasing at peak.	Financial position better.	Financial position still better.	Home ownership at peak.	Drastic cut in income.	Income still good but likely to sell home.	Same medical and product needs as other retired group; drastic cut in income.
Fashion opinion leaders.	Highest purchase rate and highest average purchase of durables.	Liquid assets low.	Some wives work.	More wives work.	Most satisfied with financial position and money saved.	Keep home.		Special need for attention, affection, and security.
Recreation oriented.	Buy: Cars, refrigerators, stoves, sensible and durable furniture, vacations.	Dissatisfied with financial position and amount of money saved.	Less influenced by advertising.	Some children get jobs.	Interested in travel, recreation, self-education.	Buy: Medical appliances, medical care, products which aid health, sleep, and digestion.		
Buy: Basic kitchen equipment, basic furniture, cars, equipment for the mating game, vacations.		Interested in new products.	Buy larger sized packages, multiple-unit deals.	Hard to influence with advertising.	Make gifts and contributions.			
		Like advertised products.	Buy: Many foods, cleaning materials, bicycles, music lessons, pianos.	High average purchase of durables.	Not interested in new products.			
		Buy: Washers, dryers, TV, baby food, chest rubs and cough medicine, vitamins, dolls, wagons, sleds, skates.		Buy: New, more tasteful furniture, auto travel, non-necessary appliances, boats, dental services, magazines.	Buy: Vacations, luxuries, home improvements.			

Source: W. D. Wells and G. Gubar, "Life Cycle Concept in Marketing Research," *Journal of Marketing Research*, November 1966, p. 362. Published by the American Marketing Association. Reprinted with permission.

primarily to those people for whom high fashion is important, to those who have budget as their most important concern, or to those who like conservative, carefully tailored clothes that they plan to wear for years.

This means of segmentation can be very important to anyone attempting to determine the likely size of a prospective business's market. The difficulty that benefit segmentation presents is that benefits that are sought are not always apparent; consequently, in-depth interviewing may be required to use this type of segmentation.

Usage Rate Segmentation.   In a highly influential study, Twedt examined the rate of use of different products and developed the concept of **usage rate segmentation.**[3] After taking out the nonusers, he split his sample into a light-user half and a heavy-user half. For example, he found 42 percent of his sample reported *no* use of lemon-lime soda, leaving 58 percent of users who were split into equal (29 percent) heavy-user and light-user groups. The 29 percent categorized as heavy users purchased 91 percent of all the lemon-lime soda sold. Other examples include beer (17 percent purchased 88 percent), dog food (17 percent purchased 87 percent), and hair tonic (24 percent purchased 87 percent). A similar pattern was found for a wide variety of products. See Illustration Capsule 4.1 for an example of how usage patterns prompted an important change in corporate strategy.

Although the heavy-user group provides the most obvious target, the light-user group or even nonuser group may provide a small business with its best opening into the market. Someone opening a travel agency may find that the heavy-user group is too hard to pull from their current agencies, whereas the light users will shift if given only minor incentive. Among the nonuser group there may be many potential customers who simply have to be told the reasons for using a travel agency. Regardless of which of these groups a business chooses to cultivate as customers, the usage pattern can be a very effective means of segmentation.

Market Grid

One way in which the various segments of a market may be used is through the use of a **market grid.** A market grid is a two- or three-dimensional view of a market. Using the Pontiac buyer information given earlier, we could construct the following two-dimensional grid, using income and age as the bases for segmentation.

Usage Rate Segmentation
Market segmentation grouping buyers according to the rate at which they use the product.

Market Grid
A two- or three-dimensional view of the market that highlights the interaction of variables affecting demand.

---

[3]Dik Warren Twedt, "How Important to Marketing Strategy Is the 'Heavy User'?" *Journal of Marketing* 28 (January 1964): 71–72.

Illustration Capsule   4.1

Marketing by Miller

Shortly after the purchase of Miller Brewing by Phillip Morris, the company's market researchers learned that Miller beer had its primary appeal within the light-user segment. The beer's slogan "The Champagne of Bottled Beer" positioned the product in such a way as to attract people with refined tastes. This group, however, consumed modest amounts of beer. Phillip Morris, knowing a thing or two about marketing, changed all that by featuring construction workers and oil field roughnecks knocking down a few after work at the saloon before heading home in their classic "It's Miller Time" television commercials. The company knew what the heavy-user group was and how to reach its members.

Age	Income		
	Under $15,000	$15,001– 25,000	Over $25,000
Young, 18–34		Sunbird	
Middle-aged, 35–39	LeMans		
Old, 60+			

If we were selling LeMans automobiles, our efforts should be directed toward middle-aged people with modest incomes since they constitute the most promising market segment. We may find, furthermore, that within this segment there is an important distinction stemming from education level, with the people with a high school education finding the car to their liking. Both higher and lower levels of education attainment seem to bring with them less interest in the car. As a result of this finding, we can build another dimension into our grid (see Figure 4.1).

The market grid allows us to describe with some precision those individuals who are most likely to be the company's customers. The dimensions used in the grid are those that best distinguish our prospective buyers from our nonbuyers. If our product clearly has appeal to the young, we will use age as a dimension. If it is a male-oriented product, we will use gender. If we have something with appeal to the highly educated, we will want to include educational level. Any of the bases of market segmentation described above can be used as dimensions of our market grid.

Figure   4.1   Market Grid for Automobiles Using Age,
Educational Level, and Annual Income

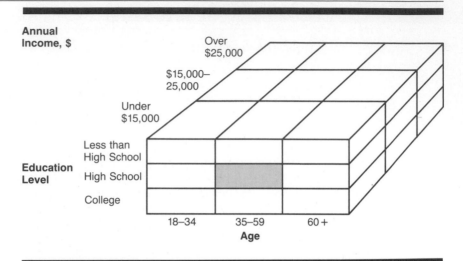

Market Research

· ·

In this section we will describe the process by which an entrepreneur can
reach an estimate of the sales volume the company is likely to achieve. Any
flaws or shortcomings in this part of the planning for a new business are likely
to be costly or catastrophic because the market shows no mercy. The process
of **market research** starts with the broadest focus, the environment, and ends
with a very specific result, the expected level of sales.

Market Research
The systematic gathering,
recording, and analyzing
of facts and opinions
concerning the market.

The Environment

The first concern of the entrepreneur is the way in which the firm's product
relates to its environment. This may be the most difficult stage in the entire
market research process because it requires close examination of some very
subtle factors. At issue here are things such as, What is the appeal of the
product? To whom does the appeal matter? Are they willing to pay? What
economic and societal changes are taking place and how might they affect
our market?

Let's use as an example a grocery buying service, one in which the customer fills out a list and the company buys and delivers the items on it for a
fee. The appeal is one of time saved, which we could reason is most important to busy people. The busy people in our society are usually working cou-
ples, particularly those with children. As to whether they will pay their hard-
earned money for the service, no one can say until some careful market

"Just how fresh are these insights?"

Source: Drawing by Lorenz; © 1984 The New Yorker Magazine, Inc.

research is conducted. Future developments must also be considered. We do not want to go into a business that may soon become obsolete. We may find groceries will be sold in the near future through computer linkages between the store and the customer.

The environment will determine whether a firm's products or services will continue to be valued or whether they will become obsolete. Information describing environmental developments can come from a variety of sources. The problem faced by most people is that of being overwhelmed by the data. Even in a small library there is so much information that it is hard to know where to look. Exhibit 4.3 lists some of the more important sources of data for environmental, as well as industrial, analysis.

In summary, the first task in conducting market research is that of determining whether the economic relationships necessary for prosperity can be expected to continue or improve. Will the traditional full-service gas station have a future in our society? Why are convenience stores prospering and mom-and-pop grocery stores failing? These are examples of issues that must

Exhibit 4.3 Information Sources for Economic Environment Research

Source	Comments
Government Publications	
Census Data	
Census of Population	Published every 10 years. Gives detailed information on population of states, counties, cities, and towns.
Census of Business	Published every 5 years, for years ending in "2" and "7." Gives data on retail and wholesale trade and selected service industries.
Census of Manufacturers	Published every 5 years. Gives data on manufacturing firms in 450 industries.
Guide to U.S. Government Publications	Published annually. Annotated guide to publications of the various U.S. government agencies.
Handbook of Basic Economic Statistics	Published monthly. Includes statistical data condensed from publications of the federal government. This source contains retail and wholesale price statistics, information concerning a variety of industries and products, and facts pinpointing significant trends in the national economy.
U.S. Industrial Outlook	Published annually by the Department of Commerce. Gives historical data, current estimates, and five-year projections for approximately 200 industries.
Business Conditions Digest	Published monthly by the Department of Commerce. Gives historical analysis and projections of various factors such as prices, wages, productivity, employment, government activities, international trade, etc.
St. Louis Federal Reserve Bank Quarterly Report	Gives monthly economic statistics, including money supply, prices, employment, production, international trade for the U.S. and nine other countries.
Predicasts	Historical and composite forecasts of major economic indicators, arranged by product, including such factors as consumption, shipments, and sales.
Survey of Buying Power	Published annually by *Sales and Marketing Management*, this publication gives estimates of population, retail sales, and other economic data for the United States and Canada.

be examined in the broadest fashion, for they are basic in nature. To paraphrase an anonymous market analyst: the quickest way to make a fortune is to sell people something they want; the quickest way to lose a fortune is to try to sell people something they do not want.

The Industry

After the industry's role in the environment has been studied, the entrepreneur's attention must turn to the nature of the industry itself. Two concerns are present here, the customers and the competitors. Put another way, we must determine how big the market is and who has it.

Exhibit 4.4   Information Sources for Industry Research

Source	Comments
*Statistical Abstracts of the United States	Published annually by the Bureau of the Census, provides an annual summary of population, prices, income, housing, etc.
*Current Population Reports	This series covers a variety of topics ranging from fertility of American women to voting and registration behavior. The data are reported for the nation, regions, and standard metropolitan statistical areas.
*Quarterly Financial Reports	Published by Securities and Exchange Commission, gives financial statistics, including profits and return on equity, by industry, by asset size, and by industry group.
*Census data for selected industries	The Bureau of the Census publishes data, usually on a 5-year cycle, for various industries including: construction, mineral industries, retail trade, transportation, and wholesale trade.
Annual Statement Studies	Published annually by Robert Morris Associates, gives composite financial data on 305 lines of business engaged in manufacturing, wholesaling, retailing, services, and contracting.
Dun and Bradstreet's Key Business Ratios	Annual publication giving financial ratios for over 800 lines of business.
Standard and Poor's Industry Survey	Published quarterly, these surveys give current and basic analysis of over 45 major industries.
Trade Association Publications	Various trade associations publish studies of their respective industries. These studies are often the most useful of all information sources. See the *Encyclopedia of Associations* or the *National Trade & Professional Associations.*

*Government publications.

The way in which the size of the market is determined depends on who our customers will be. If our prospective customers are individuals, the first task is to specify who they are in demographic terms. Will they be young, old, or both? Is there a particular income or educational level to which our product or service may have its greatest appeal? After a demographic profile has been constructed we can estimate, through census tract data, the size of the market.

The sources of data (see Exhibit 4.4) that are particularly useful in this area include the Bureau of Census' *Current Population Report,* which provides a concise summary of group trends and forecasts. The Bureau also publishes the *Statistical Abstract of the United States,* which contains annual summaries of population, housing, etc. These data are about 18 months old at the time of publication. These publications are available at libraries throughout the country. The Census Bureau also publishes an extremely useful series of guides to use of census data. The series is called "Factfinders for the Nation" and comprises 22 booklets including "Retail Trade Statistics," "Statistics on Manufacturers," "Enterprise Statistics," and "International Programs."

If a prospective company's customers are to be organizations, a different approach to market-size estimation is taken. Sometimes the estimate is made

Illustration Capsule 4.2

Cable Television Systems as a Market

You are thinking about a business that will serve the cable television industry. How many potential customers will you have in your market?

The *Statistical Abstract of the United States* might be your first stop in answering the question. Page 563 tells us that the number of cable television systems in the country has risen from 70 in 1952 to an estimated 5,600 in 1983. If your service would have its greatest appeal to small-system operators, you will be happy to learn that 80 percent of the systems have fewer than 5,000 subscribers. If you want more information, the *Statistical Abstract* provides a section on additional sources of information, which lists four publications that report on the cable television industry.

---

by using the Yellow Pages of the telephone directory to determine the identity of all of the organizations you are planning to serve. If you plan to provide a service for car dealers, for example, it is an easy matter to get the names and addresses of all such businesses from the Yellow Pages. If the product is intended for the elementary and secondary school market, the process is again straightforward: identifying the schools and/or school districts in the area to be served. See Illustration Capsule 4.2 for an example of the method of researching a broader market.

In addition to identifying the customers a prospective business might attract, an entrepreneur must analyze the competition. Some factors needed for this analysis are easily determined through the use of information sources such as those listed in Exhibit 4.4. Data from these sources are called **secondary data** because they were not generated as part of the current analysis. These data can be used to determine which firms are in the industry, the nature of their product line, what areas they serve, the population in those areas, etc.

Secondary Data
Data available from published sources.

The answer to a number of other questions may not be available in secondary data sources and will, therefore, require the generation of **primary data.** These are data gathered specifically for the researcher's purposes. Up to this point the process was one of gathering published facts. Primary data generation requires judgment regarding both the collection and the meaning of data.

Primary Data
Data collected specially for the researcher's purposes.

The kinds of competitor-oriented questions for which primary data are needed include, What will be the reaction of industry members to the entry of a new competitor? How much customer loyalty do the competitors enjoy? Do any of the competitors have a unique competitive advantage?

What the entrepreneur is looking for at this stage of the market research are insights into how the industry operates. With this as background information, the entrepreneur can move on to the next step: projecting the share of the market the proposed company can be expected to gain.

Company Market Share

This task involves assessing the relative attractiveness of the product or service being considered and translating that assessment into a numerical measure, market share.

Data Gathering.   The data may be gathered in a variety of ways. The major methods are given below in order of formality, going from the most casual to the most formal.

Observational Research
The most casual of data-gathering techniques, in which the researcher simply observes and keeps track of certain kinds of behavior.

Observational research is the observation of certain kinds of behavior. A traffic count is an example of observational research; keeping track of the percentage of shoppers stopping at a certain display is another. This research can indicate what is happening but gives no insights as to why.

Casual Interviewing
An unstructured means of determining people's impressions without the use of predetermined questions.

Casual interviewing can be used to get people's impression. This kind of data gathering is casual in that there are no predetermined questions or issues. Casual interviewing is most appropriate during the early stages of research as an aid to issue identification.

Focus Groups
A method of probing attitudes through the use of groups of 5 to 12 people.

Focus groups, another method of data gathering, are usually made up of 5 to 12 people who are asked to discuss a particular topic. The attitudes of the individuals within the group are probed by the leader. This technique is most often used to provide input for construction of a survey questionnaire. It can be a rich source of information if the group develops a relaxed atmosphere encouraging the candid opinions of every member of the group.

Survey
The most widely used means of gathering market research data, usually through the use of a questionnaire.

The most widely used means of market research data gathering is the **survey.** The instrument by which survey research is conducted is the questionnaire. Construction of the questionnaire items can be a delicate operation. Questions that seem clear to the writer can be vague or misleading to the person answering; others often ask for information that the person would rather not give, having to do with income, drinking habits, etc.; and others may be "loaded," that is, prompting a particular response from virtually everyone. Such flawed questions will keep a survey from providing much useful information.

In addition to preventing faulty questionnaire construction, the researcher must guard against bias in the group to be sampled. The classic example of the way in which bias can lead to useless survey results involved the 1936 presidential election. Based on a sample of its readers, *The Literary Digest* predicted that Alf Landon would defeat Franklin D. Roosevelt. Roosevelt won in a landslide, with Landon carrying only Maine and Vermont. What went wrong? Simply put, the magazine asked the wrong people. The people who were included were subscribers, with telephones, who participated by returning a card that the magazine had mailed to them. The surveyors could not have screened out Democrats more effectively if they had tried.

Another decision required concerns the method by which the survey is to be conducted. Three methods are available: the personal interview, the mail survey, and the telephone interview. Exhibit 4.5 summarizes the advantages and disadvantages of the three methods.

One potential shortcoming of survey research is that the people who are surveyed may be too gracious or concerned about "disappointing" the researcher. If so, they may be providing answers that are less than candid. To the extent that such bias is present in the responses gathered, the information is not valid. Because of this problem and the others just described, some firms use test marketing.

Test Marketing
The practice of actually introducing a new product or service on a limited basis to determine customer reaction.

Test marketing yields useful data because it shows what people do rather than what they say they will do. Although these data provide the best basis for making the decision whether or not to go into business, the entrepreneur usually cannot conduct such a market test because it involves actually going into business. The entry into business, even if on a small scale, can be an extremely costly way to get marketing data.

Estimating Market Share.   Whatever the means by which the market research is conducted, the data should provide some measure of the attractiveness of the proposed product relative to the other choices of the customer. These other choices include not buying at all, buying a substitute good, and buying from a competitor.

If our product is currently not available, our market research chore is a difficult one. What we are considering is the establishment of an industry. Before Walt Disney built Disneyland, theme amusement parks did not exist. Since then a number of them have been established around the country. This concept has been proven as a viable one, and yet start-up of a new industry is a very hazardous undertaking. Is there a market for religious and moral training seminars? What about Mah-Jongg lessons? This kind of case is the most unusual and the most difficult since there are no data available with which to make judgments. The data must be developed to answer the question of whether a business based on the new concept could survive.

In the next case the customer has other goods already available as alternatives to what we plan to offer. This means a change in buying habits is needed. RCA found this to be a difficult task when it tried to sell its videodisc player as an alternative to videotape machines for home entertainment. Under such conditions, our market research efforts will have to develop primary data that allow us to judge what proportion of the consumer group is likely to choose our type of product.

The final case is the most straightforward. If our product is donuts, for example, the estimate of market share is largely a matter of assessing the competitor's ability to satisfy the community's donut needs relative to our

Exhibit 4.5   Advantages and Disadvantages of Three Survey Methods

Personal Interview	Mail Survey	Telephone Interview
Advantages		
1. Obtains detailed information 2. Allows interviewer to probe 3. Obtains socioeconomic data on respondent 4. Permits use of visual aids	1. Covers widespread area cheaply 2. Eliminates interviewer bias 3. May reach otherwise inaccessible people 4. Allows respondent to answer anonymously and at leisure	1. Reaches wide area inexpensively 2. Speeds data collection 3. Allows respondent some anonymity
Disadvantages		
1. Can be expensive 2. May introduce interviewer bias 3. May raise fears for privacy	1. Can lack representativeness 2. May produce low rate of return 3. Does not allow probing or follow-up questions	1. Difficult to reach those with unlisted numbers 2. Must use short questions

Source: Taken from *Modern Marketing*, David J. Rachman and Elaine Romans, Hinsdale, Ill.: The Dryden Press, 1980. Reprinted by permission of the authors.

ability to do so. The competition's price, quality, location, service, etc., are compared with what we plan to achieve. This comparison allows us to assess the proportion of market we are likely to capture. If we are going to be about average, we should figure on a 20 percent market share after establishing our company as the fifth supplier of donuts in the local market.

To summarize, our efforts to predict what sales our business will have should start with the broadest view possible. What we have suggested here is that the industry's role in the environment first be examined. At issue here is whether the industry will prosper or stagnate. Subtle changes may be taking place within the environment that will threaten all of the members of the industry. This analysis requires the use of secondary data from a wide variety of sources, such as those given in Exhibit 4.3.

The next step in the process concerns the industry itself. The kinds of firms in the industry, the nature of competition, the important trends taking place, and the size of the market are examples of the issues explored here. The data used come from both secondary and primary sources.

The final step in the process of estimating sales volume is that of determining market share. How much of the market can the proposed business reasonably expect to gain? The data needed to answer the question must come from primary sources, that is, the data are not available from published sources and must therefore be gathered specifically for this purpose.

Exhibit   4.6   Estimated Market for Corrugated and Solid-Fiber Box by Industry Groups

Consuming Industry	Value of Box Shipments by End Use (× 1,000)	Employees	Consumption per Employee (1 ÷ 2)	Employees, Fresno Market	Estimated Sales (3 × 4) (× 1,000)
	1	2	3	4	5
Food and Kindred Products	$2,347,450	1,480,477	$1,586	5,695	$9,032
Tobacco	53,200	63,025	844	—	—
Textile Mill Products	179,550	884,485	203	950	193
Miscellaneous Manufacturing	312,550	433,937	720	295	212
All Other Industries	—	—	—	—	3,167
Total	—	—	—	—	$12,604

Source: U.S. Department of Commerce, *Measuring Markets: A Guide to the Use of Federal and State Statistical Data* (Washington, D.C.: Government Printing Office, August 1979), 58–60.

As an example of this process let's consider the case of an entrepreneur who is considering entry into an organization market, namely the corrugated and solid-fiber box industry. The analysis of the environment indicates a reasonable future rate of growth based on projections of growth and the traditional relationship between the economy as a whole and the industry. A closer look at the industry provides data on which industries use corrugated and solid-fiber boxes, how much they spend on the boxes, and the number of people they employ. The assumption we will use here is that the amount of box usage per employee, as reported nationally, will prevail in the market we plan to enter, Fresno County in California. This assumption, and data from government and industry sources, allow us to construct Exhibit 4.6. The food and kindred products industry, in which there are 1,480,477 employees in the United States (column 2), uses slightly over $2.3 billion in boxes (column 1), for an average of $1,586 per employee (column 3). In the Fresno area this industry employs 5,695 (column 4). Using the assumption just given, we multiply the employee total by the national consumption per employee to give us an estimate of slightly over $9 million in box sales to Fresno County food and kindred products processors (column 5). The same procedure is used for the other segments of the market.

The Fresno area has a $12.6 million corrugated and solid-fiber box market. The next step is to determine how much of that $12.6 million would be ours if we entered the market. As mentioned earlier, the process becomes less computational and more judgmental at this point. We must assess the nature and importance of any advantages or disadvantages we have relative to the companies already in the industry. We may use as a baseline a percentage

Mi Ranchito Mexican Food Products Inc., Phoenix, Arizona

It was his dissatisfaction with the tortilla chips he served at his Phoenix restaurant that prompted Espiridion Murillo to open a shop to make his own. The popularity of his chips in other area restaurants made him decide to go into full-time production in 1978. Sales have increased every year since then; the company now employs 90 and has a network of 35 distributors selling to retail grocery stores throughout the Southwest.

In addition to chips, the Mi Ranchito product line includes fried pork skins, picante dip, bean dip, and cheese sauces for nachos.

Source: Small Business Means Jobs (Washington, D.C.: SBA, 1984).

based simply on the number of competitors, e.g., we will get 20 percent of the market if we become the fifth company in it, 10 percent if we become the tenth. This provides a rough estimate but one that we should be able to improve on by taking into account any important factors that influence success in the industry, such as the quality of our sales effort, cost/price advantages, or location.

If our analysis leads us to conclude that we can expect a 15 percent share of the market, we simply multiply that figure by the total market to get our projected sales: $15\% \times \$12.6$ million $= \$1.89$ million.

Now our market research is complete; it has given us an estimate of sales volume. If that estimate exceeds the cost projections that we will describe in Chapter 6, we go on with the task of investigating the establishment of our small business.

K E Y Objectives Reviewed

1. A customer is an individual or organization with an interest in, and sufficient financial resources for, purchasing a firm's production services.

2. Two distinct markets, individuals and organizations, may be identified.

3.   The individual consumer engages in buying decisions that are often quite complex, with many intermediate choices being made before the purchase/no purchase point is reached. This decision process often involves inputs from people other than the individual who makes the purchase.

4.   Organizational markets consist of the producer market, the reseller market, and the government market.

5.   Market segmentation involves separating the market into groups of buyers that have something in common with one another, which causes them to have similar buying patterns.

6.   Market research is the process the entrepreneur uses to analyze the demand his or her firm has or can develop in a particular market.

Discussion Questions

1.   Identify and distinguish between the three types of organizational markets.

2.   Why do entrepreneurs make poor judgments as to sales their new companies will achieve?

3.   What makes the buying decision complicated, and why is the actual buyer often less significant than others involved in the decision?

4.   What is market segmentation and why is it advisable for a small business to use it?

5.   What is the difference between secondary and primary data?

6.   Describe the various methods of gathering market data.

CHAPTER 5

The Site

Source: Courtesy of Public Service Company of New Mexico.

K   E   Y   Objectives

1. To stress the effect of the location decision on the success of the business.

2. To identify location decisions common to all industries.

3. To identify factors that should be analyzed when completing a site analysis for:

    *   retail outlets
    *   wholesale firms
    *   service firms
    *   manufacturing plants

4. To identify factors to consider when negotiating a lease.

The market segmentation and market considerations discussed in Chapter 4 provided a framework for determining if demand for a product exists within a given area. If the entrepreneur determines that demand for a product is not being met by existing businesses, she must then decide the exact location for her business. A poor location can deter customers from purchasing from a business even if ample demand exists, so site selection requires careful attention. A site analysis will identify a location that is convenient for the customers and efficient for the business.

The Importance of a Site Analysis

For large corporations, location or relocation is a major decision that they thoroughly research. Analyzing alternative locations is a time-consuming, expensive procedure, and a final decision is made only after the business has reviewed a substantial amount of information. Firms that conduct location studies generally eliminate more than four of every five locations studied.[1] Unfortunately, too many small businesses do not approach a location decision with the same amount of caution and preparation.

---

[1]T. Lowry, *Using a Traffic Study To Select a Retail Site* (Washington, D.C.: U.S. Government Printing Office, 1976), 3.

Unique Business   5.1

Dolls and Guise Inc.

For those of you who have worried about your Cabbage Patch doll making it through those cold winter nights, help has arrived. Alper Richman Furs Ltd., a Chicago retailer, has introduced fur coats especially designed for Frieda Jean and all her shivering cousins. The price for making the best-dressed doll on the block this winter is rather steep, from $50 for a rabbit coat to $1,000 for a full-length chinchilla. The wraps are a supplement to the store's more traditional real-people lines.

Source: Inc., June 1984, 31.

In some industries, for both large and small businesses, the proper location is essential for success. For example, with retail clothing stores, location is a key factor in determining the sales volume. Conversely, for some industries (for example, an appliance repair service that goes to customers' homes), the specific location is not crucial to the business's success. However, it is still a decision the business should make only after gathering the proper information.

The information included in a site analysis varies with the type of business; a site analysis for a manufacturing plant will be substantially different than one for a retail outlet. Factors that are crucial to the success of one industry may be completely irrelevant elsewhere.

Location Decisions Common to All Industries

Trading Area

Trading Area
A geographically defined area in which the customer target market for a firm is located.

For almost any product, a specific trading area can be determined. The **trading area** is a geographically defined area containing the firm's customer target market. Therefore, the first step in determining trading area is the market segmentation process described in Chapter 4. It is critical to determine who the customers will be, their buying habits, and their preferences. In many cases, the entrepreneur can obtain very detailed information without doing any research. Many trade associations, for example, have extensively studied the "typical customer" and how this relates to site selection. Trading areas vary greatly in size, depending on the type of business. For a convenience food store, the trading area is generally quite small. Because convenience foods are purchased frequently, the consumer wants the products to be readily available; when passing a convenience food store, he may be reminded of a need and so stop to buy it. If a special trip for the item is necessary, the store should be close by. Even for convenience foods, though, other factors will affect the trading area. One study of food store purchases in a central city area indicated that "nearly 70% of the customers patronized stores within 1 to 5 blocks of their homes." For suburban locations, the majority of customers lived within 3 miles of the stores; however, the trading area did extend as far as 5 miles. In rural locations, the majority of customers lived within a 10-minute drive; however, the maximum trading area included consumers making a 20-minute drive.

Retailers of shopping goods, such as women's clothing, and of specialty goods, such as petite women's clothing, generally have a larger trading area. The consumer buys these goods less often than convenience goods and plans the purchase rather than buying by habit. Often, the consumer covers greater distances when comparison shopping. Nonetheless, a shopping goods retailer should not locate too far away from her customers. Specialty retailers have the widest trading area of all retailers, since consumers will make a special effort to shop at these stores.[2] Even wholesalers, service firms, and manufacturing plants have a definable trading area. However, the trading area for a wholesaler or manufacturing plant is obviously much larger than that of a retail or service firm and may even extend into other countries. The entrepreneur should consider the size of the trading area for the industry chosen before selecting an exact location.

Lease or Buy

All new businesses must decide whether to lease or buy a facility. For most start-ups it is best to lease with an option to buy. By doing so, the entrepreneur minimizes start up costs, and this in turn typically decreases the required down payment. Most financial institutions hesitate to lend money for the purchase of a facility when the business has no track record of success, or when there is no way to know if that location is the best choice. Therefore, the lease allows the business to learn if the location is suitable, while the option to buy may prevent a forced relocation. In most cases, the financial institutions will require that the lease have a renewal option for as long as the loan for start-up costs is outstanding. This prevents an entrepreneur from having a

---

[2]Lowry, *Using a Traffic Study*, 2.

lease expire with no suitable locations available, while still owing large amounts on the start-up loan.

Leasehold
Improvements
Renovations made on
property that is leased.

Leasehold improvements (renovations made to leased property) are often a consideration for the entrepreneur. Although leasing the property, the lessee (the entrepreneur) is often responsible for renovations. The lessor (property owner) is not required to remodel the building to the entrepreneur's specifications. This presents a dilemma for the entrepreneur since many leasehold improvements become the property of the lessor. Renovations such as tile floors, drop ceilings, or additional plumbing can not be removed by the lessee if he has to relocate. Thus, the entrepreneur must weigh the need for renovations against the knowledge that these assets belong to someone else, and that the investment will not be recouped if the business does not succeed or relocates.

Renovations are not always wise, even if the entrepreneur plans to purchase the building, because renovations will often substantially increase start-up costs. The entrepreneur often finds that he must decide between a building that originally appears to cost less but requires many renovations, and a building that has a higher initial cost but is ready to occupy.

Zoning and Licensing

For all industries, the business must obtain proper zoning and licensing. Communities enforce zoning laws to prevent the growth of establishments not compatible with the plans for the area. For example, zoning laws may prevent a used car lot from locating next to a residential area. Similarly, zoning laws have prohibited pinball arcades in shopping centers, when the existing store owners felt the arcade would become a ''hangout'' and so decrease their business.

While communities raise revenue by business licenses, they can also use licensing to keep out unwanted businesses. Communities that want to restrict the number of liquor stores or bars can do so by refusing to issue the necessary liquor licenses.

Cost per Square Foot

Whenever commercial property is leased or sold, costs per square foot are quoted. For example, a 2,000-square-foot building may lease for $36,000 per year. This building would then be said to lease for $18 per square foot ($18 × 2,000 square feet = $36,000 per year). Entrepreneurs should not allow price to dominate their decision, as the saving on rent is often made up in other costs. For example, a retail outlet and some service businesses usually find a trade-off between rental costs and advertising costs. The company with an excellent location may have to advertise less than the company with a less desirable location. Therefore, no money is saved in the long run by choosing the less expensive location. Similarly, wholesalers and manufacturers often

Unique Business   5.2

Flower Kiosks for Fliers Venture

Paul Kostoff of Dearborn, Michigan, is the founder and owner of Floraline Inc., a company that places in airport terminals automated kiosks for ordering flowers. The kiosks display a variety of floral arrangements from which customers can choose. After making the choice, the customer places the order, using a toll-free phone and charging the purchase to a major credit card. Kostoff plans to have 400 kiosks in 55 airports. Because 360 million travelers pass through U.S. airports each year, the posy potential looks mind-boggling.

Source: Venture, May 1984, 10.

find a trade-off between the cost of the facility and transportation or overhead costs.

The Ideal Location

It is often difficult for entrepreneurs to determine the best way to look for a site. Since so many factors must be considered, the entrepreneur often feels overwhelmed by the information that he needs to analyze. One helpful method entrepreneurs should consider is to imagine the perfect or ideal location before attempting to locate a site. If she lists all the factors of that perfect location, the entrepreneur has a checklist for comparing real sites to the ideal. Though no site has everything, some locations will be closer to perfect than others. This method forces the entrepreneur to consider the choices carefully, rather than taking the first location that seems "suitable." The following information should help the entrepreneur develop this checklist.

Retail Outlets

A retail consultant was asked, "What are the three factors most likely to ensure retailing success?" His reply was, "(1) Location, (2) Location, (3) Location." In his view, the impact of site selection on the success of a retail operation cannot be overstressed.[3] It is essential that potential retail entrepreneurs—a large portion of all small business owners—be familiar with the factors that determine a site's desirability. This section discusses those factors.

Type of Facility

A retail outlet's trading area (and therefore its sales volume) is determined not only by the type of product and the area (suburban, rural, urban), but also by the type of facility in which the business is located. In general, a retail business may be located in a freestanding building or in a shopping center. If the entrepreneur is considering a shopping center location, her choices are a neighborhood, community, or regional shopping center.

Freestanding Buildings. For some types of businesses, freestanding buildings are preferred to shopping centers. Freestanding buildings often have greater accessibility and visibility than a shopping center location, and therefore a shopping center location is not always the best alternative. For businesses such as convenience food stores, restaurants, or ice cream and frozen custard stands, freestanding buildings are often recommended. Consider, for example, the convenience food store customer. Typically he is in a hurry and wants to stop in, pick up an item, and continue on his way.[4] A freestanding building on a corner allows the customer easy access in and out of the parking lot, and adequate parking should not be a problem. If, however, the store were located in a shopping center, the customer might not wish to fight the additional traffic and parking problems. Also, for any business where the customers do not come to the business location (such as a pest control business), a freestanding building may offer better leasing rates, more space, and more flexibility concerning the types of renovations that can be made. Freestanding buildings are also best for businesses that have special requirements, such as auto repair shops with several bays.

Freestanding buildings are not recommended for any business that serves customers who decide to shop there on impulse. For example, a card and gift shop or a bookstore is best located in a shopping center where people browse from one store to the next. Customers often decide to stop in and purchase an item even though they did not plan the purchase. Products that are usually planned purchases, such as paint, are often found in freestanding buildings.

Neighborhood Shopping Center
A shopping center in which the anchor store is a supermarket or drugstore, and most other stores cater to the convenience needs of the area residents.

The Neighborhood Shopping Center. The typical **neighborhood shopping center** occupies approximately 4 acres and serves 7,500 to 40,000 people living within a 6- to 10-minute drive from the center. The anchor store (prime traffic generator) is a supermarket or drugstore, and most other stores in the center cater to the convenience needs of the area residents.

---

[3]Lowry, *Using a Traffic Study,* 7.
[4]Lowry, *Using a Traffic Study,* 9.

Community Shopping Center
A shopping center in which the dominant store is a large variety store or junior department store, and other stores emphasize shopping and convenience goods.

Regional Shopping Center
A shopping center that includes several large department stores, and most other stores cater to the shopping needs of the residents.

Community Shopping Center. **Community shopping centers** typically occupy approximately 10 acres and serve 40,000 to 150,000 residents living within a 10- to 20-minute drive. The dominant store is generally a large variety store or junior department store. This type of center emphasizes both shopping and convenience goods, providing more specialty shops, wider price ranges in goods, and more impulse-buy items.

Regional Shopping Center. **Regional shopping centers** serve 100,000 to 200,000 people living within a 20- to 40-minute drive. Major tenants include large department stores, often located at the ends of an enclosed mall. This type of center's major emphasis is shopping goods, although a few convenience stores may locate in the center to take advantage of the high traffic volume.[5]

Availability to Small Businesses

Although neighborhood, community, and regional centers are options as locations, the availability of space for small businesses is often limited. The developers of the shopping centers first negotiate leases with the anchor tenants. They then select other stores to complement each other and develop a variety of merchandise. For the developer to obtain the financing needed to build the center, it must obtain leases from companies with strong credit ratings. Thus, it is often very difficult for a new small business to get space in these centers. A new small business may obtain space in a neighborhood or community shopping center if the developer has most of the other spaces filled and needs smaller tenants to "fill in." However, it is very unlikely that a new small business would be given space in a regional shopping center.

The owner of a gourmet popcorn store found this to be true when she asked mall developers about leasing space. She had recently purchased the business and did not have much experience. In addition, the previous owners had not properly managed the company, and the company's credit rating was poor. Thus, developers viewed the business as a high risk and did not want to negotiate a lease. She was forced to remain in the original location for several years even though it was less desirable than what she wanted. Another example of a small business encountering difficulties in finding a suitable location is given in Illustration Capsule 5.1.

Once a small business is established, though, and has developed a good reputation, developers will welcome the small retailer. At this stage, the small business owner is in a much better position to negotiate more favorable terms. Not only will the entrepreneur be able to negotiate lease rates but she will also have more influence in obtaining an acceptable location within the center. This may be crucial, as adjacent stores are a major factor.

---

[5]T. Ross McKeever, *Factors in Considering a Shopping Center Location* (Washington, D.C.: U.S. Government Printing Office, 1979), 2.

Office Space in Short Supply

Bob Smith, president of MidPak Inc., a packaging manufacturers' representative, had every intention of renewing his lease for office space in Clayton, Missouri. But that was before he found out that the larger tenant on his floor wanted to expand. "The developer was very open about it," said Smith. "They told me if they were forced to choose between the two tenants they would have to choose to keep the larger tenant."

Although Smith did not think relocating would be a problem, it took him more than 5 months to find a place that suited his need for 800 to 1,000 square feet of quality office space.

Smith stated, "The thing that surprised me about going to occupied buildings was the only thing available was next to the furnace room. When I looked at buildings under construction . . . they were not interested in talking to me until they had leased to the large tenants . . . they are only interested in a small tenant to fill out a building . . . . It does pose a hardship on a small business."

Source: "Small Tenants Face Trouble Finding New Office Space," *St. Louis Business Journal.*

Loss of Control at Shopping Center Locations

For many retail stores, locating in a shopping center is usually more desirable than in a freestanding building. However, entrepreneurs must be aware of the loss of freedom a shopping center location brings. Many shopping centers require the stores to maintain certain hours, participate in advertising programs, and pay additional fees for maintenance of common areas. For very seasonal businesses, such as ice cream stores, a requirement to stay open all year may result in tremendous overhead costs when compared with sales volume.

Another factor that entrepreneurs must consider is the trend toward mail order or catalog shopping because of the rapid pace of life-styles. With a large number of women in the work force, the amount of time available for leisurely shopping is less than in the past. Therefore, a mall location may be less desirable than one conveniently located for quick trips.

Nature of Adjacent Stores

The sales volume of a retail business is often enhanced or diminished by the nature of the outlets surrounding it. Therefore, a major factor any entrepreneur must consider is whether the adjacent stores complement the proposed business. For certain businesses, such as card and gift shops or bookstores, the ideal conditions are those in which customers shop leisurely, browsing among many stores. Though a location next to a grocery store in a neighborhood shopping center may seem ideal because of the number of shoppers, the entrepreneur will find that the grocery store customers tend to be in a hurry and will not take time to stop and browse through a bookstore or gift shop. Adjacent stores should also keep similar hours, complementary to the proposed business.

The surrounding stores not only affect the sales of a new outlet but can also affect the sales volume of an established business. One retailer of men's apparel had successfully operated at the same location for many years with a women's clothing store and a shoe store adjacent. When the women's clothing store relocated, the shoe store noticed a drop in sales and also relocated. Although other tenants moved in, they were not complementary to the men's store. The men's apparel store experienced such a sharp drop in sales that it was forced to relocate or go out of business.

Competition

Any entrepreneur should thoroughly evaluate the competition within the trading area. He should determine not only the number of competitors but also the competitive advantage of each, their financial strength, product quality, price ranges, reputation, and so forth. Based on this information, the entrepreneur can determine how the proposed business will carve a niche in the marketplace.

Though many entrepreneurs feel that the ideal location is one where no competition exists, this is not necessarily the case. Many businesses such as car dealers, fast food stores, and shoe stores find that business increases if they locate near many competitors. In one instance, a small shoe retailer was located directly across the street from a larger shoe store. When the large store moved out, the sales volume of the small store decreased, although no competition was nearby. The customers no longer came into the area to shop for shoes but instead drove to a nearby shopping center.

Traffic Counts

Automobile and pedestrian traffic counts are often used to evaluate a location's desirability. An entrepreneur can usually learn the number of cars passing a specific location from local street departments or state highway departments. Pedestrian traffic counts may be available from shopping center developers. However, the actual number of cars or pedestrians is not sufficient information on which to base decisions. The entrepreneur needs to know not only how many people pass by, but also the characteristics of those people compared with the people who would patronize the entrepreneur's business. While a drug store may be interested in total traffic volume, a men's clothing store is more concerned with male traffic, particularly between the ages of 16 and 65 years.[6]

It may also be important to determine the reason potential customers pass a location, and the time of day, since the purpose of their trip may determine their willingness to stop. When one chain organization estimates the number of potential female customers, it considers only women passing a site between 10 a.m. and 5 p.m. to be serious shoppers.[7]

The analysis of the traffic must also include income levels, since only a percentage of the total may meet the income requirements of the desired clientele. The final analysis should include only those with the necessary buying power.

Visibility

It is also essential to consider whether the business can be easily seen from the cars or people passing by. A high traffic count or pedestrian count is of little value if no one sees the business when passing. Though poor visibility can be offset slightly by large signs, many municipalities have restrictive sign laws that prevent the entrepreneur from using large signs, neon signs, or other obtrusive signs.

Accessibility

When analyzing traffic patterns, the entrepreneur must also consider the accessibility of the proposed site. For example, is it along a major street or is it on a side street that requires extra effort of the consumers? Are there medians in the road, one-way streets, or dangerous intersections that would deter potential customers? Many previously successful businesses have found that sales volume decreased substantially when the street departments changed the flow of traffic.

Parking

Another factor to consider with traffic patterns is the availability of parking. A large flow of traffic will be useless if the parking area is not adequate. Many cities have ordinances that dictate a minimum number of spaces per

---

[6]Lowry, *Using a Traffic Study,* 4.
[7]Lowry, *Using a Traffic Study,* 4.

square foot of retail space; however, the entrepreneur must determine if these minimum standards are sufficient.

Future Population Trends

Once current conditions are assessed, it is also necessary to consider trends in the geographic area. Factors to consider include increases or decreases in population count, average age, income levels, and standard of living. It is not sufficient to consider only present conditions, as future trends may be a deciding factor. Future demographic changes must be determined and analyzed as to their impact on the proposed business.

Service

....

Method of Operation

With service businesses, much depends on whether the customers come to the service or if the service goes to the customer. If the business goes to the customers, travel time and costs would be a concern, but the actual facility would be less important. For example, a pest control business may be able to locate in a building away from the hub of the city or in a freestanding building on a side street. The dry cleaner, however, may find a side street location inadequate. As stated before, the entrepreneur must realize that even for a service firm, such as the pest control business, visibility of the facility may be advantageous. The pest control business that locates away from the traffic area may find it necessary to advertise more to keep the company name in consumers' minds. If the company is along a well-traveled road and has a visible sign, this is ''free'' advertising whenever customers drive past the office.

Reputation versus Convenience

As with retailers, the sales potential of a service firm depends on the trading area. As with any site analysis, the location of a service business often begins with determining who the customers will be and where they are located. Many service firms must be conveniently located; for others, however, the exact location is not critical to success. For example, doctors and dentists receive a substantial number of patients by referral because of a reputation for excellent service and reasonable prices. Though convenience is a factor, a customer does not necessarily go to the nearest, or most convenient, doctor or dentist. Similarly, many consumers have a favorite beautician or barber and will make a little extra effort to go to that person.

We do not mean to imply that for a service firm, such as a doctor or a dentist, location is not important. One dentist, for example, located in an upper-middle-income neighborhood with many families. His location was excellent until the community grew rapidly and the traffic count on the street in front of his office increased dramatically. Entering and exiting his parking lot became so difficult, he was forced to relocate or lose many of his clients. If convenience is as important or more important than reputation, the service firm's location decision is very similar to the retailer's. All of the factors that apply to the retail firm will most likely apply to the service firm. If, however, reputation is so important that customers will make a little extra effort to go to that business, then only some of the factors that apply to retail stores should be considered. Figure 5.1 illustrates these differences.

Manufacturing Plants

....

While it is obvious to most people that a retail outlet's location is critical to its success, the need for a proper location is no less important for manufacturing firms. A senior engineer at DuPont once stated:

> We approach the problem of site selection with the firm belief that it is one of the most critical decisions that industrial management has to make . . . Competition in industry and rising costs have made it more and more imperative that all items affecting investment and cost of operation be thoroughly analyzed and the plant located where they can be held to a minimum. Personal preference or selection at random has no place in plant site selection. Operating defects usually can be corrected at comparatively low cost, but faults of location are forever carried as a manufacturing burden.[8]

For the small firm, choosing the proper location is especially important, since the small company is less likely to relocate; the first location may also be the last location. Often, though, the manufacturer/entrepreneur does not possess enough experience to choose a site adequately. The secretary of a major city's chamber of commerce once stated that "the small manufacturer is often swayed by considerations unimportant or irrelevant to the success of the business in choosing a location, while overlooking vital considerations."[9]

Before the entrepreneur begins the search for a manufacturing site, she must complete some preliminary planning. An essential step in planning is to develop a detailed list of the firm's requirements as to area, community, and site. A good understanding of the firm's requirements not only will help prevent locational errors but will also reduce the time and expense spent on the

---

[8]James Thompson, *Methods of Plant Site Selection Available to Small Manufacturing Firms* (Morgantown, W.Va: West Virginia University, 1961), 1.
[9]Thompson, *Methods of Plant Site Selection*, 2.

Figure   5.1   Location Factors for Retail and Service Firms

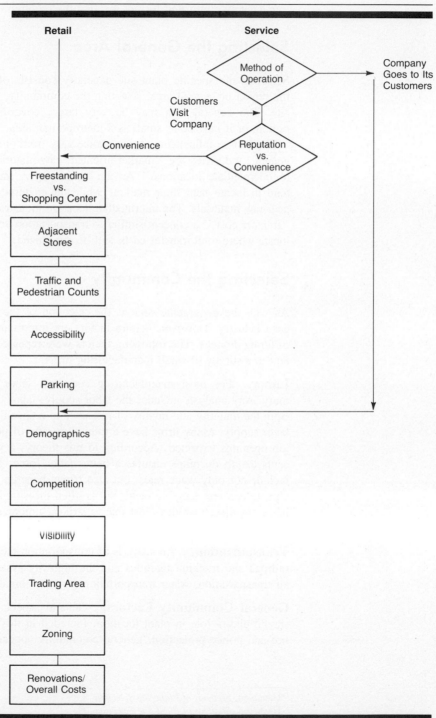

site selection. If requirements are listed, several possible locations can be immediately eliminated for not meeting the requirements.[10]

Selecting the General Area

Selecting the specific plant site generally consists of three stages: choosing the region or general area, selecting the community, and picking the specific site. The general area may be very large, covering an entire geographic region, or it may be as small as a metropolitan area.

The factors influencing region choice vary from one industry to another. In general, industries are "market-oriented, raw-material oriented, or attracted to intermediate locations." As the terms imply, market-oriented industries tend to locate near their markets while the material-oriented tend to locate near raw materials. The intermediate-location industries place an emphasis on "transfer cost," a concept similar to transportation costs. The firm will try to locate where total transfer costs will be minimized.[11]

Selecting the Community

As with the geographic region, the selection of the community varies with each industry. However, certain factors are important to all firms, though in differing degrees. The following factors were repeatedly mentioned as important in a survey of small manufacturing firms.

Labor.   For most manufacturing concerns, labor considerations are primary. Any analysis includes the labor supply, labor costs, and labor climate. Both the quantity and quality of the labor in a specific area are considered in labor supply. Many firms have a minimum ratio of possible job applicants to job openings expected. According to this theory, a very high ratio of applicants to job openings ensures a better labor force. Labor cost studies must include not only wage rates, but also fringe benefits and productivity. Labor climate is a less tangible factor but is often measured by number and type of labor disputes, man-days lost due to strikes, unionization, rates of absenteeism and turnover, and worker attitudes toward management.

Transportation.   An analysis of transportation facilities generally includes railroad and trucking facilities and the highway system. It may also include air transportation, water transportation, or a combination.

General Community Factors.   General aspects of the community also should play a role in plant location. Included in this part of the analysis are fire and police protection, general community appearance, local government

---

[10]Thompson, *Methods of Plant Site Selection*, 8.
[11]Thompson, *Methods of Plant Site Selection*, 29.

administration, and community attitudes toward the new plant. Companies should look for a ''general atmosphere of interest, enthusiasm, and a desire for additional industry.''[12] Similarly, a company may look for obvious expressions of goodwill such as a willingness of municipal leaders to make zoning changes, provide tax abatement, furnish free land, and extend utility lines free of charge.

Utilities.   An essential community factor is the availability and adequacy of utilities such as water, electric, natural gas, and sewage disposal.[13] Generally, a manufacturing firm has specific utility needs that cannot be compromised. If these utility needs cannot be met, the community can be quickly eliminated. Water supply is often of particular concern owing to water shortages in many areas of the country. Shortages result not only from climatic aberrations but sometimes from the system's failure to keep up with community development.

Other Factors.   The entrepreneur should also consider size of the community, size and character of other local industries, land and construction costs, location relative to competitors, and personal considerations.

Selecting the Specific Site

The factors affecting the selection of a specific site often overlap those that affect the choice of community; however, some factors specifically concern site.

Size and Shape of the Site.   A study of existing manufacturing plants indicated the sites ranged from one to six hundred acres, and that almost half were between twenty and fifty acres. A rectangular site was generally found, although this was subject to compromise if other factors were ideal.

Topography and Drainage.   Plant sites are usually built on comparatively level ground with enough slope to provide adequate drainage. However, exceptions do exist. One small manufacturer built his plant on a hill so that shipments and deliveries could be made on two levels.

Firms conducting a site analysis should avoid natural low spots. The possibility of flooding should be investigated by checking records of previous floods.

Soil Conditions.   Soil conditions have a substantial bearing on the foundation requirements, drainage, and development costs, so soil should not be considered unimportant. It is even more important when the plant structure requires land with a high load-bearing capacity, or when the plant is to be located in an area where foundation problems are common. Ground borings

---

[12]Thompson, *Methods of Plant Site Selection*, 47.
[13]Thompson, *Methods of Plant Site Selection*, 48.

Small Business Success 5

Dorn and Co., Encino, California

The innovative approach on which Dorn and Co. of Encino is built can be seen in the early days of its founder, Todd Dorn. As a 9-year-old, he discovered a better way to display the flowers he was selling on a street corner. He outsold his competitors, but more importantly, he learned the value of a better way in running a business. His latest use of this better-way approach is in office leasing. Dorn recognized that business owners who need more office space seldom have the time and energy to investigate. Using color videotapes and a computerized data base with current information on price, square footage, parking, and so forth, Dorn and Co. provides the tenant-client with a catalogue of all possibilities meeting their criteria.

Dorn's firm is prospering, and he has a net worth goal of $5 million by his 30th birthday.

Source: America at Work (Washington, D.C.: Small Business Administration, 1985), 40.

can provide the necessary information. "Saving the cost of test borings, even when a site appears perfect on the surface, is risking dollars to save pennies."[14]

Cost of Development versus Purchasing an Existing Building.   The cost of developing a particular site is much more important than the price of unimproved acreage. Development costs include not only the original cost of the land, but also "grading, filling, drainage, excavation, foundation construction, building access roads, constructing a railroad siding . . . when all development costs are considered, the lowest priced site turns out to be the most expensive."[15]

If the business decides to purchase or lease an existing building rather than construct a new one, this requirement is a limiting factor in selecting the community and site. The purchase of an existing building is required (1) when time is a major constraint, (2) when a branch operation is established, or (3)

[14]Thompson, *Methods of Plant Site Selection*, 53.
[15]Thompson, *Methods of Plant Site Selection*, 53.

when a brand new manufacturer cannot acquire sufficient financing to build. In many cases, the price per square foot is much less for an existing building than for a newly constructed one. However, most plant location experts do not advise the entrepreneur to purchase an existing building. "Small companies, especially, are warned not to place too high a value on existing 'brick and mortar.' An attractive, low-priced building in a poor location is no bargain in the long run."[16]

Other Factors.   In addition to the above factors, other considerations may include size of the community, size and character of other local industries, land and construction costs, location relative to competitors, and personal considerations.

Wholesalers

Choice of a City

For many wholesalers, the major decision that determines success or failure is the choice of city, rather than the choice of location within the city. Cities often serve as wholesaling centers for certain products. The wholesaler may find it best to locate within that city. However, this may result in stiff competition if several other wholesalers are already operating there; therefore, it is often possible to build a successful wholesale operation by locating in a city that does not have many other wholesalers in the same industry. One successful wholesaler of paperback books found in St. Louis a market with numerous paperback retailers but few wholesalers. Although his customers can order from out-of-town wholesalers or from the publisher, his proximity to them has allowed him to establish a reputation for good service and quick delivery.

For wholesalers, many factors affecting the choice of a city are similar to those of a manufacturer. The locations of customers and suppliers, transportation, taxes, and the labor climate will certainly influence the decision (see Figure 5.2 and Illustration Capsule 5.2)

Urban or Rural

Once he has chosen the city, the wholesaler must then decide whether to locate within its hub or on its outskirts. While an urban location may place the company closer to its customers, a location on the outskirts of the city is often less costly to lease or buy. Wholesalers need a large facility for storing inventory, so reducing the cost of the facility is desirable. If, however, the

---

[16]Thompson, *Methods of Plant Site Selection,* 56.

Figure   5.2   Location Factors for Wholesale and Manufacturing Firms

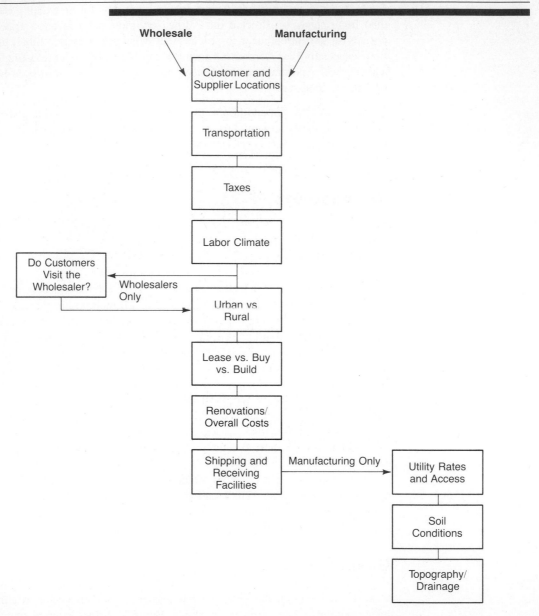

Illustration Capsule 5.2

A Great Place to Work
Reno, Nevada and Austin, Texas

Although slot machines and roulette wheels put Reno on the map, city officials saw a need to attract a variety of industries. "When three casinos closed and a number of others were showing signs of trouble," says city manager Chris Cherches, "we knew it was time to stop being a one-industry town."

Therefore, Reno officials began efforts to attract warehouses and light manufacturing plants. Reno is ideal for these industries, since it is a "hub" city with a major interstate highway, 13 airlines, 57 trucking companies, 2 freight railroads plus Amtrack, and 7 bus lines. Its location between two of the West's key cities—San Francisco is 231 miles away and Salt Lake City 521—assures overnight delivery, so critical to shippers. Tax considerations are also extremely favorable. Nevada has no personal income tax, no corporate income tax, and no franchise, inheritance, estate, gift, or inventory tax. Finally, Nevada is a right-to-work state, which means workers cannot be required to join a union.

The city officials' efforts were successful. Today, about 300 firms, ranging from the giant K mart and J.C. Penney to the smaller Shu Fly Industries and New Balance Athletic Shoe Inc., occupy 30 million square feet of warehouse and industrial space. Reno is now one of the largest central distributing points in the United States.

Since the late 1960s, about 60 firms have moved to Austin, largely because of the recruiting efforts of business leaders. From 1972 to 1982, manufacturing jobs almost tripled, to more than 33,000.

A big draw is the life-style. The undulating hills and shimmering lakes attract both the urban-weary of Texas's larger cities and those from the state's dry western plains. The slower pace contrasts to the boom-town hustle of Dallas and Houston.

One newcomer is Romeo Bachand, president of a small pharmaceutical company, who with his ten employees arrived 8 months ago from Ohio. He says he never would have considered Austin except that the computer kept spitting it out in studies of good business sites.

Source: JoAnne Davidson and Sarah Peterson, "Why Many Firms Return to Small Cities," *U.S. News and World Report,* April 2, 1984, 77.

rural location results in excessive transportation costs, no benefits have been achieved.

The Facility

Much of the decision concerning the actual facility depends on whether the customers visit the wholesaler's place of business or whether the wholesaler makes direct sales calls to the retailers. This would affect the building's location, layout, and decor. As with all other types of businesses, the overall cost of the building is a consideration, including the needed renovations, as well as zoning restrictions.

Because wholesalers are constantly receiving and shipping goods, easy access is essential in the site analysis. Loading and unloading facilities must be carefully checked, as well as the accessibility of all necessary transportation.

Negotiating a Lease

As with any legal agreement, the business owner should not sign a lease without having a lawyer review it. Because the lessor has written the lease, most of the conditions will favor the lessor, not the lessee. If the entrepreneur signs a lease without reviewing it and making changes, it is likely to contain unfavorable terms.

Although many leases are quoted at a fixed cost per square foot, some base costs on sales. For example, lease costs may be stated as $1,500 per month or 8 percent of sales, whichever is greater, or $1,200 per month plus 3 percent of sales. The entrepreneur must realize that during inflationary times when total sales volume is increasing owing to price increases, the lease rates will also be escalating. It is advisable to restrict the size of annual increases, if possible.

The entrepreneur should also build in "escape clauses" for a number of situations. Escape clauses allow the entrepreneur to terminate the lease early with no penalty. For example, an escape clause may be desired if the anchor tenant moves, if the building is sold, or if the vacancy rate in the shopping center exceeds a certain percentage. Without escape clauses, the entrepreneur is legally bound to the lease under all circumstances.

It is essential that the lease include "options to renew." This gives the entrepreneur some guarantee against a forced relocation. For example, one entrepreneur opened a store in a shopping center and signed an 18-month lease. She wanted a short-term lease to make sure that the site was excellent before she signed a longer lease. The landlord guaranteed her that she could renew the lease at the end of the 18 months. Unfortunately, the landlord sold the building one year after the entrepreneur had opened. The new owner had new plans for the building and would not renew the lease. All the money the entrepreneur had invested in leasehold improvements was lost. If she had had a 3-year lease with two 3-year options, the space would have been legally available for 9 years.

The leasehold improvements to be completed by the lessor and lessee should also be negotiated. If the lessee (entrepreneur) is expected to pay for all improvements, free rent should be negotiated in exchange for this investment. The entrepreneur must realize that, unless otherwise negotiated, lease payments may be due for several months before the business opens because of renovations being made, shelves being stocked, or machinery being installed. Several months' free rent may be necessary to keep from using up working capital funds.

Entrepreneurs leasing space in new shopping centers should be especially cautious about lease rates. Often, new shopping centers do not attract tenants as quickly as expected. The first tenants find minimal pedestrian traffic passing by the business. Some provisions must be made for reduced lease rates until the shopping center is occupied near capacity levels.

The entrepreneur must consider an almost endless list of items when reviewing a lease. The above items are merely a few examples. Because of the numerous problems that arise owing to poorly negotiated leases, the entrepreneur should have a lawyer review the lease and help negotiate changes. All changes must be in writing and initialled by the lessee and lessor to prevent future problems.

K E Y   Objectives Reviewed

1. The location decision is critical to the success of any business. Many entrepreneurs, however, do not exercise sufficient care when choosing the location. A poor location may result in a variety of serious disadvantages.

2. There are several location decisions that all industries must consider when completing a site analysis: the trading area, the decision to lease or buy, and licensing and zoning requirements.

3. For each industry, specific factors should be analyzed when completing a site analysis. For retail outlets, the type of facility, the nature of adjacent stores, competition, traffic counts, and demographics are critical. For wholesalers, the choice of a city, the area within that city, and the type of facility are often deciding factors. Service firms vary since some go to their customers, while others have the customers come to them. For manufacturers, the general area and the community are often deciding factors, as well as specific site factors such as size, drainage, and development costs.

4. Factors to consider when negotiating a lease include means of deter-
    mining lease costs, escape clauses, options to renew, leasehold
    improvements, and occupancy rates in new shopping centers.

Discussion Questions

1. Suppose an entrepreneur plans to open a retail clothing store. She
    states, ''The place I lease must have 2,000 square feet and must cost
    less than $2,000 per month.'' Why should cost per month not be a
    preliminary factor in choosing a site?

2. Discuss what types of retail and service businesses could be successful
    in freestanding buildings where there is little or no pedestrian traffic.

3. Identify some small manufacturers and wholesalers in your commu-
    nity. What factors do you feel caused them to choose their specific
    locations?

4. Identify several empty facilities in your community and determine
    which types of businesses would be most successful at those locations.

5. Identify the ''ideal'' location for the following businesses:
    • convenience food store/gas pump outlet
    • family shoe store
    • wholesale book company
    • record manufacturer

6. Identify a business in your area that you think has a poor location.
    Why is it a poor location for that type of business?

7. Identify a service firm in your area that goes to its customers and
    another in which the customers go to the service firm. How do the
    locations differ? How are they similar?

8. Contact the appropriate local agencies to determine the projected pop-
    ulation changes for your area. What effect will these changes have on
    the area businesses? Which will be favorably affected? Unfavorably
    affected? Not affected at all?

9. Identify areas in your community where competing businesses have
    purposely located near each other. Why have they done this?

CHAPTER 6

Break-Even Analysis

Source: Copyright 1986 Phyllis Woloshin.

K   E   Y   Objectives

1. To explain the role of break-even analysis in planning for business starts.

2. To describe the techniques with which break-even analysis is conducted.

3. To describe two types of errors that can occur in planning business start-ups.

4. To identify the sources of data needed for break-even analysis.

No one starts a business believing that it will fail. The entrepreneur's hopes are usually high but frequently not achieved. The failure of a business brings hardships of many types to many people. The entrepreneur suffers; the family suffers; the creditors suffer; the customers suffer. Small business failure is a very serious problem.

Small businesses often fail because of events no one could have predicted. Far more failures, however, result from ill-advised attempts to establish businesses with almost no hope of success. No planning system can guarantee that such avoidable mistakes will not be made, but the system we are about to describe can help. This system is called break-even analysis, and it is a very effective means of preventing the mistake of starting an ill-fated business. We will describe the technique and the sources of data needed to use it.

This chapter, then, is concerned with failure prevention. It has been said that the leading cause of divorce is marriage. By the same logic, it can be said that business failures are caused by business starts. By preventing starts, failures can be prevented. That statement becomes much more useful if we modify it somewhat. By preventing starts that should not be made, many failures can be prevented.

Type A and Type B Errors

Type A Error
Rejection of a plan for a business that would have succeeded.

Type B Error
Acceptance of an unsound idea as the basis for a business.

The problem is to avoid two types of errors. First, those businesses that could succeed must not be abandoned before start-up. We must not make our process of screening and evaluating ideas so stringent that only extremely promising proposals survive. Such high selectivity will result in some sound ideas being rejected. This is a **type A error.**

The second, and more obvious, error is one of leniency. Here proposals with weak prospects for success are developed into businesses. This, the acceptance of unsound ideas, is a **type B error.**

Unique Business   6.1

Business on the Move

Californians Hans Buhringer and Ann Turkel have established Now or Never, a company with five mobile fitness centers. Each unit is a customized truck, equipped with $10,000 worth of exercise equipment including weights, rowing machine, stationary cycle, heart monitors, and biofeedback machine. The $50 per hour rental includes the supervision of a trained coach.

Bette Forman, a former real estate agent in Bethesda, Maryland, replaced the seats in a school bus with video games. Since then, the Pac Van has been visiting festivals, fairs, and private parties.

Source: Nation's Business, March 1984, 66

The two types of errors are obviously related to one another. The more we take care not to reject a sound idea (type A), the greater are the chances of accepting a poor one (type B), and vice versa. There are statistics to convince us that many type B errors are made every year, but we have no way of knowing the number of type A errors because no one monitors them. For most people the consequences of going with a loser (type B) are serious enough to make this mistake their biggest concern.

Break-even analysis is a useful tool for screening ideas, and for that reason it is given a prominent place here in the early part of our text. It involves straightforward data gathering that any prospective entrepreneur can perform. The results can be extremely enlightening, despite the tool's simplicity. As an example, a couple who were considering starting a restaurant found, through break-even analysis, that they would have to average over 170 customers per day before they would realize any profits. They found this volume requirement very discouraging in light of the restaurant's 34-person seating capacity. They looked for, and found, a larger, less expensive location.

The Technique

Break-even analysis is a technique used to determine the minimum sales volume necessary for survival; at lower sales levels a company suffers losses and at higher levels it makes a profit. Two things are needed to conduct a break-

Illustration Capsule   6.1

Lowering the Cost of Doing Business

As prospective entrepreneurs weigh the possibility of going into business, they often need to trim costs to establish an attainable break-even point. In some businesses, such as restaurants, where competition is particularly keen, even a modest cost reduction can pay big dividends. Because of this, many owners of small businesses are turning to membership warehouses for a wide variety of their needs. These warehouses provide merchandise to certain individuals and to small businesses at, or near, wholesale prices, but in amounts the customer needs; there are no minimum quantities as with traditional warehouses.

One example of a business depending on purchases through a wholesale center is Top Banana Home Delivered Groceries in Baden, Maryland. Its first week of operations in 1982 brought one order and $27.86; the company's current annual gross is $130,000. The founder, Jean Guiffre, says she could not have started her business without having a center as a supply source.

Source: Sharon Welton, ''They Really Can Get It for You Wholesale,'' *Nation's Business*, March 1985, 74–76.

even analysis: an understanding of the technique and the necessary data. We will explain the technique now. Some sources of data were discussed in Chapter 4; we will discuss others later in this chapter.

Types of Costs

The first step in conducting a break-even analysis is to recognize two types of costs any business incurs. The first type of costs vary directly with the sales of the company. They are called **variable costs.** As an example of variable costs, consider the costs a store incurs in selling a $10 decal-decorated T-shirt. The company had to buy the shirt from its supplier for $3; it had to buy the decal selected by the customer for $0.40; and it must pay the salesperson a commission of $0.60. These various items cost $4, and they represent the direct costs of making the shirt. If the store sells 1,000 shirts in a month, its variable costs are $4,000 (1,000 shirts × $4 per shirt). If it sells

Variable Costs
Costs that vary directly with a company's sales.

only half that number, 500, its variable costs are also only half, $2,000 (500 shirts × $4). Variable costs rise and fall directly with the amount sold.

A business encounters other costs that are not affected by the amount of sales. These are costs that go on at more or less the same rate from week to week and month to month. The T-shirt store has to pay its rent whether it sells 1 shirt or 10,000; it must also pay its utility bills, salaries, and mortgage. These costs do not vary with sales levels; we call them **fixed costs.** By calling these fixed, we do not mean to suggest that they will never change. Indeed they will; the rent will go up, and so will salaries, utility bills, and other items in this "fixed" cost category. However, a company's fixed costs will not change as a result of a change in sales, so in that sense they are fixed. These costs are usually expressed in amount per period—$500 per month rent or $1,400 per year property taxes. For this reason such costs are sometimes called period costs.

Fixed Costs
Those costs that do not vary with sales level but are regular, ongoing obligations of a business, such as rent and utilities.

Contribution Margin

The relationship between the two types of costs is that fixed costs must be covered by the excess of sales revenue over variable expenses. Each dollar of sales requires a certain amount of variable expenses. That portion left over can be used to pay the business's fixed costs. The shirt store had $4 in direct costs for each shirt sold. Because the shirts sold for $10, the owner had $6 ($10 − $4) to use for the firm's various fixed expenses. This $6 figure has been given several names:

- **Profit.** This is incorrect because none of the store's fixed costs have been taken care of.
- **Operating profit.** This is better because it qualifies the term *profit* to indicate that there are more costs yet to be assigned.
- **Contribution margin.** This is best. The $6 is the margin of sales price less direct or variable costs, and it represents a contribution toward fixed costs and profits.

Contribution Margin
The portion of the sales revenue of an item that exceeds its variable cost and contributes toward fixed costs and/or profit.

Now that the **contribution margin (CM)** has been described, we can give it as a formula:

$$CM = \text{Sales Price} - \text{Variable Costs}.$$

An Example

Break-Even Point
The sales level at which the fixed costs have been equaled by total contribution margins.

To demonstrate how break-even analysis operates, we will use our shirt store example again, this time building in the assumption that the store has $3,000 in monthly fixed costs. Now we have everything we need to determine its **break-even point.** The process starts with the specification of the contribution margin, as given above. In our shirt store example:

$$CM = \$10 - \$4$$
$$CM = \$6$$

Figure 6.1   Break-Even Point

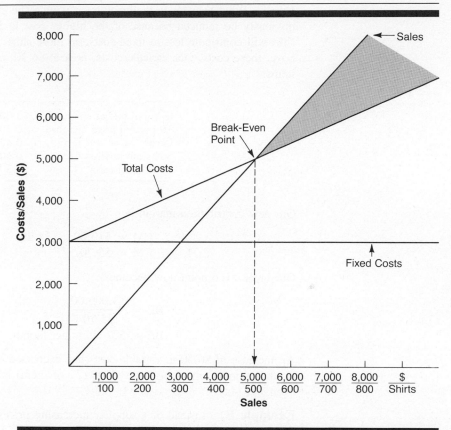

The break-even volume (BE) is determined by dividing the fixed costs (FC) by the contribution margin.

$$BE = \frac{FC}{CM}$$

$$BE = \frac{\$3,000}{\$6/shirt}$$

$$BE = 500 \text{ shirts.}$$

The store must sell 500 shirts to break even; each of these 500 shirts makes a $6 contribution to the payment of the store's fixed costs. With the sale of the 501st shirt, the profit begins. The owner makes $6 profit at that sales level and profits climb $6 for each additional sale.

Instead of these calculations we can use a graph (see Figure 6.1).

To demonstrate how changes in a firm's costs affect its break-even point, we will provide two examples.

Example A.   Suppose the T-shirt supplier announces a price increase of 10 percent. What happens to the break-even point? The contribution margin will obviously be reduced because of the higher cost level. Consequently, each shirt will contribute less to fixed costs, so more shirts will have to be sold to cover these costs. Our variable costs, now at $4.30, consist of the following items:

Original cost of shirt	$3.00
10 percent price increase	0.30
Decal	0.40
Sales commission	0.60
Total direct costs	$4.30

Our new contribution margin is

$$CM = \$10.00 - \$4.30$$
$$CM = \$5.70.$$

Our break-even point now becomes

$$BE = \frac{\$3,000.00}{\$5.70}$$
$$BE = 527 \text{ shirts per month.}$$

An increase of $0.30 in variable costs has decreased our contribution margin by that amount, meaning more shirts (27 of them) have to be sold to break even.

Example B.   Instead of a supplier increasing prices, suppose the landlord decreases the rent by $120 per month. If we use the new fixed-cost figure of $2,880 and the original variable costs, our break-even point is:

$$BE = \frac{\$2,880}{\$6}$$
$$BE = 480 \text{ shirts per month.}$$

Because the sale of each shirt contributes $6 to fixed-cost coverage, a $120 decrease in fixed costs requires 20 fewer shirts to be sold. Consequently, the break-even point goes to 480 from the original 500.

Figure 6.2 shows the impact of the two changes.

Gathering the Necessary Cost Data

By now the reader should understand the logic of break-even analysis, namely, that a business must cover its fixed costs using what is left over (contribution margin) from each sale after the variable costs of making the sale have themselves been covered. The reader should also feel comfortable

Figure   6.2   **Break-Even Point Changes**

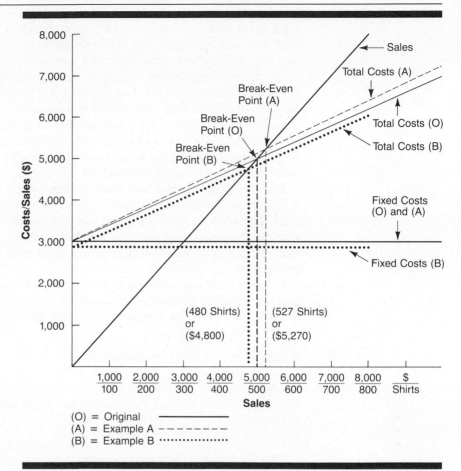

using the technique, so the next step is to describe the process of gathering the data needed to perform the analysis.

We need to know three things to determine whether a business will survive: its fixed costs, its variable costs, and the sales level it will achieve. We cover the determination of costs in the remainder of this chapter. Sales level projection was, of course, the topic of Chapter 4, "The Nature of the Market."

The distinction between fixed and variable costs, though clear in the examples given earlier in the chapter, is sometimes hard to make. For example, suppose the shirt store is air-conditioned and that the decal application process puts heat and humidity into the air. As more shirts are sold, the air conditioner uses more electricity (as does the decal machine). Consequently, part of our utilities bill (a fixed cost) varies with sales and, therefore, represents a variable cost. We seldom bother to separate that part, though, because it is small and hard to measure accurately.

Some other costs present the same problem of not being clearly fixed or variable. For example, the staffing level is roughly adjusted to anticipated sales levels, but the store manager cannot provide a corresponding unit of staff time with each shirt sold. The two are linked, but only in an indirect way, so staffing costs (other than sales commissions) are regarded as fixed costs. A large organization can adjust staffing to changes in sales volume, but a small business usually does not have that flexibility, so its labor costs are best regarded as fixed. The same is true for facilities costs. To summarize, a small, arbitrary element can come into play in designating costs as variable or fixed. The distinction is a large part of break-even analysis. The two types of costs operate in different ways, have different effects on the business, and must, therefore, be treated differently in our analysis.

Because we are dealing with small business, our approach is therefore to designate as fixed all of a business's costs other than those clearly linked to sales. These are the costs associated with the inventories and the sales commissions. For every sale made by the shirt store, the store has to have the shirt and the decal on hand in inventory and has to pay the salesperson a commission.

In using break-even analysis to evaluate a business's prospects, the first task is to establish the level of fixed costs the business will face—the costs of doing business after the firm has been established, not start-up costs. These costs include the following:

- Salaries
- Payroll taxes
- Advertising
- Rent
- Utilities
- Supplies
- Maintenance
- Insurance
- Interest
- Professional fees (legal and accounting)
- Depreciation
- Delivery expense

This list includes the typical expenses a business encounters each month. Some businesses will not face some of these, some will face them all, and still others will face additional expenses. The first step in establishing the level of fixed expenses, then, is to determine specifically the kinds of expenses that will be incurred. Some are obvious: a business needs a place from which to operate, so rent must be paid. Employees must be paid; utility expenses cannot be avoided; some kind of insurance is usually necessary. Most costs are easy to identify, but the complete listing of those a particular business will encounter can be established only on a case-by-case basis.

For every business about to start, a number of other, similar businesses already exist. Cost data from these businesses could answer our questions. Will the owners of these businesses provide the data? Certainly not to someone who may become a competitor; but if we are considering starting a drive-in movie theatre in Hannibal, Missouri, the owner of one in Hattiesburg, Mississippi may gladly share some insights. The task, of course, is to locate the owner of that similar business and get him to discuss these matters.

Exhibit   6.1   Pet Shop Costs as a Percentage of Sales

Net Cost of Goods	52.0% –58.0%
Expenses	
Advertising and promotion	2.0 – 5.0
Bad debts	0.6 – 1.0
Dues and subscriptions	0.2 – 0.3
Office expenses	0.5 – 1.0
Licenses and taxes	0.5 – 0.7
Miscellaneous	1.7 – 2.5
Rent	5.0 – 7.0
Salaries and wages	15.0 – 22.0
Supplies	1.0 – 1.5
Utilities and phone	1.5 – 2.0
Total Expenses	28.0% –43.0%

Source: "Independent Pet Shops," *Small Business Reporter* (San Francisco, Calif.: Bank of America, 1979).

There are, of course, more conventional ways of benefiting from the experiences of others. First, there are trade association publications. The *1984 Directory of National Trade and Professional Associations* lists more than 3,400 trade associations.[1] Some of these associations publish composite cost data for their members. If the potential entrepreneur is thinking about going into doors, for example, the Door and Operator Dealers of America may be able to provide some useful data. If she is going to specialize in doors of a certain material, the Fir and Hemlock Door Association or the Steel Door Institute may prove useful. Consider these other associations listed under "Doors":

- Door Operator and Remote Controls Manufacturers Association
- Garage Door Council
- Insulated Steel Door Systems Institute
- National Association of Garage Door Manufacturers
- National Sash and Door Jobbers Association
- National Woodwork Manufacturers Association

Another way to use data from existing firms is through publications such as the *Small Business Reporter* series of the Bank of America, San Francisco. The series includes profiles of various kinds of businesses, including cost data. As an example, Exhibit 6.1 gives a breakdown of expenses incurred by independent pet shops with sales of $75,000 to $175,000.

---

[1]*Directory of National Trade and Professional Associations of the United States* (Washington, D.C.: Columbia Books, 1984), 311.

El Paso Diablos Baseball Club, El Paso, Texas

Jim Paul took over the minor league baseball team in El Paso in 1973. Because of changes Paul instituted, the club doubled its attendance but still lost $22,000. The stockholders became discouraged and sold the team to him in 1974. In 1975, 80 percent of minor league baseball teams lost money, but the Diablos had crossed the break-even point, thanks to its owner's promotion efforts. Among these promotions were special nights such as "Kazoo Night" (free kazoos) and "10¢ Hot Dog Night." These and other attendance-building techniques are the basis for annual seminars Paul gives. Over 55 percent of teams represented at past seminars now show a profit. In El Paso, the turnabout has been dramatic, with attendance climbing from 62,000 in 1973 to nearly 300,000 in 1982.

Source: Small Business Means Jobs (Washington, D.C.: Small Business Administration, 1984), 18.

Two other sources of published data can be extremely helpful in projecting the costs a business is likely to incur:

- Robert Morris Associates. This is an association of bank loan and credit officers that publishes an *Annual Statement Studies* of cost data (in ratio form) for 350 different lines of business. This same group also makes available *Sources of Composite Financial Data: A Bibliography,* which lists sources for future information on costs from over 300 industries.
- Dun and Bradstreet. This organization publishes two useful annual reports: *Key Business Ratios in 125 Lines* and *Cost of Doing Business*.

One final way to benefit from the experience of existing businesses is through suppliers. The suppliers of an industry are often quite familiar with its cost structure and can provide very useful information.

When the entrepreneur has completed the search for cost data from existing businesses, she must still establish the monthly costs of running the new business. It is useful to know that the average ice cream store pays for rent 17 percent of what it takes in, but what is more important is that the actual rent of the site being considered is $300 per month. Establishing these costs is not difficult; it simply requires research. The landlord or rental agency must be

Exhibit   6.2   Gathering Cost Data

Step	Method	Information Source	Comments
1.	Library research	Small Business Administration; Financial Ratio Reports; Robert Morris Associates; Dun and Bradstreet	These sources provide general cost data (levels of profitability and various ratios).
2.	Letters	Trade associations; Bank of America; Small Business Administration; Government Printing Office	These data are a bit more specific than those gathered in step 1.
3.	Conversations and telephone calls	Neighboring businesses; competitors; similar organizations	Information gathered as a safeguard against any "hidden" costs.
4.	Conversations and telephone calls	Various "suppliers"	To determine the actual costs of various items including rent, utilities, supplies.

contacted to determine rent; the utilities companies must be asked for estimates of their monthly bill; government offices must be contacted for costs of licenses and taxes.

This process is used for the remainder of the costs of doing business identified in the earlier investigations. At this point the entrepreneur must go from the general (the experience of others) to the specific (the level of monthly expenses facing his proposed business). Exhibit 6.2 summarizes data collection by method and source. If this process is conducted completely and accurately there should be no important surprises after the business is started. If projections show $2,120 in monthly expenses, for example, they may reach $2,200 because of an overlooked item or two, but they should not go as high as $2,500. The more diligent the investigation, the greater confidence we can have that expenses will not reach $2,400, or even $2,300.

K E Y   Objectives Reviewed

1. Break-even analysis is used as a means of preliminary evaluation of a business start.
2. The technique involves the specification of fixed and variable costs and the contribution margin.

3. The two basic types of errors that can occur in planning are to start a business with no reasonable chance of success and to abandon plans for a business that would have succeeded.

4. The data sources needed for break-even analysis include publications of various types, trade associations, suppliers, competitors.

Discussion Questions

1. What are type A errors? What are type B errors? How are they related to one another?

2. What is the definition of variable costs?

3. Why are most costs a small business incurs best regarded as fixed costs?

4. In what ways can a prospective small business owner use the experiences of others?

5. How might the accuracy of cost projections be improved?

6. What are some sources of information concerning the types and amounts of fixed costs a business will incur?

Cases for Part Two

Case IIA   I'll Keep It

Three people, Judith Coleman, George McGee, and Clarence Herr, were friends in college. During that time, 1977 to 1981, Judith developed an interest in entrepreneurship, which prompted her to investigate the possibility of opening a storage facility. Her sister had used such a service and, in describing the business, made Judith interested in the line. It appeared to be a trouble-free operation and, except for start-up expenses, a low-cost one.

Judith began to think through what would be required to start such a business. Her lack of business management background prompted her to invite her friends George and Clarence to join her in the venture. Both men had graduated in business administration and were working, George in the accounting department of a local hospital and Clarence in the marketing section of an automobile parts manufacturer and distributor. Neither was married or had any important financial commitments, so each was open to Judith's proposal.

The town in which they planned the venture was the home of all three. It was the site of a major state university, with 14,000 undergraduate and 5,000 graduate students. Near the town, a large military base employed 4,500 military workers and 3,100 civilians. Also in town were the headquarters of several large corporations as well as a number of manufacturing facilities. The only other employer of significant size was an office of the state government, the work force of which varied over the past two years from 115 to the current 310.

The three friends reasoned that these employers and the university student group experienced a considerable turnover, which would mean splendid opportunities for their proposed business venture. They then set out to analyze the market and the costs associated with starting and operating a self-storage facility, as well as the revenue the business appeared capable of generating.

The Market
. . . .

The customers of self-storage facilities are people with furniture, cars, boats, and other items for which they do not have safe storage space. The minimum rental period is a month, with some firms offering 12 months' rent for the price of 11. Many customers storing boats rent for a number of years.

The city had a population of 285,000 reported in the 1980 census; the surrounding towns and villages had an additional 47,000. The partners used a figure of three people per household to determine that there were approximately 110,000 households in the area. To the partners this meant 110,000 overcrowded offices and bulging basements.

The competition included two modest-sized storage facilities, both of which appeared to be full. Their combined capacity was estimated at 170 compartments, the great majority of which were 8-, 10-, or 12-foot cubicles. One of the firms had a limited number of bays large enough for boats—no more than 12. A firm 12 miles away also offered large compartment storage, having a total of 40 to 50 bays, a third to half appearing to be vacant.

The price schedule Judith was able to determine through her investigations was as follows:

Compartment Size	Rental per Month
6 × 5 feet	$32
6 × 12	42
8 × 10	50
10 × 25	100

All compartments were 9 to 10 feet high.

Costs

. . . .

The firm would consist of four buildings that would cost the owners $330,000 to construct. This would cover the $70,000 local realtors estimated as the price of a suitable piece of ground and $65,000 for building each of the four buildings. A $50,000 down payment would leave $280,000 to borrow. The annual debt repayment would be $42,000 ($23,333 in interest and $18,667 in principal). The other large expense would be the cost of salary and benefits, estimated at $24,000, for Judith, who would run the business's daily operations. The other expected expenses, given at their annual levels, would be as follows:

Advertising	$3,000
Office supplies	1,000
Utilities	1,500
Telephone	600
Building maintenance/repair	1,000
Employee taxes	2,500
Insurance	2,400
Bad debts	1,000
Miscellaneous	1,000
Total	$14,000

Revenues

. . . .

Each of the complex's four buildings would have four large, 10-by-25-foot compartments, twelve 6-by-12-foot compartments, and twenty-four 5-by-6-foot compartments. The prospective owners conducted a market survey and interviewed owners of similar businesses in other cities, and concluded that they should reach 95 percent occupancy within two months of starting operations.

Questions

1. Should the complex be built?
2. What additional data should the prospective partners gather?
3. Who would be the best prospective customers for such a business? How might they be reached through advertising and promotion?
4. Have the partners overlooked any important expenses?

Case IIB   Gilda's Gifts

On graduating from college with a degree in business administration, Gilda Nowotmy began her career with a major department store as a department manager. After several years, she was promoted to the position of buyer, responsible for purchasing the inventory for the card and gift department. The positions of manager and buyer gave her excellent experience in product selection, inventory control, and overall department management.

Gilda eventually became disenchanted as an employee of the large company and began to consider the possibility of opening her own card and gift shop. She knew that for many retail businesses, location is critical in determining success. The card and gift industry was no exception; a poor location could cause the business to fail. Gilda began to look for locations and found three sites that she thought might serve her needs. Although the sites were very different, each had advantages and disadvantages, making a final decision difficult. Gilda researched traffic counts, census information, and the individual facilities and gathered the following information.

Site 1

. . . .

Site 1 was a freestanding building on a street containing many other small retail stores. The site had approximately 800 square feet and rented for $500 per month. It had been vacant for several months after the previous tenant, a plant shop, relocated.

Figure IIB.1   Site 1

Gilda liked the community, an older, well-established community known for small, unique retail shops along a major street. Total population in the immediate area was approximately 23,000. Median family income was $30,000, indicating middle-class living standards for most people. Census information revealed that the male-female ratio was almost even, with 51 percent women and 49 percent men. Age breakdown was as follows:

Under 20 years	19.5%
21–34	30.7
35–54	21.6
55–64	11.7
65 and over	16.5

The neighborhood was very stable, with few people moving in and out. There were no other card and gift shops in the immediate area, though the grocery store across the street sold cards, and many items in other stores could be purchased as gifts.

The proposed site was on a major street with an average daily two-way traffic count of 16,000 cars. Early morning and late afternoon traffic consisted mostly of residents commuting to and from work. Daytime traffic usually consisted of local residents shopping and attending to daily tasks.

Gilda estimated that start-up costs for this location would be approximately $60,000, of which $30,000 would be needed to purchase inventory. The remaining money would be needed for furniture, fixtures, working capital, and other normal start-up costs. The landlord of the building agreed to lease it for any number of years Gilda desired, but rent would increase to $530 per month after the first 3 years and to $600 per month after 6 years.

Figure   IIB.2   Site 2

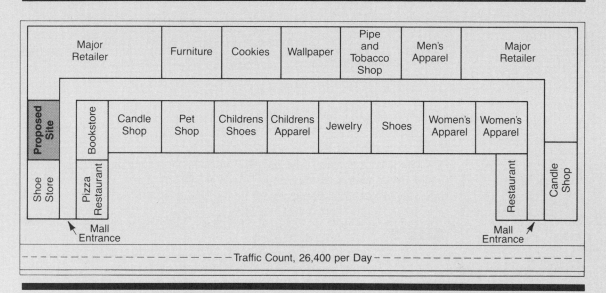

Site 2

Site 2 was an existing card and gift shop for sale. The shop was located in a medium-sized, enclosed shopping center in an older, well-established community. The owner had several other businesses and did not devote much time to this store. As a result, the merchandise selection was not as good as Gilda thought it should be, and the sales volume had not reached expected levels even though the shop had been there for several years. Income statements showed a break-even status for the past several years. Although the store had not been advertised as being for sale, the owner (a friend of Gilda's husband) informed Gilda that he might be willing to sell. The shop had 3,000 square feet and $50,000 of inventory. The owner agreed to sell the business for $100,000, including all inventory, furniture, fixtures, the cash register, and miscellaneous supplies. These assets' appraised value was $85,000. Gilda would be able to take over the previous owner's lease, which indicated rent payments of $2,500 per month with 6 years left on the lease. At the end of the lease, the mall developers would consider negotiating a new lease with Gilda.

The shopping center was on a major road with an average daily traffic count (two-way) of 26,400 cars. Morning and evening traffic was mostly commuters. Daytime traffic included many business executives traveling to nearby offices as well as community residents. The shopping center was located in a commercial area with two neighboring communities. Median family income in one area was $26,000 (42,000 people); in the other it was

$40,000 (14,000 people). The male-female ratio was approximately even, with age breakdown as follows:

	Area with Income of $26,000	Area with Income of $40,000
Under 20 Years	29.8%	30.5%
21–34	24.6	26.7
35–54	21.3	18.1
55–64	8.7	7.7
65 and Over	15.5	17.0

There were no other card and gift shops in the shopping center, but the major department store carried cards and many gift items. Products sold by other businesses in the center could be purchased as gifts.

Site 3

The third site was in a new neighborhood shopping center that had recently been built in a rapidly growing suburb. The developer was in the process of negotiating leases, and many spaces had already been taken. There was one

Figure   IIB.3   Site 3

Restaurant | Proposed Site | Major Grocery Supercenter Includes Pharmacy, Books, Small Appliances, Cards, Plants

Video Game Rental
Dry Cleaners
Dentist
Mens Apparel
Ice Cream Shop
Women's Apparel

Traffic Count, 12,400 per Day

vacant location with 800 square feet and lease payments of $600 per month. It would have a three-year lease. If at the end of the third year she wanted to, Gilda could renew the lease for another three years for $650 per month. The shopping center was located on a street that was the community's commercial area. The most recent traffic count available, three years old, indicated average daily traffic (two-way) of 12,400. Almost all traffic on the street consisted of local residents tending to daily shopping needs. Male-female population ratio was approximately 50:50. Median family income was $25,000. Age breakdown was as follows:

Under 20 years	39.5%
21–34	24.5
35–54	24.8
55–64	6.4
65 and over	4.9

There were no other card and gift shops nearby; however, the grocery store in the shopping center was very large and carried a good selection of cards. In addition, the discount store across the street from the shopping center stocked cards.

Gilda estimated start-up costs for this outlet to be $50,000 to $60,000, including all inventory, furniture, fixtures, working capital, and so forth.

Questions

1. Based on the information given, which site would you select if you were Gilda? Give reasons why you chose that site and reasons why you did not select the others.

2. Would you want other information about each site before making a final decision? If so, what information?

Case IIC   Sunshine Sawmill Inc.

In southern Missouri, many small sawmills produce lumber for housing construction, furniture, manufacturing, and general commercial and industrial use. The abundance of sawmills created a tremendous scrap wood problem for the following reasons:

- In most of the wood manufacturing processes, only 30 percent of a tree is actually used. The remaining portion is either left in the ground, trimmed during the initial refining stages, or lost as sawdust.

- Because of the large number of sawmills in southern Missouri, a large supply of sawdust is accumulating.
- The federal government prohibits the sawmills from burning the sawdust and scrap wood because of the air pollution problems this would create.
- The sawdust stockpiles eventually cause water pollution, since pollutants seep out of the sawdust into nearby rivers.

One of the sawmills, Sunshine Sawmill Inc., saw the pollution problems developing and searched for a solution. The owner, Jim Toohey, asked agricultural and engineering consultants for suggestions. One possible alternative they recommended was to convert the sawdust and scrap wood into charcoal.

Converting scrap wood to charcoal would require a major investment, the biggest portion of which would be buying a waste conversion system for $500,000. Approximately $95,000 in additional machinery and equipment would also be needed. Jim would be able to invest almost $200,000 of his own money; however, this would require him to borrow almost $400,000. Therefore, he did not want to make this major investment unless adequate profits could be generated.

Equipment and Machinery Needed

Waste conversion system	$500,000
Overhead bins	18,000
Forklift	12,000
Two buildings, 100 × 60 feet	40,000
Standby power source	1,000
Scales	22,000
Moisture tester	2,500
Total	$595,500

Because of his knowledge of the industry, Jim knew most of the owners of the sawmills in the surrounding area. He contacted them to determine how much of a sawdust stockpile they had accumulated and their willingness to give it to him free of charge. His phone calls revealed that a stockpile of approximately 57,000 tons already existed, with approximately 520 tons of additional sawdust accumulating each week. All of the sawmill owners agreed to let Toohey have the sawdust free of charge since this would solve a major problem for them. The only requirement was that Jim would have to haul it from their sawmills to his waste conversion system. Based on the information he obtained about the waste conversion system, he determined that the existing stockpile of sawdust was more than the conversion system could utilize in one year even if it operated at maximum capacity. This did not include the

Available Sawdust Free of Charge

. . . .

Sawmill	Current Stockpile (in Tons)	Weekly Accumulation (in Tons)
Sunshine Sawmill	5,000	50
PMT Sawmills Inc.	15,000	50
Treetop Sawmill	10,000	100
Ice Mueller Sawmill Inc.	5,000	100
Fred Smith Inc.	10,000	120
Lumber Products Inc.	12,000	100
Total	57,000	520

Note: Assume one ton of sawdust converts to one ton of charcoal.

additional 500 tons of sawdust being produced each week; a constant supply of free sawdust appeared to be no problem.

Based on the literature Jim obtained on the waste conversion system, its maximum output per year would be 4,690 tons of charcoal. This estimate was based on daily production of 14 tons. Only 335 working days were used in the estimate to allow for times when production would be halted for routine maintenance or repairs.

Toohey planned to sell the charcoal in bulk to a distributor who would bag and market the product under the distributor's own brand name. The distributor would pay Toohey $65 per ton.

Since Jim would obtain sawdust free of charge, he needed only to consider ongoing monthly costs to operate the system plus the costs to haul sawdust from the mills to his location. He estimated that hauling the sawdust would cut his profit on the charcoal by $15 per ton. Thus, each ton of charcoal would bring a gross profit of $50.

Monthly costs to operate at maximum capacity were estimated as follows:

Labor	$3,600	
Utilities	3,600	
Loan payment	4,462	($400,000, 20 years, 12%)
Taxes	1,000	
Delivery costs to deliver charcoal to the distributor	1,500	
Supplies	700	
Repairs	300	
Insurance	1,000	
Miscellaneous	1,500	
Accounting/legal	500	
Total	$18,162	

Questions

1. Considering the availability of free sawdust, do you think Jim should invest in the waste conversion system?

2. If Jim had to pay the sawmills $10 per ton of sawdust, would the investment be profitable?

Case IID   Scooping up Profits

Mary Cremala had obtained an associate degree in engineering when she was 20 years old and then worked as a sales representative for engineering firms while raising her family. Her 20 years in sales required substantial contact with the general public and allowed her to meet many small business owners. Although she had considered starting her own business, her need for a steady income forced her to postpone her plans.

When her children grew up and no longer depended on her for support, she again began to consider owning her own business. In 1980, she returned to college part-time to get her degree in business administration, planning to start a business after graduating. Throughout her college course work, Cremala searched for ideas for her own business.

In a marketing course she wrote a research paper on trends in the ice cream industry. Mary's research revealed the following facts about the industry in the early 1980s:

- Ice cream consumption was projected to continue to increase.
- Ice cream parlors were predicted to increase by over 20 percent.
- The International Association of Ice Cream Manufacturers estimated that 22 quarts of ice cream are produced for each American every year.
- The fastest-growing segment of the ice cream industry was the premium ice cream lines (high quality, high price).

Mary began to consider opening an ice cream store after she graduated. She began to gather information concerning locations, start-up costs, and competition. Conversations with potential suppliers and existing ice cream store owners further convinced her that her own ice cream parlor would be a lucrative business.

The Site

....

Mary began to look for a location for her ice cream parlor. She knew that managing the store would require long hours; therefore, she wanted to find a location near her home. She hoped to minimize travel time as much as possible to devote all available hours to the store.

After looking for several weeks, Mary found a location in a small neighborhood shopping center adjacent to a state park. She felt this would be an ideal location since the park had ball fields, tennis courts, and a playground area, which attracted many families as well as organized little-league ball clubs. There were no concession stands in the park and no competitors within five miles.

Mary called the lessor for information. The lessor agreed to meet with her to discuss the lease arrangements but also informed her that several other people had looked at the location with the intention of leasing it. He could not guarantee that the space would be available much longer. Mary agreed to meet with him anyway, hoping that the other prospective tenants might change their minds.

She obtained a sample copy of the proposed lease and called her attorney to have him review it. Three days later, she met with the lawyer to discuss changes that should be made in the final lease. After this meeting, she contacted the lessor to discuss the modifications, only to be informed that the owner of a clothing store had signed a lease so the space was no longer available.

Mary was disappointed but, still determined to open her ice cream parlor, began to look for another site. After several weeks, she found a site in a small shopping center in a commercial area. The shopping center was adjacent to a hospital and office buildings. There were many other businesses in the area with many employees who could stop in on their lunch hours for ice cream. Mary thought the location was excellent and contacted the lessor to determine the lease rates and terms. The initial meeting with the lessor provided the following information.

1. Lease payments would be $1,500 per month. This would include regular rent fees, a fee for parking lot maintenance, and a fee for advertising by the shopping center.

2. Mary's outlet would be 1,000 square feet.

3. The lease would be for 3 years.

4. Although there was nothing written in the lease agreement about renewing the lease at the end of the third year, the lessor told her verbally that renewing the lease would be no problem.

5. Because of the small amount of parking space in the shopping center, city ordinances would not allow more than 4 tables and 16 chairs in the outlet. Mary could operate an ice cream store as long as it was primarily carry-out.

6. Mary explained to the lessor that it would not be profitable to stay open during November through February; sales would be too low to justify opening the shop. The lessor agreed to allow the shop to close during those months.

Mary surveyed the area and found no other ice cream outlets within three miles. She felt confident that this location would be good and continued to research start-up costs and operating expenses for the new location.

Start-up Costs

Start-up costs for the proposed ice cream parlor would be as follows:

Renovations	$10,000
Equipment	23,000
Inventory—food	700
Inventory—paper supplies	1,000
Furniture/fixtures	2,000
Office equipment and supplies	600
Deposits/licenses	2,000
Working capital	13,000
Total	$52,300

In addition to the purchased equipment, Mary planned to lease one machine for $350 per month.

Mary had saved $10,500 over the years and planned to use it for part of the start-up costs. She would borrow $41,800. Her banker had informed her that loan payments would be approximately $850 per month for six years, which would include both principal and interest.

Operating Costs

Using information the lessor had given her and information from owners of other ice cream outlets, Mary projected monthly expenses as follows:

Lease on ice cream machine	$ 350 per month
Eight months' office supplies	50 per month
Advertising	400 per month for March–October only
Rent	1,500 per month
Utilities	300 per month
Telephone	75 per month
Insurance	200 per month
Repairs	50 per month
Accounting/legal	75 per month
Loan payment	850 per month
Employee wages	850 per month for March–October only
Mary's wages	850 per month (12 months/year)
Miscellaneous	100 per month
Taxes (payroll and others)	200 per month

The costs for the ice cream and necessary paper supplies (cups, dishes) were projected to be 35 percent of sales. In other words, if Mary sold an ice cream sundae for $1.00, her food and paper costs would be $0.35 and gross margin would be $0.65.

Menu

Mary began to plan the items she would offer. A tentative menu was developed as follows:

Cones (13 flavors)	One scoop
	Two scoops
	Three scoops
Sundaes	Small
	Medium
	Large
Shakes (3 flavors)	Small
	Medium
	Large
Frozen custard (13 flavors)	Small
	Medium
	Large
Sodas (5 brands)	Small
	Medium
	Large

The Last Step

Before making any final decisions, Mary contacted a business consultant for an objective opinion on her proposed business; although confident of success, she felt an outside opinion was necessary. The consultant set up an appointment and told Mary to organize all of her information so that it could be reviewed.

Questions

1. Discuss the advantages and disadvantages of the proposed site.
2. Which site do you think would be better, the site near the state park or the site near all of the businesses?
3. If you were Mary's consultant, what advice would you give her?

Case IIE

The Office Furniture Outlet

Philip Nobert had always dreamed of owning his own business. After college he had accepted a job with a major furniture manufacturing firm, planning to save his earnings for a business venture. His job required him to do extensive market research on trends in the furniture industry. He was therefore very familiar with industry sales projections, problems, and areas where growth potential existed.

An acquaintance, Nancy Southland, was impressed with Philip's knowledge of the industry and was also aware of Philip's desire to open his own business. She had inherited money from a relative and considered starting a retail office furniture outlet. She asked Philip for information on industry trends, stating that if trends were favorable she would like to open a business in partnership with him.

Philip's research indicated that the office furniture industry was rapidly changing. The industry had seen many changes in recent years. Modular office units (standardized sizes and designs) had become popular with the "open" office atmosphere, walls and doors being replaced by small cubicles. Also, research indicated that the impact of office furniture and design on productivity was becoming increasingly important to companies when they purchased office furniture. Philip gathered as much information as possible and summarized the findings for Nancy as follows:

1. The demand for office furniture will grow by approximately 8 percent per year throughout the 1980s.

2. Demand for wood furniture will increase throughout the 1980s and 1990s.

3. The demand for low-cost and used and reconditioned furniture will continue to increase due to an increasing number of people working at home.

4. Companies will need to refurbish their open-plan furniture systems in the future; therefore, a market will exist for this type of service.

5. Because of the increasing popularity of the open systems plans, the demand for regular office furniture will decrease.

6. In the early 1980s, the average furniture and equipment investment per office worker was $2,500. This will increase to $8,000 to $10,000 by 1989, owing to companies realizing that proper office design and proper office furniture greatly improve productivity.

7. Office furniture retailers will find increased competition from architectural firms, which have begun to design the office interiors as well as the office buildings.

8. Office furniture manufacturers will increase the number of direct sales to large corporations, eliminating the dealer from many large sales. The dealers, however, will get a percentage from these sales to install and maintain the furniture once the customer has purchased it.

While Philip was gathering his information, Nancy visited 20 companies (10 large corporations, 10 small) to determine what factors influence the decision to buy office furniture. She had developed a questionnaire she gave to someone at each business. If she visited a small business, the owner completed the survey, and if she visited a large business, the person responsible for purchasing office furniture completed the form. A sample questionnaire is included below along with the answers she obtained.

Questionnaire Given to Potential Customers

. . . .

1. Have you remodeled your office within the last 2 years?
   - __90%__ Yes
   - __10%__ No

2. If you were going to redesign your offices, would you
   - __70%__ Use an interior design firm?
   - __30%__ Design it yourself?

3. If you would use an interior design firm, how would you choose the firm?
   - __10%__ Lowest price
   - __40%__ Referral from another business owner
   - __10%__ Would use a design firm that has done work for the company in the past
   - __40%__ Other

4. If you wanted to buy office furniture, would you
   - __20%__ Go to the office furniture showroom of a retailer?
   - __80%__ Expect a salesperson to call on you?

Nancy also wanted to visit existing office furniture outlets to see what products and services they offered. In the telephone book she found over 100 outlets in the city. She knew there was not enough time to visit them all, so she chose five in the downtown business district. Her visits revealed the following:

1. All five companies had large showrooms.

2. All had employees skilled in interior design.

3. All carried new furniture but only one carried both new and used furniture.

After Nancy and Philip completed their research, they met to discuss the findings and decide if they should continue with their plans to open the business.

Questions

1. Based on the information Nancy and Philip gathered, what products or services do you think an office furniture outlet should offer (new furniture, used furniture, interior design, furniture refurbishing)?

2. Suppose Nancy and Philip consider opening an outlet that sells only used office furniture. In addition to existing furniture stores that sell used furniture, what other competition would exist?

3. Review Nancy's questionnaire and the results. What recommendations would you make for improving the questionnaire?

4. Do Nancy's visits to existing furniture outlets provide a good basis for the planning process?

5. If Nancy and Philip asked your advice, what would it be?

Organizing

In Part One we discussed the role of small businesses in the United States, the entrepreneurial profile, and various ways to begin a career in entrepreneurship. In Part Two, we discussed the planning process, which includes a demand analysis, a site analysis, and a break-even analysis.

If the break-even analysis indicates that the business has a good chance of being profitable, the entrepreneur then continues to gather information. This information is used to organize the business and determine as accurately as possible if the business will succeed. In Part Three we will identify major topics the entrepreneur must consider before making a final decision about the feasibility of the business.

One of the most critical steps is to refine the projected income statement that was used when determining the break-even analysis. The projected sales and expenses must be determined much more accurately to ensure that the business will be profitable. If sales are overestimated or if expenses are underestimated, the business may not be as successful as the entrepreneur anticipated. In Chapter 7 we discuss the methods for completing the necessary projected financial statements.

In Chapter 8 we will identify many of the legal aspects of business ownership. The entrepreneur must decide the organizational structure after examining the advantages and disadvantages of each option. Although most small businesses are proprietorships, many choose the partnership or corporate structure because of financing, tax, or liability factors. It may also be necessary to apply for copyrights, trademarks, or patents, to develop written contracts, or to consider other legal aspects. For this reason, the entrepreneur is advised to consult with a lawyer before the business is started.

The sources of financing must also be identified. Obtaining adequate financing is often a major problem for the entrepreneur if he has few personal assets. Though friends, relatives, or partners may be willing to invest money this option is one which the entrepreneur may wish to avoid. In Chapter 9, the sources of financing are discussed so the entrepreneur can determine the most appropriate alternative.

Finally, in Chapter 10, all of the information is compiled and expanded to complete a feasibility study. The feasibility study includes a comprehensive analysis of all the data and forms the basis for the entrepreneur's final decision. This document also forms the basis for the business plan once the business is operating.

CHAPTER 7

Financial Statement Projections

K   E   Y   Objectives

1. To review basic accounting methods—cash and accrual—and to explain their effect on the income statement.

2. To review the typical categories that appear on an income statement.

3. To review the typical categories that appear on a balance sheet.

4. To explain how to prepare an opening day balance sheet.

5. To explain how to prepare a projected income statement for the first year of operation.

6. To emphasize the difference between profit and cash flow.

Many entrepreneurs would prefer to avoid the subject of financial statements. When the topic is raised, they respond, "I'll have an accountant. I don't need to understand that aspect of the business." This is an unfortunate attitude, for no matter how small the business is, proper financial management is critical to its success. It is essential that the entrepreneur become involved in this aspect of the business and understand the basic concepts. Although accountants may provide monthly statements and some advice, the entrepreneur must understand the financial aspects to plan the future of the business. Many small business failures could have been prevented if the owners had understood their financial statements and known how to use them for decision making; many unsuccessful start-ups would never have happened had the entrepreneur prepared projected financial statements before beginning. This chapter includes three sections—first, a review of financial statements and basic terminology; second, a description of a method for developing projected financial statements for the proposed business; and third, a discussion of profit versus cash flow.

Accounting Methods

The basic financial statements a company uses include the income statement and balance sheet. These can be prepared using a variety of accounting procedures, the results varying with the method used. Therefore, it is important

Illustration Capsule 7.1

The Need for Financial Management

The need for good financial information was cited by two professors at Drake University, who stated that "although the firm may have superior product lines or provide excellent services, lack of data with respect to accounting and financial needs may have a severe detrimental effect."

Ronald C. Clute examined 359 business failures. Approximately 40 percent were in financial difficulty because of accounting problems. Among the problems identified were incomplete accounting records, poorly trained or no accounting personnel, no cash or working capital analysis, and lack of budgets or forecasts.

Source: Lynn K. Saubert and R. Wayne Saubert, "Legal and Accounting Assistance for the Small Business," Small Business Institute Directors Association Annual Conference Proceedings (February 7–10, 1984), 130.

to understand the various procedures by which the financial statements are developed.

One of the simplest methods is the **cash basis of accounting.** This procedure records sales only when the cash is received and records expenses only when they are paid. If a sale is made on January 20 but the customer pays 30 days later, the sale would be shown as a February sale even though the transaction took place in January. Similarly, if the January utility bill was actually paid in February, it would be shown as a February expense. This process is simple to use since only very basic records are needed. However, several factors must be noted. First, the cash method does not always give an accurate financial picture of the company. The profit on the income statement can be increased simply by withholding payments on bills. Similarly, the sales figure may be inaccurate, since it indicates the money received, not the volume of merchandise sold. A second important factor is that the Internal Revenue Service will not allow all businesses to use the cash method for tax purposes. Any business that maintains inventory and derives income from the sale of that inventory cannot use the cash basis in preparing income taxes. Even if this type of business maintained day-to-day records on a cash basis, it would have to change at the end of the year for tax purposes. Businesses that provide a service and do not sell inventories can use the cash method even for taxes.

Cash Basis of Accounting
An accounting method that records sales only when the money is received for the sale, and records expenses only when the expense is paid.

Unique Business   7.1

Resale Shops for Dieters

Shedding pounds can mean a slimmer you, and a slimmer wardrobe. To feed it, so that you can starve fashionably, can be expensive. Weight Loss Closets of Minneapolis and St. Paul can help; they cater to the dieter. The customer consigns the clothes that no longer fit and purchases those to be used on the journey to his or her desired weight. The stores, founded by Patty Meshbesler in late 1982, receive 50 percent of the price of the consigned items they sell.

Source: Venture, May 1984, 14.

Accrual Method
An accounting method that records sales when the transaction occurs and records expenses when the expenses are incurred.

The **accrual method** is the more common form for financial statements and presents a more accurate picture of the company's financial status. The accrual method records sales when the transaction occurs regardless of when payment is received. Expenses are recorded when they are incurred regardless of when they are paid. The exchange of money, whether for a sale or an expense, is not important. Information in this chapter assumes that the accrual method will be used.

The Income Statement

The income statement provides vital information on the profitability of the business. General categories include sales revenue, cost of goods sold, gross profit, operating expenses, and net profit or loss. The income statement covers a specific period: a month, a quarter, six months, or a year.

The format varies with the type of business. However, any direct costs generating sales revenue, such as inventory, direct labor, or direct overhead, should be included in cost of goods sold.

The gross profit is the excess of revenue (sales) over the cost of goods sold. It is an extremely important figure since it indicates the company's markup over direct costs. Thus, the company shown below—Small Business Inc.—which has a gross profit of $80,000 on sales of $200,000, has a 40 percent gross profit margin ($80,000 ÷ $200,000). The cost of goods sold ($120,000) is 60 percent of sales ($120,000 ÷ $200,000). This means that, on the average, if the company purchased an item for $0.60, it would sell that item for $1.00.

The operating expenses include all business expenses except for those included in "cost of goods sold." Often, as the company grows, the expenses are classified, such as "selling expenses" (sales salaries, advertising, shipping costs) and "administrative expenses" (office salaries, rent, office supplies, postage).

Small Business Inc.
Income Statement
January 1–December 31, 1985

Sales	$200,000	100%
Cost of goods	120,000	60
Gross profit	80,000	40
Operating expenses	65,000	32.5
Net profit before tax	$15,000	7.5%

The Balance Sheet

The balance sheet varies from the income statement in several ways. While the income statement shows the company's profit or loss over a certain period, the balance sheet shows the company's financial condition at one point in time. A balance sheet consists of three major categories: the assets, liabilities, and equity or net worth. A sample balance sheet is shown top of page 157.

Assets

Current Assets
Assets that are easily converted into cash, such as accounts receivable, inventory, prepaid expenses, and supplies.

Assets represent tangible items or intangible rights owned by the business. Assets are generally divided into three categories: current assets, fixed assets, and other assets. They are **current assets** if they are easily converted into cash. The current assets category includes cash and the following items:

- **Accounts receivable.** This includes any money owed to a business by its customers due on normal credit terms (30 days, 60 days).
- **Inventory.** The inventory is purchased by a customer and soon after becomes a paid sale. Cash is received for it within a short time.
- **Prepaid expenses.** An insurance premium paid on January 1, 1986 and covering the first 6 months of the year would be a prepaid asset until the end of the 6 months, although the amount shown as prepaid would decrease each month as the insurance is "used."

Small Business Inc.
Balance Sheet
December 31, 1985

Assets			Liabilities		
Current Assets			**Current Liabilities**		
Cash	6,000		Accounts payable	15,000	
Accounts receivable	23,000		Notes payable	3,000	
Inventory	45,000		Accrued expenses	4,000	
Prepaid expenses	3,000		Taxes payable	3,000	
Total current assets		77,000	Current maturity—long-term debt	6,000	
			Total current liabilities		31,000
Fixed Assets					
Land and building	60,000		**Long-term Liabilities**		
Less: accumulated depreciation	(15,000)		Note payable	80,000	
Land and building (net)	45,000		Less: current portion	(6,000)	
			Total long-term		74,000
Machinery and equipment	20,000				
Less: accumulated depreciation	(5,000)		Total liabilities		105,000
Machinery and equipment (net)	15,000				
Total fixed assets		60,000			
Other Assets			**Stockholders Equity**		
Deposits	2,000		Capital stock	23,400	
Patents	2,000		Retained earnings	12,600	
Total other assets		4,000	Total equity		36,000
Total Assets		141,000	Total liabilities and equity		141,000

- **Supplies.** This includes items, such as office supplies or shop supplies, that are necessary to have on hand to operate the business efficiently. These are not listed with inventory since they are not sold to customers.

Fixed Assets
Assets that are permanent or long-term in nature, such as land, building, machinery, equipment, furniture, and fixtures.

Depreciation
A method by which the cost of a fixed asset is written off over a number of years.

Fixed assets are called "fixed" generally because of the items' permanence or long-term nature. Fixed assets include land and building, machinery and equipment, furniture and fixtures, vehicles, and similar items. Fixed assets are generally not considered an expense when they are purchased but instead are depreciated as the items age or are used. **Depreciation** is an accounting method by which the cost of a fixed asset is written off over a number of years. A van a company purchases for $12,000 is not shown on the income statement. Only the depreciation for the period is shown. For this reason, the asset is shown on the balance sheet at its cost, and all depreciation is subtracted to obtain "book value." Book value and market value may vary substantially, particularly for an asset such as a building, the value of which is actually increasing even though it is being depreciated on the company's financial records.

"Other assets" often include intangible items, such as patents owned or goodwill. This category may also include deposits such as lease deposits, which will be converted into cash at a much later date.

Liabilities

A company's liabilities include all monies the company owes. Liabilities are generally divided into two categories: current and long-term.

Current Liabilities
All debts or portions of debt due within 12 months. Generally includes accounts payable, short-term notes and taxes payable, accrued expenses, and the current portion of long-term debt.

Current liabilities are all payments due within the next 12 months. If a balance sheet is prepared on December 31, 1985, the current liabilities include all payments that must be made by December 31, 1986. Current liabilities may include the following categories:

- **Accounts payable.** This includes payments due to suppliers for inventory.
- **Notes payable.** Any loans due within the next 12 months are classified under notes payable. Thus, short-term loans (90-day loans, 6-month loans) are classified as current. The figure shown usually does not include any interest due, only the amount owed.
- **Accrued expenses.** Accrued expenses include all expenses that have been incurred but not paid. Suppose a company pays its employees every two weeks and paydays fall on December 23, 1985, and January 6, 1986. If a balance sheet were prepared on December 31, 1985, the company would owe its employees one week's pay. Thus, one week's payroll would appear under "accrued wages."
- **Taxes payable.** The taxes payable account includes employee taxes, sales tax, and/or income tax due. The tax categories may be listed separately or grouped together if the amount is not large.
- **Current maturity of long-term debt.** This is the amount due, within the next 12 months, on long-term loans. Suppose a business purchases a building for $100,000, and loan payments are $14,000 per year for 15 years. This amount ($14,000) includes both the actual loan repayment and the interest costs. If the interest the first year is $11,500, the repayment would be $2,500. The current portion of long-term debt for the first year would be $2,500.

Long-term Liabilities
All debts or portions of debt due after 12 months from the date of the balance sheet.

- **Long-term liabilities. Long-term liabilities** include the amount due on all loans (excluding interest) after 12 months from the date the balance sheet was prepared. In the above example of the purchase of a building, the long-term liabilities for the first year would be:

$100,000	−	$2,500	=	$97,500
Total amount borrowed		Current maturity due in 12 months		Long-term liabilities

Net Worth or Equity

Net Worth or Equity
The owner's or stock-holders' claims on the assets of the business; the net worth or equity always equals assets minus liabilities.

The **net worth or equity** of a business represents the owner's and/or stock-holders' claims on its assets. Net worth must always equal assets minus liabilities. This category is a "paper" figure and does not necessarily represent the amount of money that could be obtained were the company liquidated or sold.

It should be apparent from the above information that a company's equity will be negative if the amount owed (liabilities) is greater than the assets. Although there are exceptions, it is generally true that a company with negative equity is in severe financial trouble. This negative equity often occurs because the company has been unprofitable for several years. If this occurs, additional owner's investment is needed along with immediate steps to correct the problems.

The Opening Day Balance Sheet

Start-up Costs
One-time costs necessary to get the business started.

Before the entrepreneur can develop projected financial statements for the proposed company, there must be a complete listing of **start-up costs** (one-time costs necessary to open the doors). Suppose start-up costs for a pet shop were as follows:

Inventory	$ 50,000
Machinery and equipment	15,000
Furniture and fixtures	8,000
Deposits (lease deposits, sales tax deposits, utility deposits)	6,000
Licenses	2,000
Professional fees (legal, accounting)	1,000
Leasehold improvements	20,000
Working capital	25,000
Total start-up costs	$127,000
(Assume) owner's down payment	−27,000
Amount of loan needed	$100,000

(If a building is to be purchased, start-up costs would be greatly increased.) This list of start-up costs and owner down payment can then be used to develop the opening day balance sheet.

Projected Assets

There is a direct correlation between the start-up costs and the opening day balance sheet. Using the start-up costs above, the assets on opening day would appear as shown at the top of page 160.

Assets		
Current Assets		
Cash (working capital)	$25,000	
Inventory	50,000	
Prepaid professional fees	1,000	
Licenses	2,000	
Total current assets		$ 78,000
Fixed Assets		
Furniture and fixtures	8,000	
Machinery and equipment	15,000	
Leasehold improvements	20,000	
Total fixed assets		43,000
Other Assets		
Deposits		6,000
Total Assets		$127,000

Notice that total assets equal total start-up costs. This is because the entrepreneur uses cash to purchase items for the business or to pay expenses before opening (prepaid expenses) and leaves the remainder in the firm as working capital.

Projected Liabilities

The opening day liabilities are generally not complex. In most cases, the entrepreneur initially pays cash for all inventory, furniture and fixtures, and so on because the company does not have a track record and cannot get credit. Thus, there are often no accounts payable for inventory or other expenses. The main liability is the loan necessary for start-up costs.

In the example, we assumed that the owner had $27,000 to invest and would borrow $100,000. Assuming the loan is for 10 years at 12 percent interest, annual payments would be approximately $17,698. Assume that, of that amount, $12,000 would be interest and $5,698 would be the actual payment on the loan. Thus, assuming no additional money is owed for accounts payable or accrued expenses, the liabilities on opening day would be as follows:

Liabilities		
Current Liabilities		
Accounts payable	0	
Accrued expenses	0	
Current maturity of long-term debt	$ 5,698	
Total current liabilities		$ 5,698
Long-term Liabilities		
Notes payable	$100,000	
Less current portion	(5,698)	
Total long-term liabilities		$ 94,302
Total liabilities		$100,000

Projected Net Worth or Equity

Each item in the list of start-up costs has appeared as either an asset or a liability, except for the owner's down payment of $27,000. This down payment is the same as the "owner's claim on assets" discussed in the review of net worth or equity. Since the initial investment is $27,000 and no other transactions affecting net worth have occurred, net worth on opening day would be $27,000.

The Completed Opening Day Balance Sheet

Using all of the above information, it is possible to construct an opening day balance sheet as shown below. Then, once the business is open, every transaction will affect the assets, liabilities, and equity of the business.

Small Pets Inc.
Projected Opening Day Balance Sheet

Assets		
Current Assets		
Cash	$25,000	
Inventory	50,000	
Prepaid professional fees	1,000	
Licenses	2,000	
Total current assets		$ 78,000
Fixed Assets		
Furniture and fixtures	8,000	
Machinery and equipment	15,000	
Leasehold improvements	20,000	
Total fixed assets		43,000
Other Assets		
Deposits		6,000
Total assets		$127,000
Liabilities		
Current Liabilities		
Accounts payable	U	
Accrued expenses	0	
Current maturity of long-term debt	$5,698	
Total current liabilities		$5,698
Long-term Liabilities		
Notes payable	100,000	
Less current portion	(5,698)	
Total long-term liabilities		$ 94,302
Total liabilities		$100,000
Equity		
Initial investment	$27,000	
Total equity		$ 27,000
Total liabilities and equity		$127,000

"I know what black is and what red is, but what's ink?"

Source: Copyright Ford Button.

The Projected Income Statement

Chapter 6 described various sources of industry cost data. Exhibit 7.1 illustrates typical information that could be obtained from Bank of America Reporters. Chapter 4 discussed demand analysis for a new business. A projected income statement for a new business combines the industry information and the information from the general demand analysis, along with information on the site and other operating costs. All of this information is combined to develop the projected income statement.

The projected sales volume is crucial since an inaccurate sales projection will cause many other numbers to be inaccurate. As a final check, the entrepreneur should verify the projected sales volume with someone knowledgeable in the industry to ensure that the projection is realistic. Once the sales potential is verified, the entrepreneur can then complete a preliminary income statement based on industry ratios.

Suppose the sales potential for our small pet store, Small Pets Inc., is determined to be $200,000. A preliminary income statement using the percentages in Exhibit 7.1 would produce the income statement below. However, this should certainly not be considered accurate, for the reasons following the income statement.

Exhibit   7.1   Pet Shop Costs as a Percentage of Sales

Net Cost of Goods	52.0%–58.0%
Expenses	
Advertising and Promotion	2.0 – 5.0
Bad Debts	0.6 – 1.0
Dues and Subscriptions	0.2 – 0.3
Office Expenses	0.5 – 1.0
Licenses and Taxes	0.5 – 0.7
Miscellaneous	1.7 – 2.5
Rent	5.0 – 7.0
Salaries and Wages	15.0 –22.0
Supplies	1.0 – 1.5
Utilities and Phone	1.5 – 2.0
Total Expenses	28.0%–43.0%

Source: Small Business Reporter: Independent Pet Shops, (San Francisco, Calif.: Bank of America, 1971), vol. 10, no. 2, 11.

Small Pets Inc.
Preliminary Projected Income Statement

Sales	$200,000	100%
Cost of goods sold	110,000	55
Gross margin	90,000	45
Expenses		
Advertising	6,000	3.0
Bad debts	1,600	0.8
Dues and subscriptions	400	0.2
Office expenses	1,400	0.7
Licenses and business taxes	1,200	0.6
Miscellaneous	4,000	2.0
Rent	13,000	6.5
Salaries and wages (including owner)	40,000	20.0
Supplies	2,400	1.2
Utilities and phone	3,400	1.7
Total expenses	$73,400	36.7
Net profit before tax	$16,600	8.3%

These figures are based on industrywide data and, as such, represent only approximations of what Small Pets Inc. is likely to experience. Following are factors that would cause deviations from the industry levels:

1. The entrepreneur for Small Pets Inc. has chosen a site that costs $1,000 per month. Rent should be $12,000 per year.

2. The owner will work in the store full-time but will not draw a salary the first year. Only $15,000 is needed for wages for employees.

3. Payroll taxes are estimated at 10 percent of payroll for social security and unemployment taxes.

4. Small Pets Inc. plans to invest $27,000 of personal money and borrow $100,000 (refer to the balance sheet). Therefore, if the $100,000 is borrowed at 12 percent, interest the first year will be approximately $12,000.

5. Depreciation is based on the $43,000 in fixed assets divided by 5 years, or $8,600 per year.

6. The sales volume the first year is not expected to reach the potential of $200,000.

7. The owner plans to run more sales and ''specials'' the first year to develop clientele. Therefore, the gross margin may be less than the average of 45 percent.

These factors would cause the actual projected income statement to materialize as shown below.

Revised Projection for Small Pets Inc.

Sales	$150,000	100%
Cost of goods	85,500	
Gross margin	$64,500	43
Expenses		
Advertising	$6,000	4.0
Bad debts	1,200	0.8
Dues and subscriptions	300	0.2
Office expenses	1,050	0.7
Licenses/taxes	900	0.6
Miscellaneous	3,000	2.0
Rent	12,000	8.0
Salaries/wages	15,000	10.0
Supplies	1,800	1.2
Utilities and phone	2,550	1.7
Payroll taxes	1,500	1.0
Depreciation	8,600	5.7
Interest	12,000	8.0
Total	$65,900	
Net profit	($1,400)	

This revised projection is more realistic for the first year of operation and should serve as a guide for controlling expenses and determining if sales estimates are being met. The projected income statement, therefore, becomes a budget to follow. It is of little use if placed in a drawer and forgotten.

To be effective, the projected income statement should be broken down into monthly budgets. Then, at the end of each month projected figures can be compared with actual figures and steps can be taken to correct anything that appears out of line. If the entrepreneur waits until year's end to compare figures, the company may be in severe financial trouble. If monthly comparisons are made, any problems can be quickly detected and handled.

Cash versus Net Profit

. . . .

Profitable but Poor

One of the most common mistakes entrepreneurs make is to assume that a profitable company will have sufficient cash on hand to meet all financial obligations. Many small business owners are shocked to learn that a very profitable company may be consistently short of cash, while an unprofitable company may have no problems paying its bills. The prospective business owner must understand cash flow since a profitable business with inadequate cash flow may be forced to slow its growth or, in the most critical situation, may be forced to close.

Some factors that require cash but do not affect profit are discussed below.

Increases in Inventory.   One of the major causes of cash flow problems in small businesses is inventory fluctuation, which is due to normal variations in inventory levels and also due to seasonal fluctuations. Even in a relatively small business, it would not be uncommon for inventory to fluctuate several thousand dollars in a given week. This does not increase or decrease profit but rather increases the inventory category on the balance sheet and simultaneously increases accounts payable. Large inventory increases quickly deplete cash reserves, since the inventory is generally paid for in 10 to 30 days. It may take longer to sell it, and once it is sold, credit may be extended to the customers. Thus, often the cash must be available to pay for the inventory long before the cash is received from the customer. The cost of inventory does not become an expense until it is sold, since it then becomes part of "cost of goods."

Credit Terms Extended.   Another major cause of cash flow problems is associated with accounts receivable. An account receivable is created each time a customer purchases inventory but does not pay immediately. Problems then occur for three reasons.

1.   The entrepreneur must pay for inventory before the customers pay for their purchases. When customers purchase merchandise, the small business owner must pay for inventory to replace the items sold and must pay employees wages. However, suppose the customers have 30 days to pay for their merchandise. If the small business owner replaces the inventory or pays wages within 10 days or 2 weeks, payment for these items is due before the customers pay for their purchases. This

Small Business Success 7

Hoyt Heater Co., Reno, Nevada

A new location saved Hoyt Heater Co. from closing. New federal regulations governing the energy efficiency of water heaters went into effect in the early 1980s. Hoyt Heater Co. had to make a decision—grow or close down.

The company, founded in 1910, manufactured water heaters in Oakland, California. Intense industry competition existed for many years, reducing the number of water heater manufacturers from 60 to 6. Hoyt Heater Co. had survived by meeting the market's changing needs.

However, in June 1980, an analysis by the Department of Energy indicated that the company could not remain in business unless it could expand and produce more products at less cost. The company obtained two Small Business Administration loans, relocated to Reno in July 1982, and increased its staff from 45 to 210. The company recorded a 60 percent increase in sales during the first part of 1983 and anticipated that a total work force of 350 would be needed by 1984.

Source: Small Business Means Jobs (Washington, D.C.: Small Business Administration, 1984), 12.

is obviously difficult, as it is similar to a person who must pay rent before he receives a paycheck.

2. Increasing accounts receivable in a growing company place a greater strain on cash flow. If accounts receivable increase because sales volume increases, even more money is necessary to replace rapidly selling inventory or to pay employee wages. Many small companies must actually slow sales growth because they do not have adequate working capital.

3. Improper management of accounts receivable can strangle cash flow. While extending 30 days' credit to customers can cause cash problems, the problem is even further aggravated by customers who do not pay on time. Although credit may be extended for 30 days, there are always customers who take longer, and some may not pay at all. If a small business allows its customers to abuse its credit policy, it may fail. (More will be said about this in Chapter 15.)

Large Loan Payments.   Recall that if Small Pets Inc. borrows $100,000 at 12 percent for 10 years, the yearly payments would be approximately $17,698. Of that amount, $12,000 is interest and $5,698 is principal. The interest is an expense, shown on the income statement. The principal portion is not an expense because it is merely repaying money given to the entrepreneur earlier. Therefore, it does not appear on the income statement. Thus, any company making large loan payments to the bank may find that it is very short of cash even if the income statement shows a profit.

Unprofitable but Rich

Just as it is possible for a profitable company to be short of cash, it is also possible for a company to appear unprofitable yet be able to pay its bills. This is possible if the company has a large depreciation expense. For example, the owner of Small Pets Inc. purchased $43,000 in fixed assets to open the business. If these assets depreciate evenly over 5 years, the depreciation expense would be $43,000 ÷ 5 = $8,600 per year. However, since there is no ''depreciation bill'' that must be paid as with rent or utilities, the depreciation expense does not affect the cash of the company. Therefore, a large depreciation expense may make the company appear unprofitable, although it has cash to spend. Small Pets, for example, actually did not ''spend'' $8,600 in cash for depreciation and, therefore, may not have cash flow problems even though it is showing a loss.

K E Y   Objectives Reviewed

1. The two most common accounting methods are the cash method and the accrual method.

2. The income statement is a financial statement that indicates the profitability of the firm.

3. The balance sheet provides a financial picture of a company on a specific date.

4. The opening day balance sheet is directly related to start-up costs.

5. The projected income statement for the first year of operation is essential in determining if the business will be a success.

6. There is no relationship between profit and cash on hand.

Discussion Questions

1. An entrepreneur states, "My accountant says I had a net profit of $10,000 last year. If I made $10,000 in profit, why don't I have any cash?" List reasons this might occur.

2. How are start-up costs and the opening day balance sheet similar?

3. Why should an entrepreneur be familiar with financial statements instead of relying on an accountant to make decisions?

4. Why is "net worth" or "equity" on a balance sheet only a "paper" figure? Why does it not represent what the business could be sold for? Why does it not represent what the owner would get were the business liquidated?

5. If net worth or equity is only a paper figure, why is it important?

6. Two companies show a depreciation expense of $25,000. One's depreciation expense, $25,000, is for the office building it owns. The other company, a delivery service, has a depreciation expense of $25,000 on its delivery vans. Which company should be concerned about its depreciation expense even though it is not a cash expense?

7. If the potential sales volume for Small Pets Inc. was estimated at $200,000, why were sales estimated at only $150,000?

8. If an entrepreneur runs specials of "Buy one, get one free," how will this affect the income statement?

9. Why is the purchase of fixed assets a good "tax write-off"?

10. Suppose start-up costs are as follows:

Inventory	$ 65,000
Furniture and fixtures	35,000
Leasehold improvements	15,000
Prepaid insurance	1,000
Prepaid grand opening advertising	2,000
Machinery and equipment	7,000
Total start-up costs	$125,000
Less owner's investment	50,000
Amount of loan	$ 75,000

The $75,000 loan will be for 7 years at 14 percent interest. Yearly loan payments will be $17,490 ($10,500 interest, $6,990 principal). Prepare an opening day balance sheet.

11. Using the industry averages in Exhibit 7.1, prepare a projected income statement for a company that projects sales of $350,000. Now assume the start-up costs for the company are those in question 10. Revise the income statement to include the interest expense on the loan.

C H A P T E R 8

Legal Aspects of Small Business

Source: Courtesy of International Business Machines Corporation.

K   E   Y   Objectives

1. To identify the alternative legal structures for a small business and the advantages and disadvantages of each.

2. To identify other legal considerations important to entrepreneurs, such as contract law and law of agency.

One of the major decisions an entrepreneur must make is the best form of organization for the firm. The entrepreneur must determine which structure will provide the necessary benefits yet present minimal legal restrictions. In addition, because many other laws will affect the business's daily operations, the entrepreneur should have a basic understanding of these laws to effectively manage the firm. This chapter provides the basic information; however, any entrepreneur should consult with an attorney before making any decisions.

Alternative Legal Structures

. . . .

Proprietorships

Sole Proprietorship
An unincorporated business owned by an individual for profit.

A **sole proprietorship** is an unincorporated business owned by an individual for profit. Proprietorships are the most common form of business organization. In 1981, there were 12.1 million U.S. proprietorships compared with only 1.4 million partnerships and 2.8 million corporations.[1] The popularity of this form is due to several advantages it enjoys, described below.

Ease of Start-up.   The proprietorship is one of the easiest and least expensive business forms to establish. The entrepreneur need only obtain the necessary state and municipal business licenses. There is little registration, few legal documents to complete, no need to establish bylaws or a board of directors. Because of its simplicity, it is preferred by many entrepreneurs who wish to minimize paperwork.

Freedom from Legal Requirements.   A proprietorship has the freedom to carry on business operations almost anywhere in the country. The business can add new services, products, and so forth without violating legal documents, whereas a corporation, for example, is limited in operations to those functions stated in the corporate charter.

Owner Has Direct Control.   Because the proprietor is a sole owner, all decision-making authority rests with her. She has no need to confer with others, no need to obtain approval from others, before taking action. Thus,

---

[1]*Statistical Abstract of the United States* (Washington, D.C.: U.S. Department of Commerce, 1982), 528.

Busy, Busy, Busy

The time pressures many executives face have provided the basis for several service companies.

In Dallas, Present Company does the executive's gift shopping, wrapping, and delivery.

Harper and Faze in Boston locates one-of-a-kind jewels to suit the tastes and budgets of corporate clients.

Another Dallas company, Cartender Inc., takes the worry out of taking the car in for repairs. They pick up the car, deal with the garage doing the work, and deliver it to the owner's office.

Finally, Red Carpet Airport Car Care, located next to Cleveland's Hopkins International Airport, will see to it that your car is repaired, serviced, or painted while you're on your trip.

Source: Inc., May 1984, 46.

---

the proprietor can make decisions quickly based entirely on personal preferences.

Total Ownership of Profits.   Because there is only one owner, all profits belong to the proprietor and can be taken for personal use or reinvested into the business. The decision rests entirely with the proprietor. Partnerships and corporations divide the profits, and the owners must share control over company income.

Possible Tax Advantages.   Because the business and the proprietor are legally viewed as one entity, the proprietor only pays income tax on the net income of the business. Therefore, if the business does not show a profit, the entrepreneur will not pay income taxes even though some money may have been taken from the company for personal use. Suppose, for example, a business has a substantial depreciation expense. It is possible that the company may show a loss yet still have enough cash flow for the owner to take money for personal use. If the company showed a "paper loss" of $5,000, but the owner took $15,000 for living expenses, no income taxes would be due on the $5,000 loss to the business or on the $15,000 the proprietor took.

Complete Responsibility for Success.   The sole proprietor derives great satisfaction from being solely responsible for the business's success. There are no other partners, no board of directors, no stockholders who share the success. Major accomplishments are obviously the result of the proprietor's business skills.

A proprietorship is not without its disadvantages, however. Our next section examines these.

Unlimited Liability.   The major disadvantage usually cited for proprietorships is **unlimited liability.** In other words, because the proprietor and the business are viewed as one entity, there is no legal distinction between personal assets and business assets. Suppose, for example, a customer files a lawsuit against the entrepreneur's business, and the court rules in favor of the customer. The entrepreneur may lose both business assets and personal assets. The entrepreneur's best protection is adequate insurance. If insurance is sufficient to cover any possible lawsuits, no assets will be lost.

Business Ceases on Death of Proprietor.   Because the proprietor and the business are one, the business ceases to exist on the owner's death. Of course, a new owner may purchase the assets and continue the business operations, but it is then considered a new company, even if it is a new proprietorship.

Financing Is Limited.   Because there is only one owner, the ability to raise equity capital depends entirely on the proprietor's personal financial situation. Unless an entrepreneur has substantial personal funds, the ability to invest a large amount of equity is limited. This low equity limits the amount of debt financing that can be obtained, since the debt-equity ratio is critical in any financing decision.

Growth of the Company May Be Limited.   Because of the limited financing ability, and because of the limits on the time and energy of one person, the company may not grow as fast or as far as it would if there were more than one owner. While the proprietor is solely responsible for the success of the company, that success may be limited owing to single ownership.

No Tax Deduction for Owner's Withdrawals.   In a proprietorship, the owner does not take a salary but instead takes a "draw" or a "withdrawal" of funds for personal use. While at first that may appear to be a minor point, it becomes a major distinction when tax returns are prepared. The funds the owner withdraws for personal use are not considered an expense of the company and are therefore not tax deductible. (This is not true for corporations, where the owner is treated as an employee and the salary is a tax-deductible expense for business.)

Partnerships

A **partnership** is an unincorporated business owned by two or more people. There are two basic types of partners—general partners and limited partners.

A **general partner** is much like a sole proprietor in that liability is not limited to business assets. A lawsuit filed against the partnership may result

Unlimited Liability
A legal arrangement in which the entrepreneur and the business are considered a single entity. Lawsuits against the business can result in loss of personal assets.

Partnership
An unincorporated business owned by two or more people.

General Partner
A partner who has unlimited liability.

Exhibit 8.1

Getting to the Handshake

Here are some principles for partnership formation based on interviews with successful partners and with search firms, venture capitalists, and others who scrutinize the viability of a partnership from the outside.

1. **Look for the chemistry.** Do the characters of the proposed partners stimulate ideas and enthusiasm in each other? The ideal partner will work with you in ways that create synergy, so that the sum of your combined efforts is greater than your individual contributions.

2. **Seek different backgrounds.** Partners should not see problems from the same perspective. ''You need to be able to play devil's advocate for each other,'' says Ken Smith, who, with his partner Rick Walsh, publishes *Multi-Level Marketing News*. ''If you just want someone to see things the same way you do you're not talking about a partner but an employee.''

3. **Be sure you share the same goals.** Each partner should write a condensed business plan for the venture with a summary of goals. Compare the goals. If they don't match and can't be merged, you are headed for trouble down the line.

4. **Check for similarity in drive and ambition.** Dave Anderson, general partner in the New York venture-capital firm of Welsh, Carson, Anderson & Stowe, calls this ''the greed equation.'' Partners need to have the same intensity of motivation and be willing to extend themselves to the same degree or there will be bickering over inequality of effort.

5. **Put your agreement in writing.** You don't need to be especially formal about this, but there are two important features that any partner-

Source: From ''Getting to the Handshake'' by Axel Madsen, which first appeared in *Success Magazine,* pp. 34–35, October 1983. © 1983, reprinted with permission.

in the loss of the partner's personal assets. All partnerships (limited and general) must have at least one general partner, but there is no maximum limit to the number of general partners.

Limited Partner
A partner whose liability cannot exceed the amount of money invested in the business.

A **limited partner** invests money into the business but cannot take an active role in its management. Because of the inactive management role, liability of a limited partner extends only to the amount of money invested, not to personal assets. This limited liability status can be lost, however, if it is determined that the limited partner has been taking an active role in management. As with general partners, there is no maximum to the number of limited partners as long as there is at least one general partner. In fact, the Delorean Motor Co., an unsuccessful car manufacturing plant established by John Delorean, had 134 limited partners, including many celebrities such as

ship contract should cover: what happens if one of the partners dies, and a buy-out clause.

6. **Agree on how soon you take income out of the business.** This can be changed later, but it's important to spell out your intent from the beginning. Most partners choose to plow money back into the business, but for how long? What will be your measure of when to start taking money out? If you don't decide until you feel the need to start taking profits, you could be in a bind that can create more problems than any other aspect of the business.

7. **Agree on expenditures.** Decide on who can spend what. You may want to place a limit on how much one partner can commit to without consulting the other. One way of keeping two partners aware of what's going on is to require two signatures on every check. This can be irritating when you write checks for $5 or $10, but it could be worth it in the long run.

8. **Draft a basic "philosophy" for the partnership.** You need consensus on your partnership's reason for existence, what market it will serve, and the image it wishes to project to the public.

9. **Define parameters for growth.** You need to avoid pursuit of opportunities that, however attractive they may be, take parts of your enterprise away from its real interest.

10. **Set up a periodic performance review for yourselves.** Partners need continually and objectively to assess whether they are pulling their own weight and correct any falloff before it becomes a problem.

Sammy Davis, Jr., and writer Ira Levin.[2] Because of their limited status, though, when the company went bankrupt, their losses could not exceed their investment; personal assets were not lost.

The Partnership Agreement. To form a partnership requires only an oral or written agreement. Except in certain situations, a general partnership requires no written partnership agreement. However, the advantages of having a written document far outweigh any legal cost of drawing up the **articles of copartnership.** Many disputes among partners could have been prevented by developing an agreement before the business began operations. The articles of copartnership include basic information such as the firm's name, when the

Articles of Copartnership
A written legal agreement for a partnership that outlines its purpose, each partner's responsibilities, financial considerations, and so forth.

---

[2]Craig Waters, "The Icarus Factor," *Inc.*, April 1983, vol. 5, no. 4, 36.

partnership will begin and end, and the nature of the business operations. It is essential that the agreement also detail monetary considerations, since money is usually the cause of disputes among partners. Any partnership agreement should state the amount of money each partner will invest, how their salaries will be determined, how profits and losses will be distributed, and so forth. Furthermore, to prevent disagreements, guidelines should be written concerning each partner's decision-making authority, the amount of time each is expected to contribute, and how disputes will be handled.

Partnerships, both limited and general, have their advantages and disadvantages. Below are some of the general partnership's advantages.

Few Legal Requirements, Ease of Start-up.   Partnerships have fewer legal requirements than corporations and generally require smaller legal fees for start-up costs. A written partnership agreement will require some legal fees, but generally less than those required for incorporating.

Shared Responsibility.   In a sole proprietorship, the owner often feels overwhelmed with the many responsibilities and tasks involved in running the business. A partnership allows the work load to be divided and so provides some relief from the daily pressures. The partnership also provides moral support; it may be easier to survive rough times if someone else shares the trouble.

Different Areas of Expertise.   One major advantage is that the partners may have expertise in different areas, providing a more balanced management. For example, successful partnerships often have one partner with a marketing and sales background and another partner with financial and accounting expertise. The need for entrepreneurs to "wear many hats" is less of a problem with several people to share the duties.

Greater Ability to Raise Capital.   In a proprietorship, the ability to raise capital depends primarily on the proprietor's personal wealth. In a partnership, the ability to raise capital is enhanced because there are two or more entrepreneurs who can invest cash or pledge personal assets as collateral. In addition, if a limited partnership is formed, partners can be added and additional capital can be raised with minimal risk to the limited partners.

No Income Taxes Due on the Partnership.   The partnership, like the proprietorship, is not taxable. The profits or losses of the business are considered as income for the owners; if the company shows a profit, this profit is taxable income for the owners. If the company shows a loss, the loss will be deducted from any other income of the owners, and taxes will then be calculated.

Partnership Status Can Be Given to Key Employees.   Many small businesses find that they are unable to offer salaries that are competitive with those of large firms. To keep key employees, the business may offer a share in the partnership. For example, in one wholesale firm, the owner felt the sales manager was so important to the firm's success, he offered the manager a partnership arrangement. Although the sales manager may have found large firms willing to pay him a greater salary, he would not find these firms offering partial ownership. Since the company was rapidly expanding, the future earning potential as a partner might actually exceed compensation offered by large firms. By offering even a small part of the partnership to the salesman, the entrepreneur was assured of maintaining a key employee.

The entrepreneur must weigh these advantages against the general partnership's disadvantages.

Lack of Continuity.   Death or withdrawal of one partner causes the partnership to end, so its existence is not indefinite. Although the business may continue to operate as a proprietorship, a new partnership, or a corporation, the original partnership is dissolved.

Unlimited Liability of General Partners.   General partners are personally liable for all debts incurred. Just as in a proprietorship, the partners' personal assets may be at risk if the business cannot pay its debts.

Liability of All Partners for Actions of One.   If one partner signs an agreement, it is binding on all partners. Similarly, if one partner borrows money in the business's name, all partners can be held responsible for repayment. Generally, unless stated otherwise in the partnership agreement, new partners will be held responsible for all debts or agreements of the partnership even though these existed before the new partners joined the company.

Partnerships Often Break Up.   One entrepreneur who had been in an unsuccessful partnership described a partnership as a "marriage without love." Just as in marriages, difficulties and disagreements often occur among partners. The division of authority creates tension because partners often do not agree on a plan of action. Two psychologists who specialize in "business therapy" for partnerships state, "One of the most common things in partnerships that have gone down the tubes is that they were very different people in personality and temperament, and they weren't able to resolve those differences."[3] Although there is no official tabulation, it is reasonable to assume that, as in divorces, estrangement among business partners is increasing. At least one statistic, the number of cases submitted to the American Arbitration Association, supports this unfortunate conclusion. Partnership disputes there rose from 130 in 1980 to 231 in 1982, or 78 percent in two years.[4]

Limited partnerships have certain advantages over general partnerships. The next section describes some of these.

---

[3]Robert Mamis, "Sparring Partners," *Inc.,* March 1984, vol. 6, no. 3, 45.
[4]Mamis, "Sparring Partners," 48.

Limited Liability for the Limited Partners.   As stated before, limited partners can only lose the money they have invested. They cannot be held liable for other debts the company incurs.

Freedom of Management by the General Partners.   Because the limited partner cannot take an active role in the company's daily management, the general partners can operate without interference from the limited partner. This is especially advantageous if there is only one general partner, since this person then has total control over daily decisions.

More Continuity than a General Partnership.   The death of a limited partner does not result in an end to the partnership. The partnership continues, and if desired, a new limited partner can be brought into the company.

Freedom of Limited Partners.   Unless otherwise stated in the agreement, the limited partners can sell their ownership in the business to other limited partners without the approval of other partners. This allows the limited partners to terminate their interest in the business without affecting its continuity.

Limited partnerships present certain disadvantages as well. These are discussed below.

More Legal Requirements.   The limited partnership must properly file a certificate of limited partnership or the company will be considered a general partnership. In addition, the limited partnership agreement is often more complicated and detailed than a general partnership agreement, resulting in greater legal costs.

Higher Tax Rates if a Large Profit Is Realized.   Limited partnerships are often formed to provide financing for the entrepreneur while providing tax advantages for the limited partners. Therefore, if the company incurs losses due to large depreciation expenses or if the company incurs research and development costs, the limited partnership is advantageous for both the entrepreneur and the investors. If, however, the company becomes very profitable, the partnership structure may result in higher taxes for the investors than if the company incorporated.

Investment in a Limited Partnership Is Not Liquid.   As stated before, ownership in a limited partnership can be sold to other limited partners without the approval of other partners. However, if someone wishes to sell the investment and no one is willing to buy it, the money may be tied up as long as the general partner deems necessary.

"Excellent Tax Shelters" Are Not Necessarily a Good Investment. Limited partnerships are often established because of the tax benefits to the investor. From the investor's standpoint, though, a business that is an excellent tax shelter may not be a financially viable business. Therefore, limited partnerships must be carefully analyzed.

Illustration Capsule 8.1

Fueling Growth through Limited Partners

In 1981, Tom Keaveney, president of Cable Management Associates, Inc., wanted to expand his cable television systems, headquartered in Hershey, Pennsylvania. An excellent opportunity arose to purchase a subscriber service near Charleston, West Virginia. This system would more than double the operations under his control.

However, two major problems had to be overcome. First, Keaveney needed to raise almost $13 million to purchase and upgrade the system. Secondly, he needed to raise that amount of money without diluting his 83% control of Cable Management Associates, Inc.

In order to accomplish his goals, Keaveney decided on a limited partnership. The limited partnership arrangement was handled by a Philadelphia brokerage firm, Butcher & Singer, Inc., who helped to find the limited partners. Because of initial costs of cable installation and high depreciation expenses, the limited partners receive substantial tax breaks. In addition, it is estimated that each investor will receive annual cash distributions of approximately $5,000.

Within five to six years, the limited partners will be able to nearly triple their investment. As the managing general partner, Keaveney will receive a fee of 6½% of gross revenues.

The limited partnership provided an excellent financing alternative for Keaveney and an excellent tax shelter for the limited partners. Through other limited partnerships, Keaveney has also raised enough capital to purchase cable television franchises in Pennsylvania, West Virginia, Virginia, Maryland and Delaware.

Source: Reprinted with permission, INC. magazine, September 1982, pp. 121–122. Copyright © 1982 by INC. Publishing Company, 38 Commercial Wharf, Boston, MA 02110.

Joint Venture
A partnership formed for a specific purpose and a specific period.

Joint Ventures. A **joint venture** is a variation of a partnership, formed for a specific purpose and for a specific period. For example, in a normal partnership, two or more people join efforts and financial resources to operate an ongoing business; it is assumed the business will operate indefinitely. However, suppose two entrepreneurs develop a product to sell at the Mardi Gras one year. This would be accomplished through a joint venture, since the legal arrangement would not need to exist once the Mardi Gras had ended.

The Northwest Shelf Joint Venture

Geoff Donaldson, owner of an obscure Australian-based firm, borrowed money from 62 separate banks for a total of $1.4 billion. Even more remarkable, the banks loaned the money based solely on future revenues.

This incredible financing arrangement was developed for a joint venture between Donaldson's firm, Woodside Petroleum, and several major firms, including Royal Dutch/Shell, Standard Oil of California, British Petroleum, and Australia's largest enterprise, Broken Hill Propriety. The joint venture was formed to process natural gas off the shores of Australia.

Although the large corporations involved own half of the joint venture, Donaldson will own half of the gas and will also serve as project operator, meaning that his company runs the joint venture. "I like to do things my own way," he says.

Source: Fortune, April 19, 1982, 114.

Incorporation

Corporation
An artificial entity created by the state that has an existence separate and apart from its owners.

The last legal structure of organization is the **corporation.** A corporation is an artificial being created by the state that has an existence separate and apart from its owners. Below we describe the advantages of this organizational form.

Limited Liability.   Limited liability is often given as a primary reason to incorporate a business; the owner's personal assets are legally separated from business assets. However, many small business owners find this does not hold true, particularly during start-up. In many start-ups, loans and other liabilities must be personally guaranteed by the entrepreneur. If the business cannot repay its debts, its owner is held personally responsible. In addition, the entrepreneur must often pledge personal assets as collateral. If the debts are not repaid, personal assets will be seized and liquidated to repay the debt. Thus, the limited liability advantage often is not realized until the business is financially secure and the owner does not need to secure the debts personally.

Existence Continues Despite Ownership Change.   Because a change in ownership can be accomplished by a stock transfer, the corporation will continue to exist as a separate entity, despite changes in ownership. Legally, the corporation's existence does not end with ownership change as it would in a proprietorship or partnership. If an entrepreneur purchases an ongoing enterprise that is incorporated, he purchases a separate legal entity that legally may have a perpetual existence.

Even this feature of a corporation, though, often is not applicable in some small businesses. Consider, for example, a doctor, dentist, or business consultant who incorporates a business. When that entrepreneur wishes to retire and sell the business, it is common for another doctor, dentist, or consultant to purchase the accounts; however, the original corporation (for example, Dr. M. Smith, D.D.S., Inc.) is ended and a new corporation (Dr. N. Jones, D.D.S., Inc.) is formed. Thus, the perpetual existence feature of corporations does not always apply to small businesses.

Ability to Raise Capital.   Because of the stock shares authorized when the corporation forms, it is often possible for the corporation to sell stock if it needs additional capital. As long as the original principals maintain ownership of the majority of stock, financing can be raised without giving up control of the company.

Board of Directors May Provide Management Assistance.   Each corporation must establish a board of directors. In some corporations, the board consists of those people directly involved in the company's daily operations. In many small corporations the board consists of the entrepreneur and family members. However, a board of directors may also consist of persons not directly connected with the daily operations. For example, local bankers and executives from large companies may become board members and provide valuable guidance to the small firm.

Tax Advantages at Very High Profit Levels.   Once a small firm begins to generate large profits, the corporate status may be preferable to proprietorship or partnership. The corporate form of organization will usually result in a smaller tax liability when profits are large, since it is taxed at a special corporate rate. (Proprietorships and partnerships are taxed at personal tax rates.)

Incorporation brings disadvantages as well, which are described below.

More Complicated Start-up, More Ongoing Legal Requirements. A major disadvantage of the corporate structure is the legal requirements for both the start-up and the ongoing business. The normal procedure for incorporating requires that the company reserve the corporate name; file articles of incorporation; develop bylaws; and obtain a corporate minute book, stock certificates, and a corporate seal. The business must maintain minutes of all corporate meetings, which must be held regularly, and must keep more detailed accounting records than a proprietorship or partnership. For many entrepreneurs, all of this record keeping becomes a burden.

There is also more ongoing regulation. Corporations are required to file more reports, file more detailed tax returns, and adhere to regulations concerning meetings of the board of directors.

More Restrictions on Expanding into Other States.   While proprietorships and partnerships can operate in almost any area of the country, states do not have to recognize a corporation. Therefore, it may be more difficult for a corporation to expand into other states. A corporation that is incorporated in one state may have to file as a "foreign corporation" to do business in another state. Proprietorships and partnerships do not have to do this.

Double Taxation
A term describing the tax liability of a corporation and its shareholders. Corporations must pay tax on net income and shareholders then pay tax on dividends.

Double Taxation.   A proprietor or partner pays income tax only on the business's net income; the corporation owner must essentially pay taxes twice. The corporation must pay taxes on the business's net income, and the owner must then pay income taxes on any dividends. This is often referred to as **double taxation.** However, as stated before, the end result may be a lower tax bill than if the company were not incorporated.

The S Corporation

S Corporation
A corporation that provides limited liability to the owner but is taxed as a proprietorship or partnership.

An **S corporation** is a unique form of organization, in which the owner enjoys the benefits of a corporation, particularly limited liability, but the company is taxed as a proprietorship (or partnership); the profits or losses of the company are recorded on the personal tax return of the owners. The S corporation, therefore, avoids double taxation. An S corporation is not a distinct legal structure but merely a special type of corporation. The state in which the S corporation is formed makes no distinction between S corporations and non-S corporations. The S corporation's major difference is its arrangement concerning taxation.

Generally, S corporations are beneficial for the following types of businesses:[5]

1.   Any start-up company that anticipates losses the first few years. The losses would be recorded on the owner's personal income tax return and would reduce personal income tax liability.

2.   A very profitable company that has no need for keeping profits in the business. For example, a profitable, stable company that is not experiencing rapid growth may not need funds for fixed assets or working capital. If the owners want to take substantial dividends, an S corporation may be best.

3.   Many service-oriented businesses that do not have large fixed assets are better as S corporations. Not all of the profits are needed for expanding the company; the owner can take substantial dividends without straining the company's cash flow.

There are restrictions on S corporations, of which the entrepreneur must be aware when considering this legal structure. An S corporation can have no

[5]Bruce Posner, "The New Lure of Subchapter S," *Inc.,* June 1982, vol. 4, no. 6, 104.

Exhibit 8.2	Effect of Legal Structure on Tax Rates

Company Net Profit before Tax	Legal Structure	Federal Taxes Due
$ 2,500	Corporation	$ 400
2,500	Partnership (2 partners, 50% ownership each)	0
2,500	Partnership (3 partners, 33% ownership each)	0
2,500	Proprietorship	0
50,000	Corporation	8,250
50,000	Partnership (2 partners, 50% ownership each)	3,565 each partner*
50,000	Partnership (3 partners, 33% ownership each)	1,860 each partner*
50,000	Proprietorship	13,972*
100,000	Corporation	25,750
100,000	Partnership (2 partners, 50% ownership each)	13,975 each partner*
100,000	Partnership (3 partners, 33% ownership each)	5,751 each partner*
$100,000	Proprietorship	$32,400*

*Amount of taxes due before personal deductions such as medical expenses, personal and charitable contributions.

more than 35 shareholders, and each shareholder must be an individual, an estate, or a specific type of trust. This is not true with non–S corporations, in which shareholders can be partnerships or other corporations. Also, an S corporation can have only one class of stock issued and outstanding even though it is legal to have more than one type authorized. This may cause problems if some investors favor common stock and others favor preferred stock. Finally, a major stockholder in an S corporation is not entitled to many tax-free benefits, such as group life insurance and health insurance, which would be available in the non–S corporation.

An Ongoing Consideration

Many businesses change organizational structure throughout the life of the business; the legal structure is not a one-time decision. Many businesses that begin as proprietorships or S corporations become non–S corporations when the company grows and net income increases. Companies that begin as partnerships may grow large and incorporate, or one partner may buy out the other and the business becomes a proprietorship.

Small Business Success   8

Industrial Machine Inc., Baltimore, Maryland

Industrial Machine Inc. has experienced a change in legal structure, a change in ownership, and many changes in profit levels.

Originally begun as a partnership in 1939, the company eventually changed to a corporation. In 1978 it was purchased by James O'Hara and James Frese, O'Hara serving as president of the corporation and Frese as vice-president. The two new owners faced an uphill climb since IMI was fraught with problems and had substantial debt. Frese and O'Hara cut the staff, established quality controls, installed new machinery, and diversified the market. The company was profitable in 1979 but then the recession and high interest rates caused it to lose money through 1981. The firm continued to struggle, working on creative solutions and purchasing state-of-the-art machinery. In 1982, IMI showed a profit; in 1983 the profit was almost $300,000. The two new owners' persistent efforts have turned a potential failure into a success.

Source: Small Business Means Jobs (Washington, D.C.: Small Business Administration, 1984), 10.

Many entrepreneurs search for specific guidelines to tell them what legal structure is most appropriate for their business and when the legal structure should be changed. As with decisions concerning financing, there are both financial and personal considerations that affect the decision. The guidelines may not be the same for each entrepreneur.

One factor in the decision is the company's tax liability. The entrepreneur should consult with a lawyer and an accountant to determine how much the tax liability would vary with changes in legal structure. She can only do this once she has prepared projected income statements and calculated projected net income. It is difficult to provide a simple comparison of tax rates for proprietorships, partnerships, and corporations for several reasons. First, because the net income of a proprietorship or partnership is treated as personal income for the owners, the amount is transferred to the entrepreneur's personal tax return. The effective tax rate will be affected by other sources of income, personal tax deductions, and filing status—whether the entrepreneur is married, single, has dependents, and so forth. Two other factors make a simple comparison difficult:

1. The corporation owner must pay taxes on any salary and dividends the company paid. The corporation then pays taxes on the company's net profit. A proprietor, though, would pay taxes only on the company's net profit no matter how much money he had taken for personal use.

2. The corporation is allowed to subtract the owner's salary as an expense, whereas the proprietorship cannot do this. If the corporation and the proprietorship operated identically, their net incomes would be different. (The proprietorship's net income would appear to be higher.)

The entrepreneur must also consider whether the profits will be taken out of the company as salary or dividends, or whether they will be reinvested in the business. This is a consideration especially when choosing between a regular corporation and an S corporation. A regular corporation pays income tax on the profit, and the stockholders pay income tax on the dividends when they are paid. If profits are paid out as dividends, double taxation occurs. In an S corporation, the owners pay personal income tax on their share of the profits but the corporation pays no corporate income tax. Therefore, in a growing company where all profits are reinvested to expand the company, a non–S corporation will probably be preferable. The company would not incur double taxation since it paid no dividends. Avoiding double taxation by establishing an S corporation is usually recommended only if the company profits exceed $100,000. If profits are less than $100,000, the non–S corporate rates are low enough to minimize the double taxation burden.[6] S corporations are more commonly used, though, when the company is incurring a loss. The loss is then subtracted from the owner's personal income tax. (More detailed information on taxes will be provided in Chapter 18.)

Because the company's income constantly changes and the entrepreneur's personal situation may change, the decision of legal structure is an ongoing consideration. The entrepreneur should constantly reevaluate the company's legal structure but should make no final decisions without the proper legal help.

Other Legal Considerations

In the daily operation of a small business, many other legal issues arise. The entrepreneur cannot expect to be expert on all legal issues but should have a general knowledge to effectively manage the business. Important legal issues include contracts, law of agency, patents, trade secrets, copyrights, and trademarks.

---

[6]Posner, ''The New Lure of Subchapter S,'' 104.

Contracts

Contract
A binding agreement between two parties that carries rights and responsibilities for the parties involved.

A **contract** is a binding agreement between two parties that carries rights and responsibilities for both. Contract law is designed to ensure that the agreements and promises will be enforced. In the free enterprise system, contracts are an essential part of most business operations. The need for contracts developed because each company conducts business differently; it is therefore impossible to establish laws to cover all possible situations. Contract law fills this void. Contracts can be simple or complex, oral or written; they can be written in detail or merely implied by conduct. Contracts range in complexity from the dry cleaner's agreement to launder a customer's clothing to a franchisor's contract with a franchisee. Entrepreneurs often find that in the business's daily operation both simple and complex contracts are necessary. These may include employment contracts, sales contracts, financing contracts, or even warranties and product guarantees. Although the remainder of this chapter will provide basic information on contract law, the entrepreneur should consult a lawyer before entering into contractual agreements.

For a contract to be valid and legally binding, it must have six elements:[7] (1) the agreement, normally consisting of an offer and an acceptance; (2) consideration, the price for a promise;[8] (3) the capacity of each of the parties to enter into a contract; (4) lawful purpose, the legality of the bargain; (5) genuine consent of both parties; and (6) the form (oral or written) specified by law.

Agreement
An essential part of a contract, consisting of an offer and an acceptance.

The Agreement.   The first element of a contract is an **agreement** between the two parties, normally one offering to do something and the other accepting the offer. The offer is defined as "a promise or commitment to do or refrain from doing some specific thing in the future." The party offering must seriously intend to become bound by the offer or no real agreement can exist. Suppose a business owner has just been informed that expensive electrical repairs must be done to the company facility. In frustration, he states to an employee, "I'm so upset, I'd *give* this building to anyone who would take it." If the employee agrees to take it, there is still no legally enforceable contract since the entrepreneur was not making a serious offer.

The second party must also accept for a binding contract. Usually the acceptance must be made in the manner requested by the offering party, must not be contingent on anything else, and must be communicated to the offering party. For example, the acceptance cannot be stated as, "I'll accept your offer if you reduce the price by 10 percent." Because the acceptance only exists if the price is reduced, it is not an unequivocal acceptance. The acceptance must be communicated. Silence alone is not sufficient acceptance unless it was previously agreed on, as in Book of the Month or Record of the Month clubs,

[7]Kenneth Clarkson, Roger LeRoy Miller, and Gaylord Jentz, *West's Business Law,* 2d ed. (St. Paul, Minn.: West Publishing Co., 1983), 100.
[8]Clarkson, Miller, and Jentz, *West's Business Law,* 136.

where the customer agrees to return a rejection card if he does not want the product shipped.

Consideration
The price for a promise.

Consideration.   As stated before, **consideration** is the price for a promise, or something exchanged for something else. Consideration requires two elements: first, something of legal value must be exchanged, and second, there must be a bargained-for exchange. If someone promises to give a gift, attend a party, or give a ride to a friend, consideration does not exist because nothing was exchanged in return for the promise.

Contractual Capacity
The legal capacity of each party to enter into a contract.

Contractual Capacity.   **Contractual capacity** refers to the competence (or legal capacity) of each party to enter into a contract. Contractual capacity was established as a required element of contracts to protect people who are too young or who are mentally incompetent. The contractual capacity clause can be used to void contracts signed by minors, intoxicated persons, insane persons, and convicts. State laws govern a person's legal capacity to enter into a contract; therefore, the rules are not identical throughout the country. In most states, legal capacity does not exist until the age of 18. If a minor signs a contract, the minor can void the contract. However, if an entrepreneur signs a contract with a minor, the entrepreneur cannot use the legal capacity clause to void the contract. It can only be voided at the minor's request.

A contract signed by an intoxicated person may or may not be valid. If the person was so intoxicated that she lacked mental capacity when signing the contract, then the contract would be void. To void the contract under these conditions, though, it is necessary to prove that the intoxicated person was incapable of comprehending the contract's legal consequences. If she signs a contract and comprehends the legal implications, the contract is binding. Because of the need to prove lack of mental capacity, intoxication is rarely a successful argument for voiding a contract.

Insane persons who have been assigned a guardian by a court of law cannot enter into contractual agreements. Only the guardian has that legal capacity. If, however, no legal guardian has been appointed, then the insane person may enter into a legal contract if the person has the mental capacity to comprehend the resulting legal implications.

State laws vary concerning the contractual capacity of convicts while they are in prison. In some states, convicts can enter into binding contracts while in prison; in other states they lose this privilege. Often, if a person is convicted of a major crime, that person will not have full contractual capacity in the eyes of the law.

Lawful Purpose and Legality.   For a contract to be valid, it must only include performances of legal acts. A contract that involves criminal or other illegal acts is not binding. The contract's legality will also be voided if certain restrictions are unduly harsh. The small business owner might face a question of lawful purpose in several instances. For example, when a business is sold, it is very common for the contract to include a ''noncompete clause.'' This prevents the seller from opening a similar business. A noncompete clause restricts time (the number of years during which the seller cannot operate a similar business) and geographic location (the area in which the similar business cannot be operated). If either restriction is determined by the courts to be unreasonable, that clause can be voided using the lawful purpose–legality requirement.

Genuine Consent.   Contracts can be voided if there is a mistake of facts by either party or if deceit, undue influence, or duress exists when the contract is made. A mistake of fact is different from a mistake in value or quality. Suppose an entrepreneur agrees to buy a building he believes is worth $100,000 when it is really worth only $75,000. This is a mistake of value or quality and does not void the contract. If, however, the entrepreneur thought the building he was buying was the one at 1709 Elm Street and it was actually at 1707 Elm Street, this is a mistake of fact and could void the contract.

Proper Form.   Although some oral contracts are legally binding, state law dictates that certain types of contracts must be in writing. This includes contracts involving an interest in land, contracts which by their terms cannot be performed within one year, and contracts for the sale of goods for more than $500. Small business owners should be aware of these situations and obtain a written contract.

The Uniform Commercial Code

Uniform Commercial Code
A uniform body of laws relating to commercial transactions.

The **Uniform Commercial Code** (UCC) is a uniform body of laws relating to commercial transactions. For entrepreneurs the UCC is important because it regulates the sale of goods and also regulates sales contracts. The code defines a sale as the "passing of title from the seller to the buyer for a price."[9] Article 2 of the code covers the sale of tangible and movable goods and therefore covers many business transactions entrepreneurs make. The code modifies many of the necessary elements of sales contracts because in business transactions some elements may not be known at the time the contract is formed. For example, contract law states that offers must be definite enough for both parties to know the terms when the contract is signed. However, in many business transactions it is necessary to leave certain terms open (for example, final price, payment schedules, and delivery dates), so the code provides for these instances.

The UCC also covers sales warranties. A warranty is the seller's guarantee to the buyer that the goods will meet certain standards. Because the warranty imposes a duty on the seller, if the warranty is not fulfilled, the buyer can sue to recover damages or can void the agreement. Warranties can be expressed or implied.[10] An express warranty exists if the seller makes a prom-

[9]Uniform Commercial Code, Section 2-106.
[10]Uniform Commercial Code, Sections 2-313 to 314.

ise to the buyer about the goods. If the seller states, "this article of clothing is machine washable and does not need to be dry cleaned," this is an express warranty. An implied warranty exists in every sale by a merchant who deals in goods of the kind sold. Merchantable goods are those "reasonably fit for the ordinary purposes for which such goods are used."[11] Thus, a sale of goods by a business owner always includes an implied warranty that results in liability for the product's safe performance.

The UCC warranty rules concerning consumer sales were modified slightly by the Magnuson-Moss Warranty Act. Under this act, a seller is not required to provide a written warranty for consumer goods covered by the act. However, if the seller makes an express written warranty, and the cost of the goods is greater than $10, the warranty must be labeled "full" or "limited." Full warranty includes the free repair or replacement of any defective part. If it cannot be repaired within a reasonable time, the consumer is entitled to a refund (or replacement free of charge). The full warranty does not necessarily cover the entire product, nor does it necessarily last for any specified time. A limited warranty covers parts only, requiring the customer to pay for labor.

Law of Agency

Agency
A legal relationship in which one party, the agent, agrees to represent or act for the other party, the principal.

All employers enter into a legal relationship known as **agency.** In this legal relationship, one party, the agent, agrees to represent or act for the other party, the principal. In matters for which the agent was retained, the principal has the right to control the agent's conduct: the principal then also becomes liable for the agent's acts. This becomes important to business owners because an employee is legally considered an agent, and therefore, the business owner can be held liable for the employee's actions on behalf of the company. If an employee making a delivery for a small firm is involved in an accident, both the employee and the business owner can be held liable. Liability is imposed on employers because it is assumed that they are in a better financial position to bear the loss. The good financial position results in a duty to be responsible for damages. Obviously, this places a substantial burden on the small business owner who is not in excellent financial condition. Although insurance helps minimize the risk, the employer may find insurance costs excessive (see Chapter 20).

Patents

As stated in Chapter 1, small businesses in the United States have been responsible for much innovation over the years. Entrepreneurs have been willing to devote time and effort to developing new products because of the opportunity to reap the financial rewards. The federal government has helped

---

[11]Uniform Commercial Code, Section 2-314.

Patent
A grant issued by the
federal government giv-
ing an inventor the right
to exclude all others from
making, using, or selling
the invention within the
United States.

to provide this opportunity through patenting. A **patent** is a grant issued by
the federal government giving the inventor the right to exclude all others from
making, using, or selling the invention within the United States.[12] A patent
is granted for 17 years, except for design patents. Design patents are for items
that have been changed to enhance their salability and are granted for 3½, 7,
or 14 years.[13] Patents are personal property and can be sold or even mort-
gaged. However, when the patent expires, it cannot be renewed, and anyone
has the right to use the invention unless it is covered by unexpired patents.

Patents can be obtained on any of the following items:

- any new, useful, and unobvious process, machine, chemical formula, or
  other product
- any new, useful, and unobvious improvements of the above
- any new and unobvious original or design change for a manufactured article
  (such as a new auto body design)
- any distinct, new variety of plant.

Patents cannot, however, be obtained for

- an idea
- a method of doing business
- printed material (this is covered by a copyright)
- a device that does not work
- an improvement in an item that is obvious or is the result of mere mechanical skill.[14]

One of the most important aspects of obtaining a patent is to establish the
item's novelty. Novelty is established by analyzing the device according to
specified standards and seeing if anyone else has patented the item. The
invention can also be tested for novelty by the following criteria:

1. Was the invention known or used by others in this country before the
    invention by the applicant?

2. Was the invention described in a printed publication in any country
    before the invention by the applicant?

3. Was the invention described in a printed publication more than one
    year before the date of application for a patent in the United States?

4. Was the invention in public use or on sale in the United States more
    than one year before the date of patent application?[15]

The above items are extremely important in determining the item's novelty.
If a new device is described in a printed publication, if it is used publicly, or

---

[12]*Q & A about Patents* (Washington, D.C.: U.S. Department of Commerce, November
1976), 3.
[13]*Introduction to Patents* (Washington, D.C.: Small Business Administration, 1979), 2.
[14]*Introduction to Patents,* 3.
[15]*Introduction to Patents,* 3.

if it is made available for sale, the inventor must apply for a patent before a year has gone by or the inventor will lose the right to a patent.

The application for a patent consists of a fee, a petition, a description of the invention including any specifications and claims about the product, an oath, and a drawing if the invention can be illustrated. The application is filed with the commissioner of patents and trademarks in Washington, D.C. When the application is received in Washington, it is given to an examiner who is trained and experienced in the appropriate industry. If any existing patents are found that show similar inventions, the claims made about the new invention may need to be changed. Once all of the examiner's objections are answered, a patent may be obtained.

The entire application and review process takes an average of 19 months.[16] If the item is publicly available during this period, the terms "patent pending" or "patent applied for" may appear on the product. This informs the public that the application is on file in the Patent and Trademark Office.[17]

The inventor must be aware of what a patent will *not* do. First, a patent does not guarantee immunity from lawsuits; in fact, sometimes it seems to invite them. As one patent lawyer stated, "a patent is merely a fighting interest in a lawsuit."[18] Second, a patent will not protect the inventor from claims of infringement on existing patents. Third, a U.S. patent provides no protection in foreign countries. To obtain a patent in foreign countries, an application must be filed with the patent office in each country. This can be very costly.[19]

Because of all of the legalities involved with patents, competent legal help is essential. Only attorneys and agents registered in the Patent and Trademark Office may handle applications; therefore, the entrepreneur should obtain a list of these people from the Department of Commerce before choosing a lawyer.

Trade Secrets

Trade Secret
A process or information that cannot be patented but that a company withholds from competitors.

Often a business will have a process or certain information that cannot be patented but that still must be withheld from competitors. Such items, known as **trade secrets,** are usually protected by law in two ways. First, theft of trade secrets is illegal; second, most companies require employees to sign a contract stating that they will never disclose the information. If an employee discloses the information, that person has broken a legal contract and has also stolen trade secrets. Each is a separate violation of the law.[20]

---

[16]*Introduction to Patents,* 7.
[17]*Q & A about Patents,* 4.
[18]*Introduction to Patents,* 4.
[19]*Q & A about Patents,* 12–13.
[20]Clarkson, Miller, and Jentz, *West's Business Law,* 74.

Trademarks

Trademark
A word, name, symbol, or device used by a business to identify its goods and distinguish them from the goods of others.

A **trademark** is a word, name, symbol, or device a business uses to identify its goods and distinguish them from those of others. Trademark rights are established by actual use of the design on goods being sold. Although it is not essential to register a trademark with the Patent and Trademark Office, the registration does provide notice of the entrepreneur's claim of ownership and exclusive right to use the trademark. Unlike patents, trademark applications have no time limit. They can be filed any time after the trademark has been used on products shipped or sold in interstate commerce. Trademark registration lasts for 20 years and can be renewed continuously as long as the trademark is still being used. As with patents, U.S. registration does not provide protection in foreign countries; a registration must be made in each foreign country where protection is desired. It is not necessary to hire a lawyer to file the trademark application. Application forms are available from the Patent and Trademark Office.[21]

Copyrights

Copyright
A form of protection given by U.S. law to authors of literary, dramatic, musical, artistic, and other intellectual works.

A **copyright** is a form of protection given by U.S. law to the authors of literary, dramatic, musical, artistic, and other intellectual works. In 1978, a new copyright law replaced a law used since 1909. The new copyright law increased the availability of creative works to the public and gave the creators of the work a fair return. The new law provided for copyright protection for the author's lifetime plus 50 years for any works created after the 1978 law was passed. Any items copyrighted prior to the 1978 law have protection for 28 years and can be renewed for another 47 years if requested.[22]

K E Y Objectives Reviewed

1. The alternative legal structures for a business include proprietorships, partnerships, and corporations. Several types of partnerships (general and limited) exist, as well as the corporation, for which there is also the S option. Proprietorship is the most common form for businesses in the United States; it exposes the entrepreneur to unlimited liability. Partnerships often provide extra financing and extra expertise, and they are relatively easy to establish, but as with proprietorships, partnerships expose the general partners to unlimited liability. Limited part-

---

[21]*Q & A about Patents*, 1–4.
[22]Clarkson, Miller, and Jentz, *West's Business Law*, 296.

ners can only lose the money they have invested; personal assets are protected. Corporations provide limited liability for entrepreneurs, although this is often lost when entrepreneurs pledge personal assets as collateral. S corporations provide limited liability as well as tax advantages similar to proprietorships and partnerships.

2. There are several other legal aspects to small business. These include contract law, the UCC, law of agency, and laws pertinent to patents, trade secrets, trademarks, and copyrights.

Discussion Questions

1. Suppose an entrepreneur plans to open a new business and tells you he plans to incorporate for ''limited liability'' reasons. How would you respond?

2. What is ''double taxation'' of corporations? If corporations incur double taxation and proprietorships do not, why is it better to incorporate when profits are high?

3. What legal structure is most common for companies in the United States? Why do you think most entrepreneurs have chosen this legal structure?

4. Why is the decision of legal structure of a small business influenced by personal factors as well as financial factors?

5. What is the difference between an S corporation and a non–S corporation? Under what general conditions is an S corporation beneficial?

6. Although corporations legally have ''perpetual existence,'' why is the existence of some corporations more like that of proprietorships? That is, why does the existence of some corporations end with the death of the owner?

7. How is a joint venture different than a normal partnership? Why might a joint venture be an alternative for someone who does not want a normal partnership?

8. The UCC modified contract law affecting business transactions. Why was this modification necessary?

9. Compare the following aspects of patent law and trademark law:
   a. length of protection granted
   b. when the protection goes into effect
   c. time limit during which the application must be filed
   d. protection granted in foreign countries

C H A P T E R 9

Sources of Financing

Source: Photograph compliments of Bank of Hinsdale, 400 E. Ogden Ave., Hinsdale, IL 60521.

K E Y   Objectives

1. To identify various sources of financing and the requirements for obtaining that financing.

2. To stress the importance of obtaining the proper length of time for repayment of financing.

3. To identify factors that influence the entrepreneur's decision in choosing financing sources.

Debt Financing
Funds that are loaned to the company and must be repaid.

Equity Financing
Funds placed in a business in exchange for partial ownership. These funds do not need to be repaid.

Highly Leveraged Company
A business that has a large amount of debt financing compared with its equity financing.

Minimally Leveraged Company
A business that has a large amount of equity financing compared with its debt financing.

There are two general categories of financing: debt financing and equity financing. **Debt financing** (sometimes called creditor financing) refers to funds given to the business that must be repaid—money loaned to the company. **Equity financing,** however, refers to funds placed in a business that do not need to be repaid. In exchange for the funds, partial or full ownership is given. Businesses are often described as highly leveraged or minimally leveraged by their amount of debt and equity financing. A firm with a large amount of debt compared with its equity is **highly leveraged.** Conversely, a business with little debt and substantial equity funds invested is **minimally leveraged.** It is essential that the new company have the proper balance of debt and equity financing, because too much debt in its early years may drain the cash flow and cause the business to fail. Properly using debt, however, the owner of a business can get more out of what has been invested. This is the reason for the use of the word *leveraged.*

The entrepreneur often encounters a number of unfamiliar terms in the search for financing. Many of these terms are defined in this chapter; however, as an additional source of information, a glossary of financing terms is given in Appendix 9A.

Debt Financing

. . . .

Banks

Banks provide debt financing for many entrepreneurs. For most companies, particularly those that are successful and continue to grow, it is essential to develop a working relationship with a bank.

Many banks prefer to lend money to those who are already their customers. An entrepreneur starting a business is often best off contacting the bank where

Unique Business   9.1

Have Headphones, Will Travel

Boston Walkabouts was formed in the spring of 1983 to provide tourists with tape-recorded guides to the city's historic Freedom Trail. Founder Jill Fallon also rents tape players for those traveling without their own. The tapes, available in four languages, are sold for $9.95 at the gift shops and hotels throughout the city. Similar guides are available in a number of other cities and tourist attractions around the country.

To help you fight the jet lag that may mean less fun for you at your destination, Capitol Hill Hospital of Washington, D.C. provides "Fitness in Flight," a program of isometric exercises.

Source: Inc., August 1984, 31.

---

he conducts personal banking. Another factor he must consider, though, is the distance from the bank to the proposed business. Most banks prefer to lend money to businesses within their servicing area; if the entrepreneur's personal bank account is with a bank far away from the proposed business site, it may be best to contact another bank.

Banks vary substantially in lending policies. If one bank refuses to lend money to an entrepreneur, another may be very willing to provide the funds. Some banks are willing to take a higher risk and are interested in lending to small businesses; others are very conservative and prefer to lend only to large companies. It is advisable to understand a bank's lending policies before applying for a loan.

Although a bank may reject a loan for many reasons, the most common follow:[1]

Undercapitalization
A situation in which the business does not have enough funds to operate the business efficiently.

Undercapitalization.   **Undercapitalization** is a condition in which the business does not have enough funds to operate efficiently. The entrepreneur does not have enough personal money invested and does not borrow enough money to run the company properly. This is one of the most common financing mistakes entrepreneurs make. Because this often leads to failure, a bank will refuse to loan money unless it is an adequate amount.

---

[1]"How Bankers View Small Business," *Inc.*, November 1981, 50.

High Debt Compared with Equity.   The bank expects the entrepreneur to raise part of the funds necessary to start the business. This can be the entrepreneur's own money or money from friends and relatives. The bank then lends money based partially on the amount of equity raised. Most banks will refuse to lend 100 percent of the start-up costs, preferring instead to loan a maximum of 80 percent. If total costs to start a company would be $100,000, it would be common for the bank to loan $80,000 and require the entrepreneur to use $20,000 of personal money.

Collateral
Personal or business assets that the entrepreneur provides as security to the lender in case the loan is not repaid.

Lack of Collateral.   **Collateral** consists of personal or business assets that the entrepreneur provides to the lender as security in case the loan is not repaid. If the loan is not repaid, the lender becomes the owner of the assets pledged as collateral. If adequate collateral is not available, the bank will usually reject the loan (see Exhibit 9.1.) Collateral often must include more than the assets being purchased with the loan proceeds. This is because the bank attempts to have enough assets to cover the loan amount if the business fails and the assets must be auctioned; usually assets are not auctioned for full value. Therefore, banks find it necessary to require more collateral than the amount of the loan (for example, $120,000 in collateral for a $100,000 loan).

Commercial Finance Companies

Commercial finance companies are another source of debt financing. The commercial finance industry is a multibillion-dollar-a-year business that provides financing to many companies that may not otherwise be able to raise necessary funds. Commercial finance companies are often willing to take a greater risk than a bank; however, their interest rates are often higher than a bank's.

Commercial finance companies offer many alternative methods of financing, including floor planning, accounts receivable financing, and leasing (see Appendix 9A). They are often more flexible in repayment terms, allowing a longer maturity than banks, and they are more willing to finance certain types of business equipment than are banks. Therefore, while a bank may be preferable because of a lower interest rate, the commercial finance company should not be eliminated from consideration. An entrepreneur may find it better to pay a slightly higher interest rate to obtain a more favorable repayment schedule.

The Small Business Administration

The Small Business Administration (SBA), established in 1953, is a government agency that provides a variety of services to small business. These services include management consulting, assistance in obtaining government contracts, and various financing programs. Several of the more common debt financing programs are described on the following pages.

Exhibit   9.1   How Bankers View Small Business

1. What were the major reasons for rejecting small business loan applications over the past year?

	% of Respondents Who Mentioned Factor
Undercapitalization or too much debt	32
Lack of collateral	20
Inability to demonstrate source of repayment	15
Poor credit history	15
Inadequate financial information	12
Weak management	8
Applicant lacks experience in his field of business	7
Poor track record or poor profitability	5
Insufficient cash flow	5
Unprofessional financial statements	2

2. How would you characterize the ideal small business borrower?

Good capitalization, decreasing debt-to-equity ratio, retains earnings in business	31
Good management	22
Good profit history	21
Good accounting or financial statements	13
Knowledge or experience in this business or product area	11

Note: This information was derived from a survey of 150 large and regional U.S. banks.

Source: "How Bankers View Small Business," reprinted with permission, *INC.* magazine, November, 1981, p. 50. Copyright © 1981 by INC. Publishing Company, 38 Commercial Wharf, Boston, MA 02110.

SBA Guaranteed Loan A loan in which the SBA guarantees the bank that 75 to 90 percent of the loan will be repaid even if the entrepreneur defaults.

SBA Guaranteed Loans.   Under the **SBA Guaranteed Loan Program,** the SBA "guarantees" the bank that the government will repay the loan if the entrepreneur defaults. The SBA will guarantee only 75 to 90 percent of the loan, but this does ensure that the bank will lose a maximum of 10 to 25 percent, even if the entrepreneur never makes a payment.

An SBA guarantee is often required for start-ups because of the high risk of new businesses. The guarantees are also required when the bank feels there is not enough collateral. Because the risk to the bank is reduced, the bank may approve a loan with a guarantee it would have otherwise rejected.

Unfortunately, the availability of a guarantee does not ensure bank approval. Many banks have experienced a high failure rate with guaranteed loans and are therefore reluctant to loan money under this program. In addi-

Good character	11
Good credit history	9
Steady growth or growth potential	9
Good cash flow	7
Strong or increasing sales revenue or market share	5
In business a reasonable length of time	5
Good collateral	5
Keeps bank informed	4
Good planning	3
Good product, market, or industry	3
Liquidity	3
Personal equity invested in company	1

3. **What are the major problems in dealing with small business?**

Undercapitalization	19
Inadequate or unreliable records	15
Lack of capable management	15
Inexperience or lack of financial knowledge	11
Inadequate credit rating	5
High interest rates	4
Do not use bank services to full advantage	4
Poor planning or overextension	3
Insufficient profit margins	3
Poor cash flow	3
Unaudited financial statements	2

tion, there is more paperwork and "red tape" for the bank, and many banks feel that the profit from the loan is not sufficient to justify the time required. Therefore, the entrepreneur should not be surprised to find that certain banks will not even consider an SBA guaranteed loan.

The guaranteed loan program offers the entrepreneur two significant advantages. First, particularly with a start-up, the entrepreneur may find that no bank will risk lending money without a guarantee. This program may provide the only possibility for obtaining bank financing. Second, in some cases, the bank may charge a slightly lower rate of interest because its risk is lower.

One of the major disadvantages, however, is the amount of paperwork. Though the bank must complete certain SBA forms, the entrepreneur must complete even more. The sight of all the application forms is often enough to discourage an entrepreneur from applying. Another disadvantage is that it is more time consuming and involves the approval of two institutions (the bank and the SBA) rather than just one. It is very possible that a bank may approve a loan and submit it to SBA for approval only to have SBA refuse to guarantee it. Then, if the bank is not willing to loan the money without the guarantee, the entrepreneur will be without financing.

SBA Direct Loan
A loan for a small business in which funds are provided completely from the government.

SBA Direct Loan Program.   The **SBA Direct Loan Program** was established to provide ''last-resort'' debt financing to entrepreneurs who could not obtain loans from any other source. Under the program, entrepreneurs whose loans are rejected by other financial institutions may apply to the SBA for a government loan. At one time, these loans were offered at very low interest rates. Recently, however, interest rates have been near market levels.

Although the program has received much criticism because of high default rates, it has provided funding for some very successful start-ups that were refused funding from all other financial institutions. Often, though, the program funding is not adequate to meet the demand, and at those times, it is not uncommon for an application to be placed on a waiting list of several months. An entrepreneur who needs funding immediately will often find that the Direct Loan Program is not a viable alternative.

SBA 503 Loan
An SBA loan program that provides long-term financing for the purchase of fixed assets.

The SBA 503 Program.   The **SBA 503 Program** provides debt financing at below-market rates for the purchase of fixed assets. This loan program provides funding to companies on a long-term basis (15 to 20 years) since the assets purchased usually include buildings or machinery with a long useful life. In addition to providing long-term financing, the program also structures interest charges in a way to protect the entrepreneur from fluctuating rates. A bank provides part of the loan and SBA provides the rest. The program is designed to provide financing to entrepreneurs who would otherwise not be able to obtain financing for large fixed-asset purchases. Because of this, it often allows small companies to expand and become more profitable.

As with other SBA loans, the 503 loan requires more paperwork and is more time consuming than a normal bank loan. However, if a regular bank loan is not available, this may be one of the few options for long-term financing. Projects that have been financed through the 503 program vary greatly: indoor soccer stadiums, restaurants, machine shops, and office condominiums for doctors and dentists.

SBA Guideline Changes.   Because it is a government agency, the SBA is subject to budget cuts and policy changes. In recent years, the amount of funding has been drastically reduced. The agency has been forced to set stricter requirements for loan approval, rejecting many applications that it would have approved in the past.

Small Business Administration programs have a substantial impact on the small business community, particularly with start-ups. Major reductions in SBA funding can prevent many new businesses from starting and existing businesses from expanding. A study by the General Accounting Office found that 13 percent of all small business lending involves an SBA guarantee. In addition, the GAO estimated that SBA guaranteed loans may account for as much as 40 percent of all long-term (six or more years) credit extended to small business.[2] The SBA's impact on the small business community should not be underestimated.

Leasing

Leasing is actually an alternative to regular financing. Under a leasing arrangement, a company (often a finance company) purchases machinery, trucks, or equipment, which it then "rents" to the entrepreneur for a specified period and payment. Leasing is similar to renting except that the payments cannot be changed until the lease agreement expires. Also, many leasing contracts allow part of the payments to be applied to the purchase price; when the lease term is over, the equipment may be purchased for a small price.

Advantages of leasing are as follows:

1. Leasing often requires little or no down payment, whereas the purchase of large assets often requires a 20 percent down payment.

2. Leasing terms are often more flexible than regular financing; it may be possible to lease a piece of equipment for five years when a purchase would only be financed for three years.

3. If an asset is likely to become obsolete, leasing provides greater flexibility for upgrading to a newer model. If the entrepreneur purchases a piece of equipment that becomes obsolete, she may not be able to resell it. If she leases it, however, the leasing company may allow her to trade it in, provided she leases a newer model.

4. Leasing maintains the entrepreneur's ability to borrow from a bank. If an entrepreneur needs funds for working capital, bank financing can be used for working capital while leasing can be used for large assets.

For example, suppose a business has the following start-up costs:

Inventory	$ 50,000
Working capital	20,000
Leasehold improvements	25,000
Machinery/equipment	35,000
Licenses/deposits	3,000
Prepaid insurance	2,000
Total	$135,000

Suppose the entrepreneur has $20,000 in personal money to invest and the bank is willing to loan only $80,000. The entrepreneur is $35,000 short of the total needed to start the business. It may be possible to

---

[2]Tom Richman, "Will the Real SBA Please Stand Up?" *Inc.,* February 1984, 85.

lease the machinery and equipment, reducing start-up costs by $35,000. Leasing can be a valuable financing source for entrepreneurs who need to reduce start-up costs.

Equity Financing
. . . .

The entrepreneur must finance his venture not only through debt but also through equity financing. As was mentioned, most lending institutions will not finance a project 100 percent; they expect the entrepreneur to provide a portion. He may obtain equity financing through personal funds, family, friends, partners, and other sources.

Personal Funds

No matter what type of business is started, or how many different sources of funds are used, the entrepreneur almost always invests personal money. Even if the amount is a small part of the total, other people are usually more willing to invest money in a project if the owner also risks some. It is an indication that the entrepreneur has confidence in the proposed project. Money the entrepreneur invests is considered equity capital. Even if the entrepreneur hopes the business will repay the investment later, it is generally not considered debt financing, because no required monthly payments will be made.

Friends and Family Members

Many entrepreneurs also receive a portion of the necessary funds from friends and relatives. This type of financing is viewed as equity when relatives do not expect to be paid back on a set schedule. It is often possible to arrange more lenient pay-back terms (such as no payments for the first year or lower interest rates) than those that would be obtained from a regular financial institution.

A major disadvantage may arise, however, if the business is not successful and no pay-back is possible. Friends may no longer be friendly, and family relationships may be strained. Friends or family members who provide funds often feel that they are entitled to help manage or make decisions concerning the business operation. To avoid any problems, it is best to clarify each party's rights and responsibilities before accepting any money.

Partners

Many entrepreneurs obtain financing by finding a partner for the business. Many partnerships are formed because one entrepreneur has the skills necessary to run the business (for example, an auto mechanic), while another has

"It's good to get away from the office. That financial world can be a jungle!"

Source: Copyright Ford Button.

business training and cash but no technical skills. The two entrepreneurs form a partnership since it accomplishes a common goal.

Partnerships are a source of equity financing since the partner is an owner and does not require repayments of the investment. However, partnerships formed because of a need for capital may develop problems once the business is operating. Unless the partners have similar goals, work ethics, and so forth, disagreements are likely. A partnership formed because of a need for money is similar to a marriage for convenience. Although it may be successful, there are obstacles to overcome.

Venture Capital Firms

Venture Capital Firm
A group of individuals or businesses that invests money in new or expanding businesses.

Venture capital firms are groups of individuals or companies that invest funds in new or expanding businesses. The unique feature of venture capital firms is that, although some provide loans, most provide equity financing. A venture capital firm will provide funding in return for partial ownership.

Venture capital is not available to all small businesses because the firms that invest the money are searching for a very high rate of return. Venture capital primarily finances companies expected to experience phenomenal growth and increases in profits.

A special report on venture capital gave the following guidelines for companies considering venture capital financing:[3]

1.   Will the company grow to $15 million or more in sales?

2.   Will the business generate a net profit of $1 million or more within the next five years?

3.   Is the business in a rapidly growing industry?

4.   Does the company have a good management team?

Companies that meet these guidelines may be able to obtain venture capital.

Unlike banks and other lending institutions, venture capital firms do not emphasize collateral and owner investment. The potential for the high rate of return and the entrepreneur's management skills are two of the most important factors. Thus, venture capital often provides large amounts of financing with the entrepreneur risking no personal assets. However, because the venture capital firm often requires a stake in the ownership (possibly more than 50 percent), the entrepreneur may find the requirements excessive.

Although venture capital firms are typically groups of individuals, large corporations also have established venture capital firms. The new businesses they finance often provide research and development for new products beneficial to the large corporation. In many cases, it has been found that businesses funded by venture capital firms are more productive and less expensive than in-house research and development departments. Many large corporations feel that establishing an independent venture capital firm will give them an edge on innovation.

Venture capital firms do not invest in a company permanently; in many cases the investment is made for less than ten years. After a specific time, the company is expected to buy its stock back from the venture capital firm. Obviously, not all investments are as profitable as anticipated. About one-fifth of the companies backed by venture capital firms go out of business. An equal number remain small, privately held corporations that make enough money to pay an annuity to the entrepreneur but not enough to pay off the investor. Two-fifths are bought out as they grow up. Only about one-fifth of venture capital–backed companies achieve a goal common to most of them: success as a corporation whose stock is publicly owned.[4] One company that successfully moved from start-up to venture capital to public ownership was

---

[3]"Is Venture Capital Right for You?" *Inc.,* September 1981, 66–67.
[4]Peter Holmes, "Ideas? The Money Is There," *Nation's Business,* September 1983, vol. 5, no. 9, 26.

Illustration Capsule 9.1

Personal Funds, Debt, or Investor Financing?

Personal funds are often used to finance business start-ups. For some businesses, personal funds are sufficient; for others, additional sources are needed.

Consider, for example, Happi-Hands, a gift and craft shop in Memphis, Tennessee. The company prospered and grew for its first 10 years using only the owners' personal savings and the profits the company generated. After 10 years of operation, when the fourth and fifth outlets were opened, bank financing was obtained.

For Alexa Betts, who wanted to open a day-care center in Washington, D.C., outside financing was necessary from the beginning. The company, named Child's Play, needed approximately $350,000 to begin operations. An SBA guaranteed loan for $200,000 was obtained, and $150,000 was raised by selling part of the ownership to a group of doctors. The doctors not only provided the additional money but also had contacts with other people and organizations that helped the company grow.

Source: "How to Bankroll Your Venture," *Changing Times*, 39, no. 9 (Washington, D.C.: Kiplinger Washington Editors, Inc., September 1985): 38–41.

Apple Computers. The rapid growth in sales and profits allowed the venture capital firm to obtain a spectacular rate of return.

Small Business Investment Corporations

Small Business Investment Corporation
A venture capital firm licensed by the SBA.

A **small business investment corporation (SBIC)** is a venture capital firm licensed by the SBA to invest in small businesses. Under this program, if a venture capital firm raises private investment funds, it can borrow additional funds from the SBA. For example, a venture capital firm may raise $500,000 in private money and borrow $1 million to $2 million from the government. This obviously allows the firm to invest in many businesses without raising all of the funds from private sources.

Generally, SBICs provide long-term loans (debt financing) or equity financing. As with the regular venture capital firm, the SBIC is interested in companies with a potential for rapid growth, a high return on investment, and a pay-back period of 10 years or less.

The Sale of Stock

One method of equity financing is to sell a portion of the company stock. In this way, the entrepreneur can raise necessary funds without being required to meet a set repayment schedule. Obviously, though, the sale of stock will result in the entrepreneur relinquishing some of the ownership of the company. It is a decision a small business owner must consider carefully.

The sale of stock may be regulated by state or federal law, or both. If the company and the stock sale are determined to be intrastate, federal laws will not regulate the sale. Suppose a company is incorporated in Texas, does business only within Texas, and plans to sell stock only to Texas residents. This would be an **intrastate stock sale** and only Texas regulations would apply.

Intrastate Stock Sale
A company with locations in only one state, doing business in only one state, selling stock only to residents of that state.

If for any reason the sale is considered interstate (involving more than one state), then the federal Securities and Exchange Commission and the appropriate state agencies will regulate the sale. The amount of regulation (and related paperwork) increases if the amount of the stock sale is large. For smaller amounts (less than $500,000), the regulation is not as complicated.

There are generally two types of stock sales, a private placement and a public placement.

Private Stock Sale or Private Placement
A sale of stock in which stock is sold only to selected individuals and cannot be purchased by the general public.

Private Placement.   A **private sale or private placement** refers to stock sold to a specific group of people, such as friends, relatives, or employees. The sale of the stock is not announced to the general public. A private sale of stock does not usually involve as much regulation as a public sale and can be completed by any incorporated company, no matter how large or small.

The private stock sale would allow the entrepreneur to raise capital without a need for immediate pay-back. In addition, it may be possible to find investors interested in long-term, rather than short-term, profits. Thus, if a company needs capital but will take several years before generating substantial profits, a private placement may provide the ideal financing arrangement. One final advantage is that several investors may become board members. If an investor has an expertise that is valuable to the company, his advice would be beneficial in making management decisions.

Public Offering
A sale of stock to the general public.

Public Offering.   Like venture capital, a public sale of stock (or **public offering**) is not a viable financing method for all small businesses. The company must be able to show that substantial profits will be made and the investors will receive a good return for their investment.

As stated in Chapter 1, when a company first offers its stock for sale to the general public, it is called an initial public offering (IPO). The number of companies able to offer a public sale of stock varies greatly from year to year. A company's ability to offer its stock for public sale depends on several factors:

1. The financial strength of the firm. Obviously, the better the financial position of the company, the easier it will be to sell the stock. The potential return on investment is an essential factor. Companies that

can successfully sell stock publicly must meet criteria similar to those that obtain venture capital. Thus, a mom and pop operation cannot sell stock publicly.

Underwriter
The stock brokerage firm that assists the small business in selling its stock to the general public.

2. The ability to find an **underwriter** (the stock brokerage firm that helps the firm sell its stock). One of the biggest hurdles a small business must overcome to sell stock publicly is obtaining an underwriter. A well-developed business plan is essential in overcoming this obstacle.

3. The general condition of the stock market. Often the chances of a successful IPO depend more on the conditions of the stock market than on specific factors of the company. For example, during the 1960s when general market conditions were good, thousands of small businesses were able to raise capital through public stock offerings. However, in the mid-1970s when general market conditions were poor, fewer than 20 businesses per year completed a new public offering.[5] Exhibit 9.2 illustrates the number of IPOs for 1980 through the third quarter of 1983. As with the 1960s, the early 1980s were spectacular years. The amount of money raised through IPOs in 1983 was greater than the total of all IPOs in the previous 10 years.

The Decision to Go Public.   The decision to go public must be considered carefully. The functions of the company owner often change dramatically once a company goes public. The entrepreneur's life is less private now. There are more meetings than before, more regulations; the entrepreneur must constantly reflect on the impact decisions will have on the price of company stock. Often the entrepreneur finds that after going public, shareholders' opinions must be considered, so the decision-making process is not as simple as in the past. Another factor to consider is the cost of going public. A substantial amount of legal work is required before the IPO is made. Therefore, unless there is a good chance of selling the stock publicly, an entrepreneur would be wise to consider other methods of financing.

If, however, the IPO is successful, the company will realize several benefits. First, the stock sale allows the business to raise a large amount of capital without the burden of loan payments. Thus, expansion without cash flow problems may be possible. Second, public image is often enhanced just because the company is publicly owned. Many people and many corporations view a publicly owned company as more stable and profitable than a privately held firm. Third, the entrepreneur often becomes a millionaire when the firm sells its stock. Consider, for example, the owner of TeleVideo Systems Inc. Mr. Hwang, who immigrated to the United States when he was 12 years old, began TeleVideo by making video games in his garage. The small company began to grow, enjoying phenomenal success, and eventually was able to sell stock publicly. This resulted in a financial windfall for Hwang, who now lives

---

[5]Roger Lopata and Ruth V. Wait, "Going Public, Making the Decision," *Inc.*, December 1983, 25.

Exhibit   9.2   Number of IPOs by Quarter (1980 through Third Quarter 1983)

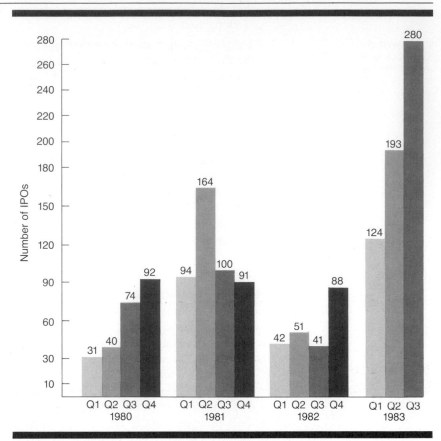

Source: Copyright © 1983 by *Going Public: The IPO Reporter,* published by Dealers Digest, Inc., December 1983. Reprinted with permission. 1983's initial public offering boom shows up dramatically when the number of initial public offerings by quarter from January 1980 through September 30, 1983 are charted.

in a Welsh castle replica that has, among other comforts, a sauna and spa in the master bedroom.[6]

Proper Financing Terms

The entrepreneur must consider not only the amount of financing necessary but also the number of years over which the loan will be repaid. If the loan repayments are not properly structured, it will create one of two situations.

---

[6]Phil Adamsak, ''100 Who Made Millions,'' *Venture,* April 1984, vol. 6, no. 4, 49.

Either it will cause a severe cash drain on the company by requiring too rapid a repayment schedule, or payments will not be quick enough and loan payments will still remain after fixed assets are no longer useful.

Suppose, for example, a company purchases a $10,000 delivery van. If the company must repay the loan within 1 year, it may not be able to do so because the monthly payments would be too high. If the loan payments are to be amortized over 3 or 4 years, the monthly loan payments will be more reasonable and will be made over the same period the van is expected to last. (If the van is used constantly, it may be worn out after only 3 or 4 years.) Suppose, though, that the loan is amortized over 10 years, and after 4 years the van is no longer useful. The company would still have 6 years left on the loan payment for the van but would need to borrow additional money to purchase another van.

Therefore, the entrepreneur must match the loan's maturity with the asset's expected life and must also consider the monthly loan payments. If the entrepreneur cannot do both simultaneously (if he needs 10 years to pay off a loan on a van), he would be wise not to borrow the funds.

Short-term Loans

Short-term Loan
A loan for a period of one year or less.

There are basically three types of loans: short-term loans, intermediate-term loans, and long-term loans. **Short-term loans** generally are for one year or less and often are used for working capital during peak seasons or to complete a contract. Suppose, for example, a retail card and gift shop needs Christmas inventory. Inventory is to be ordered in September, received in October, and paid for by November. However, the company does not begin to sell the merchandise until late November or December. It is very common for this type of business to take out a short-term loan (60 to 90 days) in November to pay the supplier. The loan is repaid after Christmas, after the goods have been sold and the cash is available.

Similarly, contractors of large construction projects often need short-term loans to pay for materials and labor costs. Even though the contractor may receive some payment after the project is partially completed, she often must pay for materials and labor before receiving payment. It is very common for a contractor to take out a short-term loan that is repaid once the project is completed and payment is received.

Intermediate-term Loans

Intermediate-term Loan
A loan amortized for a period of one to ten years.

Intermediate-term loans generally are amortized over 1 to 10 years. These loans often are for machinery and equipment, for expansion, or for starting a business. The actual length of time varies with the life of the asset and the amount borrowed. For example, a start-up loan of $30,000 may be amortized over 4 or 5 years, whereas a start-up loan of $100,000 may be amortized over

10 years. Generally, 10 years is the maximum length of time for a loan, unless the loan is for purchasing a fixed asset with a very long useful life.

Long-term Loans

Long-term Loan
A loan for a period of ten years or more.

If the loan is needed for a building or for equipment that will last longer than 10 years, a **long-term loan** (a loan of more than 10 years) is appropriate. Because fixed assets such as a building last many years, and because the purchase prices are often very high, a long-term loan is both necessary and appropriate.

The Financing Decision

. . . .

Personal Considerations

Although the first part of this chapter listed many sources of financing, entrepreneurs often find that they have few alternatives. While personal funds, friends, family members, and partners were listed as sources, none of these may be practical or desirable. Entrepreneurs often do not have enough personal money to start the business and are reluctant to ask family members or friends to risk savings or retirement money on a venture that may not succeed. Similarly, many entrepreneurs refuse to form a partnership and would rather postpone the business venture than include a partner, or refuse to sell stock because it would require that partial ownership be given to others. Entrepreneurs reject these options, desiring total independence.

Second, although banks, finance companies, and the SBA provide debt financing, the entrepreneur may not have the adequate down payment or collateral to qualify. Though this type of debt financing allows the entrepreneur to maintain full ownership, it is not always financially feasible.

Finally, venture capital firms and SBICs require such a substantial return on investment that most small businesses cannot begin to meet the requirements. Even for those businesses that may meet the necessary pay-back, this financing method requires that some ownership be given to others. Because the venture capital firm often requires controlling interest (owning 50 percent or more of company stock), many entrepreneurs will not consider this type of financing.

Profitability and Financial Stability

While personal preferences often eliminate equity capital (from family and friends) as an option, and most firms find venture capital unavailable, the impact of excessive debt financing must also be considered. Firms with substantial debt financing often find all of their profits going to the bank or finance company to repay the loan. Debt's impact on a company's profitability is shown below by illustrating the effect of varying amounts of debt on Small Pets Inc., the small business discussed in Chapter 7. As the income statements show, when debt increases, profitability and cash flow decrease.

	Small Pets Inc. Projected Income Statement at Various Levels of Debt		
	With $100,000 Loan at 12%	With $50,000 Loan at 12%	With $25,000 Loan at 12%
Sales	$150,000	$150,000	$150,000
Cost of goods	85,500	85,500	85,500
Gross margin	$ 64,500	$ 64,500	$ 64,500
Expenses			
Advertising	$ 6,000	$ 6,000	$ 6,000
Bad debts	1,200	1,200	1,200
Dues and subscriptions	300	300	300
Office expenses	1,050	1,050	1,050
Licenses/taxes	900	900	900
Miscellaneous	3,000	3,000	3,000
Rent	12,000	12,000	12,000
Salaries/wages	15,000	15,000	15,000
Supplies	1,800	1,800	1,800
Utilities and phone	2,550	2,550	2,550
Payroll taxes	1,500	1,500	1,500
Depreciation	8,600	8,600	8,600
Interest	12,000	6,000	3,000
Total expenses	$ 65,900	$ 59,900	$ 56,900
Net profit	$ (1,400)	$ 4,600	$ 7,600

Varying amounts of debt also affect the balance sheet. Substantial debt makes the firm a greater risk in the eyes of financial institutions; in businesses with substantially greater debt than owner equity, it is often stated that "the bank owns the business." Though this is not literally true, the bank would probably have all assets as collateral for the loan and, therefore, would have more of a claim against business assets than the owner. This situation is shown on page 212 by comparing opening day balance sheets for Small Pets Inc. using various levels of debt and equity.

Because of the effect of excessive debt on the company's profitability and financial stability, debt financing must often be combined with sources of equity financing. Many entrepreneurs obtain enough equity money from friends and relatives to reduce the debt needed to a manageable amount. This not only increases the firm's profitability but reduces its loan payments in the early years.

Small Pets Inc.
Opening Day Balance Sheet at Various Levels of Debt

Assets	With Loan of $100,000 for 10 Years ($27,000 Down Payment)	With Loan of $50,000 for 10 Years ($77,000 Down Payment)	With Loan of $25,000 for 10 Years ($102,000 Down Payment)
Current assets			
Cash	$ 25,000	$ 25,000	$ 25,000
Inventory	50,000	50,000	50,000
Prepaid professional fees	1,000	1,000	1,000
Licenses	2,000	2,000	2,000
Total current assets	$ 78,000	$ 78,000	$ 78,000
Fixed assets			
Furniture and fixtures	$ 8,000	$ 8,000	$ 8,000
Machinery and equipment	15,000	15,000	15,000
Leasehold improvements	20,000	20,000	20,000
Total fixed assets	$ 43,000	$ 43,000	$ 43,000
Other assets			
Deposits	$ 6,000	$ 6,000	$ 6,000
Total assets	$127,000	$127,000	$127,000
Liabilities			
Current liabilities			
Accounts payable	$ 0	$ 0	$ 0
Accrued expenses	0	0	0
Current maturity of long-term debt	5,698	2,849	1,425
Total current liabilities	$ 5,698	$ 2,849	$ 1,425
Long-term liabilities			
Notes payable	$100,000	$ 50,000	$ 25,000
Less current portion	(5,698)	(2,849)	(1,425)
Total long-term liabilities	$ 94,302	$ 47,151	$ 23,575
Total liabilities	$100,000	$ 50,000	$ 25,000
Equity			
Initial investment	$ 27,000	$ 77,000	$102,000
Total liabilities and equity	$127,000	$127,000	$127,000

Return on Investment

Return on Investment
The amount of profit generated by a business compared with the company's net worth or equity.

Another factor to consider in the financing decision is the projected amount of profit compared with the amount the entrepreneur must invest in equity money. This is known as **return on investment (ROI)** or return on equity and is computed as follows:

$$\frac{\text{Net Profit}}{\text{Net Worth (or Equity)}}$$

For example, an entrepreneur was considering opening a coin-operated car wash. The total investment for land, building, and equipment would have required $375,000. Because the bank required a 20 percent down payment,

Small Business Success   9

Components by Robert Battles Inc., Gulfport, Mississippi

Components by Robert Battles Inc. is a rapidly growing firm that has obtained two SBA loans in less than 5 years. The owner, Robert Battles, had 20 years' experience producing components for the construction industry before starting his own business. However, starting Components in 1980 was risky since the housing industry was in a deep slump and other construction-related firms were closing. Battles obtained an SBA loan for his equipment and opened the business with three employees. Within 6 months, sales reached $1.3 million and the equipment loan was completely repaid.

In March 1983, the company became the first Mississippi business to expand with funding under SBA's 503 loan program. The expansion added 18 jobs and increased production capacity 100 percent. Components by Battles now employs 80 people, and sales are projected to reach $10 million by 1986.

Source: *Small Business Means Jobs* (Washington, D.C.: Small Business Administration, 1984), 11.

the entrepreneur would have had to invest $75,000 of personal money and borrow the remaining $300,000. However, this would result in such large loan payments that the business would incur a loss. The business would show a profit of approximately $10,000 per year if the entrepreneur invested $200,000 in personal funds and borrowed the remaining $175,000. The entrepreneur, however, compared the projected profit with the necessary $200,000 investment and the potential risks and determined that the profit did not justify the huge investment.

The "proper" return on investment will vary from one entrepreneur to another. There is no right return on investment since the entrepreneur's decision is based on several factors. The entrepreneur should consider the rate of return that could be obtained if the money were invested in a certificate of deposit, in stocks and bonds, or in other possible investments. The ROI can also be viewed as a return for the entrepreneur's risk; the greater the risk, the greater the ROI desired. Financial comparisons are not the only factor to consider, though, since the entrepreneur may prefer to accept a lower rate of return in exchange for the freedom of self-employment. Thus, while ROI can be calculated, the right answer is different for every entrepreneur.

K E Y   Objectives Reviewed

1. Many sources of financing exist for potential entrepreneurs, although many of the sources have guidelines and restrictions.

2. Obtaining the proper length of time for repayment of debt financing is crucial to the business's success.

3. The entrepreneur's final choice of financing alternatives is determined by many factors.

Discussion Questions

1. Many people have argued that the SBA loan programs result in government interference in the lending market and therefore should be eliminated. Do you agree? Why or why not?

2. Identify two or three companies that have recently "gone public." How do these companies differ from privately held companies?

3. Suppose you owned a company with a high growth potential but in need of financing. Would you accept financing from a venture capital firm if they required more than 50 percent ownership? Why or why not?

4. Suppose an entrepreneur plans to start a business that will require total start-up costs of $100,000. Suppose the entrepreneur has $5,000 of his own money to invest. Why might it be difficult to find a bank loan for the remaining $95,000? Even if the loan could be obtained, why would you advise the entrepreneur that it may not be a good idea to borrow that amount?

5. What is the difference between a private sale of stock and a public sale of stock? What size companies can sell stock publicly? What size companies can sell stock privately?

6. (A) Suppose a retail store wants to borrow $30,000 to purchase extra inventory for the Christmas season. What is a reasonable length of time for this type of loan? Why? (B) Suppose the same company is currently leasing its facility and plans to purchase a building for $100,000 in the near future. What is a reasonable length of time for this loan?

7. What is ROI? Why will the proper ROI vary from one entrepreneur to another?

8. Undercapitalization is a major problem for many small businesses. Why do you think it is so common for small businesses to start out undercapitalized?

9. Suppose an entrepreneur wants to start a new business and has developed the following list of start-up costs.

Inventory	$ 50,000
Building	100,000
Delivery van	10,000
Furniture/fixtures	10,000
Working capital	25,000
Total	$195,000

If the entrepreneur wants to reduce the start-up costs, suggest methods for doing this without cutting the amounts for inventory or working capital. Why is it best not to reduce inventory or working capital?

A P P E N D I X   9A

Glossary of Financing Terms

Accounts Receivable Financing—A loan in which the financial institution extends funds to the entrepreneur based on his accounts receivable from sales.

Amortize—To repay a loan gradually by making payments over a specified period.

Balloon Note—A loan in which comparatively small periodic payments are made and one final large payment is made when the loan matures. A balloon note on a $25,000 loan may require payments of $300 per month (including principal and interest) for 3 years with a final payment of $20,000 due at the end of the third year.

Collateral—Assets the entrepreneur pledges to the financial institution until she repays the loan. If the entrepreneur does not repay the loan, the financial institution assumes ownership of the assets. These assets may be personal (home, car) or business (machinery, buildings).

Demand Note—A loan on which only interest payments are due periodically. The principal portion is due at the end of the stated loan maturity, or at any time the bank requests. Thus, even if the loan has a 1-year maturity, the bank could legally require full repayment after 1 month.

Down payment—The amount of personal money (or that of friends and relatives) invested in conjunction with a loan. If $100,000 is needed to start a business, and the owner uses $25,000 of his own money and borrows $75,000, the down payment is $25,000.

Fixed Interest Rate—An interest rate that remains the same over the life of the loan and does not vary with changes in prime rate.

Floating Interest Rate—An interest rate that increases or decreases with changes in prime rate.

Floor Planning—A type of financing in which a business assigns ownership of inventory to a financial institution in exchange for a short-term loan. Thus, while the financial institution actually owns the inventory, the entrepreneur keeps the inventory at his business. As the inventory is sold, the business repays the financial institution. This financing is used mostly by businesses that sell high-priced items (car dealers, furniture retailers, appliance retailers).

Installment Loan—A loan repaid in equal periodic payments. Each payment is partially applied to both principal and interest.

Source: Some items adapted from *Financing Small Business* (San Francisco, Calif.: Bank of America, 1976), 3.

Interest—The charge for borrowing money, usually expressed as an annual percentage of the loan amount.

Leverage—The extent to which a business is financed by debt.

Line of Credit—An agreement between the financial institution and the entrepreneur that states the amount of short-term credit the bank will make available to the entrepreneur. Interest is only charged as funds are borrowed.

Long-term Financing—Loans repaid over 10 or more years.

Maturity—The amount of time over which a loan is repaid. It may be stated, ''This loan will mature in 3 years,'' or ''This loan will mature in 1989.'' Loan maturities are generally matched to the life of the asset to be purchased. Therefore, if a loan is obtained to purchase a machine with a useful life of 3 years, the loan will have a 3-year maturity.

Prime Rate—The interest rate financial institutions charge their customers who are most credit-worthy and have the lowest risk. Usually these are large, rather than small, businesses.

Principal—The original amount of money borrowed or the unpaid balance of the original amount borrowed, not including interest.

Secured Loan—A loan for which collateral is required.

Short-term Financing—Loans that must be repaid within 1 year.

Unsecured Loan—A short-term loan for which no collateral is required. The loan is granted on the basis of the entrepreneur's credit record and previous experience with the bank.

CHAPTER 10

Feasibility Studies

Source: J. P. Morgan & Co. Incorporated. Photography by Tom Hollyman.

K   E   Y Objectives

1.   To identify topics included in feasibility studies.

2.   To provide a guide for the entrepreneur to use when completing a feasibility study.

3.   To describe the difference between a feasibility study and a business plan.

Feasibility Study
A comprehensive analysis of information on all aspects of a proposed business.

A **feasibility study** is a comprehensive analysis of all aspects of a proposed business. It is a detailed, thorough study of the marketing and financial information already discussed, as well as a careful examination of supply, personnel, and risk considerations. Thus, it is a compilation and revision of all of the information in Chapters 4 through 9, plus additional factors to be considered (see Figure 10.1). This information is compiled to assure the entrepreneur that no problems will prevent the business from becoming successful.

Figure   10.1   Preliminary Analysis Leading to a Feasibility Study

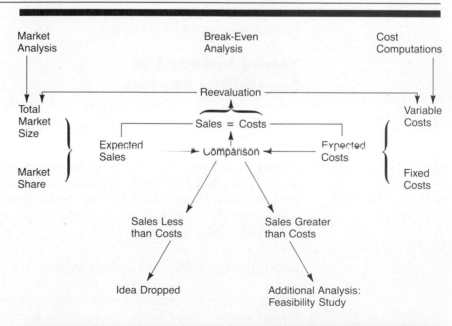

Unique Business   10.1

Color Me Profits

Anyone in Woburn, Massachusetts needing to match the color of the back bedroom or the drapes in the office can rest easy. Colorgen Ltd. has developed a computer that can analyze almost any color and specify a formula by which the shade can be duplicated. Founder John O'Brien plans to sell the computer, priced at $11,500, to businesses such as paint stores and dental practices, where color matching is critical. O'Brien projects sales of up to $10 million for his company's first year.

Source: Inc., January 1985, 19.

Because of its comprehensive nature, a feasibility study is time consuming and costly. The depth of the feasibility study varies with the type of business, the amount of investment, and the amount of risk. If start-up costs are minimal and the business is not the entrepreneur's only source of income, a less-detailed study is necessary. However, if the start-up will require resignation from full-time employment or the investment of a large amount of money, a thorough feasibility study is essential.

Topics Included in Feasibility Studies

In this chapter we will discuss some of the major topics found in feasibility studies. Not all of the topics apply to all industries; some are critical to one industry but irrelevant to others. In the second part of this chapter is a list of questions that will help itemize topics to be considered. The entrepreneur must determine whether or not the topic applies to the proposed industry. It is also necessary to decide if there are topics not covered in the general guide that must be added to the list.

Industry and Market Information

One of the most important steps in a feasibility study is an analysis of the industry and its various facets—the nature of the competition, the level of satisfaction with current members of the industry, important technological changes, possible political or legislative developments, and future trends. For example, if an entrepreneur plans to establish a business as a wholesaler of electronic products, information on this industry is vital. Because of rapid changes in technology, an industry such as electronics may have a higher risk of obsolete inventory, substantial price cuts, shortages, and so forth. A review of general industry information may result in the entrepreneur abandoning the project or it may encourage her to investigate further. This analysis was discussed in Chapter 4, "The Nature of the Market." Additional information included in a feasibility study was also described in Chapter 5, "The Site." While most of the information needed will have been collected earlier in the market analysis, it is included as part of the overall feasibility study to ensure that there are no missing pieces. The feasibility study is, after all, just that: a study to see whether it is feasible to start a particular business. There can be no missing pieces, and all the pieces must fit together.

Suppliers

Often entrepreneurs do not adequately investigate sources of supply that would be necessary for their business. However, information such as the suppliers' locations, prices, delivery schedules, discount policies, and minimum order quantities must be determined. Suppliers often require minimum order quantities impossible for a small business to meet. Therefore, this must be investigated before the business is established.

Another problem that often arises is inventory shortages. Shortages occur most often when demand jumps rapidly so that suppliers cannot meet that demand. This can be frustrating and costly to a business, since lost sales due to inventory shortages may be financially devastating. This situation occurred with video cassette recorders in early 1983. Although demand for VCRs rose dramatically, the factories could not increase production as fast as necessary. Also, because of a fear of obsolescence, the factories were hesitant to invest large sums to increase production capabilities. Thus, although the potential for a large sales volume existed, many VCR dealers lost sales because they could not find suppliers with an adequate inventory.

Personnel

Small firms are often labor-intensive (operate with many employees), whereas large firms are capital-intensive (operate with many machines). Thus, for small firms, personnel is an important area to consider. Although Chapter 14 will discuss personnel issues in more depth, the following is a summary of factors to consider in preparing a feasibility study.

The availability of qualified personnel is critical for some small businesses; for others it may present no problems. For example, if an entrepreneur plans to open a warehouse, the majority of jobs may not be highly skilled, so finding qualified employees may be relatively easy. If, however, the entrepreneur

Illustration Capsule   10.1

Great Demand—No Supply

In early 1984, Convergent Technologies, a 4-year-old business that manufactured computers, experienced "an incredible set of challenges." One of the main problems was a shortage of components for its new product line. This caused a serious "manufacturing bottleneck," resulting in production delays and inconveniences to customers.

The industry-wide shortage also drove up the prices of the components; thus, Convergent was faced with the choice of passing the increased costs on to the customers or settling for lower profits.

Therefore, although the company had $1.7 billion worth of orders, as one research analyst noted, "the challenge now is to turn those contracts into a profitable revenue stream."

Source: Business Week, March 5, 1984, 70–71.

planned to open an engineering firm, it would be necessary to determine if an adequate number of qualified applicants could be found. The availability of personnel often depends on location and economic conditions.

Once the entrepreneur has determined that an adequate labor supply exists, he should determine the cost of labor. The entrepreneur must consider the salaries offered by competing firms for comparable positions. (This information may be obtained from state employment offices or associations in the industry.) Then he must determine if the proposed business can offer competitive salaries or if other benefits will need to be offered instead. Small businesses often cannot match the high labor rates offered by large firms but instead attract employees by offering flexible work hours, profit-sharing plans, a wider variety of duties, or increased responsibility. The entrepreneur must carefully consider the personnel issues, since employees are one of the most valuable assets in small firms.

Also included in this section of the feasibility study are an organizational chart and job descriptions. Even if the staff will be small, the entrepreneur may find it beneficial to develop these documents to provide a clear picture of responsibilities to new employees. It also requires the entrepreneur to consider all functions that must be performed on a daily, weekly, or monthly basis. If this is not thoroughly developed, the entrepreneur often finds that a necessary function is not being completed consistently because no employee realized that it must be done. For example, in one dental office, no job descriptions had been developed for the office staff, hygienists, or dental assistants. Although all these employees performed specific duties, the patient files were not always refiled at the end of the day. No one really viewed this task as part of her job, and so it often was not completed. In addition, other tasks were being performed by more than one person, resulting in wasted time and effort. Job descriptions helped solve these problems.

Because the management is crucial in the success of any small business, this too must be carefully considered. It is necessary to review the management expertise of each person who will hold a management position and to identify the strengths (areas of expertise) that employee will bring to the business. This will identify areas of weakness, or management functions for which someone else must be found.

A helpful process for planning personnel needs is to develop a work schedule for a typical week during slow periods and during peak seasons. This will help to prevent underestimating the number of people needed and the related payroll costs. An entrepreneur may think, for example, that it will be possible to operate with only three employees until she attempts to schedule the employees to cover all operating hours and complete all tasks.

Financial Information

The financial information includes the start-up costs discussed in Chapter 7 and details the amounts needed for each category, such as inventory, furniture and fixtures, equipment, and working capital. It is also necessary to determine and list what is included in each. For example, what equipment is needed? How was the amount for working capital determined?

Once total start-up costs are known, the method of financing should be considered. As stated in Chapter 9, the amount of debt and equity financing substantially affects the company profits and financial stability. Therefore, the best combination of debt and equity financing should be determined to ensure that the company is not only feasible but is also financially sound. Pay-back arrangements and proposed dividends should be determined and reviewed after a projected income statement is completed for the first 3 to 5 years. This can then be compared with the break-even sales volume to determine the margin of error. This is certainly one of the most critical portions of the feasibility study, since an over-optimistic sales or net profit projection could easily lead the entrepreneur to the wrong conclusion. An opening day balance sheet should also be developed to indicate the financial position of the company when it begins operation. Finally, it is necessary to complete a cash flow projection for the first few years, to ensure that cash flow will not be a problem and that the company is not undercapitalized.

Production, Scheduling, Layout

Another factor to consider is the actual process of producing and delivering the goods and/or services of the firm. If the proposed company is a manufacturing firm, a layout of machinery and equipment would be designed as well as a typical production scheduling format. Even if the company is a small service firm, the layout of the facility should be developed to ensure the most efficient utilization of space. For retailing, proper layout is essential to maximize sales. Studies have shown that it is best for retailers to place high-gross-margin products in the front right-hand side of the outlet since approximately 20 percent of the store's revenue will be derived from this area. Thus, the layout is essential in meeting the projected sales volume. Even offices should be designed in advance for efficient information flow.

Credit Policy

For any company planning to extend credit, it is essential to establish the entire credit policy and related credit procedures. This includes terms, discounts, credit-checking procedures and costs, and methods for collection of delinquent accounts. Again, this must be compared with the credit policies of competitors to determine the new firm's ability to compete.

The effect of the credit policy on the company's cash also needs to be considered. A lenient credit policy may be needed to obtain customers, but it may also require additional financing since the money from a sale will not be obtained at the time of the transaction. This will then affect the total start-up costs, which would also affect the project's feasibility. Entrepreneurs often fail to realize this until they open the business and find that cash needs have been underestimated.

Legal Considerations

Each industry has legal factors that also must be considered. Several of these are listed below.

1. Many businesses require special licenses before the business can open. The procedures for proper licensing should be checked, since failure to obtain proper licenses will prevent the business from operating.

2. Factors such as patents or permission to use patented products should be determined along with related costs.

3. Often, legislation (federal, state, or local) can greatly affect the future of a small firm. It is essential that current and pending legislation be reviewed to determine the effect on the proposed business.

4. Tax rates vary greatly and may have an impact on the company's net profit. Tax rates should be investigated to determine if they will be a significant factor.

Dealing with Risk

Controllable Risk
An unexpected event or accident in which the effect can be minimized by purchasing adequate insurance, or a risk the entrepreneur can prevent.

Uncontrollable Risk
An unexpected event that cannot be prevented by the entrepreneur or covered by insurance.

All businesses, large and small, face controllable and uncontrollable risks that threaten profitability or survival. **Controllable risks** are unexpected events in which the effect can be minimized by purchasing adequate insurance. (More will be said about this in Chapter 20.) It is also necessary, though, to examine uncontrollable risks to establish procedures for minimizing their impact. **Uncontrollable risks** are unexpected events that the entrepreneur cannot prevent and that insurance cannot cover. Listed below are a few of the common uncontrollable risks many new small businesses face:

A Rise in Interest Rates.   When interest rates fluctuate substantially, it is difficult for businesses to plan their interest costs. A business that plans for interest costs of 14 percent must consider the effect of interest rates increasing to 18 percent. The entrepreneur must have a plan of action in the event this risk materializes.

New Competition.   A major competitor may locate nearby soon after the small business opens. A feasibility study is based on an analysis of existing competition. Therefore, even if a project was determined to be feasible, a new competitor may dramatically affect the new company's sales and profitability. Again, the entrepreneur should know what action she will take if this occurs.

Economic Conditions.   Fluctuations in general economic conditions may cause sales to be lower than the projected level. Within the past 15 years, the economy of the United States has included periods of prosperity and periods of deep recession. The economy may have a substantial effect on the sales of a new business. The entrepreneur should anticipate the effect of economic fluctuations and plan for times when sales are lower than anticipated.

Technological Change.   With rapid technological change occurring in many industries, the threat of technological obsolescence is a risk many businesses must face. Changes in technology can cause inventory to be obsolete if new products are quickly introduced in the marketplace. Companies that sell video games and computer software often encountered this problem in the early 1980s.

Similarly, new technology can create a situation in which the business owner must make a large investment or risk losing business to the competition. For example, many technological changes have been made in the automotive field that require auto repair shops to invest in new computerized equipment or eventually lose sales. Though the innovations may help increase productivity, the large initial investment often puts a strain on the company's cash flow.

These are only some examples of the risks to be considered; many more may be encountered. This portion of the feasibility study should be carefully prepared, as it may help to prevent problems that could have been avoided.

Recognition of Assumptions

Throughout any feasibility study, many assumptions are made, and often these assumptions are critical to the success or failure of the business. Therefore, it is necessary to consider these assumptions and their effect on the feasibility of the proposed project. For example, if it is assumed that the business will be at a specific location, this assumption must be stated along with the effect on the project if the site is not available. Similarly, if it is assumed that the business will open in April, what would occur if the opening were delayed until July? If it is assumed that total start-up costs will be $75,000, how much variation can occur before the project is not feasible? All assumptions must be thoroughly reviewed, and steps can then be taken to ensure that the assumptions hold true. The assumptions should be analyzed to determine which are essential if the business is to succeed and which may change without major impact on the company. It must be remembered that a conclusion of "feasible" does not mean that the proposed idea will always be successful. The project may appear to be feasible based on certain assumptions and is feasible only if all the assumptions hold true. Therefore, any changes in the information may change the final conclusion.

Completing a Feasibility Study

Remaining Objective

When completing a feasibility study, one of the most difficult tasks is to remain objective. Often the entrepreneur is so enthusiastic about the proposed business that he assumes the business is feasible and gathers information (consciously or unconsciously) that supports the "feasible" conclusion. Negative information is ignored or quickly discounted. If this happens, the feasibility study is a wasted effort.

To avoid this, one suggested method is to search for any information that proves the project will not be profitable, listing as many reasons as possible that could lead to a conclusion of "not feasible." This forces the entrepreneur to take a pessimistic view and consider negative information. This procedure may prevent the entrepreneur from being overly optimistic. If it appears that the negative information is not overwhelming, the entrepreneur can then proceed with the feasibility study aware of the negative factors and less biased in viewpoint.

Gathering Information

Entrepreneurs often find it difficult to start a feasibility study. Faced with so many facts to research and consider, it seems impossible to find an appropriate starting point, and sources of information are not obvious. Therefore, as a starting point, it is often helpful to contact associations for information as well as owners of similar businesses and potential suppliers. Since the entrepreneur would be a potential customer of the suppliers, the suppliers are often very helpful. For example, if the entrepreneur is planning to open a tanning salon, the manufacturer or wholesaler of the tanning equipment may be an excellent source of information. Similarly, the entrepreneur planning to open a grocery store will find grocery wholesalers extremely knowledgeable and willing to help. Trade magazines would also be helpful for general industry information. As mentioned in previous chapters, the Bank of America *Reporters* and other sources of financial statistics provide excellent information on the profitability of a proposed business.

Questions to Be Answered

The following list of questions is designed to serve as a guide in preparing a feasibility study. Although the information for each business will vary, the questions should serve as a helpful guide in considering important areas.

The Industry

- What are the trends for this industry for the past 5 years?
- What are projected trends?
- What risks are specific to this industry?
- What are typical markups, expenses, and profit percentages?
- How does the failure rate for this industry compare with others? Higher? Lower? The same?
- Is this industry dominated by large firms? Small firms?

Marketing

- Where will you be located? Why have you chosen that site?
- What is your primary trading area?
- Using market segmentation, define your customers.
- If you have several distinct groups of customers, list all groups.
- Describe your product—size, weight, shape, quality, service, support, delivery.
- How will your product be sold (what are the methods of selling and distribution)?
- What is your pricing structure? What is your typical markup?
- What is your competitive advantage? Why will people buy from you instead of from your competition? How does your product compare? How does your price compare?
- What type of advertising and promotion will you do?
- Is your business seasonal? What are the peak seasons? What are low seasons? How does this affect the ideal opening date of your company?

Financial

- Itemize your start-up costs.
- How much money will you invest? How much investor money will be raised?
- How much money will you need to borrow? What is the pay-back period for debt financing? What returns will be given on equity investment?
- Complete projected income statements for the first 3 years.
- Complete an opening day balance sheet.
- Complete a cash flow statement for the first year.
- What is your break-even point?

Suppliers

- Who will be your suppliers? (This can be determined by looking in the Yellow Pages and/or by asking others in the industry.)
- What are their payment terms, discount policies, minimum order quantities, delivery schedules, prices?
- Is there a risk of inventory shortages?

Your Credit Terms

- Will you extend credit to customers?
- What terms will be given to customers—length of credit, discounts, minimum order quantities?
- How do your credit terms compare with your competitors'?
- What method will be established for checking the credit of customers?
- What methods will be used to collect delinquent accounts?

Personnel

- Who will be responsible for the management of the company? Who will be responsible for major areas such as marketing, finance and accounting, employee management?
- Develop an organizational chart.
- Develop job descriptions for initial positions that need to be filled.
- Establish your compensation plans and benefit plans for all employees. How does this compare with other firms in your industry? (Typical salaries for specific jobs may be obtained from local employment offices.)
- How often will employee performance be reviewed?

Legal

- What will be your form of organization—proprietorship, partnership, corporation? Why?
- What licenses will you need?
- Can your chosen site be rezoned if necessary?

- Is there any new or pending legislation that would affect your business?
- Will your company own or need to use any patented products?

Layout and Production Process

- Design your facility for the most efficient flow of work. Explain how the best layout was determined.

Risk

- What are the major controllable risks this business faces (fire, theft, product liability)?
- What are the major uninsurable risks faced by the business (weather, economic conditions, demographic changes, price wars, political changes)?
- What steps can be taken to minimize the effects of uninsurable risks?
- How much will adequate insurance coverage cost for insurable risks?

Assumptions

- What assumptions have you made in preparing this feasibility study (rental costs, interest rates, availability of financing, specific number of competitors in your area)?

Feasible/Not Feasible

After reviewing all the above information, determine if the project is feasible. If it is feasible, remember that it is only feasible if your assumptions hold true. Therefore, determine how much your assumptions can change without changing the feasibility of the project. If the project is determined to be not feasible, then specify what factors led to this conclusion. Determine what, if anything, can be done to change the conclusion.

Although all sections must be completed before concluding that a project is feasible, it is not always necessary to complete all sections before determining that a project is not feasible. For example, a feasibility study was completed for a small grocery store in an area of St. Louis. Competition was minimal, and, using industry information concerning inventory turnover, the potential sales volume appeared to be substantial. However, after speaking with others in the industry, the entrepreneur found that, for the site he had chosen, the potential sales volume for the area could not be realized. Because the site was so small (only 2,000 square feet) he could not expect to reach the potential volume for the area or the volume necessary to meet his expenses. Thus, the entrepreneur needed only to complete the industry, marketing, and financial sections before it became apparent that the business was not feasible at the chosen location. When he identified a new location, start-up costs changed due to additional renovations, operating costs changed because of more floor space, and so forth. He then completed a new feasibility study for the new location.

Small Business Success   10

Mentor Graphics,
Beaverton, Oregon

Industry trends have created a need for electronics design automation, and Mentor Graphics Corporation is helping to meet it. The demand for highly trained electronics engineers is increasing markedly as the high-technology market and the complexity of electronic circuitry grow. In 1985, when about 20,000 new engineers graduated, industry needed an estimated 60,000, according to Thomas Bruggere, president, chief executive, and chairman of Mentor Graphics, Beaverton, Oregon. Founded in April 1981, Mentor Graphics is a pioneer in computer-aided engineering (CAE) systems. CAE reduces the time-consuming "hand work" of electronics engineers and allows for more complex and higher-performing electronic designs. Bruggere, a software engineer, started the company with $1 million in funding from venture capital firms that were early backers of Intel, Apple Computer, Prime Computer, and Qume. Mentor Graphics' customers are primarily in the semiconductor, telecommunications, aerospace, automotive, consumer, and defense industries. The company employed more than 750 people worldwide by the end of 1985, only 4½ years after being founded. Sales in 1983, the first full year of production, totaled $25.8 million, and in 1985 grew to more than $130 million. The sky is apparently the limit for sales: the CAE market is projected to be worth $1.5 billion by the end of the decade.

Source: Company press release.

The Business Plan
. . . .

Business Plan
An operational program of action stating how a business will operate.

With the completion of the feasibility study, the entrepreneur can attend to the **business plan.** The business plan is very similar to the feasibility study, using much of the same information, but is compiled only after the business is determined to be feasible. Whereas the feasibility study investigates whether or not the business should even be started, the business plan describes the way in which the firm will operate. The following points further clarify the difference between the two documents:

"You know, Mother, you could be waiting for a ship that may never come in."

Source: Drawing by Weber; © 1973 The New Yorker Magazine, Inc.

1. The feasibility study would include potential suppliers, their terms, delivery dates, and so on. The business plan would state which of those suppliers would be used and why those suppliers were chosen.

2. The feasibility study would include financing needs and may conclude that the project is feasible if debt financing is less than a specified amount (for example, less than $50,000). The business plan would state the financing plan that would actually be implemented.

3. The feasibility study would state the best types of promotion for the company to use. The business plan would include a complete advertising plan, a direct sales plan, and a plan for other promotional activities.

4. The feasibility study is written for the benefit of the entrepreneur. The business plan (especially for a start-up) is often written for potential investors as well as for the entrepreneur. Therefore, while the feasibility study would include possible pay-back methods, the business plan would include a special section on the potential earnings to investors, if investors are needed.

5. The feasibility study may be regarded as a search for the negative, that is, a search for any factor that could keep the venture from succeeding. If no such troublesome factor is uncovered, a business plan is written to state the positive. "This business is going to go and here's how it's going to happen" is the message of the business plan.

A written business plan forces the entrepreneur to detail how the business will operate on an ongoing basis. If prepared properly, it can prevent many problems from occurring and can prevent a "management by crisis" atmosphere. It also provides the entrepreneur with more credibility in the eyes of potential investors because it is obvious that the entrepreneur has given substantial thought to the proposed business. Therefore, the plan will make it easier for the entrepreneur to obtain financing.

K   E   Y   Objectives Reviewed

1. The feasibility study is a comprehensive analysis of information about the proposed business.

2. A basic checklist can be followed when completing a feasibility study. While every business has unique aspects, major topics of feasibility studies are similar for most businesses. The entrepreneur should consider all the basic questions listed and then determine what unique circumstances apply to the proposed business. This will help the entrepreneur review all areas of business operations.

3. The business plan is similar to the feasibility study but provides an operational plan once the business is determined to be feasible. The business plan is often prepared for both the entrepreneur and potential investors. While a feasibility study makes one consider several possible alternatives (such as many possible suppliers), the business plan specifies which alternative will be implemented. Also, if the business plan is written for potential investors, it would include a special section that would highlight potential rewards to investors.

Discussion Questions

1. Identify industries that have a high profit potential but also have a high risk.

2. Identify industries that, if they located in your area, might be unable to find qualified personnel.

3. What would be the best month of the year to open each of the following?
   a. an ice cream shop
   b. a wholesale toy company
   c. an insect extermination company

4. The text identified several uncontrollable risks including a rise in inter-
    est rates, a competitor locating nearby, and changes in economic con-
    ditions. Name other uncontrollable risks and ways to minimize these
    risks.

5. Certain industries are undergoing rapid changes that will force many
    small businesses to close if they do not adapt. Identify some of those
    industries.

6. After researching industry information, why is it necessary to choose a
    specific location before continuing with the remainder of the feasibility
    study?

7. What types of businesses require special licenses before opening? Why
    should these be checked at an early stage in the feasibility study?

8. Identify businesses that are "recession-proof," that is, those busi-
    nesses that do not see a large decrease in sales when the economy
    slows. Identify businesses that are severely affected by a change in the
    economy.

Cases for Part Three

Case IIIA   The Partners

Sue Sawyer and her two associates, Ben Freeze and Paula Portland, began planning for their new restaurant. The restaurant, specializing in Italian food, would be located along a major street, in a freestanding building. The facility would be leased for $2,500 per month for 3 years; initial sketches of the proposed layout showed a possible seating capacity of 60 to 75. The start-up costs would be $75,000, primarily for machinery and equipment, inventory, dishes and utensils, and working capital. Sawyer and her friends planned each to invest $25,000 of their own money, eliminating the need for debt.

For the past 7 years Sawyer had been the food service manager in a large hotel. She planned to resign to operate the new restaurant. Freeze planned to work part-time in the restaurant in the evenings in addition to his other employment. Portland was employed full-time in an advertising agency, frequently working 60 hours per week, and was often out of town on business trips. She could not devote any time to running the restaurant.

Initial discussions among the three raised several questions. First, how would ownership be divided? Second, what type of legal structure should be established? Third, how much salary should Sue take the first few years?

Because they would not borrow money, the three friends felt risk was minimal. If the business did not succeed, they would lose the money invested, but since no personal assets had to be pledged as collateral for a loan, they felt that their personal liability was not great. Sue, however, felt she was taking more risk than the other investors since she was going to give up her full-time employment, at which she was earning $30,000 per year. Because of this, she felt she was entitled to more ownership of the proposed restaurant than Ben or Paula. Ben and Paula felt they were all entitled to equal ownership because Sue did not have any personal assets to pledge as collateral and therefore could not borrow money to begin business alone. Also, Ben and Paula were reluctant to invest their money in a business if they did not have an equal vote in decision making.

The three entrepreneurs also had to determine the type of ownership they should establish. Because of depreciation expenses allowed on the machinery and equipment, they expected the restaurant to show a "paper loss" the first year. Although the company would lose money with depreciation so high, cash flow would be excellent. For this reason, Ben and Paula wanted to establish a limited partnership, which would give them limited status and would also provide tax advantages. Sue did not want to be a general partner, though, because she would be fully liable if any lawsuits occurred.

After completing projected income statements, the three investors agreed that Sue should take a salary of $20,000 the first year, $25,000 the second, and $30,000 the third. Sue was concerned, though, that if sales did not reach the projected amounts, she could not take even $20,000. If she could not take at least $20,000, she wanted greater ownership.

The three investors could not agree on the proper form of organization, nor could they agree on an ownership percentage, so they decided to see a lawyer for advice. Although all three wanted to see the restaurant become a reality, Ben and Paula were not as enthusiastic about the project as Sue. If they could not reach an agreement, they would wait until another investment opportunity developed.

Sue was determined to open a restaurant, though, even if an agreement could not be reached. She began to consider the possibility of trying to open a smaller restaurant of her own with her $25,000. She found a site where another restaurant had been located. The seating capacity was 20 to 25, and the site was located near a major university. She decided that if an agreement could not be reached with Ben and Paula she would consider the smaller restaurant. Although it would be difficult to open the restaurant with only $25,000, it appeared that it might be the only alternative.

Questions

1. Although the proposed business would have no long-term debt, what financial risk would the investors be taking?

2. Assume you are in Sue Sawyer's position. What percentage ownership do you feel you should have? What arguments can you use to justify this percentage?

3. What form of organization do you feel is best for the proposed restaurant? Why?

4. Is Sue entitled to a greater percentage of the ownership if she is not able to take the $20,000 salary owing to low sales?

5. Should Sue start the smaller restaurant instead?

Case IIIB — Financing

The following cases are brief synopses of actual entrepreneurs who sought bank financing. The entrepreneurs' names and company names are fictitious.

Questions

1. Assume you are the loan officer at a bank. Review the description of each company and decide if you would loan the amount of money

requested. Explain your reason for approving or rejecting the loan application.

2. If your decision was to loan the money, state what you would want as collateral and the appropriate maturity (years).

Painting Partners

· ·

Joseph Temple had been a painter for 5 years with a painting contractor in the Miami, Florida area. In January, Temple decided to begin his own company, Painting Partners. The company paints newly constructed offices and repaints existing buildings being remodeled. Temple has been actively bidding on contracts to ensure a steady supply of work for his crew of four. Within the first 2 months, the company has been awarded many small contracts totalling $50,000, as well as one large contract for a government office building, which is for $125,000.

Painting Partners Inc.	
Projected First Year Income	
Statement	
Sales	$350,000
Cost of goods	
Material	140,000
Labor	140,000
Total cost of goods	$280,000
Gross margin	70,000
Expenses	
Office salary	15,000
Rent	6,000
Utilities	3,000
Depreciation	3,000
Office supplies	2,400
Accounting/legal	3,600
Insurance	6,000
Telephone	2,400
Interest	8,400
Repairs	1,200
Bad debts	1,700
Miscellaneous	2,400
Taxes	2,500
Gas/oil	4,500
	$ 62,100
Net profit before	
taxes	$ 7,900

Temple invested $25,000 of his own money in the company to pay for equipment and to use as working capital for the smaller contracts. However, this is not enough working capital for the $125,000 contract.

The government project will take 4 months to complete. The government does not start paying until 120 days after work begins. Therefore, if the company begins the project in May and plans to complete it in August, 25 percent of the payment will be received in August, 25 percent in September, 25 percent in October, and 25 percent in November. The company needs $70,000 in working capital to pay for labor and materials.

Temple has prepared the projected income statement shown on page 235. Since Painting Partners has operated for only 2 months, it has few assets—$10,000 in equipment, $5,000 in accounts receivable, $10,000 in cash. There are no liabilities. Temple is willing to use his home as collateral. The market value is $60,000; he still owes $40,000 on the original mortgage.

Rhonda's Records Inc.

Rhonda's Records Inc., a record and stereo cassette shop, has been open for 5 years. During this time, the company has established a reputation for having one of the largest record selections in the area. It is well known throughout the city.

Rosemary Reel wishes to purchase Rhonda's Records for $150,000. She has $50,000 of her own money and therefore needs to borrow $100,000. Rosemary has managed another record shop for the past 7 years and has a bachelor's degree in business.

Rosemary will buy the assets in the business (assume most recent amounts shown on balance sheet are the amounts to be purchased). Rhonda paid off all loans 4 years ago; therefore, there is no long-term debt to consider. Rosemary will assume responsibility for the current liabilities shown.

In addition to business assets, Rosemary is willing to pledge her home as collateral. The market value is $70,000; the mortgage balance is $30,000.

	Rhonda's Records Inc.		
	December 31, 19X2	December 31, 19X1	December 31, 19X0
Sales	$350,000	$340,000	$330,000
Cost of goods sold	210,000	204,000	198,000
Gross profit	$140,000	$136,000	$132,000
Expenses	130,000	127,100	123,300
Net profit	$ 10,000	$ 8,900	$ 8,700

Note: Expenses include $10,000 for Rhonda's salary each year.

Balance Sheet
December 31, 19X2

Current Assets		Current Liabilities	
Cash	$15,000	Accounts payable	$15,000
Inventory	55,000	Wages payable	3,000
Prepaid expenses	6,000	Sales tax payable	1,500
	$76,000		$19,500
Fixed Assets		Long-term debt	0
Leasehold improvements	24,000	Equity	$109,500
Furniture and fixtures	25,000	Total liabilities and equity	$129,000
	$49,000		
Other			
Deposits	$ 4,000		
Total assets	$129,000		

Delivery Inc.

. . . .

Dan O'Herin has had a delivery service for the past 7 years. He began by delivering packages in St. Louis, Missouri and has now expanded to the entire state. Although he began with one truck, he now owns 25 and rents additional trucks on a short-term basis if necessary to meet demand. Sales have continually grown, and Dan has recently found that he constantly needs to rent trucks to meet demand. Therefore, he wishes to purchase five more delivery vans at a cost of $20,000 each. He will have a $20,000 down payment and therefore needs to borrow $80,000.

Delivery Inc.

	December 31, 19X2	December 31, 19X1	December 31, 19X0
Sales	$3,500,000	$2,500,000	$2,000,000
Cost of goods sold			
Direct labor	700,000	500,000	400,000
Truck depreciation	75,000	69,000	69,000
Gas/oil/repairs	175,000	160,000	145,000
Cost of goods sold	$ 950,000	$ 729,000	$ 614,000
Gross profit	2,550,000	1,771,000	1,386,000
Expenses	2,375,000	1,646,000	1,286,000
Net before tax	$ 175,000	$ 125,000	$ 100,000

Balance Sheet
December 31, 19X2

Current Assets		Current Liabilities	
Cash	$ 50,000	Current portion of long-term debt	$ 85,000
Accounts receivable	270,000	Wages payable	15,000
Prepaid expenses	12,000	Taxes payable	2,500
Total current	$332,000	Total current	$102,500
Fixed Assets		Long-term Liabilities	
Equipment (trucks)	$575,000	Notes payable	$200,000
Less accumulated depreciation	270,000	Less current portion	85,000
Equipment (net)	$305,000	Long-term liabilities	$115,000
		Total liabilities	217,500
Furniture/fixtures (net)	$ 20,000	Equity	$464,500
Leasehold improvements (net)	25,000	Total liabilities and equity	$682,000
Total fixed assets	$350,000		
Total assets	$682,000		

Case IIIC   Al's Auto Parts

Albert Olson had worked at auto parts stores for most of his career. He began working as a delivery person for an auto parts store when he was 20 years old, eventually becoming a clerk, and finally manager of a store. Albert had been able to achieve promotions even though he had only a tenth-grade education.

Throughout his career, Albert dreamed of someday owning his own auto parts outlet and had saved money to achieve that goal. By the time he was 53 years old, Albert had saved $25,000, and he began plans to open his own shop. He found a location he thought was suitable; there were no auto parts stores within five miles and rent was only $800 per month.

The auto parts distributor who would be his supplier provided substantial help. The distributor completed a market survey for Albert and felt that sales the first year would be good. This was based on an opening inventory of $45,000 (at cost) and on the population in the surrounding area. The distributor would also help Albert in choosing the proper inventory selection, designing the proper store layout, and offering grand opening specials.

Total start-up costs were estimated to be $75,000 (listed below). With Albert's savings of $25,000 he would only need to borrow $50,000. Interest rates on small business loans at the time were 14 percent. Albert's banker informed him that yearly payments on a $50,000 loan for 6 years at 14 percent would be $12,800, including principal and interest.

240 Part Three   Organizing

Mrs. Olson was employed part-time but did not earn enough money to support herself and Albert. Albert therefore determined that he would have to have a minimum salary of $750 per month for them to pay their normal living expenses. However, he wanted to have a salary of $12,500 the first year, if possible.

Albert met with the distributor to develop a projected income statement for the first 3 years. After seeing the projections, Albert felt confident that the business would succeed and continued with his plans to open. He ordered information on how to manage an auto parts store, which included industry statistics.

The following information includes Albert's projected income statements and some of the industry information.

Projected Income Statement

Sales	$290,322
Cost of goods	180,000
Gross margin	$110,322
Expenses	
Employee wages	$ 31,935
Owner wages	12,500
Rent	9,600
Taxes	4,444
Car/truck	3,000
Advertising	5,000
Insurance	3,000
Utilities	3,000
Bad debts	2,800
Depreciation	2,800
Freight postage	1,400
Office supplies	1,400
Miscellaneous	3,000
Total expenses	$ 83,879
Net Profit Before Taxes	$26,443

Start-up Costs

Inventory	$45,000 (cost)
Leasehold improvements	10,000
Working capital	15,000
Deposit on leased van	2,000
Miscellaneous	3,000
	$75,000

Industry Information

Sales	100%
Cost of goods	60–69
Gross margin	31–40

Average inventory turnover ranges from 2 to 5 times per year (average, 3.5 times per year)

Expenses

Employee wages	11.5–12.0%
Owner/manager wages	6.0–7.0
Rent	1.0–3.7
Taxes	1.4–1.9
Car/truck expenses	1.0–1.5
Advertising	0.5–2.0
Insurance	0.9–1.5
Utilities	0.5–1.7
Bad debts	0.5–1.0
Depreciation	0.5–1.0
Freight/postage	0.1–1.0
Office/store supplies	0.1–0.7
Miscellaneous	0.5–1.5
Total expenses	25.5–37.0%
Net profit	3.0–6.5%

Source: *Auto Supply Stores* (San Francisco, Calif.: Bank of America, 1976), 16.

Questions

1. How does Albert's projection compare with industry standards?

2. Do you think Albert's projection is too optimistic, too pessimistic, or about right?

3. Would you advise Albert to continue his plans for the business?

Case IIID   Struggling to Survive

In 1981, Joe Campella and two associates began making plans to establish an office supply company. Joe had managed a similar company for about 5 years, and before that he had been a clerk in another office supply firm. Even though he was only 28 years old, he had 8 years of experience in the industry and wanted to open his own firm.

Sarah and Pete, both in their early 60s, were nearing retirement and thought that a small business might provide them an income once they were no longer employed. They therefore agreed to invest $25,000 each to help start the business. Joe also invested $25,000, and the corporation stock was divided equally, each person owning 33⅓ percent of the company. Joe planned to work full-time in the business, while Sarah and Pete would not take an active part in daily operations.

Within a few years, the company's sales had grown substantially. Joe was an excellent salesman and had developed several large wholesale accounts as well as an excellent walk-in retail trade. Sales were nearly $300,000, and the company employed seven people in addition to Joe.

Unfortunately, Joe's financial management ability did not match his sales ability. The company had a phenomenal sales growth but did not have a corresponding profit level. In the 3 years the company had been open it had never shown a profit, and the most recent year ended with the greatest loss. Sarah and Pete had not been very concerned when the company did not make a profit the first 2 years. They felt that, as with many new companies, it would take time to establish itself and begin operating smoothly. However, when the third year ended with an excellent sales volume and a large loss, they became concerned. They reviewed the company's financial situation with an accountant and discovered that the company owed almost $50,000 to suppliers. Payments on some accounts had not been made for 6 months, and suppliers were threatening to stop shipping orders. Many credit sales had not been collected, and bad debts were large, yet no attempts had been made to collect them. The company had obtained loans from several banks and had been delinquent in payments several times.

Sarah and Pete were now only 1 year away from retirement, and it appeared that they might lose their investment instead of having a retirement income. The sooner they recovered their investment, the better they would be. They gave Joe an ultimatum. He could either find money from another source to buy them out or they would force him to close and sell all assets to recoup their investment. Because Sarah's and Pete's combined ownership of the company was 66⅔ percent, they had controlling interest and could force Joe to close.

Joe went to a consultant to determine a course of action. After reviewing the company's finances it was obvious that the company would not be able to borrow more money. The firm's liabilities were high and its loss had caused its equity to be low. The company could not afford another loan payment—what it needed was equity. It was therefore necessary to sell Sarah's and Pete's stock to someone else.

To try to sell the stock, Joe and the business consultant prepared a business plan to present to potential investors. When this plan was completed, Joe took it to his lawyer for review. Joe's lawyer, Samuel Trent, liked the plan so much that he agreed to buy out part of Sarah's and Pete's stock.

Joe did not want Samuel Trent to own 66 percent of the stock or he might encounter problems in the future similar to those he was trying to eliminate. The stock ownership was therefore changed; Joe invested a little more money, increasing his ownership to 50 percent, and Samuel purchased the remaining 50 percent.

Over the next 2 years, Samuel was able to help with the firm's financial management. The company continued to grow and eventually became marginally profitable. After several years of growth, the company needed more money to increase inventory and provide the necessary working capital or the company would have to slow or halt its growth. The bank agreed to loan $20,000 since the company's financial position was improving.

Joe felt that the $20,000 loan would be sufficient and was happy that the company finally appeared to be on its way to success. It had been 5 years since he had begun the company, and he had been working 60 to 80 hours per week for only a $12,000 annual salary. If the company used the loan money to obtain the necessary inventory, orders could be filled faster, sales could increase, and Joe could finally take an average salary.

The bank contacted Joe to set up an appointment for Samuel and him to sign the loan papers and pick up the money. When Joe told Samuel, Samuel informed Joe that he would not sign the loan papers unless the ownership was changed to give Samuel more than 50 percent ownership. Since this would put Joe in a situation similar to when Sarah and Pete owned stock, Joe would not agree. Samuel countered that if Joe did not give up part of his ownership, Samuel would not sign, and the loan would not be approved. The company would continue to experience inventory shortages, it would not be able to grow, and Joe could not expect a salary increase.

Samuel's personal assets were necessary for collateral since Joe did not have enough personal assets to borrow the money. Joe did not know what to do. He felt that Samuel had tricked him and was trying to force him into giving up ownership. He wished he could buy out Samuel's stock, but the bank would not loan him that much. Now he was saddled with an unreasonable stockholder and also could not get the loan he needed.

Questions

1. Do you think Samuel is being unreasonable in demanding more than 50 percent ownership?

2. Are Joe's experiences with his stockholders typical or is Joe choosing the wrong people for investors?

3. Is there any way that Joe's problems with Sarah and Pete could have been prevented? If so, how? If not, why not?

4. Is there any way that Joe's problem with Samuel could have been prevented? If so, how? If not, why not?

5. Recommend a course of action for Joe. What should he do next?

PART

Directing and Controlling

In the first three parts of this text we have examined the planning and organizing procedures that an entrepreneur must undertake when starting a business. A new business usually places many demands on the entrepreneur in terms of time and energy. The tasks that need to be completed seem overwhelming, and the variety of skills required seems endless. Many entrepreneurs mistakenly believe that this is a temporary situation that will end once the business is established. It is often thought that the business will "run itself."

In reality, though, an established, growing business places even greater demands on the entrepreneur. The entrepreneur finds he must be a "jack-of-all-trades." He must plan the future strategies of the business, make advertising and pricing decisions, manage and motivate employees, maintain an adequate cash flow, and ensure that all proper records are completed. In Part Four we identify all of these tasks and provide a framework for helping the entrepreneur gain a greater knowledge in each area.

In Chapter 11, we discuss the need for strategic management of the small firm. Many entrepreneurs do not engage in long-term planning but instead operate on a day-to-day basis. Though many entrepreneurs become successful without long-range planning, most businesses would be better managed if planning were done. Therefore, in Chapter 11, we discuss the need for strategic planning and identify ways in which the entrepreneur should approach the planning process.

In Chapters 12 through 17 we discuss the many functional areas that the entrepreneur must know. We will review the factors that affect pricing decisions and identify the pricing methods for different industries. We will also discuss promotional methods including advertising, use of a direct sales force, publicity, and so forth. This part of the text also discusses the management of human resources and its importance to the small firm since no business can be successful without good employees. Working capital management and financial analysis techniques are provided to help the entrepreneur manage the firm's assets properly. Finally, a chapter on production management is included because of its importance to the small manufacturer.

After reading this part of the text, it should be obvious to the reader that the entrepreneur must be a "generalist," with skills in a variety of areas. When the business is new, the entrepreneur usually does not have sufficient funds to hire a specialist for each area. Often he alone must be the manager of all areas. It is not sufficient to have good skills in one area without a working knowledge in all other areas. It is for this reason that we urge all entrepreneurs to understand the many areas of business management.

CHAPTER 11

Small Business Strategy

Source: Courtesy of Kelly Services, Inc.

K E Y Objectives

1. To demonstrate the relationship of strategy to the success of a small business.

2. To identify and describe the factors—the customer, the competencies of the firm, the competitors, and the culture—that must be analyzed in formulating strategy.

3. To describe techniques that can facilitate the process by which a small business determines its strategy.

Strategic Planning
The process by which an organization determines how it will attempt to achieve its long-run objectives.

In the January 1984 issue of the *Academy of Management Review,* Richard Robinson and John Pearce reviewed the literature and research studies on **strategic planning** in small business.[1] Among the conclusions that can be drawn from their results are the following:

Firms that plan are more successful than those that do not. The studies included used a wide variety of measures of success ranging from survival, to growth in sales, to profitability, to "perceived benefits from planning." In almost every case the planners outperformed the nonplanners.

With such impressive results, one might expect that strategic planning is widely used in small firms. Such is not the case, as the next conclusion indicates.

In most small businesses strategic planning is absent. Only 25 percent of the firms in one study carried out "strategic thinking." The planning small businesses use tends to be "nonsystematic" and "unstructured."

Here we have a paradox: Most business owners would like to succeed but do not engage in something (strategic planning) that promises to improve their chances of success. The evidence is clearly on the side of planning, and yet few entrepreneurs and managers bother with it. Robinson and Pearce cite four reasons strategic planning is not used:

1. Time. Managers of small businesses find the demands on their time are such that planning sessions simply cannot fit into their schedules.

2. Getting started. The planning process is something most small firm managers have not practiced. The process and the sources of needed information are new and unfamiliar.

---

[1]Richard B. Robinson and John A. Pearce II, "Research Thrusts in Small Firm Strategic Planning," *Academy of Management Review* 9, no. 1 (1984): 125–137.

Unique Business   11.1

The German Connection

Because of the vast number of calls made to U.S. embassies and consulates in Europe to contact Americans traveling in Europe, Alan Wissenberg started EurGuide Inc. The company has two offices, one in Naperville, Illinois, the other in the main train station in Munich, West Germany. In addition to sending and receiving travelers' messages, they provide travel help. The service costs $59 for six months.

Source: Inc., July 1985, 20.

3. Broad expertise. Managers tend to have broad expertise rather than the specialized skills needed for planning.
4. Lack of trust and openness. Many managers prefer to keep information to themselves. By doing so they preclude the input of subordinates and others that is so useful in the strategic planning process.

A fifth reason could be added:

5. Skepticism as to the value of strategic planning. Some small firm owners feel that the future cannot be predicted or controlled and that their efforts are therefore best centered on current activities.

Strategy
The plan used by the owner or manager of an organization to reach its long-run objectives.

Other reasons could no doubt be given, but regardless of how many are cited, the fact remains that a clear, well-conceived **strategy** can help a firm succeed. Because this is so, the question small business managers must answer is not whether to formulate strategy but how to do so. The purpose of this chapter is to describe the process of strategy formulation for small firms.

For the established business, a sound strategy formulation requires defining and redefining the business's role within its industry. This process requires closely examining the ways the firm serves its customers, the basic competencies of the business, the competition, and the culture in which the firm operates. The point of all this is to answer two simple but vital questions: "What is our business?" and "What should it be?"[2]

---

[2]The significance of these questions was first pointed out by Peter F. Drucker, *Management: Tasks, Responsibilities, Practices* (New York: Harper and Row, 1973).

Serving the Customer

Shortly after the turn of the century, the Ford Motor Company and American Telephone and Telegraph were both transforming the economy and the culture of the United States. Henry Ford defined his company's business as mass-producing inexpensive, dependable automobiles. The president of AT&T, Theodore N. Vail, said, "Our business is service." Ford's dominance lasted about 15 years, only until General Motors developed a better way to serve the needs of the motoring public. AT&T's broader, customer-oriented definition served the company well until its breakup in the early 1980s. There were, of course, many differences between Ford and AT&T, but the way a firm defines its business sets the tone for what happens internally and determines how it reacts to its environment.

The first, and clearly most important, consideration in answering the question "What is our business?" is the customer. Small firms can cope with ineptitude in many areas, but a failure to understand who the customer is, and why he or she buys the product or service, is usually fatal. Although many business owners spend a great deal of time trying to "get customers," they should remind themselves that customers create the business. This realization should not lead to a reduction in selling efforts but should prompt a close examination of how the firm helps its customers.

Putting the customer in the center of the firm's strategy is the first step. The next step is to recognize that the business is simply a vehicle by which the customer's needs can be satisfied. The customer does not buy a product because of its quality or features. The customer buys the product because of what that quality or those features do for him. Product quality or features, no matter how difficult they may have been to achieve, are meaningless until the customer has a need that they satisfy. This is what a marketing analyst had in mind when he explained disappointing sales by observing that no one wants a bullet-proof paper towel.

Exhibit 11.1 describes the satisfaction of one of Henry Ford's early customers. He obviously appreciated every mile per hour the company was able to engineer into the car.

The importance of a small business understanding its customers' reasons for buying can be demonstrated using another example from the automobile industry. The Cadillac division of General Motors was struggling during the early days of the Depression. It was only after the division's leadership realized that people bought their cars not for transportation but for status that it began to prosper. Cadillac's real competition came not from Chevrolet, Ford, or Dodge, but from mink coats and tropical cruises. This realization reoriented the division's operations and has been the cornerstone of its strategy since.

Among small businesses, this failure to understand the real concern of the customer can be seen in a variety of businesses. For example, companies that offer computer services to businesses or other organizations occasionally

Exhibit 11.1　　　　A Testimonial from a Satisfied Customer

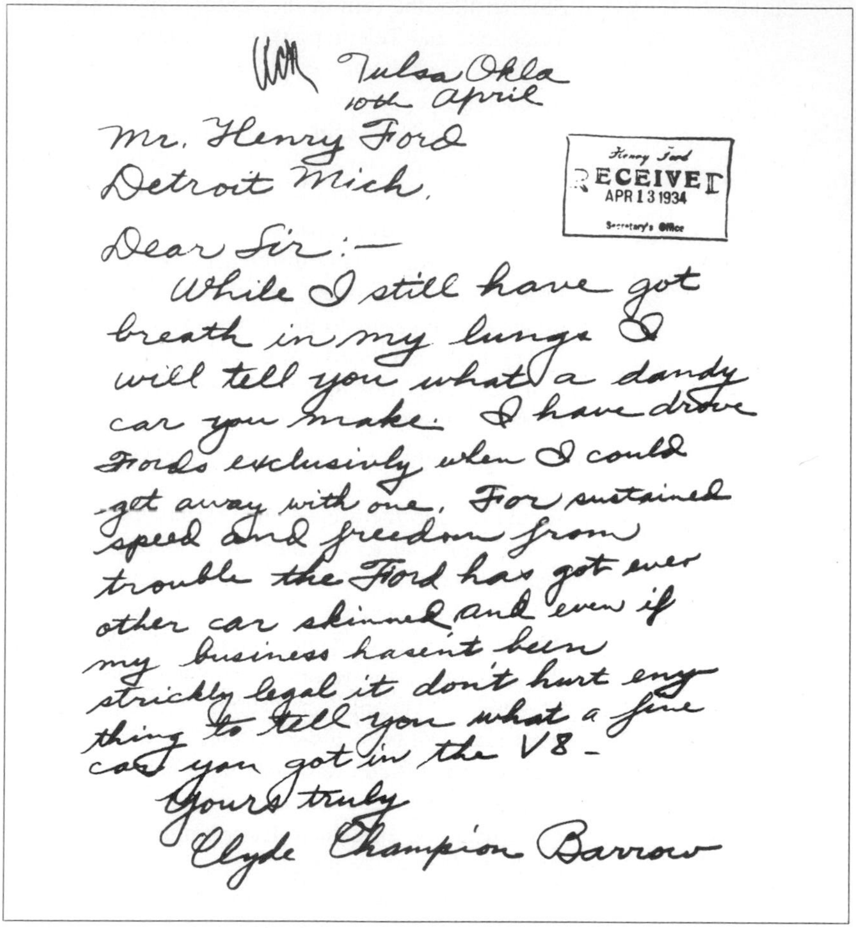

> Tulsa Okla
> 10th April
> Mr. Henry Ford
> Detroit Mich.
>
> Henry Ford
> RECEIVED
> APR 13 1934
> Secretary's Office
>
> Dear Sir:—
> While I still have got
> breath in my lungs I
> will tell you what a dandy
> car you make. I have drove
> Fords exclusivly when I could
> get away with one. For sustained
> speed and freedom from
> trouble the Ford has got ever
> other car skinned and even if
> my business hasent been
> strickly legal it don't hurt eny
> thing to tell you what a fine
> car you got in the V8 —
> Yours truly
> Clyde Champion Barrow

Source:　Courtesy of the Henry Ford Museum.

make the mistake of thinking they are hired because of their sophisticated software or powerful, up-to-date equipment. These are of little or no interest to customers unless the company can deliver timely, insightful reports that the customer can actually use. Restaurants with a family customer base will likely find no payoff in providing an extensive menu featuring exotic items. These customers want reasonably priced meals that everyone in the family will eat. In either example, the business has gone to considerable trouble only to mistake its customers' interests.

Competencies of the Firm

The customer's role in shaping the business is obviously important, but no firm can be all things to all people. Some type of specialization is always needed. For a small business, with its limited resources, the area of specialization is often narrow and carefully defined.

At this point in the strategic planning process the focus becomes internal. We have examined the customer group to learn what needs they want satisfied; now we must determine what kind of competence the firm has that will enable it to satisfy those needs. Put another way, the firm has some capability or quality that will enable it to provide better service or lower prices. Without this advantage the firm will not survive. The sources of competitive advantages a small business might enjoy include the following:

1. Production design. A unique product design can provide a firm with a competitive advantage over its competitors. In consumer markets such an advantage is less significant than in industrial markets, where a product with superior technical characteristics may capture all, or virtually all, the market.

2. Facilities. Some small firms enjoy an advantage owing to the location of their facilities. This can be extremely important for certain kinds of retail businesses (restaurants, gift shops, grocery stores). In other industries the facilities provide a strategic advantage because of the productivity level that can be achieved with them.

3. Marketing. This distinctive competence, or competitive advantage, of a firm concerns marketing capabilities, skills, and talents. Included in this category are the firm's distribution system, its promotion and advertising, its sales force, and its relationship with its customers.

In summary, somewhere in the cycle from designing the product, to making it, and finally to selling it, the firm must have unusual strength if it is to prosper.

The Competitors

After the company has determined the precise nature of its business as it currently exists, it must turn its attention to a broader concern. No company serves its customers in a vacuum. Competitors exist; so do any number of environmental factors that can affect the business-customer relationship. We will examine the role of competitors in this section. Forces within the environment will be the next section's topic.

In dealing with the question of what the business should be, the significance of competition is clear. Any firm must make its strategic plans recog-

"Now, I hear you asking yourself—'What about 1986, 1987, 1988, 1989, AND 1990?'"

Source: Copyright Ford Button.

nizing that competition will define what is possible, as well as what is advisable. What happens within an industry has much the same impact on all its members. Some factors make competition difficult and thereby drive down profits. Strategic planning must include a close examination of these industry-wide factors.

The nature of competition existing within an industry can be judged by examining five sets of forces:[3]

1. Bargaining power of suppliers. Suppliers are powerful when there is (*a*) concentration within a few companies; (*b*) a unique product being provided; (*c*) a threat of the supplier entering the business instead of simply supplying it; and (*d*) little significance of the business to the suppliers, that is, the industry as a whole is not an important customer.

2. Bargaining power of buyers. This group has the power to affect the industry when (*a*) large volumes are being purchased; (*b*) there is no differentiation between the products provided by the members of the industry; (*c*) the industry's product is a major part of the buyers' total costs; and (*d*) the buyer earns low profits.

3. Threat of substitute products. An industry with a unique product has the opportunity for high profits. Those profits, however, are likely to attract attention, and with that attention will come efforts to develop and market a substitute. When this happens a ceiling is imposed on the prices charged by the industry and profit levels suffer.

---

[3]Michael E. Porter, *Competitive Strategy* (New York: The Free Press, 1980).

4. Threat of entry. As new companies enter an industry, competition becomes more intense. The reaction of the firms already in the industry is to fight back, usually by lowering prices. The likelihood of a new firm entering into competition varies from industry to industry. Following are **barriers to entry** that determine how serious the threat of entry is.

Barriers to Entry
Those factors that hinder a firm or individual outside of an industry or market from competing with established members of the industry or market.

Economies of Scale
The cost advantages enjoyed by a firm that are the result of its large size.

Product Differentiation
The differences between products, as perceived by consumers.

Access to Distribution Channels
The availability of wholesaling and retailing opportunities with which to reach customers.

A. Economies of scale. In many manufacturing industries, the firms with large facilities have **economies of scale,** which allow them to produce at cost levels below those of smaller firms. These advantages are not limited to manufacturing, extending also to research and development, marketing, and service. A firm considering entry into an industry must choose between making a sizable early investment, competing with a cost disadvantage, or staying out.

B. Product differentiation. **Product differentiation** exists when customers perceive a difference between competing products. Customer loyalty makes it difficult for the new competitor to attract customers. This loyalty, enhanced by such things as advertising and customer service, creates a barrier that is very difficult, and expensive, to overcome.

C. Access to distribution channels. In the food industry a great deal of competition for space on the grocer's shelves exists, thereby making **access to distribution channels** difficult. Department stores also are very selective in choosing new items to carry. A new industry member is likely to encounter resistance in getting its product to the consumer.

D. Miscellaneous cost disadvantages. The established members of an industry have the experience, proprietary technology, favorable locations, best raw materials, and so forth. Each of these operates to the advantage of the firm that has existed for some time.

5. Rivalry among existing competitors. This rivalry will be intense when the following factors are present: slow industry growth; numerous competitors roughly equal in size and power; high fixed costs; high costs of leaving the industry; and no product differentiation. Under these conditions, price competition occurs. This competition will drive out any marginal firms and place limits on the surviving firms' profitability.

As the owner of the small business plans the company's future, the competition is an obviously important factor. The five forces just described will determine what that competition promises to be like. In addition to the industry conditions, the planning must assess the environment, the culture as we have labeled it.

The Payoff of Strategic Planning

When Bryan Jackson bought Superior Machine Co. of Florence, South Carolina, he liked what he saw in the standards for excellence the company had established over the years. Jackson saw his task as providing strategic planning rather than changing operations, which were already running smoothly.

That strategic planning is paying off nicely for Jackson and Superior. Sales have gone from $9 million in 1982 to $14.5 million in 1985. The company's reputation for quality has attracted international attention, with a West German firm asking Superior to build two steel furnaces in New Jersey. The company is now rebuilding two furnaces in Oregon for the same firm. Jackson's response to the problem of depending too much on the German customer was not to cut back on Superior's dealings with it, but rather to expand into other lines of business, including paper mills, rock crushing plants, and other steel mills.

Source: Tenney Griffin, ''Almost Leaving Well Enough Alone,'' *Nation's Business*, February 1985, 70.

The Culture

Most people would agree that the mom and pop grocery store has an extremely limited role in the retail food industry of the United States. Though they were vital to food distribution for much of our history, since the end of World War II, small, independent grocery stores have become less important and now are almost a thing of the past. They have been replaced by large chains of supermarkets and of convenience stores. Why has this happened? It is the result of a number of changes that have taken place in our society.

First, home refrigeration has become the rule. Virtually no home is without it. With this food storage capability, trips to the market are less frequent, so convenience of location is less important than it once was. Second, many housewives work. The daily ritual of buying fresh food has disappeared. It still thrives in countries where refrigerators tend to be smaller and shopping trips are an integral part of the social customs of housewives. Third, nearly all housewives drive. The need for a store within walking distance no longer exists. Finally, the technology of food processing and packaging, along with

Small Business Success 11

Miller/Zell,
Atlanta, Georgia

The founder and president of Miller/Zell, an Atlanta-based company specializing in turnkey programs for designing and renovating store space for large retailers, recognizes the impact of change in our society. Sandy Miller's customers, retailers of all types, must respond to these changes by continuously upgrading their places of business. Miller/Zell provides a wide variety of store planning and retailing consultation services, as well as large size graphics and point of sales material. Miller started in the printing business in 1959, and by 1977 recognized the company's need to formalize long-range planning if it was to realize its full potential. The following year the company adopted its objective of providing comprehensive renovating and merchandising service to retail chains throughout the country. Since then, the company's revenues have grown at an impressive rate, from $1,900,000 in 1977 to over $20,000,000 in 1984.

Source: The Changing World of Smaller Business (New York: Price Waterhouse, 1982), 25.

home refrigeration, has made it possible to store large amounts of food for very long periods.

The small hope for the mom and pop operation to exist as an off-hours facility was extinguished with the arrival of convenience store chains. These chains have brought the science of operations research into site selection, inventory purchase, store layout, and other areas. As a result, they have become dominant in the segment of food retailing that, because supermarkets originally ignored it, offered the mom and pop operations a niche to exploit. The niche is no longer there; neither are the mom and pop stores.

These cultural changes—housewives working, home refrigeration spreading, housewives becoming increasingly mobile—have come together to change an industry. Other examples of industries affected by cultural change include the decline of the downtown area as a shopping center with the move to the suburbs and the construction of superhighways around our cities; the emergence of unisex hair-styling salons; the growth of day-care centers because mothers work and, perhaps just as importantly, so do grandmothers.

It is the environment, or culture as we have called it, that determines whether a business can survive. Businesses that ignore, or fail to examine adequately, patterns of change in our culture do so at great risk. Even the perfect product, with flawless design and highest quality, will bring disaster in a market that shows no interest in it. Times and customer preferences change, so a product that once enjoyed widespread acceptance eventually will become obsolete.

These changes are difficult to monitor because their impact on sales is often very subtle. The owner of a business, being concerned about its competitive standing, may not notice that the demise of the entire industry is under way. When viewed in this light, the strategic planner's basic task is monitoring, and adapting to, change and innovation in the culture.

The Process of Strategic Planning

In the beginning of the chapter we pointed out that most small business owners do not engage in strategic planning despite strong evidence that they should. The following guidelines are offered to make the planning process less difficult.[4]

1. Any written planning document, no matter how brief, is better than none. Putting plans into writing forces the planner to develop her reasoning more carefully than she would simply by thinking.

2. Getting started is the hardest part. None of the process may be simple, but once a start has been made the remainder is less likely to be postponed indefinitely.

3. Concerning the use of outsiders: don't use them to do the planning. The owner must make the plans hers. The commitment required for success cannot be given to plans made by others in the same fashion as to one's own. Do use others to review your plan. Logical flaws, mistaken assumptions, and other such errors are much clearer to someone else. Best results are likely to come from professionals whose backgrounds and objectivity allow them to make the review meaningful. Among the groups that can be used are bankers, lawyers, accountants, and consultants.

4. Plans based on facts will have more value than plans lacking a factual base. Former General Motors board chairman Alfred P. Sloan had this in mind when he observed: "The big work behind business judgment is in finding and acknowledging the facts and circumstances concerning the technology, the market, and the like in their continuously changing forms." These facts are often hidden in some rather obscure places,

---

[4]These suggestions are adapted from Robert B. Buchele, *Business Policy in Growing Firms* (San Francisco: Chandler Publishing Co., 1967), 123–126.

but finding them is clearly worth the effort. Chapter 4, ''The Nature of the Market,'' provides some guidelines on how to search for them.

5. Be careful with numbers. Specifying a level of sales or profitability for some future year is easy, tempting, and often meaningless. Unless such an objective has emerged after the market has been carefully researched and after the broad goals it represents have been endorsed by the key individuals involved, any attempt at specification is futile.

K   E   Y   Objectives Reviewed

1. Strategy formulation appears to have a strong bearing on the success of a small business.

2. The major components in developing strategy include the firm's customers, its competencies, its competitors, and its environment—the culture within which it does business.

3. The process by which the owner of a small business sets strategy for the company should include a written plan, which should be based on facts rather than opinions and be reviewed by competent outsiders.

Discussion Questions

1. What are the four reasons small businesses do not engage in strategic planning?

2. Explain the statement ''business owners do not get customers, customers create the business.''

3. Why did General Motors' Cadillac division prosper only after it realized that people bought cars for status, not for transportation?

4. What forces influence the competition small businesses face?

5. What should be the role of outsiders in strategy development?

6. What role does culture have in determining the success of a business?

7. Describe the barriers to entry into an industry.

CHAPTER 12

Pricing

Source: Photograph courtesy of Wetterau Incorporated.

K E Y Objectives

1.   To identify the factors that affect the pricing decision.

2.   To identify pricing objectives.

3.   To identify pricing policies.

4.   To identify pricing methods for retailers.

5.   To identify pricing methods for service firms.

6.   To identify pricing methods for manufacturers.

7.   To identify pricing methods for wholesalers.

8.   To identify common pricing mistakes and their effects on gross margin.

   A small firm must approach pricing carefully if the business is to succeed. Pricing affects sales dollar volume, sales unit volume, and net profit and is therefore important in the company's overall strategy. To achieve its pricing objectives, the firm must set pricing policies as general guidelines to follow. There are many methods used to establish prices, since the method varies with the type of industry and the pricing objectives. The entrepreneur must consider many factors before establishing prices. These factors include competitors' prices, demand for the product, costs to produce and/or sell the product, and the firm's desired image.

Factors Affecting the Pricing Decision

Competition

In previous chapters, when discussing break-even or projected financial statements, we assumed that the entrepreneur would have a pricing structure similar to industry averages. In other words, we assumed that the entrepreneur's prices and costs would be similar to competitors'. Though this is not always completely true, the competitors' prices cannot be ignored.

Unique Business   12.1

It's One for the Money

The Bortz brothers, Joseph and Michael, of Lombard, Illinois are in the business of recreating the 1950s for customers at each of their four night-clubs. The nostalgic atmosphere comes from the music—15,000 records from that era—and the decor, which includes customized Chevies, old Coke machines, Wurlitzer jukeboxes, and Marilyn Monroe photos.

Each of the four clubs made between $500,000 and $1,000,000 in 1984 with a groovy 15 to 30 percent in net profit. The clubs are called Blue Suede Shoes.

Source: ''Rock 'N' Roll is Here to Stay,'' *Venture,* 7, no. 5 (May 1985): 10.

The number of competitors in an industry, the size of each, and the prices they charge may greatly influence the prices an entrepreneur can charge. If a small business enters an industry with numerous competitors, all relatively the same size, there may not be an industry leader that can influence pricing. In this type of industry, all businesses maintain a similar pricing structure, and no business has enough influence to change it. In many industries, though, one or two businesses may be industry leaders, holding a large percentage of the market. In this type of market, the entrepreneur may find that if the market leader increases or decreases prices, it will affect the sales of a new, small business. It is often very difficult for a small business to match the prices of larger businesses and still make a profit; therefore, the entrepreneur is forced to choose between lower sales or selling products at an unprofitable price. In many industries, even if there is no market leader, price competition is so fierce that it can cause many businesses to fail.

Many entrepreneurs are aware that they need to consider the competition but fail to realize that competitors' prices are only one of many factors to consider. If an entrepreneur sets prices only on the basis of what other businesses charge, sales and profits may be well below anticipated levels.

Demand

Elasticity of Demand
The effect of prices on the demand for a product.

A change in price often affects the number of customers wishing to purchase the product. The effect of prices on the demand for the product is called the **elasticity of demand.** If demand drops sharply when prices are raised, a

Illustration Capsule 12.1

Pricing Advertising on Cable Television

Pricing for commercials on cable television was a problem when cable networks were first being established. Because it was a "new product" it was difficult to judge the value of time on a cable network, so prices varied greatly. "Across the country, prices for cable fluctuated like the price of leather handbags in a flea market." One cable company in New York first based its prices on competition, matching the cost of local radio. This resulted in a price of about $15 for 30 seconds. Within 2 years, though, the price was increased to $30 or $40 for 30 seconds. The executive director of the network stated, "None of us know what it's worth yet."

Source: Sara Delano, "Why Bargain Prices Lure Cable Advertisers," *Inc.*, May 1983, 177.

Elastic Demand
The quantity of a product demanded by consumers drops sharply as prices are increased.

Inelastic Demand
The quantity of a product demanded by consumers changes slightly or does not change at all when prices are increased or decreased.

product is said to have an **elastic demand.** If, however, demand does not decrease as prices rise, the product is said to have an **inelastic demand.** Clothing would be a product with an elastic demand since most people would buy additional outfits if the prices decreased. However, salt is a product with an inelastic demand since people would not use more salt even if the price was cut by 50 percent. The elasticity of demand is a factor a business must consider when establishing prices. The business must be aware of how much more sales volume could be generated if prices dropped, or how much sales volume would decrease if prices were raised.

The entrepreneur must realize, also, that marketing efforts may affect the elasticity of demand for a product. When establishing prices, factors such as the level of advertising and the efforts of a direct sales force must be considered. Economic theory states that the purpose of marketing efforts is to decrease elasticity of demand. In other words, advertising and a direct sales force should create more constant consumer demand no matter what price is established.[1] Business owners can test price levels with various amounts of advertising and direct sales effort to determine the most profitable combination; however, most products will be price elastic even with marketing efforts.

[1]M. Wayne Delozier and Arch G. Woodside, *Marketing Management* (Columbus, Ohio: Charles E. Merrill Publishing Co., 1978), 275.

Costs

A major problem with considering only the competitor's prices and elasticity of demand is that no two businesses operate exactly the same; the costs incurred by each are different. A company's pricing structure must be established only after the entrepreneur considers what costs she will incur or an adequate profit will not be generated.

When a company is a wholesale or retail firm, it has a direct cost for each product (its cost of goods) plus all of the overhead expenses. The prices charged must cover both direct costs and overhead costs. One inexperienced entrepreneur failed to realize this when he began a used car business. If he purchased a car for $300 and sold it for $350, the entrepreneur thought this was fine since there was $50 profit. However, this "profit," which was actually gross profit, was not enough to cover all other expenses such as salaries or rent. This mistake was discovered too late, and the business failed.

Desired Image

Studies have shown that when customers have little knowledge of the product, price is a major factor in how they perceive the product's quality. Thus, if the entrepreneur wishes to develop an image of high quality and/or prestige, a high price is appropriate. Often, consumers are willing to pay much higher prices for prestige products. For example, designer jeans and expensive perfumes often cost much more than the competitors' products, but some consumers will pay the extra amount for the image the products create.

If, however, the entrepreneur wishes to establish a "bargain" image, then a low price is appropriate. For example, discount stores, flea markets, and garage sales wish to promote a bargain image and therefore price products with a minimal profit margin, hoping to sell a large volume.

Pricing Objectives

Pricing Objectives
Specific company goals to be achieved through pricing.

One of the first steps in establishing prices is to develop **pricing objectives,** specific company goals to be achieved through pricing. As stated before, price changes will affect sales volume (both unit volume and dollar volume) and net profit. Because of this, the entrepreneur should set objectives for the pricing structure. This is one area often completely neglected by entrepreneurs, though it is essential for a properly managed firm.

Sales Objectives

Because of the effect on sales due to elasticity of demand, pricing objectives are often sales oriented. Sales-oriented objectives may be stated in terms of actual sales or market share. Examples follow:

- Increase market share by 5 percent next year.
- Maintain the existing market share.
- Increase sales by $40,000 next year.
- Increase dollar sales by 10 percent over last year's dollar volume.
- Increase unit sales by 10 percent over the number of units sold last year.

Profit Objectives

Sales objectives, though necessary, are not sufficient. A large sales volume and large market share may be achieved by continually cutting prices. However, since profit equals revenue minus costs, if prices are set too low, the company may incur a loss even if sales volume is high. Because of this, firms will often set profit objectives in terms of a percentage of sales, a return on investment, or a fixed dollar amount. Examples follow:

- Net profit should be 10 percent of sales.
- Return on investment should be 20 percent.
- Return on investment should increase by 2 percent each year.
- Net profit should be $30,000.

Other Objectives

Often firms will have other objectives that are not directly sales or profit oriented. These objectives may include meeting the competition, following the price of the industry leader, or maintaining a certain image. Objectives will vary among industries and will also vary among businesses within the same industry.

Pricing Policies

. . . .

Pricing Policies
General guidelines and rules used when making pricing decisions.

Once pricing objectives have been established, it is necessary to establish pricing policies. **Pricing policies** are general guidelines and rules for making pricing decisions.[2] Even if entrepreneurs do not have formal, written policies, they will have unwritten ones that can be determined by observing the decisions of the company owner. Examples of pricing policy decisions follow:[3]

- If competitors cut prices will you also cut prices?
- Will you run "promotions" or "specials?" If so, how often?
- On the average, how will your prices compare with your competitors'?
- Will markdowns be necessary owing to seasonal changes?
- Will there be a single price for all customers or is price negotiable?

---

[2]Delozier and Woodside, *Marketing Management*, 264.
[3]Delozier and Woodside, *Marketing Management*, 264.

Illustration Capsule　12.2

Sample Pricing Goals of Large Companies

General Foods

- 33⅓ percent gross margin
- "⅓ to make, ⅓ to sell, ⅓ for profit"
- maintain market share

Goodyear

- meet competitors
- maintain market position
- stabilize prices

Sears Roebuck

- increase market share
- obtain return on investment of 10 to 15 percent after taxes
- maintain low margin policy

Kroger

- maintain market share
- obtain return on investment of 20 percent before taxes

Source: M. Wayne Delozier and Arch G. Woodside, *Marketing Management* (Columbus, Ohio: Charles E. Merrill Publishing Co., 1978), 265.

Introductory Prices

Introductory Prices
Temporary reductions in prices designed to increase the company's or product's acceptance in the market.

Pricing policies are often changed to accomplish long-term and short-term goals. Often this is necessary as a new product or business is accepted in the market. When a new business is established or when a business introduces a new product, it often offers **introductory prices.**[4] These are temporary reductions in prices designed to increase the company's or product's acceptance in the market. It is a short-term offer, and regular prices are established after the introductory period is over.

[4]Jerome E. McCarthy, *Essentials of Marketing* (Homewood, Ill., Richard D. Irwin, 1979), 346.

Low-Ball Pricing

Low-ball Pricing
Establishing very low prices to obtain a customer's order, hoping that future orders at higher prices will generate profits.

Another strategy using low prices is often referred to as **low-ball pricing.**[5] Low-ball pricing is often used by aggressive businesses intent on winning a customer's order. To obtain the order, the firm may set a price below the item's cost hoping that future orders at higher prices will generate profits. This strategy may work for a small business competing against a larger one if the large business is unwilling to cut prices. If the larger competitor is not concerned about the small percentage of market share a small business obtains, this strategy will often be effective. It may be risky, however, because it may begin a price war that the small business cannot survive. Also, there is no guarantee that the low-ball strategy will lead to future profits; it may just result in lower profits.

Skimming

Skimming Policy
A high initial price (compared with competitors'), gradually lowered over time, that generates high profits for the company before competitors enter the market.

A new company or a company introducing a new product often uses a **skimming policy.**[6] The company establishes a high price initially (compared with competitors') and then gradually lowers it. This is most effective if price elasticity exists for the product and more items can be sold as the price is decreased. The company benefits since the high price generates high profits and the company quickly recoups any start-up or research and development costs. The disadvantage of price skimming is that the high profits generated often encourage competitors to enter the market, and eventually the increased competition forces the prices to fall. This occurred with computers, calculators, and video games; all were initially very high priced, but as more and more competitors entered the market, the prices fell rapidly.

Penetration Price

Penetration Price Policy
A low initial price (compared with competitors') established to gain a large market share, which then allows the company to raise prices.

With a **penetration price policy,**[7] a company establishes a low price (compared with the competition) to gain a large market share, which will allow the company to raise prices. This penetration policy is the opposite of the skimming policy, since the low price yields low profits. However, if a large volume can be sold, an adequate profit may still be generated. Companies often use the low price when they expect a good deal of competition, since the low price is meant to discourage potential competitors from entering the market.

---

[5]Donald Rappaport, *Price Waterhouse, Business Review* (Washington, D.C.: National Office of Smaller Business Services, 1984), 1–2.
[6]McCarthy, *Essentials of Marketing,* 345.
[7]McCarthy, *Essentials of Marketing,* 345.

Opportunistic Pricing

Opportunistic Pricing
A pricing policy that increases prices to take advantage of temporary market conditions such as product shortages.

Prices are often changed in response to market conditions. One such change, known as **opportunistic pricing,**[8] occurs when companies raise prices during severe shortages. Because the demand for the product exceeds the supply, some customers are willing to pay a higher price, resulting in larger profits for the company. Opportunistic pricing must be used with caution, however, because customers may be aware of the price increases, and ill feelings may result. Then, when supply is more abundant, the customer may go to a competitor for the product.

Defensive Pricing

Defensive Pricing
A pricing policy a firm uses to protect its other products or to protect its market share.

Defensive pricing[9] is often used by a firm to protect the sales of its other products or the company's market share. If a company introduces a new product that competes with one of its existing products, it may give the new product a higher price. Companies often use defensive pricing by waiting until a new competitor enters the market and then cutting prices to minimize the competitor's sales.

Milking

Milking
A pricing policy in which an established company with a loyal customer base sets prices higher than those necessary to make an adequate profit.

Once a company has firmly established itself in the marketplace, it has a loyal customer base that may be willing to pay higher prices than what the company would normally charge. Taking advantage of this situation is known as **milking.**[10] A well-established firm may have lower overhead owing to depreciated products or lower debt payments and, therefore, lower required profit. However, if higher prices are maintained, greater profits may result even if some market share is lost. Often, if a company plans to drop a product line, milking provides excellent profits while market share decreases. If a small business is competing against a large firm that is using a milking strategy, the small firm may find entry into the market easier than anticipated.

Foul-Weather Pricing

Foul-Weather Pricing
A pricing policy established to minimize the effect of poor economic conditions.

Changes in general economic conditions often cause businesses to change pricing policies. During recessions, for example, a company may cut prices well below a profitable level. This strategy, used to generate revenue to cover overhead expenses, is known as **foul-weather pricing.**[11]

---

[8]Rappaport, *Price Waterhouse, Business Review,* 2.
[9]Ibid.
[10]Ibid.
[11]Ibid.

Illustration Capsule   12.3

Pricing Checklist

1. Is the relative price of this item very important to your customers?
2. Are prices based on estimates of the number of units that consumers will demand at various price levels?
3. Do you know what direct competitors are doing price-wise?
4. Do you regularly review competitors' ads to obtain information on their prices?
5. Have you estimated sales, operating expenses, and reductions for the next selling season?
6. Have you established a profit objective for the next selling season?
7. Given estimated sales, expenses, and reductions, have you planned initial markup?
8. Will cents-off coupons be used in newspaper ads or mailed to selected customers?
9. Has the impact of various sale items on profits been considered?
10. Would periodic special sales, combining reduced prices and heavier advertising, be consistent with the company image desired?
11. Should employees be given purchase discounts?
12. Have procedures for recording the dollar amounts, percentages, and probable causes of markdowns been set up?
13. Have you marked the calendar for a periodic review of your pricing decisions?

Source: Bruce J. Walker, *A Pricing Checklist for Small Retailers* (Washington, D.C.: U.S. Government Printing Office, June 1976), 2–8.

Pricing Policies and Growth

The entrepreneur must establish pricing policies when the business opens and should consistently reevaluate the policies as the company grows and is accepted in the marketplace. The policies must change as the company emerges from a new start-up to a mature firm with an established clientele. A company normally encounters four stages during its business life cycle: start-up, growth, maturity, and decline. During each of these stages, certain pricing policies are more appropriate than others. These policies follow:[12]

Stage of Growth	Appropriate Price Policy
Start-up	Skimming
Growth	Low-ball or penetration
Maturity	Defensive or milking
Decline	Milking or foul-weather

Although these strategies are recommended for certain growth stages, each company has unique circumstances it must consider when establishing price policies.

Pricing Methods for Retailers

Markup

Markup
The difference between the cost of the product and the selling price.

Most retailers use a pricing system based on a specific **markup**—the difference between the item's cost and retail selling price. This markup is gross profit and must cover all overhead costs. Confusion often exists when discussing markups because there are several ways to determine this profit margin, which is usually stated in terms of a percentage rather than an actual dollar amount. Two methods are commonly used, markup on cost and markup on selling price.

Markup on Cost
The dollar amount of profit stated as a percentage of the cost of the item.

Markup on cost[13] states the dollar amount of profit as a percentage of the item's cost. Consider a retailer who purchases calculators from the wholesaler for $12.50. The retailer adds another $12.50 to the cost to arrive at a selling price of $25.00. This is a markup on cost of 100 percent.

Markup on Selling Price
The dollar amount of profit stated as a percentage of the selling price.

Markup on selling price,[14] however, would use the same information but arrive at a markup of 50 percent as follows:

$$\$12.50 \text{ Profit} \div \$25.00 \text{ Selling Price} = 50 \text{ Percent.}$$

Markup on selling price is equal to gross margin; therefore, many small business owners understand it better. A company that maintains a markup on selling price of 50 percent will have a gross margin of 50 percent unless it makes other price adjustments (see Exhibit 12.1).

The initial markup must be high enough to cover all operating expenses plus provide the desired profit. In addition, it must be high enough to cover

---

[12]Rappaport, *Price Waterhouse, Business Review,* 2.
[13]Glen A. Welsh, Charles Zlatkovich, and Walter Harrison, *Intermediate Accounting,* 5th ed. (Homewood, Ill., Richard D. Irwin, 1979), 418.
[14]Welsh, Zlatkovich, and Harrison, *Intermediate Accounting,* 419.

Exhibit   12.1   Markup on Selling Price versus Gross Margin

Item	Cost to Produce or Buy the Product	Dollar Amount Added	Selling Price	% Markup on Cost	% Markup on Selling Price	Quantity Sold
A	$ 50.00	$10.00	$ 60.00	20%	16.67%	100
B	100.00	50.00	150.00	50	33.00	200
C	24.00	6.00	30.00	25	20.00	5,000

Sales		Cost of Goods Sold	
A 100 × 60 = $ 6,000		A 100 × 50 = $ 5,000	
B 200 × 150 = 30,000		B 200 × 100 = 20,000	
C 5,000 × 30 = 150,000		C 5,000 × 24 = 120,000	
$186,000		$145,000	

Item	Sales	Cost of Goods Sold	Gross Margin	Gross Margin Percentage (% Markup on Selling Price)
A	$ 6,000	$ 5,000	$ 1,000	16.67%
B	30,000	20,000	10,000	33.33
C	150,000	120,000	30,000	20.00
Total (or average)	$186,000 (100%)	$145,000 (78%)	$41,000 (22%)	—

any discounts or sales that will occur. Thus, the initial markup percentage can be calculated as follows:[15]

$$\text{Initial Markup Percentage} = \frac{\text{Operating Expenses} + \text{Reductions} + \text{Profit}}{\text{Net Sales} + \text{Reductions}}.$$

To use this formula, the entrepreneur must project sales, operating expenses, reductions, and projected net profit for the coming year. Suppose, for example, these projections are as follows:

- Sales, $100,000
- Operating expenses, $35,000
- Reductions, $5,000
- Profit, $6,000

The initial markup would then be calculated as follows:

$$\frac{35,000 + 5,000 + 6,000}{100,000 + 5,000} = 43.8 \text{ percent.}$$

---

[15]Bruce Walker, *A Pricing Checklist for Small Retailers* (Washington, D.C.: Small Business Administration, June 1976), 4.

Therefore, if the entrepreneur's projections are accurate, an initial markup of 43.8 percent will be necessary to make the desired profit of $6,000. It should be noted that this is the average overall markup necessary. While some items may have a greater markup and some less, the overall markup must average 43.8 percent. Once they have determined the overall markup, retailers often incorporate several other techniques into their pricing structure. These techniques include price lining, odd-ending pricing, and loss-leader pricing.

Price Lining

Price Lining
A pricing system in which categories of merchandise are established and prices are set for each category.

With **price lining,** an entrepreneur establishes categories of merchandise and then prices the merchandise by category. If the company sells men's suits, the suits may be separated by quality, type of material, and other factors. Suits may be separated into three categories—$200, $350, and $500—according to their quality. Having only three prices simplifies the entrepreneur's pricing system and also simplifies the customer's purchasing decision.

Odd-Ending Pricing

Odd-Ending Pricing
A system in which prices are set at odd numbers, based on the belief that this causes customers to buy more.

Odd-ending pricing is a system by which prices are set at odd numbers, such as $2.95, $3.99, or $9.99. This type of pricing is based on the belief that customers prefer a price of $2.99 more than $3.00. Although this type of pricing is used extensively, there is substantial disagreement as to its effectiveness in increasing demand.

Loss-Leader Pricing

Loss-Leader Pricing
The price of a particular product is set below the usual selling price, sometimes below cost, to motivate customers to shop at the store.

Many retail outlets use **loss-leader pricing** to attract customers. This practice sets the price of a particular product below the usual selling price, sometimes below its cost. This pricing technique is often used with heavy advertising and is designed to encourage people to shop at that specific outlet. Once customers are in the store they may purchase additional products or they may be persuaded to shop at that store more often. Thus, the low markup may be detrimental to profit margins in the short run but profitable in the long run.

Pricing Methods for Service Firms

Price per Hour

Pricing in a service industry presents problems because there is often no cost of materials (the physical product). In other situations, there is a minimal cost for the product. For example, in an insect exterminating business, the only

Source: Drawing by H. Martin; © 1985. The New Yorker Magazine, Inc.

cost for materials is for the chemicals used; in a secretarial service or an engineering firm the only cost of materials is for general office supplies. The major cost of providing the service is not the cost of materials but the cost of labor. Thus, in a service industry, the entrepreneur must accurately price the cost of labor. She must determine what fixed or overhead expenses will be incurred, what materials will be used, and how long it will take to complete the job. She must also determine the net profit level desired. Once she has determined these figures, she can determine the appropriate selling price.

Consider, for example, the owner of a pest control firm who had projected overhead expenses for the first year to be $66,500 and desired a net profit of $8,000. Based on his knowledge of the industry he knew that chemicals usually cost $3 for each hour of service and labor, $10 per hour. Therefore, total cost of goods sold would be $13 per hour.

It was then necessary to determine how many hours of service he could provide. Since the owner and one part-time employee would be servicing all calls, he determined that approximately 2,800 hours of service could be provided during the first year. Therefore, the revenue from 2,800 hours of service would have to be enough to cover the overhead expenses of $66,500 and generate the desired profit of $8,000. To determine the appropriate price, the owner took the following steps.

1. Determine gross margin:

$$\text{Gross Margin} = \text{Overhead Expenses} + \text{Desired Profit}$$
$$= \$66,500 + \$8,000$$
$$= \$74,500.$$

2. Determine cost of goods sold:

$$\text{CGS} = 2,800 \text{ hours} \times \$13 \text{ per hour}$$
$$= \$36,400.$$

3. Determine sales:

$$\text{Sales} = \text{CGS} + \text{Gross Margin}$$
$$= \$36,400 + \$74,500$$
$$= \$110,900.$$

Therefore sales must equal $110,900.

The price per hour to be charged is then determined by dividing the sales figure by the hours of service.

$$\frac{\text{Sales}}{\text{Hours of Service}} = \frac{110,900}{2,800} = \$39.61.$$

The owner of the new pest control firm therefore decided to charge $42 per hour to simplify billing and to allow for sales and discounts throughout the year.

Bid Pricing

Bid Pricing
A pricing system used when each customer's job or product is different, resulting in a different price for each customer.

Fixed-Cost Contract
A specific price is agreed on by the buyer and seller, and the price is not changed even if costs to complete the job are higher than expected.

For many service businesses where each customer's job or product is different, **bid pricing** is the normal method for pricing. Bid pricing consists of estimating all costs involved in completing or producing a product, then setting the desired profit margin, then setting the final price. Generally, the company that can produce the desired quality at the lowest bid price obtains the job. Bid pricing is often used in the construction industry, where each project is different, or in service industries such as office maintenance, engineering, and architectural services.

In bid pricing, two methods are common, the fixed-cost contract and the cost-plus method. With the **fixed-cost contract,** the buyer and seller agree on a final price. The selling company has legally agreed to sell a product or

Cost-Plus Contract
Instead of a specific price, the customer agrees to pay all costs incurred in producing the product or service plus a certain percentage.

service for a certain price no matter what costs are incurred. With a **cost-plus contract** the customer agrees to pay all direct costs for producing the product or service plus a certain percentage. If direct costs exceed expected levels, the customer must pay a higher price than originally anticipated. Obviously, the seller will usually prefer a cost-plus contract while the buyer prefers a fixed cost.

Pricing Methods for Manufacturing Firms

Full Absorption versus Direct Costing

Pricing for manufacturing firms must take into account all labor, materials, factory overhead, selling, and administrative expenses. Two methods are often used for determining manufacturing prices, full absorption costing and direct costing. With the full absorption method, all factory overhead costs, such as rent and utilities, are considered part of the cost of goods sold of each product. The cost of each item manufactured includes the direct materials and labor used as well as a small portion of overhead expenses. Although this method is often used in financial reports, the direct cost method is more appropriate for determining pricing.

With the direct cost method, the only overhead expenses included in the cost of goods sold are those that increase or decrease with the number of units manufactured. The expenses that do not vary, such as rent, are considered overhead expenses, not cost of goods. This is more realistic than full absorption since the manufacturer then has a clearer picture of the true cost to manufacture the product.

To determine price, the manufacturer must therefore determine direct materials, direct labor, and variable factory overhead. He then determines fixed overhead expenses, selling expenses, administrative expenses, and all other expenses that will be incurred, as well as the number of units to be produced and sold during the year. Consider a manufacturer with the following data:

Material costs per unit	$ 3.00
Labor costs per unit	6.00
Variable factory overhead per unit	1.50
Total direct costs per unit	$ 10.00
Administrative expenses projected	50,000
Selling expenses projected	60,000
All other expenses	20,000
Projected number of units produced and sold	100,000
Desired profit	$ 10,000

Then selling price is determined:

$$\text{Selling Price} = \frac{\text{Profit} + (\text{Direct Costs} \times \text{Number of Units Produced}) + \text{Fixed Costs}}{\text{Number of Units Produced}}$$

$$= \frac{\$10,000 + (10 \times 100,000) + 50,000 + 60,000 + 20,000}{100,000}$$

$$= \frac{1,140,000}{100,000}$$

$$= \$11.40.$$

Demand-Backward Pricing

Demand-Backward Pricing
A system in which a final selling price is established and intermediate markups are then "backed into" to determine price ranges at each level in the channel of distribution.

If the entrepreneur is the manufacturer or wholesaler, it is often necessary to work backward to obtain the price to be charged. This process, known as **demand-backward pricing,**[16] is used when a final selling price is known but intermediate markups have not yet been set. For example, suppose a manufacturer begins producing calculators that she wishes to be price competitive when compared with similar calculators. Suppose competing calculators have markups as follows:

Calculator	Manufacturer Cost to Produce	Sold to Wholesaler for	Add Wholesaler's Profit of	Sold to Retailer for	Add Retail Profit of	Sold to Consumer for
A	$7.00	$ 9.00	$3.50	$12.50	$12.50	$25.00
B	7.50	10.00	4.00	14.00	14.00	28.00
C	6.00	7.25	3.75	11.00	11.00	22.00

If the new manufacturer wishes to have a final selling price of $23.00, it is then possible to work backward to determine how much she will charge the wholesaler. Wholesalers will be more likely to carry and promote the new product if they make an equal or greater profit than the profits on existing product lines. If they carry calculators A, B, and C, the new product must provide a similar, or better, profit structure. Working backward, the manufacturer decides price as follows:

Desired Final Price	Retailer Purchase Price (1/2 of Final Price)	Wholesaler Price = Retailer Purchase Price Less $4.00
$23.00	$11.50	$7.50

---

[16]McCarthy, *Essentials of Marketing,* 374.

The manufacturer must then consider costs and pricing objectives to see if the $7.50 price is feasible. If she determines that this would not provide an adequate profit, she must make changes in costs, objectives, or the desired final selling price.

Pricing Methods for Wholesalers

Pricing for wholesalers is similar to pricing for retailers, because they have no variable factory overhead to consider. The method retailers use to determine markup percentage could also be used by wholesalers. However, wholesalers' pricing is often similar to manufacturers' since demand-backward pricing may be necessary and since shipping costs must be considered. The various methods of handling shipping costs discussed below are appropriate for both manufacturers and wholesalers.

FOB Pricing

FOB Pricing
A free on board pricing method used by manufacturers and wholesalers in which the seller pays to load the merchandise onto the transportation, but the buyer pays all costs for freight and legally owns the items on board.

FOB pricing is a very common method that stands for "free on board." This means the seller pays to load the merchandise onto the transportation but the buyer pays all costs for freight (and legally owns the items) on board the transportation. With this method, different customers actually pay different prices for the same merchandise because of the variation in freight costs.

Zone Pricing

Zone Pricing
A pricing system in which all buyers within a specific geographical area are charged the same rate for freight costs.

Zone pricing is a system in which all buyers within a specific geographical area are charged the same rate for freight costs. All customers within the area have the same rate for freight costs. Thus, the problems of FOB pricing are eliminated. However, since the actual freight cost varies, it may be higher or lower than the rate the purchaser pays. This results in a varying profit margin for the seller, depending on which customer purchases the product.

Uniform Delivered and Freight-Absorption Pricing

Uniform Delivered Pricing
A pricing system in which the same freight charge is applied to all customers.

Freight-Absorption Pricing
A pricing system in which the seller pays all freight costs.

Zone pricing and FOB pricing often limit sales outside a certain area because freight costs are so high; the seller cannot be price competitive with suppliers closer to the customer. Therefore, if a manufacturer or wholesaler wishes to expand its trading area, it may have to use **uniform delivered pricing,** by which it charges the same freight charge to all customers, or **freight-absorption pricing,** which means the seller pays the freight cost. This may result in a larger trading area, although it obviously reduces the profit margin on the items sold. To make either of these methods profitable, the increased volume from the larger trading area must outweigh the decreased profits from a lower margin.

Common Pricing Mistakes

Entrepreneurs commonly make pricing mistakes because not many have experience and many hidden "traps" exist. Pricing mistakes quickly affect profits; small businesses often discover that a "minor" pricing mistake creates a major problem with profitability. When reviewing markup on selling price, we stated that this markup is equal to gross margin. However, many entrepreneurs are shocked to find that although their markup on selling price was 33 percent, the year-end gross margin is substantially less. The following factors often are the reason.

Failure to Monitor Increased Costs

When first established, a business has certain direct costs (cost of goods sold) and overhead costs. It then sets prices according to these costs. However, costs are not constant, so pricing must be reviewed periodically to ensure that prices are increased as costs increase. Both direct and indirect costs must be watched.

Increases in direct costs are very common. Retailers often find that wholesalers have increased the product cost; wholesalers find the manufacturers have increased costs. Failure to raise prices accordingly will result in lower profit margins or in losses. For example, the owner of a typewriter repair service discovered, almost too late, that unnoticed rising prices can be disastrous. When the company began, he could purchase one of his products from the supplier for $6. He therefore established an $8 selling price for it. Throughout the next two years, the supplier increased prices to $7, then to $8, and finally to $9. The entrepreneur, however, did not increase his price and still sold the product to his customers for $8, resulting in a $1 loss on each sale. Though it is easy to say that this should not occur, it should be remembered that the owner of a small business generally is under tremendous time pressure owing to the enormous number of tasks to be accomplished each day. In many businesses, thousands of items may be available for sale; with everything else that needs to be done, it is easy to overlook price increases.

Increases in overhead costs must also be considered. If a 30 percent gross margin is sufficient to cover overhead costs and provide a 55 percent profit when the business is started, it may not be sufficient if rent is increased sharply or if extra office personnel are added. Either prices or sales volume will have to increase. For this reason, prices should be reviewed to ensure that the desired profit margin is maintained.

Failure to Consider Sales Promotions and Markdowns

Markdowns
Retail price reductions designed to eliminate seasonal merchandise or stimulate sales volume.

Although each product has a specific markup, the product is not always sold at the original price. Most businesses run ''specials'' or promotions to obtain new customers, eliminate seasonal merchandise, and so forth. These retail price reductions are called **markdowns.** If all items in a store have an original markup on selling price of 33 percent, the year-end income statement will probably reflect a lower gross margin because sale prices will have reduced the overall gross margin. If too many markdowns are necessary to eliminate seasonal merchandise, this indicates poor inventory buying and will be reflected on the income statement as a lower gross margin. One entrepreneur who operated a bridal shop realized this only after incurring a loss for several years. When an outside consultant reviewed the income statement, it was obvious that the gross margin was substantially below industry averages. The entrepreneur stated that traditional industry markups were used when pricing the bridal dresses. However, when the consultant looked around the shop, many sale items could be seen. Further discussions revealed that poor purchasing caused excess inventory at the end of every season. Many times the excess dresses were considered out of style the following year and were sold at cost.

Proper use of markdowns is essential in retailing; however, many entrepreneurs have not had enough experience in this area to develop the necessary skills. Markdown decisions include determining the best time to mark an item down (if it appears to move slowly after 2 weeks, 3 weeks, 4 weeks, and so on), how much of a markdown to use, and how to advertise that markdown to potential customers. Large retailers have systematic markdown procedures, but many small retailers try to use only intuition. Markdowns require a systematic method.

Inaccurate Markdowns

The confusion of markups and markdowns may cause an entrepreneur to mark a product at a sale price that is at or below cost. Suppose the entrepreneur buys a product at $20 and sells it for $25 (a markup on cost of 25 percent). Later, if the product has not sold, the entrepreneur decides to mark the product down. Since the original markup was 25 percent, the entrepreneur reduces it by 20 percent, assuming there will still be a 5 percent profit margin. However, the 20 percent markdown is then determined as follows:

$25 Selling Price × 20 Percent Markdown = $5 Markdown

$25 Selling Price − $5 Markdown = $20 Selling Price

This selling price equals the cost of the item and results in no profit at all. In some cases, depending on the percentage markup and markdown, this procedure results in selling items for less than their purchase price.

Product Mix Variations

Most companies sell many items, each at a different profit margin. The profit margin may be within a certain range (for example, 20 to 30 percent), but it will not be identical for each item. Many entrepreneurs look at their product lines and the margins and assume the overall profit margin will be an average of the figures. For example, if profit margins range from 20 to 30 percent, the entrepreneur assumes that the overall profit margin will average 25 percent. He is then surprised to find at the end of the year that gross margin averages only 22 percent. In many cases, this is due to the volume of each product sold. If a large number of items sold have the 20 percent margin, while a smaller volume of 30 percent–profit items are sold, the final margin will not average 25 percent.

The owner of a small frozen custard shop realized this after the first 6 months in business. Although the milkshakes and malts were marked to provide a 66 percent gross margin, the sundaes were priced to yield a 40 percent margin. A review of the sales records indicated a large number of sundaes sold compared with shakes and malts. The income statement at the end of 6 months showed a gross margin of only 45 percent.

Failure to Consider Waste and Spoilage

In any business that sells a perishable product, some of the inventory spoils before it is sold. Entrepreneurs often fail to consider this cost when determining necessary markups. If all inventory is marked up 33 percent, when some inventory spoils this will result in a lower ending inventory, and thus a higher cost of goods sold.

A florist with four locations found this to be true when the gross margins of each location were compared. All products were purchased through the main outlet, marked up the same amount, then distributed to the different locations. Therefore, costs and markups were identical. However, one store consistently showed a lower gross margin than others. Discussions with the owners revealed that the store had a spoilage problem. The owners then took steps to minimize the spoilage.

Bidding Errors

For any business that must submit bids, the key to profitability is properly estimating the costs. Companies usually determine all costs and then add a specific profit percentage. However, if costs are underestimated, and the contract is a fixed amount, the profit margin may be substantially reduced or a loss may result. If costs are underestimated on one large contract, the effect on overall profit margins may be dramatic.

One painting contractor consistently operated for 3 years with a profit margin of 30 percent. When business kept increasing, the owner did not have the

Small Business Success   12

Neiman Sawmill, Hulett, Wyoming

Jim Neiman, vice president of Neiman Sawmill, had to develop innovative ideas to survive recessions and industry price cuts. The sawmill, founded by Jim's grandfather, was part of Jim's life from the time he was 6 years old. In 1974, Jim took over management of the sawmill after graduating from college with a degree in agriculture. That same year, however, the market dropped and Neiman's major buyer cut the price of lumber by almost two-thirds. Jim therefore developed a new market, selling to farmers and ranchers. He also made numerous improvements to the mill, adding electrical and welding shops, boilers, dry kilns, and a planing mill. The mill has adapted and grown; despite two recessions in the lumber industry, sales have increased to over $6 million.

Source: Small Business Means Jobs (Washington, D.C.: Small Business Administration, 1984), 21.

time to bid on all of the jobs and also manage the company, so he hired an estimator to help prepare bids. Unfortunately, the estimator was not as skilled as the company owner and on several contracts grossly underestimated the costs. The company's profit margin quickly dropped to 23 percent.

Cutting Prices without Knowledge of Elasticity

It is very common for entrepreneurs to decide that decreasing prices is necessary to increase sales and profits. All too often, if sales do not reach desired levels, the entrepreneur decides to cut prices to stimulate sales. Although this strategy may be effective, it is essential first to have some knowledge of the price elasticity or the effects on profits could be severe. Suppose a company that sells a product for $10 averages sales of 10,000 units per month or a sales volume of $100,000 (10,000 × $10). Suppose the price is dropped to $9 to increase sales. The company must then sell more than 11,000 units per month just to generate the same dollar volume and profits as in the past. This can result in much more work with no change in profits. If the purpose of the price cut was a temporary reduction to generate new customers, the increased activity may be justified. If, however, the purpose was to increase dollar sales volume and profits, the price cut may have done nothing but create more work.

K E Y Objectives Reviewed

1. Several factors affect the pricing decision, including competition, demand, costs, and desired image.

2. Companies should establish pricing objectives to identify the goals of pricing strategies.

3. Pricing policies are general guidelines and rules used when making pricing decisions. These general guidelines determine whether or not promotions and specials will be run, how prices will compare with the competitors', if markdowns will be necessary, and so forth.

4. Pricing methods for retailers are usually based on markup. In addition to determining the markup, retailers may also use price lining, odd-ending pricing, and loss-leader pricing.

5. Pricing methods for service firms usually are based on a price per hour. In some service industries, bid pricing is common.

6. Pricing for manufacturing firms can be accomplished through either full absorption costing or direct costing. Demand-backward pricing may be used if a final selling price is known but intermediate markups have not been determined.

7. Pricing for wholesalers is similar to retail pricing because markups may be used. However, it is also similar to manufacturers' pricing because freight costs must be considered.

8. Many pricing mistakes result in a lower gross margin than the percentage originally established.

Discussion Questions

1. How do advertising and a direct sales force affect price elasticity? Provide some specific examples.

2. Discuss the advantages and disadvantages of pricing products based on competitors' prices. Discuss advantages and disadvantages of pricing based on costs. Which method is preferable? Why?

3. Why is pricing in a service business often more difficult than in a retail or wholesale business?

4. What is the difference between pricing objectives and pricing policies? Which must be established first? Why?

5. Compare a penetration price policy with a skimming price policy. Why is it best for the product to have price elasticity if a skimming policy is used?

6. There is substantial disagreement as to the effectiveness of odd-ending pricing. When do you feel odd prices are more effective than even prices? When would this method not make a difference?

7. Loss-leader items may be detrimental to profits in the short run but profitable in the long run. Why? How could an entrepreneur measure the effectiveness of loss-leader pricing?

8. Suppose a manufacturer is considering producing a new product. If demand-backward pricing indicates that the manufacturer's selling price would be below the desired markup, what alternatives exist?

9. Why is accurate bidding difficult? Identify controllable factors that influence the costs of producing a product or service. Identify uncontrollable factors that influence the costs of producing a product or service.

10. Suppose an entrepreneur starts a new business and tells you that the markup on selling price is 50 percent. What factors could cause the year-end gross profit to be less than 50 percent?

CHAPTER 13

Promotion

Source: Holmquists' County Market, Buffalo, MN, a successful independent retail food store serviced by Super Valu Stores, Inc., Mpls. Reprinted with permission.

K E Y Objectives

1. To identify the various elements of the promotional mix.

2. To describe essential elements of a successful personal selling program.

3. To identify the components of a successful advertising plan.

4. To discuss various types of publicity and stress its importance in company promotional plans.

5. To identify various types of sales promotion and stress its contribution to the overall promotional plan.

6. To stress the need for planning to achieve desired results.

Promotional Strategy
A plan that informs, persuades, and influences a consumer's decision.

"If you build a better mousetrap, people will beat a path to your door." This familiar advice implies that if a company has an excellent product or provides excellent service, the company will not need much effort to sell the product. Unfortunately, many entrepreneurs believe this to be true and do not realize the importance of promoting the product until sales fall below projected levels. Although a feasibility study might indicate a potential sales volume of $200,000, the sales may never reach even $100,000 if the business is not properly promoted. **Promotional strategy** informs, persuades, and influences a consumer's decision.[1] It may inform the consumer of where the company is located, persuade the consumer to believe that the company's products are superior to competitors' products, and influence the customer in making a purchase decision.

The Promotional Mix

. . . .

Types of Promotion

Personal Selling
Person-to-person presentations by a salesperson to a potential customer.

A company can promote itself or its product by several different methods. These methods include personal selling, mass selling, publicity, and sales promotion. **Personal selling** involves person-to-person presentations by the

---

[1]Louis Boone and David Kurtz, *Contemporary Business,* 4th ed. (Hinsdale, IL.: The Dryden Press, 1985), 320.

Unique Business   13.1

Babes in Consumerland

A store in San Francisco, "Desire: Sticker Headquarters for the Universe," is tapping the junior set catalog market. Owner Chuck Medlin recently sent 50,000 catalogs to children from around the world. He amassed the names and addresses from letters and visits to his store by children. The catalog features games, riddles, and, of course, stickers and related items.

Source: Leslie Schultz, "Babes in Consumerland," *Inc.*, November 1984, 46.

Mass Selling
Nonpersonal messages directed at a large number of people.

Publicity
A method in which information is presented as news to gain public attention or create company awareness.

Sales Promotion
Promotional efforts other than advertising, personal selling, or publicity.

Promotional Mix
The combination of personal selling efforts, advertising, and sales promotion used by a company.

salesperson to the potential customer. **Mass selling,** or advertising, consists of nonpersonal messages directed at a large number of people. **Publicity** is a method in which information is presented as news (published or broadcast free of charge) to create awareness of the company. **Sales promotion** includes promotional efforts other than advertising, personal selling, or publicity. This includes contests, coupons, and other methods.

The entrepreneur must decide the most effective method of promoting the new business and its products. The money allocated for advertising must be divided between regular advertising and promotion; if a personal sales force is necessary, this must be considered in personnel costs. The combination of personal selling efforts, advertising, and sales promotion is known as the **promotional mix.**[2]

The Right Blend

There is no "right" formula for deciding the promotional mix, since the most effective mix depends on the type of company, the product it sells, the price and profit margin on the item sold, the promotional efforts normal for that industry, the goal of the promotion, the nature of the target market, and so forth. For example, personal selling is more common for sales to industry, such as selling electrical components to an aircraft manufacturer. If the product is technical, the sales force may be necessary to explain the features and benefits of the product. Personal selling is also used when a product has a high price and a high markup. If the product is high priced, a personal selling

---

[2]Boone and Kurtz, *Contemporary Business*, 320.

effort may be needed to convince the customer to spend the money. A high markup justifies the use of the sales force, since it would not be cost-effective for a sales force to sell a product with a very small profit margin except in very large quantities. In certain industries, companies use personal selling as a major form of promotion. An entrepreneur trying to use a different approach may encounter an unfavorable reaction from potential customers.

Advertising or mass selling is often used both in industry and for the general public. In industry, it is often a means of support for personal selling. It can increase the customer's awareness of the company and its products and help to develop a company image. When the salesperson makes the sales call, the customer has some knowledge of the company. Advertising of this type is often through direct mail, trade shows for the industry, brochures, and so forth. For many products sold to the general public, regular advertising is essential. Since the potential target market is so large (for example, groceries or hardware items) personal selling is not practical. In addition, the profit margin on the items is too low to justify a sales force. Finally, advertising often has long-term goals, whereas personal selling is usually used to generate immediate sales.

Personal Selling

Types of Sales Efforts

Order Taker
A salesperson who accepts customers' requests for a product and delivers the goods but does not engage in any creative selling.

Creative Selling
Selling that requires the salesperson to convince and persuade the customer to buy the product.

Missionary Selling
An indirect method of selling in which the salesperson promotes the company's goodwill and image.

There are several categories of sales personnel, each involving different skills. Often the salesperson serves only as an **order taker,** merely taking the customer's request for the product and delivering the goods. This involves little selling effort by the sales representative. **Creative selling,** the type of selling most familiar to the general public, requires the salesperson to convince and persuade the customer to buy the product. **Missionary selling** is indirect selling since the sales representative sells the goodwill and image of the company. A missionary representative may also provide technical knowledge to the customer or help solve problems. In actuality, most sales jobs require a blend of all three types of efforts. The percentage of each type of effort, though, is substantially different for different sales jobs.[3]

Functions of a Salesperson

The function of a salesperson varies from company to company, but certain basic tasks are performed by most. One of the first, essential tasks is to find the potential customers. The process of finding potential customers is called

---

[3]Boone and Kurtz, *Contemporary Business,* 331.

Prospecting
The task of identifying
potential customers.

prospecting and is essential for using time effectively. If customers are not properly identified, the sales representative may spend most of the day calling on people who have no need for the product. Proper prospecting will result in a more efficient representative and higher sales.

The second task is to plan the sales presentation. Unless this is properly planned, the customer will not be given the information necessary to make a decision. The presentation must create awareness of the company and its product, and generate interest. This is usually done by explaining features, advantages, and benefits of the product and convincing the customer that objections (such as ''the price is too high'' or ''I can't spend the money right now'') are not justified. This creates a desire for the product and leads to the next task, obtaining the order. Often a sale is not made because the sales representative does not directly ask for the order; the representative must ask for the order and not be afraid of rejection.

Follow-up after the sale is also necessary to build a base of satisfied customers. Proper follow-up to solve problems, answer questions, and provide information indicates a concern for the customers, not just an interest in making the sale. Proper servicing of customer accounts increases repeated sales and establishes a strong customer base.

Managing the Direct Sales Force

Often an entrepreneur is a successful salesperson and builds the company to a certain point through personal sales efforts. As the company grows, the owner is no longer a salesperson but must assume duties of a sales manager. Sales management includes six equally important functions: recruiting, training, allocating, supervising, compensating, and evaluating.[4] Many entrepreneurs are not prepared for these tasks and find the responsibilities and necessary skills overwhelming.

Recruiting.   Contrary to what many people believe, there is not one type of personality necessary to be a good salesperson. Though some salespeople are very outgoing, those with reserved personalities are often extremely successful. Qualifications and characteristics that make a person successful in selling one product may actually be a disadvantage in selling another. Therefore, when recruiting sales personnel, it is not wise to consider only those who appear to be ''born'' salespeople. Certain guidelines have been established to help the entrepreneur in recruiting a sales force. These guidelines appear in Exhibit 13.1.

Training.   Training new sales personnel is an area entrepreneurs often neglect. Because of time pressures and budget restrictions, they may have no formal training program. A new salesperson is often ''trained'' by accompa-

[4]M. Wayne Delozier and Arch G. Woodside, *Marketing Management* (Columbus, Ohio: Charles E. Merrill Publishing Co., 1978), 499.

Exhibit 13.1   Selecting a Sales Force

Do	Don't
1. Write a job description. Define the type of selling, product knowledge necessary, abilities and qualities necessary to sell for your company.	1. Select only for selling skills. It is often easier to train a new salesperson than "untrain" someone with many years of sales experience. Bad habits are hard to break.
2. Select for initiative and perseverance. Almost all sales jobs require these two qualities. Even the best sales manager cannot develop sales ability in someone with no initiative.	2. Select for control of competitors' accounts. Some owners hire salespersons away from competitors hoping to steal business from competition. The ability to "bring customers with them" is often exaggerated by potential employees. Furthermore, if someone is willing to bring a competitor's customers to you, he would be willing to take your customers to someone else if offered a higher salary.
3. Look for reliability. A salesperson must have the trust of both the company owner and the customers. Reliability is essential.	
4. Consider mental ability. Depending on the technical nature of the product or service, imagination and intelligence may be essential.	3. Expect the impossible. Do not expect high sales volume with little or no planning of sales management functions. Also, the entrepreneur should not expect the salesperson to do something he himself would not do.
5. Select emotionally balanced people. Sales personnel must often endure rude treatment from customers, pressure of company quotas, delays in deliveries, product breakdowns. Only an emotionally balanced person will survive.	

Source: "Tips on Selecting Salesmen." (Washington, D.C.: Small Business Administration, 1976), 3–7.

nying the owner or another salesperson on calls. Though this is an essential part of the training, often it is not sufficient to provide product knowledge or develop adequate selling techniques. A small business with a direct sales force should develop a training program. This will prevent many problems and may help to prevent turnover.

For an entrepreneur to design a sales training program from start to finish would be time consuming. As an alternative, the entrepreneur may find professionally prepared programmed instruction (cassette tapes or slides) already available, or training seminars for sales personnel to attend. Programmed instructions are available through the American Management Association, Zig Ziglar Corporation, and others. Training seminars are often given by sales consultants. One of the best known is the Dale Carnegie Sales Course. These training programs are designed to teach the salesperson the following skills:

- Time management and territory management
- Effective communication
- Planning the sales call
- How to make a planned sales call
- How to utilize visual aids
- Understanding the basics of good customer relations
- Understanding the psychology of selling
- Closing the sale
- Approaching the job with a positive attitude
- Achieving a positive self-image

It should be obvious from this list that training a salesperson is not a simple process that can be completed quickly. Developing an employee into an effective salesperson takes substantial time and effort. The entrepreneur must realize that results may not be immediate, and the salesperson should be given adequate time to develop the necessary skills.

Allocating.   Allocation of sales effort refers to the number of sales calls to large, medium, and small accounts.[5] This is essential in determining the company's final sales volume. If a sales force spends too much time with small accounts and cannot devote enough time to large accounts, the loss of the large ones may devastate the firm. If, however, the sales force spends too much time with large accounts and neglects small and/or medium-sized accounts, the customer base may become too small to be profitable. In addition, large accounts may require close attention and price cutting because of competing firms trying to sell to them.

When a sales force is established, customers must be equitably distributed. It is essential to determine which salespeople will call on which customers, ensuring that one salesperson does not have a better territory than another. Customer accounts may be divided by industry, geographical area, company size, and so forth. However, proper allocation can be completed only after determining the market potential of the area and its customers. Too many small firms hire salespeople and establish quotas without having determined potential sales. When the salesperson does not meet the quotas, it is assumed that the salesperson is lazy, which can be inaccurate and unfortunate.

Supervising.   The ongoing supervision of sales personnel varies among companies depending on the amount of freedom given to the sales force. In some businesses, supervision is more complex and time consuming than in

---

[5]DeLozier and Woodside, *Marketing Management,* 518.

those whose sales personnel are "on the road" most of the time. Supervision may include any of the following:[6]

- making sales calls with sales personnel
- working with dissatisfied customers when the problem cannot be resolved by the salesperson
- communicating company information to sales personnel
- planning and holding sales meetings
- maintaining records

Successful supervision results in a motivated sales force, without direct control. Proper supervision allows the salesperson adequate freedom while it still obtains desired performance. It is common for a small business to hire a salesperson and send her out on calls, providing no direction or supervision. When sales fall short of expectations, the salesperson takes the blame. If adequate supervision is not provided, sales will not reach the potential volume.

Compensating.   Compensation of sales personnel can take one of three forms: straight salary, straight commission, or salary plus commission.

With a straight salary plan, the salesperson is more secure financially since income does not depend directly on sales. Thus, the salesperson is willing to take time to call new customers who may not provide an immediate source of revenue. However, this system provides little incentive for improving performance or reaching goals.

A straight commission plan is advantageous for the company since no money is paid unless sales are made and the company is able to maintain selling expenses at a certain percentage of sales. However, straight commission plans will frustrate the salesperson if sales are lost owing to uncontrollable factors.

Most companies find that a combination of salary and commission is most effective for both the company and the sales force. It provides a basic salary for the salesperson but also provides an incentive to improve performance. For the company, a combination may actually be less expensive than a straight commission as the sales volume increases (see Exhibit 13.2).

The business should ensure that the compensation plan is designed with company goals in mind. For example, if the company needs to obtain new customer accounts, it might set commissions on sales to new customers higher than on sales to established customers. Or, if the company wants to introduce a new product line, commissions for that product may temporarily be set higher than for other products. The compensation system can be a valuable tool to reward the salesperson and to achieve company goals. It is essential

---

[6]Delozier and Woodside, *Marketing Management*, 504.

Exhibit   13.2   Straight Commission versus Salary plus Commission

| | Sales Volume | | |
	$200,000	$500,000	$900,000
Commission 5%	$ 10,000	$ 25,000	$ 45,000
Salary of $15,000 plus 3%	21,000	30,000	42,000

that the small business owner establish the proper compensation plan or the sales force may have no motivation to achieve goals.

Evaluating.   When evaluating the performance of sales personnel, many entrepreneurs use factors that are too subjective to be properly evaluated and that have little relation to effectiveness in selling. Factors such as time spent in the office, appearance, or product knowledge are difficult to measure and may not adequately indicate performance. It is more appropriate to evaluate sales volume (or profit after expenses), number of calls made on existing accounts, number of new accounts opened, and so forth. Since actual numbers can be placed in such categories, evaluations are less subjective.

Evaluations should be based on comparing set goals with actual performance. The goals should be jointly established by the salesperson and the sales manager. If the salesperson has input in setting the goals, she will have a personal commitment to those goals. If, instead, the entrepreneur sets goals for the salesperson, there may be no commitment and results will be poor.

Goals should be established at the beginning of each year but should not be stated in annual terms. For example, setting a sales goal of $120,000 per year is not as useful as breaking it down into $10,000 per month and $2,300 per week. By breaking the goal into weekly quotas, performance can be evaluated constantly. Otherwise, the salesperson may not realize until the year is half over that the quota will not be met.

Advertising

. . . .

A company uses advertising, or mass selling, when it wishes to reach many people within a short period. Although major corporations spend an average of only 1 to 2 percent of sales on advertising, many small companies must spend a substantially larger percentage to achieve results. For some businesses, advertising is essential to success. Too often, entrepreneurs are not skilled in planning, developing, and implementing an advertising plan, and because of poor results, they conclude that advertising is a waste of money. If the entrepreneur does not have an effective advertising strategy, money will be wasted and sales will be poor. The following information is designed to acquaint the reader with the essential elements of an advertising plan.

The Customers

In Chapter 4, we discussed market segmentation. When the market is segmented, the entrepreneur often finds several distinct groups of customers, each desiring different product features, services, pricing structures, and so on. Awareness of this segmentation is essential when developing an advertising campaign because different advertising strategies may be needed for different customer segments. Suppose a company sells doors. One group of customers may be primarily interested in the energy-saving benefits of a particular door, while another group may be primarily interested in the aesthetic appearance, and still another in price. Different advertising may be needed to reach those groups—one ad stressing energy savings, another stressing beauty, another low price. In developing an advertising plan, the entrepreneur must remember that consumers do not only buy a product, they buy benefits—the "satisfactions they perceive the physical object gives them." A store that sells ice cream may actually be providing a comforting reward. A company that sells cake mixes may be selling a way to express love to a family.[7] It is essential that the entrepreneur determine the "customer's perceived benefits and how the product can fulfill the customer's hopes and dreams."[8]

For example, one small firm developed an advertising plan that appeared to be complete. However, the owner stated that the company provided an annual maintenance check free of charge to all customers, which was often their primary reason for purchasing the company's product. Yet none of the proposed ads mentioned this service. In reality, the company was selling an annual service, not just a physical product. This factor should not have been overlooked when developing the advertising.

Advertising Goals

When asked why they advertise, most entrepreneurs will reply, "to increase sales." However, there are many other reasons for advertising. The specific objectives of the advertising should be determined. Possible advertising objectives include:

- Increasing consumer awareness of the company
- Promoting or changing the company image
- Introducing a new product
- Generating new customers

The advertising objective definitely affects the type of advertising to be done. For example, if the purpose is to enhance the company image, the ads may mention the company name, its good reputation, and years in business.

---

[7]J. Douglas Johnson, *Advertising Today,* (Chicago: Science Research Associates, Inc., 1978), 119.
[8]Johnson, *Advertising Today,* 263.

Institutional Advertising
Advertising designed to
enhance the company
image and reputation.

Product Advertising
Advertising designed to
make potential customers
aware of a particular
product or service.

This type of advertising, called **institutional advertising,** is designed to keep customers conscious of the company and its reputation.

If the purpose of the advertising is to introduce a new product, then the product will be the prominent feature, the name of the company being de-emphasized. This type of advertising, known as **product advertising,** is designed to make potential customers aware of a particular product or service and of their need for it.

If a company wishes to generate new customers, the type of advertising will again be changed, two alternatives being available. The company can (1) change the customer's attitude, causing a change in buying habits, or (2) change the customer's buying habits, which will eventually cause a change in attitudes.

If a company attempts to change attitudes first, its advertising will stress the benefits of a product or service and may include a comparison with its competitors' product. For example, when one company advertises that its hamburgers are char-broiled, it is attempting to convince the consumer that its hamburgers taste better than the competitors' fried hamburgers. It is attempting to change consumers' attitude.

The alternative approach is to change the consumer's buying habits, which will eventually change attitudes. A company using this strategy often uses coupons to achieve its goal. If a coupon is offered for a new brand of soap, the customer may purchase the soap only because of the monetary savings. However, if coupons are offered several times, and the customer continues to purchase the product, he may come to prefer the new soap over the brand formerly used. The company's objective is achieved; it has obtained a new customer.

The above examples are not meant to be complete but only to illustrate how advertising goals affect the advertising method. Once the advertising goals have been clearly identified, they must be stated in specific and quanti-fiable terms. The advertising goal should not be simply "to generate new customers" but instead should be "to generate ten new customers per week during the first 6 months of 1986." Similarly, the goal should not be "to increase sales" but should be "to increase 1986 sales volume by 15 percent over 1985." Certainly a company may have more than one goal for its advertising. However, different ads may be needed for each goal.

Determining the Advertising Budget

In developing an advertising plan, the entrepreneur must determine the advertising budget. All too often, small businesses view advertising as a luxury—an expense that can be incurred if money is available and eliminated when money is tight. Almost all advertising experts, however, agree that advertising should be a fixed expense and should not vary according to general economic conditions or a company's temporary financial situation. An ongoing survey of businesses has shown that since 1958, companies that maintained advertising budgets at the same level (or increased them) during recessions found themselves in a better market position once the recession was over.[9] Those companies that did not decrease advertising during recessions were able to take customers away from the competition.

There are many methods of determining an advertising budget. Several of the more common methods are discussed below.[10]

Arbitrary Allocation of Advertising Dollars
Advertising that is not planned but is based on management intuition, emotions, or whim.

Arbitrary Allocation.   **Arbitrary allocation** is unplanned advertising. Arbitrary allocation means the budget involves management intuition, emotions, or whim. This type of advertising budget is therefore very likely to result from the personality traits, ego, or self-expression of the decision maker. Obviously, this is not the most effective method of determining a budget.

Percentage of Sales
A method of establishing an advertising budget based on a percentage of past or projected sales volume.

Percentage of Sales.   The **percentage of sales** method, one of the most common methods of determining an advertising budget, is based on a specific percentage of last year's sales, current sales, or projected sales. If a company has sales of $500,000 and generally uses 5 percent of sales, it would allocate $25,000 for advertising. This method is very easy to use. Its major disadvantage is that it may not have any relationship to advertising objectives. It may not provide enough money to accomplish objectives or it may provide too much. This is not an effective method of determining the budget.

Fixed Annual Sum
A method of establishing an advertising budget by allocating a specific dollar amount to each unit of product produced.

Fixed Annual Sum.   Some companies use the **fixed annual sum** method, particularly manufacturers of appliances. By this method, each unit produced is worth a specific dollar amount, which is allocated to the advertising budget. This allows the company to figure the cost of the advertising into the price of the product. This method is best used with products produced consistently throughout the year, because if sales of a particular item vary from season to season, this method may not provide the advertising funds needed to achieve stated objectives.

Competitive Parity
A method of establishing an advertising budget by spending the same amount as competitors.

Competitive Parity.   **Competitive parity** means that a company determines its advertising budget by spending the same amount as its competitors. Although this method ensures that an entrepreneur's level of advertising is equal to the competition's, it assumes that the competitor's level is also adequate for the entrepreneur's business. This is not necessarily true, particularly if the competition is well established and the entrepreneur's business is relatively new.

All You Can Afford
An advertising budget that treats advertising dollars as a luxury, increasing advertising when excess funds are available and decreasing advertising when cash is short.

All You Can Afford.   As stated at the beginning of this section, many businesses never develop an advertising budget. Many companies view advertising as a luxury, something increased or decreased at will, whenever funds are available or short. This is referred to as the **all you can afford** method.

---

[9]"Advertising Small Business," *Small Business Reporter,* 13, no. 8 (San Francisco: Bank of America, 1978), 3.
[10]Delozier and Woodside, *Marketing Management,* 451.

"Wilson, I want to discuss corporate image with you."

Source: Copyright Ford Button.

However, because this method results in sporadic, unplanned advertising, it is ineffective and probably produces little results even when advertising is implemented.

Objective and Task.   One of the most practical methods for a small business is the **objective and task** method. This method involves three steps:

1.   determine advertising objectives;

2.   determine how much and what type of advertising will be needed to reach the objectives;

Objective and Task
A method of determining an advertising budget by setting advertising objectives and then determining how much advertising will be needed to reach the objectives.

3.   determine the costs of the advertising and total the amounts. This is
     the necessary advertising budget.[11]

Obviously, this method is recommended over others since the amount is
based on stated objectives rather than on an arbitrary amount. This method is
based on the belief that advertising causes sales, while other methods treat
advertising as a result of sales. It also forces the entrepreneur to set specific
goals and to plan advertising. One major disadvantage is that the budget
developed may be too costly given the company's present cash flow. The
alternative then is to decrease the goals or borrow funds, hoping that the goals
and improved cash flow are realized. It is also difficult for a new entrepreneur
to determine how much advertising is needed to achieve the stated goals.
However, with practice, the entrepreneur can develop these skills.

The objective and task method may also prevent the entrepreneur from
spending too much. It may seem that if an unlimited advertising budget were
available, sales would skyrocket. This is not necessarily true. If an entrepreneur had the time and necessary funds, it would be possible to determine (as
many large companies do) an optimal advertising level. The entrepreneur will
find that after a certain level, more advertising brings only minimal increases
in sales. Past that optimal level, more advertising actually decreases profit.[12]

While it is necessary to determine objectives and allocate a specific dollar
amount to achieve each goal, it is also necessary to have an amount reserved
for unplanned, but necessary, advertising. For example, for many seasonal
businesses, advertising may be necessary at the end of a season if excess
inventory remains. The entrepreneur may also find that additional advertising
is needed to generate sales when sales are lower than expected. For these
reasons and a variety of others, unplanned advertising may be necessary. It is
generally recommended that approximately 10 to 15 percent of the total
amount spent on advertising each year be left unallocated.[13]

When to Advertise

One of the most critical factors in advertising is timing. If all other factors in
the advertising plan were properly coordinated, but the ads were not run at
the right time, the results might be very poor.

The first factor the entrepreneur must consider is whether or not demand
for the product is seasonal. If it is, there are three options:[14]

1.   Have advertising expenditures follow seasonal trends. This would
     mean that advertising is heaviest during peak seasons and drops off
     substantially in slow seasons.

---

[11]Delozier and Woodside, *Marketing Management,* 451.
[12]Delozier and Woodside, *Marketing Management,* 453.
[13]"Advertising Small Business," 10.
[14]Delozier and Woodside, *Marketing Management,* 448.

2. Have advertising expenditures run opposite the peak seasons. This would result in high expenditures in slower seasons and less advertising in peak seasons.

3. Hold advertising constant throughout the year. This would result in the same level of advertising no matter the demand for the product.

To determine which strategy is best, the entrepreneur must ask two questions:

1. Does the advertising have a carryover effect? That is, are consumers still influenced by the ads several weeks after the ad is run or are they likely to have forgotten it?

2. Do customers purchase the product by habit? In other words, is the product purchased without much thought by the customer?

If the answer to either question is yes, heavy advertising should come before the peak season and decline before the slow season. The greater the carryover effect, the longer the lead time. If a product is purchased by habit, more constant advertising should be carried out during the year;[15] however, increases would occur before the peak season. Since almost all businesses are seasonal, the entrepreneur should first chart the business's seasonality by determining the percentage of annual sales achieved each month. Then advertising can be coordinated with the seasonal fluctuations.

Three types of advertising can then be applied at various times throughout the year: maintenance, sales anticipation, and flight.[16] Maintenance advertising keeps consumers aware of the store throughout the year with a constant effort. Sales anticipation advertising is done just ahead of the peaks in sales. Flight advertising includes short bursts of advertising to fight slumps in sales during slow periods or to respond to a special situation such as a community event or increased activity by a competitor.

Determining when, and how often, to advertise also varies with the type of business. The entrepreneur should consider the following factors:

1. Amount of consumer effort required

2. Frequency of consumer visits

3. Trading area

Exhibit 13.3 identifies the frequency of advertising recommended for various types of retail outlets.

Where to Advertise

Print Media
Publications such as magazines, newspapers, flyers, posters, billboards.

The media consist of two major types, print and broadcast. **Print media** include magazines, newspapers, flyers, posters, billboards, and so forth.

---

[15]Delozier and Woodside, *Marketing Management,* 448.
[16]Johnson, *Advertising Today,* 127.

Exhibit   13.3   Factors Affecting Advertising Frequency

Trading Area	Frequency of Visit	Required Amount of Consumer Effort	Frequency of Advertising
In the neighborhood (short-trip stores) Drugstores Grocery stores Dry cleaners	One or more times per week	Little effort	Constant reminder advertising, announcements of specials
Along the way (drop-by stores) Bookstores Card shops Fast food	Weekly to monthly	Minor effort	Reminder advertising, announcements of specials
A distance away (special-trip stores) Florist Hardware store Shoe store	Weekly to several times per year	Medium effort	Frequent notice of specials
Remote (excursion store) Furniture store Jewelry store Photographic studio	Once per year	Maximum effort	Constant advertising, announcements of special prices and offerings

Source: From *Advertising Today* by J. Douglas Johnson. © 1978 by J. Douglas Johnson. Adapted and reprinted by permission of the publisher, Science Research Associates, Inc.

Broadcast Media
Radio and television.

Broadcast media include radio and television. In determining where to advertise, the entrepreneur must consider who the customers are and where they are located. The proper medium for one company may be totally ineffective for another. For example, small retailers whose customers include the general public within a 5-mile radius often use neighborhood or community papers. Large retailers may use both the metropolitan newspaper and neighborhood papers. A company that manufactures and/or sells auto repair equipment primarily to service station owners may advertise in trade magazines. Each medium is suited for certain businesses.

Selecting the best media is very difficult, and entrepreneurs often are not knowledgeable enough about marketing techniques to make the proper decision. Each type of medium should be evaluated on the following five points:[17]

1.   Reach: How many people are exposed to the advertising?

2.   Frequency: How often is the medium available to the public?

3.   Delivery: Where is the advertising message received?

---

[17]Johnson, *Advertising Today,* 140.

4. Selectivity: Who receives the message?

5. Efficiency: How much does it cost to use?

The information below identifies possible media and the advantages and disadvantages of each based on the above criteria.

Newspapers.   Newspapers are a favorite medium for many small businesses, particularly retailers.

Reach.   Depending on the type of newspaper, the reach may include only local residents or may cover the metropolitan area. The entrepreneur should therefore determine the business's trading area and, if she chooses newspaper advertising, she must then decide to use a local paper or a metropolitan paper.

Frequency.   Although frequency may vary from daily to weekly, one of the advantages of newspaper advertising is its frequency and adaptability to changes. Entrepreneurs can advertise often yet change ads on short notice.

Delivery.   Newspaper advertising may be seen at home, at work, while riding to work on a bus, and elsewhere. Where the message is received varies with the type of newspaper and the reader.

Selectivity.   One of the disadvantages of most newspapers is the lack of selectivity. Except for a few papers, most are aimed at the general population, at all demographic levels. Thus, selectivity is usually minimal.

Efficiency.   Newspapers generally offer low-cost advertising to small businesses. Because of the number of people who see a newspaper ad and the relatively low cost, papers are often one of the most efficient advertising media for small businesses.

In general, newspapers have excellent reach, great flexibility, low cost, and can provide an opportunity for written communication as well as graphics. Their disadvantages, however, include lack of selectivity, the possibility of the ad getting "lost" among all of the others, and short life, since most newspapers are quickly discarded.

Radio.   Radio advertising is best suited for businesses catering to identifiable groups, such as teens, commuters, or housewives.[18] The Radio Advertising Bureau publishes a wide variety of data on radio advertising that may benefit the entrepreneur considering this advertising medium. In addition, each radio station maintains data on its listeners that help the entrepreneur determine which station is most appropriate. We again consider the five criteria.

Reach.   Depending on the radio station, the reach may be very localized, or, particularly with AM stations, it may cover several states.

---

[18]"Advertising Small Business," 8.

Frequency.   Radio advertising is available at any time and, on many stations, is available 24 hours per day. Because the number of listeners varies throughout the day, costs will change also.

Delivery.   Radio advertising may be heard in a car, at home, or at work, depending on the time of day. Over 98 percent of U.S. homes have at least one radio and 95 percent of cars have radios.[19]

Selectivity.   Excellent selectivity is one of the advantages of radio advertising. Because each station appeals to a specific segment of the market, the advertising is not wasted on the wrong market.

Efficiency.   For many businesses, radio advertising is efficient because it reaches a large number of listeners with specific demographic characteristics many times per day.

In general, radio advertising may be advantageous because of its large reach, specific target markets, and adaptability to changes on short notice. However, as with newspaper ads, radio messages are sometimes "lost" if the listener is preoccupied with other activities. To be effective, short messages must be repeated constantly.

Television.   It is often thought that television is not practical for small business owners owing to its high costs and wide coverage. However, local advertising is becoming more common and now accounts for approximately 25 percent of all television advertising.[20]

Reach.   Television advertising may be aimed at a metropolitan area or the entire nation. Its reach is one of its major advantages.

Frequency.   As with radio advertising, the availability exists 24 hours per day. As with radio listenership, the number of viewers varies throughout the day, resulting in varying rates.

Delivery.   The delivery of television advertising is as extensive as radio. Approximately 97 percent of homes have a television set and 43 percent have more than one set. Most television viewing is done at home.

Selectivity.   One of the major disadvantages of television is its lack of selectivity. Television is a mass medium and, therefore, reaches people at all demographic levels. Though viewers vary with program type, selectivity is minimal.

Efficiency.   Television advertising is efficient if a company needs to advertise to a large number of people with varied demographic characteristics in a wide geographical area. It is not efficient if the company wishes to achieve selectivity in a small geographical area.

[19]Johnson, *Advertising Today*, 192.
[20]Johnson, *Advertising Today*, 209.

Illustration Capsule   13.1

Small Businesses Line up for Cable Advertising

When cable television became available as an advertising medium, it provided a low-cost method for many small businesses to reach a large number of potential customers. Prices for commercials were competitive with radio air time and newspaper space, yet businesses could choose specialized programming to reach target audiences. Many small businesses were pleased with the results, citing the number of customers who mentioned the advertising. At one point, Tulsa cable had a waiting list of small businesses that wanted to pay $1,000 a month to add their listing to the system's program directory. The network ran 3 hours of programming at a time, with ads rotating every 3 minutes.

Source: Sarah Delano, ''Why Bargain Prices Lure Cable Advertisers,'' *Inc.*, May 1983, 177–180.

Television advertising is advantageous because of its reach, frequency, and potential for visual impact. Its major disadvantages include lack of selectivity, high costs, short life of each ad, and the possibility of the ad being ''tuned out'' by a viewer.

Magazines.   Local magazines are an excellent advertising medium for restaurants, mail order businesses, specialty shops, and similar businesses. National magazines, like television, are best for companies that need to reach a large audience. Trade magazines are excellent for advertising to industry.

Reach.   Magazines may be limited to a metropolitan area or may be nationwide. Even for national magazines, though, ''zoned editions'' are sometimes available, which allow advertising to be limited only to copies delivered within a certain area.

Frequency.   Magazines may be published weekly, monthly, quarterly; therefore, frequency varies widely.

Delivery.   Magazines may be read at home, at the office, or while waiting for appointments at other businesses (doctors, beauty salons).

Selectivity.   Magazines have excellent selectivity because each magazine is aimed at a specific target market. Special magazines reach housewives, farmers, business executives, mothers of infants, and so forth. In addition, trade magazines reach electronics engineers, supermarket owners, mechanics, and other groups.

Efficiency.   Magazines are efficient for businesses that need to reach a large number of people in a specified target market. They are not efficient for businesses with a very small trading area.

The advantages of magazines include selectivity and long life for each ad. Many magazines are viewed several times by each reader and, in addition, may be given to friends and relatives to read. Disadvantages include a high cost even for many local magazines, a long lead time necessary for submitting the ad for printing, and the possibility of the ad getting "lost" among all of the other ads.

Direct Mail.   Direct mail is an excellent advertising medium for many businesses, particularly those that use coupons or catalogs. It is used by businesses that sell to the general public as well as those that sell to industry.

Reach.   The ability of the entrepreneur to control the reach of a direct mail campaign is one of this medium's major advantages. The reach can be limited or expanded to any number of prospective customers.

Frequency.   As with the reach, the entrepreneur can also control the frequency of the mailings. Mailings can be as often or as seldom as desired.

Delivery.   Delivery to the final consumer is usually to the home; delivery to industrial companies is to the place of business.

Selectivity.   Selectivity is also controlled by the entrepreneur. Mailing lists can be obtained for special target markets, or mailings can be made to every home or business within a certain radius. Specialized mailing lists can be purchased from many direct mail companies.

Efficiency.   Direct mail can reach many people or a special group, but costs vary widely. The costs for mailing lists are quite high, though this must be seen as an investment that will be used many times. Costs also vary greatly with the quality and weight of the information mailed.

In general, the advantages of direct mail include selectivity and reach controlled by the entrepreneur, quick results, and the ability of the entrepreneur to tailor messages to specific customers. Disadvantages include the high number of mailers discarded without being read, a high cost per thousand compared with other media, and the tendency of mailing lists to become outdated and inaccurate.

Directories.   Directories are lists of information about companies or people. Directories include the Yellow Pages, directories of minority-owned businesses, directories of suppliers of products needed by certain industries, and so on. The purpose of a directory is to match a buyer and a seller of a specific product or service. Directories are an excellent medium for companies that provide a service, for retailers of brand name items, or for specialty retailers.

Reach.   As with direct mail, the reach of a directory is controlled by the advertiser. It may cover a specific geographical area or specific types of customers.

Frequency.   Frequency is also controlled by the advertiser, although most directories are printed annually or semiannually.

Delivery.   Delivery may be to the homes of the general public, to businesses, or to both.

Selectivity.   Selectivity is controlled by the advertiser. Directories can be sent to the general public (for example, the Yellow Pages) or to specific customers (for example, purchasing agents in chemical manufacturing plants).

Efficiency.   Efficiency of directories is excellent for some businesses, such as pest control firms or locksmiths. For services such as these, Yellow Pages advertising is almost essential for a new business that needs to establish clientele. For other businesses, though, directory advertising is expensive and ineffective.

A major advantage of directories is that a directory is used by a shopper when actively seeking a specific type of business. If someone needs an air conditioner repaired, a company's listing in the Yellow Pages is extremely important. Also, directories have long lives and may often be used for more than a year. Disadvantages include infrequent publication dates, lack of flexibility for ad designs, and a probability of the ad getting "lost" among all the others.

Billboards and Transit Advertising.   Billboard advertising is an excellent form of advertising for amusement parks, tourist businesses, or brand name retailers. Though many people think billboard advertising is only for major corporations, this medium is often used by entrepreneurs whose businesses cater to tourists, such as restaurants, service stations, and tourist attractions (caves, museums, souvenir shops). Transit advertising is advertising on buses or other methods of public transportation.

Reach.   Reach may include an entire metropolitan area or only local residents, depending on the street on which the billboard is located or the route traveled by the vehicle that carries transit advertising.

Frequency.   Frequency is usually measured by the number of cars coming into contact with the billboard or transit ad; frequency is usually very high.

Delivery.   Delivery is to drivers or passengers in cars; the ad must therefore have short messages that can be read quickly.

Selectivity.   Selectivity is poor, as the ad reaches all drivers along a street, many of whom are not potential customers.

Efficiency.   Billboards are efficient for the specific types of businesses previously mentioned but are not cost-effective for companies with a specialized audience or a small trading area. Transit advertising is most cost-efficient for companies along transit routes, particularly those appealing to wage earners.[21]

Advantages of billboards include high reach and frequency, which result in a very low cost per thousand customers reached. Creative billboards capture customers' attention at a time when they are not preoccupied with many other activities. Unfortunately, for both billboards and transit advertising, the message must be extremely short. In addition, billboard sizes are restricted, and many efforts have been made to limit billboard advertising to prevent a "cluttered" look.

Trade Shows.   Trade shows are a form of advertising used by manufacturers and wholesalers. Trade shows are conventions at which companies set up booths to display and sell their products. Trade shows are held in many industries and, therefore, cater to specific customers.

Reach.   The reach of trade shows varies greatly. Though some are nationally known within the industry and attended by potential customers from all over the nation, some are local and have fewer participants and spectators.

Frequency.   Trade shows within an industry are held several times throughout the year. The entrepreneur must determine which shows will be most beneficial.

Delivery.   Delivery is always at a specified location, often convention centers or similar facilities.

Selectivity.   Selectivity is excellent since admittance to many shows is limited to those who own related businesses and are, therefore, potential customers.

Efficiency.   Efficiency varies greatly among shows. While some shows reach a large number of potential customers and produce excellent results, others bring no sales and are a waste of time, effort, and money.

Trade shows are essential for many businesses that need to reach new customers. Excellent selectivity is a major advantage. The high cost to enter trade shows, however, along with travel and lodging costs, often make trade shows an expensive advertising method for small businesses.

The Message

AIDA Concept
A communication model for advertising messages emphasizing attention, interest, desire, and action.

The advertising message must be specifically tailored to the target audience if it is to be effective. When designing the message, the entrepreneur should follow a communication model often referred to as the **AIDA concept** — an

---

[21]"Advertising Small Business," 8.

abbreviation for getting *attention,* holding *interest,* creating *desire,* and resulting in *action.*[22]

Consumers are constantly surrounded by advertising. For an ad to be effective, it must get customers' attention away from other, distracting elements. This is often done with pictures in print media, or with the words ''free'' or ''sale.'' Once the ad has the customers' attention, it must hold it long enough to ensure that the whole ad is read or heard. This is accomplished by proper wording, proper layout, and other factors. The ad must then arouse desire by telling consumers why they should buy the product. Finally, the ad must initiate action by the customer by appealing to specific needs.

Company image must also be considered when developing the message. If the entrepreneur does not formally attempt to develop an image, customers will have a ''perceived image'' of the company that may be different than what the entrepreneur desires. Business owners often fail to realize that ads convey an image even if image development was not the ads' purpose. For example, one retail clothing store carried high-quality merchandise and prided itself on the excellence of the lines it stocked. However, its advertisements always stressed sale items. The owner was shocked to find that many consumers viewed the outlet as a discount store.[23] Changes in the ads remedied this situation. The company image must always be considered when ads are designed. A professional advertising agency may be needed to accomplish the desired effect.

Measuring Results

No advertising plan is complete without measuring results. If the results of the advertising plan are not determined, it is impossible to tell if the advertising expenditures were worthwhile.

There are many methods for measuring advertising results. A first step is to compare the results with stated goals. If the advertising objective was to increase sales by 15 percent over last year's sales, the sales volume should be compared. If the advertising was designed primarily to increase store traffic, then it would be necessary to monitor the number of customers entering the store. Often the number of redeemed coupons is used to determine a particular ad's effectiveness, or a record may be kept of phone inquiries concerning an ad.

No matter what method is used to measure results, it is an essential, but often neglected, part of any advertising plan. The entrepreneur must realize that trial and error may be necessary to establish the best plan. Certain media will be effective while others may not be effective at all. The entrepreneur

---

[22]E. Jerome McCarthy, *Essentials of Marketing,* (Homewood, Ill.: Richard D. Irwin, Inc., 1979), 279.

[23]''Advertising Small Business,'' 10.

who measures results of each ad can eliminate ineffective advertising and increase what works best. An efficient advertising plan will result, and cash will not be wasted.

Cooperative Advertising

Cooperative Advertising
An arrangement in which two or more businesses share in the cost of an ad.

In **cooperative advertising,** two or more businesses share in the cost of an ad. In the past it usually referred to an arrangement between a manufacturer and a retailer. The retailer often features the manufacturer's product in an ad for the retail outlet, and the cost is shared by both businesses.

Manufacturers generally provide advertising funds based on how much inventory the retailer purchases. Generally, the manufacturer allows 1 to 5 percent of purchases for advertising. For example, if a business purchased $200,000 in inventory from the manufacturer in a year and the manufacturer provided a 3 percent allowance for ads, the retailer would receive a $6,000 credit for cooperative advertising.

More creative cooperative advertising has been developed in recent years that features several businesses but not always a manufacturer-retailer arrangement. For example, small retailers often find it advantageous to share advertising costs with other retailers (see Illustration Capsule 13.2). Shared advertising costs allow the small business to feature larger or more frequent ads than could normally be afforded. Information concerning past effectiveness can be considered, and ideas on the most effective layout examined. The results obtained are often greater than if each small retailer advertised separately.

Although no one knows exactly how much is available in cooperative funds, estimates by such media trade associations as the Newspaper Advertising Bureau and the Radio Advertising Bureau range from $6 billion to $8 billion; of that, they say at least $2.5 to $3 billion goes unused.[24] Co-op advertising can be a valuable promotional tool for a small business, and substantial funds are available. Even more funds would be available if small businesses would develop co-op advertising plans of their own. Every entrepreneur should seriously consider this opportunity when developing a promotional plan in order to reduce advertising costs and increase effectiveness.

Public Relations and Publicity

. . . .

Public relations and/or publicity is a form of advertising the entrepreneur must not overlook. While publicity is usually obtained free of charge, public relations activities may have a slight cost. However, if a fee is involved, it is not

---

[24]Sarah Delano, "How to Get a Fix on Free Ad Dollars," *Inc.,* July 1983, 94.

Illustration Capsule   13.2

Creative Cooperative Advertising

One innovative user of co-op funds is retailer Jack Mitchell, president of Ed Mitchell Inc., a family-owned retail clothing store in Westport, Connecticut. When he recently ran a magazine ad for Lord Jeff sweaters, Mitchell photographed his brother's family wearing the manufacturer's sweaters in front of a local museum. Behind the group, he parked a Ferrari from Bob Sharp Motors in nearby Danbury. Not only did the setting attract attention, but by including the Ferrari, Mitchell also reduced his costs by sharing the media bill with Bob Sharp and Lord Jeff.

Source: Sarah Delano, "How to Get a Fix on Free Ad Dollars," *Inc.*, July 1983, 94.

a direct fee for advertising but is indirectly related to the activity. The following activities are examples:

- sponsorship of local sports teams
- articles in local papers concerning the opening of the business, a new product offered, an award received
- membership in organizations such as Rotary Clubs, Lions Clubs, industry associations
- organizing a Junior Achievement group
- speaking before local community groups
- donations to charitable organizations
- appearance on local TV shows

The entrepreneur should take advantage of publicity as often as possible. When the business first opens, news stories of the grand opening should be written and sent to all newspapers. News stories can also be submitted when new product lines are added, if the company is involved in any charitable activities, or when anything newsworthy occurs.

The publicity's impact obviously will be affected by the media in which it appears. The impact should not be underestimated. For example, the *Readers Digest* published an article about the Tracer Company of America, a company that locates unclaimed bank accounts; as a result of the article the company received over 438,000 letters in 5 months.

Publicity is an excellent method for increasing awareness of a company owing to three special advantages. First, consumers regard news articles as being more truthful than regular advertising. The consumer is more likely to

Illustration Capsule   13.3

Publicity Pays

When the Mad Anthonys, a group of business and professional people in Fort Wayne, Indiana, asked Instant Copy of Indiana Inc. for $750 to help sponsor the Hoosier Celebrities Golf Tournament, Jack Caffray said no. Caffray, president of the $3.5 million printing company with ten stores in northern Indiana, had a better idea. He offered a $10,000 prize to any golfer who hit a hole in one on the ninth hole. In the event of the perfect shot, $5,000 would go to the golfer and $5,000 to the three local hospitals that the event supported.

Caffray then paid $500 for a premium from Lloyd's of London to insure himself against a potential $10,000 loss. Thus, Caffray's total expenses were $250 less than if he had been a regular sponsor. The prize was announced repeatedly by the local newspapers, television stations, and radio stations, which treated the event and the prize as news. On the day of the tournament, a sign depicting a $10,000 check was erected behind the ninth hole, a target for the television cameras during the event. The biggest winner of the day was Jack Caffray, who received a tremendous amount of publicity despite the fact that no one won the prize.

Source: Sarah Delano, "Give and You Shall Receive," *Inc.*, February 1983, 128.

believe the information presented. Second, the consumer is caught off guard and is not as defensive as if approached by a salesperson or presented with an advertisement. Finally, the publicity can present the product or company in a very favorable manner.[25]

Sales Promotion

Sales promotion includes all other promotional efforts that cannot be classified as advertising, personal selling, or publicity. These include consumer promotions, trade promotions, and sales force promotions. Consumer promotions

---

[25]Philip Kotler, *Marketing Management*, (Englewood Cliffs, N.J.: Prentice-Hall, Inc., 1972), 649.

Small Business Success   13

Tindol Services Inc.

Among his other successful ventures, Rufus "Red" Tindol, president of Tindol Services Inc. of Atlanta, Georgia, had a commercial that won an award in the 1982 U.S. Television Commercials Festival. The commercial for Tindol's pest control firm starts with footage of an extravagant royal funeral. The accompanying message says, "The only real difference between having some big company kill your termites and having Tindol kill your termites is how expensive the funeral is going to be."

Tindol has successfully launched two pest control firms. The first he sold to Orkin, where he then worked for 20 years. His second firm was started in 1967 with a $20,000 investment and now employs over 265 people; it reported sales of $3.3 million in 1984.

Tindol, a graduate of the Georgia Institute of Technology, began his pest control career in the South Pacific while controlling malaria-carrying mosquitos for the Army. He believes that small service firms enjoy the advantage of providing customers personal attention.

Source: America At Work (Washington, D.C.: Small Business Administration, 1985), 10.

include free samples, coupons, demonstrations, contests, rebate offers, and so forth. Examples of trade promotions include buying allowances, displays manufacturers give to retailers to use in the retail outlet, or dealer-listed promotions, in which an advertisement that carries a selling message also announces retailers who carry the product. Sales force promotions include bonuses, sales contests, and other incentives.

Sales promotions should be considered when developing the promotional budget. It is not uncommon for sales promotion to comprise 20 to 35 percent of a company's overall promotional budget. Therefore, if the entrepreneur does not initially plan these activities along with other advertising and personal selling costs, the amount spent on promotion will not be properly coordinated to obtain the desired results.

The results from sales promotion efforts are often more measurable and usually can be obtained more quickly than results of advertising. However, as with all other promotional efforts, the effect of each sales promotion technique should be measured to eliminate ineffective methods.

Exhibit   13.4   Typical "Advertising Calendar" for November 1985
Women's Apparel Store

Sunday	Monday	Tuesday	Wednesday	Thursday	Friday	Saturday
					1 Direct mailer to customers on mailing list featuring new arrivals for holidays. Cost—$1,200	2
3	4	5	6	7	8	9
10	11	12 Local paper Cost—$150 Theme—holiday fashions	13	14	15	16
17	18	19 Local paper— Cost—$150 Theme—holiday fashions and fashion show on 29th	20	21	22	23
24	25	26 Local paper Cost—$150 Theme—holiday fashion show on 29th	27	28 Thanksgiving	29 Fashion show—featuring holiday fashions— Cost—$100	30

The Promotional Plan

Proper management of any business function requires a definite plan rather than random decision making. Promotional decisions are no exception, although this is an area small businesses often neglect.

One of the major mistakes small business owners make is that their promotional efforts are haphazard. Often, decisions to advertise are influenced mostly by sales calls of media personnel. The entrepreneur decides to advertise in the newspaper for a few weeks primarily because a salesperson from the paper made an excellent sales presentation. A few months later, someone selling radio advertising calls, and the entrepreneur decides to try radio advertising for a few weeks. If no results are obtained, the entrepreneur decides to try newspaper advertising again. Similarly, special sales are often run because sales are low, and contests for salespersons are initiated because the results from personal selling efforts are poor. Thus, instead of a properly planned effort, the company has sporadic promotion and results are poor. A promotional plan is also necessary because it will affect the number of employees needed, the amount of inventory to be ordered, the amount of financing needed, and so forth. A well-developed promotional plan should be established to ensure that other areas of the business will be properly coordinated with the sales volume generated.

One of the best ways for an entrepreneur to develop a promotional plan is to create a promotional calendar.[26] This includes all details of proposed promotion for the coming year, including media, cost, purpose, and message. This enables the entrepreneur to have a "picture" of the plan and provides information for reference. A sample calendar is shown in Exhibit 13.4.

K E Y Objectives Reviewed

1. The promotional mix of a company includes personal selling, mass selling or advertising, publicity, and sales promotion.

2. Personal selling is often a necessary part of the promotional plan, but the type of selling effort varies among industries.

3. Mass selling, or advertising, cannot be done effectively without proper consideration of all the elements in an advertising plan.

4. Publicity is a form of promotion free to the company, whereas public relations activities may have a small cost.

5. Sales promotion is a term describing all promotional efforts that cannot be classified as personal selling, advertising, or publicity.

6. Proper planning for all elements of the promotional mix is essential to achieve the desired results.

[26]"Advertising Small Business," 11.

Discussion Questions

1. Suppose you own an auto repair shop. Give examples of cooperative advertising that could be arranged for your shop. Give examples of free publicity.

2. Suppose you own a retail outlet that sells electronic products, including video cassette recorders, stereos, home computers, and the like. Develop the theme (message) for an ad aimed at ''the customer's perceived benefits'' and how your product can fulfill the customer's ''hopes and dreams.''

3. Identify the four elements of the marketing mix and provide an example of each from companies with which you are familiar.

4. What advertising medium is best for a retailer of women's clothing if there is only one outlet? Suppose after several years, the company has three outlets. Does this change the type of media to be used? If so, how?

5. Suppose you own a pest control business and are developing an advertising plan for next year. If your advertising goal is to increase sales by 10 percent over the last year's sales volume, how would you determine how much advertising will be needed to accomplish this?

6. It is often said that the best salesperson is not necessarily the best sales manager. Compare the skills needed for each job. How are they similar? Different?

7. Suppose you owned a small firm that sold large equipment to businesses. In addition to your direct sales force, you decided to advertise the company and its products to your customers. What method of advertising would you use? What media?

8. Why do you think many entrepreneurs fail to develop a promotional plan? Why is a plan necessary to achieve results?

9. Why are results from sales promotions often easier to measure than results of advertising or publicity?

CHAPTER 14

Human Resources Management

Source: Courtesy of Honeywell Inc.

K   E   Y   Objectives

1. To explain how new employees are selected.

2. To describe the different ways new employees are trained.

3. To identify and describe the various leadership styles the entrepreneur may use in directing employees.

4. To acquaint the reader with the area of motivation theory.

5. To explain the roles of performance appraisal, rewards, and discipline in managing the firm's human resources.

6. To discuss how the law affects personnel administration in small business.

As a business prospers, the amount of work performed within it grows. Eventually the business will reach the point where the founder is unable to perform all of the work. This point is critical because it means hiring, training, directing, and motivating other people. These functions present difficulties with which the entrepreneur often is not equipped to deal. This inability can severely restrict a firm's future. Like any resource, the human resources of an organization must be managed effectively.

Hiring

The first step in the hiring process is determining what the organization needs done. Put another way, the small business manager must design the job. A job is a collection of tasks that a single employee may perform to produce some product or service. To perform these tasks, a person must have certain skills, knowledge, and abilities. The hiring process requires that these needed skills, knowledge, and abilities be identified, and that a means be developed for assessing the degree to which job candidates possess them.

Job Analysis

Job Analysis
A process for determining a job's critical components for purposes of selecting, training, and rewarding personnel.

Job Description
A document that lists the major responsibilities and tasks of the job.

Job Specification
A document listing the knowledge, skills, abilities, and personal characteristics a job holder must possess to perform effectively.

Observation-Based Techniques
A means of collecting information for job analysis consisting of observing behavior of the individual performing the job.

Interviewing
A job analysis technique in which job incumbents are asked questions concerning the job's requirements.

Critical Incidents Technique
A means of collecting information for job analysis consisting of identifying those behaviors particularly important for the job.

Job analysis is the process of determining a job's critical components for purposes of selecting, training, and rewarding personnel. Personnel management rests on effective job analysis. For example, conducting performance appraisals without clearly understanding the job being performed is likely to be futile. The same may be said of employee selection, compensation, and assignments.

Job analysis yields two types of information, **job description** or **job specification.** A job description gives the job's major responsibilities and tasks. It is a task-oriented approach. The job specification approach, on the other hand, focuses on the individual, specifying the knowledge, skills, and abilities the job holder must have to perform effectively.

A variety of techniques are available for job analysis. Most of these techniques rely on the position holder as a source and so cannot be used in analyzing new jobs. **Observation-based techniques** collect information by observing behavior. These techniques are most useful for jobs that consist of manual operations with a short cycle. **Interviewing** uses the position holder as an information source on the nature of the job. This approach can involve interviews conducted individually or in a group. The **critical incidents technique** identifies those behaviors that are particularly important to the position holder's success. By the structured questionnaire method, workers check or rate facets of their job from an extensive listing of tasks.

For jobs that do not yet exist, analysis is more difficult. It is necessary to infer what personal characteristics the new job is likely to require. The small business operator, after determining the need for a new job, must identify its component tasks and behaviors to specify the skill, knowledge, and ability necessary to carry it out.

Recruiting

Once she has established the job requirements, the manager must contact the people who might become acceptable employees. This contact can be made in a variety of ways; some of the more important follow.

Private Employment Offices.   There are approximately 10,000 private employment agencies in the United States, through which some 2½ million people find jobs each year. In most cases the employee pays the agency's fee, which usually ranges between 10 and 30 percent of the first-year salary. Some agencies specialize, dealing only with certain occupations or industries; others accept anyone. Many small businesses rely on private employment agencies because they typically have a wide range of contacts and can screen candidates effectively.

Unique Business   14.1

Ompa, pa, Profits

Donna Altieri, founder and owner of Altieri BrassPacs, showed the entrepreneurial trait of responding to opportunity as she started her firm. She said it all happened during "one of those wonderful nights drinking with musicians." One member of the group complained about the difficulty of getting about with a tuba as a traveling companion. He felt that anything that would allow him to carry the instrument on his back would lighten his load, so Altieri set to work the next day designing and sewing a backpack. Since then, she started her company and developed a line that includes packs for every standard instrument in an orchestra. The water-resistant nylon bags sell for $55 to $225 and are custom-made. She reports making a fluorescent orange bag, with gun rack attached, for a Tennessee tuba player.

Source: Inc., December 1984, 25.

United States Employment and Training Service (USETS)
A U.S. Department of Labor agency involved in testing, screening, and placing job applicants.

Public Employment Offices. The **United States Employment and Training Service (USETS),** part of the U.S. Department of Labor, is part of a nationwide system of approximately 2,400 employment offices that are run by states but supported by federal funds. These offices are used in the administration of unemployment compensation programs and therefore have a captive population, because anyone wishing to collect benefits must register with them. Because they are government funded, they are not forced to charge for their services. These offices have been criticized as being more intent on placing Vietnam veterans, minorities, and the handicapped than on serving employers. This complaint notwithstanding, the USETS system provides an effective, no-cost means of testing and screening job applicants.

Educational Institutions. Area high schools, trade schools, and colleges and universities provide candidates who have a wide variety of skills. Those institutions are also excellent sources for part-time employees. Most of these schools have placement offices that provide screening and matching services.

Walk-ins and Write-ins. Many individuals provide unsolicited applications, and although the right person seldom comes along at just the right time to suit the needs of a small business, these are no-cost prospects and should not be discouraged from showing their interest in the company.

Employee Referrals. This is a method for locating candidates that many employers favor. Some companies pay "bounties" to employees for referring

Illustration Capsule   14.1

Finding That Just-Right Employee

According to Roy A. Smith of Associated Packaging in Goodlettsville, Tennessee, the $20,000 to $40,000 his company invests in an employee during the first year makes it important to choose wisely in deciding whom to hire. Its selection methods include a telephone screening of candidates referred to the company by the local employment office or technical schools. Typically, of 50 applicants, 10 will be screened by phone and perhaps 3 invited to the company for an interview, in which two company managers will assess their attitudes and technical skills. Finally, the company checks the background of the winning candidate through contacts with former instructors and an examination of grades and other background factors.

The results of a study conducted by Opinion Research Corporation underscore the importance of a thorough background check. Approximately one-quarter of the companies surveyed reported hiring people whose resumes turned out to be inaccurate. These background investigations, along with carefully planned interviews, provide a company with reasonable assurance of being able to hire the right person for the job.

Source: Harry Bacas, "How Companies Avoid Mistakes in Hiring," *Nation's Business*, June 1985, 34–36.

candidates. Relying on this source of job candidates tends to result in a work force with less diversity than one using other sources. Companies covered by the Civil Rights Act of 1964 and Equal Employment Opportunity Act of 1972 and that have a work force in which a protected class is underrepresented, may find employee referrals an unacceptable source of candidates because this method perpetuates the underrepresentation.

Help-Wanted Ads.   This method typically generates a large number of responses, particularly if the ad is written in a nonrestrictive way. Consequently, care must be taken in composing the ad to limit the screening needed in processing the responses. Ideally, the ad should give the clearest possible description of the job to encourage the qualified and discourage the unqualified from responding.

Selection

After the manager has located the candidates, he must choose from among them. The evaluation of applicants is conducted using a number of techniques.

Preliminary Screening.   This is a review of the application blank completed by the candidate. A typical application blank requires that previous training and experience and references be listed. Many blanks also require information concerning military service and medical history. The information provided on the application should provide some indication of future job success. Candidates who do not have the necessary training or experience can be easily screened out at this point. Studies of the application blank as a prediction of job performance have indicated that it is a very useful screening device.[1]

Interviewing.   Interviews are conducted to gather information about the applicant's abilities and level of motivation. In addition, interviews are conducted to determine how the candidate will "fit into" the company. Although the interview is part of the selection process of almost all companies, there is considerable doubt of its validity as a predictor of job success. It has been characterized as a "costly, inefficient and usually invalid procedure,"[2] which "probably contributes little in the way of validity to the selection decision."[3]

Despite its shortcomings, interviewing is perhaps the most widely used selection technique in small business. Most employers feel uneasy about hiring without having talked to candidates. Consequently, almost all firms interview. Exhibit 14.1 gives some suggestions on using interviews in the selection process.

Testing.   For organizations governed by Title VII of the Civil Rights Act, the use of employee selection testing poses considerable risk. Because the act prohibits discrimination in employment because of race, color, religion, sex, or national origin, any test that has an adverse impact on any of the protected applicant groups must be a valid predictor of job performance if it is to be used. Establishing a test's validity can be difficult and costly. The last section of this chapter discusses in greater detail the legal restrictions on personnel management.

Performance Tests
Tests that measure what the candidate can already do.

Five types of tests are used for employee selection: (1) performance; (2) aptitude; (3) interest; (4) personality; and (5) intelligence. **Performance tests**

---

[1]Herbert G. Henneman, Donald P. Schwab, John A. Fossum, and Lee D. Dyer, *Personnel/Human Resource Management* (Homewood, Ill.: Richard D. Irwin, 1980), 226–277.
[2]M. D. Dunnette and B. H. Bass, "Behavioral Scientists and Personnel Management," *Industrial Relations* 2 (1963): 117.
[3]Robert E. Carlson, Paul W. Thayer, Eugene C. Mayfield, and Donald A. Peterson, "Improvement in the Selection Interview," *Personnel Journal*, April 1971, 268.

Exhibit   14.1   Guidelines on Effective Use of Interviewing in the Employment Interview

1. Structured interviews (those with predetermined questions) should be used. The "tell me about yourself" format often leads to a great deal of time spent on irrelevant information, with important issues left out of the discussion.

2. Quick decisions should be avoided. There is a strong tendency for interviewers to make a quick decision (often within 2 to 3 minutes) and spend the rest of the interview searching for supporting evidence.

3. Put aside the tendency to rate the applicant by a single trait. This is called the "halo effect," and leads to a single factor dominating the evaluation. Someone with bad grooming may be rated negatively in all respects. Someone who has participated in intercollegiate athletics, on the other hand, may be given a positive rating beyond what is deserved.

4. Do not dwell on negative information. Many interviewers give more weight to negative information than to positive.

5. Make adequate preparations for the interview. The interview will only be as useful as the interviewer's questions. Good questions take into account the position's requirements.

6. To avoid possible legal complications, the following should not be included:
   A. Inquiries that will reveal the national, ethnic, or racial origin of the applicant.
   B. Questions concerning marital status, pregnancy, future childbearing plans, or number and age of children.
   C. Questions about arrest record, unless this information is job related.

measure what the candidate can already do. These are either a work-sample test (a typist actually typing a letter; a fork-lift driver moving some pallets) or oral or written questions about the job.

Aptitude Tests
Tests measuring the applicant's ability to learn the job if given the necessary training.

Interest Tests
Tests measuring the degree of interest an individual has in a particular type of task.

Aptitude tests measure the applicant's ability to learn the job if given the necessary training. Mechanical aptitude can be measured and is useful in screening candidates for positions such as mechanical trade apprenticeships.

Interest tests are used with the assumption that people are more likely to succeed at those tasks in which they have an interest than those in which they express none. The applicant is asked questions such as, "Would you rather repair a motorcycle, practice putting on make-up, or hike through the woods?" The major shortcoming of this type of test is that the questions are often transparent, so the appropriate response is easily identified.

Personality Tests
Tests that assess traits
that appear important for
success on the job.

Professionals disagree about the usefulness of **personality tests** as a selection technique. Those attacking the tests have strong reservations on whether we can and should measure personalities. The defenders point out that personality is critical to success for some jobs and that sophisticated tests have been developed that permit reliable measurement of many traits.

Intelligence Tests
Tests that measure the
intellectual abilities of the
job applicant.

The **intelligence test** was once a standard part of the selection process of almost all companies. In recent years, however, a number of concerns have been raised about its use. Many jobs present very little intellectual challenge; for these jobs a high level of intelligence is not only unnecessary, it may be detrimental. Another criticism is that intelligence tests are "culture bound," in that they are written by and for "WASP" males, and therefore discriminate unfairly against other groups.

Few successful businesses can rely solely on the founder's efforts. Consequently, how a small business adds or replaces an employee is extremely important. We have just examined the hiring process; we will now turn our attention to managing the people who are members of the company. We will consider first training, followed by directing and motivating. Each of the three must be handled effectively if the business is to get the best out of the people it hires.

Training

It may be useful to distinguish the training needs of new employees from those of the rest of the work force. The first two types of training, though not strictly limited to new employees, are traditionally provided on entry into the company.

Orientation

The early days of employment can be rather difficult, as demonstrated by the fact that nearly 60 percent of employees who quit do so during their first 10 days. Shaping the employees' early impression of the company is important. Orientation sessions should do that by covering topics such as:

- the company's history and philosophy
- who's who in the organization
- who's who in the department and how its efforts fit in with those of the company
- personnel rules and regulations (pay, fringe benefits, attendance, discipline, parking).

Some companies use formal lectures, others use orientation handbooks, still others rely on supervisors to provide the information on a one-on-one basis. Regardless of the method used, it must meet the newcomer's need to understand her new environment.

On-the-Job Training

In addition to making the new employee feel part of the scene, he must be given the training needed to actually do the work. Some entrants require little or no training (a journeyman plumber, for example); others enter the job with no relevant skills. For this kind of employee the training usually consists of the following four steps:[4]

1. Preparation. The trainer determines how much, if anything, the new employee already knows.
2. Presentation. The job is described and demonstrated and questions solicited.
3. Performance. The trainee performs the task as the trainer observes, corrects errors, and provides further instructions.
4. Follow-up. The trainee begins the job, with frequent checks on progress.

Job Rotation

In addition to providing the basic instruction new employees need, many small businesses participate in ongoing employee development activities. One way to enhance the skills of existing employees is job rotation. Employees are allowed to perform jobs other than their own to broaden their skills and relieve boredom.

Courses

In most communities a variety of courses are available through universities and community colleges. These courses range from full-semester credit offerings to noncredit short courses. Credit courses usually have less direct applicability to the job than do those short courses designed to teach a particular skill. Courses tend to emphasize interpersonal and more general skills, whereas on-the-job training and job rotation deal primarily with the technical requirements of the job.

Regardless of its form, training represents an investment in the firm's human resources. Organizations that succeed in the long run are willing to make this investment. In addition to improving employee skills through training, however, the management of a small business must provide leadership and motivation. The remainder of this chapter will describe these two topics.

---

[4]Arthur A. Sloane, *Personnel, Managing Human Resources* (Englewood Cliffs, N.J.: Prentice-Hall, 1983), 174.

"What else can you do besides 'raising hell and fixing bikes'?"

Source: Copyright Ford Button.

Leadership

With the addition of the first employee to the business, the entrepreneur takes on the responsibility of providing direction. Put another way, the presence of another person means that the entrepreneur must exercise leadership. Various styles of leadership bring different results.

Autocratic Leadership

Autocratic Leadership
A style of leadership in which the leader makes all the decisions, not sharing the responsibility with the other members of the group.

In the **autocratic leadership** style, the leader makes all the decisions. Subordinates have no decision-making authority. This style is sometimes called "authoritarian" or "boss-centered" leadership.

The results of this, or any, style of leadership must be judged using at least two criteria: the level of productivity and its impact on subordinates. The first criterion, level of productivity, concerns accomplishment of the task and has a short-term orientation. The second concerns group members' satisfaction and has a longer orientation.

Autocratic leadership has as its primary advantage high levels of production. These high levels can only be sustained, however, by the leader's close supervision and ability to make sound decisions. Under autocratic leadership, things happen as they should only when the leader sees to it that they do.

The price of autocratic supervision is usually alienation of subordinates. Most people prefer working for someone who provides flexibility and the authority to do things as the subordinate feels they should be done. The autocratic leadership style carries the message, "Do as I say, not as you think." Over the course of a single project, this kind of approach can be quite successful, but over the long run, by precluding the development of group members as decision makers, it does not effectively use human resources.

Participative Leadership

Participative Leadership
A leadership style in which the leader involves the members of the group in decision making.

The difference between this style and autocratic is that the **participant leader** shares with the group members the decision-making authority. This style takes into account the needs of individual group members and the contributions to task accomplishment they are capable of making. The style is built on the assumptions that people want to do a good job and that the members of a group are a leader's most important resource. Using these assumptions, the leader aids and coordinates the group members' efforts.

The results of this leadership style are some early productivity problems, due in large part to coordination difficulties, and a high level of group member satisfaction.

The Best Style

Though the descriptions just given are much more positive about the participative style than the autocratic, we should not conclude that the participative is always best. The military uses the autocratic, for example, because what is needed in a crisis is dependable, not creative, behavior. Under these conditions, we cannot afford to have a mission undermined by someone who decided the orders he was given were not as good as they might be. Even in business, there are times when the situation calls for a quick, decisive response made by one person.

The safest conclusion is that there is no one best style of leadership. Different conditions dictate different leader responses. Yet in most instances in business, a participative style is most effective over the long run because it makes better use of the group's, or business's, most important resource, its members. Many entrepreneurs find this style to be uncomfortable because it requires that they rely on others in a way to which they are not accustomed.

Delegation

By delegation, a subordinate is allowed to exercise her own decision-making powers. Entrepreneurs often do not delegate, choosing instead to be involved in every phase of operations. Because of the self-confidence typical of entrepreneurs, this reluctance to delegate may be understandable, but it is nonetheless unfortunate. As an enterprise prospers and grows, its entrepreneur's time can limit its further development.

At some point in a firm's growth, even the most efficient, most dedicated person will find it necessary to involve others in making decisions. Many entrepreneurs recognize this and yet, for a variety of reasons, find delegation difficult to master. The following factors often act as barriers to delegation:

1. Lack of ability to direct. Knowing how to do something and instructing others are not the same thing; therefore, it is often much easier to do it than to see that it is done.

2. Lack of confidence in subordinates. This is often a self-fulfilling prophecy whereby failure to turn something over to subordinates stifles their development, which in turn strengthens the supervisor's belief that they are not ready for bigger challenges.

3. Aversion to taking chances. Allowing people to act on their own often brings occasional surprises, not all of which are pleasant. This is not the kind of risk taking that appeals to the typical entrepreneur.

4. The "I can do it better myself" attitude. Many entrepreneurs have confidence that knows no bounds. For these people, there is no real choice as to who will perform the important tasks.

Motivation
. . . .

Our last topic on human resource management is perhaps the most important: motivation. We may be able to hire the right people, to train them properly, and to lead them, but eventually the individual's effectiveness comes down to his or her interest in, and attitude toward, the job and the organization. That is motivation. We will consider first a general theory of human needs, followed by one explaining job motivation, and finally four topics that are not always labeled as motivation but are closely related to the topic.

A General Theory of Human Needs

Abraham Maslow provided the first major attempt to classify human needs.[5] He theorized that we have five different classes of needs, listed below.

1. Physical or physiological needs. These are our requirements as biological systems, such as food and water.

2. Safety needs. This category includes protection from physical harm, ill health, and economic disaster.

---

[5]Abraham H. Maslow, *Motivation and Personality* (New York: Harper and Row, 1954).

3. Social needs. These include our need to belong, our need for feeling accepted, and our need for companionship.

4. Esteem needs. These consist of our needs for self-respect and the respect of others.

5. Self-actualization needs. These are the needs to achieve our fullest potential, to develop in a variety of ways.

The five types of needs are related to one another in a hierarchy of importance. Unless the most basic needs are satisfied, at least to a reasonable degree, the upper-level needs are dormant. Our behavior, Maslow says, is determined by our unsatisfied needs; accordingly, the lowest level of unsatisfied need dictates our behavior. This hierarchy can be seen in Figure 14.1.

Most motivation theorists feel that people in our society have the two basic need types satisfied to the extent that they are not a major determinant of our behavior. If this is so, the upper three need types are better sources of motivation and should therefore be the primary concern of business owners and managers. This idea has contributed to a shift in emphasis from pay, working conditions, and so forth to rewards aimed at higher-level needs. The next section explains how these ideas can be used in the work place.

Figure   14.1   **Maslow's Hierarchy of Needs**

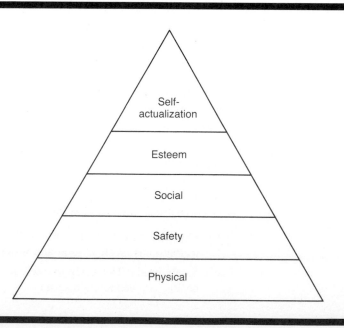

A Theory of Job Motivation

Another motivation theorist, Frederick Herzberg, made motivation on the job his primary interest.[6] His conclusions, based on results from interviews with large numbers of people from many industries, were that certain types of factors can bring satisfaction and that others can cause dissatisfaction. Consequently, Herzberg's work is often called "two-factor theory."

Motivators
Elements of the job that are intrinsic to the task and that can provide satisfaction to the individual.

The factors that can bring satisfaction are called the **motivators** and are task related, that is, they stem from what a person actually does on the job. Examples of motivators include achievement, recognition, responsibility, and advancement.

Hygiene Factors
The conditions, or context, of the job. These factors can cause dissatisfaction and are extrinsic to the task performed.

The other type of factor, called **hygiene,** is capable of causing dissatisfaction. These factors concern the conditions, or context, of the job. Pay, supervision, company policy, and working conditions are all examples of hygiene factors. Herzberg concludes that these factors are incapable of providing satisfaction, and that the best a company can hope for is the lack of dissatisfaction. The real source of motivation, he says, is the task itself.

Herzberg's message has not been lost on industry, and many companies have redesigned the jobs their workers perform. This redesigning is done in the hope of enriching the job and thereby providing the individual worker with opportunities for genuine motivation rather than simply dissatisfaction prevention. Job enrichment programs have been used with great success in jobs ranging from professional to janitorial, and in industries of all types.

Performance Appraisal

Most employees want, and need, feedback on their performance. The feedback can be used to correct ineffective or unacceptable behavior and can be used to recognize and reward a job well done. In addition to this counseling function, **performance appraisal** also serves as the means for evaluating employees. Consequently, performance appraisal information is used in all important personnel decisions including promotions, dismissals, and salaries.

Performance Appraisal
The assessment of the effectiveness of job behavior, used as a means for counseling and for rewarding employees.

For some jobs a clear, unambiguous measure of output exists. The sales man who has his own district and develops sales independently has such a job. A moment's reflection tells us, however, that few workers operate independently. Nearly everyone who works for an organization depends on others within the organization. This interdependence makes it difficult to measure an individual's contribution to the organization's overall performance.

This difficulty has led to the development and use of a variety of performance appraisal techniques based on personal characteristics. The logic behind the use of these techniques is that some traits are desirable for employ-

---

[6]Frederick Herzberg, *Work and the Nature of Man* (Cleveland: World Publishing Co., 1966).

ees, and an employee's value to the organization is reflected in the extent to which he or she has these traits. These traits might include creativity, leadership, adaptability, cooperativeness, enthusiasm, or emotional stability.

Trait assessment methods of performance appraisal have some serious shortcomings, so recent developments in the area have concentrated on behaviorally anchored techniques. These techniques identify behaviors of which good performance consists. These methods use actual behavior rather than subjectively derived traits such as those given above. This appraisal system provides a better evaluation of performance and the basis for meaningful feedback to employees or aspects of their performance where improvement is needed.

Intrinsic and Extrinsic Rewards

Intrinsic Rewards
Those rewards that an individual receives simply by doing the task.

A small business manager can influence employees' motivation through the use of rewards. Two types of rewards can be identified: **intrinsic rewards** are those an individual receives simply by doing the task. One's satisfaction and feelings of accomplishment and competence after completing a difficult task are examples of intrinsic rewards. The motivators Herzberg identified are intrinsic rewards. Certain jobs provide little or no opportunity for this kind of reward because they lack the challenge needed if any sense of accomplishment is to be experienced. Jobs must be designed so that intrinsic rewards are possible (see Figure 14.2).

Extrinsic Rewards
Those rewards that an individual is given by the supervisor or organization for doing the task.

The other kind of reward is **extrinsic.** These the supervisor or organization provides. Examples include pay, benefits, recognition, promotion, and praise. These rewards are the result of doing a good job but are not experienced as part of the task, as were intrinsic rewards. Though there are many types of extrinsic rewards, the one that overshadows the others in overall effect is money. A well-designed and properly administered compensation plan can have a powerful impact on individual performance.

Compensation

Many people equate salary and compensation, but salary is only one element of an employee's pay. The other elements, employee benefits, short-term incentives, long-term incentives, and perquisites, are important because they too affect employee motivation and performance.[7]

Employee benefits, often called fringe benefits, include paid vacation time, health care, various kinds of insurance, and retirement plans. These benefits constitute an important part of payroll costs, often as much as a third.

Short-term incentives are those typically offered to salespeople and executives to spur greater performance. These people are rewarded when a goal has

---

[7]Bruce R. Ellig, "Total Compensation Design: Elements and Issues," *Personnel* 61, no. 1 (January-February 1984): 22–30.

Figure   14.2   Job Characteristics Leading to Intrinsic Rewards

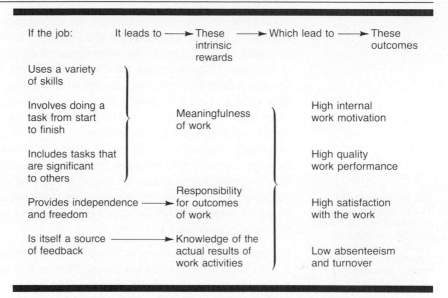

Source: Adapted from David A. Nadler, J. Richard Hackman, and Edward E. Lawler III, *Managing Organizational Behavior* (Boston: Little, Brown and Company, 1979), 83.

been met or exceeded, the amount of the payment usually varying with performance.

Long-term incentives fall into two groups: those that are linked to the market value of company stock, and those that are not. Within the first group, a wide variety of plans permit employees to benefit from increases in value of company stock. Many of these options provide important tax advantages for the employee.[8] This form of compensation is particularly useful to a cash-poor small company as a means of retaining key personnel. Long-term incentives that are independent of stock value use performance of a unit, or the entire firm, over an extended period (perhaps 2 to 5 years). The compensation level is determined by performance relative to corporate goals.

Perquisites, or "perks" as they are often called, are benefits offered only to executives. In a small business, this type of compensation is usually limited to the owner and perhaps one or two top managers. Commonly used perks are company cars, country club memberships, and special housing allowances.

Small businesses may find it difficult to compete with large organizations in salary but may nonetheless be able to offer long-term incentives such as stock option plans, which can make the business a very attractive employer.

---

[8]Robert D. Swanson, "Compensation Options for Small Business Management," *Journal of Small Business Management* 22, no. 4 (October 1984): 31–38.

Discipline

In addition to rewarding employees for appropriate behavior, the business manager must deal with inappropriate behavior. It is necessary to administer discipline. Most organizations use progressive discipline. This approach uses a minimum of punishments for the first infraction of a rule, more for the second, followed by successively higher amounts until dismissal is reached. This system is used for minor offenses such as unauthorized absences. For more serious problems, such as use of alcohol or drugs on the job, most companies dismiss on the first offense.

Although the use of discipline is often unpleasant, virtually all organizations use some system designed to control undesirable behavior. The negative, or unpleasant, effects of discipline can be minimized by using the guidelines below. These are called the **hot stove principles** because discipline based on these guidelines discourages certain behavior just as a hot stove discourages touching.

Hot Stove Principles
The guidelines for use of discipline, which state it must be clearly understood, quickly given, and consistently and impersonally administered.

- Ample and clear warning is provided. Every employee should understand what is punishable and what the punishment will be.
- Discipline is administered quickly. The shorter the time between the offense and the punishment the better.
- Each offense is given the same punishment each time. Administration of discipline is handled consistently. No one is used as an example for others.
- Discipline is administered impersonally. Everyone is given the same punishment for any offense. No apology is given.

Employee Termination

Most organizations that hire people will find, someday, that they have to get rid of some of them. This section deals with employee terminations in the forms of layoffs and firings.

Layoffs

Layoffs involve the termination of people's employment, either permanently or temporarily. This type of termination is due to economic circumstances the firm faces, rather than unsatisfactory performance or unacceptable conduct of the employee. Though layoffs are more common among the blue collar work group, clerical, technical, and managerial workers are occasionally targets for such action.

In some industries, layoffs are a regular part of doing business owing to the prevalent operating cycle. For example, winter weather means layoffs in many parts of the construction business; so do adverse economic developments. Retail stores hire workers for the holiday season and lay them off soon thereafter. Lawn service companies reduce their employee group every fall. Companies that fail to get large contracts are often forced to lay off a large part of their work force.

Clearly layoffs are not unusual, but it is also clear that layoffs are costly. They are costly to the employee because the alternatives are typically limited to unemployment or settling for a lower paying, or somehow less desirable, job. The costs to the employer should also be acknowledged. First, there is the loss of investment in hiring and training the employee. Next, layoffs often lower morale among the remaining employees. Resentment over the loss of friends from the work group and anxiety concerning further reductions are likely to damage productivity levels. Finally, the employer is likely to encounter several types of more direct costs, including higher rates for unemployment compensation insurance (see Chapter 20), severance pay settlements, and those costs associated with outplacement efforts (a service many companies offer to help the layoff victims find new positions).

The small business manager who is about to lay off workers must decide who will go and who will be kept as employees. Companies with unionized workers often have no choice because layoff procedures are clearly specified in the contract between the firm and the union. These procedures typically use worker seniority as the criterion for layoffs. For companies with no seniority provisions to abide by, the identification of employees for layoff often involves such factors as past performance, skills, and abilities. In such instances seniority is often used, but not as the sole determinant.

Firing

Firing can result from two types of situations. First, an employee may be fired for failing to perform the assigned duties satisfactorily. In most companies this move is made only after a series of steps have been taken to "salvage" the employee. These steps usually include determining the cause of the poor performance (low motivation, modest ability, poor training); counseling; retraining where appropriate; and occasionally reassigning within the company. Accurate and complete records of performance appraisals must be kept to safeguard against the possibility of the employee taking legal action.

The second instance in which termination occurs involves infraction of company rules. Two types of disciplinary termination can be identified. In the first the employee is guilty of a major offense such as theft, assault on a fellow worker or a supervisor, sabotage, or use of drugs or alcohol at work. For these offenses, once is enough; discharge is warranted.

The other type of disciplinary termination results from a record of lesser offenses. These are infractions that are not serious enough to warrant immediate discharge but that nonetheless cannot be tolerated. Included are such things as tardiness and unauthorized absences. Figure 14.3 shows the progression in discipline used for these kinds of problems.

Figure   14.3   Discipline Progression

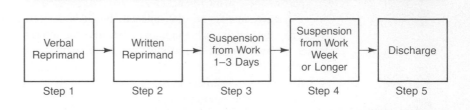

| Verbal Reprimand | → | Written Reprimand | → | Suspension from Work 1–3 Days | → | Suspension from Work Week or Longer | → | Discharge |
| Step 1 | | Step 2 | | Step 3 | | Step 4 | | Step 5 |

Source: Adapted from Keith Davis, *Human Behavior at Work: Organizational Behavior,* 6th ed. (New York: McGraw-Hill, 1981), 320.

For both layoffs and firings, the small business manager must be aware of the law and how it affects personnel management decisions. In the next section we will discuss the major legislation in the personnel management field.

Human Resources Management and the Law

Small business owners find they must deal with certain restrictions and requirements in personnel administration. The numerous restrictions come from a variety of sources; our discussion will center on the major legislation in the areas of hiring, compensation, and safety.

Hiring

Clearly the most important regulation in this area is Title VII of the Civil Rights Act of 1964, which forbids discrimination in employment on the basis of race, color, national origin, religion, or sex. An agency known as the Equal Employment Opportunity Commission (EEOC) administers the act. Through its powers, which were broadened by a 1972 amendment, the Equal Employment Opportunity Act, the EEOC investigates complaints by individuals and files suits in federal court on their behalf.

Not all small businesses are covered by these regulations; they apply to employers who are engaged in industry affecting interstate commerce and who have 15 or more employees for 20 weeks in the current or preceding year. The firms covered are prohibited from discriminating in hiring, firing, promotion, or any other terms of employment, including fringe benefits.

The effect of this legislation has been most striking in use of selection tests. Any employer using them bears the burden of proof that they predict job performance. Because such proof is typically difficult and costly to provide, the legislation and related court decisions have greatly reduced the use of some employment tests and virtually eliminated the use of others.

Small Business Success   14

The Copy Factory, San Francisco, California

Ray Tom of San Francisco recognizes the value of involving his employees in managing the firm. He believes that "the potential time savings and human creativity released will compensate a hundredfold the efforts required." The approach has worked well. Tom's printing company, "The Copy Factory," has prospered with sales growing at an astonishing 62 percent to $4.5 million in 1984. His staff now numbers 100, including employees from economically disadvantaged backgrounds. Through a combination of free pick-up and delivery, 24-hour service, and high quality, The Copy Factory has developed a strong customer base. The company's success earned it the San Francisco Chamber of Commerce's 1984 award for "Innovation in Small Business Management." In 1985 Tom was selected as the Small Business Administration's Small Business Person of the Year for the state of California and subsequently for the far western states.

Source: America at Work (Washington, D.C.: Small Business Administration, 1985), 8.

Bona Fide Occupational Qualification (BFOQ)
A situation in which a certain religion, sex, or national origin can legally be considered a qualification for a job.

Another important restriction resulting from these acts concerns the items that can be used on the application form. Questions concerning marital status, arrest record, weight and height, age, religion, ethnic origin, and race are usually illegal. Occasionally, for jobs such as acting or modeling, a **bona fide occupational qualification (BFOQ)** exists. Under such circumstances the employer may inquire about religion, sex, or national origin. Race and color are never treated as BFOQ, however.

The Federal Age Discrimination in Employment Act of 1967 prohibits discrimination against persons from 40 to 70 years of age. Employers with 20 or more employees are covered by this act, which prohibits refusing to hire, failing to promote, or firing because of age. It also prohibits mandatory retirement before age 70.

Compensation

Fair Labor Standards Act (FLSA)
The major law governing compensation.

The major law governing compensation is the **Fair Labor Standards Act (FLSA).** This law, often referred to as the wage and hour law, requires employers to pay a minimum wage to employees and to pay a minimum of

1½ of the regular wage rate for any hours beyond 40 worked in a week. Almost all small businesses are covered by this law, with exceptions mainly in the areas of seasonal businesses and small retail sales and service firms (with annual gross sales of less than $362,500). This law also stipulates the minimum age for employment of minors.

The FLSA was amended by the Equal Pay Act of 1963, which requires equal pay rates for men and women doing "equal work on jobs which require equal skill, effort, and responsibility and similar working conditions." This clearly prohibits employers from paying men and women different rates for the same work. The EEOC has pushed the concept a step further, however, in seeking "equal pay for comparable work," and in 1980 the U.S. Supreme Court ruled that women need not hold jobs identical to those held by men in order to sue employers for discrimination in pay.

Federal law also governs small business pension plans. Every employer is required to contribute to the Social Security pension plan. For 1986, employees pay 7.15 percent of their wages to the plan, up to approximately $40,000, and the employer must match this contribution. This is a plan for which neither the company nor the employee is given a choice. No employer is forced to make private pension plans available, but for those who do so, the Employment Retirement Income Security Act provides regulations that must be followed. These regulations govern eligibility, vesting rights, and insurance provisions.

Safety

The Occupational Safety and Health Act of 1970 was enacted to provide safe and healthful working conditions for every working man and woman in the nation. The legislation covers virtually every small business, since it applies to every employer with one or more employees, except those engaged in religious rites or services, those employing domestic help, or those agricultural firms employing only family members. The agency that administers the act is the Occupational Safety and Health Administration (OSHA).

Although OSHA has gained the reputation of being overzealous in dealing with violations and requiring involved and expensive solutions to minor problems, the agency provides free consultation to firms needing assistance in handling hazards and offers toll-free telephone service to businesses concerning various provisions of the law.

K   E   Y   Objectives Reviewed

1. Employee selection begins with careful analysis of the job to determine the key requirements for satisfactory performance. Recruiting of prospective employees can be accomplished through a variety of tech-

niques and channels ranging from informal contact to extensive searches through private and public placement offices. The primary means by which selection decisions are made are interviews, application blanks, and tests.

2. Employee training is accomplished through orientation, on-the-job training, job rotation, and various courses.

3. The most commonly used leadership styles are autocratic, in which the leader makes the decisions, and democratic, in which the leader shares decision-making authority with subordinates. Leadership style effectiveness depends on a number of factors, including the situation, or setting, and the subordinates. Clearly, there is no one best style of leadership.

4. The Maslow hierarchy of needs theory and Herzberg's two-factor theory are both useful in explaining human motivation at work. The Maslow theory describes motivation as consisting of five types of needs, ranging from the most basic to high-level needs. According to Herzberg's theory, two types of factors affect motivation at the workplace. Some factors, the motivators, can provide satisfaction; others, the hygiene factors, cannot provide satisfaction but, if not attended to properly, can create dissatisfaction.

5. The careful use of performance appraisals, rewards, compensation, and discipline can greatly enhance the effectiveness of a business's work group.

6. Although the law places many restrictions on the ways in which a business must manage its human resources, the law's impact is perhaps the greatest in the areas of hiring, compensation, and safety.

Discussion Questions

1. Describe the five recommendations given for improving the effectiveness of the interview as a selection technique.

2. What are the two types of leadership? Why is there no "best" leadership style?

3. What are the implications of Maslow's theory on motivation?

4. What are the implications of Herzberg's theory on motivation?

5. What is the first step in the hiring process and how might it be accomplished?

6. Describe the means by which managers may recruit, or locate, prospective employees.

7. How is the application blank used in employee selection?

CHAPTER 15

Record Keeping and Financial Analysis

Source: Courtesy of Chemical Bank, New York.

K E Y   Objectives

1. To identify records that small businesses are required to maintain and to identify common bookkeeping systems.

2. To identify the methods of a financial analysis and common ratios used.

3. To illustrate how financial information can be used for planning.

In Chapter 7, we discussed projected financial statements, including projected income statements for the first few years and the opening day balance sheet. These financial statements were estimates of what would happen in the future. Once the business is operating, it is necessary to keep records of the financial information to prepare the actual income statements and balance sheets. The financial statements must be prepared for two reasons. First, financial record keeping is legally required by the Internal Revenue Service for tax purposes. To determine "taxable income" at the end of the year, the entrepreneur must be able to document income and expenses. Second, accurate financial statements are needed for the proper management of the firm because many failures are caused by accounting problems. Often, the entrepreneur realizes too late that financial records are essential for management.

Record Keeping
....

Required Records

Several phases in the accounting process are needed to complete the financial statements. The first phase is bookkeeping, the process of recording all financial transactions. All businesses, large and small, are required by law to keep records of the following items, where applicable:

1. Sales
2. Inventory purchases and levels
3. Accounts receivable
4. Accounts payable
5. Cash receipts and disbursements
6. Payroll
7. Depreciation records

Visual Excitement in a Boardroom

Carol Nash is a person who can deal with both artists and executives. She uses this talent in her business, in which she handles the works of artists, many young and obscure. If a client wants something orange, wild, and 20 feet long, her computer identifies any pieces that may fit the bill. The client is then shown a slide of the work for early consideration. She expects to handle transactions totaling nearly $1,000,000 by 1986.

Source: "Converting Boardrooms to Galleries," *Venture*, May 1985, 16.

Not all of these records apply to all businesses. For example, some service firms do not carry inventory and so maintain no inventory records. Similarly, not all businesses extend credit to customers; an accounts receivable record would not be needed.

Accounting Systems

Shoebox Method.   There are several methods or systems for recording the above information. Unfortunately, some entrepreneurs use a method often referred to as the "shoebox method," which means they drop all receipts and documents into a box or file until the end of the year, when they take the receipts to someone who prepares tax returns. The entrepreneur operates for the whole year assuming that if there is cash in the bank, the company is making a profit; if bills start to accumulate, the company must be losing money. Unfortunately, by the time the true financial picture is determined at the end of the year, it may be too late to save the company.

Single Entry.   If a company is relatively small, with a limited number of accounts and entries, a single entry accounting system may be adequate. In a single entry system, each transaction is recorded once, like entries in a checkbook. Several standardized single entry bookkeeping systems can be purchased at office supply stores. These systems can usually be used by an entrepreneur who has little or no accounting background. The information can then be taken to an accountant at the end of each month or quarter.

Double Entry.   As a business grows, a single entry system may not be adequate. In addition, the single entry method provides few methods to check for mistakes. A wrong entry may never be discovered. Therefore, a growing company must establish a double entry system designed specifically for that particular business. The system should be tailored to the company's size and need for information; the system for a barber shop is obviously different than one for a retail or manufacturing concern. Similarly, the system for a small barber shop would vary greatly from that of a very large one or from that of a company comprising several barber shops. A bookkeeping system should not be designed once and then forgotten. As the company grows, the book-keeping system must grow along with it to provide necessary information.

The first step in setting up a customized double entry accounting system is to establish a "chart of accounts." A chart of accounts assigns a number to each balance sheet and income statement item. For example, asset categories are usually numbered first, then liabilities, owner's equity, revenue, and finally expense items. The number of accounts will usually increase as the size of the business increases. The cash accounts, for example, may be num-bered 1 to 5 or 1 to 10, depending on how many cash accounts the company needs. Similarly, a large company may have many more expense categories than a small one. A typical chart of accounts is shown below. These account numbers are then used when transactions are recorded in the books.

Sample Chart of Accounts

All Assets	1–100
Cash on hand	1
Cash in checking account	2
Cash in certificates of deposit	5
Accounts receivable from customers	15
Equipment and machinery	26
All Liabilities	101–200
Accounts payable to suppliers	101
Notes payable to banks	125
Taxes payable	115
Owner's Equity	201–205
Owner investment	201
Owner withdrawal	202
Profit/loss	203
Revenue	206–215
Sales, department 1	206
Sales, department 2	207
Sales returns	208
Interest income	209
Cost of Goods Sold	216–225
Labor	216
Material	217
Freight	218
Expenses	226–275
Rent	227
Utilities	228
Wages	229

Illustration Capsule   15.1

Small Toys Are Big Business

Lane Nemeth started a little business in her garage in Martinez, California to sell high-quality educational toys to the general public. She quickly found that accurate financial information is essential for planning. With sales projected to reach $100,000 the first year, she ordered inventory to meet that sales volume. Sales quickly exceeded the $100,000 level, and though orders continued to rush in, the company had no inventory to meet the demand. The next year, sales projections were overly optimistic, and after Christmas the company had excess inventory but no cash.

One accountant told Nemeth she didn't need to hire a high-powered bookkeeper because tiny little businesses don't need one. Nemeth replied, "I'm not going to be a tiny little business." Within eight years, sales reached $50 million.

Source: "Toying with Running a Conglomerate," *Nation's Business* (Washington, D.C.: U.S. Chamber of Commerce, May 1985), 50–51.

General Journal
A bookkeeping sheet that records all business transactions in chronological order, recording the effect of each transaction on each company account.

Ledgers
Specialized records maintained for each account, such as sales or accounts receivable.

Debit Column
Record of an increase in an asset, or a decrease in a liability or owner's equity.

Credit Column
Record of a decrease in an asset, or an increase in a liability or owner's equity.

All systems have documents consisting of a general journal and ledgers. The **general journal** records all business transactions in chronological order, recording the effect of each transaction on each company account. **Ledgers** are specialized records maintained for each account, such as sales or accounts receivable. Double entry accounting requires two entries for each transaction, since all transactions affect assets and liabilities or equity. The equation "assets equal liabilities plus equity" must always balance after each transaction. Therefore, one entry shows the effect on assets and the other entry shows the effect on liabilities or equity. Sample journals and ledgers are shown in Exhibit 15.1. Notice that both the journals and ledgers have two columns marked debit and credit. The dollar amount of the transaction is recorded in the **debit column** if an asset increases, a liability decreases, or owner's equity decreases. The **credit column** is used when an asset decreases, a liability increases, or owner's equity increases.

Many entrepreneurs find the double entry method confusing and time consuming. To simplify the process, it is often possible to develop a double entry system combining journals and ledgers, automatically recording debits and credits in the appropriate accounts. A sample of this type of system is shown in Exhibit 15.2.

Exhibit 15.1   Double Entry Ledgers and Journal

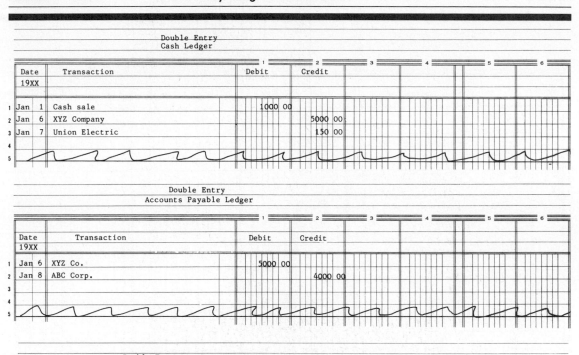

Double Entry
Cash Ledger

	Date 19XX	Transaction	Debit	Credit				
1	Jan 1	Cash sale	1000 00					
2	Jan 6	XYZ Company		5000 00				
3	Jan 7	Union Electric		150 00				
4								
5								

Double Entry
Accounts Payable Ledger

	Date 19XX	Transaction	Debit	Credit				
1	Jan 6	XYZ Co.	5000 00					
2	Jan 8	ABC Corp.		4000 00				
3								
4								
5								

Double Entry
General Journal

	Date 19XX	Transaction	Debit	Credit				
1	Jan 1	Cash	1000 00					
2		Sales Revenue		1000 00				
3		(to record cash sale)						
4								
5								
6	Jan 5	Accounts Receivable – Jones	2000 00					
7		Sales Revenue		2000 00				
8		(to record sale on account)						
9								
10								
11	Jan 6	Accounts Payable – XYZ Co.	5000 00					
12		Cash		5000 00				
13		(to pay for inventory on account)						
14								
15								
16	Jan 7	Utility Expense – Union Electric Co.	150 00					
17		Cash		150 00				
18		(to pay utility bill)						
19								
20								
21	Jan 8	Inventory	4000 00					
22		Accounts Payable to ABC Corp.		4000 00				
23		(to record inventory purchase on account)						
24								
25								

Exhibit 15.2   Automatic Double Entry Ledger

Date 19XX		Transaction Explanation	Cash	Rent	Utilities	Payroll	Insurance	Supplies	Prepaid Expenses
						All Operating Expenses			
1	1	Cash Sale	100000						
1	5	Sale on Account							
1	6	Payment for Inventory on Account	<500000>						
1	7	Payment on utility bill	< 15000>		150 00				
1	8	Purchase of Inventory on Account							
		Totals	<415000>		150 00				

Notice that using this method, an entry in a debit account has a corresponding entry in a credit account.
If both entries are made in debit accounts, or if both entries are made in credit accounts, one entry is
positive while the other is negative.

Total Debit Accounts = <4150.00> + 150.00 + 2000.00 + 4000 = $2000.00
Total Credit Accounts = $3000.00 + <1000.00> = $2000.00

At all times, the total of the debit accounts must equal the total of the credit accounts or an error has been made.

At the end of a "period" (a month, quarter, 6 months, or 1 year), closing or adjusting entries must be made. For example, if prepaid insurance totalled $200 at the beginning of a month and insurance expense is $200 per month, at the end of the month this prepaid insurance must be shown as "used up." This would be done by a debit of $200 under insurance expense and a corresponding negative entry ($200) under prepaid expenses.

Computerized.   As the company continues to grow, the amount of record-keeping time increases and the amount of information processed becomes burdensome. Often at this stage, companies find a computerized system very beneficial. Programs can be purchased that not only maintain all records but also produce income statements and balance sheets. If the system is properly designed, it can be a valuable source of information to the entrepreneur. As with all computer applications, though, the initial program design is the key to a good system. Care must be taken to purchase the appropriate hardware and software (see Chapter 19).

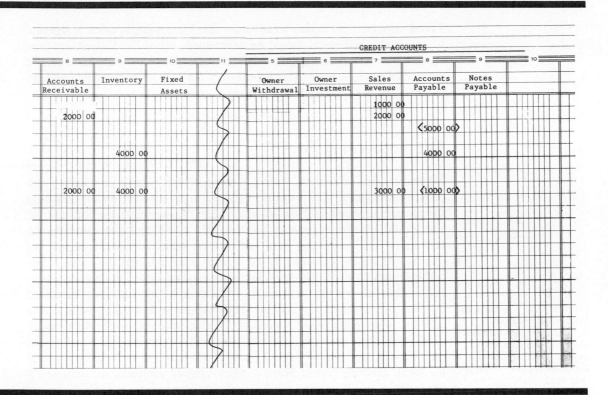

				CREDIT ACCOUNTS					
Accounts Receivable	Inventory	Fixed Assets		Owner Withdrawal	Owner Investment	Sales Revenue	Accounts Payable	Notes Payable	
						1000 00			
2000 00						2000 00			
							⟨5000 00⟩		
	4000 00						4000 00		
2000 00	4000 00					3000 00	⟨1000 00⟩		

Other Necessary Documents

Payroll.   Payroll information must be maintained to document payroll tax information, overtime pay, and so forth. This can be done with a payroll card for each employee. Most payroll checkbooks have spaces for similar information on the check stubs; however, the payroll card provides a continuous record of all wages and deductions for each employee. Then, if any questions arise, it is not necessary to sort through individual check stubs.

Sales Tax.   For businesses that sell products to the final consumer, sales tax must be charged to the customer and sent to the state. This money is not considered part of sales revenue or expenses because the entrepreneur acts only as a collector of the money; no profit or loss is incurred. However, records of sales and sales tax collected must be maintained. Though each state's rules and forms vary slightly, the process is similar in all. Additional information on payroll records and sales tax records will be included in Chapter 18.

Fixed Assets.   No matter what record-keeping system is used, a separate listing of all fixed assets should be maintained. When fixed assets are purchased or sold, the transaction should be recorded, along with the date and the sale or purchase price. This is necessary not only for depreciation and tax purposes but also for insurance purposes.

The Accounting Firm

Statement of Changes in Financial Position
A financial statement that identifies the sources money came from and the purposes for which it was used.

No matter what accounting system is used, if the journals and ledgers are properly maintained, they can then be taken to an outside firm for preparing the accounting statements: the balance sheet, the income statement, and the statement of changes in financial position. (If a computer system provides the statements, the accounting firm will review them and then prepare tax returns.) As stated in Chapter 7, the balance sheet indicates the firm's assets and liabilities on a specific day whereas the income statement shows the revenue, expenses, and net profit for a certain period. One additional statement is sometimes prepared: the **statement of changes in financial position,** also called a ''sources and uses'' statement. This statement explains where money came from (sales, owner investment, loans) and the purposes for which it was used (to pay expenses, to pay off loans). Although it is not legally required for small, privately owned firms, it often helps in analyzing the company's operation.

A good accounting firm should prepare the above statements and should also provide additional assistance. One of the most important reasons for hiring a good accountant is to obtain financial advice. It is essential that the entrepreneur find an accountant who specializes in small businesses and who understands the entrepreneur's specific industry. Other entrepreneurs in similar businesses may be willing to provide the name of their accountant. The accountant will then be able to prepare financial statements, complete tax returns, and provide assistance with tax planning and general financial management.

The Completed Year-end Statements

The completed monthly and year-end financial statements produced from the journals and ledgers include the income statement, balance sheet, and statement of changes in financial position. On page 343, the year-end income statement for Small Pets Inc. is compared with the projected income statement for this business that appeared in Chapter 7.

Small Pets Inc.
Comparison of Income Statements

	Revised Projection		Actual	
Sales	$150,000	100.0%	$152,530	100.0%
Cost of goods	85,500	57.0%	86,179	56.5%
Gross margin	$ 64,500	43.0%	$ 66,351	43.5%
Expenses				
Advertising	$ 6,000	4.0%	$ 5,600	3.7%
Bad debts	1,200	0.8	900	0.6
Dues and subscriptions	300	0.2	150	—
Office expenses	1,050	0.7	975	0.6
Licenses and taxes	900	0.6	850	0.5
Miscellaneous	3,000	2.0	3,500	2.3
Rent	12,000	8.0	12,000	7.9
Salaries and wages	15,000	10.0	14,500	9.5
Supplies	1,800	1.2	2,100	1.4
Utilities and phone	2,550	1.7	3,300	2.2
Payroll taxes	1,500	1.0	1,450	0.9
Depreciation	8,600	5.7	8,600	5.6
Interest	12,000	8.0	11,900	7.8
Total	$ 65,900	43.9%	$ 65,825	43.9%
Net profit	$ (1,400)		526	
Taxes	—		84	
Net after tax	$ (1,400)	(0.9%)	442	0.3%

Notice that the net profit after tax shown on the income statement is $442. This results in the net worth increasing by a similar amount, shown on the balance sheet on page 344. The net worth increased because the company made a profit, which was used to purchase assets and pay off debts. Because the profit was kept in the business, it is referred to as retained earnings. The balance sheet on page 344 compares the opening day balance sheet and the year-end balance sheet to demonstrate how the assets and liabilities accounts may change throughout the year. Notice that the opening day working capital (cash) amount has decreased, but several other asset accounts have increased.

A statement of changes is also shown on page 344, indicating which accounts were sources of cash and which accounts used cash. Total sources must always equal total uses.

Small Pets Inc.
Opening Day Balance Sheet and Year-end Balance Sheet

Assets	Opening Day		Year-end	
Current Assets				
Cash	$ 25,000		$11,500	
Inventory	50,000		59,000	
Supplies	0		4,730	
Prepaid expenses	1,000		4,000	
Licenses	2,000		1,500	
Total current assets		$ 78,000		$ 80,730
Fixed Assets				
Furniture and fixtures	$ 8,000		$10,000	
Machinery and equipment	15,000		15,500	
Leasehold improvements	20,000		22,300	
Less depreciation	0		(8,600)	
Total fixed assets		$ 43,000		$ 39,200
Other Assets				
Deposits	$ 6,000		$ 6,000	
Total other assets		6,000		6,000
Total assets		$127,000		$125,930
Liabilities				
Current Liabilities				
Accounts payable	$ 0		$ 3,956	
Accrued expenses	0		230	
Current maturity of long-term debt	5,698		6,000	
Total current liabilities		$ 5,698		$ 10,186
Long-term Liabilities				
Notes payable	$100,000		$94,302	
Less current portion	(5,698)		(6,000)	
Total long-term liabilities		$ 94,302		$ 88,302
Total liabilities		$100,000		$ 98,488
Equity				
Initial investment	$ 27,000		$27,000	
Retained earnings	0		442	
Total equity		$ 27,000		$ 27,442
Total liabilities and equity		$127,000		$125,930

Simplified Sources and Uses Statement

Account	Source of Money (Where Money Came From)	Account	Use of Money (Purpose for Which Money Was Used)
Profit	$ 442	Inventory increased	$ 9,000
Cash decreased	13,500	Supplies increased	4,730
Licenses decreased	500	Prepaid expenses increased	3,000
Depreciation expense	8,600	Fixed assets increased	
Accounts payable increased	3,956	(before depreciation)	4,800
Accrued expenses increased	230	Notes payable decreased	5,698
Total	$27,228	Total	$27,228

Financial Analysis

··

A financial analysis is a systematic review of a company's financial statements designed to identify its financial strengths and weaknesses and provide information necessary for financial management decisions. Both the income statement and balance sheet are analyzed.

The Income Statement

The first step is to analyze the income statement. For example, the income statements for Top Notch Apparel Inc. for 1983, 1984, and 1985 are shown below.

Top Notch Apparel Inc.
Year-end Income Statements

	1983		1984		1985	
Sales	$250,000	100.0%	257,500	100.0%	265,225	100.0%
Cost of goods	155,000	62.0	162,225	63.0	168,418	63.5
Gross profit	95,000	38.0	95,275	37.0	96,807	36.5
Expenses						
Wages	47,500	19.0	51,500	20.0	55,698	21.0
Rent	20,000	8.0	20,000	7.8	20,000	7.5
Utilities and telephone	3,000	1.2	3,600	1.4	3,710	1.4
Advertising	7,500	3.0	7,725	3.0	7,956	3.0
Insurance	2,000	0.8	2,060	0.8	2,122	0.8
Professional fees	500	0.2	575	0.2	652	0.2
Licenses and taxes	2,500	1.0	2,575	1.0	2,652	1.0
Supplies	3,000	1.2	2,575	1.0	2,652	1.0
Depreciation	1,500	0.6	1,695	0.6	1,500	0.6
Travel	200	0.8	350	0.1	948	0.3
Interest	6,000	2.4	5,500	2.1	5,000	1.9
Other	300	0.1	300	0.1	500	1.9
Total expenses	$ 94,000	37.6	98,455	38.2	103,393	39.0%
Net income before taxes	$ 1,000	0.4	(3,180)	(− 1.2%)	(6,586)	(− 2.5%)

Percentages can be calculated to determine how fast sales are growing. For example, sales volume is increasing each year by 3 percent. This is determined as follows:

$$\frac{\text{Percentage Increase in 1984}}{\text{over 1983 Sales}} = \frac{1984 - 1983 \text{ Sales}}{1983 \text{ Sales}}$$

$$= \frac{257,500 - 250,000}{250,000} = \frac{7,500}{250,000} = 3 \text{ Percent.}$$

This is a very slow growth rate and may actually indicate a decline in sales. For example, if a price increase of 8 percent had been implemented at the beginning of 1984 and the same number of units were sold, sales volume should increase 8 percent just owing to price increases. Thus, if this price increase did occur and sales volume increased only 3 percent, the company actually sold less in unit volume in 1984 than in 1983. (If no price increase was implemented, the 3 percent increase represents an increase in unit volume of 3 percent, still a very low growth rate.)

The income statements also indicate an increasing percentage for cost of goods sold. Thus, while cost of goods sold is 62 percent of sales in 1983 (equivalent to industry averages shown in Exhibit 15.3), it increases to 63 percent in 1984 and 63.5 percent in 1985. Although these increases seem minimal, each percentage increase represents a loss of over $2,000 profit ($250,000 × 1 percent = $2,500). For a small business, small increases in the cost of goods sold percentage can result in a large decrease in dollar profit.

Based on this analysis of cost of goods sold, the company owner should review the markup on goods and the inventory control system to reduce cost of goods to its original level of 62 percent of sales.

The Balance Sheet

The balance sheet for Top Notch Apparel is shown on page 347. As with the income statement, the ratios or percentages can be compared from year to year and can also be compared with industry averages (Exhibit 15.3). A quick glance at the actual dollar figures reveals the following trends:

1. The cash balance is steadily declining.
2. Inventory has increased from 58 percent of total assets to 70.5 percent.
3. The accounts payable category has increased from 29 percent of total liabilities and net worth to 34.6 percent.
4. Net worth is steadily declining both in dollar amount and as a percentage of total liabilities and net worth. (This is due to the net loss incurred each year, which is subtracted from net worth.)

The above trends definitely indicate a company in trouble. Although inventory is increasing, the cash reserves are being depleted and the company is

Assets	1983		1984		1985	
Top Notch Apparel Inc. Year-end Balance Sheet						
Current Assets						
Cash	$ 18,000	10.1%	$ 16,000	9.1%	$ 8,000	5.0%
Accounts receivable	20,000	11.2	21,000	11.9	10,000	6.3
Inventory	103,300	58.1	105,000	59.7	112,280	70.5
Prepaid expenses	3,500	1.9	3,800	2.2	2,000	1.2
Total current assets	144,800	81.4	145,800	82.9	132,280	83.0
Fixed Assets						
Furniture and fixtures	15,000	8.4	14,000	7.9	12,000	7.5
Leasehold improvements	15,000	8.4	13,000	7.4	12,000	7.5
Total fixed assets	30,000	16.8	27,000	15.3	24,000	15.1
Other assets	3,000	1.7	3,000	1.7	3,000	1.9
Total assets	$177,800	100.0	$175,800	100.0	$159,280	100.0
Liabilities						
Current Liabilities						
Notes payable	15,000	8.4	$ 14,080	8.0	$ 14,000	8.7
Current maturity, long-term debt	8,200	4.6	8,500	4.8	9,000	5.6
Accounts payable	52,000	29.2	55,000	31.2	55,146	34.6
Accrued expenses	10,000	5.6	15,000	8.5	15,000	9.4
Taxes payable	7,000	3.9	9,000	5.1	7,000	4.3
Total current liabilities	92,200	51.8	101,580	57.8	100,146	62.8
Long-term debt	50,000	28.1	41,800	23.8	33,300	20.9
Total liabilities	142,200	80.0	143,380	81.5	133,446	83.8
Net worth	35,600	20.0	32,420	18.4	25,834	16.2
Total liabilities and worth	$177,800	100.0	$175,800	100.0	$159,280	100.0

relying more and more on the sale of its inventory to pay its bills. Liabilities and debt are increasing while net worth is steadily decreasing owing to the losses incurred. If these trends continue, the company will eventually be forced to close.

Financial Ratios

The balance sheet and income statement figures are also used to calculate several ratios that provide an even greater analysis of the company. These ratios include liquidity ratios, profitability ratios, leverage ratios, and the operating cycle. As with the percentages just described, industry averages are available (see Exhibit 15.3).

Exhibit   15.3   Industry Averages for Women's Ready-to-Wear

Operating Ratios

Cost of goods	58.0–62.0%
Wages	18.0–20.0
Rent	5.0–7.0
Utilities and telephone	1.5–1.7
Advertising and promotions	2.5–3.0
Insurance	0.8–1.0
Professional services	1.0–1.5
Licenses and taxes	0.9–1.0
Supplies	1.0–1.2
Depreciation	0.7–1.0
Travel	0.6–0.9
Miscellaneous	0.5–0.7
Net income	3.0–5.5

Balance Sheet Percentages

Assets

Cash and equivalents	12.9%
Accounts and notes receivable	12.0
Inventory	52.3
All other current assets	1.6
Total current assets	78.9
Fixed assets (net of depreciation)	15.2
Intangible assets	1.1
All other noncurrent assets	4.8
Total assets	100.0

Liabilities

Notes payable, short term	9.1%
Current maturity, long-term debt	3.1
Accounts payable	18.2
Accrued expenses	5.0
All other current liabilities	3.2
Total current liabilities	38.7
Long-term debt	19.4
All other noncurrent liabilities	1.2
Net worth	40.7
Total liabilities and net worth	100.0

Financial Ratios

Current ratio	2.1
Quick ratio	0.7
Sales/receivables	37.5
Days receivables	10.0
Inventory turnover	2.9
Days inventory	126.0
EBIT/interest	3.0
Cash flow/current maturity	1.1
Debt/net worth	1.3

Sources: Annual Statement Studies (Philadelphia: Robert Morris Associates, 1979), 235; and *Apparel Stores* (San Francisco: Bank of America, 1974), 15.

Profitability Ratios
Measures of the company's financial performance.

Profitability Ratios.   The company's financial performance is measured by profitability ratios. The most common measures of performance compare net income with sales or net income with owner's equity.

$$\text{Return on Equity} = \frac{\text{Net Income}}{\text{Owner's Equity or Net Worth}}$$

Return on Equity
Comparison of the company's profit with the amount of money invested. Also called return on investment.

The **return on equity** (also called return on investment) compares the firm's net income with the owner's investment and the reinvested profits. It determines how much profit the company makes when compared with all the money that has been invested. This ratio was discussed in Chapter 9 as a method for evaluating types of financing. It was stated then that this ratio is not always appropriate for small businesses since the entrepreneur may not be concerned about large profits as long as the firm provides a certain minimum sa5 lary. However, if the salary is extremely low and the entrepreneur would like to increase it, she should identify the cause. Expenses may be too high, sales volume may be too low, or certain assets may be unproductive.

Entrepreneurial Return on Equity
Comparison of net income plus owner's pay and perquisites minus salary with the owner's equity or net worth.

$$\frac{\text{Entrepreneurial}}{\text{Return on Equity}} = \frac{\text{Net Income} + \text{Pay and Perquisites} - \text{Sacrificed Salary}}{\text{Owner's Equity or Net Worth}}$$

Because of the distortions that can be caused by the amount of pay, the value of perquisites, and the earnings sacrificed by not holding a job elsewhere, the return on equity figure should be adjusted. The **entrepreneurial return on equity** adds to the net income the pay and perquisites the owners receive and subtracts from them any salary that could have been earned in another organization.

$$\text{Return on Sales} = \frac{\text{Net Income}}{\text{Net Sales}}$$

Return on Sales
Comparison of the company's profit with the sales volume; measures profitability on sales.

The **return on sales** ratio compares the profit with the sales volume. It indicates whether the company is generating an adequate profit on its sales. This ratio also can be affected by owner preferences; for example, the owner's salary will distort this ratio if it is unusually high or unusually low. As with return on equity, though, if the return on sales is very low and the entrepreneur wishes to increase it, he must determine if sales volume is too low, if expenses are too high, or if a combination is contributing to the problem.

Liquidity Ratios
Measures of a company's ability to pay its bills as they are due.

Liquidity Ratios.   **Liquidity ratios** measure the company's ability to pay its bills as they are due. A company has high liquidity if it has substantial cash to pay bills. Conversely, it has low liquidity if it is short of cash. Typical liquidity ratios follow.

$$\text{Current Ratio} = \frac{\text{Current Assets}}{\text{Current Liabilities}}$$

Current Ratio
Measures of a company's
ability to pay bills and
debts due within the next
12 months.

The **current ratio** indicates a company's ability to pay bills and debts due within the next 12 months. With a high ratio, the company is in a good cash position; with a very low ratio, it may not be able to pay its bills on time. Though the average current ratio varies among industries, a general guideline is that a ratio of 2:1 is acceptable whereas a ratio less than 2:1 indicates possible cash shortages. As shown in Exhibit 15.3, this is the industry average for women's apparel stores. We can compute the current ratio for the Top Notch Apparel Store as follows:

$$\begin{array}{cccc} & \textbf{1983} & \textbf{1984} & \textbf{1985} \\ \dfrac{\text{Current Assets}}{\text{Current Liabilities}} = & \dfrac{\$144{,}800}{\$92{,}200} = 1.5 & \dfrac{\$145{,}800}{\$101{,}580} = 1.4 & \dfrac{\$132{,}280}{\$100{,}146} = 1.3 \end{array}$$

As with the percentages discussed previously, the cause of the steadily declining current ratio should be determined so that steps can be taken to correct the problem. A declining current ratio could be caused by a decrease in current assets, an increase in current liabilities, or a combination. In the case of Top Notch Apparel, the ratio is declining because of a combination of decreasing assets and increasing liabilities.

$$\dfrac{\text{Quick}}{\text{Ratio}} = \dfrac{\text{Cash and Cash Equivalents} + \text{Accounts and Notes Receivable}}{\text{Total Current Liabilities}}$$

Quick Ratio
A more conservative
measure of a company's
ability to pay its current
bills as they come due,
comparing only highly
liquid assets with current
liabilities.

The **quick ratio,** sometimes called the "acid test" ratio, is similar to the current ratio except that it is a more conservative measure, using only highly liquid assets. While the current ratio includes inventory and prepaid expenses, the quick ratio only includes cash and equivalents (such as marketable securities) and receivables. It eliminates prepaid assets and inventory, since the inventory must be sold before it would be converted to cash and prepaid assets usually cannot be "cashed in" if the business remains open. This ratio provides a more realistic picture of the company's cash position because a company with several bills to pay cannot use inventory for payment. If a company had little cash and few accounts receivable but a large inventory, the current ratio might appear adequate, while the quick ratio would highlight the problem. Generally, a quick ratio of 1:1 is acceptable; however, as shown in Exhibit 15.3, for women's apparel stores a ratio of 0.7 is average. For the Top Notch Apparel Store, the quick ratio would be as follows:

$$\dfrac{\text{Cash and Equivalents and Receivables}}{\text{Current Liabilities}} =$$

$$\begin{array}{ccc} \textbf{1983} & \textbf{1984} & \textbf{1985} \\ \dfrac{\$38{,}000}{\$92{,}200} = 0.4 & \dfrac{\$37{,}000}{\$101{,}580} = 0.36 & \dfrac{\$18{,}000}{\$100{,}146} = 0.18 \end{array}$$

The steady decline along with the extremely low quick ratio in 1985 further illustrates the firm's inability to pay its debts. The decline is caused by a severe drop in cash and receivables and an increase in current liabilities.

$$\text{Sales/Receivables} = \frac{\text{Sales (Less Returns)}}{\text{Accounts and Notes Receivable}}$$

Sales/Receivables Ratio
Comparison of the annual sales volume with the accounts receivable balance to determine the rate at which receivables are collected.

The **sales/receivables ratio** compares the annual sales volume with the accounts receivable balance. In general, a high number is good and a low number poor, since the high number indicates that receivables are collected properly. However, if the figure is extremely high compared with industry averages, it may be caused by too strict a credit policy. The company may not be extending credit to anyone except the best customers, or the company might be requiring customers to pay much faster than others in the same industry. The net effect of either situation is that sales might be lower than if proper credit were extended. Thus, if a very high sales/receivables ratio exists compared with industry averages, the credit policies should be reviewed. For the Top Notch Apparel Store, this ratio would be as follows:

1983	1984	1985

$$\frac{\text{Sales}}{\text{Receivables}} = \frac{\$250,000}{\$20,000} = 12.5 \qquad \frac{\$257,500}{\$21,000} = 12.2 \qquad \frac{\$265,225}{\$10,000} = 26.5$$

Compared with the industry average of 37.5, this would indicate that the company, though still below the average, has made some changes to correct the problem. The actual problem may be more obvious by looking at another ratio—days receivables.

For companies that regularly extend credit to customers, an alternative approach to this ratio is to determine the **days receivables,** which, as it sounds, calculates the average number of days it takes to collect accounts receivable. This is calculated as follows:

Days Receivables
Calculation of the average number of days it takes to collect accounts receivables.

$$365 \div \frac{\text{Sales}}{\text{Receivables}}$$

For Top Notch Apparel, in 1985, the days receivables would be

$$365 \div \frac{\$265,225}{\$10,000} = 365 \div 26.5 = 13.7 \text{ Days}$$

In 1984 and 1983, it took more than twice as long (29 days) to collect receivables. Since the industry average for collecting receivables is 10 days, this would indicate that the company has improved its collection procedures.

$$\text{Inventory Turnover} = \frac{\text{Cost of Goods Sold}}{\text{Inventory}}$$

Inventory Turnover
Measure of the number of times inventory is purchased by the entrepreneur, placed in the business, and resold to customers.

One of the crucial ratios for many small businesses is the **inventory turnover,** which measures the number of times inventory is purchased by the entrepreneur, placed in the business, and resold to customers. A low ratio may indicate too much inventory, obsolete inventory, or poor marketing resulting in low sales. On the other hand, an extremely high ratio may indicate an inventory shortage. Therefore, this ratio indicates potential problem areas but does not necessarily pinpoint the cause. If the ratio indicates that a problem exists, the entrepreneur must then determine the cause and take appropriate action. For example, in one wholesale firm, the inventory turnover ratio was calculated and was found to be extremely low compared with similar businesses. When a consultant pointed this out to the entrepreneur, the entrepreneur admitted that no inventory control system had been established and excess inventory was a problem. A physical inventory was then taken that revealed that $10,000 in excess inventory was in stock. The entrepeneur therefore returned the excess inventory to the manufacturers for credit. For the Top Notch Apparel Store, inventory turnover would be as follows:

$$\frac{\text{Cost of Goods Sold}}{\text{Inventory}} = \frac{\overset{1983}{\$155,000}}{\$103,300} = 1.5 \quad \frac{\overset{1984}{\$162,225}}{\$105,000} = 1.5 \quad \frac{\overset{1985}{\$168,418}}{\$112,280} = 1.5$$

As shown in Exhibit 15.3, the industry average for women's apparel stores is 2.9; therefore, Top Notch is turning its inventory slower than similar businesses.

Days Inventory
Calculation of the average number of days an item stays in inventory.

An alternative to the inventory turnover ratio is the **days inventory.** Similar to the days receivables ratio, this ratio computes the average number of days an item stays in a company's inventory. The ratio is computed as follows:

$$365 \div \frac{\text{Cost of Goods Sold}}{\text{Inventory}}$$

For Top Notch Apparel in 1985, this would be as follows:

$$365 \div \frac{\$168,418}{\$112,280} = 365 \div 1.5 = 243.3 \text{ Days}$$

This means that on the average, an item purchased by Top Notch stays in inventory 243 days before it is sold. Since the industry average is 126 days, Top Notch's inventory remains in the store almost twice as long as it should. This indicates a definite need to review purchasing decisions and the inventory control system.

Leverage Ratios
Indication of the extent to which a company is financed with debt financing.

Leverage ratios.   **Leverage ratios** indicate the extent to which a company is financed with debt financing. For this ratio a low figure is good, indicating a financially strong company, whereas a high ratio indicates a company in a poor financial condition. A company with a low ratio may be able to borrow additional funds, whereas financial institutions hesitate to loan money to a highly leveraged firm. Although there are several leverage ratios, the most common is debt/net worth.

$$\text{Debt/Net Worth} = \frac{\text{Total Liabilities}}{\text{Net Worth (Equity)}}$$

Debt/Equity Ratio
Comparison of all the liabilities of a company with the equity or net worth figure.

The **debt/equity ratio** compares all the liabilities of the company with the equity or net worth figure. For Top Notch this would be as follows:

	1983	1984	1985
$\dfrac{\text{Total Liabilities}}{\text{Net Worth}}$ =	$\dfrac{\$142,200}{\$35,600} = 4.0$	$\dfrac{\$143,380}{\$32,420} = 4.4$	$\dfrac{\$133,446}{\$25,834} = 5.1$

Exhibit 15.3 gives the industry average, 1.3; therefore, Top Notch has much more debt than it should compared with its equity. The problem is compounded by the decreasing net worth that results from operating losses. This ratio will improve only if the company does not borrow more money and changes its operations so that a profit is generated and reinvested back into the business. If the firm becomes profitable and the profits are reinvested in the business, this will help to increase equity. If no more money is borrowed, debt will decline while equity increases. Eventually this ratio will reach the appropriate level.

Operating Cycle
The time it takes for money invested in the business to be converted back into cash profits.

Operating Cycle.   The **operating cycle** indicates how long a business has its cash tied up in current assets. The typical operating cycle for a business is defined as the length of time it takes for money invested in the business to be converted back into cash profits. Figure 15.1 illustrates a typical cycle. The longer the operating cycle, the more cash flow problems a company will experience.

Limitations of Financial Analysis

Financial analysis is an excellent means of determining problem areas and/or providing information to make financial decisions. However, several words of caution are necessary. The ratios calculated must not be influenced by seasonal fluctuations. For example, if the year-end balance sheet is used, it is possible that inventory levels would be unusually low or receivables very high if a peak season has just ended. If "abnormal" figures are used for calculations, the ratio will be distorted and therefore useless for decision making. If figures vary greatly throughout the year, an "average" figure should be used for calculations.

Ratio analysis should be used to obtain a "total picture" of the company, after analyzing all the ratios. No single ratio should be considered by itself, as it often does not provide enough information for decision making. When

Figure   15.1   The Operating Cycle

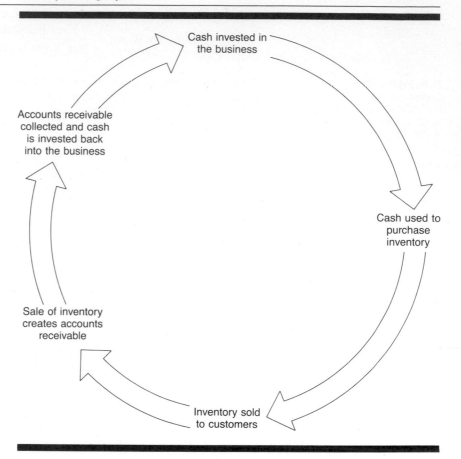

several ratios are analyzed, the information often indicates a problem and pinpoints the cause.

The entrepreneur must also realize that all calculated ratios are based on past performance—they are based on past inventory levels, past accounts receivable levels, and so forth. If the figures are outdated when the analysis is done, the results may be meaningless.

It is also advisable to analyze 3 years or more (if the figures are available) rather than only 1 year. This is true because figures during 1 year may not represent the company's normal operations. In addition, analyzing 3 years or more allows the entrepreneur to identify trends, which are often very important.

Exhibit 15.4 summarizes the ratios, the problems indicated by an abnormal ratio, and the action that should be taken to correct the problem.

Exhibit 15.4   Interpreting Financial Ratios

Ratio/Calculation	Reason for Concern (Too High/Low)	Possible Causes	Action Needed
Sales increase from 1 year to the next	Low percentage increase	No increase in sales volume; decrease in prices	Determine why sales have not increased—new competition, location, inadequate inventory selection
Expenses increase as percentage of sales	Expenses too high compared with sales	Decrease in sales; increase in expenses	If sales decrease, action taken same as above; if expenses increased, determine why and evaluate possible methods for reducing costs
Current ratio	Too low	Financing was obtained over short-term period (current maturities too high); too much short-term debt	Refinance loans over longer period
		Cash flow problems resulting in high payables; current assets too low	Determine cause of cash flow problems or reasons for low current assets
Quick ratio	Too low even though current ratio is alright	Too much of current assets tied up in inventory	Evaluate inventory control system; liquidate obsolete or excess inventory
Sales/receivables	Too low	Receivables not collected on time; large amount of bad debts carried as receivables	Establish system for collecting receivables faster; eliminate bad debts from accounts receivable
		Too much credit extended	Tighten credit policy
	Too high	Not enough credit extended	Reevaluate credit policy
		Credit policy too strict	Determine if sales are being lost to determine if more credit should be extended
Inventory turnover	Too low	Too much inventory	Evaluate inventory control system
		Obsolete inventory	Eliminate excess or obsolete inventory
	Too high	Not enough inventory	Evaluate inventory control system; determine if stockouts occur often; stock needed inventory
Debt/equity	Too high	Too much debt	Reduce debt
		Poor profit level	Improve profitability
		Profits not retained in company	Reinvest profits back into the business
Return on equity	Too low	Expenses too high	Reduce expenses where possible
		Sales too low	Evaluate marketing strategies
		Profits are reinvested in unproductive assets	Liquidate unproductive assets
		Company is underleveraged	Consider debt financing to allow more owner withdrawals

Planning with Financial Information

Financial statements and financial analysis are of little value if they are not used for planning future years. The entrepreneur should use the financial statements and analysis to prepare a budget. A budget is a plan that enables the entrepreneur to set a goal and list the steps necessary to reach it.

The most basic budget is a projection of income and expenses—a projected profit and loss sheet. Many small business owners feel that projected statements are only necessary before opening the business; however, projected statements should be completed and revised every year to guide the firm's financial planning. The entrepreneur should review the statements and analysis to determine the firm's current financial position, then set goals for the following year, then determine what steps are necessary to reach the stated financial goal.

The financial statements of Top Notch Apparel can be summarized with the following conclusions:

1. Sales growth has been minimal.

2. Cost of goods sold has been increasing.

3. The company has incurred a loss for the past several years.

4. Cash is decreasing while inventory accounts for an ever-increasing percentage of total assets.

5. Current and quick ratios show an inability to meet current bills.

6. Collection of receivables has been taking much longer than industry averages, but corrective action appears to have been taken.

7. Inventory is turning very slowly, and the dollar amount on hand has increased substantially.

8. Wages have increased as a percentage of sales although other expenses have remained at approximately the same percentages for all three years.

9. In 1985, if cost of goods had been held at 62 percent of sales and wages at 19 percent of sales, the company would have shown a profit of about $2,000 instead of a $6,000 loss.

The preceding information can then be used to analyze problems and set the following goals and plan of action.

1. Because inventory turnover appears to be a problem and the dollar amount is substantially higher in 1985 than in 1983, inventory should be reviewed to identify excess, obsolete, or slow-moving items. This inventory should be liquidated by sales and promotions. This will help

Small Business Success   15

Debenham Electric Supply Company, Anchorage, Alaska

Things looked rather bleak for Ray Debenham in 1968, when he was told that he would be out of a job as a salesman with a company closing its Alaska branch. By the middle of the next week, Debenham was in business for himself. He used his $2,800 in severance pay and a line of credit he was able to get from his ex-employer and, after a year of building a company, was able to get a Small Business Administration loan. His company, a supplier of electric products, has expanded to several sites in Alaska, Washington, and Utah. Total employment now numbers approximately 130. His advice to prospective entrepreneurs is to go into a business only after you've found a market niche not being served and only after you have some accounting background.

Source: America at Work (Washington, D.C.: Small Business Administration, 1985), 7.

provide needed cash to pay bills and will also reduce inventory to the appropriate level.

   Goal 1. Reduce inventory levels by 10 percent through eliminating excess, obsolete, or slow-moving items.

2. Cost of goods sold has increased over the past several years. Therefore, markup on goods, price increases on items purchased, and sales (markdowns) should be analyzed to determine the cause of the increase in cost of goods. The company owner should also determine if sales volume would be negatively affected if a 38 percent gross margin were maintained.

   Goal 2. Maintain a gross margin of 38 percent.

3. Because the sales increase for the past several years has been minimal, the merchandise selection, location, and promotional plan should be reviewed to determine the cause of the low sales growth. Steps should then be taken to correct the problem.

   Goal 3. The 1986 sales volume should be 7 percent higher than in 1985 ($283,790), plus an appropriate adjustment for any price increases.

4. Wages have increased from 19 to 21 percent of sales within 2 years. This trend cannot continue or any potential profits will be used up for payroll costs. Determine if the increase is due to salary increases, an increase in the number of hours worked by employees, or an increase in owner salary.

   Goal 4. Maintain wages at 19 percent of sales.

5. The company cannot survive if it continues to incur losses. Principal payments on the loan during 1986, 1987, and 1988 will be approximately $4,000 to $5,000, and additional cash will also be necessary if accounts receivable or inventory increase.

   Goal 5. Maintain a minimum cash flow (profit plus depreciation) of $5,000 for 1986 with an increasing profit and cash flow during 1987 and 1988.

A projected income statement can then be prepared for Top Notch Apparel for 1986. This is shown below.

**Top Notch Apparel
Projected 1986 Income Statement**

Sales	$283,790	100.0%
Cost of goods	175,950	62.0
Gross margin	$107,840	38.0%
Expenses		
Wages	$ 53,920	19.0%
Rent	20,000	7.0 (based on lease agreement)
Utilities	3,980	1.4
Advertising	8,513	3.0
Insurance	2,270	0.8
Professional fees	710	0.3
Licenses and taxes	2,838	1.0
Supplies	2,838	1.0
Depreciation	1,300	0.5 (no new fixed assets will
Travel	851	be purchased)
Interest	4,500	0.3
Other	567	1.6 (no additional debt)
Total expenses	$102,287	0.2
Net profit before tax	$ 5,553	
Taxes	800	
Net after tax	4,753	
Projected Cash Available		
Profit	$ 4,753	
Plus depreciation	1,300	
Cash flow	$ 6,053	

The above plan should then be used to ensure that Top Notch Apparel becomes a profitable, financially strong company.

AUTUMN IN ACCOUNTING

Source: Drawing by Leo Cullum; © 1984 The New Yorker Magazine, Inc.

K E Y Objectives Reviewed

1. All businesses must maintain certain records; many accounting systems or methods can be used.

2. A financial analysis is a systematic review of a company's financial statements to identify financial strengths and weaknesses. An analysis of the income statement and balance sheet items is completed along with various ratios.

3. Financial information should be used for planning coming years and establishing a budget. After trends and problems have been identified, goals should be set and a projected income statement developed. This should then serve as a basis for budgeted amounts for expenses to ensure that a desired profit level is reached.

Discussion Questions

1. Consider the bookkeeping systems for a restaurant and a florist. How would the systems be similar? How would they differ?

2. Suppose an entrepreneur states, ''I don't need monthly financial statements. I'll just have my tax return prepared at the end of the year.'' Respond.

3. What is the difference between the general journal and ledgers?

4. Does an increase in dollar sales volume always mean the company sold more of its products? Why or why not?

5. If a company's current ratio is equal to industry averages but the quick ratio is extremely low, what might this indicate?

6. If a company's debt/equity ratio is unusually high, why might it be difficult to obtain a bank loan?

7. Why would it be beneficial for a small business to complete a financial analysis annually? Why would it be beneficial to compare each quarter?

8. What problems may occur if a small company's ratios are compared with industry averages? Why might the comparison not provide valid information?

16

Working Capital Management

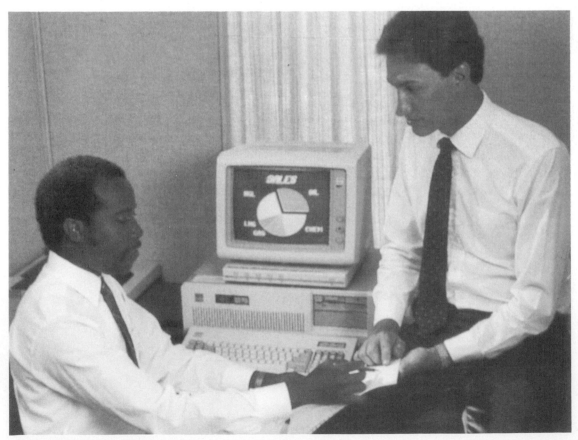

K   E   Y   Objectives

1. To discuss the effect of extending credit on a company's cash flow and to identify methods for proper credit management.

2. To describe the effect of maintaining an inventory on the company's cash flow and to identify methods for proper inventory management.

3. To illustrate the effect on cash flow when inventory and accounts receivable levels fluctuate.

Two major areas often affect the cash position of small firms — accounts receivable and inventory. Exhibit 16.1 illustrates that for companies with less than one million dollars in assets, inventory comprises 24.5 percent and receivables 26.3 percent of total assets. Improper management of these two assets can cripple a company that would otherwise be successful. Therefore, a company's credit policy and inventory control should be carefully considered and closely monitored. This chapter describes the effects of fluctuations in inventory and accounts receivable and various techniques for effectively monitoring each.

Exhibit   16.1   Working Capital Invested in Current Assets

	Assets (in Millions of Dollars)				
Working Capital Components	Under $1	$1–$5	$50–$100	$250– $1,000	Over $1,000
Cash	10.2%	7.1%	4.1%	2.8%	2.4%
Marketable Securities	1.0	1.1	2.1	1.4	3.2
Receivables	26.3	25.1	20.1	17.0	12.1
Inventories	24.5	30.8	29.8	27.0	18.3
Other Current Assets	4.2	3.4	1.9	2.5	2.3
Total Current Assets	66.2%	67.5%	58.0%	50.7%	38.4%

Source: Ernest W. Walker and T. William Petty II, *Financial Management of the Small Firm* (Englewood Cliffs, N.J.: Prentice-Hall, 1978), 230.

Unique Business   16.1

Baths for Bentleys

Steve's Detailing in New York isn't your ordinary spray-it-off, run-it-out type of car wash operation. At Steve's, your wheels get pampered and really spruced up. The car is washed, polished, degreased, and preserved in a process that takes 10 to 12 hours and costs $145. The business, a franchised outlet of a Newport, California company started by Steve Marchese, cost $5,000 in licensing fees and $30,000 to $35,000 for other start-up expenses. The New York outlet projects $125,000 to $150,000 for 1985 revenues.

Source: "Taking Care of Details," *Venture* 7, no. 3 (March 1985): 10.

Credit Management

. . . .

Consumer Credit

Consumer Credit
Credit extended to the final customer, including charge accounts and installment accounts.

Thirty-Day Account
Credit extended to customers for 30 days, requiring the entire balance to be paid at the end of the month.

Revolving Credit Account
Credit provided to customers with a minimum payment due each month.

There are two basic types of credit, trade credit and consumer credit. **Consumer credit** is credit extended to the final consumer, generally the customer of a retail or service firm. There are two basic types of consumer credit, charge account credit and installment credit, each with variations.

Charge Account Credit.   Charge account credit includes 30-day accounts (sometimes referred to as an ordinary charge account), a revolving credit account, and bank credit cards. A **30-day account** provides credit to customers for 30 days, requiring the entire balance to be paid at the end of the month. Usually, no interest is charged as long as the bill is paid in full.

A **revolving credit account** is similar to the 30-day account, but the customer does not have to pay the entire amount due at the end of the month. A minimum monthly payment is established based on the total amount the customer owes. The greater the balance due, the higher the monthly payments. Interest is charged on any unpaid balance. Although some small businesses maintain their own revolving accounts, many arrange for customers to use credit cards issued by another firm. For example, one small auto repair shop that leases space in a service station owned by Shell Oil allows customers to use their Shell Oil charge card. At the end of every month, Shell Oil sends the entrepreneur a check for the amount of purchases charged. Thus, the entrepreneur does not receive money immediately when the repair service is charged; however, Shell Oil Corp. handles all credit and collection problems.

Bank Credit Card
Credit card issued by financial institutions used to purchase a variety of products throughout the world.

Bank credit cards include MasterCard, VISA, Diners Club, American Express, and others. These cards, issued by financial institutions, can be used to purchase a variety of products in stores throughout the world. For the small business, the bank credit card is preferable to the revolving credit card because the business receives immediate credit for the charge sales. Suppose a card and gift shop sells $700 on a certain day, $300 in cash and $400 on MasterCard and VISA. When the company owner makes the daily bank deposit that evening, the $300 cash is deposited along with the charge tickets for $400. The bank immediately credits the business's account for $700.

The small business is charged a fee for the use of the bank credit card, usually 2 to 6 percent of sales, depending on sales volume. A company with a high amount of charge sales will pay a smaller percentage than the firm with only a few credit purchases.

Installment Account
Credit provided to customers for an extended period, often requiring a down payment and use of the item purchased as collateral.

Installment Accounts.   **Installment accounts** are often used for the purchase of more expensive items, such as furniture, jewelry, or cars, where credit must be extended for a longer period. The consumer is often required to provide a down payment, and the remainder of the purchase price is financed for a specified time and interest rate. Installment accounts differ from charge accounts in several ways. First, with installment accounts, the customer is often required to sign a contract specifying the interest rate, terms, and so forth. Second, the consumer often must pledge the item purchased as collateral for the financing. If the amount is not paid off, the item is repossessed. Some companies offer a variation of the installment account called a **budget account.** This is a short-term installment account, usually financed for no more than 120 days.

Budget Account
A short-term installment account usually used to finance purchases for no more than 120 days.

Though some small businesses finance their own installment accounts, it is very common for the business to sell the contracts to a bank or finance company. The financial institution charges a percentage to the small business for the discounting service. In return, the small business receives cash immediately.

Trade Credit

Trade Credit
Credit extended by manufacturers and wholesalers to their customers, generally for 30, 60, or 90 days.

Trade credit is credit manufacturers and wholesalers extend to their customers. Trade credit is generally extended for 30, 60, or 90 days for the purchase of the manufacturer's or wholesaler's products. The period for which credit is extended varies among industries and may also change with economic conditions. In many industries, specific credit terms have become accepted as standard and any new business must comply or face the consequences. For example, one entrepreneur began a business in an industry where 6 weeks' credit was the standard. The entrepreneur, however, offered only 10 days' credit. Sales volume was severely affected, reaching only 30 percent of the expected volume.

Extended Credit
Trade credit given for a longer period (6 to 9 months), often used in industries that are very seasonal.

A second type of trade credit is **extended credit,** which provides longer terms, for example 4 to 6 months. This is common in businesses that are very seasonal, having only one or two peak seasons in the year. For example, wholesalers of jewelry will often allow 6 months' credit or more to retailers. This is necessary since the retailers may purchase Christmas inventory in September. When the Christmas season is over and the retailer has the cash available from Christmas sales, the invoice for inventory is paid.

Consignment Sales
A form of trade credit where a wholesaler or manufacturer places inventory in a retail outlet and requires no payment until the item is sold.

Another, less common form of trade credit is **consignment sales,** in which a wholesaler or manufacturer places inventory in a retail outlet and requires no payment until the items are sold. This type of credit has been used by small shops that sell and service brand-name lawn mowers. The manufacturer or distributor bears the cost of carrying the inventory until the item is sold.

Purpose of Credit

The primary purpose for extending credit is to generate more sales than if cash payments were required.[1] A credit policy should be designed to increase the number of customers, the dollar volume of sales, the market share, and so forth. If extending credit does not result in more sales, the company would be in a better financial position by requiring cash. A credit policy should not be designed solely to minimize bad debts. Though the easiest way to minimize bad debts would be to require cash for all purchases (extend no credit), this would probably result in a drastic drop in sales volume. Therefore, the best credit policy maximizes sales and minimizes bad debts.

Determining Credit Risk

Character
The qualities that make a person want to pay bills on time, usually evidenced by a past record of prompt payment.

The creditor (who extends credit) must evaluate the financial position of the debtor (who is applying for credit). The four Cs — character, capacity, capital, and conditions — are the basis of the financial evaluation, the decision to extend or deny consumer or trade credit.[2] **Character** refers to the qualities that make the person or entrepreneur want to pay. The best evidence of good character is a long, consistent record of prompt payment. When previous debts have consistently been paid on time, the individual or company is likely to be a good credit risk.

Capacity
The ability to repay credit if it is extended, generally determined by comparing income with existing debt payments.

Capacity refers to the ability to repay the credit if it is extended. Generally, income is compared with debts to determine if there is adequate cash flow to pay obligations.

---

[1]Thomas Beckman and Ronald Foster, *Credit and Collections* (New York: McGraw-Hill, 1969), 82.
[2]Beckman and Foster, *Credit and Collections,* 82.

Capital
The financial strength of the company, determined by the assets that would be available to the creditor if payment on the bill were not received.

Conditions
General business conditions and state of the economy.

Capital is the net worth or financial strength of the individual or company. It compares assets and liabilities to determine what assets would be available to the creditor if payment were not received. Though character and capacity are often considered more important, a poor capital position may prevent approval of a credit application.

The final C, **conditions,** includes an analysis of general business conditions and state of the economy. While marginal businesses often can succeed when economic conditions are good, many businesses fail during bad economic times. Therefore, if the debtor appears marginal, the credit application may be approved during good economic conditions but rejected during a recession.

Costs of Extending Credit

While extending credit to customers increases sales, the entrepreneur must realize that this increase is not achieved without costs. An acceptable credit policy must encourage sales while keeping costs at a reasonable level. These costs follow.

Bad Debts.   Bad debts (customer accounts determined to be uncollectable) naturally occur when credit is extended. Though the bad debt rate for most industries is only 1 to 2 percent of sales, this still represents lost income to the firm. The bad debt rate should be monitored to ensure that it does not become excessive.

Billing and Record Keeping.   Billing and record keeping costs also increase dramatically once credit is extended. When all sales are cash sales, there is no need to send monthly statements and no need to maintain accounts receivable ledgers on each customer. Extending credit results in a substantial increase in paperwork because the sales to each customer must be recorded, each payment received must be posted, account balances must be maintained, and monthly statements must be mailed.

Credit Bureau Fees.   Creditors usually belong to a credit bureau. This bureau or association provides information (on individuals or companies) such as past payment record, financial condition, and current income. This type of association usually charges an annual fee plus charges based on the number of credit checks required. These fees are added costs to the company and should be considered carefully if a firm is deciding whether or not to extend credit.

Collection Fees.   Charges for collection fees are also incurred. These may include extra employees hired for collection functions or fees paid to a collection agency. No matter which method is used, though, collection costs will be incurred in the effort to minimize bad debts.

Opportunity Costs.   One final, less tangible cost of extending credit is that the money tied up in accounts receivable is not available for investing in

Opportunity Cost
The amount of money that could not be earned because company funds were tied up in accounts receivable.

other areas. This is known as an **opportunity cost,** since the company loses the opportunity to invest the money elsewhere and realize a return.

Since the decision to extend credit results in increased costs, it is wise for a company to extend credit only if the profit from the increased sales exceeds the total additional costs. Though it is beyond the scope of this book, specific formulas can be derived to determine exactly how much sales must increase to compensate for changes in credit policy. For example, if a company currently allows its customers 30 days to pay and is considering extending credit for 60 days, it can determine how much sales would have to increase to make this decision profitable. This allows the entrepreneur to eliminate guesswork in credit decisions.

Controlling Collections

One of the most important functions of credit management is controlling the collections on each account, ensuring that money is received on time. There are several methods to monitor cash inflows, including aging receivables, calculating days receivables, or charting a collection index.

Aging receivables generally involves categorizing accounts according to how long they have been outstanding. A sample aging is shown below. This allows the entrepreneur to determine which accounts have not been paid on time and also indicates how well the entrepreneur collects the accounts. Using this method, the entrepreneur can easily determine the percentage of overdue accounts and take steps to collect them.

Customer	0–30 Days	31–60 Days	61–90 Days	Over 90 Days
XYZ Inc.	$520	—	—	—
ABC Inc.	—	$601	—	—
Golf Greens Inc.	$330	—	—	—
Ralph's Grocery	—	—	$405	—
*Total	$18,250	$2,520	$1,520	$400
*Percentage of Total ($22,690)	80.4%	11.1%	6.7%	1.8%

*Note: The figures in this table do not add up to the totals because not all of the accounts are included.

Collection Index
A ratio that determines the rate at which receivables are collected, calculated by dividing the accounts receivable balance by the amount of money collected in a specified period.

Calculation of days receivables was discussed in Chapter 15. This allows the entrepreneur to determine the average length of time customers take to pay their bills. If the average is longer than for other businesses in the same industry, steps should be taken to increase the collection rate.

Many companies also use a **collection index** to determine the rate at which receivables are collected. The index is determined by dividing accounts receivable by the amount collected during a week. Suppose, for example, a business has an average of $20,000 in accounts receivable and usually collects $2,000 per week. The collection index would be determined as follows:

$$\frac{\text{Receivables}}{\text{Collections}} = \frac{20{,}000}{2{,}000} = 10 \text{ Times}$$

For this collection index, a lower number indicates a better collection rate. (For example, if receivables were $20,000 and weekly collections were $5,000, the index would be 4.) Companies that use this method monitor the index and watch for increases. Patterns also develop that help businesses predict the amount of cash to be collected. For example, many businesses find seasonal changes in their collection index. Therefore, while the collection index would normally be 10, it might rise around April 15, when customers must pay income tax and are short of cash. If the entrepreneur is aware of this trend, she will not be surprised when collections temporarily decrease.

No matter what method the entrepreneur uses to monitor accounts receivable, she should always watch the total amount of money tied up in accounts receivable. A simple method for tracking this information is shown below.

Accounts Receivable (AR) Control			
	May	June	October
Beginning AR	$11,000	$17,800	$20,000
+ AR Sales This Month	$13,800	15,200	16,800
− AR Collected This Month	7,000	8,000	9,000
Ending AR	$17,800	$25,000	$27,800

This method allows the entrepreneur to determine quickly how much receivables fluctuate each week or month. The accounts receivable balance continues to increase because sales are growing faster than accounts receivable are being collected.

Cash Discounts

To speed up the collection process, many businesses offer discounts if their customers pay sooner than required. A typical discount allows 2 percent off if the bill is paid within 10 days. This is often shown as "2/10 net 30," which indicates the 2 percent discount is available if the bill is paid within 10 days or the full amount is due in 30 days. If the entrepreneur bills a customer for $500 and offers 2/10 net 30 terms, the customer could pay $490 ($500 less the 2 percent discount for prompt payment) or could wait until close to the 30th day and pay the full $500.

Cash discounts give the creditor several advantages. The most obvious advantage is the increase in cash flow due to the faster collection of the receivables. However, several other benefits result. First, quicker collection of receivables often reduces the number of bad debts, because there is a direct correlation between the length of time a bill is outstanding and the likelihood of it becoming a bad debt. Thus, when receivables are collected quickly, the number of bad debts usually decreases.

The second advantage for the creditor is that a faster collection of receivables often reduces administrative costs involved with credit. If bills are paid quickly, fewer bills need to be mailed out and fewer bookkeeping entries made. Therefore, overhead costs will also decrease.

Although cash discounts benefit the creditor in several ways, they also benefit the debtor. If an entrepreneur owns a business and takes advantage of all discounts offered, this can result in a substantial savings. Even a small retail business may purchase $150,000 of inventory at cost each year. If the entrepreneur can save 2 percent by paying in 10 days, he would save $3,000 per year ($150,000 $\times$ 2 percent). For any business, a savings of $3,000 per year is welcomed; for a small business this can make a substantial difference in profit.

An unfortunate result of cash discounts is that many customers abuse the privilege. Many customers take 30 days or longer to pay their bills and still subtract the cash discount. This occurs especially when large companies buy from small companies. The large company realizes that the small business is very dependent on the large orders and knows that the small company will do nothing to jeopardize the business relationship. Discounts are often taken long after the discount period has expired.

When this occurs, the entrepreneur must decide what action, if any, to take. Taking no action is equivalent to approving the abuse, and customers will continue to take unearned discounts. If, however, the entrepreneur bills the customer for the unearned discount, he risks losing the customer owing to ill feelings. Therefore, each entrepreneur must make an individual decision.

One wholesale firm found that over the years, customers had continually taken longer to pay bills and had also taken an increasing number of unearned cash discounts. The wholesale firm decided that increased sales were not justified if the correct amount of money was not quickly received. The company therefore notified all customers that, in the future, no credit would be extended to companies that abused the credit policies. Although this decision lost a few customers, the increased cash flow and absence of unearned discounts more than compensated for lost sales.

A Collection Plan

Many small businesses fail to realize the importance of a planned approach for collections. Although it is necessary to track slow-paying accounts and offer incentives, these efforts will not eliminate collection problems. If no systematic method is established to collect receivables, slow-paying accounts are more likely to become bad debts.

The first step in efficient collection procedures is to bill the customer quickly. Often, small businesses are so concerned with selling that they do not devote adequate time to billing. If invoices are not sent until 30 days after the sale, 60 days may easily pass between the sale date and the date payment is received.

If the account is not paid when due, immediate steps should be taken. The procedure usually follows a pattern of gentle reminders, which become increasingly more firm as time elapses. After the bill has been sent and no payment is received, the second step is a gentle reminder, which assumes that the customer has overlooked the bill. If payment is not received by a specific time after the reminder was sent, a more firm reminder is sent with a request for immediate payment. At this point, the seller still assumes that the customer intends to pay and the seller also hopes to keep the customer as an active account. If the seller still does not receive payment within a specified time after the second reminder, another message is sent. At this point, the seller no longer assumes that failure to pay was an oversight but assumes something is wrong. Often, telephone calls are used as reminders; they take less time than mailing notices, and the customer cannot ignore a phone call as easily as a letter. However, some customers avoid being contacted if they know the creditor is calling. The next stage is to threaten legal action if payment is not received, and finally to follow through with any actions threatened.

Collection agencies and attorneys are often used when the small business determines that an account will not be collected. A letter from a collection agency or attorney is usually enough incentive to make the customer pay. The customer knows that, particularly with a collection agency, the agency will make money only if it collects an account. Therefore, the customer is not likely to ignore the account. If the letter does not produce results, the attorney or collection agency will help take the customer to court.

Collection agencies' and attorneys' fees are generally governed by law; the fees may run as high as 50 percent of the amount collected. Usually, the percentage charged gets lower as the amount of the bad debt increases. However, even a 50 percent collection fee is preferable to ignoring delinquent accounts and never receiving payment. Since collection fees are a tax deduction for the small business, a 50 percent fee is actually less when taxes are considered.

The Fair Debt Collection Practices Act

Many creditors and collection agencies were guilty of abuses when trying to collect debts, such as making late-night phone calls to debtors, harrassing debtors at work, threatening debtors with physical harm or jail sentences, and other tactics. To prevent these abuses, the federal government passed the Fair Debt Collection Practices Act in 1978.[3]

Among the provisions of this law were guidelines governing the actions of a debt collector. The law states that the debt collector

1. can only contact the debtor between the hours of 8 a.m. and 9 p.m. unless other arrangements have been made between the two parties;

2. may not threaten physical harm or use obscene language;

3. cannot make any false statements while trying to collect the debt or pretend to be a credit bureau, attorney, government agency, and the like;

4. may not threaten arrest or imprisonment;

5. may not threaten to garnish wages, seize assets, or take other legal action unless he intends to do so;

6. may not threaten to take any action that is not legal.

If a debt collector violates this law, the customer has the right to sue for any damages incurred and any court costs or attorney's fees associated with the suit.

Factoring

Factoring
An arrangement by which an entrepreneur can sell accounts receivable to a financial institution to speed up cash flow.

Factor
The financial institution that purchases the accounts receivable.

Factoring is an arrangement by which an entrepreneur sells accounts receivable to a financial institution to speed up cash flow. The financial institution may be a bank, a finance company, or an independent business that is a factoring company. Generally, the **factor** (the financial institution) agrees to buy the receivables for a specific period, often as long as 1 or 2 years. The factor performs many of the credit functions, including customer credit checks, bookkeeping, and collections.

For these services, the factor is paid a fee, generally a percentage of the receivables. The actual percentage depends on several criteria. Factors prefer stable industries and companies with sales volumes of one million dollars or more. A higher-percentage fee will be charged if the business is in an unstable industry, has a low sales volume, has a large number of customers with a small dollar amount per customer, or has customers with poor credit ratings.[4] The factor's fees typically range from 0.5 to 5 percent or more.

Though many large companies use factoring, small companies often find it not practical. First, the required fee is often prohibitive. For a small company

---

[3]Fair Debt Collection Practices Act, Federal Trade Commission, 1978.
[4]*Can Your Business Benefit from Factoring Services?* (Scarsdale, N.Y.: TPR Publishing Co., 1983), 16–17.

Exhibit 16.2   Why Factoring May Increase Profits

Assume two companies both produce calculators. Both have a net profit of 15 percent, establish terms of net 30 days with no discounts, and average 30 to 60 days for actual collection. Company A factors its receivables; Company B does not.

First Month	A	B
Accounts Receivable Balance	$30,000	$30,000
Net Profit on Receivables When Collected	4,500	4,500
Factoring Percentage Paid	1,500 (5% × $30,000)	—
Net Profit	$ 3,000	$ 4,500
	Uses $28,500 from Factor to Continue Production; Produces Another Shipment of $30,000	Can Only Produce $8,000 in Goods Due to Shortage of Cash
Accounts Receivable on Shipment	$30,000	$ 8,000
Net Profit	4,500	1,200
Factoring Percentage, 5%	1,500	—
Net Profit	3,000	1,200
Total Monthly Profit	$ 6,000	$ 5,700
Month 2: Same as Above	$ 6,000	$ 5,700
Total Profit for 2 Months	$12,000	$11,400

with a gross margin of 35 percent, the factor's fee may decrease the percentage to 30 to 34 percent. This decrease in revenue may be more than the business can sustain if it wants to remain profitable. Second, factoring services are usually not available to any firm that sells directly to the consumer but are available only to manufacturing or wholesaling firms; this eliminates factoring for many small businesses.

Inventory Management

As stated in the beginning of this chapter, inventory often comprises as much as 24 percent of a small firm's total assets. Proper inventory monitoring is as essential as accounts receivable monitoring. If no systematic inventory control method is established, inventory will almost always be unbalanced (too much of one item and not enough of another) and will be excessive compared with the sales level. Also, without an inventory control system, it is very difficult to detect any theft problem.

Inventory Down, Profits Up

T. D. Shea, a manufacturing firm that employs 120 people, instituted an inventory control system after its vice-president attended a seminar at Ford Motor Co. The following changes were implemented:

1. Setup time on one press was reduced by 50 percent.
2. Tote boxes and carts have been purchased to move parts easier and in smaller quantities.
3. An automatic stacking machine was purchased to stack finished products.
4. Parts inventory is coded through a card system.

The changes, which cost $25,000 to implement, are expected to save the firm $75,000 annually.

Source: Craig Waters, "Why Everybody's Talking About 'Just-In-Time,'" *Inc.*, March 1984, 77.

The Inventory Dilemma

Excessive inventory results in a substantial cost for the small business. Since inventory increases are often paid for by reinvesting profits, the entrepreneur with excessive inventory often finds the financial statements showing a good profit though the business is cash poor. In addition to tying up all profits generated, excessive inventory often results in higher storage costs, higher insurance costs, and higher taxes; profits are even less than normal owing to these costs.

The entrepreneur faces a dilemma in controlling inventory, trying to have enough inventory yet simultaneously minimizing costs. The entrepreneur often tries to satisfy all customer requests and feels that any product a customer might need should be kept in stock. This causes a large inventory level. Because of inventory costs, however, the entrepreneur wants minimal inventory levels. Thus, inventory management is like a balancing act, offsetting customer relations and the possibilities of stockouts with all inventory-associated costs.

Many of the inventory models and formulas large corporations use are too complicated to be of interest to entrepreneurs. The best inventory system is the one that is simplest to use but still provides all necessary information. All inventory systems should provide information as to how many items are on hand and how many are on order. In addition, entrepreneurs may need to know the following:

1. how many of each item sell within a specified period
2. items purchased by each customer
3. items that are back ordered
4. items that have been discontinued and are no longer available
5. the cost per item and the price for which it was sold
6. amounts paid for items taken on trade
7. which items customers returned

Buying Decisions

Replenishment Buying
Buying inventory to replace the items that have been sold.

Anticipation Buying
Buying inventory items that are expected to sell in the future.

An entrepreneur needs to consider two basic types of buying: replenishment buying and anticipation buying.[5] **Replenishment buying** is buying inventory to replace items sold. **Anticipation buying** is buying items expected to sell in the future. Anticipation buying is essential in seasonal businesses that must project how many units of each item will sell and then order accordingly. (One of the most common examples is a retail store that orders large quantities in September for the Christmas season.) Not only retailers use anticipation buying, however. Manufacturers and wholesalers must also use it when sales are very seasonal. Improper planning in anticipation buying will result in lost sales due to stockouts or large quantities of inventory remaining after the peak season is over.

Determining the Amount on Hand

Visual Method.   Many entrepreneurs, particularly in very small companies, use a visual check to determine how many items are in inventory. Although this method is simple, it is very ineffective because it is easy to overlook items and the method is extremely time consuming when a company stocks a large inventory. Also, by the time an item is so low in stock to be noticed, it may be too late to avoid stockouts because of the time it takes to get another shipment. Better methods are available.

Physical Counts.   Businesses that carry numerous seasonal product lines know which items sell fastest during each season. When an item is selling quickly, a physical count is taken at the end of each week. Items not selling quickly would be counted only at the end of each month. For example, a sporting goods store might count fishing items every week during spring and

---

[5]R. Patrick Cash, *Buying for Retail Stores* (Washington, D.C.: U.S. Government Printing Office, 1979), 1.

summer, while it would count items for the fall hunting season monthly. Then, during October and November, the hunting items would be counted weekly, the fishing items monthly.

Card System.   Another method, similar to the physical count, is a card system that records the amount of each item on hand at any given time. An initial count of each item is recorded on a card. Whenever an item is sold, the amount sold is subtracted from the total. Thus, at any given time, the exact number of each item on hand is available at a glance.

Control by Cash Register.   The preceding methods become impractical when a company carries a large number of items because all of the records are kept manually. This results in a large percentage of employee time being consumed by inventory record keeping. With the computerized cash registers available, it often becomes simpler for a retail outlet to use a cash register tied into a computer, which deducts items from inventory as they are sold. The initial cost of this system will easily be recovered by the resulting control in inventory costs.

No matter what method is used to determine how much is on hand, two other decisions must then be made: when to order more inventory and how much inventory to order.

Determining When to Order

Two basic systems can be used to determine when to order, the fixed order quantity system and the fixed order period system.[6]

Fixed Order Quantity.   When the **fixed order quantity system** is used, the entrepreneur orders the same amount of inventory each time. The time between orders will vary, though, depending on the rate of usage or sales during the period. Inventory will fall until a certain level is reached. This level, the **order point,** is obtained by first determining a minimum inventory level that should be on hand at all times and then adding the amount of the item that will be used up between the time the order is placed and the time the order is received (see Figure 16.1).

One simple system that uses the approach is called the **two-bin system.** Two bins or containers are established for an inventory item. One container holds most of the inventory, while a smaller container holds enough inventory to last from the time an order is placed until the shipment is received. When all of the inventory is used out of the large bin, an order is placed, and inventory from the smaller bin is used. When the inventory is received, both bins are replenished appropriately and the process begins again, inventory being withdrawn from the large bin.

Fixed Order Quantity System
An inventory system in which the same amount of inventory is ordered each time but the time between orders will vary.

Order Point
The time when more inventory should be ordered, calculated by adding the minimum level of inventory that should be on hand at all times plus the amount of the item used between the order time and the time the shipment is received.

Two-Bin System
A fixed order quantity inventory system in which two containers are used to hold the inventory of an item. One bin is depleted during normal operations and the other bin holds just enough to last from the time the order is placed until the time it is received.

[6]Norman Gaither, *Production and Operations Management,* 2d ed. (Hinsdale: The Dryden Press, 1984), 914.

Figure 16.1   Fixed Order Quantity System

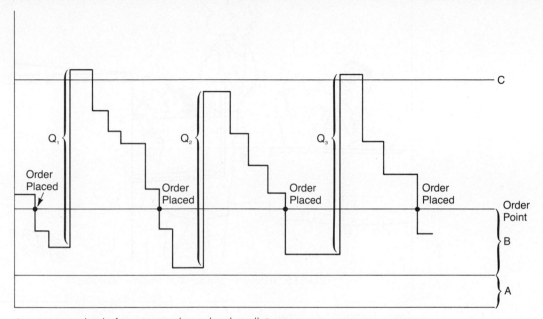

A = minimum level of inventory to be on hand at all times
B = amount used between the time an order is placed and the time the shipment is received
A + B = order point
C = maximum level of inventory
Q_1 = order quantity = Q_2 = Q_3

Source: Norman Gaither, *Production and Operations Management*, 2d ed. (Hinsdale, IL: The Dryden Press, 1984), 414.

Another method is available if a computer is used to maintain updated inventory records. If this type of perpetual inventory system is used, the computer can be programmed to print out a list of inventory items for which the order point has been reached.

Fixed Order Period System
An inventory system in which inventory is ordered at specific time intervals but the quantity ordered will vary.

Fixed Order Period.   With the **fixed order period system,** inventory is reviewed at specific intervals, and then an adequate amount is ordered to replenish inventory. Using this method, inventory will be ordered every week, every month, and so forth, but the quantity ordered will vary each time. Because demand varies during different periods, this system may require the entrepreneur to carry a larger minimum level of some inventory items than the fixed order quantity system would require. The fixed order period is often used in conjunction with a physical count method, described previously. It is often used successfully by small retail stores that do not establish a perpetual inventory method.

"I found Mr. Slackmeyer goofing off in accounts receivable!"

Source: Copyright Ford Button.

Determining How Much to Order

Determining the proper amount of inventory to order is important for all businesses, but it is crucial to small businesses because cash is usually tight. If too much inventory is ordered, the company will not only tie up cash in excess inventory but will also incur extra expenses, such as added insurance, interest on additional money borrowed, warehouse rental or space costs, and obsolescence.

If the company orders too little inventory, it may have items out of stock, resulting in lost sales or production delays. Small quantities purchased also require purchases to be made more often; thus, any costs associated with ordering (payroll time, postage, record keeping) will also increase.

Economic Order Quantity
The optimal quantity of inventory that should be ordered; the point at which annual ordering costs for an item equal annual carrying costs.

The entrepreneur must, therefore, balance the costs associated with too much inventory and the costs of too little, arriving at the optimal inventory level for each item. One of the most common methods of determining the best quantity is the **economic order quantity (EOQ).** This EOQ occurs when the annual ordering costs for an item equal the annual carrying costs.[7]

---

[7]Gaither, *Production and Operations Management,* 417–425.

To use this model, particularly at the most basic level, the entrepreneur must assume that (1) annual demand can be precisely estimated, (2) the average inventory level is equal to the maximum inventory plus the minimum inventory divided by 2, and (3) no quantity discounts exist. Given these assumptions, the following equation holds true:

$$EOQ = \sqrt{\frac{2\,DS}{C}},$$

where

D = Annual demand for an item in units per year;

S = Average cost of completing an order for the item in dollars per year; and

C = Cost of carrying one unit of the item in inventory for one year, stated in dollars per year.

Exhibit 16.3 illustrates how EOQ may save a company money when applied to many inventory items. More advanced EOQ models can be used to accommodate situations where inventory is delivered at a constant rate instead of all at once, or situations where quantity discounts exist on large orders.

Planning with the ABC Method

An entrepreneur who carries a large variety of items may feel completely overwhelmed at the thought of applying a system such as EOQ to each item. In reality, it is not necessary to establish strict controls on every inventory item, since some items are very inexpensive and do not warrant an in-depth analysis.

ABC Method
A method for determining which inventory items should be analyzed closely and which do not warrant close scrutiny.

One simple but very useful method, known as the **ABC method,** can be used to determine which items should be analyzed.[8] In a majority of inventories, 15 to 25 percent of the items will account for 75 to 85 percent of total dollars invested in inventory. These items are referred to as A items and should be analyzed and controlled closely. Another group of items, the B items, may represent 25 to 35 percent of the items but only 15 to 25 percent of total dollars invested. These B items would be analyzed and monitored, but not as closely as the A items. The final group, C items, may account for as much as 50 percent of the items, but because they are inexpensive, they will represent less than 10 percent of the total dollars invested in inventory. These items would not be analyzed closely, and might not be analyzed at all.

---

[8]Gaither, *Production and Operations Management*, 433.

Exhibit 16.3   Using EOQ in a Hardware Store

Assume a hardware store carries over 10,000 different items. The entrepreneur wishes to know if EOQ would help save money. An analysis on one of the items, screwdrivers, develops as follows.

1. Approximately 15,000 screwdrivers are sold each year.
2. The company currently orders 500 screwdrivers each time it places an order (order quantity, 500).
3. The stocking cost of each screwdriver is $0.50 per year.
4. The cost of ordering screwdrivers (wages, postage) is $6.00 per order.

Current annual stocking costs equal annual carrying costs plus annual ordering costs.

$$\text{Current Annual Stocking Costs} = \left(\frac{500}{2}\right)(\$0.50) + \left(\frac{15,000}{500}\right)(\$6.00)$$

$$= \$125.00 + \$180.00 = \$305.00.$$

$$\text{EOQ} = \sqrt{\frac{2DS}{C}} = \sqrt{\frac{2\,(15,000)\,(\$6.00)}{(\$0.50)}} = \sqrt{360,000} = 600 \text{ Units.}$$

Annual stocking costs with EOQ implemented are calculated as follows:

$$\left(\frac{600}{2}\right)(\$0.50) + \left(\frac{15,000}{600}\right)(\$6.00) = \$150.00 + \$150.00 = \$300.00.$$

Annual Savings = $305.00 − $300.00 = $5.00.

Although $5.00 may not seem worthwhile, if EOQ were applied to many of the items (considering 10,000 items are carried), the savings might be substantial.

Assigning Responsibility

Once an inventory method is established, it is essential to assign to one person the responsibility for ordering. Unless this is done, lack of communication will result in some items being ordered twice while others are not ordered at all. One restaurant, in a chain of several, found this to be a major cause of an inventory problem. The owner of the restaurants hired a consultant to help with the inventory problem. At one of the restaurants, it was discovered that four people were given the title of manager, and all four ordered inventory whenever a shortage was discovered without consulting the others. In this situation, no inventory system would be effective unless responsibility were first assigned to one person.

Small Business Success 16

Atlas Mechanical, Idaho Falls, Idaho

Lengthy periods of downtime can have a serious impact on a firm's working capital. Many of the clients of Atlas Mechanical, being in food processing, find this impact to be particularly severe because operational costs go on even though production has ceased. Because of their needs, Atlas has developed its capabilities for performing maintenance work correctly in minimum time. This service, plus fabricating pipe and duct in other settings, as well as heating, ventilation, and air conditioning work for commercial customers, have given the company a diversified base for its $6 million annual sales. The company president, Con Mahoney, is a national leader in his field and in 1983 was elected president of the National Association of Plumbing, Heating, and Cooling Contractors.

Source: Small Business Means Jobs (Washington, D.C.: Small Business Administration, 1984), 7.

Controlling Total Investment in Inventory

No matter which method is used to monitor inventory turnover, it is also essential to maintain a running account of the total amount of money tied up in inventory. Just as with receivables, a simple system can be set up to provide the necessary information to the entrepreneur. This formula can be quickly computed and yet provides vital information. Unless the entrepreneur uses a formula of this type, he has no way of knowing whether inventory is above or below the appropriate level. A typical method for monitoring the dollar value of inventory is shown below.

Inventory Control			
	May	June	October
Beginning Inventory at Cost	$50,000	$52,000	$50,000
+ Purchases This Month at Cost	13,000	12,500	29,000
+ Returned Merchandise	500	600	—
− Sales at Cost	11,500	12,000	15,000
Ending Inventory at Cost	$52,000	$53,100	$64,000

Notice the large increase in purchases in October in anticipation of the peak selling season in December. Because the inventory will not be sold for several months, ending inventory will be unusually high until January.

Cash Flow Monitoring

Control over accounts receivable and inventory ultimately results in control over cash. Because proper cash flow is so critical to a small business's survival, cash flow must be monitored constantly. Cash flow projections should be developed that indicate the anticipated cash inflows and anticipated cash outflows for expenditures. Actual revenues and expenses should then be compared with the projections to determine why any variances may have occurred. The cash flow projection shown below illustrates a typical method. If the entrepreneur consistently develops these projections and compares them with actual figures, the variances begin to decrease as the entrepreneur becomes more accurate. Accurate prediction will then prevent unexpected cash shortages.

Selected Months
Cash Flow Projection
XYZ Corp.

	May		June		October	
	Estimate	Actual	Estimate	Actual	Estimate	Actual
Cash on Hand						
Beginning of month	$15,125	$14,500	$10,035	$ 8,085	$15,000	$14,100
Cash sales	5,200	6,000	6,000	5,500	8,000	9,000
AR collected	8,500	7,000	8,500	8,000	9,500	9,000
Total cash available	$28,825	$27,500	$24,535	$21,585	$32,500	$32,100
Cash Paid Out						
Inventory purchased	$12,500	$13,000	$13,000	$12,500	$26,000	$29,000
Payroll	2,800	2,800	2,800	2,800	2,800	2,800
Owner's salary	800	800	800	800	800	800
Payroll taxes	360	360	360	360	360	360
Supplies	20	35	20	25	20	0
Repairs	100	60	100	75	100	110
Loan payment	500	500	500	500	500	500
Advertising	650	650	500	500	650	650
Utilities	250	300	350	390	350	350
Insurance	60	60	60	60	60	60
Rent	600	600	600	600	600	600
Other	150	250	200	250	200	250
Total cash out	$18,790	$19,415	$19,290	$18,860	$32,440	$35,480
Cash balance	$10,035	$ 8,085	$ 5,245	$ 2,725	$ 60	($3,380)

Notice that the dollar amounts from the inventory control chart and the accounts receivable control chart for XYZ Corp. are incorporated into the cash flow projection. The cash flow projection shows the actual effects on cash when receivables and inventory increase. For XYZ, the increase in both receivables and inventory results in a cash shortage of $3,380 by the end of October. However, if an income statement for XYZ Corp. is prepared, as shown below, it becomes obvious that the company is actually very profitable. If inventory and receivables are not monitored closely, there will not be enough cash to pay bills, even though the company is profitable.

Selected Months
Income Statement Projection
XYZ Corp.

	May	June	October
Sales			
Accounts receivable	$13,500	$15,200	$16,800
Cash	6,000	5,500	9,000
Total sales	$19,500	$20,700	$25,800
Cost of Goods Sold			
Beginning inventory	$50,000	$52,000	$50,000
Plus purchases	13,000	12,500	29,000
Minus ending inventory	52,000	53,100	64,000
Total CGS	$11,000	$11,400	$15,000
Gross profit	$ 8,500	$ 9,300	$10,800
Expenses			
Payroll	$ 2,800	$ 2,800	$ 2,800
Owner salary	800	800	800
Payroll taxes	360	360	360
Supplies	20	25	—
Repairs	100	75	110
Interest	250	200	100
Advertising	650	500	650
Utilities	250	390	350
Insurance	60	60	60
Rent	600	600	600
Other	150	250	250
Total expenses	$ 6,040	$ 6,060	$ 6,080
Net profit before taxes	$ 2,460	$ 3,240	$ 4,720

If a company's receivables and inventory are closely monitored and must still increase owing to company growth, a solution to the cash problems may be to borrow additional funds for working capital. However, this solution is recommended only if inventory balances are at the proper levels and if receivables are being collected on time. If cash balances are low owing to uncontrolled inventory growth and/or improper management of receivables, borrowing money will only be a short-term solution, and eventually the company will again be cash poor.

K E Y   Objectives Reviewed

1. Extending credit to customers will usually result in increased sales but will severely affect cash flow if the credit terms are not properly managed. The entrepreneur must evaluate the risks and costs of extending credit and determine if the benefits of extending credit offset these costs. Collections must be properly monitored either by using an aging system, a receivables turnover ratio, or a collection index, and a collection plan should be established.

2. Maintaining an inventory is essential to many businesses because cash flow can be strangled if inventory is not properly controlled. The entrepreneur must engage in two types of inventory buying: replenishment buying and anticipation buying. There are many methods for determining inventory on hand, including a visual method, a physical count, a card system, or a computerized method. The entrepreneur must also establish a method to determine when to order and how much to order.

3. Cash flow projections should be completed to determine the anticipated cash inflows and anticipated cash outflows. The entrepreneur should prepare cash flow projections incorporating anticipated changes in inventory and accounts receivable. If accurate projections are made, unexpected cash shortages will be prevented. Actual figures should be compared with projections, and the causes of variances should be determined.

Discussion Questions

1. Identify and define the two types of credit.
2. What is the primary purpose in extending credit to customers?
3. Identify and define the four Cs of credit.
4. What costs are involved in extending credit? Is it possible that the costs of extending could exceed the additional revenue generated? Why or why not?
5. There are many ways of monitoring the collection of accounts receivable, including the sales/receivables ratio, the days receivables, the collection index, or an aging schedule. Why might an entrepreneur wish to use several of these methods at the same time? (For example, why would an entrepreneur develop an aging schedule and also calculate days receivables?)

6. Define factoring. Why might factoring result in increased profits for a company even though it must pay a factoring fee?

7. What is the difference between replenishment buying and anticipation buying? In which type of buying is the entrepreneur most likely to make mistakes?

8. Explain the difference between the fixed order quantity system and the fixed order period system. Which method is utilized in the two-bin system?

9. Explain how the ABC method and EOQ method can be used jointly.

10. Explain the relationship between accounts receivable, inventory, and cash flow. How does proper monitoring of accounts receivable and inventory help a company's cash flow?

CHAPTER 17

Production and Operations Management

Source: John Blaustein for McKesson Corporation. Used with permission.

K E Y Objectives

1. To describe the elements of production.

2. To identify the various types of production systems.

3. To describe the resource requirements planning process.

4. To discuss production control methods.

5. To explore the use of robots in production.

Every business must provide a product or service that society demands. In this chapter, instead of saying "product or service" we will simply say "product." Services, though intangible, can be referred to as "products" nonetheless. For example, the product of a garbage disposal organization is trash hauling; a management consulting firm provides analysis and recommendations as its product. That product gives the firm its reason to exist. Managing the processes that produce the company's product is the core of the business. We call it production management. It means ensuring that the organization's work gets done how and when the customer requires. This calls for careful planning and controlling, topics we will discuss in this chapter.

Production System Elements

In its most basic form, a production system consists of three elements, the inputs, the transformation, and the outputs.

The Inputs

Although the specific inputs vary from firm to firm, three kinds are encountered regularly in operations of all types: human resources, money, and materials.

Human Resources. No production system operates entirely without the input of people. In some cases the skills and level of expertise are demanding, as in a corporate law consulting firm. In others, such as agricultural harvesting, there are no special skill or expertise requirements made of employees,

Unique Business   17.1

Suds and Buds

If you have dirty clothes and a bad thirst, there's a place in Austin, Texas that can fix you right up. It goes by the charming name of "Barwash" and is located in a strip shopping center near the campus of the University of Texas. The place was started by Robb Walsh and other members of his family. Barwash broke even during its third month of operation, with $12,000 in revenue. Less than a year after founding the business, the Walshes were looking into the possibility of selling franchises.

Source: "Cleaning and Drinking Up," *Venture* 7, no. 7 (July 1985): 12.

each of whom can be easily replaced. As technology becomes more complex, the required human input often decreases in terms of hours spent in production, but the skills required of the work force increase rapidly.

Money.   This input is represented by the machinery, plant and equipment, and other assets used in the production process. As automation increases and computers and related electronic devices are used more, the role of money as an input becomes more important.

Material.   The use of material in physical production is usually obvious. A sawmill must have logs to produce boards, the company that produced this book had to have paper, ink, binding glue, and material for the cover. In service organizations, material inputs are required as well; for example, medical clinics need tongue depressors and cotton swabs, among other things; auto repair shops need paint, putty, sandpaper, and other materials.

Other Inputs.   In addition to the primary inputs described above, organizations use a number of other factors in the production process, such as utilities, data processing capabilities, building maintenance, and materials handling equipment. These factors are not used in the same, direct way as the three primary inputs but are necessary nonetheless.

The Transformation

Transformation
The process by which the inputs into the production system are converted into outputs to be sold.

Now that we have identified and described the inputs, we must turn our attention to the process by which they will be transformed into the firm's product, the output. This is the **transformation,** a conversion process that may be

Analytic Conversion
A production process in which the raw material is reduced to component parts.

Synthetic Conversion
A production process in which the raw materials are combined into a finished product.

analytic or synthetic. In an **analytic conversion** the raw material is reduced to its component parts. A junkyard that buys a wrecked car breaks it down into pieces that are stored for sale as used auto parts. A butcher shop that buys a side of beef carves it into cuts of meat that its customers will find appealing. An analytic conversion, then, involves breaking up the input into small parts for output.

A **synthetic conversion** or transformation combines the raw materials or parts into a finished product. A picture framing shop takes the framing material, the glass, the mat backing, and the artwork and combines them into something the customer can hang or otherwise display. A drugstore combines a pharmaceutical company's drugs and a doctor's prescription to fill a customer's order.

Even in service businesses a transformation must take place to convert the inputs into outputs. A dry cleaning establishment, by using chemicals, machines, and personnel, transforms the dirty clothes (an input) into clean clothes (the output). A lawn care service uses as inputs its truck, chemicals, and driver, and a sick, weedy lawn and transforms them into the output, an envy-of-the-neighborhood lawn.

The Outputs

The outputs that result from the transformation process include not only the goods and services the organization intended to produce but also by-products and unintended results. From the agricultural producer may come a variety of foods, but other results, or outputs, are also generated. The water leaving the fields enters our rivers and streams containing fertilizers, herbicides, and pesticides, so pollution is an output. Farm accidents are another output. Paper mills produce useful products but also gases that pollute the air. When viewed in its entirety, then, the transformation process can be seen as creating a variety of outputs, some intended, some unintended and troublesome.

Unit or Small Batch Production
Manufacture of a product, or order, in response to customer specifications.

Large Batch Production
Production of standard items, in large quantities, in anticipation of future orders.

Continuous Production
Uninterrupted production of a single product, or a few products, to the manufacturer's own specifications.

Types of Production Systems

The means by which products are made vary greatly. Consider how a small custom builder of furniture goes about production and compare those efforts with those of a large mass-producer of low-priced furniture. In the first instance, the needs of the individual customer determine much of the materials and techniques used; in the second, the emphasis would be on uniformity and production efficiency. In contrast to both of these production systems, a third company might have a largely automated system in which machines do nearly all product handling.

The three production systems just mentioned are examples of three types of technology. They are referred to as **unit or small batch production; large batch** or repetitive production; and mass or **continuous production.**

Unit or Small Batch

Firms using this type of manufacturing make products to customer specifications. The product is nonstandard and, therefore, not produced for storage in inventory to await future orders. Firms that engage in this kind of manufacturing are called job shops.

Large Batch

Large batch or repetitive production involves making standard products in many economic-sized lots. The products are made in lots that are not large enough to justify manufacture on a continuous basis, but that are repeated from time to time without important changes in the processing methods.

Continuous

A firm with a single product, or only a few products, may use continuous manufacturing. In this system of manufacturing the company manufactures its products according to its own specifications in anticipation of future sales. Among small firms such a system is most often used in industries such as dairy and soft-drink bottling.

Resource Requirements

Regardless of the context or topic, planning is a process by which we provide for the future. In doing so, we hope to be able to deal with problems and/or take advantage of opportunities more effectively than if we had adopted a "we'll cross that bridge when we come to it" policy. To determine what course a small business will take in the months or years ahead, it must determine the future demand for its product. In Chapter 4, "The Nature of the Market," we described the methods used to make forecasts. Those forecasts, whether they are made using qualitative or quantitative methods, become the starting point for production planning. We use these forecasts, or estimates of future demand, to determine the resources needed to produce the required levels.

A moment's reflection will tell us that the demand for a company's output can be met by drawing from inventory or producing the needed items. Inventories typically provide only a portion of the goods needed for sale in a given period; production is required to provide the rest. This production in turn requires that certain inputs be available. We will separate these inputs into material requirements and capacity requirements.

Material Requirements

Material Resources Planning (MRP)
A control system, usually computerized, that generates schedule and inventory data and provides various reports concerning production performance.

Bill of Material
A listing of raw materials, parts, and subassemblies that form the item being produced.

Kanban System
A Japanese system of buying and inventory control in which inventories are kept at a minimum through just-in-time delivery schedules.

A topic receiving considerable attention as researchers and managers examine the efficiency problems of American manufacturing is **material resources planning (MRP)**. The heart of a modern MRP system is a computer program that uses as inputs the master production schedule and data from inventory and bill of material files. A **bill of material** lists the raw materials, parts, subassemblies, and so forth, that go into the product. Using these inputs, the program generates the schedule, inventory data, and various reports concerning performance.

The objectives of an MRP system are to save the company money by reducing inventory levels, to improve plant operating efficiency through better control of materials needed in production, and finally to improve customer service by allowing more reliable, and often shorter, delivery times.

The success enjoyed by Japanese firms that have put MRP into practice has prompted many large American companies to adopt some of their techniques. One example with important implications for small business manufacturers is the **"Kanban"** buying and inventory system. The innovation, refined by Toyota, allows a firm to minimize investment in inventory through a "just-in-time" system of providing materials to production. The system reduces inventories, and with the reduction come smaller storage space requirements, fewer storage racks and conveyors, and other savings. Also, because no buffer inventory exists, the emphasis on error-free parts and raw materials is constant. Many small manufacturers that supply companies going to the just-in-time system will need to be more responsive to such companies' demands. Until the company and its suppliers can develop the system, life is likely to be hectic for both, with work stoppages, rush orders, and unpredictable requirements being commonplace. See Illustration Capsule 17.1 for difficulties small Japanese firms face.

We have examined how some firms manage materials. Many small manufacturers, however, do not have a computer as the central element in their materials planning. Such companies rely on balance-of-stores ledgers and other manually prepared documents. While these procedures permit limited analysis, they answer the questions of when material should be ordered and how much should be ordered.

In addition to having the needed materials in the needed amounts, we must provide other inputs as well. These are covered in our next section.

Capacity Requirements

We use "capacity" here in a broad sense; we include not only capacity of the facility or plant, but the capacity of machines and equipment and that of the work group as well.

Machines and Equipment.   A firm's operations are limited, at least in the short run, by the number of machine hours available. Some stretching

Illustration Capsule   17.1

Pressure, Japanese Style

A big part of the Japanese automobile industry's success has been its ability to produce high-quality automobiles for far less than the American and European competition. At Toyota, this has been accomplished, in part, through relentless pressure on suppliers for price cuts. Many of these suppliers subcontract their work to small businesses that, in turn, may subcontract the work to even smaller firms, keeping on the pressure for cost reduction. At the bottom of the chain are thousands of very small organizations—many of them families working in sheds—that must deliver high-quality parts at bargain prices.

Is it efficiency or exploitation? You decide that, but we can say that it's the system.

Source: Business Week, November 7, 1985, 44.

---

may be possible by use of overtime and subcontracting with other firms, but in most cases machine capacity provides the ceiling beyond which production cannot be achieved. Machine capacity can be defined, first, as the machine's maximum output per hour times the number of hours available, or second, as the level of output that can be sustained over the course of days or weeks. This second definition is preferable because it takes into account downtime for maintenance, failures, and other problems.

Labor.   The skills of the work force represent a constraint on production in the same manner as do machines and equipment. Some flexibility may be found in the short run through scheduling overtime and pressuring workers for extra effort, but such measures are often self-defeating over the long run. Eventually, effective resource requirements planning will result in additions to the work force if needed, or in a change in the firm's man-machine mix that increases the use of machines.

Determining the labor input needed for a given production level is complicated by the variations in productivity among workers. One important source of variation is a worker's experience at a particular task. The longer we engage in an activity, the better we become. Studies of the **learning curve** phenomenon, first conducted at Wright-Patterson Air Force Base in the 1920s, have shown that with each doubling of cumulative production, the time required per unit is reduced, usually by approximately 20 percent. For

Learning Curve
The phenomenon resulting in a 20 percent reduction in time required per unit with each doubling of the cumulative production.

example, if the fourth unit a worker produced required 10 hours, the eighth unit would require 8 hours and the sixteenth 6.4 (8 hours × 0.8). Figure 17.1 shows the learning curve graphically.

Facilities. The final input the small business manager must provide is the facility. Facilities planning must closely reflect the firm's long-run strategy. What are the firm's future product plans? What technology will the firm use? What markets will it serve?

Because of the difficulty in accurately predicting future demand, many small firms develop a variety of ways to accommodate needed changes in capacity. Developing more capacity by building new facilities is only one way to respond to anticipated demand increases. Another way is through more intensive use of facilities through the schedule of second and third shifts, greater use of overtime, and various types of productivity improvements. Another alternative is using subcontractors as suppliers of parts, assemblies, or entire products. The decision to use outside sources rests on a number of considerations. Our next section examines those considerations.

Figure 17.1   **Eighty Percent Learning Curve**

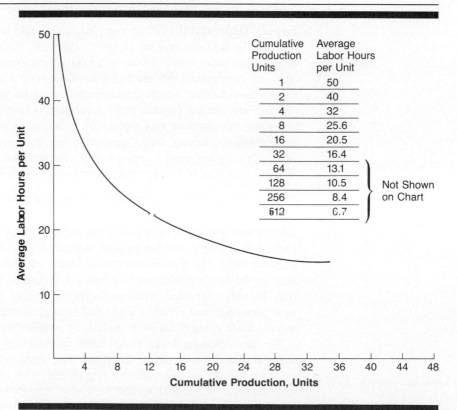

Cumulative Production Units	Average Labor Hours per Unit	
1	50	
2	40	
4	32	
8	25.6	
16	20.5	
32	16.4	
64	13.1	Not Shown on Chart
128	10.5	
256	8.4	
512	6.7	

Deciding Whether to Make or Buy

Factors that influence the "make-or-buy" choice include cost, quality level, quantity needed, supply dependability, and manufacturing requirements.

Cost.   Often a supplier's quoted price makes the decision easy. The price may be prohibitively high, clearly beyond what the firm could itself achieve. In other instances the part may be a stock item for the supplier and therefore available at a price far less than the cost the firm would incur if it were to make it.

Quality Level.   For standard parts the quality issue is seldom critical; most suppliers have suitable quality levels. For other parts, however, finding a supplier with parts of acceptable quality can be difficult. Many firms with complex technology have unique products, which makes finding high-quality suppliers difficult. In such instances, the entrepreneurial spirit of "if it has to be done right, do it yourself" seems to hold sway.

Quantity.   When only a few parts are needed, the small firm will look long and hard for an acceptable supply source. Gearing up to produce such a requirement is costly and therefore done as a last resource. The need for large quantities, on the other hand, makes self-manufacture more likely.

Supply Dependability.   In many cases the make-or-buy decision rests on whether the firm can rely on supply of the item. Interruptions in the supply of parts can mean costly delays in a firm's production process. For this reason, any components that are customized, or specially made, are candidates for self-manufacture. Standard components, or those available from a number of suppliers, do not provide these dependability concerns and therefore are items the management may decide to purchase. Another aspect of supply dependability is timing. Often production requirements call for supply variations that suppliers cannot accommodate. Deliveries delayed because of supplier inadequacies will weigh heavily in favor of in-house production.

Manufacturing Requirements.   Some components require processing that can be done only by expensive machines and/or technology. An electronically controlled valve on a pump, for example, may represent only a small part of the pump's cost but require technology that the pump manufacturer does not have. The manufacturer must decide whether to buy the valve or to gear up the firm's production to produce it in-house. The gearing-up process may be rather involved, however, with purchasing new machinery, hiring new personnel, and possibly using technical consultants. Such decisions are usually made using break-even analysis to compare the alternatives.

We have examined the components of resource requirement planning: material and capacity. Once the plans have been made, the task becomes ensuring that things take place as they should. This requires production control, the topic of our next section.

Production Control

· ·

Quality Control
The philosophy and practices a firm adopts to protect soundness of its products and production.

Long-run survival of any organization hinges on two things: its effectiveness and its efficiency. Effectiveness may be seen as an external concern, one of meeting the test of the market by providing goods and services the customer finds acceptable. Efficiency concerns the firm's internal workings. The issue is how well the company uses its resources. Production control plays an important role in the achievement of both effectiveness, through sound **quality control,** and efficiency, through scheduling practices.

Quality Control

Quality has become the rallying cry of many critics of U.S. industry. They cite examples of shoddy workmanship in domestic products and contrast them with superior foreign-made items.

Every firm must recognize the importance of the quality of its products. Unacceptable quality levels bring a variety of customer reactions, none of which management would like to see. The customer's mildest form of reaction is to complain about the product's shortcomings. Rather than simply complaining, many customers will register their dissatisfaction by no longer buying from the company. Occasionally customers' reactions to poor quality will go beyond complaining or changing suppliers and involve such activities as lawsuits and/or arranging consumer boycotts. The importance of quality is clear; unacceptable levels bring many negative results. High quality, on the other hand, can provide a company with an important strategic advantage. The issue is not whether to protect quality; the issue is how it might best be accomplished.

While the techniques of quality control to be discussed later are essential, the achievement of high quality levels requires something more. The commitment of the firm's ownership to quality as an overall organizational objective is also needed. The policies or guidelines that follow from such an objective focus and direct quality control activities throughout the company. Dr. W. Edwards Demming, a leading figure in the quality control movement in postwar Japan, faults American top management for not understanding what better quality requires within a firm and what it can do for the firm.[1]

The task of quality control is shown in Figure 17.2. The figure makes it clear that concerns for quality cannot be confined to inspecting goods about to be shipped. Each element of the production system must be included.

Except in extremely small firms, quality control involves sampling. Sampling is done as materials and parts are received, as production takes place,

---

[1]"The Roots of Quality Control in Japan," *Pacific Basin Quarterly* (Spring/Summer 1985), no. 12, 1.

Figure   17.2   Quality Control through the Production System

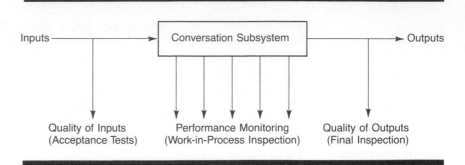

Source: Adapted from *Production and Operations Management,* Second Edition, by Norman Gaither, p. 675. Copyright © 1984 by The Dryden Press. Used by permission of CBS College Publishing.

and before finished goods are shipped to the customer. On the basis of information gained in the sampling process, decisions are made about the quality of the lots from which the samples were taken.

This sampling process generally is based on the measurement of either **attributes** or **variables.** The categories of attributes are usually defective and nondefective. The nondefective items have the attribute in question; the defective items do not. For example, inspecting a shipment of light bulbs would consist of determining the number of bulbs that light up. Variables, on the other hand, are characteristics measured on a continuous scale. The length of a part, for example, is measured against the standard.

We will next describe how sampling is used during each phase of production.

Inputs.   The importance of close attention to quality at this point is made clear in the following remarks of Dr. Demming.

> *If you have material coming in that is difficult to use . . . you will produce a lot of wasted human effort, machine time, and materials. There will be a lot of rework, with people occupying time trying to overcome the deficiencies of defective incoming material. So if you have better material coming in, you eliminate waste; production, quality and productivity go up; costs go down; and your market position is improved.*[2]

The technique used to determine whether lots of raw materials, subassemblies, or parts meet quality standards is the **acceptance plan.** In the case of attributes, the acceptance plan specifies the maximum number of defective items beyond which a sample may not go if the lot is to be accepted. For variables, the acceptance plan specifies the average values and variability that

Attribute Measurement
An approach toward sampling in which products are placed in one of two categories: defective or acceptable.

Variable Measurement
Measurement of a variable on a continuous scale; for example, the length of a part may be measured in inches and that length compared with a specified standard.

Acceptance Plan
A document that specifies the maximum number of defective items beyond which a sample may not go if a lot of raw materials, subassemblies, or parts is to be accepted.

---

[2]"The Roots of Quality Control in Japan," 1.

"Mr. Wilson, about my appointment as plant manager. . ."

Source: Copyright Ford Button.

are tolerable. This usually includes a range for the average value (1.95 to 2.05 millimeters) and an upper limit on variability (no sample group should vary by more than 0.3 millimeters). The decision that the acceptance plan allows a firm to make is whether to reject the shipment of incoming materials or accept it and release it for production. While the decision is usually acceptance or rejection, reworking the lot to improve the quality, or inspecting all of the items to save any nondefective material or parts, are also possible dispositions.

Transformation.   Even with high-quality inputs, defects are still encountered. Any manufacturing process can go wrong from time to time. For this reason, most firms use some system of work-in-process inspection. In doing

Illustration Capsule   17.2

Selling Quality throughout the Company

The problems encountered in establishing effective quality control at the Saegertown, Pennsylvania plant of Spectrum Control Inc. required changes that one worker likened to "quitting smoking, giving up drinking, and going on a diet—all at the same time." The management tried to use the statistical control models of W. Edwards Demming but found they gave little direction as to what actually to do. Through the writings of another expert, the company grasped the importance of a simple notion: Why not do things right the first time? The idea is simple, but getting it established is another matter.

According to Spectrum president and chairman Thomas Venable, very small companies do well because there's "no point in making things wrong," but "you probably lose control somewhere between 15 and 20 people." At this point, companies often develop a philosophy of acceptable quality levels (AQL) that acknowledges quality problems and a certain number of defects as inevitable. This philosophy extends throughout the organization from inspection of purchases, to control of production processes, to finished goods shipments. Once the AQL philosophy is established, the road to zero defects is long and difficult.

Source: Craig R. Walters, "Quality Begins at Home," *Inc.*, August 1985, 68–71.

so, these firms lower their costs by detecting defects before the items are processed further and by making the adjustments needed to correct the problem before too many parts are damaged.

Outputs.   The effort toward establishing quality levels is perhaps most visible at the point at which the firm decides whether its output is acceptable. Four outcomes can take place at this point. First, acceptable outputs can be approved for shipment. Second, defective goods can be rejected. In either of these cases, inspection has provided the correct decision. In either of the other two outcomes, however, an incorrect decision is made. Third, an acceptable product or a lot can be rejected. Fourth, unacceptable quality can be approved. Though sound quality control procedures can minimize the chance of either of these incorrect decisions being made, some trade-offs exist. Extremely high standards can lead to rejection of good-quality outputs, and loose requirements can mean shipment of bad products.

The likelihood of these errors taking place is largely the result of managerial attitudes toward quality. The contrasting attitudes of Japanese and American business people are reflected in these comments made by Stephen Moss, a consultant who has worked with corporations in both countries:

> *The U.S. manager sets an acceptable level of quality and then sticks to it. The Japanese are constantly upgrading their goals. The American assumes a certain rate of failure is inevitable, what the Japanese shoots for is perfection and sometimes gets close.*[3]

Scheduling

In addition to seeing to it that the "right things happen," i.e., that output of acceptable quality is produced, the management of a business must ensure that "things happen right," that the organization operates efficiently. Simply stated, efficiency is using inputs in such a way so as to minimize cost per unit of production. It means getting the maximum output from a given level of input or using minimum inputs for a given level of output.

One of the critical elements of cost is scheduling. Poor scheduling results in idle machines and human resources, excessive inventories, and uncertain deliveries. Efficiency of operations clearly depends on scheduling in the best possible way.

Scheduling is determined by the production system itself, each system having unique characteristics due to such factors as the number of products, the nature of technology, machine availability, and labor force characteristics. It is useful, nonetheless, to explore the scheduling techniques commonly encountered in both job shops and project management operations. These are the production systems small businesses most frequently use; our discussion will center on them.

Job Shops.   Job shops produce nonstandard items in response to customer orders. This kind of operation frequently encounters many orders and the need for machine changes. The following scheduling decisions must be made.

1. Sequence in which the customer orders are processed.
    Here are some rules.[4] Process first the job that
    A.   arrived first (first come, first served).
    B.   has the shortest processing time.
    C.   has the earliest due date.
    D.   is the most profitable.
    E.   belongs to the best customer.
2. Coordination of work center schedule throughout the facility.
    Most orders require multiple operations; coordination ensures that the

---

[3]J. Main, "The Battle for Quality Begins," *Fortune* 13, no. 102 (Dec. 29, 1980): 28–33.
[4]Adapted from Norman Gaither, *Production and Operations Management* (Hinsdale, Il.: The Dryden Press, 1984), 473.

Figure   17.3   Gantt Chart, Department A Weekly Schedule, Jobs A through G

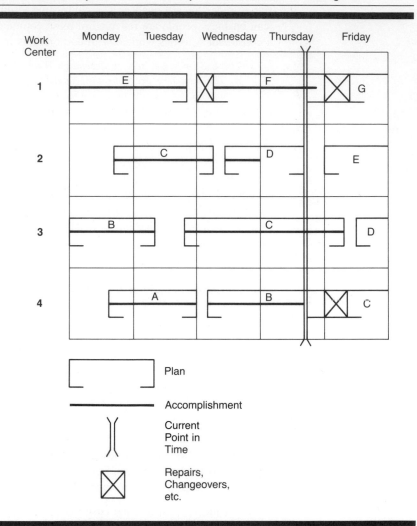

orders move smoothly and that the work load is balanced within the shop. The most common technique is the Gantt chart, an example of which is shown in Figure 17.3. The chart shows that work centers 1 and 3 are both ahead of schedule, 2 is behind, and 4 is exactly where it should be.

Project Management.   Many companies, particularly those in construction, constantly face the challenge of scheduling production of a nonrecurring project. Certain project management techniques have evolved in recent years

Figure   17.4   PERT Diagram for Building a Homecoming Float

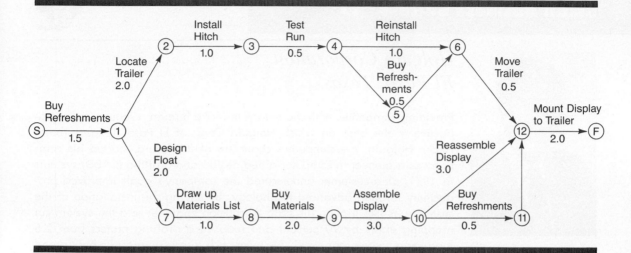

Program Evaluation and Review Technique (PERT)
A means of scheduling and monitoring progress on the events needed in completing a project.

Critical Path Method (CPM)
A method of identifying the sequence of operations in a PERT chart that requires the longest time for completion.

that are very useful in this regard. The most important is **PERT (Program Evaluation and Review Technique).** PERT aids in managing projects by breaking the project down into a series of activities, analyzing the relationships between them, and making clear the effects of any deviations from schedule. Figure 17.4 shows a simplified PERT chart for building a homecoming display.

The **Critical Path Method (CPM)** concerns the sequence of operations in the PERT diagram that requires the longest time for completion. For projects in which timing is of overriding importance, CPM can be extremely useful. By identifying the critical path, the project manager can make decisions concerning the allocation of resources to various phases of the project.

Use of Robots

Robot
A programmable machine capable of performing tasks that require the manipulation of materials and tools.

A topic that has received considerable attention in business journals as well as the popular press is the growing use of robots. A **robot** may be defined as a programmable machine capable of performing tasks that require the manipulation of materials and tools. Most robots in use today perform very simple, limited tasks. Factory use has concentrated on repetitive and/or hazardous jobs.

It appears that Japan will lead the way in the robotics movement, with more than 100 companies manufacturing industrial robots, compared with a handful of U.S. manufacturers. In number of robots in use, the United States lags as

Holguin Corporation, El Paso, Texas

Providing companies with the means to make human resources more productive is the base on which Holguin Corp. of El Paso, Texas is built. Hector Holguin, the company's chairman of the board, started his company as a pioneer in computer-aided design and drafting (CADD) systems in 1971. One customer underscored the company's goal, improved productivity through advanced technology, by saying the installation of the system was like tripling his staff. A Houston engineer said the system cut mapping errors by 90 percent and reduced a drafting project from 2.5 man-years to one man-week. News of such impressive results has spread quickly; Holguin systems are in use in 22 countries, and the company is the second largest installer of CADD systems in the United States and third largest in the world.

Source: America at Work (Washington, D.C.: Small Business Administration, 1985), 39.

well, with approximately 10 percent of the world robot population in 1982, Japan having 60 percent.[5]

Their impact on U.S. industry has been limited to date, but what about the future? Because of some obvious, very important advantages, the use of robots is certain to increase. Robots do not get sick, do not ask for more pay, and do not take vacations, coffee breaks, or offense at being ignored by the boss. As their capabilities increase and their prices decrease, they will become more and more attractive to more and more businesses. Projections of future increases in their use, though substantial, are by no means dramatic when viewed in the context of the entire economy. By 1990 we may be using as many as 100,000 robots; however, assuming one robot replaces two workers, we have a maximum potential displacement of 200,000 workers.[6] This is approximately 2 percent of our work force. The robot revolution is in reality the robot evolution.

---

[5]Charles J. Hollon and George N. Rogel, "How Robotization Affects People," *Business Horizons* 28, no. 3 (May-June 1985): 74–80.
[6]Hollon and Rogel, "How Robotization Affects People," 74–80.

K   E   Y   Objectives Reviewed

1. The production elements are the inputs, the transformation process, and the outputs.

2. Various types of production systems can be identified.

3. The resource requirements planning process consists of forecasting the level of production needed and planning for the provision of material and capacity sufficient to produce at that level.

4. Production control consists of ensuring that acceptable levels of quality be maintained throughout production and that scheduling permits efficient operations.

5. The use of robots currently is a minor, but growing, part of production.

Discussion Questions

1. Describe the inputs into the production system.

2. What two types of conversion processes may a firm use?

3. Three types of production systems can be identified; what are they?

4. What is the Kanban buying and inventory system?

5. How does the learning curve operate and how should it be taken into account in production planning?

6. What factors influence the make or buy decision?

7. Distinguish between the terms *effectiveness* and *efficiency*.

8. What effect have robots had thus far on industrial practices in the United States? How rapidly has their impact spread?

Cases for Part Four

Case IVA   Flowers Forever Inc.

Susan DiAngelo had been employed by Perfect Plants, a floral and gift shop, for 15 years. She began in high school as a part-time sales clerk and accepted a full-time position after graduating from college with a degree in horticulture. Perfect Plants was a well-established small business in San Diego, California, and Susan continually received promotions. Eventually she was promoted to store manager and was responsible for supervising all daily activities.

Susan had always dreamed of owning her own floral and gift shop but was reluctant to open a business in San Diego that would compete with Perfect Plants. Although she had not signed an employment agreement prohibiting her from opening a competing business, her loyalty to the owners prevented her from doing so. A friend in Los Angeles, however, called to inform her that a floral and gift shop there, Flowers Forever, was for sale. The business was well established, and the owner wished to retire.

After several meetings with the owner, Susan purchased the business. The business was located in downtown Los Angeles near many large corporations. The leased facility included a large display area of green plants, gifts, cards, silk flowers, and some fresh cut flowers. The location also included office space for the bookkeeping staff (two people) and for Susan's desk, as well as a shop area where flower arrangements were designed.

Susan had operated the business successfully for 5 years when a major retailer asked Susan if she would be interested in establishing a small floral shop in the department store. Susan would have to pay a commission of 11 percent of sales, which would cover rental of floor space and utilities. Susan would be responsible for all other expenses, such as employees' wages and insurance. Susan felt that the offer provided an excellent opportunity for expansion and agreed to establish the outlet. Within 6 months, another major retailer proposed a similar arrangement, offering space and utilities in exchange for a commission of 11 percent of sales. Susan agreed to the proposal, thinking that three locations would bring a substantial profit. Although some expenses would increase, some fixed expenses would remain the same and the additional revenue would increase profits.

The department store locations were small compared with the original location. All design work (flower arranging) was completed at the main location and delivered to the department stores. Because both department stores were in the downtown area, arrangements could be delivered quickly. All inventory was shipped to the main location, priced, and distributed to the other stores, eliminating the need for storage space in the department stores. Finally, bookkeeping for all three outlets was completed at the main location.

After 2 years, Susan realized that the increased profits she had expected had not materialized. Although it seemed that sales volume was adequate, the net profit was minimal. All three locations now offered several product lines, including fresh cut flowers, green plants, designed bouquets of fresh flowers, designed arrangements of silk flowers, cards, and gifts. Susan was not sure why profits were so low. She therefore reviewed the last 2 years' financial statements, which follow.

Flowers Forever Inc.
Income Statement

	Calendar 1984	Calendar 1985
Sales		
Main location	$325,000	$360,000
Department store 1	70,000	73,000
Department store 2	65,000	67,000
Total sales	460,000	500,000
Cost of Goods Sold		
Material	139,400	153,000
Freight	2,000	2,500
Total cost of goods	$141,400	$155,500
Gross Margin	318,600	344,500
Operating Expenses		
Payroll, employees	140,000	149,000
Owner salary	25,000	25,000
Rent; main location	21,000	21,000
Utilities	5,000	6,500
Maintenance and repairs	9,000	10,500
Advertising	8,000	11,000
Auto and truck expense	4,000	5,500
Delivery	23,000	27,000
Depreciation	13,000	12,000
Department store commission	14,000	15,400
Credit card fees	2,500	3,200
Bad debts	1,200	1,600
Dues and subscriptions	1,300	1,500
Insurance	4,000	5,500
Interest	5,000	4,200
Accounting and legal	6,200	7,000
Stationery, postage	5,700	6,000
Telephone	12,000	13,500
Travel and seminars	1,200	1,500
Payroll taxes	16,500	17,400
Donations	100	250
Total expenses	$318,500	$344,550
Net profit before tax	$ 100	$ (50)

Flowers Forever Inc.
Balance Sheet

	December 31, 1984	December 31, 1985
Assets		
Current Assets		
Cash	$ 8,000	$ 7,800
Accounts receivable	42,000	48,000
Inventory	28,000	32,000
Prepaid expenses	7,000	6,200
Total current assets	$ 85,000	$ 94,000
Fixed Assets		
Auto and trucks	23,000	23,000
Fixtures and equipment	29,000	29,000
Leasehold improvements	8,000	8,000
Less depreciation on assets	(41,000)	(53,000)
Total net fixed assets	$ 19,000	$ 7,000
Other assets		
Deposits	3,400	4,000
Total other assets	$ 3,400	$ 4,000
Total assets	107,400	105,000
Liabilities		
Current Liabilities		
Current maturity—long-term debt	10,000	11,500
Accounts payable	45,000	51,150
Accrued expenses	8,500	10,000
Total current liabilities	$ 63,500	$ 72,650
Long-term Debt		
Notes payable	$ 22,000	$ 12,000
Less current portion	(10,000)	(11,500)
Long-term notes payable	12,000	500
Total liabilities	75,500	73,150
Stockholders' equity		
Common stock	17,000	17,000
Retained earnings	14,900	14,850
Total stockholders' equity	$ 31,900	$ 31,850
Total liabilities and equity	$107,400	$105,000

Questions

1. Suppose Susan asked you to review her financial statements and give your opinion as to why profits are so low. How would you answer her question?

2. What changes do you think Susan should make?

Case IVB   Surefire Sales Inc.

Sam Surefire owned and operated Surefire Sales Inc. Sam and his wife Shirley were the only employees of the company, which served as manufacturers' representatives for six companies. Sam served as the salesperson, and Shirley handled the office and accounting. Both Sam and Shirley were 58 years old.

Sam had started Surefire Sales 15 years ago. Although the company began as a manufacturing representative for only two product lines, Sam had continuously expanded his territory and number of product lines. He now sold slightly over $1 million per year and received an average commission of 5 percent. Thus, the company grossed $50,000 to 60,000 per year in commissions. Expenses were minimal; office rent was only $200 per month. There were no employees' salaries, and utilities costs were minimal. After paying for travel and entertainment expenses and all overhead, Sam could easily afford to pay himself $25,000 per year. Over the years, the corporation had accumulated about $25,000 in excess funds, which was invested in stock. Sam hoped to save this for his retirement in about 5 years.

Surefire Sales Inc. sold electrical products ranging from small electronic parts to large generators, with customers located in New York, Pennsylvania, Ohio, and Massachusetts. Mr. Surefire had been asked by other manufacturers to take on additional product lines; however, he was often unable to cover his territory adequately with the current number of product lines and felt that he could not handle additional products without hiring another person.

Sam had considered hiring another person anyway, since he hoped to sell the business when he retired. If someone else worked with him for 5 years and became knowledgeable of the product lines and the customers, that person could easily buy the business and take over when Sam retired. The sale would be a smoother transition than if an outsider bought the company.

This was an important consideration for a manufacturing representative's company, because a change in ownership could result in customers canceling agreements or contracts. It would therefore be easier to sell the company to someone known to the customers.

Sam met Fredrick Platt at a dinner party. Fred was 55 years old and had worked in the electrical parts industry for a number of years, but he had never been a salesman. He had been laid off from his job and out of work for about 8 months. Mr. Surefire discussed his need for a salesperson, and Fred said he would be very interested in the job. Mr. Surefire agreed to pay Fred a salary of $20,000 plus expenses for the first year. After 1 year, Fred would switch to a commission basis and would receive 70 percent of each commission paid to Surefire Sales. For example, on a $1,000 sale, Surefire Sales would normally receive a 5 percent commission, or $50. So, if Fred sold $1,000, he would receive 70 percent of $50, or $35. The remaining 30 percent of the commission ($15) would go to Surefire Sales for administrative overhead costs. Fred would be responsible for all of his own expenses — he would not be reimbursed.

After 6 months, Fred's sales were minimal. Sam did not feel this was unusual, though, since some sales were made by submitting bids, and Sam felt that it would take Fred time to contact companies, submit bids, and then be awarded the contract. Sam did express concern that sales in one product line had not increased. Sam had expected increased sales in this line since it was Fred's area of expertise and bids were not always required.

Because of the additional expense of Fred's salary and travel expenses, the company began to lose about $2,000 per month. Cash reserves were being drained, and it would soon be necessary to use the money the corporation had invested in stocks.

Mr. Surefire knew that the company's existing cash flow would not be enough to pay the bills for the next 6 months until Fred was placed on a commission. He considered borrowing money from a bank, cashing in some of the company stock, or a combination. Sam was not sure what the best alternative would be.

Although some people felt that Mr. Surefire should fire Fred, Mr. Surefire had invested 6 months' salary and much time to train Fred. If he fired him now, that time and money would be wasted and the whole process would start over. There was no guarantee that someone else would be better, he argued, so it did not make sense to hire a new person.

Questions

1. Should Sam fire Fred and hire a new person? Why or why not?
2. Could Sam's problems with Fred have been prevented? If so, how?
3. Are the problems caused by Sam's actions or Fred's actions? Explain.

Case IVC   Inner-City Paint Corporation

History
. . . .

Stanley Walsh began Inner-City Paint Corporation in a rundown warehouse, which he rented, on the fringe of Chicago's "downtown" business area. The company is still located at the original 1976 site.

Source: Dr. Donald F. Kuratko, College of Business, Ball State University, and Norman J. Gierlasinski, DBA, CPA, School of Business, Central Washington University.

Inner-City is a small company that manufactures wall paint. It does not compete with giants such as Glidden or DuPont. There are small paint manufacturers in Chicago that supply the immediate area. The proliferation of paint manufacturers is due to the fact that the weight of the product (fifty-two and one-half pounds per five gallon container) makes the costs of shipping great distances prohibitive. Inner-City's chief product is flat white wall paint sold in five gallon plastic cans. They also produce colors on request in fifty-five gallon containers.

The primary market of Inner-City is the small to medium sized decorating company. Pricing must be competitive, and until recently, Inner-City had shown steady growth in this market. The slowdown in the housing market combined with a slowdown in the overall economy caused financial difficulty for Inner-City Paint Corporation. Inner-City's reputation had been built on fast service, frequently supplying paint to contractors within twenty-four hours. Speedy delivery to customers became difficult when Inner-City was required to pay cash on delivery (C.O.D.) for its raw materials.

Inner-City had been operating without management controls or financial controls. It had grown from a very small two person company with sales of $60,000 annually in 1976, to sales of $1,800,000 and thirty-eight employees in 1982. Stanley Walsh realized the necessity for tighter controls within his organization if the company was to survive.

Equipment

Five mixers are used in the manufacturing process. Three large mixers can produce a maximum of four hundred gallons, per batch, per mixer. The two smaller mixers can produce a maximum of one hundred gallons, per batch, per mixer.

Two lift trucks are utilized for moving raw materials. The materials are packed in one hundred pound bags. The lift trucks also move finished goods which are stacked on pallets.

A small testing lab is utilized to ensure the quality of materials received and the consistent quality of their finished product. The equipment in the lab is sufficient to handle the current volume of product manufactured.

Transportation equipment consists of two, twenty-four foot delivery trucks and two vans. This small fleet is more than sufficient because many customers pick up their orders to save delivery costs.

Facilities

Inner-City performs all operations from one building consisting of 16,400 square feet. The majority of the space is devoted to manufacturing and storage, with only 850 square feet assigned as office space. The building is forty-five years old and in disrepair. It is being leased at three year increments. The current monthly rent on this lease is $2,700. The rent is low in consideration of the poor condition of the building and its undesirable location in a run-down neighborhood (south side of Chicago). All of these conditions are suitable to Inner-City because of the dusty, dirty nature of the manufacturing process, and the small contribution of the rent to overhead costs.

Product
. . . .

Flat white paint is made with pigment (titanium dioxide and silicates), vehicle (resin) and water. The water makes up 72% of the contents of the product. To produce a color, the necessary pigment is added to the flat white paint. The pigment used to produce the color has been previously tested in the lab to ensure consistent quality of texture. Essentially the process is mixing powders with water, then tapping-off into five or fifty-five gallon containers. Color over-runs are tapped-off into two gallon containers.

Inventory records are not kept. The warehouse manager keeps a mental count of what is in stock. He documents (on a lined, yellow pad) what has been shipped for the day, and to whom. That list is given to the billing clerk at the end of each day.

The cost of materials to produce flat white paint is $2.40 per gallon. Colors are approximately 40 to 50 percent higher. Five gallon, covered plastic pails cost Inner-City $1.72 each. Fifty-five gallon drums (with lids) are $8.35 each.

Selling price varies with the quantity purchased. To the average customer, flat white sells at $27.45 for five gallons, and $182.75 for fifty-five gallons. Colors vary in selling price, due to the variety in pigment cost and quantity ordered. Customers purchase on credit and usually pay their invoices in thirty to sixty days. The customer is telephoned after sixty days of nonpayment, to inquire when payment will be made.

Management
. . . .

The president and majority stockholder is Stanley Walsh. He began his career as a house painter and advanced to become a painter for a large decorating company. Mr. Walsh primarily painted walls in large, commercial buildings and hospitals. Eventually he came to believe that he could produce a paint that was less expensive and of higher quality than what was being used. A keen desire to open his own business resulted in the creation of Inner-City Paint Corporation.

Mr. Walsh manages the corporation today much the same way he did when the business began. He personally must open *all* the mail, approve *all* payments and inspect *all* customer billings before they are mailed. He has been unable to detach himself from any detail of the operation and cannot properly delegate authority. As the company grew, the time element alone aggravated the situation. Frequently, these tasks are performed days after transactions occur and mail received.

The office is managed by Mrs. Walsh (Mr. Walsh's mother). Two part-time clerks assist her and all records are processed manually.

The plant is managed by a man in his twenties, whom Mr. Walsh hired from one of his customers. Mr. Walsh became acquainted with the man when he would pick up paint from Inner-City for his previous employer. Prior to the eight months he has been employed by Mr. Walsh as plant manager, his only other experience has been that of painter.

Employees

Thirty-five employees (twenty workers are part-time) work in various phases of the manufacturing process. The employees are nonunion, and most are unskilled laborers. They take turns making paint and driving the delivery trucks.

Stanley Walsh does all of the sales work and public relations work. He spends approximately one-half of every day making sales calls and answering complaints about defective paint. He is the only salesman. Other salesmen had been employed in the past, but Mr. Walsh felt they "could not be trusted."

Customer Perception

Customers view Inner-City as a company that provides fast service and negotiates on price and payment out of desperation. Mr. Walsh is seen as a disorganized man who may not be able to keep Inner-City afloat much longer. Paint contractors are reluctant to give Inner-City large orders out of fear that the paint may not be ready on a continual, reliable basis. Larger orders usually go to larger companies that have demonstrated their reliability and solvency.

Rumors abound that Inner-City is in financial straits, that it is unable to pay suppliers and owes a considerable sum for payment on back taxes. All of the above contribute to a serious lack of confidence in the corporation by customers.

Financial Structure

The following are the most current financial statements of Inner-City Paint Corporation for the year ended six months ago. They have been prepared by the company's accounting service. No audit has been performed as Mr. Walsh did not want to incur the expense it would have required.

Balance Sheet
June 30, 1982

Current Assets:

Cash	$ 1,535	
Accounts Receivable (net of allowance for bad debts of $63,400)	242,320	
Inventory	18,660	
Total Current Assets		$262,515
Machinery & transportation equipment	47,550	
Less: Accumulated depreciation	15,500	
Net Fixed Assets		32,050
Total Assets		$294,565

Current Liabilities:

Accounts payable	$217,820	
Salaries payable	22,480	
Notes payable	6,220	
Taxes payable	38,510	
Total Current Liabilities		$285,030
Long-term notes payable		15,000
Owners' Equity: Common stock, no par, 1,824 shares outstanding		12,400
Deficit		(17,865)
Total Liabilities & Owners' Equity		$294,565

Income Statement
For the Year Ended
June 30, 1982

Sales		$1,784,080
Cost of goods sold		1,428,730
Gross Margin		$ 355,350
Selling Expenses	$ 72,460	
Administrative Expenses	67,280	
President's Salary	132,000	
Office Manager's Salary	66,000	
Total Expenses		337,740
Net Income		$ 17,610

Future

. . . .

Stanley Walsh wishes to improve the financial situation and reputation of Inner-City Paint Corporation. He is considering the purchase of a computer to organize the business and reduce needless paperwork. He has read about consultants that are able to quickly spot problems in businesses but will not spend more than $300 on such a consultant.

The solution that Mr. Walsh favors most is one that requires him to borrow money from the bank, which he will then use to pay his current bills. He feels that as soon as business conditions improve, he will be able to pay back the loans. He believes that the problems Inner-City is experiencing are due to the overall poor economy and are only temporary.

Questions

1. a. List characteristics you feel are necessary for effective control.
   b. Indicate which of these characteristics, if any, Stanley Walsh did not utilize.
   c. How would they have helped Inner-City Paint Corporation as a management tool?

2. Did Stanley Walsh monitor the performance of the company using financial and operational controls? Explain.

3. How would a computer have aided the control process of Inner-City?

4. What, in your opinion, do the financial statements of Inner-City Paint Corporation reflect?

5. If you took over Stanley Walsh's position, what would you do to improve Inner-City Paint Corporation's financial condition?

Case IVD   The Case of the Tardy Employees

Introduction

Papenfuss Electronic Systems was founded by Jack Papenfuss shortly after leaving IBM; he had worked there for twelve years after graduating from The University of Minnesota with an engineering degree. He chose La Crosse, Wisconsin for his new firm because he grew up in this small midwestern town and wanted to stay. La Crosse has a population of 50,000 and is three hours by car from any large city (Minneapolis to the north and Madison to the

Source: The research and written case information were presented at a Case Research Symposium and were evaluated by the Case Research Association's Editorial Board. This case was prepared by Ronald G. Greenwood of GMI Engineering & Management Institute as a basis for class discussion.

Distributed by the Case Research Association. All rights reserved to the author and the Case Research Association. Permission to use the case should be obtained from the Case Research Association.

southeast). The population is unique in education and occupation in that it has a very high percentage of professional people. The city has the nation's ninth largest medical clinic (Gundersen Clinic), the largest producer of industrial air conditioners (Trane Company), sixth largest brewer (Heileman) and Viterbo College (1,000 students) and The University of Wisconsin—La Crosse (10,000 students). The number of medical professionals, engineers, and academic professionals as a percentage of the population is high. The University graduates a large number of business and computer science majors each year and Trane Company attracts many engineers. Young college trained computer people are found in high numbers in the city and, despite the relatively small job market in the area many graduates try to remain in La Crosse. La Crosse was recently picked as the nation's number one "quality of life" city for populations 50,000 to 75,000 and whose population is highly stable with few people ever moving out of the area.

Case Facts

Papenfuss Electronic Systems designs and manufactures hardware and software for computer systems. The company is fairly young, having been in business for a little over ten years. Paralleling the computer industry, the firm has experienced extremely rapid growth.

Due to this rapid growth, the firm has difficulty finding enough qualified managers. The policy is to promote from within the corporation. Unfortunately, the number of people within the corporation who are qualified for promotion to management is fewer than the number of management positions to be filled. There are many highly skilled engineers and programmers, but very few of these have management skills or training. Consequently, unqualified people have been promoted to middle management. This, in turn, has weakened the management structure.

Of the approximately 500 total employees, over 300 are engineers and programmers and 50 are managers, with the rest office staff. The morale of the engineers and programmers is very low, for a number of reasons.

One reason for low morale could be traced to the projects on which the engineers and programmers work. Lack of project direction and coordination results in inefficient use of manpower. Projects are frequently cancelled on short notice or when projects are near completion. People working on these projects are continually being shifted from project to project. When released from one project, the people are frequently used for idle tasks until a project opens up which requires their skills. Because of this anticipated constant shifting, few employees become deeply involved in their work and no "teams" seemed to be evident. Consequently, the engineers' and programmers' morale is hurt by these working and organizational problems.

Although the job related problems affect morale the most, other negative factors are also present. There are complaints about wages and management being insensitive to employees' needs. People complain about food in the small cafeteria, that there are not enough parking places with many employees parking in the street, and that their questions dropped in the employee question/suggestion box are not answered.

The low morale affects the employee work habits. Frequent bull sessions, long coffee breaks, extended noon hours and late arrival at work are common among the majority of programmers and engineers.

Upper management eventually became aware that the engineers and programmers were wasting a great deal of time. The most obvious indication of this was seeing the employees arriving at work late in the morning. In fact, one morning Jack Papenfuss stood at the front door at 8:00 a.m. to confirm his suspicion that a few were arriving habitually late. By 8:20, and blood running quite warm, he had ascertained that it was more than just a few who were late.

At 8:26 a.m. that day he requested an immediate meeting with Mary Bracken, Doug Sweetland and Bill Bingham his three-system project coordinators . . . to discuss the problem. By 8:31 a.m. he thundered, sarcastically, "Do you know how many of our loyal employees are here at 8 o'clock?" Not waiting for any answer—"Not many!"

"It doesn't take a baboon to figure the cost—if only 200 analysts are late by 15 minutes, we are losing 50 hours a week of paid work."

"Fifty hours is equivalent to over six people doing absolutely nothing for a whole day."

It was obvious that getting the employees to work on time would increase output by the efforts of six people without any increase in cost to the company.

Management's Solution

Management's solution for getting employees to work on time was to have late employees file a report with their supervisor. The report was to detail the reason for arriving late. To prevent anyone from arriving late and not filing their report, guards turned in the names of late arrivals to the employee's supervisor. Having the guards turn in names did not deviate much from standard procedure since all employees entering the building had to identify themselves to the guards with pictured I.D. badges.

If an employee was tardy for work twice in one week or three times in one month, he was to meet with the manager one level above his supervisor. At this meeting, the employee was to explain his reasons for arriving late at work and what measures were being taken to ensure his getting to work on time.

Solution Results

Solution results were disastrous. Employees did, indeed, get to work on time, but the true result was failure. Employee hostility took a quantum jump upon implementation of the reporting system. The bull sessions increased in frequency and duration. The main topic switched from sports to how management was persecuting the employees.

After less than two months, the reporting system was stopped. The increased time wasted at the bull sessions far exceeded the time saved by arriving at work on time. Employee animosity towards management from this action has lasted for three months since the solution was first tried. Tardiness continues, bull sessions continue, low morale continues, turnover is high. Management still wants to "solve" the tardiness and bull session problems, which management assumes will solve the low morale problem.

Epilogue

Employee tardiness has plagued employers for many years. One company's response is recorded in the above few paragraphs. You are to act as an outside consultant. What do you need to know and understand? How do you find out? How do you analyze? These are the real questions to which you should be addressing your attention as you read the case. You are not expected to "solve" the problem, but to find out how the underlying problem can be found, analyzed and readied for solution. In other words—what's really going on?

Case IVE   Harvey Industries

Background

Harvey Industries, a Wisconsin company, was incorporated in 1950 and specializes in the assembly of high pressure washer systems and in the sale of repair parts for these systems. The products range from small portable high

Source: This case was prepared by Donald F. Condit of the University of Detroit, Detroit, Michigan, as a basis for class discussion rather than to illustrate either effective or ineffective organizational practices. Presented at Midwest Case Writers Association Workshop, 1984 and accepted by referees of the Midwest Case Writers Association for international distribution.

pressure washers to large industrial installations for snow removal from vehicles stored outdoors during the winter months. Typical uses for high pressure water cleaning include:

- Automobiles
- Airplanes
- Building Maintenance
- Barns
- Engines
- Ice Cream Plants
- Lift Trucks
- Machinery
- Swimming Pools

Industrial customers include General Motors, Ford, Chrysler, Delta Airlines, United Parcel Service, and Shell Oil Company.

Although the industrial applications are a significant part of its sales, Harvey Industries is primarily an assembler of equipment for coin operated self-service car wash systems. The typical car wash is of concrete block construction with an equipment room in the center flanked on either side by a number of bays. The cars are driven into the bays where the owner can wash and wax the car, utilizing high pressure hot water and liquid wax. A dollar bill changer is available to provide change for the use of the equipment and the purchase of various products from dispensers. The products include towels, whitewall cleaner, and upholstery cleaner.

In recent years Harvey Industries has been in financial difficulty. The company has lost money for three of the last four years with the last year's loss being $17,174 on sales of $1,238,674. Inventory levels have been steadily increasing to their present level of $124,324.

The company employs 23 people with the management team consisting of the following key employees:

- President
- Sales Manager
- Manufacturing Manager
- Controller
- Purchasing Manager

The abbreviated organization chart reflects the reporting relationship of the key employees and the three individuals who report directly to the Manufacturing Manager.

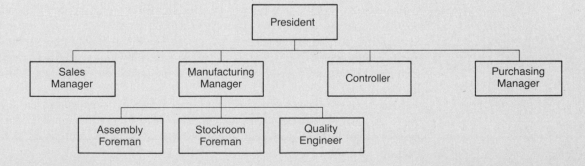

Current Inventory Control System

. . . .

The current inventory control "system" consists of orders for stock replenishment being made by the stockroom foreman, the purchasing manager, or the manufacturing manager whenever one of them notices that the inventory is low. An order for replenishment of inventory is also placed whenever someone (either a customer or an employee in the assembly area) wants an item and it is not in stock.

Some inventory is needed for the assembly of the high pressure equipment for the car wash and industrial applications. There are current and accurate bills of material for these assemblies. The material needs to support the assembly schedule are generally known well in advance of the build schedule.

The majority of inventory transactions are for repair parts and for supplies used by the car washes such as paper towels, detergent, and wax concentrate. Because of the constant and rugged use of the car wash equipment, there is a steady demand for the various repair parts.

The stockroom is well organized with parts stored in locations according to each vendor. The number of vendors is relatively limited with each vendor generally supplying many different parts. For example, the repair parts from Allen Bradley, a manufacturer of electrical motors, will be stocked in the same location. These repair parts will be used to provide service for the many electrical motors that are part of the high pressure pump and motor assembly used by all of the car washes.

Because of the heavy sales volume of repair parts, there are generally two employees working in the stockroom—a stockroom foreman who reports to the manufacturing manager and an assistant to the foreman. One of these two employees will handle customer orders. Many customers stop by and order the parts and supplies that they need. Telephone orders are also received and are shipped by United Parcel Service the same day.

The assembly area has some inventory stored on the shop floor. This inventory consists of low value items which are used every day such as nuts, bolts, screws, and washers. These purchased items do not amount to very much dollar volume throughout the year. Unfortunately, oftentimes, the assembly area is out of one of these basic items and this causes a significant amount of downtime for the assembly lines.

Paperwork is kept to a minimum. A sales slip listing the part numbers and quantities sold to a customer is generally made out for each sale. If the assembly department needs items that are not stocked on the assembly floor, someone from that department will enter the stockroom and withdraw the necessary material. There is no paperwork made out for the items needed on the assembly floor.

Nine hundred seventy-three different part numbers were purchased for stock last year. Those purchases amounted to $314,673. Although the company does not utilize a computer, it does have some accurate records on how much money was spent on each part number last year and an analysis of the data shows that $220,684 was spent on just 179 of the part numbers.

Fortunately for Harvey Industries most of the items they purchase are stocked by either the manufacturer or by a wholesaler. When it is discovered that the company is out of stock on an item, it generally takes only 2 or 3 days to replenish the stock.

Due to the company's recent losses its auditing firm has become concerned about the company's ability to continue in business. Recently the company has been selling off excess vacant land adjoining its manufacturing facility in order to generate cash to meet its financial obligations.

New President

· ·

Because of the recent death of the owner, the Trust Department of a Milwaukee bank, as trustee for the estate, has taken over the company's affairs and has appointed a new President of the company. The new President has identified many problem areas—one of which is improper inventory control. He has retained you as a consultant to make specific recommendations concerning a revised inventory control system.

Case IVF   Folk Art Inc.

Players: Mary—President and founder
         Margaret—Office Manager
         Rebecca—Production Manager
         Raymond—Advisor and member of the board of directors;
                  not directly involved with company management
         Jennifer—Credit, billings and accounts receivable

Folk Art Inc. commenced business in 1976 as a crafts shop under the name of Woodbury and was operated as a sole proprietorship for several years. The merchandise sold was characterized as unique and not readily available elsewhere in the local market. Mary did not take a salary for her services, which

Source: This case was prepared by Joseph T. Kastantin and Robin A. Alexander of the University of Wisconsin-LaCrosse and is intended to be used as a basis for class discussion. Presented to the Midwest Case Writers Association Workshop, 1985. All rights reserved to the authors and to the Midwest Case Writers Association. Copyright © 1985.

were full-time. The retail store outgrew its floorspace three times in the next nine years. Mary eventually saw the opportunity to create her own products to sell in her store. The products manufactured and sold were wooden plaques and decorations which were hand painted. Her retail sales of these products were so successful, Mary decided to market them nationally.

Mary selected the manufacturer's representative distribution method because it was the norm in the gift industry. Many of these representatives had permanent merchandise showrooms which offered increased visibility for the company's product line. Other representatives often rented booth space for the national and regional gift merchandise shows. Both groups employed on the road sales representatives who actually called on gift stores in their territories. Mary knew it was important to have representatives who worked not only the showrooms but also on the road. This balance in representation helped to even the wide fluctuations in sales due to the seasonal nature of the gift industry.

The sales volume in the manufacturing/wholesale division quickly surpassed the retail sales volume. In 1983 wholesale sales were $245,651 with a divisional, after tax profit of $16,339. Retail sales were $24,359 with a loss of $5,584. In 1984 wholesale sales were $447,390 with after tax profit of $56,020. Retail sales were $58,494 with a loss of $1,642. When Mary had the chance to buy a bargain priced building large enough to accommodate the spiraling sales of both her manufacturing company and her retail store, she capitalized on that opportunity.

The manufacturing company was labor intensive. A majority of the manufacturing employees were artists. Employee motivation was a continuing challenge. Mary, likewise, was an artist. She took great pride in the many new products which she and her staff created. This proliferation of products resulted in a price list which included several hundred available styles and colors.

The retail store flourished in the new location. Several show rooms were set up in the building, each displaying a variety of unique merchandise, including some produced by Folk Art Inc. Each room had a theme such as Christmas, gourmet treats, linens, etc. By the end of 1984 the retail store inventory was over $50,000. Combined sales in Folk Art Inc. had grown from $50,000 to $447,000 from 1982–1984. Mary determined that the new facilities had a production limit of approximately $500,000, which was nearly achieved in 1984.

Mary again capitalized on a bargain expansion opportunity. She purchased an adjacent lot and small building. The lot was large enough to accommodate a proposed 2,000 square foot building addition with ample lot space for future additions. The proposed building was completed before the end of 1984 and the manufacturing operation was moved to the new location thus allowing the retail shop to expand for the fourth time.

An intuitive entrepreneur in giftware, Mary was also very generous toward others. Her long-term business objective held Folk Art Inc. as the means by which she could convey a livelihood to her children, all of whom worked in the business.

The company designated certain family members as department managers. Each manager had limited control over an assigned area. Mary tended to allow the managers to perform until a problem surfaced at which time she usurped all subordinate control until the problem was either resolved or until it submerged from view. The company had no strategic management process, which caused many major problems.

Rebecca was a fine arts graduate who assumed supervisory responsibility for production and shipping. She was characterized by her mother as hard-working. She was also an accomplished artist.

Margaret was the eldest child. She attended university classes and acquired some skills as a bookkeeper. Margaret had a difficult time dealing with people. She had characteristics of being both aggressive and insecure which resulted in many heated confrontations between herself and Mary and other employees. Because of her bookkeeping experience Margaret assumed duties as the office manager. Margaret was unhappy with this position; however, it was uncertain where she would work if she left the company.

Jennifer attended university classes. The youngest child, Jennifer worked part-time for Folk Art. She assumed duties as accounts receivable clerk. Jennifer was diligent in her efforts to maintain accurate records on some 2,000 wholesale customers. However, there were often discrepancies between her records and those of the company's customers. Mary often said that Jennifer was the likely heir to control the company.

The gift industry consists of a nearly limitless and ever changing range of products generally classified as high, middle and low end. The high end includes glass, brass and artworks. The low end consists of cards, paper and trinkets. The middle range includes everything else from decorations to bags to jewelry. Industry sales are between $2 and 3 billion annually, are seasonally oriented, and seem to be immune to recessions. Important recurring dates are Valentine's Day, Mother's Day, graduation, Father's Day and Christmas. There are many other special recurring dates which provide minor influxes in sales. Birthdays, anniversaries and weddings provide year round sales impetus. Outlets include card shops, gift shops, department stores, mass merchandisers, discount stores and specialty shops. Wholesale sales are handled primarily through manufacturers' representatives using both showroom and road salespersons.

There were 35 employees and 15 national sales representative organizations associated with Folk Art Inc. Mary characterized business as growing frighteningly fast. She felt the company was successful but she was unable to gain the confidence she desired to control her business growth profitably. There was no evidence that any financial statements were prepared during the rapid growth period, except for the year-end tax returns. The first formal financial statements were prepared by an attorney who had done some legal work for the company. A CPA firm was retained to prepare financial statements for the

Exhibit 1

Assets	1984	1983
Current Assets:		
Cash	$ 9,694	$ 1,182
Accounts Receivable	54,008	22,601
Inventories, at lower of cost (FIFO) or market	82,956	12,781
Prepaid Expenses		1,691
Total Current Assets	$146,658	$38,255
Furniture and Equipment at cost	37,907	17,735
Less: Accumulated Depreciation	12,103	5,294
Net Furniture and Equipment	25,804	12,441
Total Assets	$172,462	$50,696
Liabilities		
Current Liabilities:		
Notes Payable Bank	$29,325	
Current Maturities of Contracts Payable	1,837	
Accounts Payable	10,422	$11,690
Accrued Commissions, Payroll Taxes and Other Expenses	19,181	9,617
Note Payable Officer	33,287	10,610
Federal and State Income Taxes Payable	5,285	352
Total Current Liabilities	$ 99,337	$32,269
Long-Term Contracts Payable, Less Current Maturities above	5,931	7,485
Deferred Income Taxes	875	
Total Liabilities	$106,143	$39,754
Stockholders' Equity		
Common Stock, no par value; 2,200 shares authorized, 375 issued, and 367 outstanding	$2,600	$1,600
Treasury Stock, 8 shares at cost	(7,000)	(7,000)
Retained Earnings	70,719	16,342
Total Stockholders' Equity	$ 66,319	$10,942
Total Liabilities and Stockholders' Equity	$172,462	$50,696

Exhibit 2

	1984	1983
Revenues:		
Sales	$507,836	$239,655
Returns and Allowance	(737)	(151)
Net Sales	$507,099	$239,504
Costs and Expenses:		
Cost of Goods Sold	207,675	92,635
Selling, General and Administrative	224,837	129,322
Depreciation	6,809	3,498
Interest on Debt	4,784	224
	$444,105	$225,679
Income Before Income Taxes	$ 62,994	$ 13,825
Provision for Income Taxes		
Current	7,741	2,451
Deferred	875	
Net Income	$ 54,378	$ 11,374

Schedule of Operating Expenses	1984	1983
Officer Salaries	$ 2,886	$
Office and Sales Salaries	33,408	64,007
Sales Commissions	64,834	
Payroll Taxes	16,952	4,115
Advertising	7,904	2,360
Auto	2,008	1,944
Bad Debts	5,602	
Collection	700	
Dues and Subscriptions	1,437	60
Insurance	11,267	1,057
Legal and Accounting	7,864	10,325
Office and Supplies	6,883	5,666
Property Taxes	2,470	3,343
Rent	29,888	14,938
Repairs and Maintenance	6,781	1,035
Telephone	4,584	2,701
Travel and Entertainment	6,181	3,622
Utilities	7,842	2,482
Directors' Fees		9,525
Contributions	44	1,456
Miscellaneous	5,302	686
Total Selling, General, and Administrative Expenses	$224,837	$129,322

year ended December 31, 1983. This same firm was to prepare monthly statements for 1984.

All accounting data were manually prepared except for the monthly financial statements beginning in January of 1984. Data to be posted were either mailed or dropped off at the CPA office and were returned with financial statements without comment each month, usually by mail. Reported profits were erratic with reported cost of goods sold fluctuating from 15% to 70% from month to month. There were over 2,000 active wholesale customers, 35 employees, 300 vendors and 400 different manufactured inventory items in addition to the 3,000–4,000 items offered for sale in the retail store. Mary estimated that as of September 30, 1984 she had $35,000 in unshipped orders on hand. A physical inspection of unshipped orders revealed that the total value of unshipped orders was actually $65,000. Many of these orders had required shipment dates in early October. Some of these orders were already past the shipment cancellation date. Mary spent most of the next eight weeks in the shipping department expediting orders, which continued to arrive at a record breaking rate.

Shipping/receiving and production were collocated. Rebecca had overall responsibility for both areas. The company had maintained very little finished goods inventory in the past. However, there had been plans for some time to build a base inventory of partially finished goods which could quickly be finished and shipped. Even though there were several hundred items on the product price list the basic wood patterns were limited. There were many variations of painted color and design and add-on pieces which made the actual total combination of products in the 300 to 400 range. Keeping partially finished blank pieces in inventory increased production and shipping turnaround efficiency. Control and valuation of this work in process inventory became a problem.

Three of 15 sales organizations accounted for 50% of Folk Art Inc sales. Mary conversed with the sales organization leaders periodically but had not prepared a sales budget or marketing plan by the end of 1984. She felt that sales would double in each of the next three years, but was leery about predicting sales beyond that period. It was estimated that the new production facility would accommodate $2.5 to $3.0 million in sales but Mary was very concerned that her internal organization would not be able to respond to the increased volume and still retain any degree of control. One sales organization had made successful contact with a national mass merchandising company which had placed several small test orders with Folk Art Inc. These orders "checked out at retail." That meant the buyer reported that the merchandise being tested sold well in the retail stores at the prices marked. There was some speculation that orders from that chain alone would exceed $150,000 during 1985.

The leading sales representative for Folk Art Inc. had proposed to Mary to become national sales manager for the company in exchange for a 3% commission override on all Folk Art Inc. sales in addition to the standard 15% sales commission paid for sales generated by his organization. Mary was concerned about this move but realized that she had spread herself too thin. She needed help in both marketing and administration. Additionally she considered arranging the retail store in such a way as to make it marketable to another investor. Mary felt this would permit her to spend more time with the manufacturing division which appeared to have considerably more overall potential than the retail store.

Mary approached the bank for funds to finance both the new building addition and a working capital line of credit for inventory and accounts receivable expansion. Her banker reluctantly turned her down. Mary planned to personally finance the building addition since she already owned the main building and land which were leased to Folk Art Inc. She had to have bank financing to handle the expansion both from a construction and a working capital viewpoint. Two banks expressed an interest in her business and a third has offered to process the loan agreement under SBA guarantee. Mary refused to consider an SBA loan because she felt there would be unwarranted governmental meddling in her business affairs.

Mary was very concerned about the coming year. The company had to decide how to handle product marketing most efficiently. The mass merchandise account could demand a delivery schedule which exceeded the company limits coupled with responding to accelerating customer requirements. Mary was both annoyed and frustrated by the rejection of her loan application by her long-time banker. In the past year many new product ideas had surfaced. Mary wanted to spend more time evaluating these and other new ideas but couldn't seem to find the time. She was very tired after spending several weeks in the production and shipping departments.

PART

Five

Contemporary Business Topics

Throughout the first four parts of the text, we have discussed functional areas of small business management. These topics have included marketing, finance, production, and personnel skills that are needed to plan, organize, and manage a business. In Part Five, we identify areas of increasing importance to the entrepreneur. These areas include interaction with the government, computerization, and insurance. In the final chapter we discuss success and failure in the small business environment.

Chapter 18 provides an overview of the many ways in which small businesses are influenced by the government. The roles of the federal government are varied, and its influence can have a substantial impact on profits. The government is often a purchaser or customer of the small business, and the contracts are often a large source of revenue. The government, however, is also a regulator, specifying standards and guidelines that businesses must follow. A third role of the federal government is as a source of assistance, providing help with both management and financing problems. Finally, the federal government is a tax collector through income taxes, employment taxes, and so forth. The last part of Chapter 18 reviews state government and its impact on small business.

Another area of increasing importance is automation. Until recently, most computers were too expensive for small businesses. However, the introduction of microcomputers has made computerization more affordable. Chapter 19, therefore, reviews computer terminology and the functions performed by computers. In addition, the advantages and disadvantages of automation are reviewed. Finally, information is provided that will help the entrepreneur determine if computerization is a feasible alternative.

In the past, insuring a business against normal business risks was a relatively easy process; one which caused little trouble for the entrepreneur. However, because of the number of lawsuits and the large settlements awarded in recent years, insurance companies are reluctant to insure certain risks. Also, the increasing insurance premiums for many risks have become burdensome for many small businesses. Chapter 20 reviews the many types of insurance that most small businesses need and describes some of the related problems faced by small business owners.

In the final chapter, we provide information concerning small business failures, providing an accurate portrayal of the extent of this problem. The "warning signals" that usually precede failure are given in order to allow the entrepreneur to identify trouble early enough to take corrective action. The legal options of bankruptcy are also discussed along with the financial, psychological, and career costs associated with bankruptcy. Finally, we recognize the persistence and endurance of entrepreneurs who fail several times but eventually succeed. We hope to encourage entrepreneurs to begin anew if they do fail, as the only true failure occurs if one refuses to try again.

Small Business and Government

Source. Courtesy of Honeywell Inc.

K E Y Objectives

1.   To describe the impact of government on the small business sector.

2.   To examine the government as a purchaser of goods and services.

3.   To explore the significance of the government's regulatory activities.

4.   To describe the government as a source of assistance.

5.   To explain the tax liabilities of small business.

6.   To discuss state government as a factor for small business to consider.

The Government as a Purchaser

The federal government spends vast amounts buying products and services each year—nearly $150 billion in 1982. Of that $150 billion, 15 percent (or about $22 billion) was spent purchasing from small businesses. The numbers are vast and so is the variety of items. Exhibit 18.1 gives a breakdown of those expenditures and lists example items.

From toiletries to tents, from fiber optics to fire control equipment, the government buys it all. Clearly, the government is an intriguing prospective customer for any small business. To make use of the sales opportunities the government presents, the management of a small business must understand the principles and procedures of government purchasing.

It is useful to think of government purchases in two broad types: those of general use and those of special use. The general-use items are those used throughout the government, including office supplies, janitorial services, telephones, and so forth. Examples of specific-use items are weapons systems for the military, seeds for the forest service, and hospital supplies for the Veterans Administration.

The General Services Administration

General Services Administration (GSA)
The federal agency that does the consolidation purchasing for the non-military agencies within the federal government.

For general-use items, the primary purchasing agent is the **General Services Administration (GSA).** The GSA does the consolidated purchasing for the civil agencies within the federal government. The GSA not only buys general-use items, it stores and distributes them throughout the government. It also

Exhibit 18.1   Federal Government Expenditures for Fiscal Year 1982

Category and Product or Service	All Business Total in Thousands	Small Business Total in Thousands	Percentage
Research and Development			
Examples:			
Agriculture	$ 7,097	$ 268	3.78
Defense systems	11,120,984	326,909	2.93
Defense—other	1,976,000	301,082	15.23
Education	23,669	4,162	17.58
Housing	538	245	45.53
Space	4,173,962	56,409	1.35
All others	2,690,667	246,660	9.17
Subtotal, research and development	19,992,902	935,735	4.68
Other Services and Construction			
Examples:			
Natural resources management	122,479	79,980	65.30
Maintenance, repair, and rebuilding of equipment	5,086,130	770,534	15.14
Architect and engineer services	1,802,892	496,813	27.56
Management and professional services	4,692,788	1,421,975	30.30
Transportation and travel	1,757,818	175,160	9.96
All others	34,372,194	6,507,123	18.93
Subtotal, other services and construction	47,834,301	9,451,585	19.76
Supplies and Equipment			
Examples:			
Guided missiles	5,808,088	69,576	1.20
Tractors	20,664	12,615	61.05
Woodworking machinery and equipment	3,575	2,451	68.56
Alarm and signal systems	30,017	9,684	32.26
Furniture	311,145	164,872	52.99
Books, maps, and other publications	71,029	18,975	26.71
All others	72,941,398	11,605,214	15.09
Subtotal, supplies and equipment	79,158,916	11,283,387	14.25
Total	$146,986,119	$21,670,707	14.74

Source: The State of Small Business: A Report of the President (Washington, D.C.: U.S. Government Printing Office, 1984), 315–320 and 458–462.

has an active role in purchasing many items for the military. Each of its six major divisions, listed below, has an area of responsibility for procurement.

1. Automated Data and Telecommunications Service (ADTS). The ADTS procures telephone and automated data processing service and equipment—computers and peripheral equipment, radio, telephone, teleme-

Unique Business   18.1

Spouse Work

When Judy Wagner's husband was being interviewed for a job, the company interested in hiring him gave Mrs. Wagner a tour of the area's shopping. She would have preferred help in finding a job. Her response to the company's mistake was to start her own company, Access Philadelphia. The company helps the spouses of prospective employees make contacts with potential employers, as well as with civic groups and real estate agents. She plans to franchise the business.

Source: Inc, May 1985, 21.

---

ter, video equipment and tape, and so forth. It buys and leases equipment and negotiates and awards service contracts.

2. Public Buildings Service (PBS). This division awards design contracts and construction contracts, leases property, maintains and repairs government-owned buildings, and conducts appraisals and land surveys.

3. Federal Supply Service (FSS). This service is responsible for supplying thousands of common-use items. It does so through its stock program; federal supply schedules, which permit agencies to order directly from suppliers; consolidated purchase contracts; and direct order purchasing.

4. Transportation and Public Utilities Service (TPUS). The TPUS buys vehicles for federal use, contracts for air and rail travel, and procures electric, water, and sewage services.

5. Federal Property Resources Service (FPRS). The maintenance, repair, and rehabilitation of office machines and furniture is the charge of the FPRS; FPRS sets aside the majority of its contracts for small and minority businesses and workshops for the blind and severely handicapped.

6. National Archives and Records Service (NARS). Most of this division's procurements are in the audiovisual field, with the primary emphasis on photographic equipment and supplies.

In addition to the purchases of the GSA, the federal government buys through other civilian agencies. Like the military, these agencies' unique requirements are not effectively met through government-wide consolidated purchasing. The GSA publication *Doing Business with the Federal Government* gives the names and addresses of offices throughout the federal government that have established their own procurement programs.

Although the government is huge, with a variety of procedures and regulations that can discourage the owner of a small business, it should be remembered that marketing is nonetheless essential to developing the government as a customer. Such marketing can take two forms, passive and active. To improve the chances of succeeding in government sales, a small business should engage in both.

Passive Marketing

Commerce Business Daily
The daily publication of the superintendent of documents, which lists the proposed buying activities and contract awards of the federal government.

The government's most important vehicle for procurement is the **Commerce Business Daily (CBD).** The CBD is published daily, Monday through Friday, to publicize proposed government procurement actions over $5,000 and contract awards over $25,000. The CBD is available in many libraries and may be purchased by subscription from the superintendent of documents.

One piece of information given in each CBD listing is whether the procurement has been "set aside" for small business. The set-aside provision means that only small firms will be given the chance to bid on the contract. To demonstrate the significance of this publication to small business, Exhibit 18.2 lists the set-aside opportunities given on a single page of a single daily issue of the CBD. The entire issue consisted of 32 pages and listed 470 opportunities.

In addition to the Small Business Set-Aside program, other preferential procurement programs have been established to encourage use of businesses owned by women, minority members, and Vietnam veterans, as well as businesses that will perform the contract work in areas with higher-than-average unemployment. Federal law requires each federal agency with procurement authority to have an Office of Small and Disadvantaged Business Utilization to promote the use of such firms.

Active Marketing

Business Service Centers
Offices of GSA, located in 13 major cities throughout the country, which serve small businesses interested in selling to the government.

In its publication, *Doing Business with the Department of Energy,* the DOE recommends that businesses go beyond passive marketing in which they simply react to notices put out by various government agencies. Active marketing requires getting to know an agency's needs and working with its personnel to serve those needs. This requires contact with technical personnel to develop an understanding of the problems the agency faces.

To facilitate a small business manager's understanding of, and access to, the federal government market, a variety of offices and programs are provided. The GSA operates **Business Service Centers (BSCs)** in 13 cities throughout the nation. The BSCs exist primarily to serve entrepreneurs in their quest for government business; BSC personnel provide information on

Exhibit   18.2   Business Opportunities Listed in the *Commerce Business Daily,*
July 23, 1984

Thinning and cleaning 126 acres of tree land, Jackson County, Oregon.
Site preparation by slash down in the Cherokee National Forest, Monroe County, Tennessee.
Hand tree planting, Idaho Panhandle National Forests.
Custodial services, Moffett Field Naval Air Station, California.
Pump and clean grease traps, Langley Air Force Base, Virginia.
Tablecloth service, Langley Air Force Base, Virginia.
Caretaker and janitorial service, Squaw Lake Recreation Site, Imperial County, California.
Falling and bucking of selected timber, Western Oregon.
Janitorial services, Ice Harbor Lock and Dam, Franklin and Walla Walla Counties, Washington.
Manual preparation of materials for mailing, St. Louis, Missouri.
Collection, removal, and disposal of refuse, Fort Huachuca, Arizona.
Installation of SVC halon systems, Davis Monthan Air Force Base, Arizona.
Plant salt-tolerant grass, Patrick Air Force Base, Florida.
Aerial fertilization, Olympic National Forest, Washington.
Photographic processing services, Denver, Colorado.
Cartographic drafting service, Salt Lake City, Utah.
Micrographic services, Denver, Colorado.
Duplicating services, Milwaukee, Wisconsin.

**Small Business
Information Officers
and Circuit Riders**
Programs of the GSA to
promote government–
small business interaction.

opportunities and required procedures in the federal government procurement area. In addition to the 13 BSCs, the GSA has 100 **Small Business Information Officers** located in federal buildings around the country, and a **"Circuit Rider Program"** in which counselors travel to remote areas to promote government business.

Advantages and Disadvantages of Government Sales

The programs and offices just described have as their central purpose the development of small businesses as suppliers to the federal government. Before responding to the opportunities of the federal government market, however, the small business should examine the advantages and disadvantages of doing so.

Advantages.   The first advantage concerns the size of the government as a customer. A government contract often means an important increase in sales for a small business, and with this increase will come an improved return on investment for the company, provided the government contract does not require the expenditure of additional capital.

Illustration Capsule   18.1

Uncle Sam as a Competitor

In recent years, the federal government has made many accommodations to small business. For example, federal purchases of less than $25,000 are reserved for small companies. In addition, the Small Business Innovation Development Act of 1982 set up research and development grant programs for small firms.

Running counter to these supportive measures are activities in direct competition with private business. The practice of federal nurseries to sell surplus seedlings, at cost, to farmers and others who need large quantities is one example of such competition. This activity has drawn the attention —and criticism—of the American Association of Nurserymen. The group also opposes a proposal to allow the government to give surplus seedlings to public spaces such as parks and school yards, which are typically serviced by private nurseries. Another form of government competition is in real estate management and leasing, where federal office complexes have taken employee offices out of privately owned commercial space.

Source: Mary-Margaret Wantuck, ''Bidding for Fair Play,'' *Nation's Business,* September 1985, 39–40.

Through government contracting, the management of a small business can negotiate an acceptable level of profit. This provides an assurance not available in other markets. Smoothing of the impact of economic cycles is another benefit arising from government contract work. The government as a customer is less vulnerable to economic ebbs and flows and for that reason is less likely to make major cutbacks as many other customers do.

Disadvantages.   There are important disadvantages to consider as well. First, and perhaps most important, the government is a unique customer, one that reserves for itself as a sovereign power the right to demand special treatment because it is acting in the public interest. This right gives the government the ability to change or cancel contracts, to insist on fair and reasonable prices through bidding procedures, and to monitor performance. In addition, the government decides what costs are allowable in reaching total contract costs, whether they are reasonable in level, and whether they can be allocated to the contract. If the contract has been inflated (even inadvertently) by incorrect cost data, the government will reduce the negotiated contract price.

Additional complications in selling to the government can arise from legislation, reflected in various provisions in the contract, which include the following objectives:

- Equal employment opportunities
- Environmental protection
- Occupational safety and health
- Balance of payment improvements (Buy American programs)

In summary, the government is a market like no other. Success in it requires an understanding of its needs as well as the rules by which it operates.

The Government as a Regulator

In addition to purchasing goods and services from small businesses, the government regulates them. In this section we will describe the growth of government regulatory activities, the impact of regulations on small business, and the recent move toward deregulation.

Growth of Regulation

Although the U.S. Constitution itself gave Congress the right to regulate interstate commerce, the first important attempt at regulation came in 1887 with the establishment of the Interstate Commerce Commission (ICC) to curb abuses in the railroad industry. The Sherman Antitrust Act, passed in 1890, outlawed economic monopolies. (Monopolies are markets with only one seller for the product and no close substitutes for it.) The Federal Trade Commission Act and the Clayton Act, both of 1914, broadened the number of prohibited business practices.

These attempts at government regulation of business were intended to protect against some of the more important evils—monopoly power and use of child labor among them—of which U.S. business was guilty during the nineteenth century. They constituted the first wave of government intervention.

The second wave of regulatory activity occurred in the 1930s and was much larger than the first. The 1930s were the years of the Great Depression and Franklin D. Roosevelt's New Deal administration. During this period a fundamental change in attitudes toward the role of government took place. The feeling of the times was that the economy cannot be allowed to operate unregulated. The disorder of the depression convinced most of the nation's leaders of the need for government intervention and regulation.

The result was the entry of government into a wide variety of regulatory activities, empowered by 42 major statutes passed during the decade. These statutes had a common theme: the belief that through government manipulation the economy could be made to operate more effectively. Governmental regulation of this period was largely economic.

During the 1970s the third, and by far the largest, wave of government regulation took place. This wave comprised 130 major legislative controls over business, covering areas such as occupational safety and health; water, air, and noise pollution; motor vehicle safety; and surface mining. Not only were the laws of the 1970s more numerous than ever before, they were often extremely costly to the economic health of industry. This is in contrast to the laws of earlier years, which were written to protect and strengthen the capitalist system. Much of the legislation of the 1970s arose out of societal concerns, for clean air, occupational safety, equal economic opportunity, and so forth. The legislation born of these objectives frequently had an adverse impact on the firms and industries it governed.[1]

The Impact of Regulations on Small Business

In the opinion of many observers, the effects of government regulations are felt disproportionately by small firms.

Often major capital expenditures are required to comply with environmental or safety standards. These expenditures are beyond the financial capacity of many firms. In a 1979 study of small firms in the forging and chemical specialty industries, 25 percent of those surveyed indicated that **Environmental Protection Agency (EPA)** or **Occupational Safety and Health Administration (OSHA)** regulations could cause them to close or sell out.[2]

The impact of minimum wage laws is felt more heavily by small than by large business, because of small firms' extensive use of unskilled and young workers.

Another way small businesses are often at a disadvantage in dealing with the government results from their inability to use the tax code effectively. In 1979, firms with less than $5 million in assets paid an average tax rate of 41 percent, while firms with over $1 billion paid 29 percent. Though there are many contributing factors, the difference is due in large part to (1) the lack of capital to take advantage of attractive depreciation schedules and tax credit plans, and (2) the lack of the kind of expertise provided by a large corporation's tax department. In the case of tax credits, 97 percent of the $20 billion in benefits from Foreign Tax Credit and 66 percent of the $2.7 billion available from Investment Tax Credit, went to 1,300 firms that constitute less than one-tenth of 1 percent of all U.S. corporations. The vast majority of firms do

Environmental Protection Agency (EPA)
The government agency charged with the enforcement of environmental protection legislation.

Occupational Safety and Health Administration (OSHA)
The government office established to enforce legislation in the safety and health areas.

---

[1]"The Past: Government," *Business Week,* September 3, 1979, 40–41.
[2]Kenneth W. Chilton and David P. Hatfield, *Big Government and Small Business: The Changing Relationship* (St. Louis: Center for the Study of American Business, October 1981), 5.

Illustration Capsule   18.2

Reg-Flex Is Moving the Mountain

The estimates of the amount of paperwork required of small businesses make it obvious that the burden is one of mountainlike proportions. The federal government's Office of Management and Budget has estimated that, in 1980, small businesses spent 2 billion hours filling out federal forms. The Regulatory Flexibility Act and its companion law, the Paperwork Reduction Act, have reduced the burden, and though the forms haven't exactly disappeared, 330 million hours have been cut.

Not all small business owners are convinced that the improvements are significant, however. Ray Morgan of Morgan Sanitation in Algona, Iowa, says, "It's like Catch 22, with each regulation or form eliminated being replaced by one or two new ones." He estimates that he spends 4 to 5 hours per week doing paperwork and keeping up with new regulations.

The chief culprit is the Internal Revenue Service, a major source of new regulations and forms, not covered by the Paperwork Reduction Act. The 1986 White House Conference on Small Business will have as one of its goals simplification of the tax system.

Source: Mary-Margaret Wantuck, "Moving the Mountain of Paperwork," *Nation's Business,* November 1985, 64–65.

not avail themselves of the credits largely because they are unfamiliar with the tax code.[3]

In summary, while government regulation was not designed to discriminate against small business, much of its impact has been more heavily on the small firm than its larger counterpart. This differential impact was in part the motivation for the Regulatory Flexibility Act of 1980. **Reg-Flex,** as it is called, requires federal agencies to analyze and publish reports on new regulations' economic impact on small firms. The act also requires agencies to tailor regulations to the size of the firm where possible.

A more important concern has been deregulation. The next section describes it.

Reg-Flex
The Regulatory Flexibility Act of 1980, which requires federal agencies to analyze, and publish reports on, the economic impact of new regulations on small firms.

[3]Chilton and Hatfield: *Big Government and Small Business,* 6–7.

Deregulation

The increasing burden of regulations prompted the government to reexamine its role in the economy, and in 1978 the first important deregulation legislation was passed, the airlines deregulation. Since then, deregulation has occurred in the financial, communications, trucking, railroad, and intercity bus industries. By 1983 the move toward deregulation had made a significant impact on the economy. *Business Week* gave the movement a ringing endorsement.

> *American business is undergoing its first redirection in 50 years. The move to deregulate, which began slowly just a decade ago, is gaining force. And the results are striking. By scrapping government regulation, the nation is not only revitalizing three basic industries—finance, telecommunications, and transportation—but boosting the economy as well.*[4]

Nowhere have the effects of deregulation been more dramatic than in the trucking industry. More than 300 trucking companies, most of them sizable, have gone bankrupt since the start of deregulation. With the deregulation, however, came opportunities for others, and over 10,000 small operators entered the industry during the same period.

Although deregulation has had dramatic results in some industries, many small businesses still encounter a variety of forms of government regulation. Perhaps the most encouraging news in this regard is that many people, in and out of the government, recognize how the regulations can especially burden small business and are looking for ways to lighten the burden.

The Government as a Source of Assistance

The federal government provides many forms of assistance to small businesses. The major vehicle of this assistance is the Small Business Administration (SBA). Congress established the SBA in 1953 "to help small businesses grow and prosper." The assistance the SBA and other federal agencies provide can be placed into three categories: assistance in managing, assistance in financing, and assistance in exporting.

Management Assistance

The SBA has offices throughout the country. At each of these offices are business development officers whose job is to counsel small businesses. Because this staff typically has a work load requiring resources beyond what

---

[4]"Deregulating America," *Business Week*, November 28, 1983, 80.

"*O.K.! So four and a half billion dollars for six hundred and eighteen guns is not a bargain-basement price, Keatley honey, but they most certainly do not need to be discussing your every decision in the 'Wall Street Journal' day after day after day!*"

Source: Drawing by Booth; © 1984 The New Yorker Magazine, Inc.

it has been given, a number of programs have been developed to supplement the staff. The most ambitious is the Small Business Institute (SBI) program. The SBI was established in 1972 to make the analytical and counseling skills of senior and graduate-level university students available to small firms. The program is available at a number of universities around the country and has provided consulting service for countless small businesses. The service is free to the firm; the university receives $400 for each case handled.

The Service Corps of Retired Executives (SCORE) provides small firms with the consulting skills of volunteer retired executives. The Active Corps of Executives (ACE) is a similar program; practicing managers assist people with small business problems.

Finally, management consultation is given through Small Business Development Centers at various universities. These centers use faculty to provide research and management expertise for small business problems.

In addition to consulting services, the SBA provides management assistance in the publications it makes available to small firms. These publications are free or of low cost and cover a wide range of topics. Three series of publications are available: Management Aids, Small Marketers Aids, and Small Business Bibliographies.

The SBA also provides management training to small business owners or operators. This training, often cosponsored with a university, includes courses or conferences that cover topics in great depth and workshops for anyone considering entry into small business.

Taken as a whole, the SBA's efforts in giving assistance are impressive. During a recent year, nearly 200,000 small businesses received consultation, over 350,000 persons received training, and over four million publications were supplied to small business. Beyond these efforts the SBA works to give special assistance to disadvantaged and minority businesses.

Disadvantaged businesses are those that are economically or socially disadvantaged or located in high-unemployment areas. Firms certified by the SBA as disadvantaged may receive help in identifying and developing new business opportunities, as well as counseling, training, and related services from organizations receiving federal project grants to provide such assistance. Minority businesses may also receive advice on financing through the Minority Small Business and Capital Ownership Development programs.

Another federal program encourages the development of small businesses' research and development capabilities: the Small Business Innovation Research Awards program. Through this program a number of federal agencies and departments are required to set aside a portion of their research budget for small business. This program, started in 1982, has given a number of small firms the opportunity to develop promising research projects. Also in the research management area, the government provides technical information through its Center for the Utilization of Federal Technology (which alerts industry to federally owned patents that show potential for commercial use) and the U.S. Patent and Trademark Office. This office maintains a public search room in Arlington, Virginia where more than four million U.S. patents and several million foreign patents are arranged by subject class.

Financial Assistance

As described in Chapter 9, the SBA provides millions of dollars in direct loans and guarantees billions in other loans, in its basic small business loan program. The government also offers financial assistance for a variety of specialized needs.

- Loans for disadvantaged small businesses. This program is for small businesses owned by low-income persons or located in areas of high unemployment.
- Physical disaster. Businesses that have suffered physical property loss as a result of floods, riots, or other catastrophies are eligible for direct loans of up to 85 percent of their loss.
- Economic injury disaster. Losses as the result of a physical disaster may be covered with a loan of up to $500,000 for working capital.
- Small business energy. These loans assist small businesses in manufacturing, designing, marketing, installing, or servicing specific energy measures.
- Small business pollution control. Guaranteed loans are provided to help small business concerns meet pollution control requirements.

In addition to the loans just described, the government provides financial assistance through two insurance programs:

- Flood insurance. This insurance protects against loss from floods, mud flow, or flood-caused erosion. A government subsidy allows premiums below the normal actuarial level.
- Crime insurance. This program, not available in all states, permits small businesses to be insured against burglary and robbery.

Assistance in Exporting

In recent years the United States has imported far more goods and services than we have exported. This is referred to as a balance of trade deficit. This deficit has government and business officials concerned, and this concern has prompted a great deal of emphasis on developing exports. The U.S. Department of Commerce actively promotes exporting for business firms of all sizes. This section summarizes the information found in *A Basic Guide to Exporting,* a publication of the International Trade Administration of the Department of Commerce.

Part 1 of the *Guide* identifies the first steps in starting an export business, first covering sources of counseling. Many sources are available; perhaps the most useful are the 47 district offices of the Commerce Department. Each of the offices can explain:

- trade and investment opportunities abroad
- foreign markets for U.S. products and services
- financial aid to exporters
- insurance assistance
- tax advantages of exporting
- international trade exhibitions
- export documentation requirements
- economic facts on foreign countries
- export licensing and import requirements

Another important source of counseling is the network of District Export Councils throughout the country. These groups, in cooperation with schools, banks, chambers of commerce, and the SBA, conduct workshops, clinics, and seminars on exporting.

The Commerce Department conducts export seminars ranging from industry- and country-specific topics to investment-oriented programs. These seminars are scheduled and presented by the Seminar and Educational Programming Section of the International Trade Administration.

The U.S. Foreign Commercial Service was created in 1980 to aid in export expansion. Its officials initiate export promotion activities and assist U.S. businesses. This agency gathers market data, identifies and evaluates prospective importers, buyers, agents, and partners, and monitors local laws and trade practices.

Part 2 of the *Guide* describes the sources of data needed in selecting markets abroad. These sources may be categorized as those with economic or demographic data and those describing sales prospects and specific opportunities.

Economic and demographic data may be found in Department of Commerce publications that track shipments to foreign countries, provide country-specific data on industrial countries, and describe, by country, total population, growth rate, life expectancy, and so on. Department publications include the *Overseas Business Report, Foreign Economic Trends and Their Implications, Global Market Surveys,* and *Country Market Sectorial Surveys.*

The primary means by which businesses are made aware of opportunities in foreign markets is the Trade Opportunities Program (TOP). Export opportunities, originating from various sources, are entered into the TOP computer in Washington, D.C. daily. Companies using this service may ask that the computer match these opportunities with their competencies or may subscribe to the *TOP Bulletin*. Exhibit 18.3 is an example of the notices appearing in the publication.

The Government and Taxes

Whether it purchases, regulates, or provides assistance, the government needs money to do its work. One important source of this money is taxes on small businesses. This section will describe the wide variety of taxes, both federal and state, that small business must pay.

In Chapter 15, we discussed the need for careful record keeping in managing a firm's finances. This record keeping is also necessary to prepare tax returns at the end of each year. However, the accounting method used to prepare financial statements will affect the net profit figure and the amount of income taxes to be paid. For example, statements prepared using the cash method will usually result in a different net income figure than if the accrual method is used. Similarly, various depreciation methods result in different net

Exhibit 18.3   Sample Page from *TOP Bulletin*

SECTION II: PRIVATE TRADE OPPORTUNITIES—Continued

NOTICE NO. 043623

THE DIAGNOSIS AND RESEARCH OF EPIDEMIC VIRUS DISEASES. CATALOGS, BROCHURES AND PRICE LISTS EX-FACTORY REQUESTED.

REPLY TO --
DR. SILBER
BUNDES ANSTALT F. VIRUSSEUCHENBEK B.H.
E. V. BEHRING-WEG 3
1231 VIENNA, AUSTRIA
--
TEL: 222/843538
--
PRODUCT CLASSIFICATIONS:
    3811XXX

PLEASE SEND COPY OF YOUR RESPONSE TO
AMERICAN EMBASSY (COM-TOP)
VIENNA, AUSTRIA
DEPT. OF STATE
WASHINGTON, D.C. 20520

U.S. GOVT. REF: 433/01/P0091

NOTICE NO. 043615   DATE: 01/24/86

AUSTRIA   DIRECT SALES TO END-USER

MEDICAL SOFTWARE, DIAGNOSIS RELATED SYSTEMS AND TRAINING PROGRAMS COMPUTER AND PERIPHERAL EQUIPMENT USED IN THE MEDICAL SECTOR # INQUIRER IS A DOCTOR OF MEDICINE AND TEACHER. CATALOGS, BROCHURES AND PRICE LISTS EX-FACTORY REQUESTED.

REPLY TO --
DR. WALTER UEBLEIS
KHEVENHUELLERSTR 30, A-9020 KLAGENFURT
AUSTRIA
--
TEL: 4222/513227
--
PRODUCT CLASSIFICATIONS:
    9921112 3573XXX

PLEASE SEND COPY OF YOUR RESPONSE TO
AMERICAN EMBASSY (COM-TOP)
VIENNA, AUSTRIA
DEPT. OF STATE
WASHINGTON, D.C. 20520

U.S. GOVT. REF: 433/01/P0090

NOTICE NO. 043616   DATE: 01/22/86

PORTUGAL   DIRECT SALES TO END-USER

AUTOMOTIVE MAINTENANCE EQUIPMENT VEHICULAR LIGHTING EQUIPMENT (INCLUDING PARTS AND ACCESSORIES) MOTOR VEHICLES SPARK PLUGS AUTOMOBILE SEAT COVERS MOTOR VEHICLE HARDWARE # FRANCISCO BAPTISTA RUSSO & IRMAO, SARL, IS A WELL-KNOWN MFR./IMPORTER/DISTRIBUTOR OF AUTOMOTIVE EQUIP. AND ACCESSORIES. FIRM EMPLOYS 1,000 WORKERS AND IS 40 YEARS OLD. THEY ARE INTERESTED IN IMPORTING PARTS AND ACCESSORIES FOR AUTOMOBILES (AMERICAN AND EUROPEAN) AND TRUCKS. FIRM HAS AN ASSEMBLY LINE AND RETAILING STORES THROUGH PORTUGAL. CATALOGOS AND PRICES ARE REQUESTED.

REPLY TO --
JOSE DOS SANTOS, MGR.
S.C.I.A. - FRANCISCO BAPTISTA RUSSO &
IRMAO, SARL, RUA AVELINO SALGADO DE
OLIVEIRA, 19 2685 CAMARATE
PORTUGAL
TEL: 2571611
TELEX: 16061 P
PRODUCT CLASSIFICATIONS:
    3549411 36470XX 3694411 2399015

PLEASE SEND COPY OF YOUR RESPONSE TO
COMMERCIAL OFFICER (TOP)
AMERICAN EMBASSY
LISBON, PORTUGAL
APO NEW YORK 09678

U.S. GOVT. REF: 471/01/P0028

NOTICE NO. 043617   DATE: 01/21/86

SPAIN   REPRESENTATION/AGENCY

FROZEN LOBSTER (PANULIRUS ARGUS) FROZEN KING CRAB FROZEN SQUID (LOLIGO PEALE) FROZEN CRAWFISH (PENEUS DUORARUM), FROZEN SALMON # MR. JOSE M. ALFONSO HAS BEEN WORKING AS AN AGENT AND IMPORTER IN THE FISH AND SHELLFISH SECTOR SINCE 1953. HE SELLS THROUGHOUT SPAIN, AND MAINTAINS A GROUP OF 25 SALESMEN TO COVER THE ENTIRE TERRITORY. HE MAINTAINS AS WELL SUBSIDIARY OFFICE IN MADRID UNDER THE TRADE MARK, INSUMAR, HIS VOLUME OF BUSSINESS IS ESTIMATED AT 100 MILLION PESE- TAS (APPROX. USD 650.000). FIN REFS.- BANCO ESPA#OL DE CREDITO, OFICINA PRINCIPAL, DEPTO. EXTRANJERO, LAS PALMAS DE G. CANARIA, (CANARIAS), SPAIN.

REPLY TO --
MR. JOSE M. ALFONSO
MR. JOSE M. ALFONSO
APARTADO 963. LEON Y CASTILLO 48
LAS PALMAS DE G. CANARIA
(CANARIAS), SPAIN
TEL: 34/28/361330
TELEX: 95684 CNSL
PRODUCT CLASSIFICATIONS:
    9973505 9973510 9973525 9973599

PLEASE SEND COPY OF YOUR RESPONSE TO
COMMERCIAL OFFICER (TOP)
BARCELONA, SPAIN
APO NEW YORK 09285

U.S. GOVT. REF: 469/02/P0080

NOTICE NO. 043619   DATE: 01/22/86

ARGENTINA   DIRECT SALES TO END-USER

HYDRAULIC SCRAP SHEARS TO RROCESS STEEL SCRAP INTO 'BAALES' OF DIFFERENT LEN- GTHS. # BUYER NEEDS THIS MACHINE TO PROVIDE METAL SCRAP PREPARATION SERVICE FOR STEEL MAKERS. MACHINE WILL REPLACE SEMI-MANUAL METHOD NOW USED. RECONDITIONED MACHINE ALSO ACCEPTABLE. SEND FULL SPECS AND QUOTATION ASAP. LINDERMAN (WEST GERMANY) IS MAIN COMPETITOR.

REPLY TO--
SR.DANIEL TIZADO, VICE-PRESIDENT
INCORFER S. A.
TEODORO GARCIA 2284 PISO 3
1426 BUENOS AIRES, ARGENTINA
--
PHONE: 208-0063 OR 773-3462
TELEX--
PRODUCT CLASSIFICATIONS:
    3542119

PLEASE SEND COPY OF YOUR RESPONSE TO
COMMERCIAL OFFICER (TOP)
AMERICAN EMBASSY
BUENOS AIRES, ARGENTINA
APO MIAMI 34034

U.S. GOVT. REF: 357/01/P0010

NOTICE NO. 043620   DATE: 01/23/86

ITALY   AGENCY

ANTHELMINTICS PREPARATION FOR VETERINARY USE ANTIBIOTICS FOR VETERINARY USE HORMONES FOR VETERINARY USE PARASITICIDES FOR VETERINARY USE VITAMINS AND MINERALS FOR VETERINARY USE # ACS IS A SMALL FIRM ENGAGED IN REPRESENTATION/IMPORT OF CHEMICALS AND PHARMACEURICALS. IT IS INTERESTED IN IMPORTING PHARMACEUTICAL PREPARATIONS FOR VETERINARY USE FOR A TOTAL ESTIMATE ANNUAL SALES VOLUME OF 1 MILLION U.S. DOLLARS. FIRM SELLS ALL OVER ITALY AND HAS ANNUAL BUSINESS TURNOVER OF 2 MILLION U.S. DOLLARS.

REPLY TO --
MR. CARLO BERTELLI
ACS
PIAZZALE MARTINI 2
20137 MILANO, ITALY
--
PHONE: 02/545988
TELEX: 312272
PRODUCT CLASSIFICATIONS:
    2834921 2834923 2834935 2834945

PLEASE SEND COPY OF YOUR RESPONSE TO
COMMERCIAL OFFICER (TOP)
AMERICAN CONSULATE GENERAL
MILAN, ITALY
C/O AMERICAN EMBASSY, BOX M

U.S. GOVT. REF: 475/04/P0001

NOTICE NO. 043622   DATE: 01/24/86

WEST GERMANY   REPRESENTATION/DISTRIBUTOR

MULTIFUNCTION TEST & MEASURING EQUIP. COMBINATION OR GROUP TEST SETS. SEMICONDUCTOR TEST EQUIPMENT. # FIRM ESTABLISHED 1979, EMPLOYS 4. ANNUAL SALES DM 1,2 MILLION. SALES AREA : EUROPE, NEAR EAST; BANK REF.: RAIFFEISENBANK, 8000 MUNICH. MR. JANOGLU IS INTERESTED IN REPRESENTING A COMPLETE RANGE OF U.S. MADE SEMICONDUCTOR PRODUCTION MATERIALS AND EQUIPMENT.

REPLY TO--
MR. IIANG JANOGLU
GARDEN ATEC BRANCH
DOM-PEDRO-STR. 9
D-8000 MUENCHEN 19, W. GERMANY
--
TEL: 089/222120
TELEX: 523286
PRODUCT CLASSIFICATIONS:
    3825244 3825246

PLEASE SEND COPY OF YOUR RESPONSE TO
COMMERCIAL OFFICER (TOP)
AMERICAN CONSULATE GENERAL
MUNICH, F.R. GERMANY
APO NEW YORK 09108

U.S. GOVT. REF: 428/07/P0178

NOTICE NO. 043623   DATE: 01/24/86

WEST GERMANY   REPRESENTATION/DISTRIBUTOR

LASER TRIMMING AND CUTTING EQUIPMENT FOR SEMICONDUCTOR PRODUCTION. # FIRM ESTABLISHED 1979, EMPLOYS 4. ANNUAL SALES DM 1,2 MILLION. SALES AREA : EUROPE, AND NEAR EAST. BANK REF.: RAIFFEISENBANK, 8000 MUNICH. MR. JANOGLU IS INTERESTED IN REPRESENTING A COMPLETE RANGE OF U.S. MADE SEMICONDUCTOR PRODUCTION MATERIALS AND EQUIPMENT.

Source: U.S. Department of Commerce, *Top Bulletin*, Trade Opportunities Program (Washington, D.C.: Government Printing Office, 1986).

income figures. The entrepreneur should realize that it is not necessary to use the same accounting method both for internal management and for tax preparation. However, the business may use only one method for taxes unless it obtains permission from the IRS to change. Thus, the entrepreneur should discuss alternative methods of preparing tax returns with an accountant to ensure that the most advantageous method is used.

Federal Income Taxes

All businesses that earn a profit must pay income taxes to both the federal and state governments. As mentioned in Chapter 8, the legal form of organization will affect how those taxes are determined and the amount that will be paid. The information below briefly explains how taxes are determined for each type of legal structure. Before we cover these taxing methods, however, we wish to remind the reader of one important fact. In each legal structure, "taxable income" is basically determined by the formula, sales − cost of goods − expenses = taxable net income. As stated in Chapters 7 and 15, there is no relationship between profit and cash on hand since many factors, such as inventory and accounts receivable increases, will affect cash but not net profit. Therefore, it is important to realize that the company showing a good net income may actually be short of cash, and the tax liability on that net profit further aggravates a cash-flow problem. Many small businesses face this situation.

The Sole Proprietorship.   As stated in Chapter 8, no legal distinction is made between the owner of a sole proprietorship and the business. In the government's view, the owner and the business are one entity; they are taxed as one entity. A proprietor must complete the tax form known as a Schedule C. (This, and all other forms mentioned, are shown in order in the Appendix to this chapter.) This form determines the business's net profit. This net profit figure is then transferred to the proprietor's personal income tax form (the 1040 form completed by all citizens), and the net profit is taxed as income to the proprietor. Thus, the company's net income is taxed as if the owner had obtained that amount of money through regular employment. Similarly, if the company shows a net loss, the amount of the loss is transferred to the 1040 form and is subtracted from any other income of the proprietor.

It is important to note one factor concerning the taxes of a proprietorship. A proprietor does not take a salary from the company but instead takes a "draw" or "withdrawal." This is the money the proprietor takes out of company funds for personal living expenses. This withdrawal is not considered a tax-deductible expense. Refer to Schedule C in the Appendix and review the expense items. Though a deduction is listed for employee wages, there is no deduction for owner's withdrawals. Thus, the net profit shown is the profit before a withdrawal was taken. It would not matter if the owner withdrew

$10,000 or $20,000, the taxable net income would remain unchanged. Because the money withdrawn is not a deductible expense for the business, the owner need not include it separately as income on which personal income tax is due.

The Partnership.   A partnership determines its taxes in a manner similar to a proprietorship because the partnership is not a separate, taxable entity from its owners. The partnership must complete and file Form 1065, which determines the net income or loss for the partnership. As with a proprietorship, this net income or loss is then transferred to the partners' personal tax returns (Form 1040 for each). The amount transferred to each partner is based on the percentage of ownership each has in the business.

Several rules for partnerships do not apply to proprietorships. First, if a partnership incurs a loss, there is a limit to the amount that can be reported on the partners' 1040 forms. The loss each partner reports on the tax form cannot exceed the value of that person's share in the partnership at year's end.

Second, payments similar to a salary are often made to a partner for tasks completed during the year. For example, two brothers owned a service station as a partnership. One of them ran the station full-time while the other was employed full-time elsewhere and only worked in the station periodically. The partner who managed the station received an annual income of $10,000 in addition to his share of the profits. The partner who worked in the station periodically only received a share of the company profits each year. The annual payment of $10,000 is known as a "guaranteed payment" and is considered a tax-deductible expense for the partnership. For the partner who receives this payment, it is treated the same as any other salary or ordinary income.

The Corporation.   Income tax for the corporation is different than for the proprietorship or partnership because the corporation is a legal, taxable entity separate from its owners. Corporations must file an income tax return on Form 1120, including an income statement and a balance sheet. (Proprietorships and partnerships do not need to file a balance sheet.) Because the corporation is a taxable entity, the tax rates differ from those of the proprietorship or partnership, where net income is transferred to personal income tax returns. Corporations' tax rates are based on increments of $25,000 as follows:

Net Income	Tax Rate
$ 0 −$25,000	15%
$25,001–$50,000	18
$50,001–$75,000	30
$75,001–$100,000	40
Over $100,000	46

Therefore, taxes on a net income of $26,000 are calculated as follows:

$$\begin{aligned} \$25,000 \times 15\% &= \$3,750 \\ 1,000 \times 18 &= \underline{\quad 180} \\ \text{Total Tax} &= \$3,930 \end{aligned}$$

One major difference in a corporation's tax return is that the owner's salary is tax deductible. Refer to Form 1120 and note the deduction listed for the owner's salary. The corporation's taxable net income is reduced by the amount of the owner's wages. The owner must then report those wages in the same manner as any employee reports wages. If the corporation paid dividends to the owner and other stockholders, they must report those dividends on their personal tax returns. (As stated in Chapter 8, the payment of taxes on net income and dividends is known as "double taxation.")

The S Corporation.   The S corporation is a corporation taxed as a proprietorship or partnership. Its net income or loss is determined and filed on Form 1120S; however, the income or loss is then transferred to the owner's personal tax return. The S corporation pays no income tax of its own. As with a partnership, there is a limit on the amount of losses that stockholders may deduct from their personal tax returns. The limit is equal to the value of each person's share of corporate stock.

State Income Taxes

State income taxes must also be paid on a business's net income, and the taxes are calculated in a manner similar to federal income taxes. In other words, the net income or loss from a proprietorship, partnership, or S corporation is transferred to the owner's personal tax return filed with the state. The corporation, however, since it is a separate legal entity, must file a state tax return separate from that of the owners.

Since each state sets its own tax rates, the rates vary. While some states have a flat tax rate for all income levels (5 percent, for example), some states have a graduated tax similar to the federal income tax rates. Finally, some states, such as Nevada, have no state income tax at all.

Estimated Taxes

Most individuals who are employees file income tax returns once each year after the year has ended. Taxes due are paid or a refund is received. Businesses, however, cannot wait until the year is over to pay income taxes. Instead, a business must estimate (early in the year) how much tax will be due for that year. It must then pay in advance, either in one large payment or in four equal installments paid on or before April 15, June 15, September 15, and January 15. If a company underestimates its tax liability for the year, it may be subject to a penalty. Estimated taxes are required for federal income taxes and are also required in most states for state income tax.

Employee Taxes

A business owner is responsible for several taxes once employees are hired. Some of these taxes are paid by the employee but collected by the employer, some are paid only by the employer, and some are paid jointly by employee and employer.

Income Tax Withholding.   While most employees do not file estimated taxes for federal and state income taxes, they are in effect paying part of their tax bill every time they receive a paycheck. From each paycheck, the employer withholds some money for federal income tax and some money for state income tax (if appropriate). The employer then transfers the money collected to the government. Many types of compensation are subject to income tax withholding, including all wages, salaries, vacation allowances, commissions, and bonuses. The amount of money to be withheld from each check depends on the employee's marital status, number of dependents claimed, how often a paycheck is received, and the amount of the paycheck. Tables for income tax withholding can be obtained from the Internal Revenue Service and state departments of revenue.

Federal Unemployment Tax Act (FUTA)
A federal law enacted to provide a minimal income and job placement assistance to those who are laid off from work.

Unemployment Taxes.   The **Federal Unemployment Tax Act (FUTA)** requires states to work with the federal government in administering an unemployment program. The unemployment program was developed to provide a minimal income and job placement assistance to those laid off from work. The unemployment tax is paid entirely by the employer; employees do not contribute. In addition to the federal unemployment tax, each state has its own unemployment tax; however, the amount paid to the state can be used as a credit against the federal tax. The federal unemployment tax rate in 1985 was 6.2 percent on the first $7,000 in wages. Each state then sets its own tax rate, so rates and benefits vary from state to state.

Federal Insurance Contributions Act (FICA)
A federal law enacted to provide disability benefits to anyone disabled for more than 12 months.

Social Security (FICA).   The Social Security program, established by the **Federal Insurance Contributions Act (FICA)** in 1935, was designed to provide retirement and disability benefits to anyone disabled for more than 12 months. As with unemployment and workers' compensation, the rate is based on wages; however, both employer and employee must contribute. Rates have consistently increased over the past several years. The percentage for both employer and employee in 1985 was 7.05 percent of wages. Therefore, an employee earning $1,000 per month must pay approximately $70 into the fund and the employer must also pay $70. The employer automatically subtracts the employee's contribution from the paycheck. The employer also writes a check at the end of each pay period, each month, or each quarter, to match the employee's contribution, then sends the entire amount to the government. As with FUTA, there is a ceiling on the wages for which FICA taxes must be paid.

Both the percentage and the ceiling have risen dramatically since the inception of the program, as shown below:

Year	Tax Rate	Ceiling on Taxable Wages
1937	1.00%	$ 3,000
1950	1.50	3,000
1960	3.00	4,800
1970	4.80	7,800
1980	6.13	25,900
1985	7.05	39,600
1986–1987	7.15	This level is now adjusted
1988–1989	7.51	using the annual cost
1990 and later	7.65	of living figures.

It should be obvious to the reader that the cost of unemployment and social security taxes can be substantial for a small business owner. Small businesses are often more severely affected than big business when the rates increase. This is because small businesses are often **labor intensive** (employing many people), whereas large businesses are often **capital intensive** (investing money in machines, which reduce personnel needs). Social security and unemployment can easily total more than 10 percent of payroll. Each time rates are increased, the small business owner must make adjustments or profits will be affected. Often, the most logical adjustment is to reduce payroll costs, which in turn reduces costs for social security and unemployment. Many people argue that this contributes to high unemployment, and that reducing the rates might allow business owners to increase payrolls.

Labor-Intensive Business
A business that needs to employ many people to produce its goods and services.

Capital-Intensive Business
A business that requires a large investment in machinery and equipment to produce its goods and services.

Self-Employment Tax

Because owners of proprietorships and partnerships are not considered employees of the company and do not take a salary, social security tax is not paid on the money withdrawn for personal use. Similarly, people employed as independent contractors do not have FICA taxes withheld from their checks. All of these people pay self-employment tax instead of social security. Recall, though, that for proprietors and partners the net income of the company is reported but not the amount of money withdrawn for personal use. Therefore, self-employment tax is calculated on the business's net profit, no matter how much money was withdrawn for personal expenses. As of 1985, the tax rate for self-employment was 11.8 percent.

Small Business Success   18

International Business Services Inc., Washington, D.C.

Marion Greene, Jr., started his computer services company in 1969. His first contract, worth $17,000, was for keypunching cards for the Equal Employment Opportunity Commission and the Labor Department. His company, International Business Services Inc. (IBS), is certified as a minority-owned firm eligible to compete for contracts under the Small Business Administration's 8(a) program. This certification plus a reputation for cost effective services has given Greene's company a sales record that places it among the top Black-owned firms in the United States. IBS now has a staff of over 500, with offices in Washington, D.C., Virginia, Florida, Colorado, and California. His clients range beyond government agencies and now include a variety of domestic and international commercial firms.

Source: America at Work (Washington, D.C.: Small Business Administration, 1985), 9.

Excise Tax

Federal excise taxes are imposed on the manufacture or sale of certain items, on certain transactions, on certain occupations, and on the use of certain items. For example, excise taxes are charged on brewers, wholesalers, and retailers of beer, wine, and other liquor; manufacturers, importers, and dealers in firearms; retailers of motor fuel; providers of air transportation; and providers of local telephone service. Because of the wide variety of businesses subject to excise tax, entrepreneurs should check with the Internal Revenue Service concerning this tax.

Sales Tax

As stated in Chapter 15, many companies are also responsible for sales tax. In most instances, if products are sold to the final consumer, the business must collect sales tax from the customer and remit it to the government. Sales tax is regulated by each state; however, many local municipalities also impose a sales tax. Therefore, even within a state, the sales tax rate will vary. Sales tax is not an expense for the company because it makes no contributions out of company funds—it merely collects the money from customers. (A sample sales tax form for Missouri is included in the Appendix.) Businesses are often required to post a cash bond or an insurance bond (called a surety bond), much like a deposit. Then, if the company does not pay the sales taxes for which it is liable, the government has the right to keep the bond.

Importance of Prompt Payment of Taxes

It is essential that the entrepreneur always make tax payments when they are due. One of the most serious mistakes entrepreneurs make is to become delinquent in tax payments. Often, if cash is short, the entrepreneur will use the sales tax money or the employee withholding taxes that have been collected. The tax money is "temporarily borrowed" to pay normal operating expenses. Then, when the due date for taxes arrives, there is no money available.

Failure to pay taxes is a serious situation for two reasons. First, both the state and federal government have the right to close a business permanently or to seize assets if it does not pay taxes. Second, the entrepreneur cannot avoid the tax liability through bankruptcy. Even if the company declares bankruptcy, the tax liability still exists and must be paid. For these reasons, entrepreneurs should not treat tax issues lightly. It is essential to determine what taxes the company is liable for and always make prompt payments.

Exhibit 18.4 is a checklist of the more commonly encountered tax liabilities of small businesses.

State Government

Although the federal government is a major factor for small businesses in long-range planning, they should recognize that state government can be an important consideration as well. Some states have gone to great lengths to create various small business support programs; other states have done very little. Some states have low tax rates, others have extremely high rates. Other factors, which vary from state to state, include the strength of the economy, the availability of capital, and the cost of labor.

Each year, in its October issue, *Inc.* magazine ranks the 50 states.[5] The ranking is a composite of five factors weighted according to their significance for small business. The factors and their respective weights follow:

1. Capital resources (25 points). This category measures levels of industrial and commercial lending, small business investment company activity, and state-provided capital resources programs.

---

[5]"Report on the States," *Inc.,* October 1985, 90–93.

Exhibit   18.4   Checklist for Selected Tax Liabilities

Tax	Required of	Appropriate Form	Due Date

Income tax	a. Sole proprietors
	b. Individuals in
	   partnerships
	c. Corporations
	d. S corporations
		a. Schedule C and 1040
		b. 1040
		
		c. 1120
		d. 1120S
			a. Same as 1040
			b–d. 15th day of 4th
			   month after tax
			   year ends

Self-employment	a. Sole proprietors b. Individuals in partnerships	a. Schedule SE b. Schedule SE	Same as 1040

Estimated tax	a. Sole proprietors
	b. Individuals in
	   partnerships
	c. Stockholders in
	   S corporations
	d. Corporations
		a–c. 1040ES
		
		d. 1120W
			a–c. 15th day of 4th,
			   6th, 9th months of
			   year, and 15th day
			   of 1st month after
			   year's end
			d. 15th day of 4th,
			   6th, 9th, and 12th
			   months of tax year

Annual return of income	a. Partnerships	a. 1065	15th day of 4th month after end of tax year

FICA tax and withholding tax	a. Proprietors
	b. Partnerships
	c. Corporations
	d. S corporations
		a–d. 941;
		   501 to make deposits;
		   W-2 to employees;
		   W-3 to Social Security
			941: 4/30, 7/31,
			10/31, 1/31
			501: b varies with
			amount owed
			W-2; 1/31
			W-3: last day of
			February

State unemployment	a. Proprietors b. Partnerships c. Corporations d. S corporations	a–d. Varies by state	Varies by state
Federal unemployment	a. Proprietors b. Partnerships c. Corporations d. S corporations	a–d. 940, 508	1/31, 4/30, 7/31, 10/31, 1/31
Sales tax (if products are sold to final customer)	a. Proprietors b. Partnerships c. Corporations d. S corporations	a–d. Varies by state	Varies by state
Excise tax	a. Proprietors b. Partnerships c. Corporations d. S corporations	a–d. Varies by product on which excise tax is charged	For most excise taxes, 4/30, 7/31, 10/31, 1/31

Exhibit 18.5   Ranking of States by *Inc.*

1. California	14. South Carolina	27. Rhode Island	39. Pennsylvania
2. Connecticut	15. Arizona	28. Idaho	40. Michigan
3. Colorado	16. Delaware	29. Louisiana	41. Missouri
4. Massachusetts	17. New Mexico	30. Arkansas	42. Mississippi
5. Virginia	18. Texas	31. Wisconsin	43. Oklahoma
6. Florida	19. Utah	32. Vermont	44. Nevada
7. Minnesota	20. Hawaii	33. North Dakota	45. Maryland
8. New Jersey	21. Washington	34. Maine	46. Tennessee
9. New York	22. New Hampshire	35. Alaska	47. Oregon
10. Illinois	23. Kansas	36. Kentucky	48. Wyoming
11. Indiana	24. Montana	37. Alabama	49. Nebraska
12. Georgia	25. Ohio	38. Iowa	50. West Virginia
13. North Carolina	26. South Dakota		

Source: Adapted from Nell Margolis, INC.'s "Fifth Annual Report on the States," pp. 90–104. Reprinted with permission, INC. magazine, October, 1985. Copyright © 1985 by INC. Publishing Company, 38 Commercial Wharf, Boston, MA 02110.

2. State support (25 points). Such state programs as procurement set-asides for small business, offices of ombudsman and advisory council, and legislative committees on small business are examined here.

3. Labor (20 points). This rating is based on the productivity levels and costs of the average worker, as well as the percentage of unionization in the work force, and proportion of workers over 25 years old who have completed high school.

4. Business activity (20 points). This measures the vitality of the state's economy using such things as changes in population, unemployment, and personal income.

5. Taxes (10 points). This is determined by the amount of state taxes per $1,000 in personal income.

Using these dimensions, the states are ranked 1 through 50. No region of the country fared better or worse than any other. The top ten states had representatives from both coasts, the South, the Midwest, and the Rockies; the bottom ten had a similar geographical dispersion. Exhibit 18.5 gives the ranking.

K E Y   Objectives Reviewed

1. The government consumes huge quantities of goods and services. Serving the government requires that a small business understand the exacting requirements and complex procedures involved in the governmental purchasing process.

2. Despite recent moves toward deregulation, the government's regulatory activities are extensive, particularly in the personnel, safety, and ecological areas.

3. The government has a vast array of assistance programs for small businesses.

4. Every business is liable for a variety of taxes. A clear understanding of their impact and the demands they place on the business operation is essential to management.

5. State governments vary considerably in attitude toward small business. Small firms operating in supportive climates have a significant advantages over those in less positive environments.

Discussion Questions

1. What are the advantages and disadvantages of government contract work?

2. What are the most important ways a business can use passive marketing in developing opportunities with the government?

3. Why does government regulation have a greater impact on small businesses than on large ones?

4. Considering the many sources of government assistance available to small business, why do many businesses not take advantage of the help available?

5. What would you advise someone to do if you learned that she planned to start an export firm?

6. What is Reg-Flex and why was it started?

7. What were the three waves of government regulation and when did they occur? What was the reason, or reasons, for each?

A P P E N D I X 18A

Sample Tax Forms

SCHEDULE C
(Form 1040)

Department of the Treasury
Internal Revenue Service (O)

Profit or (Loss) From Business or Profession
(Sole Proprietorship)
Partnerships, Joint Ventures, etc., Must File Form 1065.
▶ **Attach to Form 1040 or Form 1041.** ▶ **See Instructions for Schedule C (Form 1040).**

OMB No. 1545-0074

19 85
09

Name of proprietor | Social security number

A Principal business or profession, including product or service (see Instructions) | **B** Principal business code from page 2

C Business name and address ▶ .... | **D** Employer ID number

E Method(s) used to value closing inventory:
  (1) ☐ Cost   **(2)** ☐ Lower of cost or market   **(3)** ☐ Other (attach explanation)

F Accounting method: **(1)** ☐ Cash   **(2)** ☐ Accrual   **(3)** ☐ Other (specify) ▶ ....

	Yes	No

G Was there any change in determining quantities, costs, or valuations between opening and closing inventory?.
  If "Yes," attach explanation.

H Did you deduct expenses for an office in your home?. . . . .

Part I Income

1 a Gross receipts or sales	1a	
b Less: Returns and allowances	1b	
c Subtract line 1b from line 1a and enter the balance here	1c	
2 Cost of goods sold and/or operations (from Part III, line 8)	2	
3 Subtract line 2 from line 1c and enter the **gross profit** here	3	
4 a Windfall Profit Tax Credit or Refund received in 1985 (see Instructions) . . .	4a	
b Other income	4b	
5 Add lines 3, 4a, and 4b. This is the **gross income** . . . . ▶	5	

Part II Deductions

6 Advertising		**22** Pension and profit-sharing plans . .		
7 Bad debts from sales or services (Cash method taxpayers, see Instructions)		**23** Rent on business property		
		24 Repairs		
8 Bank service charges		**25** Supplies (not included in Part III below)		
9 Car and truck expenses		**26** Taxes (Do not include Windfall Profit Tax here. See line 30.)		
10 Commissions				
11 Depletion		**27** Travel and entertainment		
12 Depreciation and section 179 deduction from Form 4562 (not included in Part III below)		**28** Utilities and telephone		
		29 a Wages		
		b Jobs credit		
13 Dues and publications		**c** Subtract line 29b from 29a . . .		
14 Employee benefit programs		**30** Windfall Profit Tax withheld in 1985 .		
15 Freight (not included in Part III below) .		**31** Other expenses (specify):		
16 Insurance		**a**		
17 Laundry and cleaning		**b**		
18 Legal and professional services . . .		**c**		
19 Mortgage interest paid to financial institutions (see Instructions)		**d**		
		e		
20 Office expense		**f**		
21 Other interest		**g**		

32 Add amounts in columns for lines 6 through 31g. These are the **total deductions** . . . . ▶ | 32 |

33 **Net profit or (loss).** Subtract line 32 from line 5 and enter the result. If a profit, enter on Form 1040, line 12, and on Schedule SE, Part I, line 2 (or Form 1041, line 6). If a loss, you **MUST** go on to line 34 . . . . | 33 |

34 If you have a loss, you **MUST** answer this question: "Do you have amounts for which you are not at risk in this business (see Instructions)?" ☐ Yes ☐ No
If "Yes," you **MUST** attach **Form 6198.** If "No," enter the loss on Form 1040, line 12, and on Schedule SE, Part I, line 2 (or Form 1041, line 5).

Part III Cost of Goods Sold and/or Operations (See Schedule C Instructions for Part III)

1 Inventory at beginning of year (if different from last year's closing inventory, attach explanation) . . .	1	
2 Purchases less cost of items withdrawn for personal use	2	
3 Cost of labor (do not include salary paid to yourself)	3	
4 Materials and supplies	4	
5 Other costs	5	
6 Add lines 1 through 5	6	
7 Less: Inventory at end of year	7	
8 **Cost of goods sold and/or operations.** Subtract line 7 from line 6. Enter here and in Part I, line 2, above. . .	8	

For Paperwork Reduction Act Notice, see Form 1040 Instructions.   **Schedule C (Form 1040) 1985**

Form **1040**   Department of the Treasury—Internal Revenue Service   **1985**
U.S. Individual Income Tax Return   **(For VITA Use Only)**

For the year January 1-December 31, 1985, or other tax year beginning _____, 1985, ending _____, 19___   OMB No. 1545-0074

Use IRS label. Otherwise, please print or type.	Your first name and initial (if joint return, also give spouse's name and initial)	Last name	Your social security number
	Present home address (number and street, including apartment number, or rural route)		Spouse's social security number
	City, town or post office, state, and ZIP code	Your occupation	
		Spouse's occupation	

Presidential Election Campaign ▶ Do you want $1 to go to this fund? . . . . Yes ☐ No ☐   Note: Checking "Yes" will not change your tax or reduce your refund.
If joint return, does your spouse want $1 to go to this fund?. . Yes ☐ No ☐

For Privacy Act and Paperwork Reduction Act Notice, see Instructions.

Filing Status

Check only one box.

1 ☐ Single
2 ☐ Married filing joint return (even if only one had income)
3 ☐ Married filing separate return. Enter spouse's social security no. above and full name here. _____
4 ☐ Head of household (with qualifying person). (See page 5 of Instructions.) If the qualifying person is your unmarried child but not your dependent, write child's name here. _____
5 ☐ Qualifying widow(er) with dependent child (year spouse died ▶ 19___). (See page 6 of Instructions.)

Exemptions

Always check the box labeled Yourself. Check other boxes if they apply.

6a ☐ Yourself   ☐ 65 or over   ☐ Blind
b ☐ Spouse   ☐ 65 or over   ☐ Blind

Enter number of boxes checked on 6a and b ▶ ☐

c First names of your dependent children who lived with you _____
Enter number of children listed on 6c ▶ ☐

d First names of your dependent children who did not live with you (see page 6). _____ (If pre-1985 agreement, check here ▶ ☐ .)
Enter number of children listed on 6d ▶ ☐

e Other dependents:

(1) Name	(2) Relationship	(3) Number of months lived in your home	(4) Did dependent have income of $1,040 or more?	(5) Did you provide more than one-half of dependent's support?

Enter number of other dependents ▶ ☐

f Total number of exemptions claimed (also complete line 36). . . . .
Add numbers entered in boxes above ▶ ☐

Income

Please attach Copy B of your Forms W-2, W-2G, and W-2P here.

If you do not have a W-2, see page 4 of Instructions.

Please attach check or money order here.

7 Wages, salaries, tips, etc. (Attach Form(s) W-2.) **7**
8 Interest income (also attach Schedule B if over $400) **8**
9a Dividends (also attach Schedule B if over $400) _____, 9b Exclusion _____
c Subtract line 9b from line 9a and enter the result **9c**
10 Taxable refunds of state and local income taxes, if any, from the worksheet on page 9 of Instructions.   **10**
11 Alimony received **11**
12 Business income or (loss) (attach Schedule C) **12**
13 Capital gain or (loss) (attach Schedule D) **13**
14 40% of capital gain distributions not reported on line 13 (see page 9 of Instructions) **14**
15 Other gains or (losses) (attach Form 4797) **15**
16 Fully taxable pensions, IRA distributions, and annuities not reported on line 17 (see page 9).   **16**
17a Other pensions and annuities, including rollovers. Total received   17a _____
b Taxable amount, if any, from the worksheet on page 10 of Instructions **17b**
18 Rents, royalties, partnerships, estates, trusts, etc. (attach Schedule E) **18**
19 Farm income or (loss) (attach Schedule F) **19**
20a Unemployment compensation (insurance). Total received . . 20a _____
b Taxable amount, if any, from the worksheet on page 10 of Instructions **20b**
21a Social security benefits (see page 10). Total received . . . . 21a _____
b Taxable amount, if any, from worksheet on page 11. { Tax-exempt interest _____ } **21b**
22 Other income (list type and amount—see page 11 of Instructions) _____   **22**
23 Add lines 7 through 22. This is your **total income** . . . . ▶   **23**

Adjustments to Income

(See Instructions on page 11.)

24 Moving expense (attach Form 3903 or 3903F) . . . .   24 _____
25 Employee business expenses (attach Form 2106) . . . . .   25 _____
26 IRA deduction, from the worksheet on page 12 . . . . .   26 _____
27 Keogh retirement plan deduction . . . .   27 _____
28 Penalty on early withdrawal of savings . . . .   28 _____
29 Alimony paid (recipient's last name _____ and social security no. _____) . . . .   29 _____
30 Deduction for a married couple when both work (attach Schedule W)   30 _____
31 Add lines 24 through 30. These are your **total adjustments** . . . . ▶   **31**

Adjusted Gross Income

32 Subtract line 31 from line 23. This is your **adjusted gross income.** If this line is less than $11,000 and a child lived with you, see "Earned Income Credit" (line 59) on page 16 of Instructions. If you want IRS to figure your tax, see page 13 of Instructions . . . ▶   **32**

Form 1065

Form **1065**

Department of the Treasury
Internal Revenue Service

U.S. Partnership Return of Income

▶ **For Paperwork Reduction Act Notice, see Form 1065 Instructions.**

For calendar year 1985, or fiscal year beginning _____, 1985, and ending _____ 19___

OMB No. 1545-0099

1985

A Principal business activity	Use IRS label. Otherwise, please print or type.	Name	**D** Employer identification number
B Principal product or service		Number and street	**E** Date business started
C Business code number		City or town, state, and ZIP code	**F** Enter total assets at end of tax year $

G Check method of accounting: (1) ☐ Cash (2) ☐ Accrual (3) ☐ Other

H Check applicable boxes: (1) ☐ Final return (2) ☐ Change in address (3) ☐ Amended return

I Number of partners in this partnership ▶ _____

J Is this partnership a limited partnership (see page 3 of Instructions)?

K Is this partnership a partner in another partnership?

L Are any partners in this partnership also partnerships?

M Does the partnership meet **all** the requirements shown on page 5 of the Instructions under **Question M**

N Was there a distribution of property or a transfer of a partnership interest during the tax year? If "Yes," see page 5 of the Instructions concerning an election to adjust the basis of the partnership's assets under section 754.

O At any time during the tax year, did the partnership have an interest in or a signature or other authority over a bank account, securities account, or other financial account in a foreign country (see page 5 of Instructions)? If "Yes," write the name of the foreign country ▶ _____

P Was the partnership the grantor of, or transferor to, a foreign trust which existed during the current tax year, whether or not the partnership or any partner has any beneficial interest in it? If "Yes," you may have to file Forms 3520, 3520-A, or 926 (see page 5 of Instructions).

Q Check this box if the partnership has filed or is required to file **Form 8264,** Application for Registration of a Tax Shelter. ☐

Income

1a Gross receipts or sales $ _____ **1b** Minus returns and allowances $ _____ Balance ▶	**1c**	
2 Cost of goods sold and/or operations (Schedule A, line 7)	**2**	
3 Gross profit (subtract line 2 from line 1c)	**3**	
4 Ordinary income (loss) from other partnerships and fiduciaries	**4**	
5 Taxable interest and nonqualifying dividends	**5**	
6a Gross rents $ _____ **6b** Minus rental expenses (attach schedule) $ _____		
c Balance net rental income (loss) ▶	**6c**	
7 Net income (loss) from royalties (attach schedule)	**7**	
8 Net farm profit (loss) (attach Schedule F (Form 1040))	**8**	
9 Net gain (loss) (Form 4797, line 17)	**9**	
10 Other income (loss)	**10**	
11 **TOTAL** income (loss) (combine lines 3 through 10)	**11**	

Deductions

12a Salaries and wages (other than to partners) $ _____ **12b** Minus jobs credit $ _____ Balance ▶	**12c**	
13 Guaranteed payments to partners (see page 7 of Instructions)	**13**	
14 Rent	**14**	
15 Total deductible interest expense not claimed elsewhere on return (see page 7 of Instructions).	**15a**	
b Minus interest expense required to be passed through to partners on Schedule K-1(1065), lines 10, 15a (2), and 15a(3)	**15b**	
c Balance ▶	**15c**	
16 Taxes	**16**	
17 Bad debts (see page 7 of Instructions)	**17**	
18 Repairs	**18**	
19a Depreciation from Form 4562 (attach Form 4562) $ _____ **19b** Minus depreciation claimed on Schedule A and elsewhere on return $ _____ Balance ▶	**19c**	
20 Depletion (**Do not deduct oil and gas depletion.** See page 8 of Instructions.)	**20**	
21a Retirement plans, etc. (see page 8 of Instructions)	**21a**	
b Employee benefit programs (see page 8 of Instructions)	**21b**	
22 Other deductions (attach schedule)	**22**	
23 **TOTAL** deductions (add amounts in column for lines 12c through 22)	**23**	
24 Ordinary income (loss) (subtract line 23 from line 11)	**24**	

Please Sign Here

Under penalties of perjury, I declare that I have examined this return, including accompanying schedules and statements, and to the best of my knowledge and belief it is true, correct, and complete. Declaration of preparer (other than taxpayer) is based on all information of which preparer has any knowledge.

▶ _____ Signature of general partner   ▶ _____ Date

Paid Preparer's Use Only

Preparer's signature ▶	Date	Check if self-employed ▶ ☐	Preparer's social security no.
Firm's name (or yours, if self-employed) and address ▶		E.I. No. ▶	
		ZIP code ▶	

(167)

Form 1120

Department of the Treasury
Internal Revenue Service

U.S. Corporation Income Tax Return

For calendar 1985 or tax year beginning _____ , 1985, ending _____ , 19 ____

▶ For Paperwork Reduction Act Notice, see page 1 of the instructions.

OMB No. 1545-0123

1985

Check if a—

A Consolidated return ☐
B Personal Holding Co. ☐
C Business Code No. (See the list in the Instructions)

Use IRS label. Otherwise please print or type.

Name

Number and street

City or town, state, and ZIP code

D Employer identification number

E Date incorporated

F Total assets (see Specific Instructions)

G Check box if there has been a change in address from the previous year . . . . ▶ ☐ | $ | Dollars | Cents |

Income

1 a Gross receipts or sales _____ b Less returns and allowances _____ Balance ▶	1c		
2 Cost of goods sold and/or operations (Schedule A)	2		
3 Gross profit (line 1c less line 2)	3		
4 Dividends (Schedule C)	4		
5 Interest	5		
6 Gross rents	6		
7 Gross royalties	7		
8 Capital gain net income (attach separate Schedule D)	8		
9 Net gain or (loss) from Form 4797, line 17, Part II (attach Form 4797) . . .	9		
10 Other income (see instructions—attach schedule)	10		
11 TOTAL income—Add lines 3 through 10 and enter here . . . . ▶	11		

Deductions

12 Compensation of officers (Schedule E)	12		
13 a Salaries and wages _____ b Less jobs credit _____ Balance ▶	13c		
14 Repairs	14		
15 Bad debts (Schedule F if reserve method is used)	15		
16 Rents	16		
17 Taxes	17		
18 Interest	18		
19 Contributions (**see instructions for 10% limitation**)	19		
20 Depreciation (attach Form 4562)	20		
21 Less depreciation claimed in Schedule A and elsewhere on return .	21a	21b	
22 Depletion	22		
23 Advertising	23		
24 Pension, profit-sharing, etc. plans	24		
25 Employee benefit programs	25		
26 Other deductions (attach schedule)	26		
27 TOTAL deductions—Add lines 12 through 26 and enter here . . . . ▶	27		
28 Taxable income before net operating loss deduction and special deductions (line 11 less line 27) .	28		
29 Less: a Net operating loss deduction (see instructions)	29a		
b Special deductions (Schedule C)	29b	29c	

Tax and Payments

30 Taxable income (line 28 less line 29c)	30		
31 TOTAL TAX (Schedule J)	31		
32 **Payments:**			
a 1984 overpayment allowed as a credit . . .			
b 1985 estimated tax payments			
c Less 1985 refund applied for on Form 4466 . . ( )			
d Tax deposited with Form 7004			
e Credit from regulated investment companies (attach Form 2439) . .			
f Credit for Federal tax on gasoline and special fuels (attach Form 4136)	32		
33 Enter any **PENALTY** for underpayment of estimated tax—check ▶☐ if Form 2220 is attached .	33		
34 **TAX DUE**—If the total of lines 31 and 33 is larger than line 32, enter AMOUNT OWED	34		
35 **OVERPAYMENT**—If line 32 is larger than the total of lines 31 and 33, enter AMOUNT OVERPAID	35		
36 Enter amount of line 35 you want: **Credited to 1986 estimated tax** ▶ Refunded ▶	36		

Please Sign Here

Under penalties of perjury, I declare that I have examined this return, including accompanying schedules and statements, and to the best of my knowledge and belief, it is true, correct, and complete. Declaration of preparer (other than taxpayer) is based on all information of which preparer has any knowledge.

▶ _____   _____   _____
   Signature of officer   Date   Title

Paid Preparer's Use Only

Preparer's signature ▶	Date	Check if self-employed ▶ ☐	Preparer's social security number
Firm's name (or yours, if self-employed) and address		E.I. No. ▶	
		ZIP code ▶	

(215)

Form **1120S**

Department of the Treasury
Internal Revenue Service

U.S. Income Tax Return for an S Corporation

For calendar 1985 or tax year beginning _____ , 1985, ending _____ , 19 _____

▶ For Paperwork Reduction Act Notice, see page 1 of the instructions.

OMB No. 1545-0130

1985

A Date of election as an S corporation	Use IRS label. Otherwise, please print or type.	Name	**C** Employer identification number
		Number and street	**D** Date incorporated
B Business Code No. (see Specific Instructions)		City or town, state, and ZIP code	**E** Total assets (see Specific Instructions)

F. Check box if there has been a change in address from the previous year . . . . ▶ ☐ $

	Dollars	Cents

Income

1 a Gross receipts or sales _____ b Less returns and allowances _____ Balance ▶	**1c**	
2 Cost of goods sold and/or operations (Schedule A, line 7)	**2**	
3 Gross profit (subtract line 2 from line 1c)	**3**	
4 Taxable interest and nonqualifying dividends	**4**	
5 Gross rents	**5**	
6 Gross royalties	**6**	
7 Net gain or (loss) from Form 4797, line 17, Part II	**7**	
8 Other income (see instructions—attach schedule)	**8**	
9 TOTAL income (loss)—Combine lines 3 through 8 and enter here . . . . . . ▶	**9**	

Deductions

10 Compensation of officers	**10**	
11 a Salaries and wages _____ b Less jobs credit _____ Balance ▶	**11c**	
12 Repairs	**12**	
13 Bad debts (see instructions)	**13**	
14 Rents	**14**	
15 Taxes	**15**	
16 a Total deductible interest expense not claimed elsewhere on return (see instructions)	**16a**	
b Interest expense required to be passed through to shareholders on Schedule K-1, lines 9, 13a(2) and 13a(3) . . .	**16b**	
c Subtract line 16b from line 16a	**16c**	
17 a Depreciation from Form 4562 (attach Form 4562) . . .	**17a**	
b Depreciation claimed on Schedule A and elsewhere on return .	**17b**	
c Subtract line 17b from line 17a	**17c**	
18 Depletion (**Do not deduct oil and gas depletion. See instructions)**	**18**	
19 Advertising	**19**	
20 Pension, profit-sharing, etc. plans	**20**	
21 Employee benefit programs	**21**	
22 Other deductions (attach schedule)	**22**	
23 TOTAL deductions—Add lines 10 through 22 and enter here . . . . . . ▶	**23**	
24 Ordinary income (loss)—Subtract line 23 from line 9	**24**	

Tax and Payments

25 Tax:		
a Excess net passive income tax (attach schedule)	**25a**	
b Tax from Schedule D (Form 1120S), Part IV	**25b**	
c Add lines 25a and 25b	**25c**	
26 Payments:		
a Tax deposited with Form 7004	**26a**	
b Credit for Federal tax on gasoline and special fuels (attach Form 4136) .	**26b**	
c Add lines 26a and 26b	**26c**	
27 **TAX DUE** (subtract line 26c from line 25c). See instructions for Paying the Tax. . . . . . ▶	**27**	
28 **OVERPAYMENT** (subtract line 25c from line 26c) . . . . ▶	**28**	

Please Sign Here

Under penalties of perjury, I declare that I have examined this return, including accompanying schedules and statements, and to the best of my knowledge and belief, it is true, correct, and complete. Declaration of preparer (other than taxpayer) is based on all information of which preparer has any knowledge.

▶ _____ _____ ▶ _____
Signature of officer   Date   Title

Paid Preparer's Use Only

Preparer's signature ▶	Date	Check if self-employed ▶ ☐	Preparer's social security number
Firm's name (or yours, if self-employed) and address ▶		E.I. No. ▶	
		ZIP code ▶	

Form **1120S** (1985)

(233)

SCHEDULE SE
(Form 1040)

Department of the Treasury
Internal Revenue Service   (O)

Computation of Social Security Self-Employment Tax

► See Instructions for Schedule SE (Form 1040).
► Attach to Form 1040.

OMB No. 1545-0074

1985
18

Name of **self-employed** person (as shown on social security card)

Social security number of
self-employed person ►

Part I   Regular Computation of Net Earnings From Self-Employment

Note: *If you performed services for certain churches or church-controlled organizations and you are not a minister or a member of a religious order, see the instructions.*

1 Net farm profit or (loss) from Schedule F (Form 1040), line 39, and farm partnerships, Schedule K–1 (Form 1065), line 13a . . . . | 1 |

2 Net profit or (loss) from Schedule C (Form 1040), line 33, Schedule K–1 (Form 1065), line 13a (other than farming), and Form W–2 wages of $100 or more from an electing church or church-controlled organization. (See instructions for other income to report.) . . . . | 2 |

Note: ☐ *Check here if you are exempt from self-employment tax on your earnings as a minister, member of a religious order, or Christian Science practitioner because you filed Form 4361.*
See instructions for kinds of income to report. If you have other earnings of $400 or more that are subject to self-employment tax, include those earnings on line 2.

Part II   Optional Computation of Net Earnings From Self-Employment
(See "Who Can Use Schedule SE")

Generally, this part may be used **only** if you meet any of the following tests:

A   Your gross farm income (Schedule F (Form 1040), line 12) was not more than $2,400; or

B   Your gross farm income (Schedule F (Form 1040), line 12) was more than $2,400 and your net farm profits (Schedule F (Form 1040), line 39) were less than $1,600; or

C   Your net nonfarm profits (Schedule C (Form 1040), line 33) were less than $1,600 and also less than two-thirds (⅔) of your gross nonfarm income (Schedule C (Form 1040), line 5)
See instructions for other limitations.

3 Maximum income for optional methods . . . . | 3 | $1,600 | 00

4 Farm Optional Method—If you meet test A or B above, enter: the smaller of two-thirds (⅔) of gross farm income from Schedule F (Form 1040), line 12, and farm partnerships, Schedule K–1 (Form 1065), line 13b; or $1,600 . . . . | 4 |

5 Subtract line 4 from line 3 . . . . | 5 |

6 Nonfarm Optional Method—If you meet test C above, enter: the smallest of two-thirds (⅔) of gross nonfarm income from Schedule C (Form 1040), line 5, and Schedule K–1 (Form 1065), line 13c (other than farming); or $1,600; or, if you elected the farm optional method, the amount on line 5 . . . . . | 6 |

Part III   Computation of Social Security Self-Employment Tax

7 Enter the amount from Part I, line 1, or, if you elected the farm optional method, Part II, line 4 . . . . | 7 |

8 Enter the amount from Part I, line 2, or, if you elected the nonfarm optional method, Part II, line 6 . . . | 8 |

9 Add lines 7 and 8. If less than $400, do not fill in the rest of the schedule because you are not subject to self-employment tax. (**Exception:** If this line is less than $400 and you are an employee of an electing church or church-controlled organization, complete the schedule unless this line is a loss. See instructions.) . . . . | 9 |

10 The largest amount of combined wages and self-employment earnings subject to social security or railroad retirement tax (Tier 1) for 1985 is . . . . | 10 | $39,600 | 00

11 a Total social security wages and tips from Forms W–2 and railroad retirement compensation (Tier 1). **Note:** *U.S. Government employees whose wages are only subject to the 1.35% hospital insurance benefits tax (Medicare) and employees of certain church or church-controlled organizations should not include those wages on this line (see instructions)* . . . . | 11a |

   b Unreported tips subject to social security tax from Form 4137, line 9, or to railroad retirement tax (Tier 1) . . . . | 11b |

   c Add lines 11a and 11b . . . . | 11c |

12 a Subtract line 11c from line 10. | 12a |

   b Enter your "qualified" U.S. Government wages if you are required to use the worksheet in Part III of the instructions. | 12b |

   c Enter your Form W-2 wages from an electing church or church-controlled organization.
      | 12c |

13 Enter the smaller of line 9 or line 12a . . . . | 13 |

   If line 13 is $39,600, fill in $4,672.80 on line 14. Otherwise, multiply line 13 by .118 and enter the result on line 14 . . . . | .118 |

14 Self-employment tax. Enter this amount on Form 1040, line 51 . . . . | 14 |

For Paperwork Reduction Act Notice, see Form 1040 Instructions.   **Schedule SE (Form 1040) 1985**

☆U.S.GPO: 1985-463-108 E.I. NO. 43-1110209

Missouri Department of Revenue
Business Taxes Bureau
P.O. Box 840
Jefferson City, MO 65105

Do Not Write in this Space

STATE OF MISSOURI — DEPARTMENT OF REVENUE

SALES TAX RETURN

Address Correction
☐ Mailing Address
☐ Business Address

RETURN THIS COPY

ACCOUNT NUMBER __ __ __ __ __ __ __ - __   PERIOD _____
OWNER'S NAME _____
BUSINESS NAME _____
MAILING ADDRESS _____
CITY _____ STATE _____ ZIP _____
PHONE NUMBER (__ __ __) __ __ __ - __ __ __ __

*SEE INSTRUCTIONS
TAXABLE SALES
FOR THIS PERIOD
BY MONTH/QUARTER
MO/QR 1 $ _____
MO/QR 2 $ _____
MO/QR 3 $ _____
QR 4 $ _____
TOTAL $ _____

☐☐ ☐☐ ☐☐ *(DO NOT WRITE IN SHADED AREAS)*

BUSINESS LOCATION	CODE	GROSS RECEIPTS OR SALES (Circle one)	ADJUSTMENTS (Indicate + or −)	TAXABLE SALES	RATE	AMOUNT OF TAX
						1.

ADJUSTMENTS CLAIMED, IF ANY: — SEE INSTRUCTIONS —

A. Sales for resale .... −
B. Add cost of goods purchased for resale but used by you .... +
C. Goods shipped out of Missouri (export) .... −
D. Motor fuel, special fuel, other fuel .... −
E. Government, religious, educational, charitable institutions .... −
F. Drugs, insulin, prosthetic or orthopedic devices .... −
G. Farm machinery .... −
H. Water, electricity, gas, wood, coal or home heating oil (Domestic use) .... −
I. Seed, fertilizer, grain, economic poisons, livestock/poultry feed .... −
J. Labor or service charges when separately billed .... −
K. Value of trade-in .... −

CIRCLE ONE +

L. Other adjustments (attach separate sheet) ....

CIRCLE ONE

TOTAL ADJUSTMENTS .... +

SUBTRACT: 2% TIMELY PAYING ALLOWANCES (If Applicable)

TOTAL SALES TAX DUE

ADD: INTEREST FOR LATE PAYMENT (See Line 4 of Instructions)

ADD: ADDITIONS TO TAX

SUBTRACT: APPROVED CREDIT

PAY THIS AMOUNT

☐ CHECK BOX, IF FINAL RETURN (See instructions on reverse side)

2. −
3. =
4. +
5. +
6. −
7. =

Under penalties of perjury, I declare that I have examined this return, including accompanying schedules and statements, and to the best of my knowledge and belief it is true, correct and complete. RETURN MUST BE SIGNED AND DATED.

Signature of   Date _____
Taxpayer or Agent _____ Title _____ Tax Period ___ MO. ___ DAY ___ YR. Thru ___ MO. ___ DAY ___ YR.

MO 860-1153 (9-85)   DOR-53-1 (9-85)

EMPLOYEE COMPENSATION RECORD

NAME __John E. Marks__

ADDRESS __1 Elm St. Newark, N.J.__

PHONE __768-6075__

FULL TIME _____

PART TIME __X__

SOC. SEC. NO. __567-03-1973__

DATE OF BIRTH __12-21-51__

NO. OF EXEMPTIONS __Single - 1__

Pay Period Ending	Hours Worked S M T W T F S	Hours Worked S M T W T F S	Total Reg. Hours	Over-time	Earnings Regular Rate	Earnings Overtime Rate	Earnings Total	Deductions Social Security	Deductions Fed. Income Tax	Deductions State Income Tax	Deductions Other	Net Pay
1/11/xx	4 4 4 4 4	4 4 3 5 4	40		$3.57		$142.80	$8.75	$7.30	$2.85		$123.90
1/25/xx	4 4 3 4 4 2	4 3 4 4 4	40		$3.57		$142.80	$8.75	$7.30	$2.85		$123.90
			80				$285.60	$17.50	$14.60	$5.70		$247.80

QUARTERLY TOTALS

Source: U.S. Department of the Treasury, Internal Revenue Service, Recordkeeping for a Small Business, Publication 583 (Washington, D.C.: Government Printing Office, 1980), 14.

CHAPTER 19

Computers in Small Business

Source: Courtesy of Amfac, Inc.

K E Y   Objectives

1.   To review computer terminology.

2.   To identify functions often performed by computers.

3.   To discuss the advantages of computerization.

4.   To examine the disadvantages of computerization.

5.   To describe the decision process when considering computerization.

6.   To identify a recommended implementation process.

7.   To stress the need for professional advice.

Chips
Electronic circuits that
perform the functions
within a computer.

Though large corporations have used computers for many years, small businesses did not begin to do so on a widespread basis until the late 1970s. Until that time, the computers large corporations used were so expensive that small businesses could not afford them.

However, in 1971, the first microprocessors were developed. (Microprocessors—often called **chips**—are the electronic circuits that perform the functions.) As technology improved, each chip could perform more functions. This allowed smaller computers to perform more functions. Around 1975 and 1976, the first smaller computers were introduced, and by 1977, there were several small computers available to the general public. This allowed small businesses to computerize their information.[1]

Though computers can be very helpful to small business owners, the entrepreneur must be well informed and understand the computer's limitations before purchasing one. Many entrepreneurs who make a hasty or ill-informed decision find that the computer cannot provide the necessary functions. Many entrepreneurs also find that it does not solve all the problems they assumed it would solve. The entrepreneur should therefore become familiar with the different types of computers to make the best decision.

---

[1]*Microcomputers* (Price Waterhouse, January 1983), 4.

Unique Business   19.1

Finders of Lost Money

If you have an uncle smart enough to have bought Xerox stock 35 years ago, but too dumb to remember that he had done so, you may be hearing from Capital Tracing Inc. Founded in Scottsdale, Arizona by John Badger and O. Robert Meredith, the company buys lists of unclaimed monies from corporations. The individuals are tracked through a variety of means, including the use of the Mormon Church's genealogical library in Salt Lake City. CTI collects a 33 percent fee from proceeds. The company hopes to track down, annually, owners of $5 million in unclaimed securities.

Source: "Tracing Lost Money," *Venture* 7, no. 8 (August 1985): 8.

Computer Terminology

Size and Speed Distinctions

Mainframes
Large, expensive computers capable of processing information rapidly.

Minicomputers
Midsize computers that process information more slowly than mainframes and cannot handle as many users simultaneously.

Microcomputers
The smallest and least expensive computer, often portable, unable to store a large volume of information.

Bits
A shortened term for binary digits, which refers to electronic signals read by a computer.

The original computers large corporations used are known as **mainframes.** These computers are large and expensive; they perform functions very quickly, and many people can use them at the same time. The midsize computers, usually known as **minicomputers,** are smaller and less expensive but perform functions more slowly and are not able to handle as many users simultaneously. The **microcomputer** is the smallest computer and is used by many small businesses. It is less expensive and is often portable. Because the rapidly changing technology gives us increased speeds and reduced size, the distinctions between mainframes, minis, and micros are becoming blurred. Therefore, it is difficult to give specific distinctions between the types of computers or to predict the eventual outcome of computer technology.[2]

The computer's speed is determined partially by the number of electronic signals the computer can read at the same time. These electronic signals are known as **bits**—a shortened term for binary digits. The number of bits a computer can read at the same time is known as a "word." A machine that reads 32-bit words is faster than a machine that reads 16-bit words.

[2]*Microcomputers,* 6.

Hardware and Software

Hardware
The machine and circuitry of a computer.

Software
The computer program.

The actual machine—the mainframe, mini, or micro—is known as the **hardware,** whereas the actual computer program is known as the **software.** The hardware is of no value if the computer program does not provide the necessary information. The hardware-software relationship has been likened to the razor-blade relationship. The razor (hardware) represents the major expenditure, but quality blades (software) are needed to make use of it. Therefore, when purchasing a computer, the entrepreneur must consider the software each computer utilizes to determine which is most appropriate. Many software packages can be purchased for microcomputers, including programs for accounts receivable posting and aging, payroll, and accounts payable. If no standard software package is adequate for the entrepreneur's needs, it is necessary to write customized programs that provide the format and detail desired.

Some of the common languages microcomputers use include BASIC, FORTRAN, COBOL, PASCAL, and LOGO. The ultimate choice of language depends partially on what functions the entrepreneur needs performed, personal preference as to which seems easiest to use, and the types of languages the specific computer will use.

Functions Often Performed by Computers

Small businesses use computers for many applications. While some programs are necessary only for specific industries, certain programs are common to all small businesses. These include the following:

Financial Record Keeping

One of the most common applications for computers in small businesses is to process financial reports. This includes payroll, accounts receivable posting, accounts payable posting, inventory control, and complete preparation of financial statements. Financial record keeping was one of the first uses small businesses implemented when small computers became available.

Financial Statement and Ratio Analysis

Once the computer has completed the financial statement preparation, it can also quickly complete a financial analysis to determine financial ratios and analyze the company's current financial position.

Customer Billing

Because the computer posts all accounts receivable information, the next logical step is to use the computer to bill customers. With the constantly updated customer balances, the billing process is quicker and easier to complete.

Word Processing and Mailing Lists

One benefit of many computers is the possibility of printing individually addressed form letters to many customers. This saves clerical time and allows hundreds of letters to be typed quickly with no mistakes. Similarly, businesses often place customer names and addresses into the computer, which can then print them on mailing labels whenever needed. Thus, a mailing list needs to be typed only once and then updated periodically. This eliminates typing names and addresses for each mailing.

Graphics

Many computer programs provide information in a graphic format as well as in the usual printed format. Thus, a sales manager can receive graphic illustrations of each salesperson's monthly sales, total sales by territories of the country or state, sales to each customer, and so forth. Interior design firms also use graphic programs when designing offices. This allows them to make changes quickly and to have an immediate visual representation of the actual office layout.

Production Management

In manufacturing firms, proper production scheduling is critical to maintaining an efficient operation. The computer is often used to help coordinate production runs, ensure quality control, and ensure that proper levels of raw materials are on hand.

Forecasting

One of a computer's most helpful functions in managing a small firm is the ability to predict the effects of alternative decisions without actually implementing them. For example, the manager can determine the exact effect on cash flow if additional inventory is ordered, if prices increase 10 percent, or if additional employees are hired. With minimal effort, the results of decisions can be determined. This allows the entrepreneur to consider many alternatives in a short period.

Exhibit   19.1   Software Packages for Various Computers

Function	Software	List Price	Vendor
Financial record keeping	BPI Accounting	$595	BPI Systems
	Peachtree Accounting	595	Peachtree
	Dynamic Accountant	100	H & E Computronics
Forecasting and financial statement analysis	Lotus 123	495	Lotus Development
	SuperCalc 3	395	Sorcim
	Multiplan	195	Microsoft
Word processing	Wordperfect	495	Satellite
	Multimate	495	Multimate
	WordStar 2000	495	Microsoft
Graphics	Microsoft Chart	250	Microsoft
	Chart-Master	395	Decisions Resources
	Story Book	250	IBM
Customer billing and mailing lists	d Base III	695	Aston Tate
	R: Base 5000	695	Microrim
	Revelation	950	Cosmos

Software Considerations

A wide variety of software packages are available for small businesses. Exhibit 19.1 lists some choices available for each of the functions just described.

If standard programs cannot be adapted to specific needs, a specially written program can be developed. The entrepreneur should not settle for a program that is not functional. A program that provides the necessary information quickly and in the proper format is far more valuable than one that is not properly designed to meet the company's needs.

Advantages of Computerization

The installation of a computer in a small business can result in many advantages for the entrepreneur and his employees. Some of these advantages follow:

Less Time Required for Monotonous Jobs

Without a computer, a substantial amount of time is often spent in monotonous, time-consuming record keeping. Recording purchases or payments on accounts receivable requires each purchase and payment on each account to

Illustration Capsule 19.1

Investment in Computer Quickly Recouped

A small retail jewelry store in St. Louis, Missouri found the computer could save thousands of dollars within the first year it was installed.

Inventory control had been a consistent problem. With almost $200,000 in inventory comprising many individual pieces of jewelry, it was difficult to maintain records of which items sold quickly, which were out of stock, and which should not be reordered owing to poor turnover. The inventory problems were solved by purchasing a computer. The computer, which is tied into the cash register, automatically records sales and deducts the items from inventory. It also provides information on the turnover of each item.

The improved inventory control resulted in tremendous savings during the first year after installation. Cost of goods sold dropped from 51 to 40 percent of sales. Because annual sales averaged nearly $500,000, the 11 percent decrease in cost of goods sold resulted in a savings of $55,000 the first year. The entire computer system cost only $17,000.

---

be added or subtracted to each customer account. Totals must then be determined and all figures must be balanced. With an accounts receivable software program, the payments or purchases can be entered and the computer handles all calculations, totals, and balancing. The time necessary to perform this task is substantially reduced.

Information Received Faster

One of the most important benefits of computerization is that information can be processed more quickly and is therefore available to the entrepreneur for decision making. If all computations are completed manually, the entrepreneur often finds that, by the time all of the information is gathered and analyzed, it has become outdated. If this occurs, the entrepreneur is forced to make decisions with an inadequate information base.

Lower Personnel Costs

Because many tasks can be completed quickly and efficiently, the entrepreneur may be able to complete the record keeping tasks with fewer employees. Thus, the computer may help to reduce labor costs.

"You've developed a memory bank that runs on peanuts?"

Source: Copyright Ford Button.

Better Cost Controls and Cash Flow

Because the information is processed quickly, the entrepreneur can identify and correct cost increases and trends before they create financial problems for the company. Better control over inventory levels often results in substantial savings for small businesses, and better control over accounts receivable results in an increased cash flow.

Improved Customer Relations

Because computerization improves the company's overall efficiency, the company can provide customers with quicker, more accurate information. In a business such as a travel agency, the computer provides immediate information on all flights, the number of seats open, price increases, and schedule changes. Customers' inquiries can be answered immediately and accurately.

Improved Management

The increased efficiency, timeliness of information, and reduction in time required for record keeping eventually result in better overall management of the company. The owner can spend more time planning and making decisions

Management Information System
An organized method of providing past, present, and projected information on internal operations and external intelligence for use in management decision making.

instead of doing routine tasks. This is possible because a computer provides much of the internal information necessary for a management information system. A **management information system** is an "organized method of providing past, present, and projected information on internal operations and external intelligence for use in management decision making."[3] If the information from all departments within a company is computerized and constantly updated, management can quickly obtain data on changes in inventory levels, outstanding loans, employee turnover, cash flow, sales by geographic areas, and so forth. This allows management to make informed, timely decisions.

Disadvantages of Computerization
. . . .

Although the introduction of microcomputers to a business can solve many problems, it can also create a whole new set of problems. The entrepreneur must be aware of the potential problems, since awareness is the first step in prevention. Some problem areas are discussed below.[4]

Concentration of Duties

Even in very small businesses, it is common for more than one person to be involved in record keeping activities. Often cross-checks are established merely by the involvement of several people in the business's operations. Once a computer is installed, if the processes are streamlined and one person is responsible for the computer input and output, this may eliminate any cross-checks. Closer supervision may be required or a new cross-checking system may need to be established.

Change of Information Not Recorded

When information is written, changes are usually apparent. However, if information is stored in the computer, information can be changed without evidence. Unless safeguards are established, anyone familiar with the computer could alter information, such as customer account balances or cash received. This can be prevented by maintaining a record of all transactions, maintaining totals of each category (accounts receivable, payable), and having someone other than the computer operator review balances.

---

[3]Louis E. Boone and David Kurtz, *Contemporary Business,* 4th ed. (Hinsdale, IL: The Dryden Press, 1985), 372.
[4]*Microcomputers,* 8.

Easy-to-Use Languages Make Misuse More Possible

When computers were first introduced to the business world, the operations and languages were so complex that few people could use them. Safeguards naturally existed merely because of the difficulty of the system.

The new microcomputers, however, often have languages and instruction booklets specifically designed for ease of use. With limited training, many people may be able to operate the system. This creates the same situation as in a retail business that allows everyone to operate the cash register. The greater the number of people involved, the more difficult it is to identify responsibility, and the more potential problems may arise.

Some experts have said that this has created a "massive new potential for embezzlements and other frauds." Soon, approximately 10 percent of the work force will directly work with a computer. With the number of installed computers increasing rapidly, computer fraud is expected to grow proportionately.[5] Controls, therefore, need to be established to prevent unauthorized access to the information.

Information on Small Diskettes May Create Problems

With microcomputers, information is stored on small diskettes. Because of their small size, the diskettes can easily be stolen or misplaced. A backup system must exist in case the information is misplaced. For example, if accounts receivable are on a diskette and include all customer accounts, purchases, payments, and current balances, it is essential that a copy of the information be made, either on a printout or on another diskette. If this is not done, loss of the diskette would be disastrous to the company. To prevent theft, control systems must exist so that the diskettes are not easily accessible. They should remain in locked cabinets unless they are being used.

More than One Employee Must Be Trained to Use the Computer

While it is impractical for everyone to have a working knowledge of the computer, it is also unwise to have only one employee who is familiar with its use. The entrepreneur should not rely on only one person for this function, or operations may be interrupted by absences, terminations, and the like.

---

[5]Hans V. Johnson and J. Scott Hill, "Detection Controls for Minicomputers in a Small Business Environment," *Journal of Small Business Management* 19, 3 (July 1981): 33–38.

Although one person may have primary responsibility, that person should have a backup.[6]

Costs May Be More than Anticipated

Because of the variety of computers on the market, there is also a wide range of costs. Many entrepreneurs are shocked to learn that the initial price of a business system is much higher than they had anticipated. Though very inexpensive computers are available, they are designed for hobbyists, not businesses. There are also several related operating costs to consider, such as clerical costs, insurance, taxes, maintenance, and paper. When considering the ''cost'' of a computer, many entrepreneurs fail to consider all costs and then become disenchanted once the computer is purchased.[7]

Improper Software May Be Costly

Small businesses often have specific procedures that employees have followed for several years. The software package should not change these procedures any more than necessary or the employees will resist computerization.

Another software mistake is often made because the entrepreneur purchases software that cannot provide necessary information. One profitable construction firm showed a $250,000 loss the year it purchased a computer because the computer could not provide necessary data from the cost-estimating system. Similarly, a manufacturing firm computerized the accounting function but later could not retrieve necessary data for government auditors. The government, therefore, delayed paying for work completed, and the company owner had to spend substantial time correcting the problem.[8]

Assumed Accuracy of Computer Output

Because many entrepreneurs are not thoroughly familiar with computers, they often assume that computer output is accurate. Often methods are not established to verify accuracy, even though a system existed to verify information when it was produced manually. For example, a company installed a computerized inventory reordering system, which included a reorder point and a maximum allowable stock level for each item. After the computerized system was in effect for a substantial time, inventory levels on many items exceeded the maximum amounts established. It was discovered that the software was confusing maximum allowable stock and reorder points, causing excess

---

[6]*Microcomputers,* 12–15.
[7]Frederick F. Newpeck and Rosalie C. Hallbauer, ''Some Advice for the Small Business Considering Computer Acquisition,'' *Journal of Small Business Management* 19, 3 (July 1981): 17–23.
[8]Newpeck and Hallbauer, ''Some Advice for the Small Business Considering Computer Acquisition,'' 21.

inventory to be purchased. Although the mistake was eventually discovered, a substantial investment in excess inventory already existed.[9]

The Decision to Computerize

The entrepreneur must determine whether or not computerizing the company is wise. If she does not thoroughly evaluate the computer purchase, the entrepreneur may find (after purchasing the computer) that computerization is not appropriate for the business. The money invested in the computer has then been wasted. The entrepreneur should therefore determine the feasibility of computerization before making a final decision.

In general, certain situations indicate that computerization may be sensible. These situations include the following:

1. A large volume of data being processed; for example, a large number of customer accounts with constant transactions on each account.

2. A repetitive nature of the processing—constant calculations repeated many times.

3. The use of a large clerical staff.

4. The need for better planning and control, and thus for better management information.[10]

If an entrepreneur is considering computerizing company data, he must determine the benefits and costs for the company and choose an appropriate system. This is often difficult to do since it is not always easy to determine costs and benefits for a small firm; many costs are hard to measure and many benefits are intangible.[11]

The computer decision should only be made after many questions have been answered and many alternatives researched. The general procedure is to answer questions in four very important areas:[12]

1. Feasibility: Would computerization be feasible in this company? In determining the feasibility of computerization, the benefits should first be analyzed. If that analysis indicates that computerization is beneficial, the analysis must then consider five other areas—technical, economic, operational, legal, and scheduling factors. When all of these factors have been considered, the information can then be used for an

---

[9]James Senn and Virginia Gibson, "Risks of Investment in Microcomputers for Small Business Management," *Journal of Small Business Management* 19, 3 (July 1981): 24–29.

[10]K. R. Beaman, *Small Business Computers for First Time Users* (Manchester, England: The National Computing Centre Limited, 1983).

[11]Leo L. Pipino and Charles R. Necco, "A Systematic Approach to the Small Organization's Computer Decision," *Journal of Small Business Management* (July 1981): 8–16.

[12]Pipino and Necco, "A Systematic Approach to the Small Organization's Computer Decision," 9.

Small Business Success   19

Scan Optics Inc., East Hartford, Connecticut

Scan Optics Inc., which manufactures computer data entry products, attributes its success to superior technology and to understanding the customer's business. The company manufactures equipment that reads printed or handwritten information and converts it to electronic data for computer processing, storage, or retrieval. Customers have included Reader's Digest, Time-Life Books, RCA Records, insurance companies, and the U.S. Postal Service. Sales in 1984 exceeded $27 million.

Source: Small Business Means Jobs (Washington, D.C.: Small Business Administration, 1984), 5.

overall cost-benefit analysis. The answers to these questions will also provide information for determining a general system design as well as the range of costs that could be incurred.

2. Alternatives: What alternatives exist with hardware and software? What alternatives exist with in-house systems and computer service firms? Once it has been determined that computerization is feasible, the various computer systems must be analyzed. This requires an analysis of available hardware and software, the costs, the benefits, and the pertinent information available with each. The entrepreneur should also consider information on computer service firms and payroll processing companies and compare this with an in-house system.

3. System choice: What specific system should be chosen? The costs and benefits of each system should be reviewed, especially the capabilities of the hardware and software. If the entrepreneur has developed a list of functions that the system must perform, then any systems that cannot meet all requirements can be eliminated. The growth and future needs of the company must also be considered to ensure that the company will not outgrow the computer in a short time.

4. Financing: How should the computer be financed? Once the specific system has been chosen, it is necessary to decide if the computer will be rented, leased, or purchased. This includes a review of the company's own financial position, whether leasing or renting arrangements

are possible, taxes and insurance considerations, and service arrangements under each alternative.

Exhibit 19.2 gives a detailed checklist of all questions to consider in each of the above areas. Although the entrepreneur may not have the time or available information to answer all questions, the checklist provides an excellent guide to follow when making a computer decision. The more of these questions that are answered, the less likely a computer mistake will be made.

Exhibit 19.2   **Computer Feasibility Checklist**

I. FEASIBILITY (Step 1)
   A. Questions of technical feasibility:
       1. Is there hardware available to accomplish my specific processing requirement(s)?
       2. Is there software available to support the applications I desire to computerize?
       3. Do I have personnel capable of operating the computer system?
       4. Do I have personnel capable of modifying the supplied software and developing additional software as required?
       5. Are there services available for contracting the EDP operations?
   B. Questions of economic feasibility:
       1. Which applications would be computerized and in what sequence?
       2. Would any cost savings be realized by performing the data processing tasks more efficiently?
       3. What is the value of improving the accuracy of reports and documents generated by the system?
       4. What is the value of improving the timeliness of reports and documents generated by the system?
       5. Would the overall operations of the organization improve as a result of specific applications being computerized?
       6. What is the value of additional information which could be provided by the system?
       7. What is the value of the intangible benefits associated with computer use such as better customer service, improved employee morale, improved worker productivity, competitive advantages, and the like?
       8. What would be the one-time and recurring hardware costs of acquiring an appropriate computer system?
       9. What would be the site preparation costs?
     10. What are the costs of existing application packages?

(continued)

Exhibit   19.2   Computer Feasibility Checklist *(Continued)*

11. What would be the costs to develop special systems for the organization?
12. What would be the costs to maintain the computer application?
13. What would be the other operating costs?
14. What would be the personnel training costs?
15. What personnel time would be required to support the implementation of computerized applications in functional areas?
16. What are the costs of performing the necessary studies to support computerization?
17. What would be the costs to maintain security and privacy for computer systems and computerized records?
18. What would be the cost to document the system?
19. What would be the cost of computerizing additional applications?
20. With respect to the current system, what are the routine data processing costs for personnel, equipment, and supplies? What are the operating expenses?
21. What are the costs to prepare special reports using the present system?
22. How can we measure the efficiency of the data processing department?
23. How can we determine how effectively personnel use computer generated reports?
24. Will our existing investment analysis procedures be appropriate?

C. Questions of organizational feasibility:
1. Would my personnel be receptive to changes to improve the data processing systems in the organization?
2. Would my personnel be capable of interacting with computerized systems?
3. Are my present procedures systematized and documented?
4. Are my present procedures efficient?
5. Do my present data processing systems produce accurate information in a timely manner?
6. Has the growth in my organization been relatively rapid?
7. Is my organization functioning in a planned and controlled manner?
8. Are my organization's objectives clear and their attainment measurable?
9. Will my managers commit the necessary time to meaningfully support the development of computerized applications?

Exhibit   19.2   Computer Feasibility Checklist *(Continued)*

10. What would be the estimated life of the applications which were computerized?
11. Is my management system formalized?
12. Can the personnel in my organization make a long-run commitment to computerized data processing?

D. Questions of schedule feasibility:
1. Would the overall time frame for changeover to computerization be reasonable for my organization?
2. Would there be any critical time constraints or time paths with respect to when applications selected for computerization must be operative?
3. How would we plan and control the development of computerized applications?

E. Questions of legal feasibility:
1. Does the organization deal with data that is subject to privacy and confidentiality statutes?
2. Does data require special security treatment?
3. As a small business in a particular environment, are there any special reports to the federal, state, and local governments that would impact computerized operations?
4. Are there any legal constraints of a specific contractual, organizational, or operational nature that would impact a computerized system?

II. ALTERNATIVES (Step 2)
A. Questions relevant to technical hardware considerations:
1. Would the use of a service bureau where all data processing is done off the premises be appropriate?
2. Will the data processing requirements be large enough to support an in-house computer system?
3. Would a time-sharing system be appropriate for the initial computer applications?
4. Would a specialized computer organization which provides application expertise in my specific industry be appropriate?
5. Is batch processing or online processing more appropriate?
6. What alternative computer configurations could provide the necessary processing requirements?

B. Questions relevant to the operation of the computer system:
1. Should existing personnel operate the equipment after appropriate training?
2. Should personnel who have prior EDP experience be hired to operate the equipment?

(continued)

Exhibit 19.2   Computer Feasibility Checklist *(Continued)*

    3.   Should a facilities management arrangement be considered whereby personnel from the facilities management firm operate the equipment?

C.   Questions relevant to the development of computer applications:

    1.   Should applications be developed by personnel in the organization?

    2.   Should applications be developed by contract programmers and systems analysts?

    3.   Should application packages be acquired?

D.   Questions relevant to the maintenance of computer applications:

    1.   Should applications be maintained by personnel in the organization?

    2.   Should applications be maintained by personnel outside the organization? What arrangements would be available?

III. VENDOR SELECTION (Step 3)

A.   Questions relevant to the processing requirements:

    1.   Can the specific volume of data be processed appropriately?

    2.   Can the required information outputs be produced in a timely manner?

    3.   Can complex and interrelated information requests be processed?

    4.   Can significant computational demands which are imposed by the use of models be supported?

B.   Questions relevant to a specific system's costs:

    1.   What specific hardware, software, and services are provided for the cost of the basic system?

    2.   Are there delivery costs associated with the equipment?

    3.   What are the costs for individual hardware components which could be acquired to upgrade the basic computer system?

    4.   What are the costs for available application packages which the vendor has developed?

    5.   What are the costs for separate maintenance contracts?

C.   Questions relevant to the business background of the vendor:

    1.   How long has the vendor been in this business?

    2.   What other organizations are using the products and/or services of the vendor?

    3.   Is the vendor's organization financially sound?

    4.   Does the vendor have working agreements with other EDP businesses?

    5.   What is the general business reputation of the vendor?

D.   Questions relevant to the vendor's line of products and services:

Exhibit 19.2   Computer Feasibility Checklist *(Continued)*

1. Does the vendor supply a broad line of compatible equipment?
2. Does the vendor maintain the hardware and software provided?
3. How well does the vendor perform maintenance?
4. Can the vendor provide technical training and support?
5. How well does the vendor meet delivery commitments?
6. Have control and security been sufficiently emphasized?
7. Does the vendor support machine independent languages?

E. Questions relevant to the specific hardware:
1. Is the system modular so that additional primary memory and peripheral equipment can be added?
2. What is the mean time to failure for individual components of the system?
3. What is the internal processing speed in relative terms?
4. What is the size of the primary memory in relative terms?
5. What are the capabilities of the input/output devices?
6. What are the characteristics of secondary storage devices?
7. What nonstandard features does the system provide?

F. Questions relevant to the specific software:
1. What are the characteristics of the operating system provided?
2. What utility programs are available?
3. What programming languages are supported?
4. What application packages are available?
5. What data management software is provided?
6. What statistical and other special purpose software packages are available?
7. Can the software be modified easily to accommodate growth and other new requirements?

IV. SYSTEM FINANCING (Step 4)
A. Questions relevant to the expected life of the computer system:
1. When will the operational demands on the computer system change significantly?
2. When will new technology likely be introduced which would make it advantageous to upgrade this computer system?
3. What are the relative costs to buy, lease, and rent this computer system over its estimated useful life?
4. Is a combination approach of buying, leasing, and renting various components of the computer system possible?

(continued)

| Exhibit   19.2 | Computer Feasibility Checklist *(Continued)* |

B. Questions relevant to the purchase of the computer system:
   1. Are the necessary funds available?
   2. If the computer system is purchased, who will maintain the computer system and what would be the costs for maintenance contracts?
   3. What will be the taxes and the insurance costs for the computer system?
   4. What will be the resale value of the computer system?
   5. Is an investment credit on income taxes available?
C. Questions relevant to the leasing of the computer system:
   1. What alternative leasing arrangements are possible?
   2. What penalties are incurred if the lease is cancelled?
   3. If the computer system is leased, can we lease with an option to purchase?
   4. Who will maintain the computer system and what would be the costs for maintenance contracts?
D. Questions relevant to the renting of the computer system:
   1. If the computer system is rented, are there additional charges if computer usage exceeds the prime shift hours?
   2. What will be the availability of a vendor's representative in the event of a system failure?
   3. In what length of time can the rental agreement be modified to add and/or replace components of the computer system?
   4. Is there an option to purchase, with a portion of the rental payments applicable to the purchase price of the computer system?

Source: From "A Systematic Approach to the Small Organization's Computer Decision," by Leo L. Pipino and Charles R. Necco, *Journal of Small Business Management* July 1981, p. 12–15. Used with permission.

Implementing the Computer

Once the entrepreneur has determined to buy a computer, he must plan its implementation. Computerization of any firm, even a small one, cannot occur overnight. Therefore, the entrepreneur must realize that several months may be needed before the system is completely functional and free of errors.

Price Waterhouse, a large accounting firm, recommends developing a "computer implementation plan."[13] The purpose is to provide an overview

---

[13]*Microcomputers*, 18.

Illustration Capsule   19.2

The Video Blues

When one company switched from a file card system to a computer, the change resulted in more problems than solutions. One employee stated, "The equipment was just thrown at us. They put one machine in the back of the office and told us to practice in our spare time. Everybody resented it . . . All we could think of was, they really don't care about us."

Many experts have begun calling this problem "the video blues." The video blues include headaches, backaches, and many other symptoms related to being under stress and unhappy. Video blues can only be avoided if (1) the work area is redesigned for computers, (2) employees are given enough breaks away from the machines, (3) workers are sufficiently trained to feel comfortable with the computers, (4) workers are given opportunities to voice concerns, and (5) employees still have a chance to work and talk together instead of spending 8 hours with a machine.

Source: Judith Newmark, *St. Louis Post Dispatch,* July 18, 1985, sec. E, 1.

of the computer activities that will be implemented over a specific period. The entrepreneur must be flexible with this plan and must realize that it may change. The implementation plan, therefore, includes the type of information to be computerized, the importance of each set of information (priority), the timing of the implementation, the impact of the computer on other business areas, the responsibility for implementing each group of information, and how personnel will be trained for computer use.

For example, the plan may begin as follows:

- Week 1. Familiarization with the computer.
- Weeks 2 and 3. Computerization of accounts receivable information.
- Weeks 4 and 5. Computerization of inventory.[14]

Only one application (for example, accounts receivable) should be computerized at a time, and the second block of information should be computerized only when the first is thoroughly implemented.

[14]*Microcomputers,* 18.

It is important to realize that all regular work continues while computerization is occurring. This often means that overtime hours are necessary to complete the implementation. Employees should be involved in the computerization decision before the implementation step, or they could present substantial resistance when asked to work overtime to accomplish a goal they do not share.[15]

Obtaining Professional Advice

To determine whether or not to computerize, to determine the proper hardware and software, to implement the system, and to prevent problems, the entrepreneur may need professional advice. Though the sales personnel in computer stores are generally very helpful and knowledgeable, they obviously feel their system is superior to the competition's. Therefore, it may not be best to rely solely on their advice, unless visits are made to many stores before a decision is made.

Professional advice may be obtained through some accounting firms, independent consultants, or universities and colleges that emphasize computer studies. The entrepreneur may also consider contacting other small businesses that have computerized systems to obtain names of qualified consultants. Although the cost for the service may seem unwarranted, it is much less costly than purchasing the wrong computer or implementing the system haphazardly.

K E Y Objectives Reviewed

1. The entrepreneur considering computerization should be familiar with the terminology to make an informed decision. Computers range in size from the large mainframes to the midsize ones known as minicomputers to the smallest, which are microcomputers.

2. Computers perform many functions that businesses often need. Even in small businesses, computers can perform the functions of financial record keeping, preparation of financial statements and ratio analysis, customer billing, word processing and mailing lists, graphics, production management, and forecasting.

---

[15]Frank Greenwood, ''The Ten Commandments of Small Business Computerization,'' *Journal of Small Business Management*, 19, 2 (April 1981): 61–67.

3. The installation of a computer can be very advantageous for a small business. If a company is computerized, the employees will spend less time on monotonous jobs, leaving more time for more productive tasks. Information is received faster, allowing management to make more informed, timely decisions.

4. Although the introduction of a computer may solve many problems, it may also create a whole new set of problems. The elimination of cross-checks, and the ability to change information without leaving evidence, can create internal control problems. Costs to computerize may be more than anticipated, often because the entrepreneur is not aware of the limited capabilities of the "hobbyist" computers.

5. When considering whether or not to computerize, the entrepreneur should complete a thorough analysis before making any decision. The analysis should center around four major topics, which include feasibility, the specific system and vendor to be chosen, and the method of financing.

6. The implementation process must be planned carefully to ensure an orderly transition from the manual to the computerized system. An implementation plan should be developed to provide an overview of computer activities established over a period. Only one computer application should be implemented at a time, ensuring that one application is thoroughly functioning before the next is implemented.

7. The entrepreneur may need professional advice when considering whether or not to computerize. Because of a lack of time and because of the complexity of a computer decision, the entrepreneur may need a consultant's services. Paying a consultant may seem unnecessary, but the money is well spent if it prevents a poor purchase decision or haphazard implementation.

Discussion Questions

1. Define the words *bit, hardware,* and *software*.

2. Identify common functions a computer could perform in a small business.

3. Identify some of the advantages and disadvantages of computerization. What steps can be taken to offset some of the common disadvantages?

4. What situations in a business may indicate that computerization is sensible?

5. The decision to computerize should be made only after an in-depth analysis of four questions. Identify these four questions.

6. When purchasing a computer system, why must the entrepreneur first analyze the software?

7. What personnel problems may arise from computerization? How can these problems be prevented or minimized?

8. What is a microcomputer implementation plan? What problems are likely to occur if no plan exists?

CHAPTER 20

Insurance

Source: Photo courtesy of Nationwide Insurance Group.

K   E   Y   Objectives

1. To identify insurance that businesses are legally required to carry as well as the types of insurance small businesses most often need.

2. To identify ways of preventing risks.

The outline for feasibility studies discussed in Chapter 10 included a section on risks—both insurable risks and uninsurable risks. That part of the feasibility study is necessary to identify risks and establish methods for minimizing those that are uninsurable. The entrepreneur, however, must then determine what insurance is necessary to minimize the effects of risks that are insurable.

Insurable risks include those related to property or company assets, those related to employees, and those related to customers. General categories of insurance include property; earnings; liability; and health, disability, and life. Certain types of insurance may overlap two areas. For example, theft of company property can occur by employees (**embezzlement),** by customers (shoplifting), or by strangers (theft, burglary, or robbery). Exhibit 20.1 provides a listing of insurance types and whether they are property, earnings, employee, or customer related.

Embezzlement
Theft of company property or money by employees.

Insuring the Risk

. . . .

Risk Management
A planned approach by company owners to avoid loss of assets or earning power.

The term *risk management* is often used in discussions of insurance. **Risk management** is a planned approach by company owners to avoid loss of assets or earning power. Risk may be "managed" in four basic ways—it can be avoided, reduced, self-insured, or shifted to someone else. Some companies avoid risk altogether by deciding not to manufacture or sell risky products. (More will be said about this later.) Risk can be reduced by establishing internal controls such as an adequate inventory control system, a cash reconciliation system, an employee safety program, and so on. Some risks are self-insured, in which case the company periodically sets aside a specified amount of money to be used only to replace assets lost to a risk. The final, and most common, method of managing risk is to shift it to someone else—an insurance company.

One of the major benefits in having adequate insurance is that the entrepreneur thereby purchases free legal help in case a lawsuit occurs. If someone sues the small business for an insured claim, and the insurance company feels the claim is not justified, the insurance company's lawyers will defend the

Exhibit 20.1   Insurance Classifications

	Property	Earnings	Employee	Customer
Unemployment			X	
Workers' Compensation			X	
Social Security			X	
Fire	X			
Business Interruption		X		
Vehicle	X			
Marine	X			X
Theft, Burglary, Robbery	X			
Fidelity Bond			X	
Product Liability			X	X
Premises and Operations				X
Completed Operations				X
Officers and Directors	X			
Health, Disability, and Life	X		X	
Bad Debt		X		

entrepreneur in court. Without insurance, the entrepreneur could incur substantial legal costs for defense.

Risk management and insurance costs are rapidly becoming a major concern for the small business owner. Insurance used to be a minor consideration; it now may represent a major expense. For many businesses classified as high risks, insurance costs may cause the business to close or prevent it from ever getting started. The insurance topics in this chapter include workers' compensation (which is legally required) as well as other types of insurance that most small businesses need. The general categories include property, earnings, liability, and health, disability, and life insurance.

Workers' Compensation

The law requires most businesses to carry three types of insurance. Two of these—unemployment and social security—were discussed in Chapter 18 because they are federally mandated taxes. The third, workers' compensation, is usually included on an income statement with other insurance costs.

Workers' Compensation
Insurance that provides an income, as well as payment for medical and rehabilitation costs, to workers who are injured on the job.

Workers' compensation is insurance that provides income, as well as payments for medical and rehabilitation costs, to workers injured on the job. As with unemployment insurance, workers' compensation is governed by state law; the laws vary among the states. Many states require workers' compensation to be carried only if a company employs a certain number of people or pays a minimum payroll each month (for example, five or more employees or

Unique Business   20.1

Gimme a V–C–R

For those trying to perfect those excitement-inducing cartwheels and splits, help has at last arrived. Jerry Colclazier of Norman, Oklahoma has developed a library of videotapes featuring top cheerleading instructors from the National Cheerleaders Association. Mr. Colclazier's primary promotion vehicle is the catalog of the NCA, *Cheerleader Supply,* which reached 400 cheerleading camps and 50,000 schools. The projected revenues for 1985 are $240,000.

Source: "Rah-Rah Tapes Sell to Camps," *Venture* (May 1985): 11.

---

a monthly payroll of $10,000). However, even if a business falls below the minimum standards and is not legally required to carry this insurance, it is advisable to carry it. When employers carry workers' compensation insurance, they accept "liability without fault," paying all injured workers' medical expenses and lost wages. In return, workers typically give up their right to sue.[1] In certain instances, though, courts have allowed employees to sue even though the company was covered by workers' compensation. Recent court rulings indicate this to be an increasing trend; thus, employers should not feel that workers' compensation will protect them from litigation.

The company's workers' compensation rates depend on the payroll amount, the job's hazards, and the company's safety record. For example, the owner of a sawmill paid a very high percentage of wages to insure the employees who worked near the large saws, but paid a much smaller percentage to insure the clerical staff. If many accidents occurred at the company, the rate would increase; if no accidents occurred, the rate would decline. As with unemployment insurance, the employer pays the full cost of the insurance; the employees are not required to contribute.

Property

Property Insurance
Insurance that protects the entrepreneur against loss of assets.

Property insurance protects the entrepreneur against the loss of assets, including buildings, equipment, vehicles, inventory, and so forth. The entrepreneur should always maintain an updated list of all assets. Insurance can be

---

[1]William Steele, "The Product Liability Trap," *Inc.,* July 1982, 93–96.

Fire Insurance
Insurance that covers losses due to fires and can be extended to include smoke damage, storms, hail, and even riots.

Vehicle Insurance
Insurance that covers damage to cars, trucks, or other vehicles due to fire, theft, and collision, and damage the vehicle causes to other property.

Comprehensive Vehicle Insurance
Provides coverage of the vehicles against fire, theft, hail, falling objects, and so forth.

Collision Vehicle Insurance
Insures a vehicle against damage caused by accidents.

Liability Vehicle Insurance
Provides coverage for property damage and bodily injury by accidents in the vehicle.

Uninsured Motorist Insurance
Provides coverage in cases where the policyholder is involved in an accident caused by a driver who does not carry liability insurance.

No-Fault Insurance Laws
Laws that require insurance companies to pay claims regardless of who caused the accident.

Ocean Marine Insurance
Covers loss of property that occurs while the property is being transported by ship.

Inland Marine Insurance
Covers damage to, or loss of, property being transported by truck, rail, or plane.

purchased that will pay the amount needed to replace items lost (current replacement value), the cost less depreciation (book value), or what the item could have been sold for (market value). Insurance costs vary with the method chosen. The most common forms of property insurance follow.

Fire.   **Fire insurance** covers losses due to fires and can be extended to include smoke damage, storms, hail, and even riots. Rates for fire insurance depend on the value of the assets covered, the location of the business, the type of structure (brick, frame, steel), and the quality of the fire protection in the area.

Vehicle.   **Vehicle insurance** covers damage to cars and trucks or other vehicles, caused by fire, theft, or collision, and it also covers damage of other property by the vehicle. All business vehicles should be insured, especially since employees as well as the company owner may be driving them. There are several types of vehicle insurance, including **comprehensive coverage, collision insurance,** and **liability insurance.** Comprehensive coverage protects against damage caused by fire, theft, hail, falling objects, and so on. Often it will also cover the contents of the car in case of theft, as long as the car was locked.

Collision insurance covers any damage caused by an accident with another vehicle or with a stationary object. It should be noted that collision insurance covers the insured person's car, not the other vehicle or object involved in the accident. Therefore, a company's collision insurance on its vans will cover the vans but not damage to other vehicles or objects. Liability insurance is necessary to cover damage done to other vehicles or objects and also covers bodily injury caused in the accident.

In most states it is legal to drive without liability insurance; thus, an entrepreneur may also want **uninsured motorist insurance,** which will provide coverage in case a business vehicle is involved in an accident with someone who does not carry liability insurance. Uninsured motorist insurance also provides coverage in case of hit-and-run accidents. Some states have enacted **no-fault insurance laws.** These vary from state to state but have a few similar provisions. These provisions require insurance companies to pay claims regardless of who caused the accident, and accident victims can only sue in certain instances (for example, if medical expenses are excessive, or in cases of death or serious injuries). States with no-fault laws require all drivers to carry liability insurance to cover medical expenses for themselves and their passengers.

Marine Insurance.   Marine insurance may be necessary if a small business transports goods, whether by land, water, or air. Insurance that covers loss of property on a ship is known as **ocean marine insurance.** Although this may be necessary for some small businesses, a more common form would be **inland marine insurance,** which covers damage to, or loss of, property while goods are being transported by truck, rail, or plane. For example, a moving and storage company would need to insure the customer's furnishings

Illustration Capsule 20.1

High-Tech Insurance

While insurance decisions and risk management on earth may seem complicated, the insurance industry has become more complex since it now provides "space insurance." Space insurance is a general term encompassing several policies available to owners of commercial satellites. Examples of such satellites include the Westar VI and the Palapa B-2 communications satellites, which were drifting in space after unsuccessful launchings. When the crew of the shuttle orbiter Discovery rescued the satellites, the insurance company (Lloyds of London) that provided the space insurance breathed a sigh of relief.

In 1984, when the Westar and Palapa satellites failed to reach their proper orbits, the insurance companies were required to pay $180 million to the satellites' owners. NASA agreed to attempt the retrieval of the satellites for $5.5 million, and the recovered satellites then became the property of the insurance companies. The insurance companies then repaired the satellites so they could be resold and the $180 million pay-out could be recouped.

Source: Les Dorr, Jr., "Satellite Insurance In the 80's" *Space World*, V-2-254 (Amherst, Wis.: Palmer Publications, February 1985), 28–30.

---

while they are in transit from one location to the next. Similarly, a tour operator would need to protect customers' luggage while being transported from hotels to buses, or buses to planes.

Theft, Burglary, and Robbery. Although most people think theft, burglary, and robbery insurance are the same, each is different and the rates vary for each.[2] **Theft insurance,** which covers all losses due to the unlawful taking of property, is the most expensive because it provides the broadest coverage. **Burglary insurance** will only reimburse the company if property loss occurs with forcible entry. **Robbery insurance** will only provide for losses due to the unlawful taking of property from another person by force or threat of force. Although theft insurance is the most expensive, it is often worth the increased rate because the small business cannot sustain a major loss without

Theft Insurance
Covers all losses due to the unlawful taking of property.

Burglary Insurance
Covers loss of property that occurs with forcible entry.

Robbery Insurance
Covers loss of property due to the unlawful taking of property from another person by force or threat of force.

[2]Louis Boone and David Kurtz, *Contemporary Business,* 4th ed. (Hinsdale, IL: The Dryden Press, 1985), 516.

severe financial effects. The financial loss is no less severe just because it did not occur with forcible entry or threat to someone's life.

Fidelity Bonds.   Anyone who has worked as a cashier in a major department store or as a sales clerk in a jewelry store has probably been bonded. **Fidelity bonds** are insurance policies that protect employers from losses due to employee theft.

Employee theft is a problem for both large and small employers; however, small businesses often do not have proper internal controls to detect employee theft. In addition, it is common for a small business to neglect to bond its employees. Without internal controls theft is likely, and without bonding a substantial financial loss may be incurred.

Consider the following examples of companies that were not bonded:

- In one small business that had gross sales of $3 million, the bookkeeper embezzled $250,000 over several years. By the time the embezzlement was discovered, the company was nearly bankrupt, and the bookkeeper had disappeared.
- During the first year of operation, the owner of a small restaurant noticed a rapid decrease in the liquor inventory, even though liquor sales were not high. Employees were caught taking liquor out the back door to their cars, but only after the company had incurred losses of several thousand dollars.
- The receptionist of a beauty salon periodically took customers' payments, without writing up receipts, for several years before being discovered. The total amount stolen was estimated to be modest but equal to approximately one week's sales.

Bonding may also be necessary to provide for any employee theft of customers' property. For example, a cleaning service in which employees enter customers' homes or offices should bond the employees to cover any theft. Similarly, home remodeling companies, appliance repair companies, and the like should bond employees since there is a possibility of theft. One cleaning service obtained a major contract with a large department store. The employees were not bonded and were not screened properly before they were hired. When one of the employees was caught "shoplifting" while cleaning, the cleaning company almost lost the contract. Bonding may have prevented the dishonest employee from being hired and would have saved the small cleaning service from an embarrassing situation.

In addition to reimbursing losses due to theft, the bonding process also serves as an excellent screening device, often eliminating a potential embezzler before the person is hired. The bonding company requires careful background checks on those employees it bonds and will prosecute any employee caught stealing. Also, the potential embezzler, who knows that the bonding company will prosecute in the case of theft, will not be able to convince the small business owner to drop the prosecution. The bonding company will also require that proper internal controls be established, forcing the entrepreneur to safeguard against theft. Thus, the bonding company serves as a watchdog to ensure that good internal controls are used.

Fidelity Bonds
Insurance policies that protect employers from any losses due to employee theft.

Illustration Capsule   20.2

Insurable Baseball Strikes

When the baseball players went on strike for 50 days in 1981, the team owners had business interruption insurance that covered strikes. The owners had paid a total of $2 million for the insurance but collected $47 million as compensation for the strike. This strike insurance placed the owners in an excellent bargaining position, since they were under much less pressure to settle.

In 1985, the owners had no strike insurance, and the threat of a strike caused them more concern. Without insurance, loss of just the playoffs' and World Series' revenues would total $80 million from television alone. The owners could not sustain a long strike, and the players were therefore in a better bargaining position. The strike was settled after 2 days.

Source: Barry Stavro, ''Strike Three?'' *Forbes*, July 1, 1985, 70.

Earnings Insurance

Business Interruption Insurance
Provides coverage for loss of income or to pay for specified expenses while a business is temporarily shut down.

Business Interruption.   Although fire insurance will replace assets lost in a fire, if a business is closed owing to a fire or storm, it may lose much more than the value of the assets. Consider a small men's apparel store destroyed by fire. Although insurance paid to remodel the building and replace all fixtures and inventory, the business was closed for 8 months before all remodeling was finished and inventory was restocked. Meanwhile, loan payments continued, the owner and employees had no income, and all of the profits that would have been made were lost. **Business interruption insurance** can be purchased to cover such losses. The kind of business interruption insurance needed depends on the type of business, its location, and its ownership structure. Insurance can be obtained that will pay monthly net profit, a specified amount for each day the business is closed, or just fixed costs, such as rent or employee wages.

Business interruption insurance can also be purchased in case the small business is closed owing to a shutdown of another business (a supplier is forced to close temporarily), a strike by employees, an interruption in utilities, or many other reasons.

Bad Debt Insurance
Provides reimbursement to the entrepreneur for any customer accounts receivable determined to be uncollectible.

Bad Debt Insurance.   **Bad debt insurance** or credit insurance provides reimbursement for customer accounts receivable that prove to be uncollectible. This insurance is usually not available to businesses that sell to the final consumer but is available to businesses that sell to other businesses. The insurance is similar to other insurance in that a ''deductible'' is established. In this case, the deductible is the annual maximum amount of bad debts the business is willing to incur. The insurance company will reimburse any bad debts in excess of that amount. The higher the deductible, the lower the cost of the policy.

Liability

A major concern for many small businesses is liability insurance. Liability insurance protects businesses from lawsuits resulting from injuries to others or to others' property. The following types are those most often needed by small businesses.

Premises and Operations Insurance
Covers injuries done to others while they are visiting the company location.

Premises and Operations.   **Premises and operations insurance** will cover injuries others suffer while they are visiting the company location. Suppose that while a customer is shopping at a grocery store, a display falls on the person, causing injury. Premises and operations insurance will cover injuries up to a stated amount.

Completed Operations Insurance
Covers damage done to others' property while the entrepreneur is performing a service.

Completed Operations.   **Completed operations insurance** is often needed by companies that provide a service instead of selling a product. Completed operations insurance will cover damage done to others' property while the company performs the service. For example, while a contracting company was building a new restaurant, a fire erupted and destroyed the entire facility. Preliminary evidence indicated that the fire may have been caused by a welding torch left on by a construction firm employee. Since this was eventually proven to be the cause, the construction firm was held liable for the damage.

Surety Bonds
Protect against losses that occur if a contract is not satisfactorily completed.

Service firms often purchase **surety bonds** to protect against losses that occur if a contract is not satisfactorily completed. For example, if a general construction contractor subcontracts with a plumber, the general contractor often requires the plumber to obtain a surety bond. Then, in case the plumber does not complete the job for any reason, the general contractor will not lose money when a new plumber is hired.

Officers and Directors Insurance
Protects officers and directors of incorporated businesses from loss of personal assets.

Officers and Directors.   Even though a small company incorporates, this does not completely protect the corporation owners and officers from liability. Many entrepreneurs are surprised to find that corporation officers and directors may be sued if their decisions are not within the law or if it can be proven that they neglectfully erred in judgment. Therefore, **officers and directors insurance** is available for owners of small corporations to protect personal assets in case of a lawsuit. Officers and directors of corporations should obtain this insurance even if they do not own the company.

Product Liability Insurance
Protects businesses against claims for damages resulting from the use of company products.

Product.   **Product liability insurance** protects businesses against claims for damages resulting from the use of company products.[3] Product liability

---

[3]Boone and Kurtz, *Contemporary Business*, 518.

Illustration Capsule   20.3

Officers and Directors Risk Personal Liability

Lawsuits against the directors of corporations increased approximately 20 percent between 1982 and 1985. Because of the increase in lawsuits and large amounts awarded, costs for officers and directors insurance have also skyrocketed. Even with the increase in premiums, some insurance companies have completely stopped providing this type of insurance. One insurance expert stated that even if prices increased by 300 to 400 percent, this would just result in an "adequate" price in the eyes of the insurance company.

Source: "Protecting Directors Suddenly Gets Costly," *Fortune,* March 18, 1985, 61.

has become a major concern for both large and small businesses owing to the rapid increase in insurance premiums for liability protection. For many businesses, large and small, the cost of premiums has resulted in the company withdrawing a product from the market or closing completely. Premiums have continued to increase because courts continue to broaden the liability burden of businesses. In some cases, companies have been completely unable to purchase insurance at any cost. The following examples illustrate the liability burden, the rapid increase in costs, and the resulting effect.

> *One manufacturer has been held liable for defects in a 50-year-old machine. Another was held liable for injuries because warnings were not duplicated in Spanish.*
>
> *One manufacturer was found liable when an adhesive exploded in a poorly ventilated, windowless room, even though instructions warned that the product was flammable and windows should be open. The court held the manufacturer liable because the instructions did not state what should be done if the container was opened in a room with no windows.*
>
> *In 1970, the average liability premium in the metal cutting industry was $1,900. In 1978, it was $139,000, an increase of over 7,000%.*
>
> *A National Machine Tool Builders Association survey in the late 1970s found that about 20 percent of its members could not afford liability insurance, or could not obtain it at any price. Most of those companies (70 percent) were small businesses.*
>
> *A small instrument manufacturer had developed a small black box that attached to construction cranes to warn the operator of unsafe conditions. The president of the company discovered that if the crane malfunc-*

> *tioned for any reason and injury occurred, his company would be included in the lawsuit. He therefore took the product off the market.*[4]
>
> *A number of small manufacturing firms were forced to liquidate because they could not obtain product liability insurance.*[5]

Liability insurance is needed not only by manufacturers but also by wholesalers, retailers, and service firms. Normal consumer products often cause injury, and the firms selling or distributing them may be held liable. A study completed by the National Commission on Product Safety found that each year 30,000 Americans were killed, 110,000 were permanently disabled, and more than 20 million were injured in connection with using consumer products. The consumer products most often involved included color television sets, hot water vaporizers, infant furniture, and toys. Service firms, such as pest control firms, construction firms, restaurants, and travel agencies, also risk liability suits for a variety of reasons.[6] Many such firms have experienced dramatic increases in insurance premiums, mostly hazardous wastes handlers, architects and contractors, doctors, truck and bus companies, restaurants, hotels, and anyone else who deals with the public or has a high probability of being involved in a liability suit.

One asbestos-removal contractor in Belleville, Illinois saw liability insurance increase from $10,000 to $153,000 in one year. If business increases more than expected, he will have to pay an additional $100,000 before the year's end. Unfortunately, the contractor's problems do not end there. Because the new insurance policy provides less coverage than the previous ones, several customers have cancelled jobs, forcing the contractor to lay off seven employees.

Similarly, a trucking company's liability rates rose from $6,000 to $27,000 in one year, and a bus company's rates increased $1,400 for each bus operated. A small tourist attraction that includes rides on a ski lift was forced to close temporarily because the company was unable to find an insurance company willing to write a liability policy.[7]

Although some companies attempt to limit their liability by posting disclaimers (such as a motorbike rental firm posting "ride at your own risk"), there is no way to guarantee that the disclaimer will be of any use in court. One disclaimer has been upheld by courts in one state and thrown out in another. However, warning signs should certainly be used. Experts suggest that all warning signs and instructions should first be reviewed by a lawyer. Entrepreneurs should make sure that the company lawyer is completely familiar with product liability law or retain a specialist. Product liability is a very specialized field and requires an expert to provide adequate counsel.[8]

---

[4]Steele, "The Product Liability Trap," 93–95.
[5]William Trombetta, "Products Liability from the Small Manufacturer Industrial Distributor's Perspective," *Journal of Small Business Management* 15, 4 (October 1977), 31–36.
[6]Lonnie Ostron and John Schlacter, "Product Liability: An Awakening Giant," *Journal of Small Business Management* 13, 2 (April 1975): 10.
[7]Bill Smith, "Firms Crying Over Insurance," *St. Louis Post Dispatch,* October 30, 1985, 1.
[8]Steele, "The Product Liability Trap," 99.

Professional Liability Insurance
Provides coverage for professionals against claims of malpractice.

Professional (Malpractice).   Liability insurance is necessary not only for those selling a product but also for those selling a service or giving advice. For example, business consultants, psychologists, and even ministers carry **professional liability insurance** to protect themselves from lawsuits claiming malpractice.

Professional liability insurance for the medical profession has skyrocketed in recent years owing to the increasing number of lawsuits and the large monetary awards. For example, in 1985, New York State approved a 52 percent increase in medical malpractice insurance rates. For a neurosurgeon on Long Island, annual premiums for malpractice insurance increased from $66,000 to $101,000. Nationally, rates increased by 15 to 20 percent per year from 1980 to 1984, and in 1985 rates increased an average of 25 to 30 percent. These rate increases are eventually passed on to patients, forcing medical costs up rapidly.[9]

The problems with liability insurance have not only created problems for existing businesses, but the high costs or inability to obtain insurance have also affected some possible business starts. Reports from Silicon Valley in California have indicated that many possible start-ups did not materialize because of insurance problems.[10]

Health, Disability, Life Insurance

Health and disability insurance is a concern for both the owner of a small business and the employees. In many small businesses, the owner is the driving force; if she is hospitalized or disabled, there may be a severe effect on the company's financial condition. It is therefore essential to obtain adequate **health insurance** to cover expenses due to sickness or accidents and **disability insurance** to cover loss of income due to sickness or disability.

Health Insurance
Covers expenses due to sickness or accidents.

Disability Insurance
Covers loss of income due to sickness or disability.

Providing health insurance for the small firm's owner and employees can be a substantial expense, so employees are often asked to pay part or all of the cost. However, to attract good employees, the employer often must provide or at least subsidize the benefits.

Life insurance for the company owner or for key employees is recommended to reimburse the company for the loss of services and to help the company until a replacement is found. This type of insurance, called **key executive insurance,** may keep a small business from closing when the owner, a partner, or a key employee dies. Key executive insurance is essential if a business has substantial debt. The surviving spouse of an entrepreneur should not have to worry about meeting large financial obligations soon after the spouse's death. Consider a gift shop in which the proprietor had borrowed $200,000. The company was very successful until the owner passed away,

Key Executive Insurance
Covers loss of income or services due to the death of the company owner or significant employee.

---

[9]"Malpractice Malaise," *Fortune* 111, no. 4 (February 18, 1985): 9–10.
[10]Eric Gelman, Ann Hughes, Mark Miller, Peter McAlevey, Elisa Williams, Nadine Joseph, "Insurance: Now It's a Risky Business." *Newsweek,* November 4, 1985, 49.

leaving the company to the spouse, who was not skilled in business management. The business soon began to lose money, and the $200,000 debt created a great financial strain. The company was forced into a bankruptcy, which probably could have been prevented if life insurance had been purchased to pay off the loan in the event of the owner's death.

The Insurance Purchase

The proper insurance coverage should be obtained using a systematic method as carefully planned as all other business decisions. The following suggestions are provided as a guide in choosing the proper coverage.

1. Write a statement of the company's insurance philosophy. While this may seem unnecessary, it provides direction for the insurance purchase and helps the insurance agent to serve the company's needs better. It will also prevent haphazard insurance purchases. For example, if a company is established to provide day care for children, the insurance philosophy must address whether the insurance purchase is only a business decision, or whether the company owners feel morally obligated to insure risks to a greater extent than that justified from a purely business viewpoint. That is, are the owners willing to pay more for insurance (thereby reducing profits) to carry extra insurance? What risks, if any, does the entrepreneur wish to insure at any cost?

2. It is essential for the entrepreneur to choose an insurance agent who can provide advice as well as sell the insurance. All too often, an entrepreneur does not plan his approach to insurance coverage but instead purchases insurance for specific items (for example, company trucks). This often results in the entrepreneur having insurance to cover some possible losses but leaving other risks completely uninsured. A knowledgeable agent will help the entrepreneur identify all possible insurable risks and will provide advice as well as the insurance coverage.

3. There are two basic types of firms, mutual companies and stock companies. Mutual companies are nonprofit and are owned by the policyholders. Stock companies are for-profit and the stockholders are not necessarily policyholders. Both have advantages and disadvantages, and the entrepreneur must determine which company can provide the best insurance package. However, one firm should provide the entire package, since a piecemeal approach may leave many risks uninsured.

4. Develop an insurance budget to ensure that insurance costs do not become unrealistic. The insurance budget must be realistic and must provide enough funds to purchase adequate coverage. Insurance purchases without a budget may result in unnecessarily high costs.

5. Purchase insurance for the greatest risks first, then use remaining dollars in the insurance budget to cover less-catastrophic events. Deter-

"First, the good news—our sales were up 22% in the past fiscal year.
The bad news is our treasurer is somewhere in South America."

Source: Copyright Ford Button.

mine how much the company can afford to pay for insurance and allocate that budgeted amount over the various insurance needs. Insurance costs should be decreased by using deductibles whenever possible.

Preventing the Risk

While insurance purchases will help protect the owner from major losses, no risk management program is complete without appropriate prevention measures. As stated before, a bonding company will require that a good internal control system be established. Similarly, insurance companies will require certain preventive measures before providing any fire, workers' compensation, or product liability insurance.

On the following pages we provide some brief guidelines for risk prevention. The lists are not meant to be comprehensive but instead provide a guide for action and further thought by the entrepreneur. Additional checklists in each area can be obtained from insurance companies, fire departments, the Department of Labor, and other sources. The entrepreneur should obtain these lists because it is difficult to think of all necessary preventive measures without guidelines.

Preventing Embezzlement of Cash

1. Set a good example. If the entrepreneur "borrows" from the petty cash fund or cash register, exaggerates expense accounts, or uses company funds for personal items, employees may feel free to do the same.

2. Hold employees accountable for their actions and mistakes. Do not appear indifferent concerning financial matters.

3. Develop an adequate accounting system with appropriate internal control measures. Obtain monthly statements; look for variations and unexplainable figures.

4. Maintain a separation of duties. For example, the person receiving checks should not be responsible for entries in the accounts receivable ledger. Similarly, one person should prepare the payroll and another should give the employees their checks.

5. Check the backgrounds of prospective employees.

6. Carefully monitor daily bank deposits and compare them with what the amounts should be. Determine reasons for any discrepancies. Examine all cancelled checks to look for anything unusual.

7. Do not sign blank checks.

8. Always watch for clues, which include
   A. unusual increases in sales returns (often used to hide payments on accounts receivable);
   B. unusual bad debt write-offs;
   C. any decrease or minimal increase in sales (often because sales are not being recorded);
   D. inventory shortages (caused by fictitious purchases, unrecorded sales, or employee pilferage);
   E. profit declines or increasing expenses (caused by theft of cash);
   F. increases in collection times of accounts receivable (often caused by methods to hide embezzlement).[11]

Preventing Theft and Burglary of Assets

1. Always price items by machine or rubber stamp — never by handwriting.

2. Permit only authorized employees to set prices and mark merchandise.

---

[11]Christopher Moran, *Preventing Embezzlement* (Washington, D.C.: Small Business Administration, 1975), 5.

3. Watch for over-rings on the cash register to ensure that they are not covering up shortages due to theft.

4. Have a secondary check by a worker or salesperson on all incoming shipments.

5. Prohibit employees from parking near receiving doors or the dock.

6. Keep the receiving door locked when not in use.

7. Distribute door keys carefully and keep a record of them. Change locks whenever an employee leaves without returning a key.

8. Install and maintain excellent burglar alarms and locks.

9. Keep only a minimal amount of cash on hand at any time. Do not leave money in the business overnight unless absolutely necessary. Purchase an adequate safe if all money is not deposited daily.

10. Maintain adequate lighting inside and outside.[12]

Protecting Against Shoplifters

1. Post antishoplifting signs warning of prosecution.

2. Install convex mirrors that allow company personnel to see around corners or one-way mirrors for monitoring daily operations.

3. If very expensive items are sold, consider using electronic devices that signal when a shoplifter tries to leave the store with the merchandise.

4. Small, easily stolen items should be placed near the cash register or in cases.

5. For soft goods such as clothing, use hard-to-break plastic strings.

6. Maintain enough personnel so that floor space is adequately covered.

7. Prosecute all shoplifters, even first offenders. Failure to do so encourages the shoplifter to try again.[13]

Preventing Injuries to Workers

1. Allow only trained personnel to operate hazardous machinery or heavy equipment.

2. Use approved containers for any flammable liquids, toxic materials, and so forth.

3. Ensure that exits are not blocked.

---

[12]Saul Astor, *Preventing Retail Theft* (Washington, D.C.: Small Business Administration, 1975), 5–6.
[13]Addison H. Verrill, *Reducing Shoplifting Losses* (Washington, D.C.: Small Business Administration, 1975), 5.

Small Business Success   20

Optikem International/Optacryl Inc., Denver, Colorado

Optikem International/Optacryl Inc. produced its first product, a cleaner for hard contact lenses, in a garage in 1977. Barbara Johnson, one of the original company founders, diligently contacted doctors to market the product. She was so successful that she soon needed help filling incoming orders. Then, in 1981, the company introduced the first hand soap for contact lens wearers, a soap that leaves no film on the hands. This product has developed a secondary market with photographers, allergists, and veterinarians. Sales grew from $5,608 in 1977 to $2 million in 1983. The rapid growth is attributed to an expanded product line, product innovations, and a sales force hired to sell nationwide.

Source: Small Business Means Jobs (Washington, D.C.: Small Business Administration, 1984), 5.

---

4. Keep the work place clean at all times.

5. Check for proper ventilation.

6. Establish a maintenance program for all machinery, vehicles, hand tools, and power tools.

7. Provide protective goggles or other protective equipment when needed.

8. Keep first aid supplies on hand at all times.

9. Post emergency telephone numbers and instruct all employees on procedures to be followed in case of emergency.[14]

Preventing Losses Due to Fire

1. Purchase and maintain an adequate number of portable fire extinguishers.

2. Install a fire alarm system or individual fire alarms throughout the building.

---

[14]*OSHA Handbook for Small Businesses* (Washington, D.C.: U.S. Department of Labor, 1977), 19–25.

3. Instruct all employees in the proper use of fire extinguishers.

4. Post "no smoking" signs in areas that are unsafe.

5. Routinely check all electrical outlets, wires, plugs, and the like.

Preventing Product Liability Claims

1. Develop a quality control program to prevent defective merchandise from being sold.

2. Provide adequate instructions for using all products.

3. Post disclaimers or have customers sign disclaimers when appropriate.

4. Post any necessary warnings.

5. Consult with an attorney to determine the extent of the company's liability and ways to reduce it.

K   E   Y   Objectives Reviewed

1. Businesses are often legally required by state law to carry workers' compensation. In addition, businesses may choose to carry other insurance such as property; earnings; liability; and health, disability, life insurance.

2. Proper risk management includes more than simply purchasing insurance. It extends to establishing procedures to prevent risks. Specific steps can be taken to prevent embezzlement, theft, or burglary of assets, shoplifting, worker injuries, losses due to fire, and product liability claims.

Discussion Questions

1. One of the major benefits of purchasing proper insurance is that the entrepreneur may then be entitled to free legal help in certain situations. Explain.

2. What is the difference between embezzlement and burglary or robbery?

3. What factors affect the rate of workers' compensation a company pays?

4. Explain the difference between theft, burglary, and robbery insurance.

5. A small, very profitable gift store, located in a shopping mall, was forced to close for 13 months owing to major mall renovation and

expansion. What type of insurance might cover loss of income during those 13 months?

6. If a company incorporates, the owners are said to have limited liability. Why, then, is officers and directors insurance needed?

7. Manufacturers often argue that the increase in successful product liability lawsuits has reduced research and development efforts and will limit new product introduction. Why? Do you agree? Why or why not?

8. Why is key executive insurance important to a small firm with a large debt?

9. Why should an entrepreneur develop a written insurance philosophy?

CHAPTER 21

Small Businesses:
Successes and Failures

K E Y   Objectives

1. To identify and examine the myths concerning the successes and failures of small businesses.

2. To describe symptoms of failure.

3. To identify legal options available for financially troubled firms.

4. To identify the costs of failing.

5. To recognize the persistence of entrepreneurs and the desire to begin again after a failure.

Those considering entrepreneurship as a career must consider the possibility of failure. It is unwise to be overly optimistic, to assume failure cannot happen, or to be unaware of options in the event of failure. It is common for the entrepreneur's first business to be a learning experience, a training period for future businesses that will be more successful. The entrepreneur should, therefore, have a realistic view of the possibilities of failure, a knowledge of options in case failure occurs, and a determination to try again until success is realized.

The Extent of the Problem

Several myths concerning small business failures distort the true picture of the small business environment. If the potential entrepreneur believes these myths, the chance of success appears unrealistically remote. Following are several of the most common myths of small business failure.

Myth 1: Most Small Businesses Fail

Whenever the phrase "small business failure" appears, it is almost always followed by statistics of doom. One source states that "35% of all businesses fail within three years, 55% within five years and 80% within ten years. In any given year, the failure rate actually runs about 90% in that for every ten new firms started, nine existing ones fail."[1] Another source continues the

---

[1] Norman Land, "Too Much Emphasis on Management Assistance," *Journal of Small Business Management* 13, 3 (July 1975): 1.

Illustration Capsule   21.1

Business Closure — Not Business Failure

Mollie Parnis opened her dress business in 1933. After 50 years of operation, she closed the $9 million business. Why close such a successful business? "It was a sudden decision," she said. "My lease was up. The whole fashion business has changed. It's not the business I knew. I don't like talking to a computer. Now it's a whole new world, and that's as it should be. But I was bored. I decided I should be doing something else."

She started the company, called Parnis-Livingston, with her husband, Leon Livingston, who ran the business while she did the designing. "We had very little money," she said, "but were fortunate. We walked in where angels feared to tread and made money from the beginning."

Miss Parnis, who appears to be in her mid-sixties, is said to be around 80 years of age. Closing the business was a "traumatic" experience, but Miss Parnis did not retire. Instead, she became a consultant for Christian Dior Lingerie.

Source: St. Louis Post Dispatch, October 28, 1984, 1J.

---

tales of doom: "Everyone in the public sector is concerned about the small business . . . the reason behind this concern is that 1,000 businesses quit every day. They simply close their doors, swallow their losses, pocket their pride and give up."[2] Statistics about bankruptcies are then cited, leading one to believe that if a small business is started, the chances of great financial loss are very high. A closer examination of statistics proves this to be quite misleading.

Many sources use the terms "business failures" and "business discontinuances" synonymously, which leads one to believe that all businesses that are discontinued are financial failures. However, businesses that are discontinued were often financial successes. In fact, 90 percent of the approximately 400,000 businesses that dissolve each year do so for voluntary reasons, such as the owner retiring or desiring to enter a more profitable field.[3]

[2]Joseph Schabacker, *Strengthening Small Business Management: Selections from Papers of L. T. White* (Washington, D.C.: Small Business Administration, 1971), 36.
[3]*State of Small Business: Report of the President* (Washington, D.C.: U.S. Government Printing Office, 1984), 36.

While it may seem unwise to close a profitable company, it may be terminated for many reasons, including the following:

1.   Small business ownership (especially of a new business) often requires long work hours, leaving little time for family. Consequently, an entrepreneur often decides that the family requires more attention and closes or sells the business.

2.   Many entrepreneurs start a business or purchase an existing business with the intention of selling it within a few years, often realizing substantial profits. However, if the business was a proprietorship or partnership, the change of ownership would be counted as a business discontinuance and a new start-up. Consider, for example, one entrepreneur who invested only $2,000 of his own money to start a business, operated it for 3 years, and sold it at a $30,000 profit. The business had provided a salary for 3 years and generated a substantial return on the original investment. While this was a business closure, it was by no means a business failure.

3.   Profitable businesses often close because no successor is available. As with the business described above, though, the business may have been very successful. The National Federation of Independent Business estimated in 1981 that 50 percent of all small businesses had no employees.[4] Thus, while the business provides income to the entrepreneur, it may simply end when the entrepreneur retires.

The following facts should also be noted:

1.   The number of businesses that fail with substantial financial loss is actually very minimal. Dun & Bradstreet consistently monitors a sample of approximately three million businesses (approximately 20 percent of the 14 million businesses in existence). Of the sample monitored, the number of financial failures per year usually ranges from 8,000 to 10,000. From 1946 to 1981, financial failures for the Dun & Bradstreet sample never exceeded 61 per 10,000 businesses in existence.[5] *This is approximately one-half of 1 percent.* Unless the 20 percent monitored by Dun & Bradstreet is a misrepresentation of the business population, substantial financial losses are not common.

2.   The number of bankruptcies is minimal compared with the number of businesses in existence. From 1972 to 1981, business bankruptcies filed in court ranged from 18,000 to 66,000 per year for the entire nation.[6] This level of failure must be compared with the base of 14

[4]*Small Business in America* (San Mateo, Calif.: National Federation of Independent Business Research and Education Foundation, 1981).
[5]*Statistical Abstract of the United States* (Washington, D.C.: U.S. Department of Commerce, Bureau of the Census), 532.
[6]*Statistical Abstract of the United States,* 533.

Unique Business   21.1

Test Kits Tap the Hypochondria Market

Worried about that sore throat being a case of strep? A kit developed by Personal Diagnostics of Whippany, N.J. will provide the diagnosis without a trip to the doctor. The kit, which costs $10, requires that you mix a sample from your throat with some chemicals in a small container. In a few hours you'll know. Some of the company's other products are kits that aid in conception, a test for urinary-tract infections, and a kit to diagnose diabetic blood glucose imbalance.

Source: Virginia Inman, "Test Kits Tap the Hypochondria Market," *Inc.*, November 1984, 44.

million existing businesses, giving a bankruptcy rate of less than one-half of 1 percent.

3. The statement that most businesses close within 3 to 5 years of opening is also misleading. The Dun & Bradstreet statistics show that, *"Of the businesses which fail,* most have been in business less than five years." This is substantially different than saying "most businesses fail within 3 to 5 years." Suppose, for example, a class of 100 students (50 men, 50 women) takes a test. Suppose also that six people fail, three men and three women. A true statement would be, "Fifty percent of those who failed were men." Clearly it cannot be said that 50 percent of the men failed the test, yet a distortion of this type often creates confusion over the topic of small business failures.

4. Entrepreneurs often start and operate several businesses throughout their lifetimes, just as most people change jobs several times throughout their careers. When someone changes jobs, it is not automatically assumed that they were a failure in the first job. However, when someone "changes businesses," the earlier one is often supposed a failure.

Myth 2: Business Failures Are High during Recessions and Low during Good Economic Times

When the country's economy is in a recessionary period, constant reference is made to the poor economy and the number of business failures. The impression is that poor economies cause large numbers of failures whereas

"*Obviously, some people here do not appreciate the gravity of our situation.*"

Source: Drawing by Modell; © 1985 The New Yorker Magazine, Inc.

rapidly expanding economies produce few failures. Again, however, a review of the statistics indicates this to be misleading.

In 1961, the economy was beginning a period of sustained growth. That year is considered to be the "springboard year of the boom," yet 17,075 business failures were recorded. In 1981, though, when the economy was very poor, only 16,794 business failures were recorded. Similarly, in 1922, the economy was expanding at an incredible rate of 16 percent, and business failures totalled 23,676. In 1924, the economy slowed slightly, but business failures declined to 20,615.[7] Thus, although recessionary times may be bad for business, it cannot be assumed that boom periods are necessarily prosperous.

If recessions and business failures are compared, one finds that failures often rise 1 to 2 years after the recession is over. One reason this occurs is that business owners are often walking financial tightropes during recessions. They deplete cash reserves below the proper level and find themselves deep in debt. Then, when the recession is over, the economy expands rapidly, demand for the product jumps dramatically, and the company does not have, and cannot borrow, sufficient working capital to meet demand. Competitors in a better cash position, therefore, can take customers away from the ailing

[7]"A History of Failure," *Time*, October 26, 1981, 61.

firm. Loss of customers compounded by cash shortages eventually causes failure.

Businesses also fail during boom periods because the prices they must pay for goods and services rise faster than what they can pass on to their customers.[8] Thus, although demand for the product increases, the profit per sale is less, and again the result is a severe strain on cash that can result in the business failing. As one associate research director stated during the recession in the early 1980s, "You will have corporations coming out of this recession staggering like a boxer after the 15th round. . . . They could easily fall flat on their faces after the fight is officially over."[9]

Figure 21.1 illustrates the trends of financial failures from 1965 through 1985. During this 20-year period, there were two major recessions, one during 1973 to 1974 and another in 1981 and 1982. Notice that business failures peaked in 1975 and in 1983 even though the recessions had ended. The extremely high failure rate in 1983 was due to the length and severity of the recession in the early 1980s. Although the rate began to decline by 1984 and 1985, only a sustained period of economic growth and low interest rates will allow rates to fall back to previous levels.

Myth 3: Small Business Failures Are Caused by Factors Beyond the Entrepreneur's Control

The majority of small business failures are not caused by the economy, a bad product, high interest rates, and so forth. Most small business failures are caused by the owner's incompetence or lack of experience in specific areas. Entrepreneurs who fail often have an excellent technical background but no business skills or knowledge. For example, an auto mechanic may have excellent skills for repairing vehicles but know little about financing, motivating employees, or keeping records. A dentist may have excellent dental skills but no knowledge of marketing strategies to obtain new patients. Thus, although highly qualified in technical knowledge, the entrepreneur's lack of business skills causes the business to fail. The successful entrepreneur must wear a "variety of hats." Unless the entrepreneur has a general knowledge of many business skills, managing the business may overwhelm him.

Peter Principle Syndrome
A failure because the business grows beyond the skills and expertise of the owner.

Another test of business skills often occurs after the business is several years old. In many cases, the entrepreneur is capable of operating the business when it is first started, but the business continues to grow and eventually expands beyond the owner's skills and expertise. Two business consultants, Goldstick and Schreiber, refer to this as the **Peter Principle syndrome**[10] (a reference to the original Peter Principle, which states that people are promoted

[8]"A History of Failure," 61.
[9]Ipson Pauly, "The Bankruptcy Syndromes," *Newsweek,* April 26, 1982, 68.
[10]John Banazewski, "Thirteen Ways To Get a Company in Trouble," *Inc.,* September 1981, 98.

Figure   21.1   Trends of Financial Business Failures

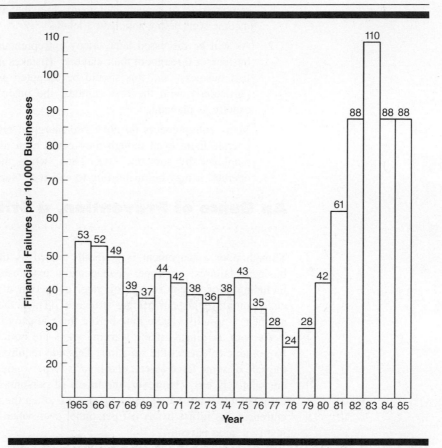

Source   U.S. Department of Commerce, *Statistical Abstract of the United States* (Washington, D.C.: Government Printing Office, December 1984), 519.
Note: The 1984 and 1985 figures are authors' estimates based on preliminary available information.

to their level of incompetence). Though the owner could profitably operate the business at one level, if she does not restrict the business to a manageable size, the growth actually causes failure. Goldstick and Schreiber see this problem recurring in many troubled businesses.

Maintaining a Realistic Perspective

We hope that the information presented above provides a more optimistic picture of small business. However, it would be a disservice to imply that success is nearly automatic if one opens a small business. Therefore, the following facts should also be noted:

1. Many entrepreneurs start a business assuming they will make a substantial sum of money, but many find that the business provides an
   income well below anticipated levels.

2. As will be discussed later, many entrepreneurs start (or own) several
   businesses throughout their careers. Mistakes are always made with the
   first business, and this should be accepted as a learning experience.
   Particularly with the first venture, the business may not materialize
   exactly as planned.

3. Many entrepreneurs do not close marginal businesses but continue to
   operate them even though they could earn more money if they were
   employed by someone else. Thus, while the business continues to
   operate, it may be misleading to call it a "success."

An Ounce of Prevention, a Stitch in Time

Though poor management is generally stated as the major cause of small
business failures, improper management manifests itself in many ways,
including poor inventory control, poor collection of receivables, poor financial planning, and poor pricing structures. Thus, the evidence of poor management is usually visible long before the company is in financial trouble.

As with an illness, if the warning signs are noticed early enough, it may
be possible to correct the situation. This can require drastic cuts in expenses,
the sale of some fixed assets, and layoffs in personnel. Cuts in some expenses
are relatively easy. However, the layoff of personnel is often the step that is
essential to the business's survival, yet it is often the step most resisted. Many
entrepreneurs refuse to lay off personnel even when the sales volume cannot
justify a large payroll.

It is essential for a financially ailing company to receive expert advice to
save the company. Often entrepreneurs use available cash unwisely, paying
bills that could have been paid later while ignoring payments to essential
suppliers or banks. In addition to giving advice on proper cash management,
outside consultants can help identify methods of streamlining operations, cutting costs, and reducing overhead.

If the entrepreneur heeds this advice, the company may survive and prosper. If, however, the entrepreneur waits too long before seeking help and
taking action, danger signals will begin to appear.

Symptoms of Failure

Failure usually is not an overnight occurrence but a very slow, agonizing
process for the entrepreneur. Typical symptoms of a business in trouble are
given below.

Declining Inventory Level.   For any business that carries inventory, a
declining inventory balance is often one of the first warning signals. Since

working capital problems occur early in the failure process, inventories cannot be replaced as needed. This decline is not always noticeable but instead may happen gradually over several years. If the dollar figures are not closely watched, and the losses incurred are not huge, the decline may not be obvious to the casual observer for quite some time. Only accurate inventory records will reveal the problem. While inventory levels will constantly fluctuate in an ongoing business, a consistent decline is cause for alarm.

Declining Accounts Receivable Balance.   As with the inventory balance, accounts receivable balances also decline if a business is in trouble. Because of the cash shortages, most of the payments received on accounts are used to pay bills and are not reinvested into assets to generate additional sales. For example, when money is received, most of the funds are used to pay utilities, loans, and rent and very little or none may be used to purchase more inventory. The amount of money owed to the failing firm slowly decreases. As the accounts receivable decline, the cash inflow into the business declines, further aggravating the worsening condition.

Increasing Accounts Payable Balance.   Because of the cash shortage, the company cannot pay its bills on time, and the accounts payable begin to accumulate. In the early stages of failure, the company's suppliers continue to extend credit; however, credit is eventually discontinued. At this point, the company is often forced to pay cash when goods are delivered. This puts a further strain on cash and increases the decline in inventory levels.

Delinquencies on Taxes and Loan Payments.   Just as with late payments on accounts payable, the cash shortage also results in delinquent payments on taxes or loans. When companies begin to run short of cash, money that should be set aside for sales tax and payroll tax is often used for operating capital. Then when the payment for the sales or payroll tax is due, the company has no funds to make the payment. In the beginning of the failure this results in substantial penalties and interest charges. If adequate payment is not made, the state's department of revenue has the authority to close the business for failure to pay sales tax. Similarly, the Internal Revenue Service has the authority to close the business if payroll taxes are not paid. As the situation worsens, the entrepreneur is at odds not only with suppliers but also with government agencies.

Simultaneously, the company is usually delinquent in loan payments to the bank. As do other creditors, the bank often tries to negotiate with the company, allowing payments of interest without principle. If the company cannot meet the interest payments or if the situation continues to worsen, the bank threatens to seize assets that were pledged as collateral. Often this includes the entrepreneur's home, creating a tremendous psychological strain.

Borrowing to Solve Money Problems.   At this point in the failure process, it is very common for the entrepreneur to attempt to borrow money. This is commonly referred to as an attempt to ''borrow one's way out of debt.'' In other words, there is a mistaken belief that borrowing money will solve the problems. Obviously, this is not the solution. Unless changes are made to ensure that the company operates at a profit, more debt would only postpone the inevitable. Eventually, the borrowed funds would be exhausted and the same cycle would be repeated.

The entrepreneur must be aware of the danger signals to catch problems early, when corrective action can be taken. Ignoring the symptoms of trouble only makes a solution less likely. The warning signals are simple enough for all entrepreneurs to understand. It is not necessary to completely understand finance or accounting but merely to observe the business's basic accounts.

Legal Options

. . . .

If the entrepreneur does not seek help quickly, the debts will become unmanageable. There are several options available to businesses that are in severe financial trouble. A discussion of these options follows.

Informal Arrangements

Chapter 11 Bankruptcy
A type of bankruptcy that allows the business to work out a payment plan with creditors while continuing to operate.

If the company cannot be salvaged, it is often possible for the entrepreneur to work out a settlement with creditors without ever entering bankruptcy court. Generally, this can be arranged if the company owes only a few creditors, and if the amounts owed are not extensive. Therefore, closing a business while still owing money does not automatically result in bankruptcy proceedings.

Reorganization Bankruptcy

Extension
A method used in Chapter 11 bankruptcy in which the bankrupt firm is given more time to pay debts than the terms originally agreed on.

Substitution
A method used in Chapter 11 bankruptcy in which the failing company gives creditors company assets (such as machinery or inventory) as payment for debts.

Composition Settlement
A method used in Chapter 11 bankruptcy in which the debtor pays only a portion of each debt owed (for example, $0.50 on each $1.00 owed).

If an entrepreneur allows the company to deteriorate too much, it may be so delinquent in payments to suppliers, banks, and government agencies that it is not feasible to repay these debts under normal circumstances. If no informal arrangements can be developed, one option is to file for a special type of bankruptcy that allows the business to continue operating. This bankruptcy, known as **Chapter 11 bankruptcy,** is named for the chapter of the bankruptcy code that regulates business "reorganizations." When a business is reorganized owing to excessive debt, several options exist to pay off creditors. One method allows the bankrupt firm to pay the debt but take longer to pay than originally set forth. This is known as **extension.** An alternative is for the failing company to pay creditors with assets other than cash, a procedure known as **substitution.** For example, the failing company may give the creditors machinery or equipment, stock, or inventory in payment of debts. A more common alternative, though, is to pay a portion of the total amount owed, for example, $0.50 for every $1.00 owed. This type of agreement is known as a **composition settlement.**

Liquidation

Chapter 7 Bankruptcy
Bankruptcy in which the business is closed and assets are liquidated.

If no Chapter 11 plan or informal agreements can be agreed on, or if the failing company waits too long before seeking help, it may have no alternative but to declare complete bankruptcy and liquidate assets to pay creditors. This is known as **Chapter 7 bankruptcy.** If assets are liquidated (often auctioned), the funds generated often do not cover all debts owed. If this occurs, funds are distributed in the following order:

- Secured creditors. Secured creditors are entitled to take the assets pledged to them as collateral.
- Legal and administrative fees. Any legal and administrative fees arising from the bankruptcy are then paid from funds provided through liquidation. Although court costs are relatively minor, legal fees and administration may be quite substantial. Legal fees for a simple bankruptcy may be only $500, but for anything other than the simplest bankruptcy, fees may be considerably higher.
- Taxes. After the secured debts and the legal and administrative fees have all been satisfied, taxes (generally payroll tax and sales tax) are paid from any funds still available. It is important to note that tax liability cannot be eliminated by declaring bankruptcy. If the sale of a company's assets does not result in enough funds to pay administrative fees and all taxes, the administrative fees will be paid first, and the company owners will be personally liable for any taxes owed.
- Priority claims. Debts such as payroll owed to employees are paid next. This type of debt is given priority over debts arising between the company and regular creditors.
- Unsecured creditors. If funds remain after administrative fees, taxes, and priority claims are paid, unsecured creditors will be paid. Typically, this group will receive only a fraction of the total amount owed to them.
- Stockholder and equity claims. Finally, if any money remains, it is distributed to stockholders and/or the company owner. There is rarely any money left for this group.

The Costs of Failing

A business failure involves financial, psychological, and career costs.

Financial

The financial costs of failing may include the loss of funds invested, loss of other personal assets, and a detrimental effect on the entrepreneur's personal credit record. If the entrepreneur invested personal funds, or funds from friends and relatives, this money will probably not be recouped when the

Small Business Success   21

Scott Air,
Alamogordo, New Mexico

After completing a contract with the Army in 1973, Harold C. Scott, president of Scott Air of Alamogordo, New Mexico, faced the unenviable position of having no orders, no potential customers, and no financing. The oil embargo was on and things looked a bit bleak. Scott's response was to hit the road—not for purposes of quitting, but rather to search for business. He bought an old school bus, then painted, refurbished, and air-conditioned it. He used the vehicle to capture $100,000 in orders from bus companies around the country. His bus air-conditioning has caught on in a big way, with orders from companies as far away as India and sales totalling $7.5 million in 1984.

Source: America at Work (Washington, D.C.: Small Business Administration, 1985), 19.

---

company is liquidated. Often, entrepreneurs invest all available money when the business is started. If the business fails, the entrepreneur may have no personal funds remaining. In addition, the loss of friends' and relatives' money can have a detrimental effect on their financial situations as well as the entrepreneur's.

Often the failure of a small business results in the loss of personal assets such as the entrepreneur's home. Many people mistakenly believe that declaring bankruptcy will protect them from losing personal property. However, if any personal assets are pledged as collateral, bankruptcy will not protect against loss. Even if an entrepreneur incorporates and does not pledge personal assets, financial institutions quite often require a **personal guarantee** when loaning money. This makes the entrepreneur personally responsible for the loan if the company cannot repay it. If the entrepreneur signs a personal guarantee, company bankruptcy may also result in personal bankruptcy.

The effect of the business failure on the entrepreneur's credit record should also be considered. If the business failure results in personal bankruptcy, the entrepreneur's ability to borrow money (even for personal needs) in future years may be lessened. Since a proprietorship and partnership are legally the same entity as the owner or owners, bankruptcy or credit problems of the business will affect the credit rating of the entrepreneur. Complete separation of the business's finances and the owner's requires that the owner incorporate,

Personal Guarantee
A legal agreement in which the entrepreneur agrees to be personally responsible for repaying business debts.

Illustration Capsule   21.2

An Entrepreneur's Struggle to Keep His Business Alive

"I put out a 'rumor control' memorandum last week. I write them from time to time, whenever it seems to me that the mill is being overcome with fears about the company closing . . . This one, however, didn't soothe the fears."

"In 1981, the company slid into bankruptcy, and operated under Chapter 11 for a year before we bought it. During that year, the machines . . . were patched. They weren't repaired because no one wanted to buy replacement parts."

"On Monday our annealing furnace blew out one of its tubes and was turned off for 24 hours of intensive repairs. On Tuesday a chain broke . . . On Wednesday it was a finish line where a mysterious electrical problem was causing a scratch on an industrial tube. On Thursday, a high pressure pump began to vibrate dangerously."

"People yell at me all the time. They're angry all the time."

"The wife of one of the men in the plant called me last week. She was crying because her husband is carrying home the rumor that he may be laid off."

"We're not going to close the company or sell it unless we fail and if management skill makes a difference, we won't fail."

Source: Excerpts from Mark Furstenberg, "In Search of Survival," *Inc.*, January 1984, 67–74.

---

pledge no personal assets, and sign no personal guarantees. This is not usually possible, though, for the owner of a small business who needs financing.

Psychological

The psychological strain associated with failure can be equally devastating. Even if the entrepreneur can escape personal financial ruin, closing the business often takes a psychological toll. The entrepreneur has worked tremendously long hours, totally committed to the business. To see the business fail is to see a personal dream disappear. Also, the psychological stress caused by business failure can result in additional strains in the entrepreneur's family life. While successful entrepreneurs' marriages are strained owing to long working hours, those of unsuccessful entrepreneurs are strained even more. The loss of a business may also result in the loss of one's marriage.

Career

Often, the entrepreneur left a career in one industry to begin a business in another. If so, it may be difficult to reenter the original career field. Often, within a few years, technology has changed rapidly, and retraining would be necessary. Even if it is possible to return, the entrepreneur may be several years behind others who never left the field, in terms of knowledge, wages, and so forth.

Even those who begin businesses in the same industry as their previous career may find it difficult to obtain employment after business ownership. Many employers feel that entrepreneurs are too independent and may not adapt to life as an employee.

Starting Over

Many entrepreneurs start more than one business during their lifetime. The experience of a business failure, although stressful, does not result in total abandonment of the entrepreneurial dream. In fact, it often serves as a learning experience and prevents the entrepreneur from making the same mistakes in the next business.

Because the first business is often undercapitalized, the entrepreneur begins the second with more money. More personal money is invested as a down payment and more money is borrowed for operating capital. The second business often does not suffer from cash shortages as many first businesses do.

Also, the entrepreneur usually realizes that being a good ''technician'' is not enough; a variety of business skills is necessary. Through the experiences of the first business, the entrepreneur usually learns what specific areas of expertise need to be improved. Before beginning the second business, additional management skills may be obtained through college courses or other seminars. The entrepreneur realizes that it is necessary to be a professional business manager as well as an expert in the industry.

The entrepreneur's persistence to try again, often after several failures, is a tribute to the entrepreneurial spirit. Many well-known entrepreneurs failed several times before eventually succeeding. Henry Ford failed twice. Walt Disney failed many times. Often the failure of one venture serves as a springboard for a successful one. The entrepreneur's perserverance and need for achievement eventually overcome the obstacles, and a dream becomes reality.

K   E   Y   Objectives Reviewed

1. Several myths are commonly associated with small business failures. These myths exaggerate the likelihood of a business failing.

2. Several symptoms of failure are common in businesses in financial trouble; if they are closely monitored, failure may be prevented.

3. The legal options available to financially troubled firms range from informal arrangements with creditors to court proceedings.

4. There are financial, psychological, and career costs that result when a small business fails.

5. Entrepreneurs often start more than one business even if they have experienced failure.

Discussion Questions

1. Why do you think the "myths" about business failures exist?

2. Why is the distinction between business closures and business failures important? Identify reasons a successful business may close or end.

3. Why do business failures increase after a recession is over?

4. What is the Peter Principle syndrome? How can it be prevented?

5. Identify the symptoms of failure. Why is it important for entrepreneurs to be aware of these symptoms?

6. Why will borrowing money only be a temporary solution to a financially troubled firm?

7. What is Chapter 11 bankruptcy? Identify and define the three common reorganization methods.

8. If a business is liquidated, many people may be entitled to payment for debts. Identify the order in which funds are distributed after liquidation.

Cases for Part Five

Case V A   The Collapse of the Bushnell Empire

Summary of the Growth of the Bushnell Companies

In the early 1970s, Nolan Bushnell's Atari Company, which developed and sold video games, began to grow rapidly. By 1976, the company was so successful that Warner Communications purchased it from Bushnell for $28 million, although Bushnell remained with Atari as a director. Soon after this buy-out, Atari opened its first Chuck E. Cheese Pizza Time Theatre, a business that combined a pizza restaurant with video games and mechanical animals performing on stage. Eighteen months later, the pizza parlors' growth was well below expectations, and Bushnell was arguing with Atari over other matters. Bushnell therefore resigned his position with Atari in 1978 and purchased the rights to the Pizza Time Theatres. Under his direction, Pizza Time Theatres grew rapidly, numbering 88 in 1980 and 204 by 1982. At that point, Bushnell turned his attention to developing other companies. Catalyst Technologies, a company designed to help new businesses get started, was developed in 1981, as well as Androbot Inc., which would design, produce, and sell robots for home use. In 1983, Bushnell formed Sente Technologies to design and sell video games to Pizza Time Theatres, distributors, and retailers. Bushnell's empire appeared to be taking shape.

Problems at Pizza Time

By summer and fall of 1982, the phenomenal growth of Pizza Time had disappeared and sales began to level off. January through March of 1983 were even worse, with sales dropping 20 percent from the previous year. The situation continued to worsen; in the next 3 months (April through June) the company lost $3 million. This drop in sales and profits followed the trend of the entire video game industry. (In only a few years, video game industry sales fell by $4 million per year.) To try to stop this trend, unprofitable stores

Source: Steve Coll, "When the Magic Goes," *Inc.*, October 1984, 83–97.

were closed and other changes were made. Most Pizza Time executives felt that the declining interest in video games would place more emphasis on the restaurant part of the business, so an improved pizza was introduced. Bushnell, however, had never planned for the theaters to be considered restaurants and thought that developing better video games through Sente Technologies was the answer.

Problems at Sente Technologies

In the fall of 1982 and early 1983, Sente Technologies had enough of its own problems without adding Pizza Time's. Atari had filed a lawsuit against Bushnell charging that he had violated the 7-year noncompetition agreement when he organized Sente Technologies. Even though Sente did not operate before the end of the agreement, Atari felt that Bushnell's developing Sente constituted a violation. Bushnell eventually settled the lawsuit, but the result was that Sente developed much more slowly than expected. Because of the slower development and Pizza Time's losses, more cash was used than anticipated. When payments to suppliers for parts and tools became delinquent, the suppliers stopped shipping Sente's orders. Sente engineers, pressured to develop the company's first video game by a specific date, found the task impossible.

Problems at Androbot Inc.

At the same time that Sente and Pizza Time were fighting for survival, Androbot was struggling. Engineering problems developed, and it was becoming obvious that the planned selling price of $2,000 may have been unrealistically low. Adding to that problem, there had never been final agreement by Androbot management as to what the robots should actually do. Some engineers began to think that it would take 6 years to develop the robots, although they had been given a 6-month deadline. Quality control problems and arguments among engineers resulted. The company, which had 105 employees, four product lines, and no money, was spending hundreds of thousands of dollars each month.

Problems at Catalyst

Catalyst Technologies did not produce successful businesses as originally planned. Catalyst had sponsored several companies, including Cinemavision, a big-screen television company, and Axlon, which was supposed to develop a data communications device, but neither company was successful.

The Collapse

. . . .

Eventually Pizza Time was losing approximately $20 million per month. The number of customers continued to drop dramatically. Although Bushnell began to call weekly meetings of his board of directors, it seemed he rarely took their advice, and several board members resigned. Because of the problems at Androbot, huge layoffs were necessary, including members of the management team. Most people felt that Sente would have to be sold to avoid bankruptcy.

Bushnell, however, remained optimistic, insisting that December 1983 would be the beginning of the turnaround. December was always one of the best months for Pizza Time, and Sente's new video game would be released that month, causing an even greater number of customers to come to the Pizza Time Theatres. Unfortunately, this did not occur. Although Sente's first game was available by December, it was not an incredible success. The number of customers at Pizza Time Theatres did not increase dramatically, and Bushnell began to realize that success would not come in the near future. On March 28, 1984, Pizza Time Theatres filed Chapter 11 bankruptcy, owing creditors more than $100 million. Nolan Bushnell lost more than $5 million he had invested as well as hundreds of millions of investors' dollars.

Figure   V A.1   The Development and Failure of the Bushnell Empire

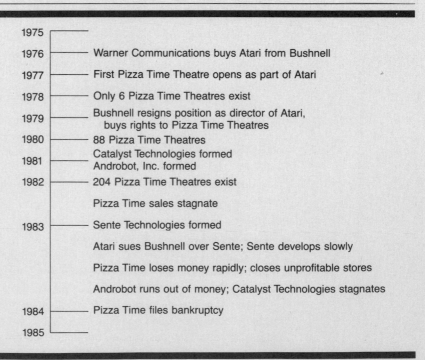

1975

1976 ——— Warner Communications buys Atari from Bushnell

1977 ——— First Pizza Time Theatre opens as part of Atari

1978 ——— Only 6 Pizza Time Theatres exist

1979 ——— Bushnell resigns position as director of Atari, buys rights to Pizza Time Theatres

1980 ——— 88 Pizza Time Theatres

1981 ——— Catalyst Technologies formed
Androbot, Inc. formed

1982 ——— 204 Pizza Time Theatres exist

Pizza Time sales stagnate

1983 ——— Sente Technologies formed

Atari sues Bushnell over Sente; Sente develops slowly

Pizza Time loses money rapidly; closes unprofitable stores

Androbot runs out of money; Catalyst Technologies stagnates

1984 ——— Pizza Time files bankruptcy

1985

Persistence

Despite the bleak situation, Bushnell persisted in developing his ideas. Sente Technologies was sold to a manufacturing firm in Chicago. A small crew of engineers continued at Androbot, hoping eventually to produce a successful robot, and several Catalyst companies were still developing products that would be introduced within a few years.

Questions

1. What do you think caused the collapse of Bushnell's empire?
2. Could this failure have been prevented? If so, how?
3. Looking back on the success and failure of Bushnell's companies, what do you feel are his strengths and weaknesses?

Case V B   Successes and Failures of Walt Disney

An Entrepreneurial Background

Although most people would classify Walt Disney as an extremely successful entrepreneur, many are unaware of the fact that he failed many times before succeeding. Only through perseverance did the Disney dream become reality.

Walt Disney was born December 5, 1901 to an entrepreneurial family. At a very early age he began working long hours on his father's farm. Despite the Disney family's long hours of hard work, the farm did not succeed.

His father then tried to support the family by operating a newspaper route. Walt started at 3:30 a.m. every day to help with the route. Because he received no money for helping his father, Walt searched for ways to make money for himself. Therefore, when he returned home every day at 6:30 a.m., he began selling his own papers. He also worked in a candy store during his school's noon recess, although his father was not aware of it.

He began his art training at a very early age, working under a cartoonist for a newspaper. This career was soon interrupted when World War I began and all able men enlisted. Although Walt Disney was not yet 17 years of age, he wanted to serve in the armed forces. Though he was too young to serve in

---

Source: Richard Schickel, *The Disney Version* (New York: Simon and Schuster, 1968).

many branches of the service, the Red Cross Ambulance Corps accepted him. His passion for art continued, and while serving in the Ambulance Corps he began selling artwork to other servicemen.

The First Business
....

After his service, Disney accepted a job in a commercial art studio in Kansas City. He was hired as an apprentice to help with the advertising rush during the Christmas season; as soon as the rush was over, he was laid off. At that point, Disney and another employee of the agency began their own business.

The partnership was relatively successful from the start, earning more in the first few weeks than the partners' combined former salaries. However, soon after the business began, a job arose at the Kansas City Film Ad Company, which Disney accepted. Although his partner attempted to keep the business operating, without Disney's talents, the business failed quickly.

Although employed by the Kansas City Film Ad Company, Disney continued to experiment with his own ideas. He developed Laugh-O-Gram segments, which consisted of jokes and announcements to be shown in theaters. When one theater owner expressed an interest and asked Disney how much the segments would sell for, Disney forgot to include a profit margin in his price. The theater owner accepted the stated price, so Disney made a sale but no profits.

The Second Business
....

Disney eventually left his job at the Kansas City Film Ad Company to start the Laugh-O-Gram Company. The company produced regular features plus animated fairy tales, including Puss 'n Boots and Little Red Riding Hood. Unfortunately, the motion picture industry was very corrupt, and Disney was naive. He had a representative in New York selling his Laugh-O-Gram segments and fairy tales. Although sales were good, the money never seemed to get back to Disney in Kansas City. The shortage of money forced Disney to lay off employees and cut expenses. In an effort to save the company, Disney gave up his apartment and lived at the office, often existing on a meager diet. These valiant attempts were not enough, however, and the business was eventually forced to close. At that point, Disney was only 21 years old and had already had two businesses fail.

Disney decided that if he was going to succeed in the film industry, he would have to move to the West Coast where all the other filmmakers were. However, he did not have money to pay for the trip. He therefore sold his camera and left for California.

The Third Business

On Disney's arrival in California, a film distributor offered him a contract for the Alice in Cartoonland series that Disney had begun with his Laugh-O-Gram Company. Though not an immediate success, the series eventually improved and began selling well. Disney then developed an Oswald the Rabbit series, which was very successful.

When it was time to renew the contract with the film distributor, Disney was confident that he would be offered a modest price increase. The distributor, however, tried to force Disney to take a decrease in price, saying that since the distributor owned the rights to the series, Disney could take the offer or end the contract completely. Disney ended the contract and went back home to Kansas City, determined never again to give up the ownership of any series.

The Fourth Business

Although other people might have given up at this point, Disney began to plan his next venture while he was on the train back to Kansas City. The concept of Mickey Mouse began to develop during the trip back home, and once home, Disney started a studio and developed Mouse films, including *Steamboat Willie*.

Repeating past mistakes, however, Disney signed a contract with a New York film distributor who agreed to sell the films. As with the other representative, the money from the film sales was never sent back to Kansas City. Disney therefore searched for a new distributor and was successful in signing with Columbia Pictures.

Disney's attempts always to produce a perfect product resulted in long work hours and constantly rising costs. Disney would redo portions of films until they were perfect, even if costs became excessive, therefore merely breaking even. The break-even status combined with incredibly long work hours took their toll on Disney's mental health. He became irritable and unable to sleep, pushing himself near to collapse. His doctor suggested a long trip, and Disney agreed.

Success

A year later Disney returned and signed a contract with United Artists. His temporary break was apparently the key to success, as the company now became profitable; only 2 years later, in 1934, the company earned $660,000. Profits were consistently reinvested into the business, generating unexpected growth. By 1935, Mickey Mouse was said to be the "international symbol of goodwill," and Disney was known throughout the world.

The company was now growing rapidly and consequently experienced management problems. Within 5 years, it had grown from 150 to 750 employees. Disney, who would spend any amount necessary to produce a perfect film, was notorious for paying low wages, a constant source of conflict between Disney and his employees. For example, though the cost to produce *Snow White* was estimated at $250,000, the actual cost totaled $1.7 million, causing rough times for the studio until the picture was released. Once it was released, the film grossed $8.5 million on its first run. This eventual success caused Disney to try to grow too fast. Three films — *Pinnochio, Bambi,* and *Fantasia* — were being produced at the same time. In addition, Disney spent $3.8 million building his "dream studio." By 1940, Disney had spent all of the profits from *Snow White* and owed $4.5 million to banks. Adding to his problems, overseas sales of films, which normally accounted for 45 percent of his returns, were stopped because of World War II. Added to all of this were personnel problems, technical problems with *Bambi,* and a temporary financial disaster with *Fantasia.* By early 1940, the banks stopped Disney's line of credit and he was forced to sell stock publicly to raise money.

Personnel problems continued to plague Disney. Many of the employees resented the amount Disney had spent on the new studio when their wages were still extremely low. They also resented the layout of the new studio, which separated production units from each other. To add to their grievance, anyone leaving a work area had to provide an explanation to the person stationed at the front of each group of offices. Threats of layoffs circulated as well as rumors of time clocks being installed. Low wages persisted and the employees unionized. Some participated in a strike, and several layoffs occurred.

Successful Again

. . . .

Disney temporarily removed himself from the company's daily management, and the strike was eventually settled. Disney Studios then produced *Dumbo,* which was a tremendous hit. Despite its success, the company was still in debt.

In the late 1940s, the studio began making several films, including *Cinderella, Alice in Wonderland, Peter Pan,* and a series of successful nature films. In 1950, *Treasure Island* was released, and the company finally showed a profit after 2 years of losses. The studio continued to produce hit films, including *The Shaggy Dog, The Absent Minded Professor, 20,000 Leagues Under the Sea,* and many more.

By 1955, Disney's dream of the ultimate amusement park materialized with the opening of Disneyland. In 1985, Disneyland celebrated its 30th anniversary.

Questions

1. In what ways is Disney typical of successful entrepreneurs?
2. What is the major reason for Disney's success?
3. What were Disney's major strengths? Major weaknesses?

Case V C   Korvettes

When the Korvettes stores in the United States closed in 1980, an uninformed observer would only have been aware that a major retailer had gone bankrupt. Those who knew Korvettes' history, though, knew of its tremendous success when it was a new small business, and knew that the business failure was the end to one man's dream.

Eugene Ferkauf grew up in an entrepreneurial family, his father the owner of two successful luggage shops in New York. Eugene's father had always wanted him to run one of the shops when he grew up, but when Eugene returned from the service in the mid-1940s, he had an idea of his own. Eugene and his friends planned to start a business—a discount business that would sell not only luggage but housewares, jewelry, clocks, and many other items. At that point in the history of retailing, discounting was an unfamiliar concept.

Unbelievable Success

Eugene planned for his business to be small and simple. He chose a location of only 400 square feet on the second floor of a New York building, renting for $550 per month. One month before opening, Ferkauf and his friends distributed discount cards and price sheets to many businesses and individuals in the area.

The first day the company opened for business, the customers were lined up, waiting to get in; inside, the store was jammed. This was not just opening-day curiosity, though, since the crowds continued all week long. By the end of the first week, all of the merchandise had been sold.

The business had no formal organizational structure or job descriptions. If something needed to be done, someone would see that it was done right. The only employees were Ferkauf, his two friends, and one new employee. Fer-

---

Source: Isadore Barmash, *More Than They Bargained for: The Rise and Fall of Korvettes* (New York: Chain Store Publishing Corp., 1981).

kauf drove his car to the distributor every day to pick up merchandise and unloaded it outside the store. Often the customers would help him carry the merchandise up the stairs to the showroom.

The Christmas season proved even more phenomenal, though the store was only open from 8 a.m. to 6 p.m. and had not done any formal advertising. The employees were so busy and the room was so crowded that it was often impossible to get to the cash register. The four employees would just put the money in their pockets until they had time to ring up the sale. When the business closed at 6 p.m., the employees worked all night to get the business ready for the next day. Daily sales during the first Christmas season (1948) averaged $13,000. In the first year of business, the company grossed $1 million in sales, and inventory sold five times faster than at other retail businesses. The small, simple business that sold name brand merchandise at discounted prices experienced more success than anyone had believed possible.

Suppliers of major appliances such as refrigerators and washing machines then approached Eugene to sell their products. Because the large appliances could not be carried up and down the stairs, Ferkauf and his employees would merely take the customer's order, and the distributor would deliver the appliance directly to the customer. Within a short time, the small store was selling 60 washing machines per week.

When Ferkauf decided more employees were needed, he hired friends or friends of friends. There were no college graduates, no experienced retailers. Within 2 years, the company employed 12 people, all working together as a family.

The company continued its phenomenal success and by 1951 opened a second store. The new store, seven blocks from the original store, was 3,000 square feet and rented for $15,000 per year. From the day it opened, it was an incredible success. During the same year, the first store moved down to street level, further enhancing its success. The two stores' combined sales totaled $5 million, resulting in a net profit of approximately $500,000. The company employed 30 people.

Signs of Trouble

Korvettes continued its growth and within a few years had six successful stores, five small stores and one large one. The large store sold $138,000 in merchandise the day it opened, more than $2 million its first 23 days, and $20 million its first year. Incredibly, the family atmosphere still existed despite the growth. Most employees were 20 to 30 years old and willing to work long hours. Although the pay was not high, the year-end bonuses were often tremendous. Eugene was often seen visiting the stores, talking to customers and employees, noting which items were selling well and which were not.

Eventually the company expanded into separate carpet and furniture show-rooms, which also proved successful. Ferkauf and his group of advisors then began to consider closing the five small discount stores and concentrating on building more large stores. He therefore began to look for suitable sites.

By 1956, the small stores were closed and three new large stores were opened. The large stores were successful, and expansion continued. A new store averaging 200,000 square feet was opened almost every 6 weeks, total-ing 25 new stores in 3 years. For a while, there were growing pains. Costs rose dramatically, profits fell, and inventory control was difficult. Eugene and his group pulled together and tightened controls, and the company was back on course. The company continued its success, branching out into records, tapes, cosmetics, and books. Eugene Ferkauf was considered one of the six greatest merchants in U.S. history.

Eugene then brought in a new top man to help him, Jack Schwadron, the first "outsider" in the company's top management. A second outsider, Hil-liard Coan, was added to management when Korvettes merged with Coan's food chain to add a food line. At that point Ferkauf stepped aside and Coan became chairman of Korvettes. Ferkauf remained chairman of the executive committee. To the general public, the threesome appeared to work well together, but signs of trouble soon became evident when Schwadron unex-pectedly resigned and employees were ordered not to talk to the press. At many of the planning meetings, Eugene did not appear and Coan made many of the decisions.

In 1966, Korvettes merged with Spartans Industries Inc., an apparel man-ufacturing firm. This fulfilled one of Eugene's dreams—to merge with a major corporation. As part of the merger, Ferkauf received $20 million, and Charlie Bassine, owner of Spartans Industries, took over management of both companies.

The company now faced increased competition from many major retailers, such as Kmart, that had copied the discounting concept. With the large Kor-vettes stores averaging 200,000 square feet, increased costs made the dis-counting concept difficult to continue. The stores outside of New York were experiencing other management problems, and the entire corporation was described as suffering from problems of "distribution, supervision, customer identity and lack of market dominance."

In 1968, at the age of 47, Ferkauf retired and left Bassine to direct the struggling company. Sales continued to drop 15 percent per year, and profits were only about $1 million. Bassine felt the only answer was to increase markups, emphasize apparel, and phase out large appliances, housewares, and so forth. Despite signs of trouble, three new stores were opened.

In 1971, the company again merged, this time with a real estate develop-ment company that had built many of the Korvettes stores. The merger was intended to provide excellent tax benefits to Korvettes and growth opportuni-ties to the real estate firm. In 1972, the real estate company showed a profit of $21 million, though Korvettes still floundered. Bassine decided to leave, and another management group took over Korvettes.

Rapid Decline

· ·

The merger with the real estate firm resulted in double trouble. The mid-1970s were very bad years for the real estate industry owing to high interest rates. The real estate firm began losing money in 1973 and by 1978 had accumulated losses of $275 million in 6 years. Meanwhile Korvettes' sales were stagnant and profits low. In 1977, Korvettes began its own trend of losses. Losses in 1977 were $4 million, and 1978 losses were $5.4 million.

In mid-1978, Korvettes employees were shocked to learn that the company had been purchased by a French company, which again caused a change in management. Losses accelerated to $25 million in 1979, as sales continued to fall. The French management closed unprofitable stores, reducing the number of stores from a high of 58 to 35, resulting in 7,000 people being laid off. The French company then changed management, but no improvement developed. Creditors had not been paid in many months and refused to ship more merchandise. Arrangements with banks to make payments on delinquent loans were discussed but not implemented owing to a difference of opinion within the French management. On Christmas Eve 1980, all Korvettes stores were closed. In July 1981, Korvettes filed for Chapter 11 bankruptcy with $113 million in debts and only $27 million in assets.

Eugene Ferkauf owned several other businesses after his retirement from Korvettes in 1968. In 1981, he owned a retail consulting and management company in New York and a chain of apparel stores in the South. Then in 1983, Eugene and some of his original employees began a membership discount store in Manhattan where only cardholders were admitted. Ferkauf's one regret is that throughout Korvettes' troubled years after he retired, no one asked him to return, even to provide advice.

Questions

1. What were the reasons for the incredible success of Korvettes in its early years?

2. Do you think Korvettes would have failed if Eugene Ferkauf had remained manager?

3. Would the early Korvettes strategy be successful today — a small, independently owned store with low overhead and large discounts? Why or why not?

Case V D   Central Auto Parts

In 1983, Tom Mellick opened Central Auto Parts, a store that would sell to area auto repair shops and to the general public. The store was located on a well-traveled street, had no competition within 5 miles, and was relatively successful from the start.

Both Mr. and Mrs. Mellick worked in the business full-time along with their son, who worked in the store part-time. There were no other employees. Mellick and his son were responsible for helping customers, ringing up purchases, making deliveries to auto repair shops, and ordering inventory. Mrs. Mellick helped customers, rang up purchases, and was responsible for the bookkeeping on a daily basis; however, the Mellicks planned to have an accountant prepare the income taxes each year.

Within the first year the business grew much faster than the Mellicks had anticipated and the record keeping requirements consumed almost all of Mrs. Mellick's time. It was obvious that if the business continued its current growth, the record keeping would require at least two people. The accountant who completed the tax returns for the first year informed the Mellicks that their bookkeeping system was not as complete as it should be and suggested that they establish a good general journal. Mrs. Mellick therefore designed a general journal with the help of the accountant and recorded all transactions each day. This only added to her bookkeeping duties, though, and the entries were not being posted quickly because a backlog of work quickly developed.

Mr. Mellick had considered getting a computer, but Mrs. Mellick did not want one because she had no training and was not sure of her ability to operate a computer. She was concerned that it would take substantial time for her to comprehend the computer operations and her work would get even more backlogged. Because of Mrs. Mellick's reluctance to computerize, Mr. Mellick thought it would be good to get an inexpensive computer for record keeping. Then, if Mrs. Mellick did not like it, no major investment would have been wasted.

Mr. Mellick's brother, Charles, had purchased a computer in 1980, primarily as a hobby, but did not use it as much as he had hoped. He was willing to give it to Tom to see if it would help. Tom decided to take Charles's computer on an experimental basis.

Tom went to a software store to purchase the record keeping programs he would need. He discovered, though, that the program he needed would not run on Charles's computer. The sales consultant at the software store suggested that Tom either have a customized program written or purchase a different computer. The consultant gave Tom a list of programmers who could write a customized program.

After contacting several of the programmers, Tom chose one to design a bookkeeping package, although he was upset over spending the additional money for programming fees. The programmer designed a system that would provide a general journal and all necessary ledgers, helped to implement the programs, and also provided Mrs. Mellick with some training to acquaint her with the programs.

Throughout the next 6 months, Mrs. Mellick worked with the computer and became comfortable with its operation. Although it reduced the time needed for each entry, the business's sales volume continued to expand rapidly so Mrs. Mellick still spent a substantial amount of time keeping records.

Because of the growth of the business, the Mellicks had continually expanded the inventory, which after only 2 years had increased from $50,000 to almost $100,000. The computerized system maintained an ongoing record of the total dollar amount of inventory on hand but did not include an inventory control system. All inventory counting and ordering was completed manually. The owner of another auto parts store suggested that a card system of inventory control might help the Mellicks with their problem. Tom therefore purchased a card system specially designed for auto parts stores. Mr. and Mrs. Mellick spent several weeks implementing the card system. Once it was in place, they began to use the system, recording each transaction on the appropriate card. It soon became evident, though, that with the large number of daily transactions, the card system was very time-consuming. The Mellicks felt that it was almost a full-time job to keep the system accurate. After several months, the Mellicks agreed that the card system was not a practical solution.

Tom decided that a computerized inventory system might be a good solution and visited a software store to purchase one. The sales consultant asked Tom basic questions about his store, including the number of suppliers, the number of different inventory lines he carried, the number of transactions per day, and so forth. He then informed Tom that, although inventory control programs were available, Tom's computer was not large enough to handle the type of program he needed. Even if Tom had a customized inventory control program written, he would need a larger computer. The sales consultant told Tom that he had three options — continue to use a manual system, write a customized program providing some inventory information but less than the Mellicks needed to maintain good control, or purchase a larger computer system.

Mr. and Mrs. Mellick were reluctant to buy a bigger system since the computerized bookkeeping system had finally been perfected and no more problems occurred. If a new system were implemented, it would be necessary to begin the process all over again. Also, the Mellicks were reluctant to change systems so soon because of the money they had invested to have the customized bookkeeping system written. Mr. Mellick therefore considered purchasing a larger computer for the inventory control system and leaving the bookkeeping system on the smaller computer.

Questions

1. Do you think the Mellicks took the proper steps in computerizing their information? Was it wise to use Charles's computer on an experimental basis to familiarize Mrs. Mellick with automation?

2. Should the Mellicks get a larger computer for the inventory control system? If so, should the bookkeeping be implemented on the new system or remain on the old one?

3. How could the Mellicks' computer problems have been prevented?

Index